Second Edition

LAND RESOURCE ECONOMICS

The Economics
of Real Property

Raleigh Barlowe

Michigan State University

DOES ECOLOGY PROVIDE A SET
GOALS for RESOURCE POLICY?
DOES ECONOMICS?

PRENTICE-HALL, INC., Englewood Cliffs, N.J.

ISBN: 0-13-522557-4

Library of Congress Number: 76-179905

10 9 8 7 6 5 4

Printed in the United States of America

PRENTICE-HALL INTERNATIONAL, INC., *London*
PRENTICE-HALL OF AUSTRALIA, PTY. LTD., *Sydney*
PRENTICE-HALL OF CANADA, LTD., *Toronto*
PRENTICE-HALL OF INDIA PRIVATE LIMITED, *New Delhi*
PRENTICE-HALL OF JAPAN, INC., *Tokyo*

To

the memory of

GEORGE S. WEHRWEIN

gifted teacher, scholar, and public
servant—sincere and humble friend
of man and land

Handwritten annotations:

THE END OF THIS CLASS,
ANT TO HAVE A BIG FIELD
: WE WANT TO LOOK AT THE
ST (NOT THE TREES) AND THE PEOPLE
INDIVIDUALS OR POLITICS) TO LOOK AT THE
BROKEN CHAIN."

TO BEGIN WITH
NEED READINGS ON THE
MECHANISMS —
1ST ALSTON'S HISTORY
2ND ALLISON'S CEPTUAL MODEL
OF THE BUREAUCRACY.

THE THEME OF THE CLASS IS
THAT NO ONE KNOWS HOW TO MAKE
POLICY FOR RESOURCE USE
[DO 10 min TRIP ON CURRENT CONGRESSIONAL
MECHANISM

FOCUS IN ON
1) PUBLIC LANDS
ECONOMICS GOVERNS PRIVATE LAND MNGMNT)
2) US FOREST SERVICE
HE ONLY CLEARLY DEFINED LAND
MNGMNT AGENCY)
—ORGANIC ACT
—MOST EFFECTIVE
—POSSESS MOST
SIGNIFICANT % OF
PUBLICALLY-OWNED NATURAL
RESOURCES,

SO, WE'RE GOING TO LOOK AT THE
CONCEPTUAL MODELS, TOOLS + MTDS
BEING TRIED,
PLUS A LITTLE HISTORY

SOMETIME LATER — COUNTERACT
BARLOW WITH SCHUMPTER:

2 OVERVIEW LECTURE ON THE COURSE
ITS CONDUCT (TUES 30TH)

3 1ST LECTURE ON HOW WE THINK
WE'RE DOING IT & HOW WE'RE NOT
REALLY — BECAUSE WE DON'T KNOW WHAT
WE WANT OR HOW TO DO IT IN THE POLICY
SENSE.

4 READINGS AFTER RAUPP

5 2ND LECTURE : GOAL IDENTI(+ FORMATION

6 2ND SET OF READINGS IS ETHICS STUFF

3D LECTURE : RISK + UNCERTAINTY (RATIONAL CHOICE THEORY)

3D SET OF READINGS IS THIS BOOK'S 1ST TEN
CHAPTERS
[BASIC CONCEPTS + TERMS]

7

Contents

Preface

Man's relationships with the earth-oriented resources that pro- ~~LAYER CEPT~~
vide his natural endowment and environment are both basic and
fundamental. In a primitive world, many of these relationships
are simple and easily perceived. In modern society, they have
been vastly complicated by man-to-man relationships involving
population pressures, economic considerations, and a web of
institutional arrangements. These developments have in no way
changed the basic nature of man's ties to his land resource base,
but they have brought considerable confusion in the ideas
people hold concerning land.

My objective with this edition of *Land Resource Economics,*
as earlier, has been to help clear away some of this confusion by
presenting a straightforward and systematic description of the
economic concepts that affect man in his use and possession of
land resources. With this purpose in mind, emphasis has been
given to the threefold framework within which man's use of
land takes place. Consideration is given in the first chapters to
the physical and biological factors that help to determine our
supply of and demand for land resources. This discussion is
followed by six chapters that deal with the economic principles
that affect man in his use of land resources. A third group of
chapters stresses the impact of institutional factors on land use
and upon the manner in which people hold and enjoy rights in
real property. Emphasis in the final chapters is focused on issues
associated with the social direction of land use.

This book could not have been written without the help of others. Much of my thinking as a land economist is rooted in our rich heritage of ideas. Much of it stems from my reading of the literature and from my contacts as a student with three great teachers of land economics: Lewis C. Gray, George S. Wehrwein, and Leonard A. Salter, Jr. My association with other teachers, with colleagues in university life, with fellow land and resource economists, and with students both in and outside the classroom also has added to my understanding of the issues described here.

Special credit is due to a number of people who have assisted this project in various ways. Among my colleagues at Michigan State University, Milton H. Steinmueller, Myles Boylan, Daniel E. Chappelle, Leighton L. Leighty, and A. Allan Schmid have provided valuable suggestions that are incorporated in this edition. J. Paul Schneider has been most helpful in assisting in the preparation of charts and diagrams. A grateful vote of thanks also is due to my good wife, Jean, and to my son for the tolerance and forbearance they have shown while urging this project to completion.

Raleigh Barlowe

1

Land
Economics:
A Study of Man and Land

Much can be said about the basic importance of land resources in the modern world. They provide people with living space, with the raw materials necessary for filling material needs, and with opportunities for satisfactions dear to the heart of man. People look to land for their physical environment, for the food they eat, for fibers and the other materials needed to clothe their bodies and to provide housing and manufactured goods, for building sites, for recreation opportunities, and for scenery and open space.

History speaks eloquently of the high regard with which man has viewed land in times past. The ancient Minoans and Greeks prayed to an earth goddess, a reverence that has come down to us in the respect we show for Mother Earth. For long centuries, most wars were fought for the possession of land, and the average man everywhere lived in close association with the soil, fields, forests, and fishing grounds that provided him with sustenance. Rights in land were often the key factor that determined an individual's economic, social, and political status. Hunger for land and for land ownership brought thousands of immigrants to the Americas and still affects the thinking of people in many places.

Concern over the intimate relationship between man, land, and food supplies has influenced the writings and teachings of many of the world's great thinkers, including the early economists who viewed land as a key factor in production. This concern over man's ties to land and his natural environment is somewhat less evident now in many parts of the world, but land resources still play a role of elemental significance. Without them, man's civilization and very existence would speedily end.

Average Americans often tend to take their relationship to land for granted. Urbanization has separated the great bulk of the nation's population from intimate contact with land as a producer of food and raw materials. Technological advance has removed the threat of famine and hunger, and comparative affluence has centered the concerns of most people on issues only indirectly related to land resources.

It is not unfair to say that most Americans have lost much of the land hunger felt by their ancestors. Except for expressions of concern over the quality of their environment, most people now tend to view land resources as a dependable and thus routine input in their scheme of values. The fact that the supply of land resources is fixed while population numbers and new technology are increasing and creating new capital developments and products has prompted some decline in the proportionate importance of the role land resources play in the whole society. This does not mean, however, that land resources are expendable or unimportant. Their significance in absolute terms grows steadily with each passing year.

The basic and underlying significance of land resources to mankind can never be gauged simply in terms of their relative economic contributions to a nation's economy. Yet measures of this order can be used to illustrate the current significance of land resources. Investments in land and land improvements account for two-thirds of the wealth of the United States, while proprietor and rental incomes account for approximately a sixth of the personal income realized. New structures on land accounted for annual expenditures that ranged from 9.6 to 11.3 percent of the nation's gross national product during the 1960-1970 period. Expenditures on housing represent the most important single item in most family budgets; real estate loans account for between 35 and 40 percent of the private credit in the United States; and taxes on land resources provide most of the revenue for the operation of local governments.

Much of the high standard of life enjoyed in the United States and Canada can be credited in part to the rich land-resource base these nations possess. The situation in these countries differs from that in many parts of the world. On the world front, many people feel that the need for additional food supplies is the leading problem of our time. Two-thirds of the world's people still live in the shadow of want and hunger; and with the current upward surge in world population numbers, this over-all situation could easily become worse rather than better. This problem calls for development of new agricultural lands and for more productive use of many areas already in cultivation.

Other land-resource problems of world scope include the emphasis most nations now give to economic development, the programs they are using to develop and settle new areas, and their continuing need for land-reform measures that will bring a better distribution of the rights people hold in land. Still other problems stem from increasing international competition for certain basic resources and from worldwide demands for nonfood products—fibers, building materials, minerals, and energy resources.

Throughout the United States, Canada, and much of the western world, the major land problem is more one of marshalling land resources so that they might be used effectively and efficiently to help provide people with high levels of living than it is of providing people with food and basic sustenance. Highly important urban land problems are associated with the succession of land uses that takes place with urban growth; the operations of the real estate market; the provision of needed housing, recreation, open space, rapid-transit, parking, and other facilities; enhancement of the urban environment; the redevelopment of blighted areas; and planning for the future growth of cities.

With the sprawling outward growth of most cities, these problems have spilled over into the suburban and urban-fringe communities. Many areas regarded as rural a few years ago now face problems comparable to those of nearby cities. In addition, they face the expense of providing schools, water and sewerage systems, paved streets and other public services. Action is needed to prevent undesired developments and to integrate certain local programs with those of the metropolitan communities.

Rural residents who own and operate farms, forests, and other rural lands also face numerous land problems involving the acquisition, management, improvement, conservation, and eventual transfer of their properties. Some of these problems center on the individual operator's choice of enterprises, his managerial decisions, and his willingness to bring new areas into use. Others deal with land appraisal methods, the use of credit financing, the determination of fair rental rates, and the development of satisfactory tenure and property-inheritance arrangements.

Land resource problems are also an important province of government. Various units of government in the United States now control and administer 38 per cent of the nation's land area. They depend upon property and other land-oriented taxes for much of their revenue. They are carrying on active research and educational programs dealing with land problems. They have sponsored reclamation, urban development and highway construction programs and have concerned themselves with reforestation, flood control, public housing, rent control, area development and many other problems involving land use. They have taken important steps to plan for the more orderly and effective use of our land resources and to use zoning ordinances and other public measures to control and direct land-use practices in the public interest.

The discussion in the chapters that follow centers for the most part on the principles and problems that affect man in his use of land resources. In the balance of this chapter, emphasis is focused on the scope and content of land economics and on some basic land economic concepts.

SCOPE AND CONTENT OF LAND ECONOMICS

Land economics may be described simply as the field of study that deals with *man's economic relationships with others respecting land.*[1] It is concerned with man's economic use of the surface resources of the earth and the physical and biological, economic, and institutional factors that affect, condition, and control his use of these resources. As Leonard A. Salter once observed: "Land economics is a social science that deals with those problems in which social conduct is strategically affected by the physical, locational or property attributes of whole surface units."[2]

Like general economics, land economics is concerned with the allocation and use of scarce resources. Its chief focus of interest centers on one particular type of resource: land. But the land economist can never give exclusive attention to the land factor for the simple reason that this concept has very little economic value until it is related to other productive factors. Land economics involves a wide variety of economic relationships; but it is always concerned with problems and situations in which land, its use, or its control, is regarded as a factor of strategic or limiting importance. This factoral approach can be compared with the attention given to the factors of capital, labor, and management in the fields of money and banking, labor economics, and business management, respectively.

Land Economics: A Branch of Political Economy

Land economics is ordinarily regarded as an applied branch of economics. This designation springs from the fact that land economists are usually

[1] Land economics was first recognized as a course for collegiate study in 1892 when Richard T. Ely started his seminar on Landed Property at the University of Wisconsin. Formal recognition as a separate field came in 1919 when a Division of Land Economics was established in the U. S. Department of Agriculture. Foundations were established in the 1920s for much of the work in urban and rural land economics that has followed. The first course materials dealing specifically with this field were published in 1922.

For more detailed accounts of the history of land economics see Leonard A. Salter, Jr., *A Critical Review of Research in Land Economics* (Minneapolis: University of Minnesota Press, 1948), chap. II; Coleman Woodbury, "Richard T. Ely and the Beginnings of Research in Urban Land and Housing Economics," *Land Economics,* Vol. 25, February, 1949, pp. 55-66; V. Webster Johnson, "Twenty-five Years of Progress: Division of Land Economics," *The Journal of Land and Public Utility Economics,* Vol. 31, February, 1945, pp. 54-64; and Henry C. and Anne D. Taylor, *The Story of Agricultural Economics in the United States* (Ames: Iowa State College Press, 1952), Part VI.

[2] Leonard A. Salter, Jr., "The Content of Land Economics and Research Methods Adapted to Its Needs," *Journal of Farm Economics,* Vol. 24, February, 1942, p. 235.

more interested in working with and finding solutions to land problems than in developing new theories.

Because of the nature of their work, land economists are naturally interested in the application of economic theory to land problems. They are concerned with all those economic factors and concepts such as cost, returns, prices, profits, and value that affect man in his economic use of land. At the same time, however, they must assume a very practical attitude regarding the application of economic concepts under real-life conditions. Like the nineteenth-century economist Richard Jones, the land economist must "look and see." He cannot ignore the importance of economic theory; but at the same time he must always recognize that economic activity never takes place within a vacuum and that it seldom takes place under the fixed assumptions often used in economic analysis.

Land economics is often characterized by its practical, institutional, and problem-solving approach. In his attempt to explain man's behavior with respect to land, the land economist frequently finds it meaningful to use concepts developed in the other social sciences and in other related disciplines. When he tries to explain certain happenings or particular patterns of behavior, for example, he often finds it expedient to use working tools that come from history, law, political science, psychology, and sociology as well as economics. Similarly, when he considers land-resource problems, he often uses concepts developed by geographers, soil scientists, planners, architects, engineers, foresters, and geologists. In their use and integration of these various lines of thought, land economists often step beyond the bounds of economics to operate as social-science land specialists in the broader field of political economy.

Threefold framework of land economics. The broad scope of land economics is illustrated by the threefold context or framework within which most land economists see man's use of land resources as taking place. These three frameworks involve the physical and biological, the economic, and the institutional factors that affect man in his use of land resources. In actual practice these three frameworks operate together. For analytical purposes, however, their separate consideration often helps one to understand the effect each of these groups of factors has in influencing man's behavior with respect to land.

Briefly stated, the *physical and biological framework* is concerned with the natural environment in which man finds himself and with the nature and characteristics of the various resources with which he must work. The physical and biological factors involved in this framework provide the physical support, the site, and the raw materials for man's activities. At the same time they provide not only the inanimate resources of the earth but also the vegetative, bacterial, insect, fish, animal, and human resources that both help and hinder man in his use of land. This framework has an important effect both upon the total supply of land resources and upon the demands made against these resources.

The *economic framework* is concerned with the operation of the price system as it affects each individual in his attempt to make profitable use of his land-resource base. This framework deals with man's tendency to maximize his returns. It is concerned with the effect that economic concepts such as value, costs, returns, and profits have upon his allocation and distribution of land resources and upon his use of these resources for production and consumption purposes. As later discussion will indicate, most land economics thinking is oriented within this framework.

The *institutional framework* is concerned with the role man's cultural environment and the forces of social and collective action play in influencing his behavior as an individual and as a member of his family, his various groups, and his community. It is concerned with the impact of cultural attitudes, custom and tradition, habitual ways of thinking and doing things, legal arrangements, government programs, religious beliefs, and other similar factors upon man-to-man and man-to-land behavior. Among its many facets, it also involves the effect of personal and household considerations—an individual's nonmonetary goals or his family obligations—upon one's decisions as a business operator. Almost every type of human activity is influenced or conditioned to some extent by the institutional factors that operate within this framework.

Together with the level of technology, these three factors set the stage within which man's use of land takes place at any given time. In his work with this threefold framework, the land economist finds that he must deal with the full gamut of factors that affect land-resource use. Much as he may wish to limit himself to the application of economic principles, he frequently finds that the solution of his problems requires consideration of the physical and biological nature of his land-resource base. In like manner, his problem-solving approach also requires an understanding of the various institutional and man-to-man relationships that influence human behavior in matters involving the ownership and use of land.

Content of Land Economics

Almost from the beginning, workers in land economics have assumed a broad definition of their field of endeavor. They have concerned themselves with all problems in which the land factor plays a significant or strategic role. Sometimes these problems involve resource developments and the economics of production. At times, they are concerned with the marketing, distribution, or consumption of land or its products; and in many instances they deal with questions of public policy. In their work with this wide range of subject matter, most land economists consider both the efficiency and the welfare goals of economics. Many, however, have tended to give more weight to the concept of social welfare than to that of strict economic efficiency.

The subject matter of land economics is often divided between two subfields: rural land economics and urban land economics. Where this division exists, rural land economics is usually considered as a phase of agricultural economics, while urban land economics is regarded as a branch of general economics or business. From a research standpoint, urban land economists have given most of their attention to the problems of housing, urbanization, urban land development and redevelopment, industrial and commercial location, and urban real estate marketing and finance. The rural land economists have concentrated on issues such as land and water utilization, land settlement and development, reclamation, land classification, land valuation, land market trends, land tenure, conservation, tax delinquency and land abandonment, land-use planning, zoning and land-use controls, and public land acquisition and management.

Organization of book. This volume deals with the political economy of urban and rural land-resource use. From the standpoint of overall organization, the chapters that follow are divided into four parts. Chapters 2, 3, and 4 deal mostly with the physical and biological framework and the effect it has upon the economic supply of land resources, the over-all demand for land and its products, and future land requirements.

Chapters 5 through 10 are concerned with the economic framework within which land resources are used. Consideration is given in these chapters to the economic roles that input-output relationships, land rent, resource development and conservation decisions, and location factors play in influencing decisions concerning land use and investments in land resources.

The institutional framework is examined in Chapters 11 through 15. Emphasis is given in these chapters to the general impact of institutional factors on land use, the nature of the rights people hold in property, and some of the land-tenure problems that arise with the acquisition, transfer, leasing, and mortgaging of land holdings.

Chapters 16, 17, and 18 deal with the social control of land use. Attention is given in these chapters to the nature of the land-resource planning process, to some leading measures that governments use in their direction of land use, and to the taxation of landed property.

SOME BASIC LAND ECONOMIC CONCEPTS

Like most fields, land economics has several specialized concepts and terms that one must understand if he is to appreciate their significance and usefulness as tools of analysis. Most of these concepts will be introduced and explained in the chapters that follow. At this point, however, special attention should be given to four basic land economic concepts: (1) the economic concept of land and land resources, (2) the classification of land uses by type, (3) the concept of land use-capacity, and (4) the concept of highest and best use.

Economic Concept of Land

The term "land" suggests different things to different people, depending upon their outlook and their interests at the moment. In its most widely accepted use, this term refers to the solid portion of the earth's surface. But it may also apply to a nation, a people, or a political division of the earth's surface. People often refer to ground, soil, or earth as land and speak of land as something on which they can walk, build a house, plant a garden, or grow a crop. These commonly accepted definitions of land should not be confused with the more technical concepts used by lawyers and economists.

From a legal standpoint, land (or real estate) may be considered as any portion of the earth's surface over which ownership rights might be exercised. These rights relate not just to surface area but also to things such as trees, which have been attached to the surface by nature, to buildings and other improvements attached by man, and to those objects of value that lie either above or below the surface.

Because of their concern over the distinction between land and capital, economists often differ in their opinions regarding the nature of land. Many economists accept broad definitions similar to those used by lawyers; others treat certain aspects of this broad concept as capital. For our purposes, the economic concept of land can be defined as *the sum total of the natural and man-made resources over which possession of the earth's surface gives control.*

This broad concept of land includes all of the earth's surface, water and ice as well as ground. In addition to building sites, farm soil, growing forests, mineral deposits, and water resources, it also involves such natural phenomena as access to sunlight, rain, wind, and changing temperatures and location with respect to markets and other areas. Moreover, it includes all those man-made improvements that are attached to the surface of the earth and cannot be easily separated from it.

Concepts of land. For illustrative and discussion purposes, this broad concept of land can be subdivided into several more limited but still overlapping concepts. Important among these are the concepts of land as (1) space, (2) nature, (3) a factor of production, (4) a consumption good, (5) situation, (6) property, and (7) capital.[3]

Land may be thought of as *space*—as room and surface within which and upon which life takes place. In this sense, land is fixed in quantity and

[3] Two other facets of land—concepts of land as a deity and land as a community—may also be noted. Some cultural groups view land as a deity that possesses itself and that can exercise certain inherent controls over the people who use it. [Cf. J. A. Umeh, *Development of a Land Market in Eastern Nigeria,* unpublished dissertation (Cambridge University, 1967).] Land also is associated in some areas with concept of a community or fatherland to which individuals have special responsibilities.

is indestructible because space cannot be destroyed or increased. Land as space includes not only the surface of the earth with the oceans, mountains, valleys, and plains, which provide physical support for man and his works, but also cubic space. Land thus involves the space beneath the surface within which minerals are found and from which they might be removed, the space that man occupies in his daily living, and the space above and about him.

When land is considered as *nature*, it may be identified rather closely with the natural environment. As such, it is conditioned by its access to sunlight, rainfall, wind, changing climatic conditions, and different evaporation, soil, and topographic conditions. Because of the past and present workings of nature, some areas are rich in soil, forest, fish, and other resources while other areas appear bleak and barren. Man can change or modify many of the characteristics of land as nature. Many of the basic features of this concept, however, still lie beyond the tampering hand of man.

Economists frequently refer to land along with labor, capital, and management as one of the basic factors of production. When land is considered as *a factor of production*, it is usually thought of as the nature-given source of the food, fibers, building materials, minerals, energy resources, and other raw materials used in modern society. This concept of land is closely allied to that of land as *a consumption good*. Land is often held and coveted not only because it adds directly to man's production but because it has value as a consumer's good in its own right. Building lots, parks, recreation and residential properties are frequently treated as consumption goods even though they might also be regarded as factors of production.

Considerable importance is attached in the modern world to the concept of land as *situation*. This concept involves location with respect to markets, geographic features, other resources, and other countries. It is significant not only because the value and use of most land is largely determined by its location and accessibility but also because of the strategic importance of the location factor in modern economic affairs and world politics.

The concept of land as *property* has legal connotations. It is concerned both with the areas over which individuals, groups, or sovereign powers exercise rights of ownership and use and with the nature of the rights and responsibilities they hold in land. This concept of land is important because of the strong conditioning effect it has on human attitudes and activities regarding land use all over the world. Property institutions change with time, but the institutions that prevail at any one time always exert a powerful influence upon our attitudes and actions regarding land.

Despite the fact that land is frequently regarded as a separate factor of production, it is often realistic to speak of land as *capital*. This situation arises because of the close relationship between the concepts of land and capital. From an economic standpoint, it is often difficult if not im-

Land Economics: A Study of Man and Land

possible to clearly distinguish between land and capital. Following the assertions of the early classical economists, one might say that land is a free gift of nature while capital is man-made and represents past savings and stored-up production, or that land is durable while capital tends to be expendable.

These distinctions are applicable in a broad sense, but they break down and tend to shade into each other when they are applied in marginal or twilight cases. One might ask, for instance, if one farm is land because its owner settled on productive soils while a second farm is capital because the owner started with poor soil and built up a productive farm unit. Similarly, one may question how free land actually is and how durable soil, forest, and mineral resources are in comparison with certain types of capital goods. The nature of this problem has led many economists to regard land as a species of capital while others assert that space and situation are the only singular characteristics of land.

Whether or not land should be clearly separated from capital is an academic issue and has no particular bearing upon the problem considered here. Suffice it to say that the characteristics of land are often very similar to those of capital. Land may be fixed in quantity, durable in nature, and a "free good" from the standpoint of society; but from the standpoint of the average investor, land must be purchased or leased like other capital goods. In this sense land is capital to the individual even though it may be viewed differently from the standpoint of society.

Land resources. Because of the frequent confusion and widespread lack of agreement regarding the precise meaning of the term "land" when applied in economics, it is often desirable to speak of land resources (or real estate) rather than land. With this substitution of terms, it is possible to clarify the general meaning of this central concept and at the same time avoid quibbling over details. As used here, the concept of *land resources* will be considered as roughly comparable to the economic concept of land and the legal concept of real estate described above. It represents a merging of the economic and legal concepts of land and definitely includes buildings and other capital improvements attached to the land as well as the natural characteristics of land.[4]

As a descriptive term in economics, "land resources" is both broader and narrower than "natural resources." It is broader because it includes all man-made improvements that are attached to land. "Natural resources" can involve a broader concept in that it includes all nature-given resources from the center of the earth to the highest heavens while the term "land resources," when treated as an economic concept, is limited to surface resources together with the thin layer of subsurface and suprasurface resources that man uses in his daily life.

[4]The terms "land" and "land resources" are used interchangeably throughout this book with no distinction as to meaning.

Principal Types of Land Use

Various classification schemes can be used to describe the principal types of land use found throughout the world. One of the more workable and more inclusive of these—and the system followed throughout this book—calls for the following tenfold classification of land uses:[5]

Residential lands	Mineral land
Commercial and industrial sites	Recreation land
Cropland	Transportation lands
Pasture and grazing land	Service areas
Forest land	Barren and waste

Residential lands and commercial and industrial sites account for most of the land area of cities but cover only a small proportion of the earth's surface. These uses and their various subclasses are particularly important in the modern world because they represent the areas where most people live and work and where most productive activity takes place. They involve the areas most subject to intensive human use and the sites of highest market value.

Because of their contributions to agricultural production, the next three of these classifications are often grouped together as agricultural uses. These types of land use account for by far the largest proportion of the total area that may be said to have economic value. Cropland includes all of the cultivated areas used in the production of food, feed, fibers, and other crops. As a land-use concept, it includes not only cropland harvested but also planted areas that have suffered from crop failure and cropland areas that are temporarily idle or fallow.

The concept of pasture and grazing land is somewhat more complicated because it really involves two types of land use—arable pasture plus range and grazing land. Arable pasture includes all those improved and rotation pasture areas that are considered plowable and that might easily be shifted into cropland use. Areas of this type frequently are interspersed with and sometimes rotated with croplands. As a result, these two uses overlap, and it is often desirable to treat them together under the designation of arable farm land.

[5] For other discussions of land use classification cf. Marion Clawson and Charles L. Stewart, *Land Use Information* (Baltimore: The Johns Hopkins Press and Resources for the Future, Inc., 1965), chaps. VII-VIII; *Standard Land Use Coding Manual,* Urban Renewal Administration and Bureau of Public Roads (Washington: Government Printing Office, 1965); *The Canada Land Inventory,* Canadian Department of Regional Economic Expansion Report No. 1, 2nd ed. (Ottawa, 1970); *A Review of the New York State Land Use and Natural Resources Inventory,* Cornell University Center for Aerial Photographic Studies, (Ithaca, 1970); and James R. Anderson, "Land-Use Classification Schemes," *Photogrammetric Engineering,* Vol. 37, April, 1971, pp. 379-87.

As one might expect, the concept of pasture land also overlaps with that of range and grazing land. The term "range" is ordinarily associated with the large, naturally vegetated, and often unfenced grazing lands found in the low-rainfall areas of the West. This term is also applied at times to natural grazing lands in other areas such as the South. Some range lands have a cropland potential, particularly if they can be irrigated; but most of them are best adapted to permanent grazing use. Generally speaking, the concept of range and grazing land applies to those lands that produce forage cover for grazing by domestic animals and game mammals, but which are generally unsuited for cultivation because of inadequate rainfall, rough topography, or high altitude. This subclassification includes not only range lands but also many smaller nonarable areas, such as the nonplowable rough pasture lands found on some farms.

Forest land includes the areas used for commercial timber production together with noncommercial woodlands, farm woodlots, cutover lands with a timber growth potential, and some brushland areas. This classification occasionally overlaps certain other agricultural uses. Grazed woodlands, for example, may be treated as either grazing or forest land. Similarly, a number of tree crops have value for food as well as for timber production purposes.

Aside from the residual class of barren and waste lands, most of the remaining types of land use might be grouped together as special-use areas. Mineral lands vary from open-pit sources of coal or iron ore to the much smaller surface areas required to support the operation of oil wells and underground mines. Recreation lands include parks, beaches, resort areas, racetracks, game preserves, and open space and scenic areas that are used largely for recreation and closely related purposes. Transportation lands include those areas used for highways, streets, alleys, parking purposes, railroads, airports, harbors, and wharves. The concept of service areas overlaps somewhat with other special-use areas but applies specifically to uses such as military reservations, prisons, cemeteries, reservoirs, and hydroelectric power sites.

It should be noted that this classification of land uses applies primarily to surface land. When it is remembered that the economic concept of land includes water as well as solid surface, an additional classification may be argued for water resources. The fact that the use of water for purposes such as irrigation, domestic and municipal water supplies, navigation, recreation, and power may be treated quite adequately under the existing classifications makes this new classification unnecessary.

Schemes for clear-cut classifications of land uses are often complicated by the presence of overlapping and multiple-use patterns. Most lands are used primarily for one purpose and accordingly can be classified as residential sites, cropland, or some other use. Many lands, however, are used simultaneously for more than one purpose. Many western lands, for example, are used for forestry purposes but at the same time have value for grazing, recreation, and watershed uses. Similarly, the site occupied by a hotel may be used primarily for residential purposes but at the same time provide commercial, recreation, transportation, and service-area facilities.

Clear-cut delineations of land-use types is often complicated by the complementary nature of most typical land-use patterns. Many areas enjoy natural and man-made advantages that favor their use for particular purposes. Man's need for different uses of land often causes combinations of uses to be found in close proximity to each other even in those areas where comparative advantage favors one type of land use above all others. Farmers in specialized crop production areas often use substantial acreages for other crops, pastures, woodlots, and for farmsteads, farm roads, and fence lines. Woodsmen and ranchers frequently carry on some arable farming even though their land is primarily suited for forestry or grazing. Similarly, most cities have large areas that are used for gardens, recreation, transportation, and service purposes as well as for residential, commercial, and industrial uses.

Land Use-Capacity

The concept of land use-capacity refers to the *relative ability of a given unit of land resource to produce a surplus of returns and/or satisfactions above its cost of utilization*. This concept applies to the productivity of given tracts or units of land when utilized for a given use at some assumed moment in time and with a given technology and given production conditions. The amount of net return or satisfactions secured provides an index of relative use-capacity. When these indices are compared for particular tracts or units of land resources, the concept of use-capacity provides a common measure of the quality or excellence of the units considered. For example, one might assume a comparison of three land areas of equal size, each of which is used for the same purpose. If the first area produces a net return of $50, the second $100, and the third $15, the second area naturally has the highest economic use-capacity.

Use-capacity has two major components—accessibility and resource quality. *Accessibility* involves the location of a land resource, its position with respect to markets and transportation facilities, and its site in relation to other land resources. It involves transportation and communication costs and time-distance considerations.

Resource quality involves the relative ability of a land resource to produce desired products, returns, or satisfactions. With agricultural lands, quality is usually viewed in terms of native fertility or fertility in combination with ability to respond to fertilizer inputs. Quality involves climatic advantages—temperature and precipitation levels, wind velocity, and frequency and severity of storms. It also involves esthetic considerations such as scenery, presence of trees and water attractions, nearness to parks or open space, access to schools and cultural opportunities. In urban areas, quality can include items such as functional area planning, attractiveness of neighborhoods, architectural styling of buildings, and other conditions that may favor or discourage land uses that give rise to net returns and satisfactions.

The concept of use-capacity is often used in land economics to distinguish between the comparative abilities of different units of land resources to provide their operators with net returns and other satisfactions. From an over-all point of view, this concept involves all the factors that affect the ability of a unit of land resource to produce a net return as compared with some other unit. In practice, however, it is often employed with examples that involve a single criterion of accessibility or quality—all other factors being assumed as constant. With discussions of the productivity of farm lands, for example, use-capacity is often identified with differences in fertility. In discussions of site location advantages, it is frequently associated with trasnportation costs. Similarly in examples involving urban location differences, use-capacity may be thought of in terms of the relative amounts of time and effort required to transport persons or things from particular sites to other sites such as the downtown business district.

Comparisons involving use-capacities assume a given instant of time. Observations based on particular comparisons can remain unchanged for long periods. Shifts take place, however, with changes in the resource base, changes in man's know-how, and changes in the uses to which he puts his land resources. Factors such as urban blight or the depletion of a mine, can downgrade the use-capacity of land while resource-development programs usually increase the use-capacity of particular resources. In similar fashion, new inventions, the building of railroads, and the development of new markets often raise the use-capacity of some lands— sometimes at the expense of others. Changing opportunities and the shift of land areas to new uses, such as the movement of land from farming to suburban residential use, also can have a marked effect upon observations of the relative use-capacities of individual properties.

Highest and Best Use

Most land areas are suited for a variety of uses. The areas found in the highest-value sections of central business districts, for example, could very well be used for forestry or grazing purposes, crop production, residential purposes, or commercial use. In the absence of a definite system indicating the importance-priorities of various types of land use, it is not unusual to find wide differences in individual choices concerning the uses to which different areas are put. As a general rule, however, land owners tend to use their land resource for those purposes that promise them the highest return. In this respect, they tend to allocate their land resources in accordance with the concept of highest and best use.

Land resources are at their highest and best use when they are used in such a manner as to provide the optimum return to their operators or to society. Depending upon the criteria used, this return may be measured in strictly monetary terms, in intangible and social values, or in some combination of these values. Land is ordinarily considered at its highest and best use when it is used for that purpose or that combination of purposes for which it has the highest comparative advantage or least comparative disadvantage relative to other uses. This concept necessarily calls for consideration of both the use-capacity of the land and the relative demand for the various uses to which it might be put. Large areas are sometimes suited for high-priority uses such as industrial or residential sites; but the limited need for these sites often causes many qualified tracts to find their highest and best use in lower-priority uses.

The highest and best use of any particular site is often subject to change. Like the concept of use-capacity, it can shift with changes in the quality of the land resource, with changes in technology, and with changes in the demand picture. Sometimes it is affected by zoning ordinances and other public policies. Under most circumstances, a certain amount of shifting also can be expected to take place in response to the bidding and counterbidding that goes on between various operators.

In modern society, land resources usually earn a higher return when used for commercial or industrial purposes than for any other type of use. As a result, these uses are often able to outbid other uses for almost any site. Residential uses ordinarily have next priority, followed by various types of cropland, pasture, grazing, and forest uses. This simple ordering of land uses suggests a definite profile such as that depicted in Figure 1-1 in which the highest-value lands at the center of our cities are used for

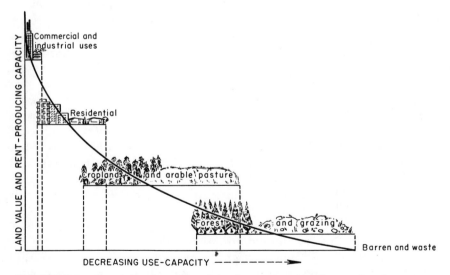

FIGURE 1-1. Generalized profile of land uses showing the overlapping ranges within which selected uses may be regarded as the highest and best use.

commercial purposes while the areas with successively lower values are used for residential, cropland, grazing, and forestry purposes, respectively.

Profiles of this type naturally represent a generalized average; and they are never as fixed or static as they may at first appear. To begin with, there are wide gradations within each type of use class, and there is a distinct tendency for the various use classes to overlap. Also, numerous exceptions can usually be found. Some industrial and commercial uses deliberately seek low-cost sites; and some residential uses such as apartment houses occasionally outbid commercial and industrial uses for particular sites. Similarly, in areas such as the oasis communities of the Sahara Desert where the supply of arable land is extremely limited, residential quarters may be located on the edge of the desert while the arable land they could occupy is used for food production purposes.

Considerable overlapping is found within the agricultural uses. The high productivity and value of some farm pastures together with the fact that they 'are usually intermingled with cultivated fields logically favors the combination of arable pasture with cropland as a type of land use. Arable farm land usually commands a higher priority than either grazing or forest land and accordingly has first claim on the areas suitable for these uses. The residual lands are then allocated between grazing or forest uses depending upon their location, natural cover, rainfall, and the needs for these uses. Both of these types of land use will upon occasion outbid some types of farming for the highest and best use of particular tracts. Similarly, with good management, they sometimes prove profitable on lands that could be classified as barren and waste.

Wide variations exist in the priorities associated with special-use areas. Mining sites often have a top priority, particularly when the prospects are good for their profitable use. Recreation lands vary from low-priority wilderness and residual areas to urban park areas that may be reclaimed or redeveloped at great expense. Lands used for transportation purposes may be low in value in some instances but involve considerable cost in the case of street-widening projects, new parking lot developments, or new metropolitan airport facilities. A similar wide range in use priorities applies to service areas. Some of these land uses, such as watershed protection areas, reservoirs, and hydroelectric power sites, are closely associated with special characteristics provided by nature. This gives these uses a first choice of these particular sites. Where competition exists for these lands, this may lead to high land values. Where less demand exists, site values may be low in spite of the high priorities claimed by particular uses.

Though the highest and best use of a given unit of land resource at any one time can usually be computed in monetary terms, differences of opinion frequently arise when weight is given to welfare considerations and nonmonetary satisfactions. One land owner may keep a forested area as a woodlot. His successor in ownership may choose to convert it into

BS TODAY!

farm land, residential lots, or possibly a public park. An individual may feel that his entire lot should be retained for residential or commercial purposes while a city may insist that part of it be given up for a street-widening project. One public-spirited group may insist that a virgin forest be maintained as a public park, while other groups may argue that it be cut to provide timber resources for a growing nation. These examples show that the concept of highest and best use is at most a relative concept. It provides a worthy objective in land use. But it is a goal that man must continually strive toward and one that he has little hope of ever attaining in an absolute sense.

GOAL IDENTIF PROBLEM

—SUGGESTED READINGS

Ely, Richard T., and George S. Wehrwein, *Land Economics* (Madison: The University of Wisconsin Press, 1964), Preface and pp. 25-28. Originally published by The Macmillan Company, 1940.

Johnson, V. Webster, and Raleigh Barlowe, *Land Problems and Policies* (New York: McGraw-Hill Book Company, Inc., 1954), chap. I.

Renne, Roland R., *Land Economics,* 2nd ed. (New York: Harper & Brothers, 1958), chap. I.

Salter, Leonard A., Jr., "The Content of Land Economics," *Journal of Farm Economics,* February, 1942, pp. 226-36.

2

The
Supply of Land
for Economic Use

Man has always evidenced a keen interest in his prospects for survival and for the future maintenance and improvement of his level of life. With this interest, it is only natural that questions should arise from time to time regarding the ability of our natural environment to supply the food and other raw materials needed by an expanding population.

Answers to the questions *will* the world be able to feed its people and *will* it provide them with higher levels of life always hinge upon economic, social, and political considerations. These answers necessarily start with the question of *can* the world meet its emerging requirements for food and other resources. This question concerns the long-run balance between our over-all capacity to produce and the sum total of our human needs. As such, it involves the interrelationship of the supply and demand factors that affect land resources; and its answers are found largely in the physical and biological framework within which land use takes place.

Most of the discussion in this chapter and the two chapters that follow centers on the physical and biological factors that affect the over-all supply and demand for various land resources. Our discussion begins with a general examination of the economic concepts of supply and demand—after which consideration is given to (1) some leading factors that affect the economic supplies of land, (2) the importance of the fixed location of land resources, and (3) the present land-use situation. The next two chapters continue this discussion by emphasizing the effects of population pressure and other related factors on the over-all demand for land resources and the nature of our future land requirements and our prospects for meeting them.

INTERRELATIONSHIPS OF SUPPLY AND DEMAND FACTORS

/PRICE

Supply and demand—these two concepts play a key role in economic thinking. At the same time, they also symbolize two basic aspects of the physical and biological framework. On the supply side, this framework is concerned with the quantity and quality of the land resources that are or can be made available for man's use. On the demand side, it is concerned both with the factors that affect the growing need for land and land products and with our ability to provide for these needs. In our discussion here, we will first examine the nature of the concepts of supply and demand as they involve land resources and then consider the principal factors that affect the interrelationship of these two concepts.

Concepts of Supply and Demand

Like many other common words used by economists, the terms "supply" and "demand" do double duty in the sense that they have been assigned more than one meaning. Economists often use these terms in a highly specialized sense.[1] Throughout our discussion, however, we will follow popular usage in speaking of supply as the *quantity of goods or resources available for use* and of demand as the *amounts of a commodity people want and are willing to buy.*

As we look at the supply side of the land-resource picture, two factors bear notice. The over-all supply of land resources is limited to the sum total of the resources provided by the earth's surface. The amounts of land resources available for use by individual operators, by nations, and by mankind as a whole, however, tend to vary with changing circumstances. This situation suggests need for a distinction between the physical and the economic concepts of supply.

When we speak of the *physical* supply of land, we are concerned with the physical existence of land resources. This concept of supply can be

---

[1] Economists frequently speak of "supply" as the schedule of amounts of a good or service sellers will offer on the market at different prices during any given time period, all other factors being equal. In similar fashion, the term "demand" is used to describe the schedule of amounts of a commodity buyers are willing to purchase at all possible prices during any given time period, all other factors being equal. These specialized concepts have their place in rigorous economic analysis. However, economists often revert to the popular usage of these terms (1) when they talk generally about amounts of goods or resources rather than specific supply or demand schedules, and (2) when they are concerned with supply or demand conditions over time or in periods during which other relevant conditions may change.

applied to particular resources, such as the physical supply of forests, mineral fuels, or areas with selected soil types. It can also be applied to area units, as when we speak of the sum total of the land resources found in individual ownership units, counties, nations, or the entire world.

The *economic* supply of land concerns only that portion of the physical supply that man uses. Land resources become a matter of economic significance whenever man shows sufficient interest in them to actually use them and whenever he exhibits a demand for their use, places a value upon them, or indicates willingness to undertake the costs involved in their development. The economic supply of land resources is responsive to price and demand factors, and it reflects the scarcity or abundance of physical land resources, their relative accessibility, and their general use-capacity. This supply can be expanded or contracted; and in an ultimate sense, it is limited only by the total physical supply of land.

The concept of demand is analogous to that of supply. As a strictly physical concept, the term "demand" is sometimes associated with desires, needs, or requirements for certain commodities and services. Concepts of *resource requirements*—need for better diets, more adequate housing, more school and recreation facilities, better highways, more parking space—often play an important role in program planning and in public social policy. They also affect the economic concept of demand. From an economic standpoint, however, this physical concept of demand has only limited value. The operation of the price system in allocating resources in the economy makes it necessary for us to emphasize *effective* demand—the willingness and ability of people to buy—rather than the mere existence of unsatisfied needs or desires for products.

As an additional refinement of the concept of demand, it should be noted that most demand for land resources involves a derived type of demand. People often compete for the ownership of particular tracts of land, such as building lots or farms. Except for possible sentimental attachments, however, they are usually interested in the productive potential of land or in its location, scenery, or other advantages rather than in the land itself. Most of us want land resources because they represent a means to an end. We want them because they offer opportunities for income and employment, because they supply our needs for food and housing, and because they open the way for the realization of various human satisfactions.

Interaction of Supply and Demand

Though the factors of supply and demand are often treated separately, they normally operate in close conjunction with each other. It is the interaction of these factors that gives us the concept of a market. Under free market conditions, it is through this interaction that prices are established.

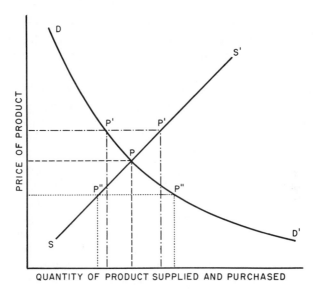

FIGURE 2-1. Interaction of supply and demand factors in determining market prices under free market conditions.

This situation can be illustrated by a model such as that depicted in Figure 2-1. In this model, the supply curve *SS′* represents a schedule of the increasing quantities of a product sellers would offer in the market at some given time at a series of rising price levels. The demand curve *DD′* in turn represents the schedule of increasing quantities of the product buyers would take in the same market at the same time at a series of decreasing prices. With these supply and demand schedules, the only possible equilibrium price occurs at *P,* the point of intersection between *SS′* and *DD′.* At this price, the quantity of product offered and the quantity buyers are willing to purchase are equal. If the price were set at a higher point such as *P′,* the sellers would be willing to supply a larger quantity of product, but some buyers would take less and some would probably drop out of the market. With a lower price such as *P″,* the reverse situation would hold.

Under real market conditions, supply and demand factors usually tend to follow the model of the perfect market. Complications often arise, however, because of variations in the knowledge and market expectations of individual buyers and sellers and because of the linkage and inter-dependence of various factors in the economy. Variations from this model also come with differences in the elasticity of supply and the elasticity of demand. These concepts measure the relative response of various levels of supply and various levels of demand to price changes within their respective supply and demand schedules.[2] By indicating the relative

[2] A supply or demand is said to be *elastic* when a given change in price results in a more-than-proportionate change in the quantity of product supplied or purchased. When a given price change results in less than a proportionate change in quantity, the supply or demand is *inelastic.*

location and slope of the supply and demand schedules (or curves) found in various markets, they help to indicate both the points of price intersection between supply and demand and the quantities of product sold at these points.

The concepts of elasticity of supply and elasticity of demand are most meaningful when they are applied to products produced for a definite market. In this respect, they have far more application to land products such as wheat, milk, or coal than to particular types of land resources. The supplies of most types of land are responsive to price changes. When prices are high relative to costs and the market outlook is favorable, grazing lands are often plowed for wheat production, new mines are opened up, new subdivisions are brought in, and considerable sums are ordinarily spent on housing and other construction projects. When prices drop, land uses are sometimes abandoned and areas often shift to lower uses. Despite this relationship, however, the supply response of most types of land to price changes is definitely inelastic. It is a rare occasion when a short-run price-prompted addition to the economic supply of any type of land accounts for more than a minor portion of its total supply.

A similar condition arises with the elasticity of demand. This situation exists because most people have somewhat limited and routine demands and needs for most land resources. The demand for cemetery lots seldom extends beyond one lot per person. The range of man's needs for the land areas used to produce food and living space are limited even though he often demands more and better food and living accommodations when incomes are high than when they are low.

Over-All Supply and Over-All Demand

The foregoing discussion of the interaction of supply and demand centers mainly on the market activities of buyers and sellers. These activities have an important impact upon the operation of the price and market system. Most discussions of land resources are less concerned with these activities than they are with the quantity and quality of the land resources available for society's use over time and with society's changing need and demand for these resources. Unlike the concepts of supply and demand schedules, these over-all concepts of supply and demand are often used without specific assumptions as to time, place, or level of technology. Their relationships with other factors are often vague and accordingly differ from those experienced by the individuals, firms, and groups of firms that operate as buyers and sellers in the world's markets.

The concept of over-all supply can be used to indicate the sum total of the economic supplies of various types of land resources. One can also speak of the over-all demand for various types of land resources. With both of these concepts it is usually meaningful to distinguish between different types of land resources. Thus, one can speak of the over-all supply of crop or forest land and of the over-all demand for housing or for recreation areas.

Secular supply relationships are sometimes visualized for different types of land use. These relationships ordinarily call for assumptions concerning (1) the relative demand for the particular type of land use, (2) the total area already devoted to this use, (3) the approaching physical limit on the total area suited to this use, (4) the impact of competing uses on the availability of lands for this use, and (5) the costs associated with new land developments. With assumptions concerning these items, it is possible to visualize secular or long-run supply curves for particular types of land resources such as the secular supply curve for agricultural land hypothesized in Figure 2-2.

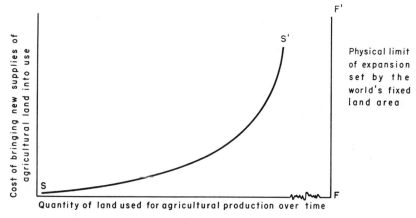

FIGURE 2-2. Long-run supply curve for agricultural land (assuming a fairly uniform rate of population increase and gradual but steady improvements in technology over time).

In this particular example, the secular supply curve *SS′* indicates the increasing quantity of land that will be brought into agricultural use over time assuming a fairly uniform rate of population increase and gradual but relatively steady improvements in technology. Along the early portion of this curve, the supply tends to be elastic. This situation exists because only a small total area is already in agricultural use, a relatively plentiful supply of land is naturally adapted to this use, and large additions can be made to the total economic supply with little increase in developmental costs. This supply becomes more and more inelastic, however, as the better lands are brought into use and as the relative cost of developing new farm lands increases. An ultimate limit on the quantity of land that can be added to the economic supply (represented by the line *FF′*) is always set by the world's fixed land area. The rising cost of new land developments discourages further additions to the economic supply long before this limit is reached.

Shifts in the over-all supply situations for the various land uses are often prompted by changes in demand. The extent and nature of the over-all demand for each type of land and its products varies at every point along the secular supply curve. Generally speaking, these changing demand conditions reflect the current situation regarding population numbers, income levels, individual needs and choices, and the impact of technology both in stimulating additional demand and in providing possible substitutes.

FACTORS AFFECTING THE ECONOMIC SUPPLY OF LAND RESOURCES

The quantity of land resources available for particular uses at any given time ordinarily depends upon the interaction of a variety of factors. Emphasis is given here to four major types of factors that play significant roles in conditioning and determining the economic supplies of land that are available for different uses. These include the natural physical characteristics of land and the economic, institutional, and technological settings within which land-resource use takes place.

Natural Limits on the Land Supply

Nature has provided man with a vast resource heritage. But the gifts of nature are not scattered evenly; and as often as not, they are cloaked with characteristics that tax the ingenuity of man. In his age-old effort to find, develop, and utilize new land resources, man has often found that he must cope with the problems of uneven resource distribution and unfavorable climate, topography, and location.

He has also found that the resources of different areas vary both in their natural characteristics and in their general use-capacities. These variations usually stem from differences in (1) sunlight and temperature, (2) precipitation and access to water supplies, (3) topography and drainage, (4) soil conditions, subsurface strata, and presence of minerals, and (5) physical location with respect to markets and transportation facilities.

Limitations involving these characteristics definitely limit the area suited for particular uses. Fortunately, however, man has found that the purposes for which he uses land vary almost as much in their need for particular land characteristics as do the characteristics of the land resource base with which he works. Thanks to this happy circumstance, most of the earth's surface has potential value for some use or group of uses, although the total area suited for any one use is often quite limited.

Agricultural uses. Almost all of the earth's surface affords sufficient access to sunlight to permit some type of crop, range, or forest use.

Optimum use of this possible access to sunlight, however, is prevented by temperature extremes—primarily by the problem of short growing seasons and unseasonable frosts. Baker has estimated that around one-fourth of the earth's land surface is too cold for wheat culture.[3] Much of this area has value for forestry purposes as is attested by the northern forests of Alaska, Canada, the Scandinavian countries, and the Soviet Union. Some of it also has commercial value for summer range, for the pasturing of sheep and cattle, and for the provision of forage for wildlife and reindeer. Yet large areas such as the icy expanses of the Arctic and Antarctic must be written off as waste so far as current agricultural use is concerned.

The supply of moisture for plant use also presents a varied picture. Pearson and Harper have indicated that only 34 percent of the world's land area enjoys both an adequate and reliable supply of rainfall, and that only 200 million acres—considerably less than 1 percent of the world's surface land area—benefits from irrigation.[4] Baker's estimates show that only 11 million square miles, 20 percent of the earth's land surface, have suitable temperature and moisture conditions to permit wheat culture.[5] Of the 41 million square miles with suitable temperature conditions for wheat, Baker found that 17 million were too dry while 13 million were too wet for wheat culture.

Most of the world's cropland is found in areas that boast both an adequate and a relatively reliable supply of plant moisture. Large areas with these characteristics still await development for agricultural use in many parts of the world. Yet rather than reach out to these lands, man has often found it convenient to use other lands less favorably endowed by nature. Large areas in the United States, for example, have been opened up for wheat culture in the drier sections of the Great Plains even though the prospect of frequent crop failures makes farming in these areas a high-risk enterprise.

In adapting themselves to the problems of too much or too little

---

[3] Cf. O. E. Baker, "The Potential Supply of Wheat," *Economic Geography*, Vol. 1, March, 1925, p. 31; also O. E. Baker, "The Population Prospect in Relation to the World's Agricultural Resources," *Maryland,* alumni publication of the University of Maryland, 1947. Baker indicated that only 41 million square miles, 79 percent of the earth's surface area, excluding the polar continents, had temperature conditions suitable for wheat production. When his calculations are adjusted to include the polar areas, it appears that 25.5 per cent of the earth's surface area is too cold for wheat.

[4] Cf. Frank A. Pearson and Floyd A. Harper, *The World's Hunger* (Ithaca: Cornell University Press, 1945), pp. 27-28. They define an adequate and reliable supply of rainfall as a minimum of 15 inches of precipitation annually in temperate areas (40 inches in equatorial areas of high evaporation) varying from year to year by less than 20 percent from the normal average. They found that 79 percent of Europe, 70 percent of South America, 38 percent of North America, 29 percent of Asia, 25 percent of Africa, and only 9 percent of Oceania enjoy both an adequate and reliable supply of rainfall.

[5] Cf. Baker, *loc. cit.,* pp. 27 and 31.

moisture, farmers have found that wet lands can be used productively for the culture of water-loving crops, such as rice, and for forestry. Summer-fallowing practices can be used in the more arid regions to store two years' precipitation in the ground for use during a single crop season. Irrigation developments can be used to bring water to large areas with inadequate supplies of moisture for normal crop growth. And many areas considered unsuited for cultivation can be used for ranching and grazing.

Much of the land area climatically suited for crop use is too hilly, mountainous, steep, or rough for successful cultivation. Pearson and Harper have indicated that only 64 percent of the world's land has favorable topography for crop use, while Baker estimates that 4 of the 11 million square miles of earth surface climatically available for wheat culture are unfit for this use because of hilly or rough land.[6] Extensive terracing programs are used in many rough land areas to augment the limited supply of agricultural land. Mountainsides in Southeast Asia are often covered with small patches and fields that have been reclaimed in this manner. Similar conditions exist in some of the Andes valleys of Peru where the ordering of successive tiers of terraces along the mountainsides suggests what is sometimes called "staircase farming." This type of development calls for large expenditures of capital, time, and effort. Where these expenditures are economically impractical, steep, rough, and mountainous areas often find a residual use in either forestry or grazing.

The soils that cover the earth's surface vary considerably in color, structure, texture, physical constitution, chemical composition, and in their other natural characteristics. They range from light-colored soils to black earth, from heavy clay to sand and gravel, from shallow soils to deep formations, from soils that tend to be acid to those that are alkaline, and from soils that provide plants with little more than space and foundation to soils of high inherent productive capacity. Agricultural uses vary somewhat in their soil requirements; but most crops are responsive to fertile and productive soils. The same may be said of grazing and forest uses, even though these uses are often relegated to the less fertile and less desirable lands.

Pearson and Harper have indicated that around 46 percent of the earth's surface is covered with "good soils," which are suitable for crop use.[7] This estimate may be taken as a general measure of the world's soil characteristics. It must be remembered, however, that soil conditions vary a great deal, that the supply of the more productive soils is relatively limited, that man is continually drawing upon less and less fertile areas, and that the decision as to what is "good soil" involves value judgments that may change with time and circumstances. Furthermore, the require-ment of "good soils" for cropland use is not an unwavering one because

---

[6] Pearson and Harper, *op. cit.*, p. 42; and Baker, *loc. cit.*, pp. 28 and 31.
[7] Pearson and Harper, *op. cit.*, p. 46.

numerous soil deficiencies can be overcome with fertilization, soil-building practices, irrigation, draining, and other measures.

Urban uses. Climate, topography, and soils have an all-important effect upon the use of land for agriculture. The location factor also is important, particularly in cases of commercial crop production, but it is of little significance in the absence of a suitable physical resource base. Almost the reverse situation applies with urban uses. Climatic and soil conditions ordinarily play a relatively minor role in limiting the supplies of land available for these uses. Location factors in turn usually have a dominant effect upon both the rise of cities and the allocation of land uses within cities.

Urban growth usually requires a strong commercial, trade, or industrial base. This calls for locating cities near sources of raw materials and near the consumers who will eventually buy and consume the products processed in cities. Since agriculture has long provided a high proportion of the raw materials used in cities plus a market for processed and manufactured goods, it is only natural that most urban centers are found in or near areas also used for agricultural purposes. Sites around harbors, along navigable streams and railroads, and in other spots that offer natural trade advantages also provide favored locations for cities.

As human beings, most of us prefer to live in areas that are neither too hot nor too cold for agricultural use. From a strictly functional standpoint, however, urban areas are not subject to the same range of climatic controls as crops. Sunshine is desirable; but numerous urban functions are carried on with the use of artificial light. Access to water supplies is necessary; but most cities could get along quite well without torrential rains, snow, sleet, or fog.

As long as the subsurface strata provide a firm foundation for buildings and other structures, soil conditions usually have little bearing on the use of urban land. True, most home owners want productive soils for their lawns and flower beds. Quite frequently their original topsoil is covered with subsoil deposits in the building process, and they finally resort to the purchase of topsoil from outside sources.

Topography is the one natural factor that does have an important impact upon the location and desirability of urban residential, commercial, and industrial sites. Residential and other property owners usually prefer high and well-drained sites to low-lying areas that may be subject to occasional floods. Yet important as this preference factor may be, many cities have been built in low, swampy areas, and considerable urban property still suffers from occasional flood damage. In many established cities, high land values have made it practicable to drain, dike, or fill low-lying areas so that they might be developed for commercial and residential uses.

Mountainous and rough terrain may also discourage the use of land for urban purposes. But building and public works contractors have shown remarkable ability to smooth rough areas, fill in or bridge gullies, and either move hills and mountains or capitalize upon the altitude and site advantages they afford. Cities such as Pittsburgh and San Francisco provide excellent examples of areas of rough terrain that have been developed for urban use.

Recreation uses. Recreation areas differ more in their natural characteristics than most types of land use. High values are ascribed to such diverse features as desert sand dunes, underground caverns, mountain lakes, wilderness areas, fishing streams, hunting marshes, pleasant country vistas, warm ocean beaches, tropical splendors, winter wonderlands, pollen-free air during the summer, and dry desert air during the winter.

As one might expect, the most intensively used recreation lands are found in and around metropolitan centers. Municipal parks, playgrounds, gymnasiums, athletic fields, swimming pools, golf courses and sports palaces ordinarily are located where they are primarily because of their proximity to large numbers of people. This same factor helps explain the location of many other public and private recreation developments. In the selection of recreation sites, emphasis is usually given to the development or provision of characteristics that appeal to potential users. Scenic wonders and sites of historical significance have definite advantages along this line. Other desirable characteristics include items such as a variety of flora and fauna; water resources that permit swimming, boating, fishing, and other recreation uses; and a favorable climate for the type of development contemplated.

Transportation, service-area, and mining uses. Location and topography are the most important natural characteristics that affect the use of land for transportation purposes. Harbor and dock facilities are found where nature provides the best natural sites or where population and other pressures dictate that man-made harbors should exist. Most airports, railroads, streets, and highways are located where it is hoped they will facilitate commerce or convenience. Large bodies of water and mountainous or rough terrain often make it expedient to direct roads over something other than the shortest or most direct route between points. But while barriers of this type complicate transportation developments, they seldom prevent the linking of cities and other centers. Rain, snow, sleet, and fog conditions can create transportation-use problems; but it is a rare occasion when these factors play more than a minor role in influencing the location of transportation routes.

Service areas call for a wide variety of natural characteristics. Urban-associated uses, such as public buildings, cemeteries, and water-filtering areas, must usually be located within or at least close to the cities they serve. These uses ordinarily call for well-drained locations. City dumps, on the other hand, can use low-lying areas and areas of rough terrain. Other service areas such as military reservations may involve sizable tracts of land that have been deliberately selected because of their location, type of climate, tree or plant cover, or topography. Multiple-use areas, such as reservoir sites and watershed areas, may also call for particular rainfall, soil, land-cover, and topographic conditions and in many cases represent the only sites available for these uses.

Of the various types of land use, mineral lands are the least dependent upon favorable location, climate, topography, and soils. Mining activity takes place in locations where commercial deposits of mineral resources are known or believed to exist. Because of the potential value and need for mineral resources, it is often economic to go to the far ends of the earth for them. As a result, oil wells and mining camps may be located far from the industrial centers of modern civilization, and pipelines may be laid or railroads may be built across hundreds of miles of desolate territory. Location and accessibility factors may prevent the development of mineral and energy resources, however, if the potential supply does not promise sufficient return to more than pay for the cost of their capture and transportation to market.

Other Factors Affecting Supplies

Natural characteristics determine the physical suitability of resources for various uses. Within the limits set by these characteristics, economic, institutional, and technological factors usually play dominant roles in determining the actual amounts of land resources that will be used at any given time. More detailed attention will be given to the roles played by these factors in future chapters. A few comments are in order at this point, however, concerning the impact these factors have upon land resource supplies.

Importance of economic factors. Land resources become a matter of economic significance whenever people begin to use them, compete with others for their use or control, put a price or value on them, or assume the costs associated with their development—in short, whenever they become the subject of economic demand. These same concepts—demand, price, cost, and competition—also have an important effect upon the extent and nature of the supplies of various types of land resources.

In his use of land for agriculture and other purposes, man is naturally inclined to make first use of those areas with the highest use-capacity for his intended use. His need for additional land products causes him to gradually resort to the use of lower and lower grades of land. Higher product prices are needed to cover the higher production costs per output unit encountered on the lower-quality lands. Those buyers who want more products bid market prices up to the level necessary to bring forth the production they need; and these higher prices logically lead both to more intensive use of the existing supply of developed land and to the addition of new areas to the total supply.

Most programs that add to the economic supplies of land call for the development and use of the less productive, less favorably located, and harder-to-develop lands. When the pressure for new land development is strong enough, drainage, irrigation, terracing, and greenhouse practices are used to "create" agricultural lands, and leveling, filling, landscaping, and multistory building practices are used to "create" urban and recreation sites. Each of these types of development has its price tag, and its feasibility always depends upon the willingness of buyers and of society to pay the market prices and possible subsidies associated with this cost.

Competition between individuals and between land uses also has its effects on the land-resource supply picture. It is the bidding and counterbidding that goes on between different buyers and users of land resources that provides the basis for land values and land-product prices. This competition, or the lack of it, is often responsible for the chain of causation that leads to an expanding or contracting land supply.

In this bidding and counterbidding between individual operators and uses, resources normally go to those operators and those uses that offer the highest prices and enjoy the greatest prospects for their remunerative use. From an over-all standpoint, the supply of land resources available to each individual operator is limited only by his willingness and ability to pay the going price asked for the resources he needs. In actual practice, however, individuals are often forced to use fewer or lower-quality resources than they desire because they lack adequate financing or because they have only limited opportunities to make optimum use of the resources they could acquire through the bidding process.

Much the same situation applies in the competition between various types of land use. No serious supply problem develops as long as each type of land use can expand without impinging upon the areas used for other purposes. But real problems arise as soon as conflicting uses begin to compete for the same land areas. At this point, the more highly valued and economically more productive uses usually take precedence, thus crowding the lower-priority uses into outlying or lower-quality areas.

Once the maximum amount of land has been brought into use, any continued expansion of the areas put to urban, cropland, and other high-premium uses must come at the expense of the residual areas previously put to grazing, forestry, wilderness, and other lower-priority uses. In this respect, continued expansion of the high-priority uses inevitably leads to a diminution of the secular supplies of land resources available for lower uses.

Institutional determinants of supply. In addition to the physical and economic factors listed above, institutional factors also have an important impact upon the supplies of land resources. These factors involve several aspects of our culture and of group action such as custom, government, law, public opinion, and the concept of property rights. Their impact can best be illustrated by a few simple examples.

Much of our incentive for the development, maintenance, and improvement of land resources is rooted in the concept of property rights. This concept provides the complex of rules and procedures under which property is owned, leased, mortgaged, and legally transferred to others. As such, it underlies the whole existence and operation of our economic system.

Another far-reaching example of the impact institutional factors have upon land supplies is often found in the activities of government. A series of favorable land laws stimulated the early settlement and development of the lands along the western frontier of the United States and Canada. Reclamation projects, protective tariffs, farm and home credit programs, flood control, and urban renewal and highway construction programs are examples of the measures governments can use to promote the development and expansion of certain types of land use. Zoning ordinances and building codes are used in many communities to guide and control future land-use development. Still other measures involving restrictive legislation, repressive taxation, acreage controls, and court injunctions can be used to limit particular land-use practices and to stimulate the shift of certain areas to new uses.

Laws often limit the opportunities some individuals have to control, exploit, and use land resources while they may expand and enlarge the opportunities available to others. Customary practices such as the medieval two- and three-field system of community crop culture can discourage the use of improved farming methods and even the bringing of new areas into use. Other practices such as the widespread use of coffee and tea may require the use of large areas for the production of these products. Public opinion also can serve as an institutional factor in stimulating interest in environmental quality, in resource conservation programs, and in the public acquisition of recreation areas.

Another land-supply problem with institutional ramifications involves the impact some types of land developments have upon the utilization and value of adjacent properties. Large public buildings, parks, and church properties frequently provide buffer areas for urban commercial districts and in reality constitute barriers to the further extension of commercial developments in their directions. Cemeteries, parks, and college campuses sometimes contain or regiment the growth of cities by forcing them to develop in different directions than they logically would if these tracts were available for private use and development. The proximity of railroad yards and industrial districts also discourages certain types of urban development and at times contributes to the blighting of already developed neighborhoods.

Impact of technological factors. Most of the value we ascribe to land resources is directly related to our ability to use them. In this sense, the economic supplies of land resources always reflect the current level of technological development. With his limited know-how, primitive man had no conception of the worth of iron, coal, and petroleum and accordingly placed no economic value upon these resources. He valued fertile valleys mostly for hunting purposes until he learned the art of agriculture.

Technological developments have a tremendous impact upon the interaction of supply and demand. They often give rise to new demands and help stimulate the search for new land-resource supplies. They affect the extent and nature of our economic supplies of various resources by pointing the way for the fuller and more extended use of existing supplies and by facilitating the discovery and development of new sources of supply. At times, they also provide substitutes that may enhance the value of some resources while reducing the need for others.

Numerous examples can be cited to illustrate the impact changing technology has had on various land supplies. The steam engine revolutionized industry, increased the demand for coal and other raw materials, and stimulated the growth and expansion of many cities. Railroad building programs have opened many remote areas for commercial cropland, forestry, and other uses. The cotton gin made cotton production economically practicable and prompted the widescale development of new areas for this purpose. Improved oil drilling techniques paved the way for the rise of the automobile industry; and this development in turn prompted an increased demand for oil and mineral resources and for more and better highways. The substitution of steel girders for solid masonry construction permitted an expansion of the supplies of usable space in downtown commercial areas by making it possible for buildings to rise above a six- to ten-story maximum height.

Technology, in meeting the problem of scarce supplies, has frequently provided substitutes superior to the products replaced. The use of coal and petroleum products has freed us from much of our earlier dependence upon water power. The development of the synthetic dye industry during the late 1800s virtually wiped out the market for the two million acres that had been used to produce indigo and madder, the age-old sources for blue and red dyes. In similar fashion, our use of automobiles, trucks, and farm tractors has freed some 80 million acres in the United States that were once used to produce feed for horses and mules.

IMPORTANCE OF THE FIXED-LOCATION FACTOR

One of the most fundamental characteristics of land is its fixed location in space. Particular land resources such as mineral deposits, soil, forest products, and houses may be moved about; but land as space remains fixed, immobile, and industructible. As Alfred Marshall has indicated:

> ... the fundamental attribute of land is its extension. ... The area of the earth is fixed; the geographic relations in which any particular part of it stands to other parts are fixed. Man has no control over them; they are wholly unaffected

by demand; they have no cost of production; there is no supply price at which they can be produced.[8]

This fixed-location characteristic has an important impact upon the supply of land available for economic use. Evidence of this importance may be seen in the manner in which it (1) affects human decisions regarding the value and use-capacity of various sites; (2) influences land-utilization practices; (3) facilitates private ownership and ties land values, uses, and ownership conditions to the local environment; and (4) affects the legal description of properties.

Economic Location

As has been mentioned, location and accessibility often play an important role in determining the uses for which various tracts of land are suited. This situation springs largely from three factors: (1) the fact that man prefers and usually finds it more profitable to concentrate his use efforts on some portions of the earth's surface rather than on others; (2) the need for expending time, effort, and material supplies in providing transportation facilities to bridge the fixed geographic or spatial relationships that separate various areas; and (3) the effect the principle of diminishing returns has in forcing man to spread his productive activities over extensive areas of land.[9]

Whenever groups of individuals start to use or show a preference for using certain areas, these sites acquire economic significance. Man's original choice of one area over another is usually associated with natural or man-made advantages such as soil fertility, location near a harbor or water-power site, or location along a railroad or near a good market area. The fact that many people recognize these advantages and have enough regard for these sites to compete for their use gives them economic value. In this process, human choice is combined with physical location to create situs or economic location.[10]

The concept of economic location assumes that some areas enjoy locational advantages over others. This advantage often involves savings in transportation costs and time; and it stems partly from the fact that the law of diminishing returns makes it both physically impossible and economically impracticable for man to produce all his market goods at

---

[8]Alfred Marshall, *Principles of Economics,* 8th ed. (New York: The Macmillan Company, 1938), pp. 144-45.

[9]The operations of this principle are discussed in Chapter 5.

[10]Cf. H. B. Dorau and A. G. Hinman, *Urban Land Economics* (New York: The Macmillan Company, 1928), pp. 167-69; also Richard T. Ely and George S. Wehrwein, *Land Economics* (Madison: The University of Wisconsin Press, 1964), p. 65. Originally published by The Macmillan Company, 1940.

points adjacent to a central market. Location advantages also result from the higher productivity and lower production costs associated with particular sites.

Since most sites can accommodate only one use at a time, competition naturally exists for their possession and control. Under free market conditions, this control usually goes to those uses with the highest prospects for profit and the highest capacity to bid up market values. This bidding and counterbidding process goes on continuously. It tends to assign economic values to different areas and in so doing indicates that some areas are regarded as prime spots for certain types of economic activity. In urban areas, the prime spots for commercial activity are frequently referred to as "100 percent" spots.

Economic location or situs involves location with respect to other economic factors. For the businessman, this usually means location with respect to the 100 percent spot—the spot where he might expect the biggest flow of customers and trade and thus the highest profit. For the agricultural producer, it usually means location with respect to market; for the urban resident, it may mean location with respect to employment opportunities; and for industry, it means location with respect to both the sources of supply and the consumers' market.

Effects of Location on Land Utilization

It is difficult to discuss the effect of fixed location upon land utilization without making some cross reference to the economic factors that affect intensity of land use, competition between land uses, and the location of enterprises.[11] However, this relationship can be viewed in physical as well as economic terms. When production sites are located at varying distances from market and from the homes of their operators, differential advantages arise because of the time, trouble, and effort involved in commuting to and from these sites and in transporting supplies to the sites and produce to market. Possibilities for saving time and avoiding unnecessary physical effort favor the location of those uses that call for considerable commuting near the homes of their operators. Similarly, those uses that involve the hauling of heavy, bulky, or perishable products are frequently located near the market.

Von Thunen's model. One of the first analyses of the relationship between differences in spatial location and land-utilization patterns was developed by Johann Heinrich von Thunen, a German land owner and economist, in his book *Der isolierte Staat,* written in 1826. Von Thunen illustrated this concept by assuming the case of an isolated state with a single European-type village or city located in the midst of a level pro-

---

[11] These subjects will be discussed in Chapters 5, 6, and 9, respectively.

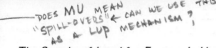
ductive plain, which in turn is surrounded by a wilderness area that separates it from other markets.[12]

In his model, von Thunen assumed not only an isolated state (which freed his example from the possible effects of other city markets) and a village type of settlement (with most of the farm families living in the central city rather than in the open country) but also uniform climate and soils, uniform topography, and relatively uniform transportation facilities. Since railroads and superhighways were not as yet known, he assumed that the products produced around the city would be hauled to market in horse- or ox-drawn wagons, be carried by man, or be driven in the case of livestock.

Except for location and distance to market, von Thunen's analysis held constant all of the natural factors affecting land use. Differences in land use could be attributed directly to variations in transportation costs. These in turn were dependent upon such factors as distance to market, ease of transportation, and bulk, weight, and perishability of the products sent to market. The land-use pattern envisaged by von Thunen (Figure 2-3A) assumed that lands near the market would be used in an intensive

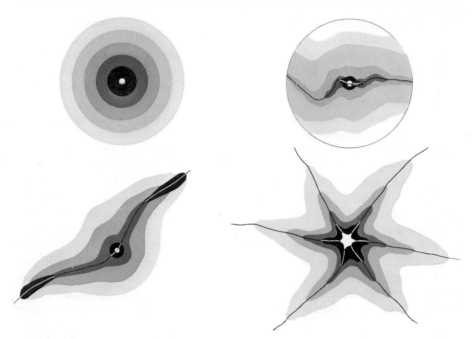

FIGURE 2-3. Modified presentation of von Thunen's theory of the relationship between resource location and land utilization.

[12]One of the earliest discussions of von Thunen's concepts in English appears in Ely and Wehrwein, *op. cit.,* pp. 66-71. The first English translation of his work was published in 1966. Cf. Peter Hall, ed., *Von Thunen's Isolated State* (London: Pergamon Press, 1966).

manner and would be used to produce crop and livestock products that are highly perishable or heavy and bulky to transport. Because of the tendency for wagon transportation costs to increase with distance, the lands located farther away would suffer an economic handicap that would dictate their use for enterprises involving lower transportation costs.

Following von Thunen's line of reasoning, one might assume that the first concentric zone around the city would be used mostly for gardens, truck crops, and some of the facilities needed for stall-fed milk cows and laying hens. This use is appropriate because the area would be subject to intensive use, would be visited frequently, and a high proportion of the products would probably be carried to the city by man. This zone grades into a second zone, which in von Thunen's time would have been used for the production of forest products. Though this use may seem unusual today, it must be remembered that forest products provided both fuel and a source of building materials. And since this product is both bulky and heavy to haul, it seemed important that it be produced near the city.

Immediately beyond the forest zone the land would be used for the more intensively cultivated field crops—for bulky and heavy crops such as potatoes, root crops, and hay, and for grain grown in rotation with these crops. As one works out to and through zone 4, more and more land would be planted to cereal grains or would be used for fallow or pasture. Zone 5 would be used primarily for grazing purposes, with the sheep and cattle produced or fed in this area being driven to market. Finally, the surrounding wilderness area might be classified as a sixth zone with possible value for hunting.

Von Thunen's simple model can be modified by adjustments in its many assumptions. For example, if one assumes that a navigable stream flows through the "isolated state," the opportunity for water transportation may very well bring changes in land utilization. With some series of uses, each zone may be expected to take on the elongated pattern suggested in Figure 2-3B. With the example described above, however, zone 1 would probably remain pretty much unchanged, while it would become practicable to center the areas used for forest production along the navigable stream at greater distance from the city (Figure 2-3C). The introduction of additional improved transportation routes, as in Figure 2-3D, would lead to star-shaped land-utilization patterns. Still other adjustments are needed when one relaxes von Thunen's assumptions to allow differences in fertility, topography, the number of city markets, or variations in the settlement pattern.[13]

Von Thunen's concept clearly illustrates the effect transportation facilities and location with respect to market can have upon land-utilization practices. Naturally many of the transportation problems of von Thunen's time have been simplified by the development of railroads, automobiles, trucks, modern highways, and other travel and transport

[13]These adjustments are discussed in more detail in chapter 9.

facilities. By speeding up the transportation process and by reducing transport costs, these developments have made it economic to use many areas for production purposes, which would not have been practicable in times past. These changes, however, have not shaken the significance of von Thunen's conclusions regarding the importance of transportation costs as a factor affecting the allocation of land uses. As Ely and Wehrwein have observed:

> No matter how much transportation is perfected it can never become instantaneous, effortless, or costless. There will always be a cost of overcoming friction, gravitation, and loss of time in moving goods and people. Farmers near a city will always have some advantage over those farther from the market who are raising the same crops and who have identical transportation facilities. . . . The distance from which people can commute comfortably is still a matter of time, convenience, and costs, complicated many times by the congestion caused by modern transportation.[14]

Effects on Ownership and Community Ties

The fixed location of land makes it easy for man to establish and exercise ownership rights over the surface units of the earth. In his exercise of these rights, however, man must use land where he finds it. Some substitution of fields or tracts is always possible in the production process. A businessman may have a choice between several prospective commercial sites, all of which appear to fit his needs. But he has no alternative of moving low-value land to high-value sites. The fact that surface space may be idle or cheap in Nevada or in northern Michigan means very little to those individuals who compete for the use of commercial space on Manhattan Island or in the Chicago Loop. Businessmen operating in these areas must either pay the going price for the space they need or move out to other areas where land values are lower and where the land may or may not be suited to their purposes.

One of the peculiar characteristics of land is that it cannot be standardized. Most commercial products such as canned peas, automobile parts, and rifle shells are standardized to a considerable extent and usually can be substituted for each other with ease. This degree of standardization is never possible with tracts of land because even when they have the same size, shape, and soil types, they always differ in location and have different neighbors and different spatial relationships with respect to other properties and facilities.

Not only does the fixed-location factor prevent standardization of properties, it also tends to tie land values, uses, and ownership conditions to the local environment. Land owners usually find it difficult to disassociate themselves and their land-use operations from their local

---

[14]Ely and Wehrwein, *op. cit.*, p. 71.

communities. They enjoy the same climate as their neighbors and very often the same marketing, social and governmental services. Ordinarily, they carry on the types of farming for which their areas have some comparative advantage or find that their use of land for residential, commercial, and other purposes tends to complement other land uses carried on in their areas.   SPILL OVERS

When a land owner wishes to sell his property, he usually expects to find a market among local buyers. If his community has a high property tax levy, he suffers the consequences because he does not have the alternative of picking up his land and moving elsewhere. Whole groups of property owners are adversely affected when their communities are hit by floods, storms, droughts, insect invasions, industrial stagnation, loss of established markets, or possible urban or rural blight.

Legal Description of Properties

In addition to its other effects upon land use, the fixed-location factor provides an important basis for the concept of property rights in land. It makes it possible for one to describe the location of various land holdings in very specific terms. These descriptions facilitate the legal registration of land titles and also the identification, location, and measurement of the surface extent of different properties. Three principal systems of land measurement are used in the United States. These systems involve measurement by metes and bounds, by rectangular survey, and by platting.

In most of the older settled areas of the United States, properties are described by *metes and bounds*—that is, in terms of their location with respect to local landmarks and natural objects such as streams, rock formations, and trees. Metes-and-bounds descriptions ordinarily start with a reference to some carefully identified monument, such as a stone, tree, body of water, building, or piece of pipe driven into the earth. They then indicate the distance and direction to each boundary corner so that a surveyor might accurately locate the property boundaries. For example, the property that later became Washington's Mount Vernon estate was described by metes and bounds in 1726 as:

> ...a moiete or half of five thousand acres formerly Lay'd Out for Collo Nicholas Spencer and the father of Capt. Lawrence Washington. Bounded as follows Beginning by the River Side at the Mouth of Little Hunting Creek according to the several courses and Meanders thereof nine hundred Eighty and Six Poles to a mark'd A Corner Tree standing on the West side of the South Branch being the main branch of said Hunting Creek. From there by a lyne of Mark'd trees west eighteen Degrees South across a Woods to the Dividing Lyne as formerly made Between Madam Francis Spencer and Captain Lawrence Washington and from hence W by the said Lyne to ye River and with the River and all the Courses and Meanders of the said River to the Mouth of the Creek afor'sd.

Metes-and-bounds descriptions are often somewhat involved—partly because of their tendency to fit property boundaries to local topographic features such as streams or mountain ridges. Despite their cumbersome nature, however, these descriptions fill their purpose as long as the various boundaries and corner monuments can be easily identified. Real problems arise when the boundary descriptions are vague, when property owners mentioned in the description have been forgotten, when original monuments have been moved or destroyed, or when properties have been subdivided. When complications of this type develop, the title clearance process often becomes both time-consuming and expensive.

A second type of land measurement, the *rectangular system*, applies in the thirty public domain states and also in parts of some other states. Under this system principal meridians running north and south and base lines running east and west have been established in various parts of the country. Working out from the intersection of these two lines, additional meridians and parallels have been surveyed at six-mile intervals. The intersection of these lines suggests a huge gridiron with each six-mile square representing a township of thirty-six square miles. Each township is numbered according to the number of ranges it is from the principal meridian and the number of tiers of townships it is from the base line. The township with the cross-hatching of section lines in Figure 2-4 can be described as Township 2 North, Range 3 West of the Sixth Principal Meridian.

Every full township is divided into 36 sections. These are a mile square in size and contain 640 acres. In the United States, these sections are numbered from 1 to 36 beginning in the northeast corner as in Figure 2-4. Each section can then be divided into quarters containing 160 acres and each quarter section can be divided into "forties" and sometimes even smaller units.[15] The 20-acre parcel designated in Figure 2-4 has the following description: W½ of SW¼ of Section 12 of T 2 N, R 3 W of the Sixth Principal Meridian.

On the whole, the rectangular-survey approach has provided a workable and systematic method of land measurement. In those parts of the United States and Canada where it has been applied, it has had a pronounced effect upon the size and shape of rural land holdings. It has also influenced the legal boundaries of local units of government and the location of many public roads. Despite its numerous advantages, this approach has some weaknesses: (1) frequent "correction lines" are needed to compensate for the curvature of the earth; (2) the presence of streams and bodies of water in surveyed areas occasionally prevents the designation of full descriptions; (3) section lines often provide illogical property boundaries; and (4) complications have resulted from errors in the original surveys.

[15] For a more detailed description of the rectangular-survey system, cf. William G. Murray, *Farm Appraisal and Valuation*, 5th ed. (Ames: Iowa State University Press, 1969), chap. IV.

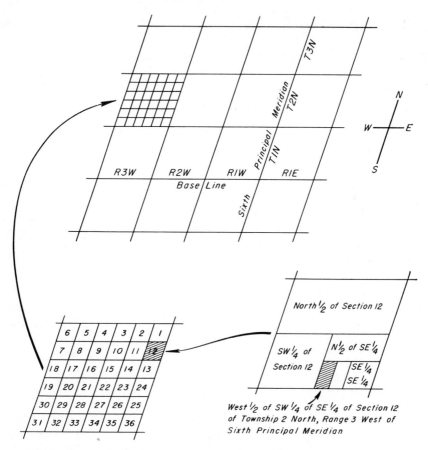

FIGURE 2-4. Legal description of areas under the rectangular survey system.

A third system of land measurement known as *platting* is used in the legal description of most urban and suburban properties. The areas subdivided for these uses are first located according to their metes-and-bounds or rectangular-survey descriptions. Careful surveys are then made, corner monuments are established, and information concerning the size and location of each lot and the areas dedicated for streets and public purposes is recorded on a map that is filed with the proper local authorities. Thereafter, each tract of land may be legally described for tax and other purposes by lot number rather than by metes-and-bounds or rectangular-survey descriptions. A tract might thus be described as Lot 3, Block 5 of the Wellsley subdivision or as Lot 187 in Glencairn subdivision number 4.

THE PRESENT LAND-USE SITUATION

Almost all of the earth's surface has been explored by man and most of its visible resources have been appropriated for various types of human use. From an over-all standpoint, these different uses present a widely varied and highly complex land-use pattern. In our examination of the present land-use situation, let us first look at some of the major differences in land-use patterns found on the world scene and then at the land-use situation in the United States.

World Land-Use Picture

Altogether, the world has a total surface area of approximately 197 million square miles of which 55 million square miles or 35.7 billion acres are land surface. When a deduction is made for the ice-covered wastes of Antarctica, it appears that the six major continents have a total surface area of slightly under 33.1 billion acres (Table 2-1). Approximately 3.6 billion acres or 10.8 percent of this total area can be classified as arable land. An additional 7.1 billion acres (21.6 percent) are used for meadows and pasture while 9.9 billion acres (29.8 percent) are used as forest land. This leaves 12.5 billion acres (37.8 percent), which are classified by the Food and Agriculture Organization of the United Nations as "built upon, unused but potentially productive, wasteland, and other."

As one might expect, this land-use distribution pattern varies considerably by world regions and by individual nations. Almost a third of the surface land of Europe (excluding the Soviet Union) is classified as arable land. This compares with only 4.9 percent of Oceania (Australia, New Zealand, and the Pacific Islands) and only 5.8 percent of Latin America. At the same time, 58.2 percent of Oceania is classed as meadow or pasture while only 10.0 percent of the Near East and 14.2 percent of North America falls into this classification; and 48.7 percent of Latin America but only 9.6 percent of Oceania is classed as forest land.

Greater differences exist between individual nations. Australia, Brazil, and the United Arab Republic reported one-twentieth or less of their areas as arable cropland as compared with half of the land area of Italy and India. Nigeria and India reported no meadow or pasture land while 58.2 percent of Australia is used for this purpose. The U.A.R. reported no forest land while more than half of Brazil and Sweden are forested. The residual classification accounts for only 12 to 15 percent of France, Italy, and the United Kingdom but for more than half of the area of Canada, China, and the U.A.R.

Many reasons can be given for these wide differences between continents and between countries. Relatively favorable climatic, topographic, and soil conditions favor agricultural developments in Western Europe and the United States. In contrast, the use of land for crops is regimented by deserts in the U.A.R. and Australia, by a short growing season in the northern parts of Canada and the Soviet Union, by mountainous topography in parts of Latin America, and by tropical jungles in countries such as Brazil. Population pressure over long periods of time also has had its

TABLE 2-1. Major Land Uses by World Regions and Selected Nations

Area	Total area*	Arable cropland	Meadows and pasture	Forest land	Built upon, unused but potentially productive, wasteland, and other
	(millions of acres)	(percentages)			
	33,099	10.8	21.6	29.8	37.8
World regions:					
Europe	1,218	30.4	18.5	28.2	22.9
North America	4,870	11.1	14.2	37.5	37.1
Latin America	5,083	5.8	24.3	48.7	21.2
Near East	2,982	6.2	16.2	10.4	67.2
Far East	2,760	24.6	10.0	37.6	27.8
Africa	6,185	8.6	28.0	19.9	43.4
Oceania	2,103	4.9	54.2	9.6	31.3
U.S.S.R.	5,535	10.8	16.7	40.6	31.9
Selected nations:					
Australia	1,899	5.2	58.2	4.6	32.0
Brazil	2,103	3.5	12.6	60.8	23.1
Canada	2,465	4.4	2.1	44.4	49.1
China	2,363	11.4	18.6	8.0	61.9
France	135	36.9	24.9	23.2	14.9
India	808	49.7	4.5	18.7	27.1
Italy	74	50.5	17.2	20.3	12.0
Japan	91	15.4	2.7	69.2	12.7
Mexico	487	12.1	40.1	22.2	25.7
Nigeria	228	23.6	–	34.2	42.2
Sweden	111	7.1	1.2	50.7	41.1
United Arab Rep.	247	2.8	–	–	97.2
United Kingdom	60	30.3	49.7	7.4	12.6
United States	2,314	18.8	27.7	31.6	21.9

*Totals include reported area within boundaries, not total surface area.

Source: Food and Agriculture Organization of the United Nations, *Production Yearbook-1968,* Vol. 22 (Rome: 1969), pp. 3-8. The data reported by countries represent the latest official reports from each nation. All totals have been converted from hectares to acres.

effect in countries such as India, Italy, and Japan in favoring the terracing and reclamation of areas that might pass as wasteland in other countries.

Use of Land in the United States

Approximately a fifth of the surface land area of the United States can be classified as arable cropland, slightly under half as pasture and grazing land, and almost a third as forest land. These classifications overlap, and each involves a considerable area that is used for more than one purpose. When these multiple-use lands are arbitrarily assigned to a single major

TABLE 2-2.   Major Land Uses in the United States, 1970

	Millions of acres	Percentage of total area
Total land area	2,263.6	100.0
Area in private ownership	1,377	60.8
Area in public ownership	887	39.2
Land area in farms	1,063.3	47.0
Land not in farms	1,200.3	53.0
Land Use		
Cropland		
Cropland harvested	273.0	12.1
Other cropland	97.8	4.3
Total cropland	370.8	16.4
Pasture and grazing		
Pasture in farms	445.8	19.7
Cropland used as pasture	88.2	3.9
Nonforested grazing land	293	12.9
Total pasture and grazing	827	36.5
Forest and woodland		
Farm woodland, not grazed	52	2.3
Grazed farm woodland	70	3.1
Forest land, not grazed	464	20.5
Grazed forest land	140	6.2
Total forest and woodland	726	32.1
Miscellaneous farm areas		
Farmsteads, roads and lanes	8.5	.4
Other farm land, wasteland	36.5	1.6
Total miscellaneous farm land	45	2.0
Nonagricultural uses		1.4
Urban areas	32	1.0
Highways and roads	22	.14
Railroad rights-of-way	3.2	.07
Airports	1.6	1.5
State and national parks	33	
State and national wildlife refuges	30	1.3
National defense areas	23.6	1.0
Miscellaneous nonfarm uses, idle areas, and wasteland	150	6.6
Total nonagricultural uses	295	13.0

Source: Totals approximated from data reported in United States Census of Agriculture, 1969; U.S. Department of Interior, *Selected Outdoor Recreation Statistics,* 1971; and by H. Thomas Frey *et al., Major Uses of Land and Water in the United States with Special Reference to Agriculture: Summary for 1964,* U.S. Department of Agriculture, Economic Research Service, Agricultural Economic Report No. 149 (Washington, 1968).

use, it appears that 16.4 percent of the total area was used as cropland in 1970, 36.5 percent as pasture and grazing land, 32.1 percent as forest land, 2.0 percent as miscellaneous areas in farms, and 13.0 percent as land used for nonagricultural purposes. (Table 2-2.)

As these data indicate, around 87 percent of the nation's surface land was used for cropland, pasture, grazing, forestry, and other agricultural purposes. Of this total area, some 1,063 million acres (47 percent of the total area) were included in farms in 1969.

Agricultural uses. The U.S. Census of Agriculture for 1969 classified 459 million acres as cropland within farms.[16] Of this total, 273.0 million acres involved cropland harvested in 1969 while 88.2 million acres represented cropland used for pasture. Approximately half of the remaining 97.8 million acres were summer fallowed in 1969 while smaller acreages stood idle, were planted to nongrazed cover and soil building crops, or were the victims of crop failures.

Around 1,037 million acres or 46 percent of the nation's area was used for pasture and grazing purposes in 1969. This total included 739 million acres of farm pasture and open-range grazing areas, plus 88 million acres of cropland used for pasture, and 210 million acres of grazed farm woodland and grazed forest land. In addition, a substantial area of harvested cropland was grazed after the principal crops had been removed. Approximately a third of the area used for grazing is publicly owned. Most of this land is found in the open range and grazed forest areas of the West.

Forest lands account for approximately 726 million acres or slightly less than one-third of the total area of the United States. Around two-thirds of this area is regarded as commercial forest land. The remaining third has little commercial forest value though much of it is used for production of fuelwood and posts and for grazing, recreation, cover, and other multipurpose uses. About a third of the forest lands are publicly owned.

Forty-five million acres may be classified as miscellaneous farm areas. Some 8.5 million acres of this total are used for farm homesteads, yards, lanes, and roads. The remaining 36.5 million acres reported in farms includes farm service areas and wasteland.

The information reported in Table 2-2 gives a generalized picture of the land-use situation in the United States in 1970. But as Figure 2-5 suggests, this picture varies considerably by regions. Cropland accounts for a very high proportion of the total land area in the Corn Belt, the Northern Plains, and the Lake States, but for less than a fourth of the area of the other regions. Pasture and grazing land is most important in the Mountain, Northern and Southern Plains, and Pacific States. Forest land, on the other hand, is the predominant use in the Southeast, Mississippi Delta, Northeast, Appalachian, Pacific, and Lake States regions.

[16] Approximately 99.9 percent of the nation's cropland is located in the 48 contiguous states. This land represents 24.1 percent of the area of the 48 states as compared with 20.3 percent of the total national area. Land in farms accounted for around 56 percent of the area of the 48 states in 1970 and land in public ownership for 28 percent.

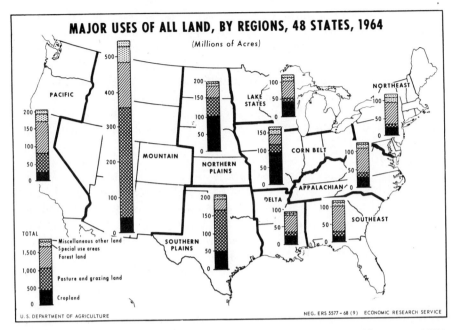

FIGURE 2-5. Comparison of major uses of land by regions, 48 states, 1964.

TABLE 2-3. Land Utilization Trends for the United States, 1880-1970*

Year	Land in farms	Cropland harvested	Other cropland	Pasture & grazing	Forest & woodland	Other uses
		(Millions of acres)				
1880	536	166	22	935	628	153
1890	623	220	28	892	604	160
1900	841	283	36	831	579	175
1910	881	311	36	814	562	181
1920	959	349	53	750	567	185
1930	990	359	54	708	607	176
1940	1,065	321	78	723	602	180
1950	1,161	344	64	700	606	189
1959	1,124	311	71	798	747	339
1970	1,063	273	98	827	726	346

*Data for years prior to 1959 are for the 48 contiguous states only. Alaska and Hawaii are counted in the 1959 and 1970 totals.
Source: Adapted from United States Census of Agriculture, 1969 and Hugh H. Wooten and James R. Anderson, Major Uses of Land in the United States, U. S. Department of Agriculture Information Bulletin 168, 1957, pp. 36-37.

As the trend data reported in Table 2-3 indicate, the agricultural land-utilization picture has changed considerably since 1880. The total area in farms has more than doubled since 1880, and the acreage used for crops increased from 188 million to over 400 million acres in the 40 years between 1880 and 1920. This upward trend in cropland area reached a peak during the late 1920s around which it remained until the 1950s, after which it declined. This leveling off and decline in cropland area has not been accompanied with a similar trend in crop production. More intensive use of croplands, improvements in cultural practices, and a shifting of 80 million acres once used to produce food for horses and mules to food production has permitted a doubling of agricultural production since 1920.

From 25 to 30 million acres of new cropland were brought into use by land clearing, drainage, and irrigation between 1930 and 1970. The addition of these areas was more than balanced, however, by the abandonment and shifting of large areas of cropland to pasture, woodland, and nonfarm uses. This shifting process has been going on for a long time. Many farming areas in the eastern part of the country reached their peaks in cropland use before the turn of the present century; and more than 46 million acres cultivated at the time of these peaks have since shifted to other uses.[17]

Most of the increase in cropland prior to 1920 came at the expense of grazing areas and to a lesser extent from the clearing of forested areas. The total area used for pasture and grazing purposes has fluctuated considerably in recent decades. In the case of forest lands, the reforestation movement and the tendency for some cleared lands to revert to forest use has more than balanced the clearing of forest lands for crop and pasture use. An upward trend in forest and woodland acreage started around 1910 and boosted the total forest land acreage to the 605 million acre level around which it remained from 1930 until the forested areas of Alaska and Hawaii were added to the total in 1959.

Nonagricultural uses. Tables 2-2 and 2-3 treat the lands used for nonagricultural uses as a residual area. This area includes lands used for residential, industrial and commercial, mining, recreation, transportation, and service areas plus the wastelands not included in farms. Unlike the agricultural areas, very few census data have been collected for these lands. Available estimates, however, indicate that the total area used for these purposes increased from approximately 40 million acres in 1920 to 270 million acres in 1964. (Table 2-4.)

---

[17]New Hampshire, for example, reached its peak in 1860. Between 1860 and 1950, its area of tillable land in farms dropped from 2,367,000 to 451,000 acres. Cf. W. K. Burkett, *New Hampshire's Idle Farm Land,* New Hampshire Agricultural Experiment Station Bulletin 339, 1953. In some sections of the East and the South, forest lands have been cleared, cultivated for awhile, then allowed to revert to forestry, only to be recleared later. Wooten (Hugh H. Wooten, *Major Uses of Land in the United States,* U.S. Department of Agriculture Technical Bulletin 1082, 1953, p. 5) estimates that around "150 million acres have been involved in this long-time rotation of forest, cultivated crops, and pasture."

TABLE 2-4.   Approximate Acreage of Lands in Principal Nonagricultural Land Uses, 1920, 1930, 1945, 1950, 1959, and 1964

Types of Use	1920[1]	1930[2]	1945[3]	1950[4]	1959[5]	1964[6]
	(millions of acres)					
Urban areas	10.0	12.0	15.0	18.3	27.2	29.3
Highways and roads	15.0	19.0	19.1	19.4	20.5	21.2
Railroad rights-of-way	4.0	4.0	3.4	3.4	3.4	3.3
Airports	—*	—*	1.3	1.3	1.4	1.5
State and national parks	8.0	12.0	17.9	18.7	29.7	31.9
Wildlife areas	—*	1.0	4.7	8.9	17.2	29.0
National defense areas	2.0	2.0	24.8	21.4	24.4	23.6
Total	39.0	49.0	86.2	91.4	123.8	139.8

*Not separately reported.
[1]U.S. Department of Agriculture, *Yearbook of Agriculture*, 1923.
[2]National Resources Board, *Land Planning Committee Report*, 1934.
[3]Ruess, Wooten, and Marschner, *Inventory of Major Land Uses*, U.S. Department of Agriculture Miscellaneous Publication No. 663, 1948.
[4]Wooten, *Major Uses of Land in the United States*, U.S. Department of Agriculture Technical Bulletin No. 1082, 1953.
[5]Wooten, Gertel, and Pendleton, *Major Uses of Land and Water in the United States: Summary for 1959*, U.S. Department of Agriculture, Agricultural Economics Report 13, 1962, p. 10.
[6]Frey, Krause, and Dickason, *Major Uses of Land and Water in the United States With Special Reference to Agriculture*, U. S. Department of Agriculture, Agricultural Economic Report 149, 1968, p. 26.

Frey, Krause, and Dickason indicated that 29.3 million acres were occupied by incorporated and unincorporated urban places with 1,000 or more persons in 1964.[18] This total represents a three-fold increase in urban land area since 1920. Significantly larger areas also were used for highways, airports, state and national parks, wildlife areas, and national defense sites in 1964 than in 1920.

Nation-wide data unfortunately are lacking concerning the use breakdown of the land uses found in urban areas. A 1955 study of land uses in 86 American cities indicates that around two-fifths of the developed area in each of three classifications of cities is used for residential purposes. [19]

[18]Cf. H. Thomas Frey, Orville E. Krause, and Clifford Dickason, *Major Uses of Land and Water in the United States With Special Reference to Agriculture: Summary for 1964*, U.S. Department of Agriculture, Agricultural Economic Report 149, 1968, pp. 26 and 68.

[19]Cf. Harland Bartholemew, *Land Uses in American Cities* (Cambridge: Harvard University Press, 1955), Tables 3 and 7. John H. Niedercorn and Edward F. R. Hearle, "Recent Land Use Trends in Forty-eight Large American Cities," *Land Economics*, Vol. 40, February, 1964, pp. 105-10, found that 39.0 percent of the developed area of 48 large cities studied in 1963 was used for residential purposes, 10.9 percent for industrial uses, 4.8 percent for commercial uses, 25.7 percent for roads and highways, and 19.7 percent for other public uses.

An additional third of the area is used for railroads, streets, and alleys. Approximately a tenth of the developed area in each classification group is used for commercial and industrial purposes; and a sixth of the area is used for parks, playgrounds, and other public and semipublic uses.

Specific data also are lacking on the extent of the areas utilized for several other uses. Millions of acres of forested and nonforested land are now used primarily for recreation purposes. Large areas also are used for mining and service purposes. Sizable areas of nonurban land, for example, are used for schools and public buildings, cemeteries, golf courses, storage areas, power sites, reservoirs, flowage and watershed protection areas, dumping grounds, and other service purposes. Large areas also are used as sand or gravel pits, stone quarries, open pit mines, and as the service areas for oil and gas wells and underground mines.

—SELECTED READINGS

Ely, Richard T., and George S. Wehrwein, *Land Economics* (Madison: The University of Wisconsin Press, 1964), chaps. II and III. Originally published by The Macmillan Company, 1940.

Frey, H. Thomas, Orville E. Krause, and Clifford Dickason, *Major Uses of Land and Water in the United States With Special Reference to Agriculture: Summary for 1964,* U. S. Department of Agriculture, Agricultural Economic Report No. 149 (Washington, 1968).

Hall, Peter (ed.), *Von Thunen's Isolated State* (London: Pergamon Press, 1966).

Renne, Roland R., *Land Economics*, 2nd ed.(New York: Harper & Brothers, 1958), chap. III.

Zimmermann, Erich W., *World Resources and Industries,* rev. ed. (New York: Harper & Brothers, 1951), chap. VII.

3

Population Pressure
and the Demand for Land

When we speak of the demand for land, we are concerned for the most part with a derived type of demand. Few individuals seek land for its own sake. Instead, they want it because of what it produces. The products of land vary from the food we eat, the clothes we wear, and the materials we use in our daily life to the scenery we enjoy and the prestige and other satisfactions associated with land ownership.

Man's over-all demand for land resources finds its roots in the needs and aspirations of the many individuals who make up society. These people have different wants and desires. Up to a certain point, they are all primarily concerned with the physical need to secure sufficient food and other materials to sustain life. Beyond this point, their demand for land and its products is influenced largely by technological developments, custom and tradition, their educational and cultural backgrounds, their incomes and spending power, individual tastes and personal goals, and by the changing attitudes that come with advancing age. Each of these factors helps to condition the over-all demand picture. But the basic factor affecting the demand for land is that of population numbers. It is imperative, therefore, that we begin this discussion with some consideration of the problems of population pressure and population growth.

POPULATION TRENDS AND OUTLOOK

Considerable controversy surrounds the problem of increasing population pressure and the question of what, if anything, should be done about it. In newly settled areas and rapidly developing economies, popular opinion has often favored large families and an increasing population. Similar attitudes have won acceptance in areas where religious dogma or social prestige have favored large families or several sons. This attitude also has been fostered in military-minded nations by public policies oriented toward the provision of more troops for the armed services.

At the other extreme, the effect of increasing population numbers upon the sufficiency of man's food supply is often regarded as a matter of critical importance. Recognition of this problem in times past has prompted many cultures to accept a variety of population control measures involving practices such as sex taboos, delayed marriage, birth control, infanticide, and senicide.[1] Religious and moral restraints now prevent popular acceptance of population control measures that involve the taking of human life. Strong public and private programs are being pushed, however, for the acceptance of practices that will check the rate of population increase.[2]

Regardless of the position one takes on the controversial question of population control, it must be recognized that the problem of increasing population pressure has a considerable impact upon the demand for land and its products. Accordingly, careful consideration should be given to the population situation in various parts of the world, to current trends in population growth, and to the future outlook for population increase.

The World Population Picture

Population reports for the pre-modern era are both fragmentary and incomplete. Most demographers agree that the world's total population probably did not pass the 500-million mark until some time after 1500 A.D. The population problem during this early period was characterized by high birth rates, high mortality rates, and a relatively short average span of life.

Naturally there was some increase in population numbers during this period. Yet almost every upward surge resulting from the high birth rate was counterchecked by the doleful effects of famine, plague, or war. Some 600 famines were recorded in Europe in the first 18 centuries after Christ. Nearly three times this number have been reported for China.

---

[1] Cf. Warren S. Thompson and David T. Lewis, *Population Problems,* 5th ed. (New York: McGraw-Hill Book Company, 1965), pp. 238-39.

[2] Cf. J. Mayone Stycos, "Effective Implementation of Fertility Control Programs," and Stephen Enke, "Monetary Incentives for Accepting Birth Control," published as chap. XIV-XV in David M. Heer, *Readings on Population* (Englewood Cliffs, N.J.: Prentice-Hall, Inc., 1968).

Plagues such as the Black Death of the fourteenth century wiped out more than two-thirds of the population of some countries and probably claimed between a fifth and a fourth of all the lives in Europe. Intermittent warfare also provided a strong check against population increase. The Thirty Years' War, for example, reduced the population of Bohemia and the German States to between a third and a half of their former numbers.

The over-all importance of these checks against population increase may be illustrated by a simple comparison between conditions now and in times past. The average child born in the United States or Canada in 1970 had a life expectancy of around 71 years. This is approximately double the life expectancy of American children born in 1789 and probably three times the life expectancy of children born in Europe during the Middle Ages. An average of 2.38 children per marriage is now sufficient to maintain the total population.[3] During the late Middle Ages in the plague-ridden years that followed the appearance of the Black Death, population maintenance called for 10 or 11 children per family.[4]

With the beginnings of the agricultural revolution in Western Europe around 1700, the somewhat static population situation that had prevailed began to change. The increase in food production provided more sustenance for human life and paved the way for an upward trend in population numbers. This trend was accelerated by the industrial and sanitary-medical revolutions of the next two centuries. Increasing trade and commerce, the settlement of new areas, the trend toward industrialization and higher productivity per man, and the success with which modern medical science tackled the problem of high mortality rates—all added up to new incentives for population increase.

Between 1650 and 1850 the population of Europe and the world more than doubled. These totals doubled again in the next century; and by 1970, the world had a total population of around 3.6 billion persons. Between 1950 and 1970, the world's population increased at a rate of around 1.9 percent a year—between 40 and 60 million persons per year. Continuation of this rate will give the world a population of around 6 billion persons by the end of the present century.

The general trend in world population growth by continents from 1650 to 1970 is summarized in Table 3-1. As this tabulation suggests, more than half of the world's people live in Asia while less than a fifth live in Europe (including the U.S.S.R.) and only a seventh live in the two Americas. The significance of this distribution may be visualized in terms of the individual prospects faced by the thousands of new babies born into the world each day. Only about one in eighteen will be born in the United States and one in fifteen in the Soviet Union. About one in four will be Chinese and one in every eleven will be born in India. Only one in four will be born a Christian and only one in three will be white.

[3] Cf. Thompson and Lewis, *op. cit.,* pp. 270-71.
[4] Cf. J. C. Russell, "Demographic Pattern in History," *Population Studies*, Vol. 1, March, 1948, pp. 393-94.

TABLE 3-1.   World Population Growth, 1650-1970 (in millions)

Area	1650	1750	1800	1850	1900	1930	1940	1950	1960	1970
Africa	100	95	90	95	120	164	191	222	278	344
America	13	12	25	59	144	242	274	329	412	511
Asia*	330	479	602	749	937	1,120	1,244	1,381	1,660	2,056
Europe*	100	140	187	266	401	534	575	572	639	705
Oceania	2	2	2	2	6	10	11	13	16	19
World total	545	728	906	1,171	1,608	2,070	2,295	2,517	3,005	3,632

*The entire population of the Soviet Union is included in the total for Europe for the period since 1900.

Source: Estimates for 1650 through 1900 from A. M. Carr-Saunders, *World Population: Past Growth and Present Trends,* 1936, p. 42. By permission of the Clarendon Press, Oxford. Population estimates for 1930 through 1960 from *Demographic Yearbook,* 1968 (New York: Statistical Office of the United Nations, 1969), p. 83. Population estimates for mid-1970 from 1970 World Population Data Sheet. (Used with the permission of the Population Reference Bureau, Inc., Washington.)

Distribution of Population in Relation to Land Resources

Most of the world's people live on a very small proportion of its surface area. (Figure 3-1.) The total population is not distributed between regions or nations in accordance with their land areas or their population carrying capacities. Some parts of the world are far better endowed on a per capita unit basis with food and other land resources than others. Some are approaching the limits of their population-carrying capacity (assuming existing levels of technology) while others are capable of supplying high levels of living for somewhat larger populations than they now have.

Population density. The relationship between population numbers and land resources is often stated quantitatively in terms of *population density* or number of persons per square mile or other area unit. As Table 3-2 indicates, wide differences exist in the average population densities reported for various countries. Some areas such as Belgium, the Netherlands, Puerto Rico, and Taiwan have densities of more than 300 people per square kilometer while others such as Canada and Australia have averages of 2.3 and 1.6 persons per square kilometer, respectively.

Population distribution patterns often differ as much within countries as between countries; and it is usually unwise to generalize from an area's population density figure to conclusions regarding its population-land resource relationships. With the United Arab Republic, for example, the average density figure of 33.3 persons per square kilometer suggests a population distribution similar to that found in the United States, which has an average density of 37.3 in its contiguous 48 states. The situation

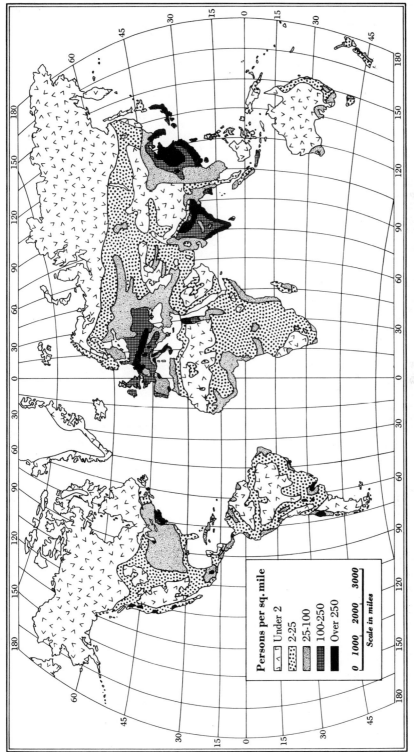

FIGURE 3-1. The distribution of world population. (From Oliver H. Heintzelman and Richard M. Highsmith, Jr., *World Regional Geography*, p. 25. Englewood Cliffs, N.J.: Prentice-Hall, Inc., 1967.)

Persons per sq. mile

Under 2
2-25
25-100
100-250
Over 250

Scale in miles

0   1000   2000   3000

TABLE 3-2. Population, Population per Square Kilometer, Birth and Mortality Rates, Average per Capita Supplies of Calories and Proteins, Average per Capita Consumption of Commercial Energy Resources, and Average per Capita Gross National Product for 50 Selected Countries, 1970

Selected countries	Midyear estimate of population 1970 (millions)	Population density per square kilometer	Crude birth rate	Mortality rate	Per capita daily supplies of: Calories	Per capita daily supplies of: Proteins (grams)	Per capita annual consumption of energy resources (kgms. of coal equiv.)	Per capita share of gross national product in U. S. dollars
Algeria	14.0	5.9	44	14	1,950	55.4	415	250
Argentina	24.4	8.8	22	8	3,130	87.6	1,411	800
Australia	12.3	1.6	20.0	9.1	3,110	91.6	5,124	1,970
Belgium	9.7	317.9	14.8	12.8	3,150	88.6	5,236	1,740
Brazil	95.3	11.3	39	11	2,700	66.5	364	250
Canada	21.4	2.3	17.7	7.4	3,180	95.4	8,483	2,380
Chile	9.8	12.9	34	11	2,720	77.8	1,048	470
China (Mainland)	759.6	79.4	34	15	2,050	57.4	458	90
China (Taiwan)	14.0	395.9	29	6	2,510	64.8	816	250
Colombia	21.1	18.5	44	11	2,280	53.3	576	300
Costa Rica	1.7	33.5	45	8	2,610	57.9	346	410
Czechoslovakia	14.5	115.4	14.9	10.7	2,990	83.3	5,776	1,110
Denmark	4.9	115.6	16.8	9.7	3,180	89.2	4,690	1,950
Finland	4.7	15.4	16.0	9.6	2,890	87.8	3,339	1,660
France	50.8	92.9	16.8	11.0	3,180	99.8	3,282	1,950
Germany, Fed. Rep.	59.6	239.9	19.7	11.9	2,960	80.5	4,484	1,750
Greece	8.9	68.8	18.2	8.3	2,900	98.9	1,017	700
Haiti	4.9	181.5	45	20	—	46.3	32	70
Honduras	2.6	23.6	49	16	2,010	51.0	217	240
India	550.4	168.2	42	17	1,900	47.8	184	90
Indonesia	121.2	63.6	49	21	1,870	41.4	99	100
Iran	28.7	17.4	48	18	1,950	52.1	478	280
Ireland	2.9	42.1	20.9	11.3	3,450	93.2	2,882	910
Israel	2.9	143.1	26	7	2,930	88.9	2,014	1,200
Italy	53.7	182.6	17.6	10.1	2,940	87.2	2,215	1,120

Japan	103.5	279.9	19	7	2,460	75.7	2,515	1,000
Kenya	10.9	19.1	50	20	2,240	67.9	144	120
Mexico	50.7	25.7	44	10	2,600	66.8	1,064	490
Netherlands	13.0	389.3	18.6	8.2	3,030	84.2	4,012	1,520
New Zealand	2.8	10.5	22.6	8.9	3,290	107.3	2,678	1,890
Nigeria	55.1	59.6	50	25	2,170	59.5	29	80
Pakistan	136.9	144.6	50	18	2,230	50.6	96	90
Peru	13.6	10.6	44	12	2,300	55.4	633	350
Philippines	38.5	129.5	50	–	2,010	51.9	248	180
Poland	32.8	108.0	16.2	7.6	3,110	93.2	3,826	780
Puerto Rico	2.8	316.0	25	6	2,460	63.3	2,719	1,210
Saudi Arabia	7.7	3.6	–	–	1,830	49.8	510	350
South Africa	20.1	16.4	40	16	2,870	78.2	2,721	590
Spain	33.3	66.0	20.5	8.7	2,680	81.9	1,313	680
Sweden	8.1	19.7	14.3	10.4	2,880	80.7	5,360	2,500
Syria	6.1	33.0	47	15	2,480	74.5	434	180
Thailand	35.8	70.0	46	13	2,100	43.8	198	130
Tunisia	5.1	32.7	45	16	2,190	66.2	235	210
Turkey	35.2	45.6	43	16	2,860	78.2	450	290
U.S.S.R.	242.8	10.8	17.9	7.7	3,150	91.5	4,059	970
United Arab Rep.	33.3	33.3	43	15	2,960	76.3	298	160
United Kingdom	55.7	231.2	17.1	11.9	3,180	88.0	5,004	1,700
United States	205.4	22.3	17.6	9.6	3,240	96.1	10,331	3,670
Venezuela	10.4	11.8	46	10	2,490	65.9	2,543	880
Yugoslavia	20.5	80.1	18.9	8.6	3,200	93.3	1,247	530

Source: Estimates of midyear populations for 1970 for all countries except Pakistan and Saudi Arabia are from the United Nations *Monthly Bulletin of Statistics,* September 1971, pp. 1-5. Data on crude birth rates, mortality rates, and average per capita shares of gross national product for all countries and 1970 midyear population estimates for Pakistan and Saudi Arabia are based upon tabulations of the Population Reference Bureau, Inc., as reported on the *1970 World Population Data Sheet.* (Used with permission of the Population Reference Bureau, Inc..) Population densities computed from 1970 populations and surface land areas reported in Food and Agriculture Organization, *Production Yearbook, 1969.* Data on average per capita net daily supplies of food calories and protein nutrients are for latest years reported in FAO, *Production Yearbook, 1969,* Vol. 23, pp. 438-51. Data on per capita consumption of energy resources is measured in kilograms of coal equivalent for 1968 as reported by the United Nations, *Statistical Yearbook, 1969,* pp. 324-27.

appears differently, however, when it is noted that 98 percent of Egypt's population is concentrated on about 3 percent of its land area and that the Nile Valley has what is probably the highest density of agricultural population in the world.

Comparable differences in population distribution patterns can be found in Algeria, Australia, Canada, the Soviet Union, and several other countries. Population densities in the United States in 1970 ranged from highs of 953 persons per square mile in New Jersey and 898 in Rhode Island to 3.4 in Wyoming and 0.53 in Alaska. On a still smaller unit basis, these densities ranged from the 67,160 persons per square mile reported on Manhattan Island to the zero densities found in the uninhabited portions of the Nevada and Arizona deserts.

Though the concept of population density has value as a quantitative measure of the number of persons per area unit, it does not provide a truly adequate measure of man's real relationship to his land-resource base. This relationship must be viewed in qualitative as well as quantitative terms. Consideration must be given both to differences in population distribution and to the carrying capacity of the land-resource base. When one considers the problem of dense population pressures, for example, it should be recognized that some populations such as those found in Haiti, Java, and the Nile Valley depend almost entirely upon local agriculture while others such as those found in England and Holland depend more upon industry and world trade for their livelihood.

Man-land ratio. When the relationship between man and his resource base is viewed in qualitative terms, it is often described as a *man-land ratio*—as the ratio between the total population or some segment of the population and the particular supply of land resources with which it works or upon which it depends. In a broad general sense, this concept is concerned with all of the factors that affect the per capita returns and satisfactions man receives from his use of land resources.

Man-land ratios may be applied in various ways. They are frequently used in a very specific sense to describe the areas of cropland per farmer or the average "arable cropland equivalent" per person. Data on average per capita availability of food calories or nutrients provide a general measure of the ability of an area to supply its residents with food resources up to an optimum level of consumption. Indices of average per capita consumption of energy resources provide another man-resource ratio that helps to indicate the ability of a resource base to support an industrial society.

Comparisons of the man-land ratios found in different areas are often complicated by the assumptions or lack of assumptions associated with their use. In a realistic sense, one cannot speak of a man-land ratio without definite assumptions regarding the population that uses the land and its products, its resource-use objectives, its stock of technological know-how, and the social institutions that affect its use of land resources.

The problems that arise when comparisons are made between areas involving differences in these assumptions can be illustrated by a simple example of two countries with land-resource bases of comparable size and use-potential but with one country making more use of modern technology and having a somewhat larger population than its less-developed counterpart. A comparison of the production records of these two countries would probably show that the more industrialized country secures the higher per capita return from its resource base and thus suggests that it enjoys a higher man-land ratio. When consideration is centered on potential rather than current production, however, the advantage could easily lie with the less-developed country because of its smaller population.

Per capita levels of food consumption. Ability to provide people with adequate diets is a basic requisite for economic growth and development in the modern world. No nation can make much progress in raising the living standards of its citizenry until it meets this first requirement. Indices of average per capita levels of availability of food calories and nutrients accordingly can be viewed both as a type of man-food land-resource ratio and also as an indicator of an area's relative ability to emphasize goals beyond the provision of minimum levels of living for its people.

International emphasis on the average per capita availability of food calories was highlighted by the Food and Agriculture Organization of the United Nations in 1946 when it established some provisional nutritional targets designed to bring world food production up to a minimum per capita average of 2600 calories per day.[5] Data at the time showed that only 30.6 percent of the world's people had enjoyed access to more than 2700 calories daily in the 1934-38 period and that these average high calorie diets were limited to Europe, the U.S.S.R., Australia, New Zealand, Argentina, Canada, and the United States. Some 38.6 percent of the world's people—found mostly in Africa, southern Asia, and South America—had low calorie diets with averages of less than 2200 calories per person each day. This food situation deteriorated considerably during World War II, particularly in the war-torn areas of Europe.

Considerable progress was made in increasing food production in the early post World War II period, but only 27.8 percent of the world's people had access to diets averaging 2700 calories or more a day in 1951-52 while 59.5 percent had access to averages of less than 2200 calories per day.[6] Since the 1952-56 period, per capita food supplies have increased substantially in all of the developed countries except the United States and Canada, where production control programs have been used to

---

[5] Cf. *World Food Survey* (Washington: Food and Agriculture Organization, 1946).
[6] Cf. *The State of Food and Agriculture: Review and Outlook, 1952* (Rome: Food and Agriculture Organization, 1952), p. 36.

discourage excess production. Meanwhile, food production in the developing areas of Latin America, the Far East, and Africa has barely held its own in the race with increasing population numbers. As Table 3-3 indicates, the FAO index of food production rose from 100 during the 1952-56 base period to 125 in 1969 for the developed countries while it rose to only 104 for the developing countries.

TABLE 3-3. Trends in Indices of Per Capita Food Production, 1948-1970

World region	1948-52	1952-56	1960	1965	1970
World (excluding China)	93	100	107	108	112
Developed countries	92	100	111	116	125
Western Europe	87	100	113	118	128
Eastern Europe and USSR	87	100	122	128	147
North America	99	100	100	102	103
Oceania	102	100	106	107	118
Others (Japan, South Africa, Israel)	87	100	114	121	142
Developing countries	94	100	104	104	106
Latin America	97	100	99	104	105
Far East (excluding Japan)	94	100	107	104	110
Near East (excluding Israel)	90	100	104	106	104
Africa (excluding S. Africa)	97	100	102	99	95

Source: The State of Food and Agriculture: 1971 (Rome: Food and Agriculture Organization, 1971), p. 2.

Use of the average per capita daily supplies of food calories available at the retail level as a measure of the man-food land-resource ratio may be criticized on several counts. It may be argued, for example, that the availability of calories at the retail level does not provide a measure of calories consumed. This is true. With average diets at the 2750 calorie level, it is usually assumed that around 400 calories are lost in food preparation or as spoilage or waste.[7] Greater losses are common when higher calorie levels are available and smaller losses can be assumed when fewer calories are available. These losses, however, do not detract from the value of this index as a measure of an area's ability to provide adequate food supplies for its people.

A second criticism stems from the fact that the calorie needs of different people vary with differences in their normal body size, level of

[7]Cf. Gove Hambridge, *The Story of FAO* (New York: D. Van Nostrand Company, Inc., 1955), p. 30.

activity, sex, and age.[8] Mature workers who are five feet tall and who have a normal body weight of 120 pounds naturally have lower calorie requirements than workers who are six feet tall and who weigh 180 pounds. Manual workers ordinarily have higher requirements than sedentary workers; and moderately active men usually eat more than women, small children, or the aged. Also, the people who live in warm climates ordinarily need fewer calories for body warmth than is the case in cooler areas.

This index also has been criticized for the overemphasis it gives to calories. Diets can be rich in calories and still be quite deficient in the quantities of proteins, fats, minerals, and vitamins they provide. Indices involving these other components of balanced diets are important in discussions of nutritional standards. In practice, however, the levels of these components in average diets by nations are usually highly correlated with calorie levels. Examination of the national averages on the availability of food calories and food proteins reported in Table 3-2, for example, shows that all of the nations with average calorie levels of 2700 or more had average protein levels of 80 grams or higher while nearly all of those with calorie levels of less than 2200 calories had protein levels of less than 60 grams of protein per capita daily.

Average per capita use of energy resources. The above comparison of average dietary levels provides a meaningful measure of the man-food resource relationships found in different countries. But its exclusive concern with food resources makes it only a partial measure of the complete man-land relationship. Before one generalizes from the average daily food supplies of a people to their use of other land resources, it should be noted that dietary levels always range between definite limits. A

---

[8]These differences were recognized by FAO in its report, *Calorie Requirements, FAO Nutritional Studies*, No. 15 (Rome: 1957). This report speaks of a Reference Man and Woman with minimum daily requirements of 3200 and 2300 calories, respectively. Significant adjustments upward and downward from these norms are suggested with variations in body weights. The reference levels assume individuals in the 20 to 30 age bracket and requirements drop to 69 percent of this level by the age of 70. The reference levels assume mean outside annual temperatures of 10 degrees Centigrade. Caloric requirements rise 1.5 percent with each drop of 5 degrees in this temperature and drop 2.5 percent with each 5 degrees of increased temperature. Calorie requirements for children range from 1150 calories daily for infants to 2650 for 12-year-olds. Cf. also Richard I. Meier, *Science and Economic Development*, 2nd ed. (Cambridge: The M.I.T. Press, 1966), pp. 4-6.

Colin Clark suggests substantially lower minimum calorie requirements in his discussion of the caloric needs of people in Central Africa, India, and North China. [Cf. Colin Clark, *Population Growth and Land Use* (London: Macmillan, 1967), p. 129]. For individuals with average male adult weights of 110 pounds in India and 121 pounds in North China, he indicates minimum daily caloric requirements of 400 and 433 for children, 447 and 528 for women, 582 and 626 for men leading sedentary lives, and 1821 and 2011 for men working eight hours daily in India and China, respectively.

lower limit is set by the minimum nutritional requirements needed for human survival while an upper limit is set by the capacity of the human stomach. These limits together with man's paramount need for at least minimum supplies of food often cause countries with low dietary levels to devote major portions of their resources to food production. Other countries with more adequate supplies of food can utilize higher proportions of their resources for purposes other than food production. These countries are usually more industrialized and enjoy higher average levels of living with better housing, more worldly goods per family, and greater opportunities for the enjoyment of leisure.

No complete index has yet been developed to indicate the comparative amounts of nonfood land resources that the people of different countries use in their daily lives. An index of this type would be concerned both with the land resources used on a consumption basis for residential, recreation, service, and other associated uses and with the raw materials and energy resources used for production purposes.

A general measure of man's use of this second group of resources is suggested by the comparative data on the average per capita consumption of energy resources by countries reported in Table 3-2. As this tabulation indicates, the average person in Australia, Belgium, Canada, Denmark, France, West Germany, the Netherlands, Poland, Sweden, the Soviet Union, the United Kingdom, and the United States used 3,000 or more kilogram-equivalent units of energy in 1966. Average per capita consumption levels of less than one-tenth of this amount were reported for Algeria, Haiti, Hondorus, India, Indonesia, Kenya, Nigeria, Pakistan, the Philippines, and Thailand. Some of this difference stems from the fact that little energy is used for space heating purposes in the warmer countries. Even when allowances are made for this use, however, it is obvious that levels of energy consumption are closely correlated both with national levels of industrialization and with the per capita shares of gross national product reported for the various countries.

Area Differences in Population Growth

In addition to the wide differences in man-land ratios found around the world, notable differences also exist in the net rates of population growth experienced in different areas. World regional comparisons (cf. Table 3-1) show that all the continents have experienced rapid rates of population growth since 1900. Some countries such as the United States, Canada, Japan, and the Soviet Union have experienced faster rates of growth than others.

Population growth in the United States. The United States provides an excellent example of a nation that has experienced tremendous population growth. In 1800 it had a population of 5.3 million. Between then and 1850 this total increased more than fourfold to 23.2 million. It then more than tripled to a total of 76.2 million in 1900; it almost doubled in the next half century to a total of 151.3 in 1950; and by 1970, it had increased to 204.8 million.

Much of this rapid rate of increase can be credited to the land settlement and development opportunities associated with the nation's bountiful land resource base. It also has been facilitated by relatively high birth rates, early progress in the reduction of mortality rates, and immigration policies favorable to settlement. Between 1830 and 1970 some 45.2 million immigrants officially entered the country; and, except for the 1930s, this flood of immigrants passed the one million mark in every decade between 1841 and 1970.

As Table 3-4 indicates, population increases of between 25 and 36 percent were reported for every decade from 1790 to 1890. This rate of increase declined somewhat between 1890 and 1910, dropped to 14.9 percent for the decade during which World War I was fought, climbed to 16.1 percent during the 1920s and then dropped to a low of 7.2 percent during the 1930s. The low rate of increase of the 1930s can be credited largely to conditions associated with the Great Depression. Partly as a result of these conditions, the marriage rate dropped to a low of 7.9 marriages per thousand people in 1932. (Figure 3-2.) At the same time, the birth rate dropped from the level of 20 to 25 births per thousand people, which had existed between 1915 and 1927, to a low of 16.4 births per thousand in 1933. Immigration was limited during this decade to 528,000 persons or to less than 13 percent of the number of immigrants

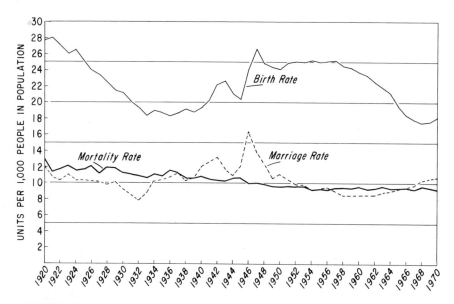

FIGURE 3-2. Trends in birth, mortality, and marriage rates, United States. 1920-1970.

TABLE 3-4. Population Trends in the United States, 1790 to 1970

Year	Total population in millions	Amount of increase in millions	Per cent of increase	Immigration by decades* (thousands)	Percentage distribution of population			Percentage distribution		
					Native white	Foreign-born white	Non-white	Urban	Rural nonfarm	Rural farm
1790	3.9	—	—	—	80.7		19.3	5.1		94.9
1800	5.3	1.4	35.1	—	81.1		18.9	6.1		93.9
1810	7.2	1.9	36.4	—	81.0		19.0	7.3		92.7
1820	9.6	2.4	33.1		81.6		18.4	7.2		92.8
1830	12.9	3.2	33.5	152	81.9		18.1	8.8		91.2
1840	17.1	4.2	32.7	599	83.2		16.8	10.8		89.2
1850	23.2	6.1	35.9	1,713	74.6	9.7	15.7	15.3		84.7
1860	31.4	8.3	35.6	2,598	72.6	13.0	14.4	19.8		80.2
1870	38.6	7.1	22.6	2,315	72.8	14.3	12.9	25.7		74.3
1880	50.2	11.6	30.2	2,812	73.5	13.1	13.5	28.2		71.8
1890	62.9	12.8	25.5	5,247	73.0	14.5	12.5	35.1		64.9
1900	76.2	13.2	21.0	3,688	74.5	13.4	12.1	39.7		60.3
1910	92.2	16.0	21.0	8,795	74.4	14.5	11.1	45.7		54.3
1920	106.0	13.8	15.0	5,736	76.7	13.0	10.3	51.2	18.7	29.9
1930	123.2	17.2	16.2	4,107	78.4	11.4	10.2	56.2	19.0	24.8
1940	132.2	9.0	7.3	528	81.2	8.6	10.2	56.5	20.3	23.2
1950	151.3	19.2	14.5	1,035	82.8	6.7	10.5	64.0†	20.7	15.3
1960	179.3	28.0	18.5	2,515	83.4	5.2	11.4	69.9	21.4	8.7
1970	203.2	23.9	13.3	3,322	83.4	4.3	12.3	73.5	21.7	4.8

*Immigration data for 1830 cover period from Oct. 1, 1819 to Sept. 30, 1830, for 1840 cover period from Oct. 1, 1830 to Dec. 21, 1840, for 1850 and 1860 cover calendar years, for 1870 cover Jan. 1, 1860 to June 30, 1870, and for the decades since then cover periods beginning on July 1 and ending June 30.
† Part of the increase in the urban percentage for 1950 resulted from a change in definition which included much urbanized unincorporated area, previously classed as rural nonfarm, in the urban classification.

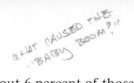

admitted during the 1920s and to only about 6 percent of those admitted during between 1900 and 1910.

During the 1940s population increased by 19 million persons or by 14.5 percent. Most of this increase was associated with the "population explosion" that followed World War II. The birth rate rose to 25.7 per thousand people in 1946 and remained at a high level until the middle 1960s. High births in combination with a low mortality rate and a resurgence of immigration brought an increase of 28.0 million people, an 18.5 percent rate of increase, during the 1950s. This trend caused some observers to predict a national population of 400 million by 2000.

The population boom tapered off in the 1960s as the small "baby crop" of the 1930s came into their child-bearing years. The birth rate dropped below 20 in 1965 and then to a 17-births-per-thousand level in 1967. By 1970, many of the children born in the early post-World War II period were married and ready to have families of their own. Yet birth rates remained low, for the time being at least, for a number of reasons. Important among these were the popular acceptance of family planning measures and widespread concerns over the problems of population increase.

Population trends in other countries. The rapid rate of population increase noted in the United States has counterparts in the cases of Canada, Japan, and the Soviet Union. The population of Canada increased from 2.4 million in 1851 to 5.4 million in 1901, 8.8 million in 1921, 13.8 million in 1951, 18.2 million in 1961, and an estimated 21.4 million in 1970. These totals are smaller than those for the United States; but it should be noted that Canada experienced a significantly higher rate of increase between 1901 and 1970 than did its neighbor to the south. This increase was prompted by Canada's expanding economy, its liberal immigration policy, and the fact that its birth rate has been consistently higher and its death rate lower than the rates experienced in the United States. (Table 3-5.)

From 1721 until 1853—throughout the long period during which the Japanese people isolated themselves from contact with the rest of the world—Japan maintained a population balance of between 28 and 30 million persons. Beginning around 1850, this population total began to increase; and with the Meiji Restoration of 1868 and the period of industrialization that followed, this upward trend became more and more perceptible. By the 1920s the population had doubled from its 1850 level; in 1950 it reached a total of 83.2 million, in 1960 a total of 93.2 million, and in 1970 a total of 103.5 million. Unlike the United States and Canada, Japan has been troubled by a limited food supply and has had to rely heavily upon industry and commerce to provide sustenance for its population. This fact has caused the government to actively push birth control measures in recent years as a means of alleviating future population problems.

Czarist Russia had a population of around 38 million persons in 1800,

TABLE 3-5.   Comparative Trends in Birth and Mortality Rates, Selected Countries, 1905-1970

Time period	Canada	England and Wales	France	Japan	United States	U.S.S.R.
Crude birth rates						
1905-09 average	–	26.7	20.1	31.9	–	45.5
1911-13	–	24.1	18.1	34.1	25.1*	–
1920-24	28.1	21.3	19.9	35.0	22.8	44.1
1925-29	24.5	17.1	18.5	34.0	20.1	43.4 (1927)
1930-34	22.2	15.3	17.3	31.8	17.6	–
1935-39	20.4	14.9	15.1	29.2	17.2	–
1940-44	23.2	15.5	16.3	30.1	19.9	31.7 (1940)
1945-49	27.0	18.0	20.3	30.1	23.4	26.5
1950-54	28.2	15.5	19.5	23.7	24.4	26.4
1960	26.7	17.2	18.0	17.2	23.7	24.9
1965	21.4	18.1	17.8	18.4	19.4	18.4
1970	17.6	16.2	16.7	18.9	18.2	17.2 (1968)
Mortality rates						
1905-09	-	15.1	19.5	20.9	15.4	29.4
1920-24	12.3	12.2	17.3	23.0	12.0	24.1
1930-34	10.0	12.0	16.0	18.1	11.0	–
1940	9.8	14.6	19.1	16.4	10.7	18.3
1950	9.0	11.6	12.8	10.9	9.6	–
1960	7.8	11.5	11.4	7.6	9.5	7.1
1965	7.6	11.5	11.2	7.2	9.4	7.3
1970	7.3	11.8	10.6	6.9	9.4	7.7 (1968)

*Figure is for 1915. It is estimated that the United States had a crude birth rate of around 50-55 in 1800.

Source: United Nations, *Demographic Yearbooks* for 1950, 1954, 1959, 1962, and United Nations *Monthly Bulletin of Statistics,* 1971.

77 million in 1870, and 140 million in 1914. Boundary adjustments, external and internal warfare, and famine brought the total population down to 133 million in 1922. The population of the new Soviet Union then increased rapidly to 147 million in 1927 and 170 million in 1939. This trend was reversed by the Nazi invasion of World War II, which left the nation with 27 million fewer people than it had at the beginning of the war. Postwar increases brought the total population up to 200 million in 1956 and an estimated 242.6 million in 1970. The Soviet Union has only recently broken away from a pattern of high birth and high mortality rates. As a result, it has a relatively young population and a considerable potential for further population increase.

The slower rates of population growth reported in England and Wales and in France throughout the past century stand in marked contrast to the cases just discussed. Throughout the nineteenth century, the population of England and Wales increased quite rapidly from around 9 million in 1801 to 17.9 million in 1851 and 32.5 million in 1901. Near the end of the century birth rates as well as mortality rates declined and the spread between these two rates narrowed. The result was a slower rate of population increase as is indicated by the totals of 37.9 million in 1921, 41.7 million in 1941, 43.7 million in 1951, 46.1 in 1961, and an estimated 49.2 million in 1970. Much of this change may be attributed to factors such as Britain's participation in two world wars, its changing position as an economic and commercial power, and the continued out-migration of English settlers to other areas.

France provides another example of a nation with a relatively stable population. In 1801 France had a population of 27.3 million. This total increased to 35.8 million in 1851, 38.4 million (excluding Alsace-Lorraine) in 1901, 38.8 million in 1921, 41.9 million in 1936, dropped to 39.8 million in 1946, and then increased to 42.8 million in 1954, 46.5 million in 1962, and to an estimated 50.8 million in 1970. France lost population during World War I, had a relatively stable population during the 1930s, and lost population again during World War II. The nation experienced its most rapid rate of population increase of the past century during the 1946-70 period. Declining birth rates in the late 1960s, however, suggest a return to relative population stability.

Changing Characteristics of the Population

While population numbers provide an important index of the demand for land and its products, differences in demand are often associated with population characteristics. This is particularly true in the United States, where increasing urbanization and changes in household characteristics, the age composition of the population, and the education and family income status of the population are exerting a significant influence on the over-all demand for land resources.

Urbanization. In 1790 only about one person in 20 in the newly constituted United States lived in an urban community. (Table 3-4.) By 1970, three out of every four Americans lived in urban places while only one in 21 still lived on a farm. As a result of this change, the thinking of most people is no longer as farm-oriented as it has been in times past. Urbanization has divorced the interests of most city folks, particularly those who have not grown up on farms, from any intimate use of agricultural land resources. As consumers, they are greatly interested in food, fibers, fuels, and building materials and in the prices at which they retail in their processed form. They have a distinct tendency, however, to associate milk with the sanitary container in which it is delivered to one's door or fresh vegetables with the well-lighted greens department of the local supermarket rather than with the cow or truck garden from which they came. So long as there is no threat to their supply of food and other land products, members of this increasing segment of the population show little interest in the direct demand for agricultural land. Their direct interests are expressed more in the demand for housing, commercial and industrial developments, parking space, and recreation areas.

Continued urbanization also has brought significant changes in the composition of the urban population. The proportion of the urban population reported as Negroes, for example, rose from 6.3 percent in 1910 to 12.3 percent in 1970 while the proportion of blacks among the population of the nation's central cities increased from 12.3 percent in 1950 to 20.5 percent in 1970. Meanwhile, the share of the urban population made up of foreign-born whites declined considerably, decreasing from 22.6 percent in 1910 to 6.8 percent in 1960.

Number and size of households. As Table 3-6 indicates, there has been a considerable increase since 1890 in the proportion of the adult population who are or have been married. This trend coupled with increasing population numbers has brought the creation of millions of new households, each with its independent need for living quarters, furnishings, and other products. Between 1890 and 1970 the number of households in the United States increased from 12.7 to 63 million, or at a rate more than half again as high as the increase in population numbers. During this same time period, the size of the average household dropped from 4.9 to 3.2 persons.

TABLE 3-6.   **Trends in Proportion of Adult Married Population, Number and Size of Households, and Median Age of Population, United States, 1820-1970**

Year	Percentage of population 14 years old or over who are or who have been married		Number of households (millions)	Average number of persons per household	Median age of population
	Males	Females			
1820	–	–	–	–	16.7
1890	56.4	65.9	12.7	4.9	22.0
1900	58.0	66.7	16.0	4.8	22.9
1910	59.6	68.2	20.3	4.5	24.1
1920	63.1	70.6	24.4	4.3	25.3
1930	64.2	71.6	29.9	4.1	26.5
1940	65.2	72.4	34.9	3.8	29.0
1950	73.8	80.4	42.9	3.5	30.2
1960	74.7	81.0	53.0	3.3	29.5
1970	71.8	77.9	62.9	3.2	28.3

Source: Statistical Abstract of the United States, 1971, pp. 26, 32, and 36.

In past decades the nation's farms have provided a reservoir of surplus population for industrial employment while the urban areas have been occupied largely by adults and have had less than their proportionate share of people under the age of 20. This situation has changed somewhat with the decline in the number of farms and in the size of the average farm family. Central cities still have less than their proportionate shares of pre-school and school-aged children, however, because large numbers of urban workers prefer to live with their families in the suburbs.[9] This situation helps to explain the fact that the median age of the nation's urban population was 30.3 in 1960 as compared with 26.8 in the suburban and rural nonfarm areas and 29.6 in the farm areas.

Changing age distribution of population. The median age of the American population was 16.7 years in 1820. Since then people have been living longer with the result that the median age went up to 22.9 years in 1900 and 30.2 years in 1950, after which the large number of young people in the population caused it to decline to 28.3 years in 1970. The effect of this changing age distribution is illustrated by the age-sex pyramids for 1900, 1950, and 1970 shown in Figure 3-3. In 1900 the proportion of males and females found in each successively older age bracket declined in such a manner that the age-sex distribution could be portrayed by a pyramidal-type diagram. Changes in the age distribution of the nation's population explain the patterns shown for 1950 and 1970. It may be noted that significantly larger proportions of the individuals of both sexes lived beyond the ages of 50 and 65 in 1950 and 1970 than in 1900. A slight bulge in the 25-29 age bracket for 1950 and the 45-49 age bracket for 1970 shows the impact of the "baby boom" of the early 1920s on later age distributions. This group was followed by the short crop of persons born during the 1930s (the 15-19 age bracket in 1950 and the 35-39 age bracket in 1970) and then by the "population explosion" of the 1946-1965 period.

These age distribution patterns can and have had a considerable impact upon the demand for land and its products, upon the nation's manpower resources, and upon population trends. The large number of children born in the post-World War II period guarantees a large and growing demand for food, fibers, housing, and other land products for years to come. It will also supply the nation with an abundant supply of manpower. Also, just as the surplus babies born in the 1920s became parents in the 1940s and 1950s and as the smaller number of children born during the 1930s contributed to the decline in birth rates in the 1960s, the large number of young people in the 0-24 age brackets in 1970 portends a future avalanche

[9] This situation is more true with whites than with the blacks who live in metropolitan areas. The Bureau of Census has found that only 41 percent of the white families who lived in Standard Metropolitan Statistical Areas in 1969 lived in the central cities as compared with 80 percent of the blacks. Approximately 18 percent of the families in the central cities as compared with less than 4 percent in the suburbs were blacks. Cf. *Household and Family Characteristics, March, 1969,* Bureau of the Census Current Population Reports Series P-20, No. 200 (Washington: 1970), pp. 12-13.

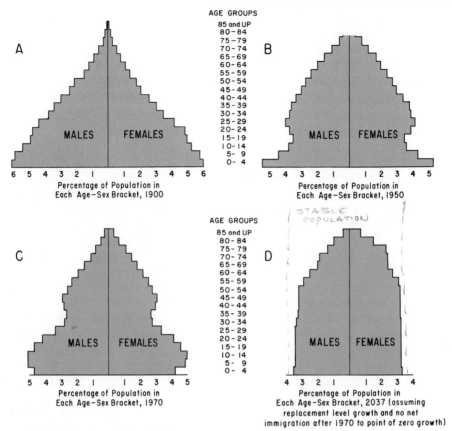

FIGURE 3-3. Comparison of age-sex distributions of population of the United States for 1900, 1950, and 1970 with a projection, assuming growth at a replacement level after 1970, to 2037.

of births if steps are not taken to keep the rate of population increase under control.

Reductions in the mortality rate explain the fact that far larger proportions of the people born in the United States now live through infancy and childhood to become productive workers than was once the case. This trend has added to the size and productivity of the nation's working force. From an economic and social point of view, it has greatly enhanced the returns the nation can expect from its investment in the nurture and training of the young. From the standpoint of land resource demand, it means that almost every baby born now will consume and use land products as a child and as a youth, then as a working adult and parent, and probably later as a retiree.

Attainment of population stability (cf. Figure 3-3D) calls both for a reduction of birth rates to a level commensurate with mortality rates and stabilization of the size of the pre-retirement age groups in the population.

The United States is approaching but has not yet reached this age-sex distribution pattern. Considerable progress has been realized, however, in extending average life expectancies and in greatly increasing the proportion of the population who live to their "golden years." By 1970, one person in every 11 in the United States was 65 or over as compared with only one in 25 in 1900. With this upward trend, more and more attention is being given to the care and provisioning of older people. Social security benefits and other pension plans now make it possible for most of them to retire or at least take life easier during their declining years. This financial assistance has brought an increasing demand on the part of oldsters for small modern homes, travel opportunities, and retirement sites that combine a favorable climate with opportunities for gardening, relaxation, and other interests.

Educational levels. Most Americans of post-school age now have more educational training than did their fathers or grandfathers. The average person in the 25-29 age bracket in 1968 had a median of 12.5 years of education as compared with medians of 10.3 years for those in the 55-64 age bracket and 8.4 years for those in the 75 and over age bracket.[10] Some 73.1 percent of those in the 25-29 age bracket had four years of high school whereas 14.7 percent had an additional four or more years of college. These totals compare with the 37.8 percent of the people in the 25-29 age bracket in 1940 who had four years of high school and 5.8 percent who had four or more years of college. By 1985, it is expected that 84.9 percent of the population in the 25-29 age bracket will have four years of high school and 21.1 percent will have four or more years of college.[11]

The upward trend in levels of educational attainment is illustrated by the fact that approximately the same proportion of young people now graduate from college as graduated from high school 50 years ago. This trend has delayed the entry of large numbers of potential workers into the labor market. At the same time, however, it has increased their productive potential. It also has opened new horizons to them in awakening desires for enjoyment of the material and amenity benefits of modern life. High among these benefits are those associated with opportunities to use, own, and control various land resources and land products.

Income status. Technological advance and rising worker productivity

---

[10] Cf. *Educational Attainment: March 1968*, Bureau of the Census Population Characteristics Report Series P-20, No. 182 (Washington: 1969) p. 9.

[11] Cf. *Projections of Educational Attainment to 1970 and 1985*, Bureau of the Census Current Population Reports Series P-25, No. 390 (Washington: 1968), p. 15. Another indication of rising educational levels is found in the fact that approximately 85 percent of the young people in the 15 to 17 year bracket and approximately 37 percent in the 18 to 20 year bracket were enrolled in school in 1960 as compared with 66.3 and 21.4 percent in 1930 and 14.4 and 3.9 percent, respectively, in 1900.

in the United States has permitted a substantial increase in average real incomes. Calculated in terms of 1958 prices, the average annual disposable income for each person in the United States rose from $1,145 in 1929 and $897 in 1933, to $1,178 in 1940, $1,520 in 1950, and $1,749 in 1960 to approximately $2,600 in 1970.[12] The median income per family rose from $3,031 in 1947 to $5,620 in 1960 and $8,632 in 1968 when measured in current dollars and from $4,716 in 1947 and $6,604 in 1960 to $8,632 in 1968 when measured in 1968 dollars.[13]

This rise in real incomes has been associated with a reduction in the average work week from 60.2 hours per week in 1900 and 49.7 hours per week in 1920 to approximately 40 hours per week since 1950.[14] Paid vacations have become a common phenomenon with most jobs since 1946. The combination of higher real incomes with increased leisure has made it possible for the great majority of American families to care for their subsistence needs and still have additional income for better housing, household luxuries, a second car and sometimes a second home, vacation trips and travel, college educations, and investments and savings. These additional expenditures and particularly the demands for better housing, recreation opportunities, and improved highways have had direct impacts upon the demand for land resources as well as upon the over-all demand for land products.

World Outlook for Population Increase

World population numbers have been increasing at a rate of 1.9 percent annually in recent years. Continuation of this rate could bring a 6.5-fold increase in world population numbers in the next century. This spectre of "standing room only" has prompted many predictions of dire consequences. The world obviously has room for some additional people. It must be recognized, however, that there are limits to the number of people it can accomodate. Population pressure is already pressing against the food supply in many areas; and although great potentialities exist for increasing food production, it is neither logical nor practical to assume that the world can go on indefinitely providing adequate sustenance for an ever-increasing population. Some point of stability in population numbers must be reached. The real question is when or at what level will population stabilize. Will this level permit improvements in the living standards

[12]Cf. *Statistical Abstract of the United States: 1969* and *Survey of Current Business*, July, 1970.

[13]Cf. *Income in 1968 of Families and Persons in the United States*, Bureau of the Census Current Population Reports Series P-60, No. 66 (Washington: 1969), pp. 19-20.

[14]Cf. J. Frederic Dewhurst and Associates, *America's Needs and Resources* (New York: Twentieth Century Fund, 1955), p. 40.

of the great mass of the world's people or will the pressure of population numbers force a vast majority to live at a subsistence level?

Malthusian Doctrine. A very gloomy answer to this question is suggested by the now-famous Mathusian doctrine of population growth. This doctrine—first introduced by the Reverend Thomas Robert Malthus in 1789—asserts that "population invariably increases where the means of subsistence increases . . . unless prevented by some very powerful and objective checks." Malthus was deeply concerned with the problems of human welfare; but he was not at all optimistic about man's future prospects in the world he saw. His fears and forebodings are illustrated in shocking fashion by his assumption that population tends to increase in a geometric ratio—1, 2, 4, 8, 16, 32, and so on—while the means of subsistence tend to increase in arithmetic ratio—1, 2, 3, 4, 5, 6, and so on. The example of the American colonies led Malthus to believe that population would double every 25 years were it not held back by lack of subsistence. Over a two-century period, this trend would bring a 256-fold increase in population numbers but only a 9-fold increase in food supplies.

As Professor Warren S. Thompson has observed:

Clearly, this is an impossible situation, but Malthus explained that the fact that man's numbers did not generally show this rapid increase was due to vice and misery, which operated to produce a high death rate. He recognized from the very first, however, two types of checks to population growth—the positive and the preventive. The only form of the latter that he ever contemplated was abstention—either temporary or permanent—from marriage. He did not believe, however, that this would so reduce the rate of increase of any people that the former—that is, the positive checks—would be rendered inoperative; consequently, he did not believe that schemes for improving human institutions, of themselves, were ever likely to do much to increase man's happiness. It seemed to him that, however good human institutions became, they would serve to mitigate the positive checks for only a short time, until man's numbers grew up to his productive capacity under his new institutions. Then he would suffer from hunger, disease, war, and a host of other ills as he had always done in the past.[15]

Malthus modified some of his views in later editions of his essay. His basic concept of the tendency of mankind to breed to the limit provided by the means of subsistence still stands, however, as one widely accepted answer to the question of how far population will increase.

The Malthusian doctrine provided a reasonable interpretation of population trends at the time of Malthus and has since demonstrated itself time after time in many parts of the world. But while this doctrine has a certain logic in theory, it has not always held up in practice. Throughout much of the world, modern technology has made it possible for man to raise his level of life far above his subsistence requirements. A true

[15] By permission from *Population Problems,* by Warren S. Thompson. Copyright, 1942, McGraw-Hill Book Co., Inc., pp. 21-22.

Malthusian would probably argue that this victory of production over increasing population pressure is temporary and that in the years to come population will eventually outrun production and again force the mass of mankind down to a subsistence level. This view—and with it the future of the Malthusian doctrine—is subject to one important modification. Experience shows that where man has been able to raise himself above a subsistence standard of life, he frequently has also shown a willingness and a desire to reduce the birth rate to a lower level.

Cultural and social approach.   This observation suggests a cultural and social approach to the problem of population growth that stands in marked contrast to the naturalistic approach accepted by Malthus and his followers. It indicates that there is no need for passive or fatalistic acceptance of the inevitability of a Malthusian balance between population numbers and the means of subsistence. With suitable incentives and with appropriate cultural and social adjustments, man has shown both willingness and ability to limit his rate of population increase.

Recent history shows that the rising standards of life and reduced mortality rates found in the more industrialized areas have usually led to a gradual decline in the birth rate. This decline normally lags some years behind the drop in mortality rates and thus provides a large potential source of population increase. As long as birth rates follow the downward trend in mortality rates, however, there is hope that whole populations can be moved from low Malthusian levels of existence to higher plateaus where better levels of life can be maintained through relative balance between reduced birth and mortality rates.

Part of the reason for this decline in birth rates may be attributed to the fact that mankind needs fewer births for replacement purposes when mortality rates are low than when they are high. Another important reason involves the changing attitudes regarding optimum family size and the place of children in modern society. As families become accustomed to the advantages of modern life, they seldom show any desire to return to subsistence levels of existence. Instead they often willingly accept family limitation as a means of insuring continued high living standards for themselves and their children. This attitude may be prompted to some extent by the fact that children are less and less the economic asset they have been in times past when child labor was more common; but it stems mostly from the desires of modern families to improve rather than lower their levels of living.

The presence of children in many families is now regarded as a deliberate matter of choice and planning. In these families one might say that children are no longer accepted as a matter of fate but instead are treated as an integral part of the family's standard of living. Children are added to the family because they are desired for their own sake and because they add to the satisfactions and fullness of life. Yet from a cost standpoint, they compete with other items that also constitute a part of the family's standard of living. Family size in these cases depends not only upon ability of parents to have children and their willingness to limit family size but also upon budgetary considerations and the attitudes of husbands and wives regarding the effect of children upon their living standards both now and in the future. During some periods such as the 1930s, competition between wants for babies and wants for goods may favor family limitation. In periods of business prosperity and economic expansion, the typical worker may choose to take the fruits of his higher productivity in the form of more goods and services, better housing, a more pleasing environment, fewer hours of labor, "earlier marriage, somewhat more living children per family, and greater ease in old age."[16]

Classification of nations by population-growth potential. One of the biggest problems demographers face in forecasting world population trends is that of estimating how fast various peoples will shift from a Malthusian balance of high birth rates and high mortality rates to a more rational balance of low birth rates and low mortality rates. A rapid shift from one level to the other could involve a relatively small increase in population numbers. Tremendous increases in population can result, however, when the decline in birth rates lags far behind the reduction in mortality rates.

Demographic forecasts of future population levels are usually based on careful analyses of the age-group profiles of the present population and interpolation of known or assumed mortality, fertility, and immigration rates into the future.[17] This approach is often applied with individual countries. Its application on a world-wide basis, however, is complicated by the wide divergence between the average fertility and mortality rates found in different countries and by widespread differences in cultural attitudes regarding family size.

Meaningful analysis of the prospects for world population increase calls for classification of the people of different nations into the five groups or stages depicted in Figure 3-4. The first of these involves a situation in which high mortality rates counterbalance high birth rates and provide a "Malthusian balance" in population numbers. Stage 2 involves a "high growth potential" group of nations that still have high birth rates but are experiencing a decline in mortality rates. Stage 3 is characterized by a "transitional growth" group of nations that have already benefited from declining mortality rates and can expect considerable population growth before the now declining birth rates drop to the same plateau as mortality

[16]Joseph S. Davis, "Our Changed Population Outlook and Its Significance," *The American Economic Review*, Vol. 42, June, 1952, p. 318.

[17]In this process, particular consideration is usually given to fertility rates—the number of children under 5 years of age for every thousand women of child-bearing age (usually all women between 15 and 44)—because these rates provide a better means for predicting trends in births than the birth rate, which measures the number of live births per thousand people of all ages in the population.

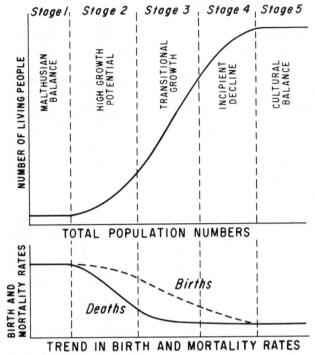

FIGURE 3-4. The five stages of national population growth.

rates. A fourth group, called the "incipient decline" group, occupies stage 4. Mortality rates already are at a low level with this group, and birth rates have declined to such a point that population stability could be attained rather easily if the circumstances so warranted. Stage 5 involves a "cultural balance" at which population numbers are relatively stable and births and deaths are approximately in balance at the same low level.

Few if any nations can now be said to operate in the first Malthusian balance stage even though the conditions associated with this stage are those that characterized the population situation in most countries until comparatively recent times. At the other extreme, no nation has yet definitely shifted to the cultural balance grouping. All of the present countries of the world fit into the second, third, or fourth groupings. At the end of World War II, three-fifths of the world's people were classified as in the high growth potential group, one fifth in the transitional growth group, and a final fifth in the incipient decline group.[18] In the period that

18Cf. Frank W. Notestein, "Population—The Long View," *Food for the World* (Chicago: University of Chicago Press, 1945), pp. 42-57. The incipient decline group included in the countries of northwestern and central Europe, Australia, New Zealand, Canada, the United States, and the white population of South Africa. The transitional growth group included the Soviet Union, eastern and southern Europe, Japan, and parts of South America. Most of the remaining countries were classified as high growth potential areas.

followed, some incipient decline areas such as the United States seemed to shift back temporarily to the transitional growth classification. More recently, the worldwide trend toward lower mortality and birth rates has brought the shift of transitional growth countries such as Japan and the Soviet Union to the incipient decline group and the shift of numerous high growth potential areas to the transitional growth category.

The relevance of the five stages for future world population growth may be illustrated with the examples of the countries reported in Table 3-7. High growth potential areas such as Bolivia, Cameroon, Liberia, and

TABLE 3-7. Comparison of Birth, Mortality, and Population Growth Rates for Three Groups of Nations, 1970

Selected nations	Birth rate	Mortality rate	Growth rate
High growth potential areas			
Bolivia	44	20	2.4
Cameroon	50	26	2.2
Liberia	44	25	1.9
Nepal	41	21	2.2
Transitional growth areas			
Colombia	44	11	3.4
Iran	48	15	3.4
Mexico	44	10	3.4
Morocco	46	15	3.3
Thailand	46	13	3.3
Incipient decline areas			
Belgium	14.8	12.8	0.4
Czechoslovakia	14.9	10.7	0.7
Hungary	15.1	11.2	0.4
Sweden	14.3	10.4	0.8

Source: 1970 World Population Data Sheet. (Data used with permission of the Population Reference Bureau, Inc.)

Nepal still have high birth and mortality rates. For them, the Malthusian devil is still unchained. Mortality rates can be expected to drop; but tremendous population growth is probable during the time it will take for birth rates to drop to the same lower level. Transitional growth countries such as Colombia, Mexico, and Thailand have already enjoyed the benefits of medical services that have helped them to reduce their mortality rates. Population will continue to increase rapidly in these nations until their birth rates also decline. In the incipient decline nations, the period of rapid population increase hopefully is over. Birth rates have declined to levels only slightly above the mortality rates, and population stability can be achieved within a short time if attainment of this goal appears desirable.

The extent to which world population numbers will increase in the future will depend upon the progress individual countries make in shifting from the second, third, and fourth to the fifth stage of population growth. Tremendous progress has been realized during the present century in bringing medical knowledge and expertise to most people of the world and in lowering mortality rates. This trend has been followed by sizable reductions in birth and fertility rates in many countries. Over time, all countries can be expected to shift to stage 5.

The large increase in world population that can occur while this shifting process is taking place has brought widespread support for policies that will implement early reductions in birth rates. Family planning and birth control measures are advanced as logical means for avoiding the famine, privation, environmental pollution, and other undesired consequences of undue population pressure on land resources. Indeed, without some miracle answer that will involve either a vast increase in food supplies or a near-simultaneous reduction of mortality and birth rates, it is questionable whether the people of some countries in the high growth potential and transitional growth categories will ever be able to raise themselves much above a subsistence level of living.

Population projections. Popular interest in the subject of population growth has prompted numerous predictions of future population levels. One prominent planner has suggested a world population of 20 billion by 2050.[19] A British physicist has calculated a possibility of the world's population doubling every 37 years to a total of 400 billion in another 260 years.[20] This population presumably could be supported through extremely intensive use of the earth's present land resources. New technology, including dependence upon photosynthetic plankton, synthesizing of food, and use of satellite mirrors to reflect sunlight to the polar regions, would then permit the earth to support a maximum of 60 million billion people living in air-conditioned 2,000 storied-buildings that would cover all the earth in another 890 years. These predictions are not apt to come about for the simple reason that man, as a rational being, can be expected to take such actions as are necessary to keep his numbers from rising to these levels.

Two studies of world population trends were prepared for the United Nations in 1963 and 1968. The first of these projects future trends at four assumed rates of growth while the second study distinguishes between growth rates in different groups of countries. These projections are as follows:[21]

[19]Cf. Constaninos Doxiadis, "Water and Human Environment," *Proceedings of International Conference on Water for Peace* (Washington: 1967).

[20]Cf. John M. Fremlin, "How Many People Can the World Support?" *New Scientist*, Vol. 24, October 29, 1964, pp. 285-87.

[21]Cf. *World Population Prospects* (New York: United Nations, 1966), pp. 15 and 126; and *Growth of the World's Urban and Rural Population, 1920-2000* (New York: United Nations, 1968), p. 56.

	1970	1980	1990	2000
1963 projections		(millions of people)		
Low variant	3,545	4,147	4,783	5,449
Medium variant	3,592	4,330	5,188	6,130
High variant	3,692	4,551	5,680	6,994
"Constant fertility" variant	3,641	4,519	5,764	7,522
1968 projections				
World total	3,584	4,318	5,174	6,112
Developed areas (including Europe, USSR, North America, and Oceania)	946	1,042	1,153	1,266
Less developed areas	2,638	3,276	4,021	4,846

As these data indicate, world population was increasing at less than the medium variant rate of 1963 by 1968, and most of the population increase expected by the end of the century will come in the less developed areas. These projections have been criticized as unduly pessimistic by Donald J. Bogue.[22] He cites the fact that birth rates are falling more rapidly on the world front than mortality rates and that national rates of population increase are beginning to decelerate as reasons for expecting future population levels somewhat below the United Nations' low variant assumption.

Numerous population projections also have been made for the United States. These are sometimes high, sometimes on target, and sometimes low depending upon the accuracy of their assumptions. Abraham Lincoln, for example, was overly optimistic when he extended the eight-fold national growth rate of the 1790-1860 period in projecting a national population of 250 million for 1930.[23] At the other extreme, an often-quoted projection of the 1930s was unduly pessimistic when it indicated that the nation's population would reach a peak of slightly more than 139 million around 1960 and thereafter decline. More recently, several people have extended the national growth rate of the 1950s to predict totals of 400 million or more by 2000.

An authoritative series of projections based upon analysis of known and expected demographic trends was published by the Bureau of the Census in 1970.[24] These projections assume four possible rates of

[22]Cf. Donald J. Bogue, *Principles of Demography* (New York: John Wiley and Sons, Inc., 1969), pp. 881-83. Professor Bogue has suggested world populations of 4.1 billion in 1980 and 4.5 billion in 2000 with zero population growth by 2000.

[23]Cf. Abraham Lincoln, *Message to Congress of December 3, 1861*, Senate Executive Documents, Vol. 1, p. 20, 37th Congress, 2nd Session.

[24]*Projections of the Population of the United States, by Age and Sex (Interim Revisions): 1970 to 2020*, Bureau of the Census Current Population Reports Series P-25, No. 448 (Washington, 1970), p. 1. A slowing down of the national rate of population increase prompted the dropping of the Series A rate and the adding of the Series E rate for these projections.

national population increase. Averages of 3.1 children per woman were assumed with Series B, 2.775 with Series C, 2.45 with Series D, and 2.11 with Series E. The future populations projected at these rates are:

Year	Series B	Series C	Series D	Series E
1970	205.5 m.	205.4 m.	205.2 m.	205.1 million
1980	236.8	232.4	227.5	225.5
1990	277.3	266.3	254.7	247.7
2000	320.8	300.8	280.7	266.3
2010	376.3	341.0	307.4	283.7
2020	440.3	386.0	335.9	299.2

The nation's population was increasing at approximately the Series D rate in 1970. A drop to the Series E rate, which corresponds to the population's replacement rate, in combination with a total cessation of immigration would permit a leveling off of the total population at around 276 million people once the age structure of the population could be stabilized around 2037. Zero levels of population increase can be achieved with or without immigration at earlier dates through lower birth rates. With the acceptance of a uniform replacement level of births, however, several decades must be allowed for age structure stabilization before total population numbers can reach a relatively constant level.

INTERRELATION WITH OTHER DEMAND FACTORS

Increasing population pressure always suggests increasing need for food and other land products. After all, every new birth means a new mouth to feed, a new body to clothe and house, and a new person whose health and happiness calls for the use of land and land products. The question of how much land is needed in different areas to fill these needs varies with the productivity of the land, the level of technological development, and the consumption and buying habits of the people. These differences have an important impact upon the actual areas needed for the production of food, feed, fibers, and forest products. They also have considerable influence upon the acreages needed for nonagricultural uses and upon the extent to which various land uses compete for particular sites.

Demand for Agricultural Lands

Agricultural land requirements ordinarily reflect the operation of three principal factors—population numbers, nutritional and other consumption standards, and land productivity. Because of the impact of these last two factors, it is not always possible to generalize directly from an indication of population increase to an assumption of increasing agricultural land requirements. Ordinarily, an increase in population numbers means a need for more production. But the question of how much more production always depends upon food consumption and land-use practices. In similar fashion, the question of how much land is needed to provide this production depends upon the trend in crop and livestock yields.

Consumption and nutritional standards. Human stomachs have approximately the same average capacity all over the world. From the standpoint of quantity of food consumed, there are no great differences between people or nations. Pearson and Harper report a world average per capita consumption of 558 pounds of food (dry weight) each year with the difference between continents ranging from a low of 543 pounds per capita in Asia to a high of 587 pounds per capita in Europe.[25]

Greater differences exist in the quality of diets. More emphasis is placed on the consumption of meat, dairy products, fruits, and vegetables in Canada, the United States, Australia, New Zealand, and western Europe than in most parts of the world. The people in these countries consume more calories and usually enjoy diets more varied and often better balanced from a nutritional standpoint than is the case in those areas where major reliance is placed on the use of cereals and pulses with limited use of animal products.

Dietary tastes and nutritional differences have a considerable effect upon the amounts of land needed for food-production purposes. Some types of food provide a large output of food nutrients from relatively small areas. Others call for the extensive—and sometimes luxurious—use of considerably larger areas. As the data presented in Table 3-8 suggest, the calorie requirements of a moderately active man can be supplied for a period of one year by the sugar produced on a fraction of an acre of sugar beets. These same energy requirements can be met by slightly less than an acre used to produce apples, wheat, or beans, while larger acreages are required with livestock products. It takes around 7.5 acres for feed crops plus 2.3 acres of pasture to produce enough dressed beef to provide the annual food-energy requirements of a moderately active man. This makes beef one of the most expensive foods from the standpoint of land requirements. Among the cereals, wheat is most expensive. This explains why wheat is usually displaced in heavily populated areas by rice or potatoes or by crops such as oats and rye, which yield more grain per acre, particularly on the less fertile lands.

[25] Cf. Frank A. Pearson and Floyd A. Harper, *The World's Hunger* (Ithaca: Cornell University Press, 1945), p. 12. They list the average per capita consumption for North America as 576 pounds a year (dry weight). Between 1909 and 1968 the average annual per capita consumption of food products in the United States varied from a low of 1,414 pounds (retail weight equivalent) in 1963 to 1,651 pounds in 1945. Except for the 1942-47 period this average never exceeded 1,600 pounds. It has averaged less than 1,450 pounds annually since 1958 and was never below this level prior to that year. Cf. *Agricultural Statistics, 1967,* p. 693 and *Agricultural Statistics, 1969,* p. 580.

TABLE 3-8.　Average Outputs of Food Nutrients per Acre of Land (Assuming 1941-45 Average Yields) Computed in Number of Days They Could Supply A Moderately Active Man with an Adequate Daily Allowance for Selected Food Products*

Farm product and food use	Food energy (days)	Protein (days)	Fat (days)	Calcium (days)	Five vitamins† (days)
Livestock products:					
Cattle, all	27	77	88	4	47
Eggs	54	188	158	70	98
Hogs	183	129	765	7	228
Milk, whole	108	236	245	696	157
Field crops:					
Beans, dry edible	414	1,116	71	656	483
Corn, cornmeal	725	773	294	136	740
Potatoes	806	812	43	391	2,247
Rice, brown	855	772	163	351	754
Sugar beets, sugar	2,199	0	0	0	0
Wheat, white flour	405	527	41	81	77
Vegetables, fresh:					
Cabbage	373	773	110	2,235	6,303
Carrots	878	1,009	235	2,869	30,500
Onions	769	951	133	1,900	1,639
Peas, green	170	486	27	140	964
Tomatoes	141	266	74	255	2,346
Fruit, fresh:					
Apples	401	80	100	140	484
Oranges	769	582	131	1,898	7,154
Strawberries	120	101	70	308	1,552

*Daily allowances are those recommended by the National Research Council for a moderately active man and are as follows: Food energy—3,000 calories; protein—70 grams; calcium—800 milligrams; iron—12 milligrams; vitamin A—5,000 International Units; thiamine—1.5 milligrams; riboflavin—2.0 milligrams; niacin—15 milligrams; and ascorbic acid—75 milligrams. No recommended allowance is given for fat, but it is considered desirable that 20 to 25 per cent of the food energy be in this form.

†A simple average of the number of days computed separately for vitamin A, ascorbic acid, thiamine, riboflavin, and niacin.

Source: Raymond P. Christensen, *Efficient Use of Food Resources in the United States,* U.S. Department of Agriculture Technical Bulletin No. 963, October, 1948, pp. 26, 70-76.

The high emphasis placed upon livestock products in the diets of the western world means that large areas must be used for feed crops, pasture, and range. In areas of high population pressure, this could represent a wasteful practice because crops fed to livestock lose 80 to 90 percent of their food value before they re-emerge as meat, milk, or eggs. Observations of this type suggest that areas such as the United States could support three or more times as many people under Asiatic dietary standards as under its present prevailing standards.[26] It must be recognized, however, that nutritional values are associated with diets rich in livestock products. Also, the fact that crops fed to livestock lose much of their caloric value:

> ... does not mean that for every calorie produced in the form of livestock products, four or five calories could have been produced in other forms of human food. To a considerable extent animal and crop production are supplementary rather than competitive and under the climatic and other conditions prevailing in many parts of the world, a system of mixed farming based in part on grazing or grass production gives best results for both crops and livestock products. In some parts of the world animals constitute the main form of draft power, in the absence of which crop production would seriously suffer.[27]

The preceding discussion applies primarily to food production. Much the same conditions apply to the areas needed for the production of fibers and forest products. As long as the per capita demand for these products remains unchanged and as long as there are no changes in yield rates, every increase in population numbers means a commensurate increase in land requirements. These other factors, however, have shown little tendency to remain constant. With forest products, for example, higher prices and the increased use of substitutes have brought a marked decline in per capita consumption rates. In 1907 when the average price of sawed lumber was around $16.50 per 1,000 board feet, f.o.b. mill, the average person in the United States used around 107 cubic feet of this product. By 1968 the price of sawed lumber had quadrupled and the average per capita consumption rate was down to 33 cubic feet. This downward adjustment in individual consumption has been associated with a reduction in total production.

Changes in land productivity. Although the demand for agricultural land and its products ordinarily increases with population numbers, the amount of land needed to meet this demand always reflects changes in crop and livestock yields. Decreasing yields resulting from past exploitation practices can lead to higher land requirements and in some cases may force a tightening of the nation's belt. Increasing productivity, on the other hand, may make it possible for a nation to supply a growing population with more agricultural products per capita without any increase in the area used in production.

The United States provides an excellent example of this relationship between productivity trends, land requirements, and total food supplies.

---

[26]Colin Clark, *op. cit.*, pp. 152-53, indicates that the average American-type diet requires three times as much land per capita as the average Japanese standard. He calculates that by use of all of the world's surface land at the average American level that the world could support 47 billion people. At the Japanese level, this projected carrying capacity rises to 157 billion people.

[27]*The State of Food and Agriculture: Review and Outlook, 1952* (Rome: Food and Agricultural Organization of the United Nations, 1952), p. 36.

Total farm output almost doubled between 1900 and 1950 and then increased another 40 percent by 1970.[28] The nation's farms produced 48 percent more produce from 20.5 percent less harvested cropland (74 million acres less) in 1964 than in 1944. Some of this increase resulted from the displacement of horses and mules on farms but most of it can be credited to higher crop yields and greater efficiency in the conversion of feed into livestock products.

This same situation applies with the production of fibers and other nonfood crops. Approximately one-third as much land was used for cotton production in 1968 as in 1910. Total production was down slightly because of changes in export and per capita demands, but average yields were up from 176 to 516 pounds per acre.

Nonagricultural Land-Resource Needs

Higher total population numbers mean more demand for nonagricultural as well as agricultural land. With anticipated increases in population, nations need millions of new houses, automobiles, television sets, refrigerators, and other consumer goods. In addition, needs also arise for hundreds of new schools, factories, shopping centers, streets, and parks. These needs herald a tremendous demand for building materials, minerals, energy resources, and additional water supplies. They also call for new residential, commercial, and industrial developments and for additional areas to be used for recreation, transportation, and service purposes.

While the over-all demand for nonagricultural land is strongly influenced by population trends, it is also conditioned by per capita consumption rates and by our ability to better utilize the resources we have at our disposal. Technological developments have had an extremely important impact upon demand. Primitive man had little appreciation or use for many of the energy and mineral resources we now hold in great esteem. But as man has acquired additional technical knowledge, he has found it increasingly possible to convert these resources into goods we can use in our daily life. This has stimulated an increasing demand for many types of raw materials. With the invention of the steam engine, the automobile, and the telephone, for example, tremendous new demands have risen for mineral and energy resources.

Among the many factors that affect the increasing per capita consumption of nonagricultural products, mention should be made of the role played by the increasing productivity of many workers. Low labor productivity frequently means that the average worker must spend most of his time producing food or other subsistence items. With increasing productivity, the production of subsistence items can be handled by a smaller portion of the total labor force and increasing numbers of workers

[28]Cf. Harold F. Breimyer, "Sources of Our Increased Food Supply," *Journal of Farm Economics,* May, 1954, pp. 228-42.

can be freed to produce the nonsubsistence items associated with high levels of life.

Higher worker productivity also means higher real incomes and increased consumer purchasing power. Much of the increased purchasing power associated with increasing labor productivity in this country has gone for nonfood items—for new houses, shiny automobiles, household goods, recreation, and travel. These expenditures, together with our exposure to a continuous barrage of advertising, have stimulated a widespread desire for more goods and for still higher living standards. In this sense, we have come to regard yesterday's luxuries as the necessities of today.

Effects of increasing urbanization. Aside from the growing need for mineral and material resources, most of the increasing demand for nonagricultural resources is directly associated with the phenomena of increasing urbanization. During the past century, the United States has been transformed from a predominantly rural, farm-minded country into an urban-oriented nation. This trend will probably continue, with an increasing proportion of the total population devoting itself to nonfarm pursuits. With this increase in nonfarm population, it is only natural to assume a substantial increase in the areas used for residential, commercial, industrial, and other urban-associated uses.

From a historical point of view, the areas used for urban purposes have usually been small. Less than 1.5 percent of the land area of the United States was used for residential and urban purposes in 1970. This total represents a significant increase over the typical situation in times past. Except for a few great political centers such as Rome and Constantinople, the leading cities of the premodern period were ordinarily small by present standards. Defense considerations kept the fortified areas within the city walls compact. Other factors such as the primitive transportation facilities of the time, an almost pitiful lack of sanitation facilities, the absence of a strong urban industrial and commercial base, and the high labor requirements associated with agricultural production also had important discouraging effects in keeping most cities small in area.

Up until recent decades, urban traffic moved at ox-cart pace. Most urban residents faced the necessity of walking to and from work and to and from the market. Since man usually walks at a rate of about three miles per hour, this definitely limited the area over which the larger cities extended. Residences, barns, and courtyards could be spread out in the smaller cities and villages; but in the larger cities, a high premium was placed upon space.

Ancient Rome may be cited as an example of the crowded quarters found in most early cities. At the height of its grandeur, Rome had many more palaces, temples, public squares, and baths than the average city. Yet for every villa or private house there were 26 blocks of teeming apartment houses.[29] These buildings were located along dark, crooked, and narrow streets (sometimes only a few feet across) and frequently stood six or seven stories in height. Inside these structures the bulk of the Roman populace found themselves quartered in small apartments or single rooms with only primitive lighting, heating, and sanitary facilities.

The crowded conditions found in Rome have been duplicated time after time in other cities and still may be found in the older sections of many cities. It took the development of modern transportation facilities to free the cities from the necessity of this congestion. With the development of carriages, those families that could afford this mode of travel often found it possible to build their houses farther out from the urban center. Trolley cars speeded up transportation to a 10- to 15-mile-an-hour pace. Buses and commuter trains contributed further to this conquest of distance. The automobile and the development of networks of highways have done more than anything else, however, to encourage the sprawling outward growth of the modern city with its scatteration of "bedroom" satellites.

Coupled with this new freedom in transportation has come a trend toward single-floor homes and a desire for larger lots, more outdoor living space, and sometimes country living. This has ended the popularity of the narrow 25- to 40-foot lots found in many cities. The average family seeking a new homesite now looks for a lot that has more frontage and greater total area. Between increasing urbanization and the trend toward larger lots and building sites, the growing demand for residential lands will undoubtedly call for large additions to the areas now used for this purpose. During the 1960's an estimated one-half million acres were converted to this use each year in the United States.

Urbanization and the increasing affluence of the population also are contributing significantly to new demands for recreation, transportation, and service lands. With more leisure time and higher real incomes, urban man demands opportunities for outdoor recreation seldom dreamed of by average workers in earlier times. Parks, playing fields, golf courses, and other user-oriented facilities are needed in urban areas while millions of acres must be set aside and developed for national and state parks, recreation areas, and metropolitan area parks outside the cities. Urbanization also has brought new demands for highway and airport facilities and various service areas. Important among the service areas are those required for the provision of municipal and industrial water supplies. These

[29]Cf. Jerome Carcopino, *Daily Life in Ancient Rome* (New Haven: Yale University Press, 1940), p. 23. Because of their shoddy construction the *insulae* or apartment houses often had a tendency to crumble and collapse. In one of the first building codes on record, Augustus Caesar decreed a maximum height of around 60 feet for these buildings and specified certain minimum standards in construction. Another regulation prohibited vehicular traffic during daylight hours on most Roman streets. This regulation relieved traffic congestion during the day, but made it necessary for tradesmen to transport their supplies at night.

supplies often call for the construction of reservoirs, canals, and conduits as well as pumping stations and treatment plants, for the development of watershed protection systems, and sometimes for the diversion of water resources now used for other purposes.

Competition Between Land Uses

With increasing population growth and the increasing material requirements of modern life, the area needs of almost every type of land use are bound to increase. The problem of meeting these additional land requirements would be greatly simplified if each use could expand without impinging upon lands needed or used for other purposes. Unfortunately, the fixed nature of the world's land-resource base makes this an idle dream. Accordingly, each new upward spurt in the demand for land may be expected to contribute further to the competition and possible conflicts between existing and emerging land uses.

The emerging land-use picture suggests numerous widespread conflicts of interest both within and between the various types of land use. Most cities experience continual competition between commercial, industrial, residential, and other uses for the control of particular sites. Individual operators are often willing and anxious to bid against each other for the use of these sites. This same situation exists in agriculture when various crop and livestock enterprises compete for the use of certain fields and when various individuals compete against each other for the privilege of owning or operating particular farms.

Some of the most talked-of competition between land uses comes with the encroachment of residential, recreation, and other consumption uses on areas used for production purposes. Much of the sprawling outward growth of our cities has come at the expense of areas once used for agriculture. This shift from agricultural to suburban and urban uses frequently involves a wasteful use of land resources. Lots in premature subdivisions often remain idle for many years before houses are built on them. Lands attached to rural residences and other properties waiting for future subdivision may also lie idle or, if farmed, may be utilized on a far less efficient basis than would be the case if their owners felt that their lands had a long-time future in farming.

Once an area shifts to urban use, conflicts often develop concerning the future use of open spaces. Most authorities agree that substantial areas of open space are needed around built-up sections for parks, playgrounds, parking areas, and other similar uses. Yet there is always a temptation to use these open areas for various building projects. A variation of this problem often occurs in subdivisions where once-open spaces are converted into building sites with little or no provision for future parks and other open areas. Public funds frequently are not available to insure the reservation of needed open areas at the time when they might be secured at least cost. As a result, it is often necessary to spend considerable sums at later dates for the purchase of built-up areas that are then redeveloped as open spaces.

Expanding urban uses are not the only types of land use that infringe upon agricultural areas. Oil drilling and open pit mining operations, recreation attractions such as golf courses, and new highway and airport developments often bite into the nation's stock of productive farm land. Cropland in its turn tends to outbid and displace lower types of use. Arable grazing lands may be plowed for crop use and forested or cutover areas may be cleared for farming. Irrigation converts arid grazing or waste areas into arable farm land; and drainage projects favor the cultivation of wet land areas that may have value for wildlife purposes.

Under free market conditions, the control of land resources normally goes to the highest bidders. These bidders are then free to put their lands to those uses that offer the highest returns. In most cases, these uses coincide with—or at least are not contrary to—the long-run welfare of society. Operators frequently find it profitable, however, to either exploit their land resources or to use them in ways not compatible with the long-run interests of society.

Exploitive practices and the encroachment of consumption uses on lands that could be held for long-run production purposes are often tolerated by society, particularly when it enjoys a plentiful supply of land resources. Changes in this situation can occur when governments and people become fully conscious of the effects of questionable resource use practices on the environment, on the costs that may be shifted to society, and on their implications for needed uses of land resources. At this point, priorities may be established in land resource use. Resource use standards may be developed to protect the quality of environmental resources. Productive farmlands and natural areas may be protected against urban and residential encroachments. Programs also may be instituted to encourage long-term forest management and the redevelopment and renewal of blighted urban areas.

As population pressure increases and as people strive for higher standards of life, more and more competition can be expected between land uses. This competition will favor more intensive land-use practices; and it will also lead to significant shifts in land use and to the subjugation and nonfulfillment of many land requirements. At the same time, it will probably bring additional controversies and conflicts of interest. In the final analysis, the arbitration and resolution of these conflicts by society will call for a larger measure of institutional and governmental control over land-use practices.

——SELECTED READINGS

Bogue, Donald J., *Principles of Demography* (New York: John Wiley and Sons, Inc., 1969).

Clark, Colin, *Population Growth and Land Use* (London: Macmillan, 1967).

Davis, Joseph S., "Our Changed Population Outlook," *American Economic Review,* Vol. 42, June, 1952.

Johnson, V. Webster, and Raleigh Barlowe, *Land Problems and Policies* (New York: McGraw-Hill Book Company, Inc., 1954), chap. VIII.

Ratcliff, Richard U., *Urban Land Economics* (New York: McGraw-Hill Book Company, Inc., 1949), chaps. III-V.

Renne, Roland R., *Land Economics,* 2nd ed. (New York: Harper & Brothers, 1958), chap. V.

Thompson, Warren S., and David T. Lewis, *Population Problems,* rev. ed. (New York: McGraw-Hill Book Company, Inc., 1965).

United Nations, *Demographic Yearbook,* current years (New York, United Nations).

4

Land

Resource Requirements

Questions concerning the adequacy of the world's land-resource supply necessarily go beyond the present situation. Obviously, the world has sufficient land and productive capacity now in use to do the job it is doing in providing living space, food, fibers, and other land products for its present population. But is this land-resource base adequate to provide a high standard of life for all the world's people? Can it care for the needs of an expanding population? And can it meet the increasing needs that will come with continued technological advance?

These questions can be answered only in a general way. As yet, we have far too little data concerning the present and expected future land requirements of different peoples to more than guess at the world's future needs. Considerable thought has been given to this problem in the United States, however; and projections of the future land-resource requirements of this country are presented here to illustrate the nature of the land-resource requirements problem. This presentation is followed with a discussion of the prospects both in the United States and in other countries for meeting these future needs.

LAND-RESOURCE REQUIREMENTS IN THE UNITED STATES

Wide differences exist between the present and future land-resource needs of different peoples. The average per capita needs of some nations are relatively simple. Most typical consumers in the United States, however, demand diets rich in fruits, vegetables, and livestock products.[1] They demand more and better housing and use more forest products, more mineral and energy resources, more water, and more land for recreation and transportation purposes than the people of most countries.

With the rate of population increase experienced in the United States since 1950, it has been realistic to talk of setting additional plates at the nation's table and building additional houses for the millions of new citizens soon to be born. The increasing affluence of the citizenry has brought higher levels of per capita food consumption and demands for better housing, more opportunities for outdoor recreation, and greater awareness of environmental concerns. This combination of a growing population and rising consumption levels poses a real challenge for those who work with future land-resource needs. It calls for higher productivity standards with the land resources now in use and in many cases for the addition of new land resources to those currently in use.

Crop and Pasture Land Requirements

History shows that man has always been more or less concerned with the adequacy of his food supply. Frequent experience with the pangs of involuntary hunger has often made him food-conscious—a condition well expressed by the first request in the Lord's Prayer: "Give us this day our daily bread." This concern over whether we have food enough has been tempered somewhat in the western world during modern times. But it still remains a chronic problem of persistent importance in many parts of the world. It can be likened in some ways to a smouldering volcano. On many occasions, it lies almost dormant. Sometimes its fires flare up in localized areas. And at times, particularly during and after wars, it erupts in almost epidemic proportions as a problem of world-wide concern.

The problem of food supplies has never been as serious in the United States as in many other countries. The nation has been concerned much more with problems of food surpluses than with shortages. Its experiences during and immediately after World Wars I and II when it tried to supply

[1] Most of the world still clings to a cereal-potato standard in its food consumption. Dr. Bennett's studies of the composition of typical average national diets for the 1934-38 period show that more than four-fifths of the world's people depended upon starchy staples (cereals, potatoes, manioc, and plantain) for more than half of their total calorie intake. Starchy staples accounted for more than three-fourths of the average total calorie intake in Bulgaria, China, Indochina, Indonesia, Japan, the Soviet Union, and Yugoslavia. Cf. M. K. Bennett, *The World's Hunger* (New York: Harper and Brothers, 1954), pp. 214-15. This study indicates that the relative dependence upon starchy staples declines with increasing average per capita incomes. Starchy staples accounted for only 30 to 35 percent of the average total calorie intake in New Zealand, the United States, Australia, the Netherlands, and the United Kingdom.

food for the deficit-producing nations have had their sobering effect, however, and have given rise to numerous questions concerning long-run crop and pasture land needs.

Several estimates have been made of the approximate cropland acreage the United States will need for future production purposes. Some of these involve simple projections of the current average acreage of cropland per person to fit the needs of an assumed future population. Some emphasize the effects different levels of food consumption can have on over-all demand, while others highlight the role improved production practices can play in increasing the productivity of lands currently in use.

Realistic projections of future land requirements call for careful consideration of five sets of variables. These include: (1) assumptions as to future population levels, (2) levels of resource use or consumption, (3) production trends and costs, (4) allowances for imports and exports, and (5) possible changes in production and in levels and types of demand. Regardless of whether one is considering the future land requirements for food, fibers, minerals, housing, recreation, or some other land product, all of these factors should be considered.

Applications of the first four of these variables are highlighted in the crude illustrative projection of cropland requirements reported in Table 4-1. This example assumes a future population of 250 million persons—a total that might well be reached sometime during the 1980s. As a first step in this computation, the average acreage of cropland used per person in the United States in the 1967-69 period is projected to indicate the total cropland area needed to support 250 million people at three different levels of food and crop fiber consumption. These three projections are then added to an estimated 60 million acres of cropland, which will be needed for export crops and feed for horses and mules to indicate the total area of cropland that will be required. Factors indicating the areas planted to cover and soil-improvement crops and the cropland equivalent of the pasture and grazing lands in use could be added at this point but are omitted here as this projection deals only with cropland requirements.

Table 4-1 shows that the provision of a low level of food and crop fiber consumption (10 percent per capita below the 1967-69 level) for a population of 250 million people could call for 324 million acres of cropland or about 8 percent more than was used for this purpose in 1967-69. Maintenance of the 1967-69 level of per capita consumption would call for 353 million acres or 18 percent more cropland, and a 10 percent higher level of consumption would call for 383 million acres or a 28 percent increase in cropland area.

These three projections assume that crop and livestock yields will remain at their 1967-69 level. In practice, however, one cannot ignore the prospects for increased agricultural productivity. As Table 4-2 indicates, the average yields associated with several crops have risen substantially in recent decades and further increases may be anticipated in the future. The

TABLE 4-1. Illustrative Projection of Cropland Requirements in the United States for a Future Population of 250 Million Persons (all figures in millions)

Item	1947-49	1967-69	Levels of food consumption[a]		
			Low	Medium	High
Average total population	147	201	250	250	250
Cropland requirements:*					
Cropland for domestic consumption of food and nonfood products[b]	286	236	264	293	323
Export crops[c]	46	60	56	56	56
Feed for horses and mules[d]	24	4	4	4	4
Total cropland requirements	357	300	324	353	383
Total cropland requirements assuming a 15 percent increase in productivity			275	300	326
Total cropland requirements assuming a 30 percent increase in productivity			227	247	268

*Cropland requirements are measured in acres.

[a]The medium level of food consumption assumes a continuation of the average level of food and crop fiber consumption of the 1967-69 period. The low level assumes consumption at a 10 percent lower level or at a level roughly comparable to that of the 1935-39 period. The high level assumes consumption at an average per capita rate 10 percent above the 1967-69 average. This could involve significantly higher consumption by the nation's poor.

[b]This acreage represents the area reported by the U.S. Department of Agriculture as planted for the production of food and nonfood crops for domestic consumption.

[c]A slight decline in the acreage used for production of crops for export is assumed for this illustrative projection.

[d]Around 1915 a total of 91 million acres was needed to produce feed for the 26 million horses and mules on farms plus the horses found in nonfarm areas. By 1964 the number of horses and mules had dropped to such a low number that they were no longer counted in the Census of Agriculture.

TABLE 4-2. Average Yields per Acre of Selected Crops in the United States, 1937-39 to 1967-69 with Projections to 1980

Crop	1937-39	1947-49	1957-59	1967-69	Projection to 1980
Cotton, lbs.	253	287	438	466	560
Corn, bu.	28.6	36.6	51.4	80.4	109
Hay, tons	1.28	1.34	1.68	2.0	2.3
Peanuts, lbs.	733	721	1,076	1,767	2,470
Rice, lbs.	2,270	2,126	3,250	4,416	5,700
Wheat, bu.	13.6	16.9	23.6	28.4	35

Source: Agricultural Statistics, 1969 (Washington: U. S. Department of Agriculture, 1970); and David W. Culver, "A View of Food and Agriculture in 1980," Agricultural Economics Research, Vol. 22, July, 1970, p. 67.

U. S. Department of Agriculture's index of farm productivity increased from 63 in 1930 (1957-59 = 100) to 85 in 1950 and 108 in 1969. Its index of total farm output doubled between 1930 and 1968 (cf. Figure 4-1) while its indices of crop production per acre, total crop production, and total livestock product production rose 74, 63, and 69 percent, respectively, in the 30 years between 1939 and 1969.

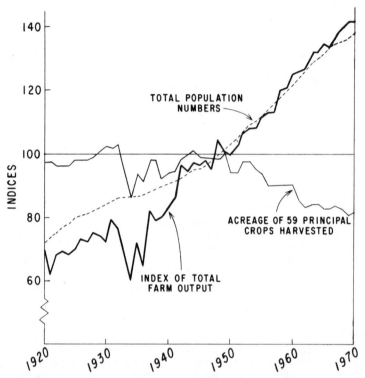

FIGURE 4-1.. Comparison of trends of indices on total population growth, total farm output, and acreage of 59 principal crops harvested, United States, 1920-1970 (1947-49 = 100).

Naturally, it is difficult to predict the net effect new technology and improved production practices will have on crop and livestock yields in the future. However, if productivity increases 15 percent above the 1967-69 level, it will be possible to provide for the nation's domestic cropland requirements at a medium level of consumption with approximately the same acreage as was in use in 1967-69. Should productivity increase by 30 percent, the nation will be able to supply its domestic needs at a medium consumption level from 18 percent less cropland than it had in use in the 1967-69 period and at a high consumption level from 11 percent less cropland than was used in the 1967-69 period.

This simple projection of future cropland requirements is presented for illustrative purposes only. As an indicator of actual future cropland requirements, its value is definitely limited by its implicit assumption that agricultural lands will be distributed between specific crop and livestock uses in approximately the same way in the future as during the 1967-69 period. Important shifts will undoubtedly take place as the demand pattern for agricultural products responds to changes in the nation's eating and other consumption habits and as improved production practices affect some types of land use more than others. A realistic analysis of the impact of these and other relevant factors on future cropland requirements calls for setting up aggregate models in which detailed attention is given to incomes, changing buying patterns and other factors that affect the supply and demand for each type of agricultural production.[2]

Despite its obvious deficiencies, Table 4-1 highlights the general nature of the nation's future cropland needs together with some leading factors that will affect them. Assuming peacetime conditions and no major catastrophes, it indicates that the American people are in no imminent danger of starvation. A cropland shortage may develop over the long run; but with the use of improved production practices and its backlog of cropland reserves, the nation should experience few food problems within the foreseeable future. Far from suggesting a Malthusian balance, the widespread acceptance and use of new technology by farmers and the nonreversible impact of this technology on total farm output signals the probable continuation of a farm-surplus problem for many years to come.

Forest Land Requirements

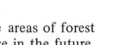

Several factors must be considered in projections of the areas of forest land needed to provide adequate supplies of this resource in the future. Important among these are the long-run nature of the forest production process, the character of the demand for forest products, and the difficulties that arise when one attempts to translate projections of forest-product requirements into forest-land requirements.

[2]For examples of this type of analysis, cf. *Land and Water Resources—A Policy Guide* (Washington: U. S. Department of Agriculture, 1962); and Hans H. Landsberg, Leonard L. Fischman, and Joseph L. Fisher, *Resources in America's Future* (Baltimore: Resources for the Future, Inc. and the Johns Hopkins Press, 1963). Changing-trends in food consumption provide a dramatic example of one of the factors that must be considered in these models. The average per capita annual consumption of meat, poultry, and fish in the United States rose from 177.9 pounds in 1909 to 221.3 pounds in 1968 and is expected to rise to 245 pounds by 2000. Meanwhile, average consumption of potatoes and sweet potatoes and of flour and cereal products dropped from 211.9 and 300 pounds in 1909 to 105.7 and 143 pounds in 1968 and are expected to decline farther to 95 and 120 pounds, respectively, by 2000. For additional discussion of changing food consumption patterns in the United States, cf. National Advisory Commission on Food and Fiber, *Food and Fiber for the Future* (Washington: U. S. Government Printing Office, 1967), pp. 161-68.

Because of the long-term nature of the forest production process, many of the decisions affecting future production must be made years in advance. The quantity and quality of the land areas reserved for future forest use are always affected by current estimates of future supply and demand conditions. On the demand side, every forest-land owner speculates regarding future price levels. His prospects for profit are affected by possible changes in the need for forest products, by the threat of increasing competition with substitute materials, and by the possible development of new uses and new markets for his product. On the supply side, he must consider his prospective forest yield, his probable production costs, and the effect of the import-export situation upon his competitive position. He must also consider the relative pressure to use forest lands for food production and other uses, the alternative uses he could make of his land, and the numerous management and risk factors that affect the willingness of public and private owners to engage in this long-term enterprise.

The United States used approximately 11.8 billion cubic feet of forest products in 1962 of which 10.3 billion came from domestic sources. (Cf. Table 4-3.) According to the projections made by the U. S. Forest Service in its study for forest production trends in the early 1960s, the nation will need 15.4 billion cubic feet of forest products in 1980, 17.9 billion cubic feet in 1990, and 21.3 billion cubic feet in 2000.[3] Sawlogs accounted for about half of the domestic production and consumption in 1962. Their proportionate importance is expected to decline slightly in future decades as pulpwood becomes the most important user of timber.

Sufficient young and maturing timber is now growing in the United States to meet the projected needs until 1990. Questions exist, however, as to the ability of the nation's forests to supply the projected needs for 2000 without some over-cutting of its growing reserves.[4] The present inventory of old-growth stands will be exhausted by that date, and the nation will depend upon younger growth stands, which in the case of saw timber and veneer logs should already be growing. Around 1970 the amount of new timber growth exceeded the amount of annual forest drain caused by cutting operations. Much of this growing timber was young, and a high proportion involved the less desirable species. If this situation continues and the projected annual cut increases as expected, the drain on the nation's forest inventory will exceed new growth after 1990.

---

[3]Cf. *Timber Trends,* U. S. Forest Service Forest Resource Report No. 17, 1965, pp. 5-74. This study assumes future populations of 208 million people in 1970, 241 million in 1980, 280 million in 1990, and 325 million people in 2000. In a separate projection, which assumes populations of 245 million in 1980 and 331 million in 2000, the staff of Resources for the Future, Inc. has projected future needs for lumber from 36.8 billion board feet in 1960 to 61.9 billion in 1980 and 97.6 billion board feet in 2000 and wood pulp from 26.6 million short tons in 1960 to 56.4 million in 1980 and 110.1 million short tons in 2000. (Cf. Landsberg et al., *op. cit.,* p. 812.)

[4]*Ibid.,* pp. 110-37.

TABLE 4-3. Domestic Production, Net Imports, and Consumption of Roundwood in the United States, 1952-2000

Product	1952	1962	Projections to: 1970	1980	1990	2000
			(millions of cubic feet)			
Domestic production						
Sawlogs	6,146	5,271	5,500	5,960	6,560	7,340
Veneer logs	422	857	1,300	1,540	1,840	2,160
Pulpwood	1,823	2,603	3,250	4,640	6,110	8,170
Miscellaneous industrial wood	699	466	460	460	460	460
Fuelwood	2,008	1,123	990	810	680	540
Total	11,098	10,320	11,500	13,410	15,650	18,670
Net imports						
Sawlogs	270	650	800	910	1,020	1,090
Veneer logs	30	110	190	300	380	490
Pulpwood	870	720	760	780	830	1,060
Total	1,170	1,480	1,750	1,990	2,230	2,640
Total consumption	12,268	11,800	13,250	15,400	17,880	21,310

Source: Timber Trends, U. S. Forest Service Forest Resource Report No. 17, 1965, pp. 64-65.

Several factors can operate to change this situation. Applications of improved forest management practices on the nation's 509 million acres of public and private commercial forest lands can lead to greater forest productivity and to a fulfilling of the expected timber requirements. Improved technology in the use of timber products such as increased use of hardboard, particle-board and plastic laminates as substitutes for high quality timber and veneer also can help stretch the nation's timber supplies. Substitution of other resources for forest products and a slowing down of the rate of population growth can have similar effects. Diversions of extensive areas now used for commercial timber production to other uses such as farming, recreation, or residential developments can have an opposite effect.

Housing and Residential Site Requirements

The housing shortage of the early post-World War II period stimulated considerable discussion of the housing problem in the United States and prompted numerous estimates of present and future housing requirements. These estimates varied over a wide range, partly because of differences in assumptions and partly because some estimates were concerned with probable construction while others were concerned more with the problem of social need.[5]

One of the best indices of the nation's future housing needs is provided by recent population trends. A few calculations concerning the children born since 1940 indicates that the nation can expect between 75 and 77 million households in 1980 and between 81 and 84 million in 1985 as compared with 63 million in 1970.[6] Each of these households will provide demand for one residential unit and some will be financially able to own or lease additional units.

Two projections of future residential needs in the United States are reported in Table 4-4. As this tabulation shows, the nation had 68.6 million residential units in 1970, 67.6 million of which were year-round units. Of this total, 63.4 million were occupied units, 46.9 million were single family homes, 18.9 million were parts of two- or more family units and 1.8 million were mobile home units.

The two projections of future trends indicate that the nation should have between 81 and 83 million dwelling units in 1980 and between 112 and 116 million units in 2000. Both projections assume that the great bulk of the increase will involve construction similar to that accepted in the past. Both also assume a considerable increase in the number of unoccupied units by 2000. Some of these will be vacant units but most will represent second homes used for vacation and weekend recreation purposes.

Attainment of these housing objectives can be affected by future population and household formation trends. The slowing down of the rate of population increase will reduce the over-all need for new residential construction, and population stability would call for new construction for replacement purposes only. Most of the people who will make up the household units that will require new housing before 2000 have already been born, and future increases or reductions in the birth rate will have little effect on housing needs until after 2000.

A second factor that will have a significant effect upon the attainment

[5] The National Association of Real Estate Boards estimated in 1944 that an average of 300,000 units a year would be built in urban areas in the first postwar decade. Charles Abrams, on the other extreme, estimated that 18.6 million new housing units would be needed during this same 10-year period. Cf. Charles Abrams, *The Future of Housing* (New York: Harper and Row, 1946), p. 70. Cf. also *The Housing Situation: The Factual Background*, Appendix B, "Estimates of Housing Requirements," a mimeographed report of the Housing and Home Finance Agency, Washington, 1948. One of the more widely quoted estimates was provided by the Congressional Joint Committee on Housing in 1948, which concluded "that for many years at least 1,500,000 houses should be built annually in the United States." Cf.. *Housing Study and Investigation,* Final Majority Report of the Joint Committee on Housing, House Report No. 1564, 80th Congress, 2nd Session, 1948, p. 8.

[6] Cf. *Projections of the Number of Households and Families 1967 to 1985,* Bureau of the Census Current Population Reports Series P-25, No. 394. June, 1968, p.2.

TABLE 4-4. Number of Residential Units in the United States, 1920-1970, With Projections to 2000

Year	Total number of dwelling units	Number of occupied units	Average new units annually	Average annual additions to total stock from:[a]			Mobile home units
				New construction		New additions from conversions	
				All starts	Single-family units		
	(thousands of dwelling units)						
1920	24,552	24,352	909	803	527	106	—
1930	32,495	29,905	593	365	305	227	—
1940	37,325	34,855	1,089	865	719	196	28
1950	46,137	42,969	1,686	1,460	1,216	186	40
1960	58,468	52,955		1,453	925		206
1970	68,627	63,417		1,467	815		401

Timber Trends Report

Projection year	Number of dwelling units	Number of occupied units	Average annual rate of new additions[a]
	(millions of dwelling units)		
1970	69.4	62.5	1.9
1980	81.7	73.5	2.2
1990	95.8	86.2	2.55
2000	112.2	101.0	3.0

Resources for the Future Report

Projection year	Number of dwelling units	Number of occupied units	Average annual rate of new additions[b]
	(millions of dwelling units)		
1970-75	68.8	61.2	2.2
1980-85	83.0	73.0	2.5
1990-95	96.9	84.3	3.1
2000	115.6	99.4	—

[a]Average annual rates are for the full decade (e.g. 1920-29) except for 1970 which is for 1970 only.
[b]Average annual rates are for the first five years of the decade only.
Sources: *Timber Trends*, pp. 14-17; and Landsburg *et al.*, *op. cit.*, p. 621.

of future housing goals involves the nation's ability to provide the number of housing units that are assumed to be needed. High interest rates and the tight real estate mortgage money situation in 1970 permitted construction starts for only 1.47 million new housing units in 1970. This total fell far short of the projected needs of 1.9 and 2.2 million new units annually reported in Table 4-4. Continuation of this trend can lead to a national housing shortage and pressures for a housing boom once credit becomes more readily available.

The question of housing requirements is logically associated with that of residential site needs. Between the time of the stock market crash of 1929 and the building boom that followed World War II, the problem of residential sites was more one of a surplus supply of vacant lots and premature subdivisions than one of new residential land requirements.[7] Most of these vacant lots were swallowed up in the building boom that started in 1946. As a result, the problem of site requirements has become increasingly one of outward urban expansion plus a need for the redevelopment of decadent built-up areas.

Many of the new housing units that will be constructed by 1990 will be built on vacant lands now within established city limits. Thousands of other units will come with apartment projects in redeveloped areas. Most of the new construction, however, will likely come in suburban areas, unincorporated subdivisions, and in areas now classified as open country. This trend will call for the shifting of extensive now rural areas to urban and suburban developments.

Just as the total area needed for new residential sites is affected by population and household trends, so also is it affected by unit area requirements. The Garden City movement and the current architectural emphasis on rambling ranch-type houses has stimulated a demand for lots of considerable size and width. Many prospective owners now seek lots with from 70 to 150 or more feet of frontage and with up to an acre or more of total area. If one assumes that half of the 28 million housing units that should be built between 1970 and 1990 are built outside of present incorporated areas and that the average unit takes only one-third of an acre, this building trend will account for almost 5 million acres. If the average suburban and rural building site covers one-half of an acre, 7 million acres will be needed for this use.

Industrial and Commercial Site Needs

Commercial and industrial sites have an importance that far exceeds their actual area requirements. Generally speaking, the proportion of any city's area that is used for these purposes is usually small. From 10 to 16

---

[7]For a more detailed discussion of this subject, cf. Miles Colean, *American Housing* (New York: Twentieth Century Fund, 1944), chap. I.

percent of the urban area usually suffices for these purposes.[8] The trend, however, is in the direction of more extensive use of land for these purposes. With the continued expansion of the national economy and of the areas used for urban and suburban residential purposes, more and more land will be needed for commercial and industrial sites.[9] Some of these sites will be provided by the redevelopment of urban areas now used for residential purposes. However, the lure of lower land values, more space, and suburban markets will undoubtedly favor a marked expansion of these uses in suburban and now rural areas.

Hundreds of suburban neighborhood shopping areas have been developed in recent years. These areas vary in size from congested centers that cover a few acres to spacious developments that occupy 100 or more acres. In most instances they are laid out on a single-floor level with considerable allowance for adjacent parking space. The Urban Land Institute has suggested that approximately one acre of store space be used in these centers for each 1,000 persons (300 families) in the shopping area.[10] Substantial additional areas are suggested for wide sidewalks, streets, adequate parking, buffer areas, and possible landscaping.

Industrial space needs also reflect the trend toward decentralization. No longer is it as necessary as it once was to locate industries next to railroads or navigable waters or to seek sites that provide natural water power. The widespread use of motor trucks for transport purposes and the use of electricity and mineral fuel for power and energy has freed industry from the "tyranny of site." This change in site requirements, together with the relative scarcity of new or vacant industrial sites within urban centers and rural areas, has made it practicable for many industries to locate in areas where they can spread out over sizable areas.

No well-developed criteria exist for the projection of future com-

---

[8] John H. Niedercorn and Edward F. R. Hearle, "Recent Land Use Trends in Forty-eight Large American Cities," *Land Economics*, Vol. 40, February 1964, pp. 105-110, found that 4.8 percent of the area of their sample of cities was used for commercial purposes and 10.9 percent for industrial uses in 1963. These totals vary slightly from the 2.5 to 3.4 percent for commercial uses and 2.8 to 16.3 percent for industrial and railroad uses reported by Harland Bartholemew, *Land Uses in American Cities* (Cambridge: Harvard University Press, 1955), Tables 3 and 7, from his study of three different groups of cities.

[9] *Timber Trends*, p. 23, projects nonresidential construction expenditures of $42.6 billion in 1970, $57.4 billion in 1980, $75.9 billion in 1990, and $101.8 billion in 2000 as compared with $33.9 in 1962. Of these totals, expenditures for commercial and hotel-motel construction are projected to rise from $6.5 billion in 1962 to $6.8 billion in 1970, $9.2 billion in 1980, $12.1 billion in 1990, and $16.7 billion in 2000 while investments in industrial building construction are expected to rise from $2.8 billion in 1962 to $3.4 billion in 1970, $4.6 billion in 1980, $6.5 billion in 1990, and $8.7 billion in 2000.

[10] Cf. Seward H. Mott and Max S. Wehrly, *The Community Builder's Handbook* (Washington: Urban Land Institute, 1947), p. 193.

mercial and industrial land requirements. Yet the assumptions of an increasing population and a dynamic developing economy logically suggest a tremendous increase in area requirements. This conclusion is supported by the tendency of new commercial and industrial developments to make more lavish use of the land factor than has been the general case in times past. It must be remembered, however, that the area requirements for retailing, wholesaling, office space, and industrial uses depend upon the types of enterprises undertaken, the competition for desirable sites, and the size, shape, location, and value of the land parcels involved.[11] The demand for these sites also will be affected to a considerable extent by business conditions and by the existence of a present or potential market for the goods and services produced.

Land Requirements for Recreation

Land requirements for recreation was a subject of secondary interest in the United States until the middle 1950s. True, the nation had its natural and man-made parks, scenic drives, and recreation areas at the local, state, and national levels. It had a dedicated group of park and recreation workers and also its share of outdoor recreation devotees. Yet the subject of recreation land resource requirements was usually viewed as a miscellaneous residual need. This situation suddenly changed when the burgeoning population of the nation's urban areas found with their new affluence and their increase in leisure that there was a shortage of opportunities for outdoor recreation activities. An Outdoor Recreation Resource Review Commission was appointed to study the problem, and public programs were soon initiated to acquire and develop more lands for public recreation use.

The problem of future recreation land requirements is somewhat elusive. To begin with, individuals differ a great deal in their recreation likes and dislikes. Some people choose to take practically all of their recreation in their homes, in night clubs, taverns, and theaters. The per capita recreation-land-area requirements of this group are very low. Others make considerable use of city parks, beaches, and golf courses. Their per capita land requirements also are relatively small but involve intensively used properties of high value. At the other extreme, many people go in for transcontinental tours and for camping, hunting, and fishing trips, which give them a chance to "rough it," commune with nature, and visit wilderness areas.

Recreation lands also vary over a wide range. The intensively used tot-lots, parks, playing fields, and golf courses found in and around cities

---

[11] Cf. Richard U. Ratcliff, *Urban Land Economics* (New York: McGraw-Hill Book Company, 1949), chap. V.

are sometimes described as user-oriented facilities.[12] Many of the facilities associated with wilderness areas, national parks, some state parks, and the recreation areas in national forests, on the other hand, are resource-based in the sense that they feature and try to protect natural wonders of nature along with the flora and fauna. These facilities are ordinarily used on an infrequent vacation basis and often entail considerable travel by the users. Between these two classes is an intermediate classification of parks and recreation areas, which involves natural and man-made developments located within a few hours driving time of most of their users. Emphasis has been given to the development of all three of these types of facilities. It is obvious, however, that the nation can soon run out of wonders of nature and that much of the future acquisition and development of parks and recreation areas should come at sites located within easy commuting distance of the using populations.

The question of how much land should be reserved for recreation uses depends mostly upon the needs of the urban population. A widely quoted rule of thumb regarding municipal recreation-land requirements was suggested around 1923 by the National Recreation Association. This group recommended that cities of 10,000 or more have 10 acres of recreation land for every 1,000 people and that smaller cities use a sliding scale, which goes up to one acre for every 40 persons in villages with 1,000 residents. Most recreation land-use authorities regard this formula as inadequate. Some would expand the National Recreation Association standards to require 10 acres of county and metropolitan-area parks and an additional 10 acres of state and federal recreation lands (located within a two-hour drive of the central cities) for every 1,000 people in the metropolitan centers.[13] These standards call for somewhat larger holdings of municipal and county or regional recreation lands than the nation now has.[14]

[12] Cf. Marion Clawson, R. Burnell Held, and Charles H. Stoddard, *Land for the Future* (Baltimore: The Johns Hopkins Press, 1960), pp. 153-83; Marion Clawson, "The Crisis in Outdoor Recreation," *American Forests*, Vol. 65, March 1959; pp. 30 and 40, and Marion Clawson and Jack Knetsch, *The Economics of Outdoor Recreation* (Baltimore: The Johns Hopkins Press, 1966), pp. 36-40.

[13] Acreage standards of this type can be viewed as arbitrary. They ignore the intensity with which different types of recreation areas are used. By linking recreation area needs to population numbers, they can also provide unrealistic goals in urban regions with rapidly increasing populations. Goals defined in terms of some specific percentage of an urban region's total area provide a more workable standard over time for public planning purposes

[14] Reports of the Bureau of Outdoor Recreation indicate that cities had 805,336 acres of parks and recreation areas plus 96,965 acres of school recreation areas in 1965 while the counties had an additional 691,042 acres of parks and recreation areas and 19,741 acres of school recreation lands. Cf. *Recreation and Parks Yearbook, 1966* (Washington: National Recreation and Park Association, 1967). In addition to this total, state agencies administered 32.9 million acres of land, 1.9 million acres of

More fire was added to the demand for additional recreation lands in 1959 when Marion Clawson argued that rising population numbers, higher family incomes, increases in leisure time, and transportation improvements could call for a 5- to 15-fold increase in the demand for outdoor recreation by the end of the century.[15] The U. S. Forest Service projected a 4-fold increase in demand in its Operation Out-of-Doors program while the Outdoor Recreation Resources Review Commission projected a 3-fold increase in outdoor recreational activity-participation by 2000.[16]

Considerable progress has been realized since 1960 by federal, state, and local agencies under their own programs and in cooperation with the Land and Water Conservation Fund and the Open Space Lands Acquisition programs in reserving and acquiring public wilderness, recreation, and open space lands. A high proportion of these lands are held for single purpose wilderness or recreation use. In many instances, however, recreation is treated as one of two or more uses in multiple-use programs. With the competition that can be expected in a populous amenity-oriented society for land areas that provide trees, scenic attractions, and access to lakes or streams, more emphasis probably should be given to the treatment of recreation as a multiple use, particularly with the resource-based and intermediate area classifications of recreation areas. In this sense, much of the public and private land now classified as in forest, mountain grazing, or marginal farming uses perhaps should be reclassified as recreation multiple-use areas. Some of the less unique public resource-based lands now reserved exclusively for wilderness or recreation uses may also shift, if national priorities so dictate, to multiple-use areas.

Transportation and Service Area Needs

No discussion of over-all land requirements would be complete without some consideration of the areas needed for transportation and service purposes. Approximately 37 million acres were used for transportation purposes in 1964.[17] This estimate includes 21.2 million acres in rural

---

water surface, and 4.9 million acres of wetland as outdoor recreation areas of which 67,291 acres were classified as high density recreation areas. The National Park Service administered 26.5 million acres of national park and recreation areas in 1965. Additional large areas used for recreation were included within the areas administered by the U. S. Forest Service, the Bureau of Land Management, the Bureau of Reclamation, the Bureau of Sport Fisheries and Wildlife, and the Army Corps of Engineers.

[15] Clawson, "The Crisis in Outdoor Recreation," *loc. cit.,* Vol. 65, March and April 1959.

[16] Outdoor Recreation Resources Review Commission, *Outdoor Recreation for America* (Washington: U. S. Government Printing Office, 1962), pp. 32 and 221.

[17] Cf. H. Thomas Frey, Orville E. Krause, and Clifford Dickason, *Major Uses of Land and Water in the United States,* U. S. Department of Agriculture, Agricultural Economic Report No. 149, 1968, p. 26.

highways and roads, 3.3 million acres in railroad rural rights-of-way, 1.8 million acres in farm roads and lanes, 1.5 million acres in airport sites, and an allowance of 9.5 million acres for streets, alleys, parking areas, and railroad lands in cities, villages, and unincorporated subdivisions.

By and large, the boom period of railroad and local highway building in the United States has passed. Significant areas will be needed in the future, however, for the construction of limited-access highways and turnpikes; and additional rights-of-way will be required for highway widening, rebuilding, and improvement projects. The national road building program authorized by the Federal-Aid Highway Act of 1956 called for construction of 41,000 miles of interstate highways and for the improvement, rebuilding, or replacement of some 200,000 miles of state highways and 508,000 miles of rural roads. The new limited-access roads and interchanges envisaged in this program have required upwards of 35 to 40 acres of land per mile of highway. This requirement together with the new areas needed for the improvement, widening, and relocation of existing highways has called for a shift of approximately 2.5 million acres to highway uses.

Substantial additional acreages also have been needed for the construction of new and wider streets in cities and new subdivisions and for the provision of off-street parking facilities in urban areas. Around a third of the developed land area of most cities is now used for streets, alleys, and railroad purposes. Less land is used for this purpose in most new subdivisions. Still, the emphasis on street widening projects and the provision of new parking areas suggests that this proportion will probably continue to provide an index of the urban area needed for transportation purposes.

Serious problems are arising in many cities because of the need for more adequate parking facilities. Most projects for this purpose involve an expensive type of urban redevelopment. Yet city residents and merchants often support this type of action in the hope that it will attract new business and prevent migration of their present trade to suburban shopping centers. Comparable problems are associated with the provision of new or improved airport facilities. With the development of large commercial planes, every large city has felt a need for enlarging its airport facilities. Inasmuch as these larger airports usually involve tracts of substantial size, which must be located within reasonable commuting distance of the city, they ordinarily involve expensive land-acquisition programs and the frequent displacement of other desired uses.

Land requirements for service areas. Service areas tend to fall into two groups, those which exist primarily for single service purposes and those which fit into multiple-use patterns. Military reservations rank most important area-wise in the first group (23.6 million acres in 1970). Other important examples include the sites used for cemeteries, schools and public buildings, water-filtering operations, power plants, and public dumping grounds. The area requirements for most of these uses will probably increase with population growth. Future military reservation needs will depend upon international politics and the future course of peace and war.

Watershed protection areas and large storage reservoirs provide leading examples of service areas that often are associated with other land uses. The need for multiple-use projects involving these types of service areas will in all probability increase with population numbers and with society's need for additional water supplies.

Water Resource Needs

Water resource needs and water quality have become subjects of widespread public awareness and concern since the late 1950s. Interest in the increasing water resource needs of a growing population and an expanding economy prompted the appointment of a United States Senate Select Committee on National Water Resources in 1959. This committee issued a series of reports, which projected a 2.5-fold increase in municipal water supply needs and an 8-fold increase in industrial water supply needs for the nation between 1954 and 2000. These reports were followed by the creation of a United States Water Resources Council and the launching and expansion of several public programs for the development and treatment of water supplies, improvement of desalinization processes, and the enhancement and protection of water quality.

In a first national assessment of the nation's water resources, the Water Resources Council projected a 3-fold increase in water withdrawals between 1965 and 2000. and a doubling of the rate of water consumption.[18] (Cf. Table 4-5.) It found that the nation was withdrawing 270 billion gallons daily and making consumptive use of 78 billion gallons of this daily total. Almost 90 percent of the water withdrawn is used for irrigation, thermal power generation, and industrial uses, while agricultural irrigation accounts for more than 80 percent of the consumptive use. Most of the water withdrawn is used and then returned to streams, lakes, or the ocean for possible reuse.

The nation has sufficient access to water supplies to meet its projected demands. Unfortunately, however, water supplies are not always found at the places where they are needed at the specific times and in the quantities and quality desired. In a very practical sense, most of the nation's water use plans must be built around the supplies that are normally available at specific sites under the operations of the hydrologic cycle. Additional supplies can be secured by pumping from greater depths, by conducting waters through canals or conduits from greater distances, by transforming saline waters into fresh water supplies, and by treating

[18] Cf. *The Nation's Water Resources:* The First National Assessment of the Water Resources Council (Washington: U.S. Government Printing Office, 1968), pp. 1-8.

TABLE 4-5. Water Uses by Major Purposes in the United States in 1965 with Projections to 1980, 2000, and 2020 (million gallons daily)

Type of use	Used 1965	Projected requirements		
		1980	2000	2020
		Withdrawals		
Rural domestic	2,351	2,474	2,852	3,334
Municipal (public-supplied)	25,745	33,596	50,724	74,256
Industrial (self-supplied)	46,405	75,026	127,365	210,767
Steam-electric power:				
Fresh	62,738	133,963	259,208	410,553
Saline	21,800	59,340	211,240	503,540
Agriculture:				
Irrigation	110,852	135,852	149,824	160,978
Livestock	1,726	2,375	3,397	4,660
Total	269,617	442,626	804,610	1,368,088
		Consumptive use		
Rural domestic	1,636	1,792	2,102	2,481
Municipal (public-supplied)	5,244	10,581	16,478	24,643
Industrial (self-supplied)	3,764	6,126	10,011	15,619
Steam-electric power:				
Fresh	659	1,685	4,552	8,002
Saline	157	498	2,022	5,183
Agriculture:				
Irrigation	64,696	81,559	89,964	96,919
Livestock	1,626	2,177	3,077	4,238
Total	77,782	104,418	128,206	157,085

Source: Water Resources Council, *The Nation's Water Resources* (Washington: U.S. Government Printing Office, 1968), pp. 1-8.

used waters for reuse. These practices involve costs that should be borne by the water users and that can discourage the use of high-cost water supplies for low-value uses.

Water resource and watershed management practices are needed to protect water supplies, to minimize damage from floods, to facilitate retention of water supplies for use in low-flow periods, to minimize pollution problems, and to enhance quality maintenance. Like other fixed supplies of free natural resources, which have appeared more than adequate in times past, water supplies must now be stretched to supply the needs of larger numbers of users. This stretching process calls for discipline in water use, new regulations affecting individual use rights, water quality maintenance programs, and emphasis on recycling practices that permit the use of the same water resource many times.

Mineral and Energy Requirements

Great quantities of mineral and energy inputs are needed to keep the wheels of modern industry moving. As one of the industrial powers of the present world, the United States uses considerably more minerals and energy resources on an average per capita basis than does the average country. Projections of future resource requirements, however, indicate that the nation will need more rather than less of these resources in the years ahead.

Table 4-6 reports the consumption rates for selected minerals and energy resources in the United States in 1968 together with the projected consumption rates for 1985. These data show that increases in demand are expected with almost every item. The demand for aluminum, copper, cement, and electric power is expected to double, while increases of 50 percent or more apply with zinc, sand and gravel, bituminous coal, petroleum, and natural gas.

TABLE 4-6.   Consumption of Selected Minerals and Energy Resources in the United States in 1968 With Projections to 1985

Mineral and energy resources	Consumption in United States in 1968	Projected rate of consumption in 1985
Iron ore, thou. lg tons	131,753	176,000
Raw steel, thou. short tons	131,462	162,000
Aluminum, thou. short tons	4,656	12,300
Copper, thou. short tons	1,880	3,750
Lead, thou. sh. tons	1,329	1,430
Zinc, thou. sh. tons	1,728	3,000
Cement, mil. barrels	403	890
Sand and gravel, mil. sh. tons	917	1,510
Bituminous coal, mil. sh. tons	499	755-925
Anthracite coal, mil. sh. tons	10	5
Petroleum, mil. barrels	4,900	8,000
Natural gas, dry, bil. cu. ft.	18,957	31,000
Electric generation, bil. kt. hrs.	1,433	n. a.
Hyrdo, bil. kilowatt hrs.	222	376
Nuclear, bil. kilowatt hrs.	12	796-1,256
Thermal, bil. kilowatt hrs.	1,092	1,928-2,392
Energy resource inputs, trillion B T U's	62,308	110,300

Source: U. S. Department of Interior, Minerals Yearbook, 1968, Vol. I - II, (Washington: U.S. Government Printing Office, 1969), pp. 21-22.

In meeting these resource needs, the United States will depend both upon domestic and world sources of supply. Some indication of the extent of this dependence upon foreign sources is suggested by Table 4-7,

TABLE 4-7. Production of Selected Minerals in the United States in 1968, United States Production as a Share of World Production, and United States Production and Imports as a Share of World Production

Selected minerals	Total production in United States in 1968	United States production as a percentage share of world production	United States production and imports as a share of world production
Bauxite, thou. lg. tons	1,665	3.9 percent	29.5 percent
Copper, thou. sh. tons	1,205	20.4	26.3
Iron ore, thou. lg. tons	81,934	12.8	19.3
Lead, thou. lg. tons	359	10.8	13.4
Nickel, thou. lg. tons	17	3.2	25.3
Tungsten, thou. sh. tons	11	14.0	17.3
Zinc, thou. lg. tons	529	9.7	18.0
Cement, mil. barrels	412	14.0	14.3
Nitrogen, agricultural	6,872	27.9	32.5
Phosphate rock, thou. lg. tons	41,251	44.4	44.5
Potash,	2,722	15.9	28.6
Salt,	41,274	33.1	35.9
Sulfur, thou. lg. tons	9,770	52.8	61.2
Crude petroleum, mil. barrels	3,329	23.6	31.0

Source: U. S. Department of Interior, *Minerals Yearbook, 1968,* Vol. I - II (Washington: U. S. Government Printing Office, 1969), p. 59.

which reports the production of selected minerals in the United States in 1968, the proportion that this production represented of world production, and the proportion of the world's production produced in and imported by the United States. This table shows that the United States was heavily dependent upon foreign imports of bauxite and nickel and that it received 25 percent or more of its supplies of copper, iron ore, zinc, and potash from other countries while it produced almost all of the cement, phosphate rock, and salt it used. A comparable pattern of dependence on foreign sources may be anticipated in the future.

A major problem associated with the filling of future demands is that of providing new and additional sources of supply. Minerals are scattered in fairly good supply throughout the earth's crust. Most of the surface sources, however, have already been discovered and exploited. Man's problem is that of discovering and developing new subsurface supplies in adequate time to provide for his current needs. With a steadily increasing rate of drain against known reserves, this problem is becoming more and more critical and may logically lead to higher costs and some material shortages.

As the report of the President's Materials Policy Commission observed in 1952:

The nature of the problem can perhaps be successfully oversimplified by saying that the consumption of almost all materials is expanding at compound rates and thus is pressing harder and harder against resources which, whatever else they may be doing, are not similarly expanding. [19]

All of the minerals may be classified as fund or stock resources. None are renewable, and although some of the metals are not destroyed by use—as is the case with the mineral fuels—their recovery for future use involves time, trouble, and a certain amount of conscious planning.

It is estimated that the United States used more metals and mineral fuels between 1918 and 1950 than the entire world used prior to 1941. It also has been estimated that if all nations were to use minerals at the same per capita rate as the United States, total consumption would increase about sixfold and would exhaust the known reserves of chromite, copper, lead, tin, and zinc in less than a decade. [20]

Statements of this order raise the spectre of a minerals famine. It should be recognized, however, that the concept of "known reserves" refers only to publicly announced reserves of ore or other deposits of sufficient quality to justify their present economic exploitation. By this standard, the United States has run out of oil and other minerals several times in the past century. Each time, however, new resources have been discovered or developed so that the nation now has more known reserves than at any time in its past history.

Viewed realistically, it may be noted that much of the earth's surface is composed of minerals, although most of them are present in concentrations too low to justify their current economic exploitation. Once mining operations begin to press upon actual reserves, the interrelationship of supply and demand leads to higher resource prices. These higher prices help to correct the shortage problem by generating three types of activities. They create (1) higher incentives for the discovery and development of new mineral sources, (2) opportunities for the profitable processing of lower grades of ores, and (3) shifts to possible alternative resources that could not compete with the minerals in question when their prices were lower.

It is true that the United States has skimmed the cream from its stock of mineral resources insofar as it has been able to find them. There has been nothing unnatural in this process. Bounteous supplies made it economically feasible for the nation's copper producers to pass up ores with concentrations of less than 5 percent copper around 1900. Ores were being smelted in 1968 with concentrations as low as 0.4 percent copper

[19]Cf. President's Materials Policy Commission, *Resources for Freedom* (Washington: U.S. Government Printing Office, 1952), Summary of Vol. 1, p. 2.

[20]Cf. Elmer W. Pehrson, "Estimates of Selected World Mineral Supplies by Cost Range," in United Nations Scientific Conference on the Conservation and Utilization of Resources, *Proceedings* (New York: United Nations, 1950), Vol. 2, p. 2.

and new processing efficiencies can make the mining of even lower concentrations economically feasible in the future. [21] The same situation applies with other minerals.

Higher mineral prices or greater efficiencies are needed to justify the resort to lower grade resources. As long as prices are the hurdle, the public cannot be expected to pay the prices needed to bring lower grade resources into use as long as adequate supplies can be secured at lower cost either here or abroad. This situation can change as the richer deposits of minerals are used, but consumers can still expect to find sufficient minerals produced to fill their needs. The prices they will pay for these resources, however, will probably be somewhat higher than those they have paid in the past.

PROSPECTS FOR MEETING FUTURE NEEDS

Few problems provide a bigger challenge than that of meeting the world's future requirements for food and other land resources. With food, as with other land products, the problem of increasing supplies is always one of expanding production where the people live, transporting the food from where it can be produced to the people, or moving the people to the food supply. Problems arise with each of these alternatives. Factors such as a limited resource base, operation of the law of diminishing returns, and present production and ownership patterns may discourage efforts to increase production in the areas where people live. High transportation costs, limited consumer purchasing power, trade barriers, and international exchange problems frequently prevent the use of areas located away from the market for this purpose. The movement of people to areas of potential surplus production in turn is often stymied by immigration barriers, migration costs and restrictions, or the reluctance of people to move.

Opportunities for Better Man-Land Relationships

Nations or communities that desire a better or more rational balance

21 Cf. Thomas S. Lovering, "Mineral Resources from the Land," National Academy of Sciences-National Research Council Committee on Resources and Man, *Resources and Man* (San Francisco: W. H. Freeman and Company, 1969), p. 111. On this point, Harrison Brown has observed that "if at some future time the average concentration of copper in copper ore were to drop to 0.01 percent, and if there were still an acute need for copper, there would be little question but that the metal could be extracted in high yield. . . . Given the brainpower and the energy, the people of the world could, if need be, support themselves entirely with the leanest of ores, the waters of the oceans, the rocks of the earth's crust, and the very air around them." Cf. Harrison Brown, James Bonner, and John Weir, *The Next Hundred Years* (New York: The Viking Press, 1957), pp. 90 and 92.

between their supplies of land products and the demand for these products can pursue three principal types of programs for this purpose. They can enlarge their resource base and bring new lands into use. They can make more intensive use of the lands they have available. They might also shift to lower man-land ratios by reducing their population numbers or by making downward adjustments in dietary standards.

Bringing new resources into use.   Almost every country has areas that can be brought into agricultural or other uses should the price and demand situation so warrant. The area used for cropland can be supplemented by the clearing, draining, irrigation, or terracing of new lands. Sometimes these lands represent areas of high potential productivity whose development has been delayed because of imperfect human knowledge, lack of accessibility to market, or the high costs involved in bringing them into use. Changed demand and price situations may also justify the cultivation of lower grade lands, the development of grazing areas, or the planting of trees in cutover and wasteland areas.

Agricultural lands are frequently used when the need arises for commercial and industrial, residential, transportation, recreation, and service area uses. Additional sites for these uses can be created by filling in swampy and submerged lands and by building dikes and levees in lowland and flood plain areas. More mineral reserves can be tapped once they are discovered and developed for human use.

Individuals and nations have long since found that it is possible for them to extend their controls over new resources without going through the land development process. Individuals can buy the already developed resources of others. Nations have frequently used brute force and military power to acquire control and sovereignty over additional resources. This method is frowned upon in the modern world, but it has been used quite extensively in times past by most of the world's great powers. World War II was precipitated by the expansionist policies of the Axis Powers; and many tensions in international politics still spring from national ambitions for control, exploitation, and use of the resources found in other countries.

Many nations have also found that they, or their citizens, can exert considerable economic power over the development and use of the resources found in other countries without exercising political domination. This type of control usually involves large investments in resource development and frequently ties the economy of the developed areas to the home country from which the investment funds have come.

Industrialization and extensive use of international trade provides another means that some nations have used to enlarge the resource base upon which they draw. Nations such as Great Britain, Belgium, and Japan have found it profitable to market the products of their labor and manufacturing skill in a world market. In this process they import a high proportion of their supplies and raw materials. By processing these materials at home, selling a high proportion of the finished products

[handwritten annotations in top margin: "BETTER PUBLIC INVOLVEMENT: SHORT-TERM. PROCEDURES ARE JUST A FORMAL 'FIX': NEED MTDS of CONFLICT RESOLUTION (SIM MODELS) AS WELL (DECISION AS BETTER BARGAINING (POLITICAL) PROCESSES. ← ASSUMING BASIC INFO GATHERING MECHANISMS"]

abroad, and then reinvesting in raw materials, they have found it possible to expand their accessible resource base far beyond their geographic and political boundaries.

Intensifying the use of available land resources. Higher production can come from the more intensive use of lands currently in use as well as from the development of new land areas. Up to a certain point, most types of land yield a higher and higher total production with increasing inputs of capital and labor per unit of land. These inputs naturally add to production costs, and it is seldom economic to push production to or even near the point of diminishing physical returns. Nevertheless, it is often profitable to use land resources somewhat more intensively than they have been used. This is particularly true in periods of rising prices and on those occasions when new technological developments can be used to increase production or to reduce costs.

Numerous examples of intensification practices may be listed. With croplands, these may involve the use of improved cultural practices, better seed, insecticides, more fertilizer, irrigation water, and possibly some double-cropping. Pasture and grazing lands can often be planted to improved grass species, fertilized, irrigated, and stocked with better livestock. Forest-land use can often be intensified through the use of timber-stand improvement and selective cutting practices.

The high property values and concentration of economic and group activities around urban sites ordinarily favors the intensive use of these sites. Leading examples of this intensification are provided by the use of skyscrapers and other multistoried structures, and by the leveling, filling, and bridging operations used in the development of urban areas.

Intensification practices also have an important impact on the use of mineral resources. Higher prices and technical improvements frequently make it profitable for operators to capture a higher proportion of their known reserves of ores, coal, and oil. This condition leads to more intensive mining operations and in so doing reduces the amount of physical waste by favoring use of the lower-grade or less-accessible deposits, which might otherwise be discarded or by-passed. Minerals are also used more intensively when means are developed to make them work harder and longer than they have in the past and when emphasis is given to programs designed to reclaim scrap materials for reprocessing and reuse.

More effective land use can also be secured by actions designed to overcome or at least partially offset present barriers to intensive land use. Highways, railroads, and other transportation and communication developments have helped to make areas more accessible to one another. Canals and aqueducts bring water to thirsty cities and fields. Sewers and drainage ditches take away urban wastes and the surplus waters found in agricultural areas. Flood control programs protect many land uses from possible flood damage. Commercial fertilizers are used to overcome soil-nutrient deficiencies.

Considerable progress has been made in removing obstacles in the past, but much remains to be done. With new demands, man can use his existing know-how to overcome numerous barriers to effective land use and to facilitate new and improved uses of land in many parts of the world. New scientific and technological developments will undoubtedly open doors for new resource-utilization possibilities. Some much discussed possibilities such as the processing of food from algae and the synthesizing of food and other products may even work miracles in greatly reducing the amount of land needed per capita to support human habitation.

Downward adjustments in demand. Nations with limited opportunities for increasing their economic supplies of land sometimes find it necessary to adjust their land requirements to their available supplies of land resources. During emergency periods this situation may call for the rationing of food and other products or for the allocation of priorities for the use of critical materials.

Over longer periods, forced rationing can bring adjustments in attitudes concerning need for the products in short supply. People may reconcile themselves to the changed situation and gradually accept downward adjustments in their consumption patterns. With an increasing demand for food, they may find it logical to cut down on livestock production while they shift more and more of their available arable land into food crops. This would result in less human consumption of livestock products and bring a downward adjustment in dietary standards.

Migration and population-control programs provide another possible means for stabilizing or reducing the total demand for land products. Several countries in times past have encouraged the migration of their citizens to frontier, colonial, or other areas and have thereby improved the man-land ratio situation at home. Population-control programs also have received some emphasis. One of the best modern examples of population control is suggested by the example of Ireland, a nation that now has only slightly more than half the population it had before the potato famine of the 1840s. *yes   But, take a closer look at their m/o of pop control.*

Outlook for New Land Development

A considerable portion of the earth's land surface can still be developed for agricultural and other uses. The Food and Agriculture Organization has classified 3.57 billion acres, 10.8 percent of the world's land surface, as arable cropland, and an additional 1.1 billion acres as unused but potentially arable land. Considerable areas now used for pasture, meadows, and forest might also be shifted to agricultural uses. Large tracts of both arable and nonarable land can be drawn upon for urban, transportation, recreation, and service-area uses. The area used for mining can also increase as new deposits are discovered and opened up for exploitation.

Most of the world's easy-to-develop fertile soils have already been brought into agricultural use. Soil classification and climatological studies, however, show that the earth has 7.86 billion acres of potentially arable land and that an additional 9.02 billion acres have a potential for grazing. [22] Most of the land that has an arable use potential but is not now used for that purpose is found in Africa and South America. Still, almost one billion acres are found in North America, Australia, and New Zealand, while smaller areas are located in Europe and Asia. [23] Irrigation is needed for the production of even a single crop with 850 million of the 7.86 billion acres while land-clearing, irrigation, drainage, and other land-development practices are necessary for optimum use of much of the remaining area.

More land can be brought into cropland use even in the world's great "bread basket" areas. A nationwide inventory of soil and water conservation needs conducted in the United States in 1958, for example, found that the 48 mainland states had 637.1 million acres of rural lands suited for cropland use plus an additional 168.7 million acres suited for occasional cultivation. [24] It found that 25.4 million acres then in cultivation needed to be retired to grass, trees, wildlife, or other similar uses because they were eroded, too steep, or were otherwise unsuited for cultivated crops. This means that the 459 million acres of cropland reported by the Agricultural Census of 1969 (371 million acres of cropland plus 88 million acres of cropland used for pasture) could be increased by around 178 million acres without resort to the lands suited only for occasional cultivation. While this large area has definite potential as additional cropland, it is logical to assume that most of it is now used for pasture, grazing, and woodland purposes within farms and will probably remain in these uses.

[22] Cf. President's Science Advisory Committee, Panel on the World Food Supply, *The World Food Problem* (Washington: 1967), Vol. 2, p. 423. Without irrigation, multiple cropping could increase the gross cropped-area (the cultivated area times the number of crops) to 9.8 billion acres annually or about three times the world's present cultivated area. Use of irrigation and double and triple cropping in those areas where it is feasible would permit a maximum gross cropped-area of 16.3 billion acres. (Cf. *ibid.*, p. 434.)

[23] These totals are somewhat higher than earlier estimates of the world's gross area of potential cropland. During the 1940s, for example, Charles E. Kellogg ["Food Production Potentialities and Problems," *Journal of Farm Economics*, Vol. 31, February, 1949, pp. 251-62; and "World Food Prospects and Potentials: A Long-run Look," *Alternatives for Balancing World Food Production and Needs*, (Ames: Iowa State University Press, 1967), pp. 98-111] estimated that 1.3 billion acres (one billion acres of tropical soils and 300 million acres of temperate area podzol soils) could be shifted into food production. In 1964, he reported a soil classification study that showed the world had 6.59 billion acres of potential arable land. [Cf. Kellogg, "Potentials for Food Production," *Farmer's World: The Yearbook of Agriculture, 1964* (Washington: GPO, 1964), pp. 57-69.]

[24] Cf. *Soil and Water Conservation Needs—A National Inventory*, U. S. Department of Agriculture Miscellaneous Publication No. 971, 1965.

A false sense of security often accompanies the knowledge that a large physical supply of land is available for possible cropland use. Before these "available areas" acquire economic value, they must be "produced." This calls for favorable economic, social, political, and institutional conditions. A variety of cost outlays are usually involved, and the justification of these expenditures may call for much higher food prices than now exist.

In areas such as the tropics, for example, the development of new croplands will call for more than just land clearing, drainage, and terracing activities. Suitable transportation and communication, sanitation and health, and housing facilities must be provided. Consideration must be given to the nature of the local social services, to marketing and international trade problems, to local tax systems, to possible governmental restrictions, and to the problem of growing nationalism. Attention must also be given to problems of tropical soil management, to the financing of land settlement and development projects, to the relationships between outsiders and the native populations; to the impact commercial agriculture will have upon a subsistence and barter economy; and to the adjustments that must be made to local problems of poverty, disease, and illiteracy. The scope of these problems suggests the risks and headaches often associated with new land developments. These factors together with the problem of economic uncertainty provide effective barriers to the development of new areas.

The Promise of Technology

Technological developments have played a very important role, particularly in the western world, in helping man to keep ahead in the race between population and the food supply. They have also made great contributions to the building of cities, to the construction and conveniences of modern houses, to the manufacture of thousands of commercial and industrial products, and to the more effective exploitation and use of the world's energy and mineral resources.

Because of this help in times past, many people have come to regard the flow of new technology as endless. Without doubt, new technological developments can go a long way in solving man's future land-requirement problems. Yet the assumption of continuous technological improvement is a tenuous one. One cannot be certain that new technology will unlock the doors to new resource potentialities as fast in the future as in recent decades. Serious questions can thus be asked concerning the extent to which public planners and policy makers should depend upon hoped for answers to emerging resource needs.

Secular law of diminishing returns. Long before the full impact of technology upon production was clearly understood, the economists of the early classical school formulated what is now known as the "secular law of diminishing returns." As stated by Marshall, this law proclaims that "whatever may be the future developments of the arts of agriculture, a continued increase in the application of capital and labor to land must ultimately result in a diminution of the extra produce which can be obtained by a given amount of capital and labor."[25]

As this statement suggests, over the long run man must expect to eventually reach a point of over-all diminishing returns.[26] New technological advances have helped man to increase production and to expand his productive capacity far beyond his earlier potential. In the western world in particular, he has been able to enjoy the rising standards of life that come with operations during periods of increasing returns. Present prospects suggest that further increases in technology are probable and that all of the world's people can share in the opportunities for higher levels of living. No one knows how long this process might continue. Simple logic, however, indicates that if population continues to increase, man must either accomplish the highly unlikely miracle of producing more or better goods, services, and amenities to satisfy both the quantitative and qualitative aspects of man's mounting desires or someday face the problem of diminishing returns.

The phenomenon of increasing production costs and decreasing returns per unit of cost outlay is not at all uncommon in the world today. Already it is exerting an important impact upon man's efforts to develop and secure additional economic supplies of many land resources. Since the best and most accessible supplies of most of these resources have already been put to use, society often finds that it faces the increasingly difficult task of drawing upon a residual resource base which is dwindling both in quantity and quality. As a result, increasing outlays of human labor and capital are often needed to secure set quantities of land or materials. With increasing demands for resource development and use, this problem will probably become more rather than less serious.

Outlook for new technology. Despite the possible limits on technological advance, the present situation suggests no need for the posting of storm warnings. True, there is some evidence that the rate of increase in the supply of new technological developments has started to decline. There are suggestions that fewer new patents are being issued and less new

---

[25] Alfred Marshall, *Principles of Economics*, 8th ed. (New York: The Macmillan Company, 1938), p. 153.

[26] While the secular law appears to be logically consistent, there are those who question its validity. Harold J. Barnett and Chandler Morris, *Scarcity and Growth: The Economics of Natural Resource Availability* (Baltimore: The Johns Hopkins Press, 1963), p. 236, for example, indicate that "a strong case can be made for the view that the cumulation of knowledge and technological progress is automatic and self-reproductive in modern economies, and obeys a law of increasing returns. Every cost-reducing innovation opens up possibilities of application in so many new directions that the stock of knowledge, so far from being depleted by new developments, may even expand geometrically."

technology is being developed than at times in the past.[27] But a great backlog of already developed technology still awaits general acceptance and use; and the horizon is still bright with the promise of tremendous new developments to come.

The President's Materials Policy Commission has suggested the following six tasks for technology:

1. To foster new techniques for discovery.
2. To bring into use materials that thus far have evaded our efforts.
3. To apply the principle of recycling more and more broadly.
4. To learn how to deal with low concentrations of useful materials.
5. To develop and use more economically the resources that nature can renew.
6. To lessen or eliminate the need for a scarce material by substituting a more abundant one.[28]

Big and challenging as these tasks are, there is every indication that tremendous strides are being made toward their achievement. Numerous research organizations and individuals are now at work developing and testing a wide variety of new production methods and techniques, which undoubtedly will have significant effects upon many types of land resource use.

Agricultural production in the United States could be increased significantly if every farmer made full and effective use of the present stock of technical and managerial know-how in his operations. The stock of know-how is still growing, and it is reasonable to suppose that many new biological, chemical, and mechanical developments will facilitate the future production and processing of food, fiber, and forest products. An indication of the impact of technological and other factors on expected future production is provided by the U. S. Department of Agriculture's projection of an increase of approximately a fourth in crop production by 1980 from the 1967-69 average and increases of a third and a half in beef and poultry production, respectively.[29]

[27] For typical discussions of this point, cf. Alfred B. Stafford, "Is the Rate of Invention Declining?" *The American Journal of Sociology*, Vol. 36, May, 1952, pp. 539-45; Jacob Schmookler, "The Level of Inventive Activity," *Review of Economics and Statistics*, Vol. 57, May, 1954, pp. 183-90; Harry C. Trelogan and Neil W. Johnson, "The Inevitability of Technological Advance," *Journal of Farm Economics*, Vol. 35, November, 1953, pp. 599-605; and Byron T. Shaw, "The Role of Research in Meeting Future Agricultural Requirements," *Agronomy Journal*, Vol. 45, March, 1953, pp. 85-92.

[28] Cf. President's Materials Policy Commission, *op. cit.* Vol. 1, pp. 132-9. Vol. 4 of this report deals with "The Promise of Technology" as applied to mineral and energy resources.

[29] Cf. Culver, "A View of Food and Agriculture in 1980," *loc. cit.*, p. 67. Earl O. Heady and Howard Madsen, "Agricultural Land Diversion Programs: Problems, Potentials, and Trade-offs," *Journal of Soil and Water Conservation*, Vol. 25, March-April, 1970, p. 37, indicate that farmers will be able to feed a larger population in the United States in 1980, with some increase in per capita food consumption, with 50 to 60 million fewer acres of cropland than were in use in 1970.

Science has much to offer in helping man to meet his requirements for agricultural, building, energy, and other materials. It can help him further utilize the resources of the air and the ocean as well as those of the earth and teach him how to use these resources without impairing the environment. Science may also help man synthesize not only new fibers and plastics but also food and metals. It most certainly will open the way to new opportunities for resource use and development.

From a hard-headed practical point of view, however, it is important that man keep his balance and not be carried away by his dreams of the future. It is easy to talk of a world of "inexhaustible resources" and of a "chemistic society" in which all of man's food is synthesized and in which plants are used for decorative purposes only.[30] Visions such as these must be regarded as fanciful dreams until they are demonstrated in reality. Encouragement should be given for research and experimentations; but society must play the game safely and refuse to count its chicks before they are hatched.

The Problem of the Future

When one considers the future problem of satisfying the expanding needs of a growing population for food, minerals, and other land products, it is hard not to be impressed by the divergent views expressed on this subject. On the one extreme, writers of the neo-Malthusian school speak of the future with dire forebodings. To them the threat of overpopulation is real and suggests future shortages, famine, and a "road to survival."[31] As they see it, over the long-run "the avalanche of births will outweigh all possible scientific advance unless factors enter the situation that cannot now be foreseen, factors on which we dare not count."[32] On the opposite extreme, the optimists predict an age of industrial synthesis, which will transform the world into a new Garden of Eden. In their enthusiasm, they talk almost glibly of a chemistic world in which "notions like 'hunger,' 'food problems' and 'over-population' will become things belonging to a past barbaric age."[33]

---

[30] Cf. Jacob Rosin and Max Eastman, *The Road to Abundance* (New York: McGraw-Hill Book Company, 1953); and Eugene Holman, "Our Inexhaustible Resources," *Atlantic Monthly*, Vol. 189, No. 6, June, 1952, pp. 29-32.

[31] For examples of this point of view, cf. Georg Borgstrom, *The Hungry Planet* (New York: The Macmillan Company, 1965); Paul E. Ehrlich, *The Population Bomb* (New York: Ballantine Books, 1968); William and Paul Paddock, *Famine, 1975!* (Boston: Little, Brown and Company, 1967); William Vogt, *Road to Survival* (New York: Wm. Sloan Associates, 1948); Fairfield Osborn, *Our Plundered Planet* (Boston: Little, Brown, and Company, 1948); Frank A. Pearson and Floyd A. Harper, *The World's Hunger* (Ithaca: Cornell University Press, 1945); and Edward M. East, *Mankind at the Crossroads* (New York: Charles Scribner's Sons, 1923).

[32] Bruce Bliven, *Preview for Tomorrow* (New York: Alfred A. Knopf, 1953), p. 14.

[33] Rosin and Eastman, *op. cit.*, p. 57.

In all probability, the world will follow a middle course between these extreme points of view. The problem of supplying the world's growing needs for food, minerals, and other products will likely continue to loom large on the horizon. But it is not a hopeless problem. Countries such as the United States and Canada face no imminent danger of famine or starvation. Indeed, barring emergencies or a major catastrophe, their problem during the next few decades is more apt to involve food surpluses than shortages. For many overweight individuals in these countries, the major nutritional problem will continue to be that of excessive food consumption in relation to the decreasing muscular-energy requirements of a pushbutton civilization.

Happy as the food situation may be in some areas, the problem of want and hunger still remains acute on the world front. Properly used, the world's present resource base will suffice to provide increasing supplies of food and other materials for its present population. With the development of some new lands and a greater use of technological know-how, the world's resources can provide for the needs of a considerably larger population than it now has. Still it must be remembered that there are limits to the carrying capacity of the world's resource base. No one knows just where these limits are; but it is obvious that man cannot enjoy the fuller life promised by science on a standing-room-only basis. This means that over the long run, population numbers must level off or society will suffer the squeeze of diminishing returns.

The real problem at the present time is not "Can the world produce enough?" but rather "At what cost?" and "With what adjustments?" As man attempts to convert his ability to produce into actual production, more and more attention must be given to economic and institutional considerations. This may create only minor problems in some countries. On the world front, however, it may call for new policies affecting trade and immigration as well as for the industrialization and economic development of many underdeveloped areas. These adjustments sound simple; but in the final analysis, they may require sweeping changes in national attitudes and policies. They almost inevitably will involve sacrifices on the part of some peoples together with some reallocation of the world's resources and wealth.

Finally, man must plan for the future in terms of his available resources. In this process, he must recognize the need for maintaining and conserving his present resource base. He must do what he can to prevent waste and to discourage further use of those exploitive practices that undermine his future productive capacity. Much as he might wish it, he cannot depend upon technology to come to his aid if he dissipates and wastes his resource heritage. If he insists upon strangling the goose that lays his golden egg, he must expect to find himself reduced to a state of poverty.

—SUGGESTED READINGS

Barnett, Harold J., and Chandler Morris, *Scarcity and Growth: The Economics of Natural Resource Availability* (Baltimore: The Johns Hopkins Press, 1963).

Clawson, Marion, R. Burnell Held, and Charles H. Stoddard, *Land for the Future* (Baltimore: The Johns Hopkins Press, 1960).

Landsberg, Hans H., Leonard L. Fischman, and Joseph L. Fisher, *Resources in America's Future* (Baltimore: The Johns Hopkins Press, 1963).

Ottoson, Howard W. (ed.), *Land Use Policy and Problems in the United States* (Lincoln: University of Nebraska Press, 1963), chaps. VIII-X.

Outdoor Recreation Resources Review Commission, *Outdoor Recreation in America* (Washington: U. S. Government Printing Office, 1962).

President's Materials Resources Policy Commission, *Resources for Freedom* (Washington: U. S. Government Printing Office, 1952).

U. S. Forest Service, *Timber Trends*, Forest Resource Report No. 17 (Washington: U. S. Government Printing Office, 1965).

Water Resources Council, *The Nation's Water Resources* (Washington: U. S. Government Printing Office, 1968).

OUGHT TO READ A LITTLE ABOUT THE T— AND PRACTICE of "SPECULATION" if THAT'S WHAT FORESTRY IS ABOUT.

— GO THRU THE TIMBER OUTLOOK 1ST, THO

5

Input-Output
Relationships
Affecting Land Use

Land economics deals with man's attitudes, behavior, and decisions concerning the use of land resources. Some of its most significant aspects involve the workings of the economic framework within which land use takes place. This framework can be described largely in terms of the principles that affect, condition, and control (1) the response of land as a factor of production to varying input combinations of capital, labor, and management; (2) the economic returns that accrue to land in the production process; (3) the factors that influence land resource development and resource conservation decisions; (4) the location considerations that affect land use; and (5) the concept of land resource value and its measurement. Emphasis will be given to these economic aspects of land-resource utilization in this chapter and in the five chapters that follow.

BASIC ASSUMPTIONS OF ECONOMIC ANALYSIS

Realistic economic analysis calls for a broad understanding of the multitude of factors that influence economic behavior. In his search for explanations, the economic theorist ordinarily employs an inductive approach. He recognizes that the limitations of the human mind complicate the analysis of interrelations involving more than a few variables at any one time. Accordingly, he identifies and isolates those factors that appear to have the most important effects upon behavior. He then assumes an idealized situation in which the operation of other factors can be ignored or held constant. With these assumed controls in effect, he can proceed with the construction and manipulation of economic models and with the development of theories and explanations of the relationships that affect economic behavior.

This approach is basic to fundamental economic analysis. As a method of analysis, it has the advantage of focusing attention upon important relationships that would otherwise be hidden by the simultaneous operation of the vast maze of variables that complicate everyday life. The validity of this approach is always conditioned by the nature of the assumptions upon which it is premised. Unrealistic assumptions can easily give rise to unrealistic theories. Because of this situation it is always desirable to examine theories in the light of reality and to appraise their worth in terms of their usefulness in explaining day-to-day problems.

Like most theoretical concepts, the body of economic thought that has been developed to explain the patterns and processes of land utilization rests upon a number of basic assumptions. The most important of these is the assumption that man is a rational being who behaves in a logical and reasonable manner. This is probably the most basic assumption in all economic analysis. As such, it underlies a number of other important assumptions. Two of the most important of these involve the assumption that man normally attempts to maximize his self-interests and that prices tend to allocate resources.

Before turning to a more detailed discussion of these two basic concepts, it may be noted that economic analysis and the development of economic concepts often calls for other basic assumptions. Many conclusions in economic analysis involve simple cause-and-effect reasoning with the assumption of "other things being equal."[1] Frequent use also is made of economic models and examples that assume conditions of perfect competition with perfect knowledge on the part of buyers and sellers, perfect mobility of goods and productive factors, and a perfectly elastic supply of productive factors. These assumptions can be criticized as unrealistic. But if they seem to provide an artificial "test-tube" atmosphere, it should be remembered that they are used primarily as a means of holding most factors constant while attention is focused on particular factors that may have significance in the explanation of economic and social behavior.

[1] The far-reaching nature of this assumption can be illustrated by the simple statement that: "Other things being equal, people will buy more of a good at a lower price than at a higher price." The condition of "other things being equal" in this case assumes: (1) no appreciable change in consumer income or consumer tastes, (2) no change in the price of other goods, (3) no anticipation on the part of buyers of further price reductions, (4) no new substitute for the good in the market, and (5) no complications of prestige value, which may lead buyers to purchase products simply because they are high in price. Cf. Albert L. Meyers, *Elements of Modern Economics*, 3rd ed. (Englewood Cliffs, N.J.: Prentice-Hall, Inc., 1948), pp. 3-4.

Maximization of Individual Self-Interests

The so-called economic man, who is often set up as the prime mover in economic society, is motivated by a desire to maximize his economic returns. He also is equipped with an uncanny knowledge of his alternative opportunities and of what he might logically expect under varying production, price, and cost situations. The assumption of perfect knowledge gives the economic man a tremendous advantage over his contemporaries in everyday life. The principle of individual self-interest, however, is generally realistic. Up to a certain point, it is descriptive of most economic activity. Businessmen are interested in pushing plant production to its optimum level; farmers attempt to combine their productive factors in such a way as to enjoy the maximum income from their activities; workers demand the highest wages they can get for their labor.

The production response of business-minded producers to higher prices and the migration of workers to areas of greater economic opportunity give evidence of the importance and validity of this basic assumption. One must remember, however, that people place emphasis on noneconomic as well as strictly economic returns. Human behavior is motivated by a desire for leisure time, for self-expression, for the enjoyment of nature and the arts, and for many other types of psychic income as well as for monetary returns.

All rational individuals try to maximize their value returns and the satisfactions they derive from life. But wide differences exist between individuals in the extent to which they measure their satisfactions in monetary returns. Some people place a high value on profits and the maximization of monetary returns *per se.* Most people, however, regard monetary returns as an intermediate rather than a final goal. For them, money is a means to the attainment of more ultimate ends. And when the profit-maximization process conflicts with these ends, they will often settle for less money and more leisure, more security, or more of some other goal. Recognition of this factor is important, because it explains why land owners frequently fail to behave in a strictly economic manner even when it might be clearly to their financial interest to use their land resources in a different manner than they do.

The real-life problem of maximizing returns would be much simpler if individual operators really did possess perfect foresight and knowledge—if they could predict in advance what combination of factors and what economic decisions would prove most profitable. Unfortunately, this is not a human trait. Operators seldom enjoy perfect security in their economic expectations. Risk and uncertainty factors often cause even the best-laid plans to go astray. As a result, practically all individuals find that they must operate partly in the dark. Even when they are well supplied with information, they must make numerous decisions with no certainty concerning the net outcome. Yet in making these decisions, they and their families must usually stand ready to bear the consequences—be they good or bad.

People differ considerably in their reactions to this situation. Some are inclined to take calculated risks or perhaps even to gamble on an occasional long shot. Others place much more emphasis on security. This basic difference in willingness to take risks often has an important effect upon economic behavior. Some operators who take long chances succeed in parlaying their earnings into substantial fortunes; many others end up without their shirts. On the other extreme, security-minded businessmen often act too conservatively. They may muddle along with old, tested, and proved practices while other more aggressive operators profit by accepting new techniques and by readily adapting themselves to new and changing situations.

Successful operators in the modern economic world must make decisions and must bear the consequences of their decisions. There is no simple formula for success in the decision-making process. Even the most skilled operators expect an occasional set-back. But experience shows that most successful operators find that they can best maximize their returns by plotting a course between the extremes of overconservativism and outright gambling. These operators are interested in profits; but they also accept the concept of the "minimax."[2] They seek to maximize their returns but at the same time attempt to minimize any potential losses.

In following this policy, they take a forward view in their decisions and carefully consider and weigh the available facts before they act. Their knowledge and willingness to take risks steers them beyond a policy of inaction. At the same time, their intuition frequently holds them back from long-shot decisions that could lead to fortune but which are more likely to result in failure. This middle-road policy often results in less spectacular economic action; but it provides most operators with a reasonable return, and it saves many from possible financial ruin.

Prices and the Allocation of Resources

Economics is sometimes described as the science that deals with the allocation of scarce resources. In this sense, it deals with prices, because in our society prices—or the amounts people are willing to pay—usually determine who gets what. Under ordinary conditions, any person who desires a larger supply of a product can increase his supply by offering to buy more. If the supply of goods is short in relation to current demand, he can usually secure the supply he wishes by offering to pay more for the product than his competitors. Upward adjustments in the demand for

[2]Cf. John McDonald, *Strategy in Poker, Business and War* (New York: W. W. Norton and Co., Inc., 1950); also John von Newman and Oskar Morganstern, *Theory of Games and Economic Behavior* (Princeton, N. J.: Princeton University Press, 1944).

products such as food, housing, or building lots usually result in higher prices. These in turn encourage increased production.

The general assumption that prices allocate production and determine the distribution of resources permeates much of our economic thinking. This assumption is entirely logical under free market conditions. No economic man can be expected to sell his resources, products, or services for less than he can get elsewhere. The rights to use land resources ordinarily go to those buyers who can bid up and pay the highest prices. Land resources normally gravitate to those uses that command the highest market prices and offer the highest net returns. They seldom move into production without some promise of a suitable market for their products. Rising price levels often favor the bringing of additional land into use and the more intensive use of areas already in use. Declining price levels, on the other hand, can force retrenchment policies, shifts to lower uses, and sometimes land abandonment.

Though prices tend to allocate resources under free market conditions, there are numerous occasions when other factors interfere. Factors such as haste, ignorance of the facts, custom, conspicuous consumption, or the maximizing of other than monetary returns often prevent prices from playing their normal role in the allocation of resources. The frequent failure of prices to allocate resources in accordance with accepted concepts of distributive justice sometimes results in ameliorative measures. Merchants sometimes ration their sales of scarce commodities. During wars and periods of emergency, governments often follow a similar pattern by instituting price control and rationing programs and by assigning priorities for the purchase and use of vital materials. Community chest, charity, and public relief and welfare programs often make resources available to people who have difficulty in commanding their use in the open market. Most of the tax-supported services provided by government involve some reallocation of the assets held by individuals in society.

THE CONCEPT OF PROPORTIONALITY

Among the economic principles that affect land utilization, first mention should be made of the concept of proportionality. This concept involves the operator's concerns and decisions in securing an optimum combination or proportioning of his various factors of production.

As Ely and Wehrwein have observed, "Land in itself is not productive. It yields wheat, forest products, or office space only when labor and capital are applied to it."[3] In the normal production process, operators must always add various inputs of capital, labor, and management to their

[3] Richard T. Ely and George S. Wehrwein, *Land Economics* (Madison: The University of Wisconsin Press, 1964), p. 50. Originally published by The Macmillan Company, 1940.

land if they want it to produce the products they desire. The farmer cannot expect to live off his idle fields. He must prepare his seedbed, plant his seed, and fertilize, cultivate, and sometimes irrigate his crop before he can reap a harvest. This process ordinarily involves use of considerable machinery and other capital plus application of the operator's own labor and possibly the hired labor of others.

Operators of forest, urban, and other land areas also find it necessary to combine capital and labor with their land resources in the economic production process. The amounts of capital and labor needed vary somewhat with the type of land use. On the one extreme, forest and grazing operators benefit from the fact that their trees and grass often grow with little help from man. In contrast, large inputs of capital and labor per unit of area are normally involved with commercial and industrial developments. Regardless of which type of land use one considers, some input of capital and labor is necessary; and the operator's success in realizing a profit almost always depends upon the quality of the judgment and management he uses in proportioning his various productive factors.

Producers ordinarily try to secure the most profitable or highest profit combination of their productive factors. Their actions along this line are prompted by their desire to maximize their returns. Sometimes their efforts in this direction are limited by ignorance of the facts, lack of know-how, shortages of capital or labor, or perhaps a limited desire for more income. Within the bounds of these limitations, most individuals try to secure those yields and prices that will give them the highest net return. Success along these lines ordinarily calls for awareness and appreciation of the workings of the law of diminishing returns plus ability to recognize and adjust to the strategic roles that limiting factors play in the production process.

The Law of Diminishing Returns

Man has long observed that whenever successive inputs of a productive factor are added to a limited fixed factor, a point is soon reached after which the additional or marginal output of product per unit of input decreases and eventually becomes a negative quantity. This principle is known as the law of diminishing returns. By its very nature, it is one of the most important factors that affect man in his use of land. Without the operation of this principle, man would be able to concentrate all of his production in one spot. He would be able to raise his entire food supply in a flower pot.

The concept of diminishing returns can best be illustrated by use of an example such as that reported in Table 5-1. This table assumes a single unit of land as the fixed input factor (column 1) with composite homogeneous units of capital and labor treated as variable input factors

TABLE 5-1.   Illustration of Operation of Law of Diminishing Returns

Inputs of fixed factor (land)	Inputs of variable factor (capital-labor)	Units of total output (total physical product)	Average units of output per variable input unit (average physical product)	Increase in output per additional variable input (marginal physical product)	Value of marginal product at: 50¢ per unit	80¢ per unit	$1.20 per unit
(col. 1)	(col. 2)	(col. 3)	(col. 4)	(col. 5)	(col. 6)	(col. 7)	(col. 8)
1	1	2	2	2	$1.00	$ 1.60	$ 2.40
1	2	6	3	4	2.00	3.20	4.80
1	3	13	4.333	7	3.50	5.60	8.40
1	4	23	5.75	10	5.00	8.00	12.00
1	5	35	7	12	6.00	9.60	14.40
1	6	49	8.167	14	7.00	11.20	16.80
1	7	64	9.143	15	7.50	12.50	18.00
1	8	78	9.75	14	7.00	11.20	16.80
1	9	91	10.111	13	6.50	10.40	15.60
1	10	102	10.2	11	5.50	8.80	13.20
1	11	111	10.091	9	4.50	7.20	10.80
1	12	118	9.833	7	3.50	5.60	8.40
1	13	122	9.385	4	2.00	3.20	4.80
1	14	123	8.786	1	.50	.80	1.20
1	15	121	8.07	−2	−1.00	−1.60	−2.40

(column 2). Up to a certain point (the fourteenth variable input unit), the addition of each successive input of capital-labor to the fixed factor results in an increase in total output (column 3). This total is called the *total physical product.*

The average yield or output of product per variable input unit is known as the *average physical product* (column 4). This measure is determined by simply dividing the total physical product by the number of variable inputs used in its production. For example, the use of the eighth variable input unit in Table 5-1 brings a total physical product of 78 and thus results in an average product of 9.75 (78 divided by 8 = 9.75). The point of highest average return in this illustration comes with the tenth variable input unit.

In addition to the concepts of total and average physical product, operators also are interested in the amount of output associated with the use of each successive additional input unit. This concept is known as the *marginal physical product* (column 5). In the example, the use of six variable inputs results in a total physical product of 49 while a seventh input pushes total production up to 64. The difference between these two totals (64-49=15) represents the additional yield or marginal physical product associated with the use of the seventh variable input.

The concepts of total, average, and marginal physical product are often symbolized by the letters TPP, APP, and MPP, respectively. These concepts may be depicted graphically as in Figure 5-1. As this diagram indicates, the changes in total production associated with the use of each successive variable input unit suggests a series of steps that go up to a peak level and then start down again. For analytical purposes, these steps are usually smoothed out and depicted by production curves. The TPP curve in Figure 5-1 shows the cumulative increase in total physical product (measured on the vertical axis) that comes with the addition of each successive input of variable factor (measured on the horizontal axis). Whenever an input-output relationship can be described by a continuous curve of this type, it may be described as a *production function.*

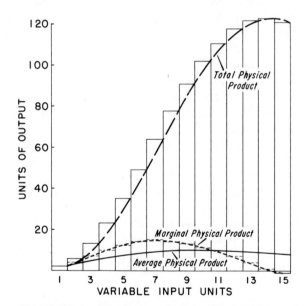

FIGURE 5-1. Illustration of production function and input-output relationships involved in operation of physical law of diminishing returns.

As Figure 5-1 indicates, every production function involves three points of diminishing return. Total production increases at an increasing rate until the MPP curve reaches its peak. From this point on, the marginal physical product diminishes while the total physical product continues to increase at a decreasing rate. The TPP curve reaches its highest level—the point of total diminishing returns—at the same point on the variable input scale as that at which the MPP curve intersects the base line and becomes zero. Any additional application of variable inputs beyond this point results in both a decrease in total physical product and a negative marginal return.

The APP curve always reaches its maximum height at the point at which it intersects the declining MPP curve. Beyond this point, the average physical product gradually decreases. Unlike the MPP curve, the APP curve always remains above the base line as long as there is any total product. Operators can add so many inputs of sunlight, water, or other variable inputs that they end up with no total product and thus have an average product of zero. Situations of this type seldom occur in real life.

Economic Law of Diminishing Returns

Our discussion thus far has dealt primarily with the physical law of diminishing returns. This physical concept is basic in production. Profit-oriented businessmen must recognize this concept but they also find it both logical and desirable to view their input-output possibilities in monetary terms. They think not only of physical inputs and outputs but also of the costs and returns associated with these units. They are concerned not so much with the maximization of physical output as with the maximization of economic net returns. In short, they are concerned with the economic law of diminishing returns.[4]

The transition from the physical to the economic concept of diminishing returns can be achieved simply by assigning a cost to each of the input factors and a market value or price to each unit of product produced. With this adjustment, one can speak of the total, average, and marginal returns secured in the production process and of the total, average, and marginal costs associated with these respective measures of return. Once this transition is made, operators ordinarily find it most profitable to push production to the point at which the value of their marginal product equals or just exceeds the cost associated with its production. This is the point of diminishing economic returns. As long as an operator combines his variable input factors around his scarce or limiting factor, he can always expect his highest net return at this point.[5]

---

[4] Different terms are frequently used in discussions of this concept. Some authors describe the physical concept as the "law of diminishing productivity" or as the "law of diminishing physical outputs." The economic concept is often referred to simply as the "law of diminishing returns," the "law of variable proportions," or as the "law of proportionality." Some writers limit the concept of diminishing returns to combinations in which land is treated as the central or limiting factor and use the concept of variable proportions to signify other types of combinations.

[5] The difference between an operator's total production costs and the value of his total product is referred to here as "net return." Depending upon one's point of view and one's assumptions concerning the nature of the fixed factor and the items treated

Most of our economic analysis involving production problems stems directly from the economic concept of diminishing returns. In their application of this concept, economists sometimes find it desirable to calculate costs and returns on an input-unit basis. On other occasions they find it more appropriate to deal with the costs and returns associated with units of output. Both of these approaches have merit; both have numerous applications in land economics analysis; and both involve applications of the same basic principle.

Input-unit approach. As long as costs and returns are computed on an input-unit basis, one can shift from the physical to the economic concept of diminishing returns simply by assigning a value to each unit of physical product and a production cost to each unit of variable input factor. With this adjustment, the value of the marginal physical product may be described as the marginal return per input unit or more simply as the *marginal value product* (MVP). Similarly, the concepts of *total value product* (TVP) and *average value product* (AVP) are used to describe the value of the total and average physical products, respectively.

On the cost side, the term *factor cost* is ordinarily used to describe the costs associated with the use of the variable factor inputs. Thus, the additional cost associated with each successive input unit is known as the *marginal factor cost* (MFC) while the average variable cost per input unit is known as the *average factor cost* (AFC).

One can illustrate the *value product* or input-unit approach for explaining economic input-output relationships simply by assuming a value of $1 for each of the physical output and variable input units listed in Table 5-1. With this assumption, and assuming that land is the fixed factor, the operator will find it profitable to push production to his 13th input unit. At this point, he receives a marginal value product of $4 at a marginal factor cost of $1 and thus realizes a net return of $3 on his last variable input unit. If he adds a 14th input, his marginal value product of $1 just equals his marginal factor cost and he neither gains nor loses. He may decide to add the 14th input; but he may also choose to withhold this last input because it contributes nothing to his net returns. Should the operator push to the 15th input, his marginal factor cost would still be $1 while his marginal value product would become a negative quantity.

If the operator in this example thinks in terms of total net returns, he may ask himself why he should push production to the point at which his marginal value product equals or just exceeds the cost of his last variable input. Why not stop at some point of higher marginal return? A few simple calculations involving the above cost assumptions and the production data reported in Table 5-1 show why it is most profitable to push

---

as variable inputs, this net above cost can also be described as an economic surplus, as land rent, or as operator's profit. As will be explained in the next chapter, this surplus is viewed as land rent in those instances in which land resources are treated as the fixed factor. It is operator's profit only when management is treated as the fixed factor.

production to the point at which MFC = MVP. If the operator stops with his tenth input, he will have a net return of $92 (total physical product valued at $102 less $10 in variable input costs). The use of an 11th input brings his net return up to $100. Total net returns rise to $106 with the 12th variable input and $109 with the 13th input. The 14th input barely pays for itself, and total net returns drop to $106 if a 15th input is applied.

The exact number of variable inputs an operator finds it profitable to combine with his fixed factor always depends upon existing cost and price conditions. If one assumes that each variable input factor costs $4.75, it will pay the operator to push production only to the tenth input when his units of product are priced at 50 cents each (cf. the last three columns in Table 5-1). At a price of 80 cents, it will pay to push production to the 12th input; and at a price of $1.20 it will be most profitable to apply 13 inputs of variable factor. If the unit cost of the variable inputs is raised to $7, the operator will reduce the number of variable inputs he uses. Conversely, if variable input unit costs are lowered, it will pay to apply additional inputs of capital and labor.

Value product analysis highlights the choices available to operators as they make decisions concerning combinations of successive numbers of variable inputs with their fixed factor. Operators want to maximize their net returns. They can accomplish this goal by using the number of variable inputs that permits the maximum spread between their total value product and their total factor cost. As Figure 5-2A shows, this maximum spread always comes at the point at which MVP equals or just exceeds MFC. This mathematical truism favors the focusing of economic analysis on the relationships between marginal value products and marginal factor costs and between average value products and average factor costs.

Figure 5-2B provides a diagramatic example of the simplest form of value product analysis. In common with similar value product or input unit diagrams, it assumes a single fixed factor (land), a single type of homogeneous variable input, a fixed price per unit of product, and a fixed cost per variable input.[6] This particular example assumes the production

[6]Modification of these assumptions calls for significant changes in the basic value product diagram. When two fixed factors are assumed, for example, it is sometimes expedient to assign fixed or overhead costs to one of them. This assumption can call for spreading the overhead costs over the number of variable inputs used and for drawing average overhead or fixed cost and average input unit cost curves comparable to those often used in cost curve analysis. As will be pointed out later, the assumption of two or more variable inputs with different production functions complicates the analysis. Two types of variable inputs can call for three-dimensional diagrams in which value product surfaces are substituted for product curves.

An assumption of declining product prices with increased production requires adjustments in the slopes of the MVP and AVP curves. Similarly, an assumption that factor costs will increase as more factors are used in production calls for separate MFC and AVC curves. Assumptions of this order are often realistic. For our purposes, however, it is not necessary to complicate the basic assumptions accepted in Figure 5-2.

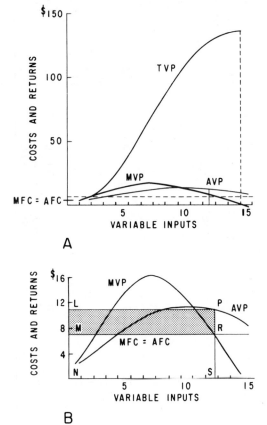

FIGURE 5-2. Use of value product curves to determine net return to fixed input factor at most profitable point of operations.

function reported in Table 5-1, an average factor cost of $7 per variable input unit, and an average market value of $1.10 for each unit of product. (Cf. Table 5-2). With this combination of factors, the operator finds it advantageous to stop with his twelfth variable input because this is the last logical breaking point before *MFC = MVP*. At this point, his total value product (*AVP* times the number of variable inputs used) is represented by the large rectangle *LNSP* while his total factor costs (*AFC* times the number of variable inputs used) are represented by the lower small rectangle *MNSR*. The shaded rectangle *LMRP* represents the share of the total value product above factor costs that may be credited to the fixed factor.

Computed in arithmetic terms, the operator secures a total value product of $10.817 X 12 (*AVP* X number of variable inputs used) = $129.80. His total factor costs are $7 X 12 (*AFC* X number of variable inputs used) = $84 and his net return is $129.80 - $84.00 = $45.80. If he used only eleven variable inputs his net return would be $45.10, and if he used 13 it would be $43.20.

Transition to cost curves. Economists make frequent use of the

TABLE 5-2. Illustration of Economic Costs and Returns Calculated on an Input-Unit and on an Output-Unit Basis Assuming the Production Function Reported in Table 5-1, a Standard Price of $1.10 per Unit of Output, and a Uniform Cost of $7.00 per Variable Input-Unit

Number of variable inputs used with fixed factor	Total units of physical product produced (TPP)	Marginal physical product (MPP)	Standard price per unit of output (AR and MR)	Value of total physical product (TVP and TR)	Marginal value product (MVP)	Average value product (AVP)	Uniform cost of variable input (AFC and MFC)	Total cost of variable inputs used (TFC and TC)	Average cost per unit of output (ATUC or AC)	Marginal cost per output unit (MC)
1	2	2	$1.10	$ 2.20	$ 2.20	$ 2.20	$7.00	$ 7.00	$3.50	$3.50
2	6	4	1.10	6.60	4.40	3.30	7.00	14.00	2.333	1.75
3	13	7	1.10	14.30	7.70	4.77	7.00	21.00	1.615	1.00
4	23	10	1.10	25.30	11.00	6.33	7.00	28.00	1.217	.70
5	35	12	1.10	38.50	13.20	7.70	7.00	35.00	1.00	.583
6	49	14	1.10	53.90	15.40	8.98	7.00	42.00	.857	.50
7	64	15	1.10	70.40	16.50	10.06	7.00	49.00	.766	.467
8	78	14	1.10	85.80	15.40	10.73	7.00	56.00	.718	.50
9	91	13	1.10	100.10	14.30	11.12	7.00	63.00	.692	.538
10	102	11	1.10	112.20	12.10	11.22	7.00	70.00	.686	.636
11	111	9	1.10	122.10	9.90	11.10	7.00	77.00	.694	.778
12	118	7	1.10	129.80	7.70	10.82	7.00	84.00	.712	1.00
13	122	4	1.10	134.20	4.40	10.32	7.00	91.00	.746	1.75
14	123	1	1.10	135.30	1.10	9.66	7.00	98.00	.797	7.00
15	121	-1	1.10	133.10	-1.10	8.87	7.00	105.00	.868	7.00

input-unit or value product approach particularly when they deal with production and management situations. They also have considerable need for viewing production in terms of the price and cost assumptions associated with units of output or product. This approach is commonly called the *cost curve* approach. Like the input-unit approach, it has its own set of production concepts.

When product values are computed on an output-unit basis they are ordinarily called *returns* or *revenue*. The value of the total physical product may thus be called *total return,* while the average value associated with each output unit is *average return*. In similar fashion, the value of the marginal or last additional unit of production is called *marginal return*. With this approach and the assumption of a uniform price for all product units, the concepts of average return and marginal return can be depicted in diagrams by a horizontal line, which represents the price level.

Three cost concepts—total cost, average cost, and marginal cost—also play significant roles in cost curve analysis. *Total cost* represents a sum of all the production costs incurred at any given point in the production process. With the example assumed in Table 5-2, total cost is equal to total factor cost and involves the cost associated with the use of x number of variable inputs. The term *average cost* (or average total unit cost) is used to describe the proration of total costs among the various units of output (total costs divided by the number of units of output).[7] *Marginal cost* represents the addition to total costs associated with the production of each last additional unit of output (cost of the last variable input divided by the marginal physical product).[8]

---

[7] It is common practice in production analysis to distinguish between variable costs and fixed costs as components of the concepts of total and average costs. When this practice is followed, total cost represents the sum of the total variable and fixed costs and average cost the sum of the average variable and fixed costs. Variable cost in this case represents the aggregate cost of the variable inputs used in production. When plotted in a diagram, average variable costs decline with the increasing output secured from use of the initial units of variable inputs and reach their lowest level at the point of highest physical product per input unit. Beyond this low-cost level, they rise with the higher marginal costs per unit of output associated with the decreasing physical product secured by each successive additional variable input.

Fixed costs involve costs associated with overhead and other outlays, which are viewed as fixed throughout the production process. These costs are fixed for the production period and are just as high when one variable input is used to produce two units of product as when 14 inputs are used to produce 123 units. Average fixed costs decline steadily as production mounts to its maximum level.

Overhead and fixed cost assumptions involve identification of two or more fixed factors in production. This approach is frequently used when some factor other than land is treated as the fixed factor, in which case an allowance of a fixed payment for land and taxes is often viewed as an overhead cost. No assumption of fixed costs is used in Table 5-2 or Figures 5-2 or 5-3 for the simple reason that land is treated here as the single fixed factor in the analysis.

[8] When plotted in a diagram as in Figure 5-3, the marginal cost of each successive output unit declines rapidly with the increasing production per unit experienced at the

With these concepts of returns and costs and the basic production data reported in Table 5-2, one can illustrate input-output relationships with cost curve diagrams such as those presented in Figures 5-3A and 5-3B.

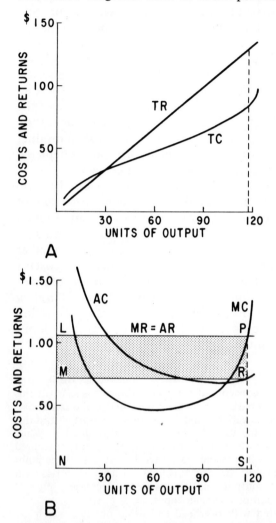

FIGURE 5-3. Use of cost curves to determine the net return to a fixed input factor at the most profitable point of operations.

beginning of the production process. The MC curve then levels off, reaches its lowest level at the point of highest physical product, and then rises—gradually at first and then at an accelerating rate—until it goes straight up at the point of total diminishing returns. In its upward swing the marginal-cost curve intersects both the average variable cost curve (if computed separately) and the average cost curve at their lowest points.

The marginal cost curves shown in most diagrams suggest continuous input-output relationships. In practice, a discontinuous relationship normally exists with whole groups of output units being associated with the cost of successive input factors. Marginal cost in these cases represents the average cost of each last group of output units.

Again the operator seeks to maximize his net returns and finds that he can do so by pushing production to that point at which he secures the maximum spread between his total returns and total costs. (Figure 5-3A.) This point corresponds with the number of units of output secured in Figure 5-3B at the point at which $MC = MR$. This is the point of diminishing economic returns and as such it corresponds with the point at which $MFC = MVP$ in Figure 5-2.

As the cost curve diagram shown in Figure 5-3B shows, the operator should produce to his 118th unit of output because this is the last unit of output that can be produced at a cost less than its product value. The 118th unit has a value of $1.10 and a marginal cost of $1.00 while the 119th unit would cost $1.75. The operator's total returns (total units produced times the average return per unit) are represented in the diagram by the large rectangle $LNSP$. Production cost (total units produced times the average cost per unit) is represented by the smaller rectangle $MNSR$ while the return to the fixed factor is represented by the shaded rectangle $LMRP$. This net return also may be calculated by subtracting the operator's average costs from his average return and then multiplying the difference by his number of output units. Measured in this way ($1.10 - .7119 = .3881 X 118 = $45.80), the net return in Figure 5-3B corresponds with that reported with the value product diagram in Figure 5-2B.

SOME APPLICATIONS OF PROPORTIONALITY

At this point, one might well ask how much consideration the average operator gives to the concept of proportionality. Is it a fancy theory or does it have real-life significance? In answering this question, first consideration should be given to the over-all importance of the proportionality concept as it affects managerial decisions. Other examples of its importance include its effect on the fixed and variable nature of land costs, its recognition of the need for adjustments to limiting factors in production, and its application under secular conditions.

Use in Managerial Decisions

The central goal in proportionality is the combination of the resources used in production in such a manner as to provide a maximum return. All producers are concerned to a greater or lesser degree with this objective. True, many of them have never heard of "proportionality" and some still pattern their practices on those of their fathers. But most of the more successful operators have a definite feel for this concept and realize that their success depends in large part upon the skill with which they proportion the production factors they have at their disposal.

Examples of the day-to-day application of proportionality occur with almost every type of land use. Industrialists employ proportionality when they decide how much raw material to use, how many workmen they should hire, and what adjustments they should make for changing costs or prices. Commercial businessmen apply this concept when they consider how much floor space they will use, how much they should spend on advertising, and what types of goods and services they will offer. Farmers use this concept when they decide how much seed or fertilizer to use, how often they should cultivate their crops, and how much grain it pays them to feed their cattle.

Foresters consider proportionality when they decide how much they can afford to spend on reforestation and stand-improvement measures and whether they should cut their trees for pulp or hold them until they are ready for use as saw timber. Miners use this concept when they determine the maximum depth it pays to go for ore and the minimum grade of ore they can afford to handle. Proportionality affects the real estate investor who wants to know the optimum height and size of the office building he proposes to build. It presents important problems to the land subdivider who asks himself how much he can spend on the acquisition, development, and improvement of a possible residential site and still sell his lots at the going market price with some profit for his efforts.

Proportionality is by no means limited to decisions involving the maximization of economic returns. It is also used by operators who are motivated, at least in part, by noneconomic goals. Architects and planners use this concept when they attempt to combine the factors in their plans in such a way as to achieve the highest standards of quality possible within the limits of their budget specifications. Public administrators and engineers use this approach when they determine the optimum allocation and use of the funds placed at their disposal. Public agencies and private benevolent groups use proportionality to work out combinations of programs and arrangements that promise the maximum social return from their activities.

The success with which operators apply the proportionality concept is conditioned both by the clarity of their reasoning and by their response to the problems of uncertainty and imperfect knowledge. With perfect knowledge and foresight, the average operator would find it relatively easy to use static input-output models in proportioning his inputs to the exact point of maximum returns. But these assumptions seldom apply in the real world. Instead, the average businessman operates with only a limited knowledge of the production conditions that affect his enterprise. Beyond his known facts, he operates within a realm of expectations, which involves some assumptions of high probability and others that are beclouded by uncertainty. In adjusting to this situation, he sometimes makes blind decisions without having a firm factual basis for predicting their outcome. Most of his decisions, however, involve calculated risks that fit within a reasonable range of expectations.

Most real-life operators find it impossible to predict in advance the exact combinations of output that will bring them the highest net return. When an operator tries out a new enterprise, he must experiment with various input combinations; and he is rarely in a position to recognize his point of highest economic or physical return until this point is passed. Even when he has the necessary experience or experimental data to guide him in the choice of an optimum combination of his factors, he must still concern himself with the vagaries of climate and nature and with the uncertainties occasioned by changing cost, price, market supply, and consumer demand relationships.

With this complicated situation, one might logically ask how an operator can apply the proportionality concept in his decision making process. How can he determine the optimum combination of his factors when he lacks perfect knowledge and foresight and when he must always speculate concerning the cost, price, and yield situations he will encounter throughout the production process? How can he adjust to the dynamic changing conditions of the business world; and how can he adjust to the simultaneous operation of two or more production functions? The impact of these factors upon an operator's use of proportionality can best be considered in terms of (1) his attempt to keep his operations within the zone of rational action, (2) his problem in adjusting to dynamic conditions, (3) his response to the problem of multiple production functions, and (4) his acceptance of the equi-marginal principle in operations involving two or more enterprises.

Zone of rational action. Most successful businessmen operate within what is known as the zone of rational action. This zone represents the range of possible input-output combinations with any given production function within which a producer can reasonably expect to maximize his returns. With his human limitations, the operator usually finds it impossible to gauge his inputs to the exact point of diminishing economic returns. But by following an economic input-output model for his particular enterprise, he can usually push production to points near his economic optimum. In this sense, he can visualize the production point at which $MFC = MVP$ as the bull's-eye on a marksman's target. In aiming at this economic target, the operator may sometimes overshoot his mark, sometimes undershoot it. As long as he keeps his operations within a reasonable range, however, he finds that he can use his knowledge and feel for proportionality to keep his operations generally on target and profitable even though he may seldom register a direct hit on the bull's-eye.

The concept of a rational action zone is closely associated with the production function and value productivity analysis. As Figure 5-4 shows, the usual production function can be divided into three segments or stages. Stage 1 covers the production response of the enterprise to the first variable resource inputs. Throughout this stage, production increases steadily from zero to the point of highest average physical product per

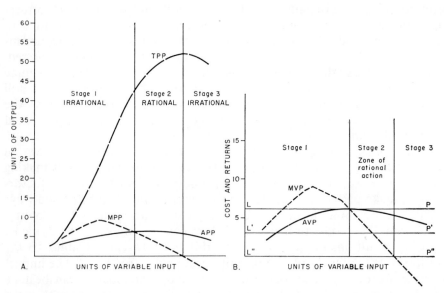

FIGURE 5-4.   The three stages of production showing the limits of the zone of rational action.

input unit. Stage 2 starts at the point of highest average physical product and goes to the point of total diminishing physical returns. Total production continues to increase throughout this stage but the average physical product declines and the marginal physical product drops to zero. This stage is known as the "zone of rational action." Stage 3 covers the irrational situation that arises when an operator continues to apply inputs beyond the point of total diminishing physical returns.

When values and costs are attributed to the physical production data depicted in Figure 5-4A, the point of highest profit always occurs in Stage 2. When the cost of each successive input is depicted by *L'P'* (Figure 5-4B), the point at which MFC = MVP comes near the center of this zone. Operators can continue to operate as long as their input unit costs do not rise above *LP,* the level at which their average costs coincide with the point of highest average return. At any cost above this level, the operator's variable costs will exceed his returns, and he will usually find it irrational to continue operations. Conversely, even if his cost level dropped to zero (the *L"P"* base line), he would not find it rational to operate beyond the point of total diminishing physical returns.

Those operators who produce in Stage 1 ordinarily find it to their advantage either to add more variable inputs or, if the supply of these is limited, to concentrate their use on a smaller portion of the fixed factor. As long as they have a sufficient supply of variable inputs, producers find it irrational to halt production in this stage because they can easily increase their average returns by using additional inputs. Operators in

Stage 3, on the other hand, ordinarily find it desirable to reduce the number of variable inputs they use per unit of fixed factor.

Most operators try to enhance their prospects of profit by operating within the zone of rational action. Many frequently undershoot or overshoot this goal. Their failure to operate in the rational stage can sometimes be attributed to ignorance, a lack of know-how or managerial ability, or a malallocation of resources. Unexpected changes in factor costs and sudden changes in market prices can cause a firm to produce for a time at an uneconomic level. Natural catastrophes such as floods, drought, hail, or forest fires also have this effect upon some types of operations.

Adjustments to dynamic conditions. In his attempt to stay within the zone of rational action, the average operator must always cope with the problem of uncertainty. Unlike the "economic man" whose perfect knowledge permits him to work with a certainty model, the operator in real life must always be ready to adjust his decisions to the changing conditions of a dynamic world. The decisions he makes at any one time are based partly on his understanding of certain known facts and partly on his expectations regarding future cost, price, and yield conditions.

With the passing of time and the unfolding of the production process, an operator's original expectations may or may not materialize. When they materialize as expected, he can often continue with his original course of action. When they change, the alert operator will often reconsider his production plan and make those adjustments that seem expedient. An increase in the market-price outlook for a given market product after the beginning of its production process, for example, usually favors additional use of those types of inputs that contribute to higher production. Similarly, a drop in market prices may cause a producer to store his product for later sale.

Most business managers continually adjust and readjust their plans and expectations as they proceed with their production operations. In this adjustment process, they usually find that they must treat the inputs they have already applied as fixed. Any changes they make in a production program already under way must revolve around those variable inputs they have not as yet applied. A manufacturer who finds that there is a disappointing market for his product may cut off new production, offer his existing inventory at bargain prices, or try to salvage what value he can from alternative uses of his product. Similarly, a farmer who discovers midway through the crop season that he faces the prospect of either low yields or low prices may adjust to this situation by harvesting his crop for what it is worth, converting it into cattle feed, or possibly plowing it under as a soil-building crop. Neither operator has the alternative of stepping back in time to reclaim his original inputs.

The necessity for treating past inputs as fixed naturally narrows the alternatives available to the operator as he approaches the end of his production process. The significance of this situation may be illustrated by the example of a speculative house builder. At the time the builder starts his building operations he can ordinarily choose between several styles and types of residential structures. Once he has laid his foundation and framed in his structure, however, he usually finds that he is bound by the general pattern of his plan. At this stage, he is still free to modify many details. He can substitute some types of inputs for others and within limits he can either downgrade or upgrade his house to meet particular levels of market demand. But as the production process proceeds, he is seldom willing to backtrack and make sweeping changes in work already completed; and the closer he comes to the completion of his house the fewer become the modifications he is willing to make.

Multiple production functions. Throughout the above discussion it has been possible to think in terms of simple input-output or resource-product relationships that involve the application of successive inputs of some standardized or homogeneous factor to a fixed factor such as land. This centering of attention on a single production function has facilitated the isolation and recognition of the leading principles involved in proportionality. A look at the real world, however, indicates that very few operators deal with a single production function.

Most producers deal with situations that call for the joint operation of several production functions. These situations can stem from enterprises that involve the joint production of two or more products (*e.g.,* the joint processing of gasoline and other petroleum products, the joint production of mutton and wool) or joint use of the same durable fixed factor in two or more enterprises. Under typical circumstances, however, the problem of multiple production functions springs simply from the nonhomogeneous nature of the wide variety of variable input factors used even with single-product enterprises. Sometimes these various inputs are complementary and must be used together; sometimes they may be regarded as substitutes for each other. Sometimes they are indivisible and must be used as whole units; at other times they can be divided for smaller applications. As a rule, they are applied separately at different times and often in different sequences, have different costs, and can be combined differently with other factors with different results.

Each of the several types of variable inputs used in combination with the fixed factor in production has its own production function. Fortunately, many of these parallel and complement the production functions of other necessary inputs. Because of their number and concomitant use, operators ordinarily find it necessary to deal with whole groups of production functions at the same time. In this process, they may find that the optimum use of various inputs calls for different scales of operation and that the highest profit combination for their enterprise may not represent the optimum use point for any one factor.

Operators faced with this problem ordinarily view the use of each factor in terms of its contribution to the total.[9] Sometimes they operate on a hit-or-miss basis. Usually, however, they find it expedient to experiment with various combinations and to observe the activities of others so that they might determine the resource combinations that work best for them. In this way, they are guided by reasonable judgment; and they use their feel for proportionality to develop workable and profitable combinations of their resource factors.

Equi-marginal principle. Up to this point, we have assumed that the average operator deals primarily with one enterprise and that he has a plentiful supply of variable input factors he can combine with his single fixed factor. With these two assumptions, one might logically expect him to push production to the point of diminishing economic returns. Under practical conditions, however, the average operator has a limited supply of productive factors and he can usually put these factors to a variety of alternative uses. This combination of circumstances calls for some modification of the operator's production goals. Instead of always pushing production to the point at which MC = MR (or MFC = MVP), the operator with limited resources tends to push production in any particular enterprise only to the point at which his marginal value product equals or promises to drop below the return he could secure from the use of his marginal inputs in some recognized alternative use.

In this equalizing process, the operator with limited resources applies the *equi-marginal principle.* This principle asserts that maximum profit can be secured only when each input of land, capital, labor or management is used in such a way as to add the most to total return and when the various resources used in any one enterprise produce a marginal value product at least equal to that which they could secure from their best alternative use.

This principle encourages operators to shift to those enterprises that promise the most net returns and to allocate their inputs between enterprises in such a way as to maximize their total returns. For instance, if a producer of shoes and handbags has comparable inputs and costs with both products but finds that his last variable inputs provide a marginal value product of $5 with handbags as compared with $12 with shoes, he will normally shift some of his variable inputs from handbags to shoes to the point at which his marginal value products are more equal.

The land-use problem that arises in equating marginal value products

[9] Various techniques have been developed in production economic theory for the analysis of multiple production functions. Simple cases involving one or two variables can be depicted in geometric diagrams and can usually be handled with simple reasoning. Any further increase in the number of variables usually taxes the reasoning capacity of the human mind. Cases involving four variables, for example, call for five-dimensional diagrams. Higher mathematics can often be used in the analysis of multiple production functions of this type; but very few operators think in these terms.

can be illustrated with the example reported in Table 5-3, which assumes an operator with 30 units of variable input costing $3 each, which he expects to apply to three tracts of land, each of which has a different production function. If he had an unlimited supply of variable inputs, it would pay him to push production to the point at which MFC = MVP or to the 16th input on the first tract, the 13th input on the second tract, and the 9th input on the third tract. Production at these points would call for 36 inputs, however, and he can use only 30 inputs.

TABLE 5-3.   Illustration of Application of the Equi-Marginal Principle in the Allocation of 30 Variable Inputs Costing $3 Each to Three Tracts of Land with Different Production Functions When the Product Has a Market Value of $1 per Unit

Number of Variable Inputs	First Tract		Second Tract		Third Tract	
	TVP	MVP	TVP	MVP	TVP	MVP
6	$ 47	$11	$45	$10	$42	$9
7	59	12	56	11	49	7
8	72	13	65	9	54	5
9	84	12	73	8	57	3
10	95	11	80	7	59	2
11	104	9	86	6	60	1
12	112	8	90	4	60	0
13	119	7	93	3		
14	124	5	95	2		
15	128	4	95	0		
16	131	3				
17	133	2				

In his search for an optimum proportioning of his variable inputs, he could apply an equal number (ten inputs) to each tract. This would give him a total value product of $95 + $80 + $59 = $234. This obviously is not his best combination because the 10th input on the third tract does not pay for itself. By shifting this last input from the third tract to the first tract, he can secure a marginal value product of $9 instead of $2 and thereby increase his total value product to $104 + $80 + $57 = $241. Further experimentation in shifting marginal inputs to sites where they can earn higher marginal products shows that the operator can maximize his returns by so proportioning them that he can secure approximately equal marginal value products from the last variable inputs used on each tract. By using 13 inputs on the first tract, 10 on the second, and 7 on the third, he receives marginal value products of 7 from each tract and secures a maximum total value product of $119 + $80 + $49 = $248.

Fixed and Variable Nature of Land Costs

Our discussion up to this point has assumed production under short-run conditions—the *short run* being defined as any production period during which the operator is limited by the fixed supply of particular inputs. Under short-run conditions, land resources are almost always regarded as a fixed production factor; and the costs associated with the acquisition and holding of land resources—property taxes, insurance payments, and commitments to pay cash rent—are classified as fixed costs. This situation stems from the relative immobility of land resources, from our concept of property rights, which ties ownership to fixed locations, and from the natural tendency of most enterprises to be tied to some location during their productive period.

Since operators must normally plan their enterprises in terms of the land resources they have at hand, the duration of any short-run period depends upon the conditions under which land is held and used. For many enterprises, it may also involve the time needed to grow a marketable crop, to complete a production cycle, or to justify certain operating expenditures.

Individual producers normally operate in a series of short-run periods during which they are limited by various fixed factors such as land. When these periods are treated together as part of the long-run situation, all fixed factors become variables. The supply of land resources available to individual operators over this longer run can change with individual adjustments. Industries secure new plant locations; commercial operators relocate, remodel or rebuild their establishments; tenants renegotiate their leases; and operators often reduce or add to their land holdings. Changes also occur in the ownership, size, and value of holdings and in the rental rates, tax, insurance, and other charges associated with the holding of land-resource units.

As one shifts from this long-run situation to the shorter-run periods under which production takes place, most variable factors eventually become fixed. At one stage in this process—the occasion when an operator decides upon the location and size of his lot, commercial site, or farm—the land factor is the key variable. At this point, the operator considers the possible advantages and profits associated with each of his alternative choices, and he ordinarily chooses a site that promises to more than pay for its cost. Once he has committed himself, however, his land factor becomes relatively fixed and the cost of acquiring and holding the land may be treated as a fixed or "sunk" cost.

As the production process continues, other costs become fixed as capital outlays are made for labor and supplies. These accumulated costs always have an important effect upon total and average production costs. Yet regardless of their amount, each of these fixed-cost items becomes of historical importance only once the cost has been incurred. From this point forward, the operator can do little if anything to reduce these costs; and he usually finds that they represent investments of limited salvage value. Accordingly, he finds it advisable to ignore them in his operation planning while he continues to push production to the point at which his current marginal variable inputs just pay for themselves. Operators sometimes suffer financial losses when past inputs involve unwise expenditures, but they can usually realize a higher return or a smaller loss over time by maximizing their returns from any given moment to the end of the production process than by stopping at some lower level of production.

Economies of size and scale. The long-run variable nature of land makes it possible for operators to adjust the size and scale of their enterprises to an optimum level at which they can secure the highest possible net return from their combinations of outputs. But what is the optimum economic size of a factory, an apartment house or a farm? And assuming that such an optimum can be determined, how might an operator move to this optimum? To determine the optimum size of his enterprise, an operator should consider the effect of different scales of operation upon his returns and also upon his cost structure. If he can secure more than proportionate increases in total output from use of additional inputs in his present production combination, he is said to enjoy increasing returns to scale. With this situation and even with constant returns to scale, the operator has an economic incentive to increase the size of his enterprise. Once he experiences a decreasing rate of return in response to increasing scale, he knows he has passed his optimum size and that he can find it profitable to reduce the scale of his operations.

Operators are keenly aware of the cost outlays and expenditures they must make for additional land, labor, and materials if they are to increase their scales of operation. Insofar as their resources permit, they are often willing to expand their scale as long as this action leads to production efficiencies and to a lowering of their average production cost per unit of output. In this respect, they are concerned with the possible economies and diseconomies of scale associated with enterprises of varying sizes.

Cost economies occur whenever an operator finds that a larger scale of operations makes it possible for him to make more effective use of his managerial ability or to better utilize the underused capacity of particular factors such as specialized machinery. Similar economies result when expanded operations permit job specialization, work-simplification techniques, the increased use of labor-saving machinery, and the savings that can come with bulk purchase of materials and supplies. In addition to these internal economies, operators may also benefit from various external economies. A producer may benefit, for example, from the improved processing or marketing facilities attracted by his larger volume of production. In similar fashion, a large subdivision and apartment development may benefit from the improved bus, school, and community shopping facilities it may attract.

In addition to the cost economies that often come with increasing scale, certain diseconomies also are associated with the enlargement of enterprises. Some of these result from the operator's delegation of managerial responsibilities to individuals of less ability. Others may arise when the operator substitutes impersonal dealings with hundreds of employees for his one-time personal contacts with a small labor force; when he copes with the communication and transport problems that arise as enterprises are spread over larger areas; when his enlarged scale of operations entails greater risks from disease, fire, and other hazards; or when his increase in size and labor specialization makes his operations more vulnerable to work stoppages caused by occasional limiting factors. External diseconomies also develop when the expanded needs of an enterprise force it to bid up the prices it pays for the factors it uses in production.

Over the long run, an operator should always seek that size or scale level at which his cost economies most exceed his diseconomies of scale. He should visualize a planning curve (Figure 5-5), which connects the

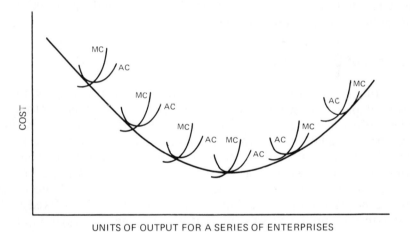

UNITS OF OUTPUT FOR A SERIES OF ENTERPRISES
OF INCREASING SIZE

FIGURE 5-5.   Use of a planning curve to indicate effects of economies and diseconomies of scale upon the optimum operating size of an enterprise.

various cost curve combinations associated with the optimum proportioning of his productive factors in a series of enterprises of increasing size. With this model in mind, he can then adjust the size of his factory, farm, or other business to that scale which has the lowest average cost curve. If he stops with an enterprise of smaller scale, he will always find that he could have enjoyed greater economies of scale with a larger enterprise. Should he go beyond this optimum size, he will find that his diseconomies of scale outweigh any cost economies that can come with additional size.

Most of the operators who use land resources in various parts of the world today work with production combinations of less than optimum size. Some of them shift to larger enterprises over time. Numerous others appear to be only slightly motivated by the comparative economies and diseconomies of scale. Several reasons can be advanced for this situation. Many operators see the advantages of larger scale but fail to shift because they lack the initial capital outlay needed to finance this line of action. Others are held back by lack of imagination, initiative, or ability. Still others remain at their present scale because their personal goals call for the maximization of particular satisfactions, such as the provision and enjoyment of leisure time, which may not be compatible with the operation of larger enterprises.

Institutional factors also have an important impact upon individual operator decisions regarding shifts in scale. In many peasant communities of the Old World, the average land worker operates only slightly above the subsistence level. His desire to shift to a higher scale is frequently limited by custom, by his lack of capital and know-how, by his relative inability to acquire additional land in his home community, and by the absence of public policies and programs for this purpose.

Importance of Limiting and Strategic Factors

One of the most important problems with proportionality is that of identifying and making adjustments for limiting and strategic factors. This problem arises because of the scarce and frequently indivisible nature of the resources available to individual producers. Every operator deals with a limited supply of productive resources and ordinarily treats some one limiting factor, such as land, as the fixed factor around which he proportions his variable inputs. Sometimes he has access to all of the variable inputs he needs for optimum input combinations with his fixed factor. But the scarce supply or strategic nature of some particular input will frequently cause it to stand out as a "bottleneck" factor, which holds up the normal functioning of the production process.

All things considered, man's lack of know-how is probably the most limiting factor with which he must deal. Throughout time, man has often done things the hard way because he has not known how to better use the earth's resources for his benefit. Modern science has made tremendous progress in its conquest of the unknown; and this progress has permitted greater labor efficiency and higher levels of life. Yet man's productivity is still hampered to a considerable extent by his lack of know-how and by his failure, refusal, or inability to use much of the knowledge now at his disposal.

The average producer's primary problem is often that of making better use of his available stock of know-how in working out more productive combinations of his resource factors. In this process, he must often adjust his operations to the strategic roles played by particular input factors while recognizing that some factors may be of strategic importance at a particular moment or during some season and yet be of no more than routine importance on other occasions. An adequate supply of water or moisture for industrial or crop use, for example, may be more or less taken for granted under ordinary circumstances. It may suddenly loom as a critical factor, however, if a well runs dry, a water main bursts, or if an area is affected by drought.

A successful operator must be able to identify his limiting factors and be ready to shape his production decisions around these factors. When his supply of some particular factor such as water is scarce, he must ration his use of this resource and try to combine his inputs so as to secure the highest return to his critical factor. Similarly, when his supplies of capital, labor, or management are limited, he may find it advisable to treat these factors rather than land as the fixed factors around which he proportions his productive factors.

Indivisible inputs. An important example of limiting and strategic factors in production is provided by the indivisible inputs found in most production combinations. Because of their indivisible nature, these inputs often make it necessary for operators to choose between using a larger supply of a resource than they need or being content with a smaller supply than that needed for most effective use.

Many resource inputs are highly divisible. Productive factors such as chemicals, fertilizer, or water may be used in minute quantities or may be added by the ton. Numerous other resources, however, may be quite indivisible, or, if divisible, come in large units. Labor, for example, may be calculated in hours and minutes; but a hired man or a skilled laborer must usually be treated as a unit whose services are sold by the day, week, or month. Similarly, it may be possible for two industrialists to share a single drop forge or for two farmers to share a field chopper. The desire for individual ownership and control is such that both operators frequently choose between whole units even though this may mean that each must choose between the diseconomies of operating with insufficient or inadequate equipment and the unused capacity associated with full ownership of the needed equipment.

Land is often thought of as an easily divided factor, and it is true that fields and lots can be divided and easily added to each other. Yet farms, lots, and buildings are usually sold as units, not as separate 10-acre tracts, so many square feet, or as separate rooms. Because of this factor the industrialist or the retailer will often content himself with his present cramped quarters because no adjacent space is available for expansion. Farmers also may content themselves with farm units of uneconomic size because they cannot enlarge their present units or because they would have to acquire entire farms in the enlargement process. Similarly, the operator of a small factory or shop may hesitate to enlarge his scale of operations because of the costs associated with the enlargement or replacement of his present building.

Resource substitution in production. Producers frequently find that they can use different combinations of input factors to secure approximately the same net return. This means that they can often adjust to their limiting factors by substituting other resources for those in short supply. When an operator's supply of labor is short, he can sometimes substitute capital for labor in the form of labor-saving machinery. Similarly, when he has only a limited supply of land resources at his disposal, he can often substitute capital and labor for the land factor by making more intensive use of the land resources he has.

Most producers are quite mindful of their opportunities for substituting resource factors for each other. As businessmen, they are intensely interested in ways and means for securing more production at less cost. They are always on the lookout for new materials, processes, and techniques they can use to cut costs or increase production. This interest naturally causes them to favor resource substitution whenever it promises higher net returns.

On an individual-operator basis, the relative scarcity of any particular input factor is usually gauged by the operator's opportunity to find a satisfactory substitute. When the price of a resource input increases relative to the price of a possible substitute, and when the substitution process involves only nominal cost and trouble, operators ordinarily shift to the substitute. Thus, an increase in labor costs relative to machinery costs will often cause operators to consider installations of automated equipment. Changes in input costs may cause livestock feeders to adjust their feeding formulas so that they might draw upon less expensive sources of protein and other digestive nutrients. Similarly, the high value of land relative to other input costs in the land-hungry areas of the world often favors the substitution of capital and labor for land in the production process.

Opportunities for resource substitution also play an important part in favoring technological development. With the progress of the Industrial Revolution, man has found it possible to substitute many new materials and devices for other factors in the production process. The steam engine and the gasoline engine have displaced millions of units of animal and man labor. Mass production techniques in industry have been widely substituted for the far less efficient use of labor in cottage industries. The combine harvester and other types of farm machinery have saved great quantities of farm labor for other uses. These examples merely suggest the tremendous impact new technology has had upon resource substitution in production. Far greater developments may be expected in the future as man acquires the ability and know-how for dealing with the limiting factors that now hold him back.

Secular Aspects of Proportionality

Throughout this discussion, proportionality has been treated as a concept that applies primarily to the operating decisions of individual businessmen and firms. This is the sense in which the concept most often is used. It should be noted, however, that the concept of proportionality can be applied to entire industries and also to the resource problems of society at large.

In this respect one might again refer to the secular law of diminishing returns. As was pointed out in chapter 4, the classical economists who developed this concept regarded land as the fixed factor in production. Their reasoning led them to suppose that increasing population pressure would force more and more intensive use of the land factor, that this use would be associated with diminishing returns to society, and that the net result would be higher land values and higher returns to land owners. This concept has operated in many land-hungry areas of the world in times past.

Modern science and technology have prevented—or at least postponed—the operation of this concept throughout the western world. Science and technology have pointed the way for thousands of improvements in the proportioning process. New techniques have been developed, little-used resources have acquired new value in production, mechanical means have been used to free men for still more productive jobs, and great progress has been made in identifying and overcoming the limiting factors in production.

The tremendous progress enjoyed by western man during the past two centuries may be credited in large measure to the success he has enjoyed in better proportioning his resource factors. This progress has permitted him to shift from what appeared to be a constant or diminishing-return stage of the secular production curve to a stage of increasing returns. Over the distant long run it appears entirely probable that mankind may sometime encounter the problem of constant or diminishing secular returns. Present prospects with regard to technological development, however, indicate that this problem is not imminent. New technology is being developed at a rapid rate; and, even if this flow of new developments were cut off tomorrow, the stockpile of unused technological know-how now on hand would still permit tremendous improvements in future production.

INTENSITY OF LAND USE

A high proportion of our economic theory regarding land use is rooted in the concept of proportionality. This central concept—with its emphasis upon marginal analysis, input-output relationships, and those factors that affect operators in their decisions concerning the proportioning and combination of resource factors—provides the keystone for most of our production economic theory. As such, it involves not only the use of land resources in production but also a number of other land economic concepts such as rent, land values, highest and best use, and the allocation of land resources between competing uses. One of the simplest and most direct applications of proportionality arises when one considers the intensity with which land resources are used.

When applied to land use, the term *intensity* refers to the relative amounts of capital and labor combined with units of land in the productive process.[10] People speak of those types of land use that involve high ratios of capital and labor inputs per land unit as intensive uses. Those enterprises involving large land areas relative to the amounts of capital and labor used are described as extensive uses.

Land areas differ a great deal in the intensity with which they are used. Urban lands, particularly those found in central commercial districts, are usually subject to very intensive use, farm lands are ordinarily the subject of somewhat less intensive use, while forest and grazing lands receive still less intensive treatment. This wide range of intensities stems mostly from variations in the input-output responses associated with different types of land use and with the different use-capacities of the land areas devoted to particular uses.

Intensive and Extensive Margins of Land Use

When one considers the intensity of land use, it is important to distinguish between intensive and extensive *uses* and the intensive and extensive *margins of land use.* The intensive margin in agricultural land use has been defined as "the point in the cultivation of a given piece of land at which the labor and capital used barely pay their cost."[11] This concept is applicable to urban, mining, transportation, and other land uses as well as to agriculture. The intensive margin is reached with the last successive variable input that can be applied before marginal costs exceed marginal returns.

---

[10]This concept may be divided into the twin concepts of primary intensity (or intensity of primary production) and secondary intensity (or intensity of secondary production). Primary intensity refers to direct applications of capital and labor to land in the production of land products such as crops, minerals, office or housing space, and highways. Secondary intensity involves applications of capital and labor in the processing of land products which takes place at particular sites. This concept may be applied to livestock enterprises on a farm, the smelting of mineral ores, manufacturing and commercial operations, and even the residential use of housing space. When used without a qualifying prefix, the term "intensity" usually assumes both primary and secondary intensity. Cf. Arthur C. Bunce, *The Economics of Soil Conservation* (Ames: Iowa State College Press, 1945), p. 29.

[11]John Ise, *Economics* (New York: Harper & Brothers, 1946), p. 440.

In contrast to the intensive margin, the extensive margin in land use may be thought of as the no-rent margin at which land under optimum conditions will barely yield enough to cover the costs of production. Unlike the intensive margin, which applies in all cases of land use, the extensive margin affects only those producers who find it impossible to more than break even in their operations. The intensive margin represents the general case in society, while the location of the extensive margin always depends upon the breakeven point at which the effective demand for various land products favors the economic use of a land resource.

The concept of intensive and extensive margins in land use can be illustrated with value product curves and also with cost curves. The examples of these two approaches presented in Figure 5-6 assume the

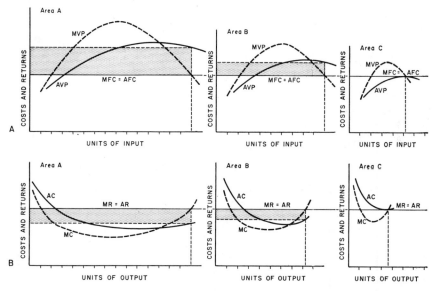

FIGURE 5-6. Use of value product and cost curves to illustrate location of intensive and extensive margins of land use on three areas of differing use-capacities.

same enterprise on three land areas of different use-capacities. Area *A* has the ability or *economic capacity* to absorb 15 variable input units to advantage while area *B* can absorb 10 inputs and the operator in area *C* barely breaks even with an optimum combination of five variable inputs with his fixed factor. With this difference in the economic capacities of the three sites, the operator finds himself at the intensive margin with the addition of the fifteenth input in area *A*, the tenth input in area *B*, and the fifth input unit in area *C*. With area *C*, it takes five inputs to bring the area into use. Any land area of lower use-capacity would prove uneconomic in production; and since the operator can no more than break even at this point, area *C* represents the extensive or no-rent margin of land use.

When this situation is pictured through the use of value product curves as in Figure 5-6A the intensive margin for each grade of land comes at the point at which MFC = MVP. Similarly, when cost curves are used as in Figure 5-6B, the intensive margin comes at the point at which $MC = MR$. With both of these approaches, the lack of any net return above cost on the grade *C* land indicates that the intensive margin has intersected the no-rent or extensive margin of land use.

The situation portrayed in Figure 5-6 may also be visualized as a continuum such as that pictured in Figure 5-7. In this illustration, the horizontal axis measures decreasing use-capacity while the vertical axis indicates the economic capacity or number of variable inputs that can be used to advantage with each successive grade of land. It will be noted that area *A* uses 15 inputs at its intensive margin, while *B* uses 10 inputs and *C* uses 5 inputs. Other land areas with use-capacities between *O* and *R* could also be located along *OR* and would find their intensive margins along *MN*.

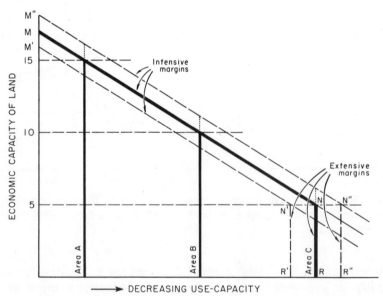

FIGURE 5-7. Illustration of intensive and extensive margins of land use.

The line *NR* may be identified in this example as the no-rent or extensive margin of land use. This line is called the "no-rent margin" because it intersects those points on the horizontal axis and on the *MN* line beyond which it does not pay to bring new units of land into use. In simple terms, the intensive margin represents the economic point with each grade of land beyond which it does not pay to apply additional variable inputs. The extensive margin represents the point in a continuum of land areas with decreasing use-capacities beyond which it does not pay to bring additional land into production.

With changing price and cost conditions, there is usually some shift in the location of both the intensive and extensive margins. If production costs increase or if product prices drop, it may no longer pay the operator on area A to add his fifteenth input. In such an event he may find it more economic to apply only 14 units. The operator on area B in this case may find it profitable to stop with his ninth input and the operator on area C would probably discontinue production entirely. With this situation, the intensive margin would drop to $M'N'$ while the extensive margin would shrink back to $N'R'$. A drop in production costs or an increase in product prices could have the opposite effect in encouraging A to add a sixteenth input, B to add an eleventh input, and C to go to six inputs. Under this circumstance, the intensive margin would rise to $M''N''$ while the extensive margin would move out to $N''R''$.

Marginal and submarginal land. Economists frequently speak of some land areas as being marginal or submarginal for particular types of use. The usual inference with these statements is that the areas fall either at or below the no-rent or extensive margins for the particular uses considered.

Past experience shows that operators sometimes exercise bad judgment in bringing new lands into production or in shifting already developed lands from lower to higher uses only to find them unsuited for the uses contemplated. These examples frequently involve a malallocation of resources. Once this fact is established, the submarginal uses are usually abandoned and the lands revert to lower types of use.

Changing price conditions provide a second major cause of submarginality. During the depression of the 1930s, large areas that had paid their way in production under more favorable price and business conditions suddenly became submarginal when lower product prices forced a leftward shift of the extensive or no-rent margin. These conditions forced some operators out of production. In numerous instances, however, land operators continued to produce at a financial loss. Sometimes they maintained themselves by drawing upon personal or family reserves, by accepting a lower labor income and thus reducing their level of living, by borrowing funds from others, or by accepting financial aid or subsidies from various public and private agencies.

With the passing of the 1930s, much less was heard about marginal and submarginal lands. The reason for this change was simple. With higher price levels and better business conditions, the extensive margin again shifted to the right; and it again became profitable to shift many of the afflicted lands of the 1930s back into production. This experience has far-reaching implications for the future because it indicates the effect higher prices can have in fostering the extension of various land uses to areas now considered submarginal for these purposes.

Some Factors Affecting Intensity of Use

Many factors affect the intensity with which land is used. If a tract is selected for industrial or commercial development, it normally receives more intensive use than when it is used for farm, grazing, or forest purposes. As a rule, its intensity of use also reflects its natural characteristics, its location with respect to markets, and its general use-capacity.

As has been pointed out, when product prices go up operators often find it profitable to intensify their use of already developed lands and to bring new lands into use on the extensive margin. A decrease in product prices often has the reverse effect. Changes in production and marketing costs can also affect land-use intensity. With higher costs and no change in price, operators ordinarily find it necessary to cut back production. A reduction in production or marketing costs with no change in price, on the other hand, usually favors the more intensive use that comes with the application of additional inputs up to the new point at which marginal costs equal marginal revenues.

Increasing population pressure usually suggests more intensive land use. Sometimes this results from the effects of increased demand upon product prices. In a Malthusian sense, it might also result from the effects population pressure can have in forcing labor costs down to a subsistence level.

Limiting factors in production frequently have an important effect upon the intensity with which land is used. When the supply of land or space included in a farm, industrial establishment, or commercial shop is the limiting factor, operators have every economic incentive to push their operations to the intensive margin. But when some nonland resource such as the operator's managerial capacity, an insufficient supply of operating capital, or a fixed labor force is the limiting factor, operators find it most profitable to proportion their factors around their scarce resources even though this may result in less intensive land use.

Family and operator attitudes also have an important impact upon intensification practices. Several immigrant groups and religious communities have at times displayed a willingness to accept hard labor and low levels of living. With this set of values, these operators have often found it possible to push production further than most of the operators with whom they have had to compete. This willingness to accept the lower marginal returns to labor and management that have come with their intensive land-use practices has frequently made it possible for these operators to outbid other prospective buyers in the purchase of land.

All things considered, the intensity with which land is used always involves the interrelationship of several contributing factors. Areas of high use-capacity can ordinarily be used more intensively than areas of lower productive potential. Whether this relationship follows in actual practice depends upon the impact and interrelationship of other conditioning factors such as population pressure, the stage of economic development, availability of capital and labor, and the attitudes and goals of those who own and operate the land. Differences involving these factors sometimes result in the intensive use of areas of limited use-capacity while nearby areas of greater productive potential remain underdeveloped or underutilized.[12]

—SUGGESTED READINGS

Black, John D., *An Introduction to Production Economics* (New York: Henry Holt & Company, Inc., 1926), chaps. XI-XIII.

Bober, Mandell M., *Intermediate Price and Income Theory* (New York: W. W. North & Co., Inc., revised 1962), chaps. V-VII.

Clough, Donald C., *Concepts in Management Science* (Englewood Cliffs, N.J.: Prentice-Hall, Inc., 1963), chap. VIII.

Doll, John P., V. James Rhodes, and Jerry G. West, *Economics of Agricultural Production, Markets, and Policy* (Homewood, Ill.: Richard D. Irwin, Inc., 1968), chaps. III-V.

Heady, Earl O., *Economics of Agricultural Production and Resource Use* (Englewood Cliffs, N.J.: Prentice-Hall, Inc., 1952), chaps. II-VII.

Leftwich, Richard H., *The Price System and Resource Allocation,* (New York: Rinehart and Company, Inc., 1960), chaps. VII-VIII.

Nemmers, Erwin E., *Managerial Economics* (New York: John Wiley & Sons, 1962), Part III.

---

[12]Cf. C. H. Hammar and J. H. Muntzell, "Intensity of Land Use and Resettlement Problems," *Journal of Farm Economics*, Vol. 17, August, 1935, pp. 409-22; and Conrad Hammar, "Intensity and Land Rent," *Journal of Farm Economics*, Vol. 20, November, 1938, pp. 776-91.

6

Economic Returns to Land Resources

History shows that rental payments have been made for the use of land resources almost since the beginnings of organized land settlement. These payments provide a measure of the economic return that goes to land resources for their use in production. This economic return was described in the last chapter as "net return" and as the net surplus of total value product above the operator's total factor costs, which should be credited to the fixed factor. Hereafter, it will be referred to simply as land rent.

Land rent is the key concept in land economic theory. It provides a theoretical base for explaining the value we place on land resources and much of the incentive we have for their ownership. It influences the allocation of land resources between individuals and between competing uses. It also has important effects upon leasing arrangements, taxation policies, the economics of land development and conservation, and several other aspects of land-resource use.

THE NATURE OF LAND RENT

"Rent" is another of those common words for which the economist has a specialized meaning. In his day-to-day use of this term, the average layman ordinarily thinks of the payments made to property owners for the use of their lands and buildings. Thus he speaks of house rent, room rent, and the rent paid for commercial sites and farms.

Like other people, economists often use the term "rent" in its popular sense. When they think in economic terms and more particularly when they consider the economic returns to land resources, they find it appropriate to differentiate between three concepts of rent—contract rent, land rent, and economic rent.

Contract rent refers to the actual payments tenants make for their use of the property of others. The amount of these payments is normally agreed to by the landlord and tenant in advance of the period of property use and thus stems from mutual contractual arrangements. This concept is more or less synonymous with the popular meaning ascribed to the term "rent."

Land rent is a more specialized concept. It represents the theoretical earnings of land resources and may be defined simply as the *economic return that accrues or should accrue to land for its use in production.* This concept applies to all of the theoretical earnings of land and, as used here, applies to the combined earnings of land sites and their improvements. When distinctions are made between classes of land rent, it is sometimes expedient to distinguish between ground rents or site rents—the returns associated with building sites, bare ground, and raw land—and the improvement rents, which can be associated with buildings and other man-made real estate improvements.[1] Distinctions also can be made between location rents or rents that arise because of the favorable location of a particular tract of land and fertility or site-quality rents.

Economic rent also is a specialized economic concept. For over a hundred years, this term was used by economists to describe the economic earnings of land and had a meaning more or less synonomous with the present concept of land rent. With the refinements in economic thinking that have come during the past century, the tendency of more and more economic discussions to center around topics other than land, and the frequent tendency of economists to view land resource investments as a type of capital, a new meaning has been ascribed to the term "economic

[1] Some economists favor a narrower concept of land rent than that employed here and prefer to think in terms of what is here called ground rent. Von Thunen, for example, accepted this more narrow definition of land rent and used the term "estate rent" to describe economic returns to land and land improvements. Cf. Peter Hall (ed.), *Von Thunen's Isolated State* (New York: Pergamon Press, 1966), p. 18-19. The broader concept of land rent appears more meaningful today and is accepted here because (1) nearly all land sites have benefited from some man-made improvements, (2) it is often difficult to distinguish between the shares of land rent that should go to sites or raw land as compared with improvements, and (3) the focus of this study is on a broad concept of land resources, which includes both land sites and the improvements legally attached to them, rather than on a narrower natural concept of land.

rent." It is now defined as the surplus of income above the minimum supply price it takes to bring a factor into production.[2]

Economic rent, as now defined, can be viewed largely as a short-run economic surplus that a productive factor or an operator can earn because of unexpected demand or supply conditions. Over longer time periods, the supply and demand for the commodity in question come into balance, and the phenomenon of economic rent disappears.[3] A land resource such as an apartment house development, for example, can earn an economic rent above its normal land and contract rents when a sudden demand for housing makes it possible for the owner to raise his rental rates. This temporary advantage disappears over time as the demand situation changes or as new housing is produced. Elements of economic rent may also be associated with the returns received by capital, labor, and management.[4]

Land rent and contract rent are the two important rent concepts used in land economics. These concepts differ from each other in one significant respect. Contract rent involves an actual payment to the property

---

[2]Cf. Joan Robinson, *The Economics of Imperfect Competition* (London: The Macmillan Company, 1933), p. 102; and Kenneth E. Boulding, *Economics Analysis,* 4th ed. (New York: Harper and Row, 1966), Vol. 1, p. 265. This modern concept of economic rent is an outgrowth of Marshall's views on "quasi-rents" [Alfred Marshall, *Principles of Economics,* 8th ed. (London: Macmillan & Co., Ltd., 1938), pp. 421-27.] and has gained common acceptance among economic theorists.

Economic rent, as defined above, may be considered as synonomous with land rent as long as one is willing to treat land as a free gift of nature. With this assumption, all of the earnings of land above the necessary payments for property taxes and insurance of improvements can be classified as land rent and also as economic rent. Difficulties arise in the application of this concept when one recognizes that very few operators are willing to view the minimum supply price of their land resources as zero. In practice, there is no more justification for assuming a minimum short-run supply price of zero for land than for any other type of input. Operators generally equate the minimum supply prices of the land resources they use in production with their current contract rental values.

This situation highlights the need for distinguishing between land rent and the modern concept of economic rent, for recognizing the fact that "economic rent" no longer embraces its original meaning, and for employing a term such as "land rent" to describe the return attributable to land resources for their use in production. Cf. Robert H. Wessel, "A Note on Economic Rent," *American Economic Review,* Vol. 57, December, 1967, pp. 1221-26; and Joseph S. Keiper *et al., Theory and Measurement of Rent* (New York: Chilton Company), 1961, pp. 108-113.

[3]Cf. Richard H. Leftwich, *The Price System and Resource Allocation,* rev. ed. (New York: Holt, Rinehart and Winston, 1963), pp. 294-96.

[4]Wages include an element of economic rent when they exceed the minimum supply price at which workers are willing to sell their services. Thus if one's minimum supply price is $150 a week but he receives a weekly wage of $175, the $25 of surplus return may be identified as an economic rent to labor. Other types of economic rent appear when an investor is willing to loan money at 5 percent interest but finds that he can get 7 percent (a surplus of 2 percent) or when a contractor or concert artist is willing to provide his services for $500 but finds that he can collect $1,000.

owner. This payment may either exceed or fall below the amount of land rent theoretically earned by the property. When it exceeds the amount that should be paid as land rent, the tenant must contribute the difference from the returns that should go to his capital, labor, or managerial inputs. When it falls below this amount, the tenant is able to pocket part of the land rent.

With this background, further emphasis should be given to the theoretical concept of land rent. Attention can first be focused on the value-productivity explanation of land rent associated with present day production analysis. Consideration will then be given to some earlier formulations of the rent concept and to some criticisms and suggested modifications of rent theory that have helped to shape the present concept of land rent.

Land Rent As An Economic Surplus

Land rent can be treated simply as a residual economic surplus—as that portion of the total value product or of the total returns that remains after payment is made for the total factor costs or total costs, respectively.[5] This concept is illustrated by the value product and cost curve diagrams presented in Figure 6-1. The total value of the product produced is represented in these diagrams by the large rectangles *LNSP*, and the total cost of the variable inputs by the lower rectangles *MNSR*, and the residual surplus or land rent by the shaded rectangles *LMRP*.

This simple formulation is both flexible and all-inclusive in its consideration of the factors that influence rental levels. Cost curves may be used, for example, to explain differences in the amounts of land rent that accrue on different grades of land. As Figure 6-2 indicates, the units of output secured from three different grades of land can be assumed to have the same market value. Meanwhile, the average cost of production per output unit is lower on the grade *A* tract than on the grade *B* and *C* tracts because the total cost of production is spread over more units. With these differences in average unit production costs, the grade *A* tract yields considerable land rent, the grade *B* tract a smaller amount of rent, and the grade *C* tract produces barely enough to pay its production costs. As this example suggests, the amount of rent that accrues on each grade of land depends upon the relationship between price levels and costs. With higher prices or lower costs, rents rise all along the line—even on the grade *C* land. Lower prices or higher costs, in turn, would lower the rents secured on the *A* and *B* tracts and force the grade *C* land out of use.

[5] Malthus recognized this relationship during the early 1800s when he defined rent as "the excess value of the whole produce, or if estimated in money, the excess price of the whole produce, above what is necessary to pay the wages of labor and the profits of capital employed in cultivation." Cf. Thomas Robert Malthus, *Principles of Political Economy* (London: William Pickering, 1836), p. 136. Malthus outlined this same concept earlier in his 1815 essay on "The Nature and Progress of Rent."

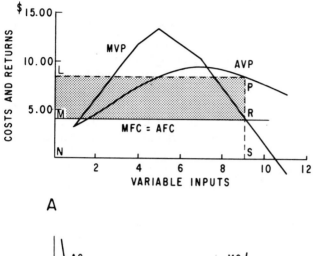

A

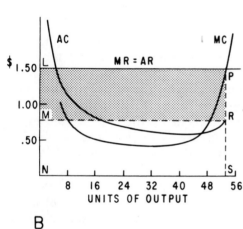

B

FIGURE 6-1. Use of value product and cost curve diagrams to illustrate concept of land rent as a residual economic surplus which remains after the payment of production costs.

A similar comparative approach may be used to illustrate the effects of differences in location upon the land rent produced on tracts of comparable quality. The first diagram in Figure 6-3 indicates the amount of land rent that can be expected on a grade *A* site located at the market. Lands located at greater distances must pay a shipping cost to get their products to market. Since this cost is proportional to the number of units of output sold, it may be treated as a price-depressing factor, which lowers the actual prices received at outlying production points.

As Figure 6-3 indicates, the lower net price received by producers located 250 and 500 miles from market has a considerable effect in reducing the amount of land rent received at these locations. These areas are just as productive as those located at the market; but with a transportation-cost handicap, the operators located at these distances must gear their production to a lower net price level. The lower land rents associated with the less advantageous locations may be attributed both to the lower net prices received by the operators at these locations and to the effect of

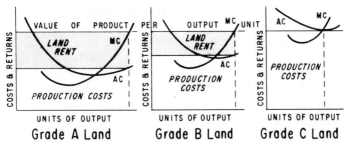

Grade A Land   Grade B Land   Grade C Land

FIGURE 6-2. Illustration of the effects differences in land quality have upon the amounts of land rent which accrue to three grades of land.

this lower price level in cutting back the number of variable inputs operators can profitably employ in production.

With marginal productivity analysis, one can use either the input- or the output-unit approach to secure clear-cut and highly meaningful explanations of land rent. Along with its many advantages, however, this method of analysis has one important weakness. In its treatment of land rent as the residual surplus that remains after payment is made for the

NET VALUE OF PRICE PER UNIT OF OUTPUT (AFTER
DEDUCTION OF SHIPPING COSTS) AT POINT OF PRODUCTION

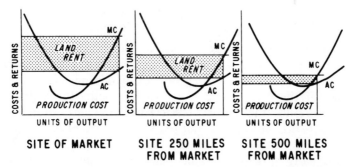

SITE OF MARKET   SITE 250 MILES   SITE 500 MILES
                   FROM MARKET   FROM MARKET

FIGURE 6-3. Illustration of the effects of differences in accessibility upon the amounts of land rent which accrue to three tracts of land of comparable quality located at different distances from market.

other factors of production, marginal productivity analysis assumes that the return to the other factors can be determined with some precision. This assumption is often unwarranted. The returns attributed to nonland factors in calculations of land rent are usually arrived at through an accounting process. They may represent the actual cash payments made for these factors, the going rates for these payments, or estimates of what a fair or normal return should be. Each of these methods gives value figures that bear the same relationship to actual productivity as contract rent bears to land rent.

The marginal-productivity approach can be used to measure the economic return attributable to nonland factors as well as to land. When it is used for this purpose, it is usual practice to impute a fair return to land just as fair returns are imputed to nonland factors when this approach is used to measure land rent. As this situation suggests, the accuracy of the final answers secured by this approach depend upon the basic data used in the calculations. In cases involving superior management, the income assigned to land may easily be too high if the return to management is calculated at a going rate. Conversely, with mediocre combinations of productive factors, too little return may be attributed to land if all of the other factors are compensated at their going rates.

It should also be recognized that land rent is not always treated as a residual surplus. Rent may be regarded in this light from the standpoint of society and some individuals. Under real-life conditions, however, many individuals—and most particularly those who make contract rental payments—tend to view rent as a fixed item among their production costs. Management or labor are treated as the fixed factor in these cases, and the residual surplus is viewed as either profit or labor income.

Classical Formulations of Rent Theory

Little consideration was given to economic explanations of the nature of land rent until relatively recent times. Sir William Petty made some pertinent observations concerning rent in 1662 as did several other writers in the next 150 years.[6] The beginnings of classical rent theory are usually associated, however, with the writings of a group of English economists at the conclusion of the Napoleonic Wars. At that time, the British Parliament was considering the controversial Corn Law question; and the attention given to this problem prompted several writers to publish their views regarding the nature of rent and certain related subjects.[7] Three writers of this early post-Napoleonic period—Thomas Robert Malthus, David Ricardo, and Johann Heinrich von Thunen—made significant contributions to present land rent theory. Malthus outlined a residual surplus concept, which was largely ignored at the time but which fore-

---

[6]Other important contributors to the early conceptualization of rent theory include Richard Cantillon (1730), Francois Quesnay (1756), A. R. J. Turgot (1770), Adam Smith (1776), James Anderson (1777), and James Mill (1804). Anderson was the only one of these writers to present a reasonably complete theory of rent. Cf. Keiper *et al., op. cit.*, pp. 4-21; and Edmund Whittaker, *A History of Economic Ideas* (New York: Longmans, Green & Co., Inc., 1940), pp. 487-99.

[7]Thomas R. Malthus, David Ricardo, Robert Torrens, and James West published important pamphlets on rent in 1814 and 1815. Cf. Keiper *et al., op. cit.*, pp. 21-34; and Whittaker, *op cit.*, pp. 499-503.

shadowed the marginal productivity concept of rent described in the last section. Ricardo attributed rent to differences in fertility and presented his views with such force and clarity that they were soon widely accepted as the basis for the classical concept of rent. Von Thunen authored an independently developed and complementary theory, which explained rent in terms of differences in location with respect to a central market.

Ricardo's emphasis upon differences in fertility. In formulating his theory of rent, Ricardo was concerned almost entirely with the problem of agricultural rents. He started his analysis by assuming a newly settled country with "an abundance of rich and fertile land, a very small proportion of which is required to be cultivated for the support of the actual population."[8] He then argued that only the most fertile lands would be brought into cultivation and that no payment of rent would be associated with their use. Rents arise on these lands only when increases in population numbers and in the demand for land make it necessary for society to bring less fertile lands into use. In Ricardo's words:

> If all land had the same properties, if it were unlimited in quantity, and uniform in quality, no charge could be made for its use, unless where it possessed peculiar advantages of situation. It is only, then, because land is not unlimited in quantity and uniform in quality, and because, in the progress of population, land of an inferior quality, or less advantageously situated, is called into cultivation, that rent is ever paid for the use of it. When, in the progress of society, land of the second degree of fertility is taken into cultivation, rent immediately commences on that of the first quality, and the amount of that rent will depend on the difference in the quality of these two portions of land.
>
> When land of the third quality is taken into cultivation, rent immediately commences on the second, and it is regulated as before by the differences in their productive powers. At the same time, the rent of the first quality will rise, for that must always be above the rent of the second by the difference between the produce which they yield with a given quantity of capital and labour. With every step in the progress of population, which shall oblige a country to have recourse to land of a worse quality, to enable it to raise its supply of food, rent, on all the more fertile land, will rise.[9]

[8]David Ricardo, *The Principles of Political Economy and Taxation* (London: 1817: Everyman's edition, London: J. M. Dent & Sons, Ltd., 1911), p. 34.

[9]*Ibid.,* p. 35. James Anderson expressed generally the same concept in 1777 when he wrote:

> In every country there are various soils which are endured with different degrees of fertility; and hence it must happen, that the farmer who cultivates the most fertile of these can afford to bring his corn to market at a lower price than others who cultivate poorer fields. But if the corn that grows on these fertile spots be not sufficient fully to supply the market, the price will naturally be raised to such a height as to indemnify others for the expense of cultivating poorer soils. The farmer, however, who cultivates the rich spots, will be able to sell his corn at the same rate with those who occupy poorer fields; he will

Ricardo's theory of rent determination is often illustrated by an example such as that portrayed in Figure 6-4. In this example, one might assume four grades of land with yield capacities of 50, 40, 30, and 25 units of product for a given input of capital and labor. As long as only the

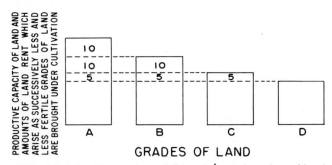

FIGURE 6-4. Illustration of Ricardo's explanation of land rent.

grade *A* land is needed in production, the market price of the product corresponds with the cost of production and no rent is paid because every land user is able to bring new equally fertile areas into use. Before any grade *B* lands can be brought into use, product prices must increase enough to cover the higher unit-production costs encountered on these lands. Once prices rise to this level, the extensive margin of cultivation shifts to the grade *B* land, and these lands become available for economic use. At the same time, the value of the 10 additional units of product secured on the *A* lands, as compared with the *B* lands, becomes an economic surplus. This surplus is unnecessary from the standpoint of continued production; but since it exists, it goes as rent to the owners of the grade *A* land. When the *C* lands come into use, rent arises on the *B* lands while additional rent occurs on the *A* lands. When the *D* lands are brought into use, rent commences on the *C* lands and increases on the *A* and *B* lands.

A more meaningful formulation of the same concept results when the productivity of the four tracts is viewed in terms of costs and returns per unit of output as in Figure 6-5. It is assumed with this example that the inputs of capital and labor used on each tract have a cost of $100 and that

consequently, receive more than the intrinsic value of the corn he raises. Many persons will, therefore, be desirous of obtaining possession of these fertile fields; being content to give a certain premium for an exclusive privilege to cultivate them, varying, of course, according to the more or less fertility of the soil. It is this premium which we now call *rent;* a medium by which the expense of cultivating soils of different degrees of fertility is reduced to a perfect equality.

From Anderson's essay, "Observations on the Means of exciting a Spirit of Industry," as reported by J. R. McCulloch, *Principles of Political Economy* (Edinburgh: 1843), p. 442.

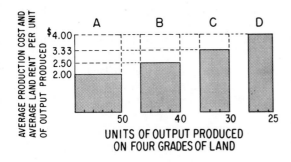

FIGURE 6-5. Alternate presentation of Ricardo's explanation of land rent.

use of the four grades of land entails minimum costs of $2.00, $2.50, $3.33, and $4.00, per output unit, respectively. As long as there is enough grade A land to provide all the needed output, the market price of the product can correspond with the $2 per unit cost of production. No rent needs to be paid because every land user is able to bring new equally fertile areas into use, and any operator who attempts to raise his product price will be undersold by other producers.

This situation changes when grade B lands must be brought into use to provide products for the growing population. At this point, product prices must rise to the $2.50 level to cover the cost of production at the new extensive margin of cultivation. The higher product price, which encourages operators to cultivate the grade B lands, provides an economic surplus of 50 cents per unit of output to the operators of the A lands. This surplus is unnecessary from the standpoint of continued production; but since it exists, it goes as an economic return or as land rent to the owners of the grade A lands.

Product prices must rise to the $3.33 level if the grade C lands are to be cultivated. This price increase provides an economic surplus or land rent equivalent to 63 cents for every unit of output produced on the B lands and an additional land rent equivalent to 63 cents for each unit of output produced on the A lands. A price of $4.00 per unit of output is needed to bring the D lands into use. At this point, a land rent equal to 67 cents for each unit of output arises on the C lands and additional land rents arise on the B and A lands.

Ricardo believed that farm product prices are determined by the production costs associated with the highest-cost portions of the total supply needed by society. His theory assumes that prices are set by production costs at the intensive and extensive margins of cultivation. He recognized that product prices must rise with the outward shift of the extensive margin of cultivation and that these higher prices at the same time raise the intensive margin on the more fertile lands and thus favor their more intensive use. In his words:

> It often, and, indeed, commonly happens, that before No. 2, 3, 4, or 5, or the inferior lands are cultivated, capital can be employed more productively on those lands which are already in cultivation. It may perhaps be found that by

doubling the original capital employed on No. 1, though the produce will not be doubled, will not be increased by 100 quarters, it may be increased by 85 quarters, and that this quantity exceeds what could be obtained by employing the same capital on land No. 3.

In such case, capital will be preferably employed on the old land, and will equally create a rent; for rent is always the difference between the produce obtained by the employment of two equal quantities of capital and labour.[10]

Ricardo's thesis can best be illustrated through the use of cost curves as in Figure 6-6. When only the *A* lands are used, operators find it profitable to produce *p* units of output. At this point no rent arises. When the *B* lands come into use, the operators of these lands find it profitable to produce *j* units of output at which point they experience an extensive no-rent margin. Their production at this price level creates a land rent for the owners of the *A* lands on the *p* units of output and also makes it profitable to increase production to a new intensive margin at *q* units of output. Similarly, when the *C* lands are brought under cultivation, the operators of the *B* lands secure a land rent on *j* units of output and find it profitable to increase production to the *k* units of output level while the operators of the *A* lands secure larger land rents at the *p* and *q* levels and find it profitable to push to their new intensive margin with *r* units of output. A similar chain reaction takes place when the *D* lands are brought into use and the operators of the more fertile lands find that their rents increase on their present units of output and that they can move on to new intensive margins involving additional units of output.

As a final observation concerning the Ricardian doctrine of rent, it may be noted that Ricardo held that rent was price-determined and that it

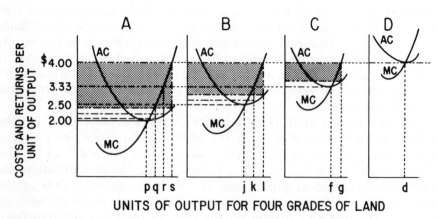

FIGURE 6-6. Alternate presentation of Ricardo's explanation of land rent.

[10]*Ibid.*, p. 36.

"does not and cannot enter in the least degree as a component part of its price."[11] He argued:

> The reason, then, why raw produce rises in comparative value is because more labour is employed in the production of the last portion obtained, and not because a rent is paid to the landlord. The value of corn is regulated by the quantity of labour bestowed on its production on that quality of land, or with that portion of capital, which pays no rent. Corn is not high because a rent is paid, but a rent is paid because corn is high; and it has been justly observed that no reduction would take place in the price of corn although landlords should forego the whole of their rent. Such a measure would only enable some farmers to live like gentlemen, but would not diminish the quantity of labour necessary to raise raw produce on the least productive land in cultivation.[12]

Rent arising from location. Ricardo's explanation of rent in terms of differences in land quality deals with only one factor that affects rent-paying capacity. Location is another important rent-determinant. The importance of this factor was stressed by Petty and von Thunen but received little more than passing attention from Ricardo and his English contemporaries.

Von Thunen in particular observed that when crops produced for a central city market are grown on lands of like fertility, the lands located nearest the city enjoy a definite rent advantage over those located at greater distance. The extent of this rent advantage corresponds with the difference between the transportation costs that arise in the shipment of products from the two areas to market.

In the days of ox-cart and wagon transportation, shipping costs often restricted the areas within which products could be produced on a commercial scale. The transportation costs associated with cereal crops such as wheat, for example, were often so high that they discouraged the commercial production of these crops at distances of more than 25 to 40 miles from market. Technological developments have fostered a tremendous change in this situation. Yet transportation costs still have important effects upon rent-paying capacity and the extent of the area within which many products can be profitably produced.

The importance of the transportation costs associated with different locations may be illustrated by the example of a heavy and bulky product such as sugar beets. If sugar beets are worth $15 a ton delivered at a factory and can be produced at an average cost of $13.80 a ton (including loading costs and a fair return on the operator's capital, labor, and management), a surplus of $1.20 a ton will be available as land rent on those lands located at the market. With an average yield of 10 tons per acre this would result in a land rent of $12 per acre at this location.

Fields located at greater distances from market naturally have higher

[11] *Ibid.*, p. 41.
[12] *Ibid.*, pp. 38-39.

transportation costs and thus produce less land rent. With an average transportation cost of 3 cents per ton-mile (once the beets are loaded in trucks), the amount of land rent attributable to a site drops 3 cents a ton, or 30 cents an acre with every additional mile between the location of the production site and the factory. (Figure 6-7.) This means that there can be only $6 in land rent per acre at locations 20 miles from the factory and that this rent drops to the zero or no-rent point 40 miles from the factory. Some production may be carried on beyond the no-rent point but only with a reduction in the payments that normally would go to labor and management.

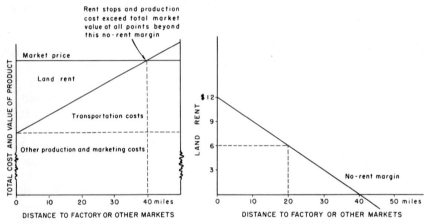

FIGURE 6-7. Effects of transportation costs associated with shipment of products from various locations to market upon land rent.

Fortunately, the no-rent points for different crops and land uses occur at different distances from market. This factor together with the multitude of markets found in modern society gives almost every tract of land some rent-producing capacity. Lands located near a market or near the 100 percent spot of a central business district may have a high income- and rent-producing capacity for any of several alternative uses. Lands located in more distant or remote spots are often beyond the no-rent margins for many uses. The operators of these lands usually have a limited choice of enterprises and frequently find it most profitable to concentrate on extensive-type land-use operations such as ranching.

Use-capacity and rent paying ability. Differences in rent-paying capacity can often be explained in terms of variations in either soil fertility or location. By themselves, neither of these factors provides a completely satisfactory explanation of the ability of land to pay rent; and even when the two are considered together, they can leave significant aspects of rent-paying capacity unexplained. Operator choices concerning enterprises and the impact of good or poor management often affect the level of land rent.[13]   Land quality factors such as levels of capital improvements, property improvement practices, and amenity considerations such as a desirable neighborhood, a pleasing view, ready access to water supplies, or nearness to educational and recreation facilities can have significant effects on rental values. Convenience of access and possible savings in time-distance of travel also can influence the rent potential of various sites.

The cumulative impact of the various factors including soil fertility that affect land quality and of the items including location that affect accessibility are measured by the concept of use-capacity. This concept has particular value when applied to land resources because it permits relatively complete comparisons of the income-producing potential of various sites. Those areas with the highest use-capacity ordinarily have the highest value, the greatest production potential, and yield the most land rent. The general relationship between land use-capacity and the appearance of land rent may be visualized as in Figure 6-8. This diagram assumes

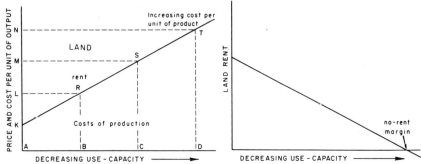

FIGURE 6-8.   Illustration of relationship between use-capacity of land resources, production costs, and the appearance of land rent.

a continuum of lands of decreasing use-capacity ranging from areas of highest use-capacity at *A* to lands of much lower use-potential at *D*. As society resorts to the use of the lower-grade, less productive, and less advantageously situated lands—as the extensive margin of land use shifts to the right—unit production costs gradually increase and the price level rises enough to command whatever additional production is needed. When only the lands between *A* and *B* are used, prices are pegged at the *LR* level

[13]Management is treated here as a constant factor. Any increase in the returns attributable to superior management should go as a payment to management. In actual practice, however, it is difficult to give the exact credit due to each factor for changes in production. For example, if the better areas are operated by superior managers while prices are set at the margin by the operations of average managers, some of the products of superior management may easily be credited as economic return to land. Conversely, poor management on the better lands may result in an unwarranted reduction in the amount of economic return credited to land.

and the surplus above production costs available for land rent is small. When the extensive margin of land use shifts from *B* to *D*, prices climb to *NT* and the total volume of land rent increases from the area included within the triangle *KLR* to the area included within the triangle *KNT.*

Figure 6-8A assumes a continuum of lands of diminishing use-capacity and shows the quantities of land rent that arise at different sites as prices rise to meet the cost of utilizing lands at the extensive margin for some given use. The triangles *KLR* at price *LR, KMS* at price *MS,* and *KNT* at price *NT* are indicative of the amounts of land rent produced as the assumed use is extended out from *A* to points *B, C,* and *D,* respectively. For analytical purposes, these land rent triangles can be detached from the remainder of the diagram, turned over, and shown as land rent triangles such as that pictured in Figure 6-8B.[14] Land rent triangles or profiles of this type can be utilized to show the relationship between decreasing use-capacity and the amounts of rent produced for any land use.

This analysis assumes some abstraction from reality. The concept of a continuum of lands of decreasing use-capacity involves two important assumptions: (1) that society proceeds in its use of land resources from those sites and areas of highest use-capacity to those of lower potential, and (2) that areas with various levels of use-capacity are distributed more or less uniformly along the horizontal axis. Neither of these assumptions is completely valid under real-life conditions. This situation naturally complicates the use of this approach. As long as these limitations are recognized, however, this approach can be used to provide a meaningful explanation of the effect of various levels of use-capacity on land rent. More important, it supplies an analytical basis for the concept of the land rent triangle.

Other Views Concerning Rent

Numerous criticisms have been made of the earlier theories of land rent. Some of these attacked Ricardo's assumptions concerning the order of

---

[14]Each land rent triangle can be visualized as a cross-section of a land rent cone, which surrounds a central market point (the site of highest use-capacity). Various terms have been used to describe the surface of the land rent cone, which is shown in Figure 6-8B simply as the hypotenuse or slope of the land rent triangle. Edgar M. Hoover, *Location Theory and the Shoe and Leather Industries* (Cambridge: Harvard University Press, 1937), p. 23, uses the term "rent surface." Edgar S. Dunn, Jr., *The Location of Agricultural Production* (Gainesville: University of Florida Press, 1954), p. 34, and Walter Isard, *Location and Space-Economy* (New York: John Wiley & Sons, 1956), pp. 194-95, speak of a "rent function." William Alonso, *Location and Land Use* (Cambridge: Harvard University Press, 1964), pp. 40-41, describes it as a "bid rent function." Alonso sees the slope of the rent triangle for each use as being determined by the highest bid-prices offered by land users at various sites. The total length of the hypotenuse from its high rent point on the vertical axis to the no-rent margin on the horizontal axis represents a family of bid-rent functions, which permits any user to be indifferent as to his precise location along the function (p. 41).

land development; some stressed the application of rent to factors other than land; and some criticized the assumption that rent does not enter into price. The more important of the modifications occasioned by these views have been noted in the above discussion. Attention should be given, however, to two alternative views of the nature of land rent. These are the concept of rent as an *unearned increment* and the concept of rent as a *return on capital investment.*

Rent as an unearned increment. Ricardo treated rent as an economic surplus, as a payment to the land owner that is not required to keep land in production. With this approach, it was an easy step for later observers to conclude that rent is an unearned increment or windfall return for which the land owner does nothing and that he receives only because of his favored "monopoly" position.

This view of rent was accepted by three important nineteenth-century economists. John Stuart Mill regarded rent in this light and suggested that this unearned increment be taxed for public use. Henry George accepted this point of view and used it as the basis for his crusade favoring the single tax. Karl Marx also tended to regard rent as an unearned increment or monopoly return.

There is no necessary conflict or inconsistency between land rent and the concept of rent as an unearned increment. In some instances, rent may even be regarded as something akin to a monopoly income. This is particularly true in those areas where vestiges of feudal land-ownership systems persist, where a high proportion of the land is controlled by a few families, or where factors such as tradition and prestige of ownership discourage market transactions. In an economic sense, however, the presence of other owners holding similar property ownership rights prevents the existence of a true monopoly. Land ownership frequently confers a differential advantage upon particular individuals but rarely confers monopoly rights in the usual sense of the word.

Rent can be viewed as an unearned increment any time it arises from the mere holding of land. Whenever a property owner enjoys an increase in his land rent from the acts of others in the economy and not because of his own improvements or actions, he enjoys an unearned increment. Unearned increments of this type are associated with the returns to most factors of production and are often hard to identify. This identification problem is complicated in the case of land resources by the tendency of owners to improve their properties—a situation that gives the owner a claim to part of the increase in rent—and by the frequent sale of properties.

Unearned increments ordinarily are capitalized into the selling price of properties at time of sale; and their value thus goes to the seller. New owners then start out with properties that supposedly are worth no more than their purchase price. Should the buyer's purchase funds involve savings earned through past sweat and toil, he may well reject the view that all or part of his land rental return is an unearned increment. To him, it represents a fair return on his investment outlay.

Rent as a return on investment. It is both logical and proper to view land rent as the economic return to land resources when one considers input-output relationships from the standpoint of society at large. This approach is necessary if one is to treat land or land resources as a separate and unique factor of production. Most investors, owners, and tenants, however, tend to treat land rent as a return on investment.

These operators are not particularly concerned with the fact that land resources usually involve intermixtures of land—a free gift of nature—and man-made improvements. To their way of thinking, the land resources they work with are a type of capital. They realize that the development of land resources calls for sizable investments in time, effort, and money and that the acquisition and use of already developed properties calls for purchase or leasing arrangements. For them, land resources are a capital good that can be leased, bought, or sold in the market, and the land rent is a return on the capital investment made in land resources. The typical tenant, for example, views his contract rental payments as an operating cost, not as a residual economic surplus due to landowners because of the particular income-producing advantages associated with their properties. Landlords and owners in turn think of their rental returns as returns on the capital value of their investments and compare these returns with those they could receive in alternative investments.

SIGNIFICANCE OF LAND RENT

Theoretical concepts such as land rent have little importance in and of themselves. Their real significance arises because of their value as tools of analysis that can be used in explanations of real-life conditions. The concept of land rent is highly significant in this respect because of its application to different land economic problems. Four of the more important of these applications involve its relationship to contract rental arrangements, to property values, to land resource investment and development decisions, and to the allocation of land resources between different types of use.

Effects upon Rental Arrangements

No rental arrangement is complete without some agreement concerning the amount of rent that will be paid for the use of the property involved. The effect of land rent on the determination of contract rental rates is best observed in the workings of the rental bargaining process. Under ideal bargaining conditions, both the landlord and the tenant have accurate knowledge concerning the fair economic return that should be paid for the use of land resources. The landlord under these circumstances finds it to his advantage to demand the full land rent plus any additional payment he can get. The tenant in turn insists that he should pay no more than the recognized land rent and naturally favors payments of less than this amount. Should the tenant agree to a higher payment rate than that necessary to provide the fair land rent, he would find it necessary to sacrifice part of the return that should go to his labor, management, and capital. On the other hand, should the land owner accept a lower rental payment, his willingness to share his land rent would redound to the benefit of the tenant.

This ideal pooling of perfect knowledge seldom exists in practice. Sometimes landlords and tenants do have fairly accurate ideas concerning the income- and rent-producing capacities of the properties with which they are concerned. Assuming fairly equal bargaining positions, the contract rents agreed upon under these conditions often approximate the amounts needed to cover land rent. However, frequent deviations occur from this model. Sometimes the tenant has only fragmentary knowledge concerning the rent-producing capacity of the land; sometimes neither party is apprized of the facts; and sometimes institutional arrangements such as custom, a semifeudal landlord system, special landlord-tenant regulations, or rent controls give landlords and tenants little opportunity to bargain as equals. Even when landlords and tenants enjoy equal knowledge and equal bargaining power, contract rental rates may differ from the theoretical land rent because of the failure of future production and income to match the conditions anticipated at the time of rental agreement.

The rental bargaining process may involve sharp negotiations in which each party argues his position, or it may involve the placid acceptance of terms already determined by the landlord. In either case, the problem of inadequate knowledge causes many landlords and tenants to guess at what is a fair rental rate. This guessing process can easily result in inequitable arrangements. Partly because of this situation, landlords and tenants long ago started modeling their rental arrangements upon practices that had proved satisfactory in their areas. The acceptance and following of these precedents often results in customary and traditional rental systems such as the "half and half" sharecropping and the "third and fourth" share rent systems used in the South and the prevailing housing rental rates that apply in many residential areas.

Customary rental arrangements often start with payments that correspond closely with the theoretical land rent. As these customary systems continue and spread, however, they may be applied under conditions that no longer fit the original assumptions. This situation can result in definite inequities for either the landlord or the tenant. Generally speaking, once these systems are established they often resist change or modification. But adjustments can be and often are made for changing supply and demand conditions. Landlords tend to make rental concessions during those periods when the supply of tenants is low. When the opposite set of conditions prevails, landlords often increase their demands and tenants may actually assist them by bidding up contract rental levels.

Numerous examples may be cited to illustrate these two extremes. At the time of the Black Death in England, serfs frequently used their strong bargaining position to secure more desirable tenure conditions and in some cases to work out extremely favorable long-term leasing arrangements. Comparable benefits are often enjoyed by residential tenants. During the 1930s, for example, many apartment and office-building owners cut their rental rates and then used special inducements—such as periods of free rent or agreements to redecorate—to attract new tenants.

History also provides numerous examples of the impact of increasing competition between tenants upon the development of landlord rental markets. This has been a common phenomenon in the land-hungry areas of the world and has often been a contributing cause of peasant unrest. Counterbidding between tenants together with landlord greed gave rise to the famous "rack rents" of nineteenth-century Ireland. Exorbitant rental arrangements of a comparable nature have also persisted for long periods in countries such as Egypt and India.

The pressure for land and housing has seldom been great enough to create conditions of this type in the United States. This does not mean that supply and demand conditions have had no effect upon American rental rates. Landlords often raise their rents during periods of favorable business conditions and increasing demand. The housing shortage of World War II gave many property owners an opportunity to increase rents. Even after public rent controls were put into effect, special bonuses and black market payments were sometimes associated with the leasing of residential properties. The high demand for tenant farms in some areas during the 1930s also gave rise to a system of bonus rents. Under this system, tenants paid the customary share rent plus a bonus for features such as pasture land, an above-average house, or other improvements that might have been included in the rental bargain without extra charge in earlier periods.

Short-run changes in supply and demand conditions often result in wide disparities between contract and land rents. Over the long run, however, contract and land rental levels ordinarily move in the same direction. When contract rents decline because of a decrease in the relative demand for land resources, land rents also tend to decline because of the lower income attributable to land resources. With the reverse situation, land rent tends to rise. These adjustments may be attributed in part to changes in the income-producing capacity of land, but they also involve the relative bargaining position of landlords and tenants.

The impact of the bargaining position of landlords and tenants on the interrelationship between land rent and contract rent may be illustrated by the two tracts of land of comparable productivity, which are producing for the same market but are located in different areas, shown in Figure 6-9. The tenants on tract *A* enjoy a favorable rental market and a wide

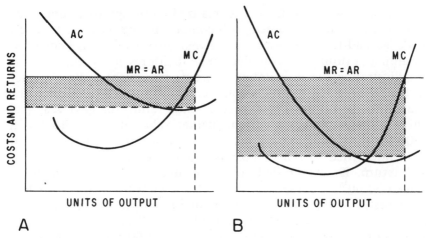

FIGURE 6-9. Illustration of effects of high and low tenant bargaining power upon land rental levels.

choice of alternative employment opportunities. This situation gives them a strong bargaining position, which allows them to insist upon high returns to their labor and management inputs with consequent lower returns to land resources. Limited outside employment opportunities and intense competition between large numbers of tenants for a limited number of rental opportunities on the *B* tract, on the other hand, favors an opposite trend. These tenants have little bargaining ability and are willing to sacrifice virtually all of the return to their labor and management above its subsistence cost with the result that a far larger portion of the total return is paid as contract rent. Continuation of this situation can result in incorporation of the short run economic rents—the additional contract rent the tenants pay—into the accepted long run structure of land rents.

Relation of Land Rent to Land Values

Some types of land resources such as farms or forest land may be viewed as productive factors with almost unlimited productive lives. Others such as housing and office buildings have more limited economic lives but can be utilized over extended periods. Both types can and usually do produce a predictable future flow of reoccurring land rents. This situation makes it possible for owners and investors to visualize the future as well as the present use-capacity and rent-producing advantages associated with particular tracts of land when they consider the purchase and sales prices associated with land resources.

From a theoretical point of view, land resources have a current market value equal to the present value of their expected future land rents. Determinations of current values call for estimates of the expected average annual levels of land rent and for calculations of the present value of rental returns, which will not be realized until specified times in the future. The first of these processes is complicated by man's lack of perfect knowledge and foresight while the second involves what is known as the discounting of future values to determine their present worth.

In illustrating the discounting concept, one might assume a tract of land that is expected to produce net rental returns of $1,000 annually for *x* years into the future. The expected rental return for next year and for each year thereafter has a current market value of something less than $1,000 for the simple reason that the operator must wait to receive it. If the operator tried to sell or borrow money against his expected future rental return, he would find that the buyer or lender would tend to calculate its present value in terms of the amount of money it would take when invested at an acceptable compound interest rate to yield $1,000 in the year in which the rental return would be realized. When discounted at five percent, an expected rental return of $1,000 one year hence has a current market value of $952.40, a return due in ten years has a current market value of $613.90, and a return due in 20 years a current market value of $376.90. With a five percent discount rate, an expected flow of annual net rents of $1,000 annually would have current values equal to those shown in the shaded portion of Figure 6-10.[15]

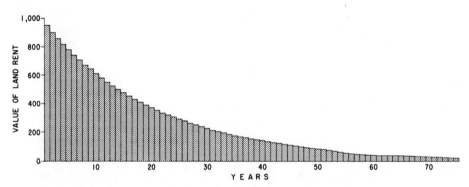

FIGURE 6-10. Present values of an expected flow of land rents of $1,000 annually for 75 years, discounted at five percent.

For property valuation purposes, a capitalization formula is commonly used to indicate the discounting of expected future annual net rents that takes place in the computation of land values. This formula may be expressed as

$$V = \frac{a}{(1+r)} + \frac{a}{(1+r)^2} + \frac{a}{(1+r)^3} + \cdots + \frac{a}{(1+r)^n}$$

[15] The present value of the future flow of returns can be charted infinitely into the future. However, as Figure 6-10 indicates, the present value of future returns becomes very small in a matter of 40 to 50 years when discounted at five percent. Values decline more rapidly when higher interest rates are used and more slowly with lower rates.

in which V = the value of the property, a = the expected average annual land rent, and r = the capitalization interest rate.[16] This formula reduces to $V = a/r$. By way of illustration, if one assumes an expected average annual land rent of $1,000 and uses a five percent capitalization rate, the land resource in question has a value of $1,000 divided by 0.05 or $20,000. Similarly, with a four percent capitalization rate the property would have a value of $25,000 and with a ten percent capitalization rate it would have a value of $10,000.

Despite its theoretical soundness, this income capitalization approach presents some very real problems.[17] The capitalization formula can be modified to handle properties of limited production life such as coal mines. It can also be modified to account for anticipated future changes in annual income and for value adjustments necessitated by the presence of amenity or blighting factors. Yet even with these adjustments, the capitalization approach is plagued with numerous problems of a subjective nature. Questions arise in the determination of the appropriate level of land rent and the choice of an appropriate capitalization rate. Wide differences exist between people in their estimates of present and future property values. And in the case of market-value appraisals, attention must always be given to the impact of changing supply and demand conditions on current market values.

Applications to Land Resource Development Decisions

The expected future flows of net land rents associated with various land uses also provides an incentive and a guide for investments in existing and possible future land resource developments. When operators consider the prospect of undertaking new land developments, they ordinarily visualize a future pay-off. They assume that the developments under consideration will produce sufficient additional return to the land resources to at least repay their cost. Prospective buyers of existing developments also think in terms of a sufficient flow of future land rents to justify their investment outlays.

Benefit-cost analysis is a formal technique that public agencies and some private operators use in evaluating proposed developments from the

[16]The term "capitalization rate" may be defined as the rate needed to convert a given periodic payment into a given cash value. As used here, it may be noted that the concepts of compound interest, discounting, and capitalization often involve different applications of the same interest rate. With compound interest, one starts with a present value and works toward a larger future value as accumulating interest payments are added to an initial amount of principal. Discounting involves a reversal of this process as one works back from an expected future value or return to a calculation of its present worth. The same interest rate can be used in the capitalization process to indicate the current market value of a property that promises to provide a given flow of future land rents.

[17]This subject will be discussed in more detail in chapter 10.

standpoint of their prospects for producing a surplus of economic returns or benefits above their expected costs. Less sophisticated evaluation techniques are used by many investors, but the marshalling of their impressions in the decision making process nevertheless involves a type of benefit-cost analysis, and the emphasis they place on securing a surplus of benefits, measured either in economic returns or satisfactions, really involves an appraisal of future land rents.

Various relationships between expected benefits and costs may be assumed as one appraises the future income-producing potential of particular developments. Production, product prices, costs, and land rents may be expected to rise, remain constant, or fall. In the first of the two typical evaluation models shown in Figure 6-11 A and B, total returns (AR'), operating costs (DR) and the surplus of returns available for the payment of rent and profits are expected to remain relatively constant into the future. This expectation gives the investor an indication of how much he can safely invest in the development and may provide him with an economic incentive to buy the property or proceed with a contemplated development.

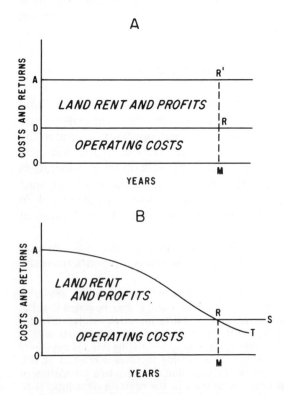

FIGURE 6-11. Illustration of effects of expected costs, returns, and net land rents on resource development and investment decisions.

Many land resource developments involve investments with a limited economic future such as that portrayed in Figure 6-11B. The investor in this instance may visualize considerable land rent and profits in the immediate future with a reduction and eventual disappearance of the returns to land as his enterprise reaches the end of its economic life. Whether or not the prospective investor will proceed with his contemplated development will depend in large measure upon his evaluation of the relationship between his expected investment costs and the amount of land rent he anticipates.

Expected flows of land rent and calculations of their discounted present values influence a wide variety of investment decisions. As has been indicated, the most common examples involve decisions to undertake new land developments or to purchase existing developments. They play a significant role in property redevelopment decisions. They exert some influence on decisions to engage in land speculation. They also have a significant impact on decisions affecting the timing of conservation management decisions. With each of these decisions, investors need some measure of probable rental returns to judge the economic potential of individual investments and to compare them with possible alternative investment opportunities.

Effects upon Land-use Allocation

Areas of high use-capacity and high income-producing potential usually produce high land rents. Conversely, as man resorts to lands of lower use-capacity (cf. Figure 6-8), land rent tends to decline. This close correlation between use-capacity and land rent makes the amount of land rent a site can command for a particular use an index of its use-capacity for that use.

Our discussion of the economic returns to land resources to this point has assumed only one type of enterprise or land use. In actual practice, most operators choose among a number of alternatives. Sometimes they concentrate on the enterprise or use that offers them the greatest opportunity for profit. They may also work with complementary enterprises or divide their attention among a variety of enterprises. Choices between alternatives usually reflect a number of factors including consideration of personal aptitudes, individual likes and dislikes, and the capital and labor requirements of various alternatives. With due allowances for imperfect knowledge and other associated factors, operators tend to concentrate upon those uses that will maximize their returns at their particular locations and with their particular combinations of productive factors.

In their choice of enterprises, operators are always interested in comparisons of the income-producing potentials of their various alternatives. These comparisons may be based upon general observations or may involve calculations of the probable economic returns to land and management they can expect from each alternative. From an economic standpoint, comparisons of this type, particularly those involving both uses and locations, may be thought of in terms of overlapping rent triangles. The individual rent triangles for different land uses vary considerably in size and shape for different land uses. With the example used in Figure 6-12, they range from the high narrow triangle *EOP'*, which depicts the land rent secured from use *A*, to the low broad triangle *HOT* which represents use *D*.

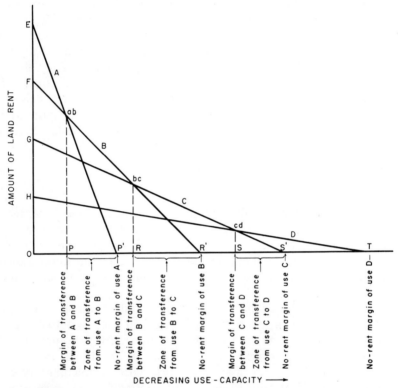

FIGURE 6-12. Illustration of relationship between land rent and allocation of land resources between competing uses.

The four land rent triangles pictured in Figure 6-12 (*EOP'*, *FOR'*, *GOS'*, and *HOT*) may be used to describe the competition between four types of land use. With an agricultural example, the four triangles may represent the use of land for milk production, potatoes, wheat, and ranching, respectively. Under urban conditions, they may apply to a large department store, a light industry, a used-car lot, and the use of land for middle-class homes. This example may also be applied to selected industrial uses ranging from heavy industry to the manufacture of lace or to a composite picture of all land uses. When considered from an over-all standpoint, the four uses may represent industrial and commercial areas, residential uses, arable farming, and grazing and forestry, respectively.

With each of these examples, those uses producing the highest land rents ordinarily have first claim upon the areas of highest use-capacity. The lower uses can always be carried on to advantage on the better lands, near the market, or at the 100 percent spot. But their lower comparative rent-producing capacity makes it impossible for them to compete with the more productive uses. As a result, they are crowded toward the outskirts to those locations where they can compete successfully with other uses. At any one location, some use can always return a higher land rent than any alternative use. From the economic standpoint of the individual operator, this is always the highest and best use for his land.

When Figure 6-12 is examined in detail, it may be noted that the hypotenuse of each of the four land rent triangles represents the intensive margin for that particular use. The intensive margin for use *A* follows the line *EP'* and the intensive margins for uses *B, C,* and *D* follow the lines *FR', GS',* and *HT,* respectively. The points at which these intensive margins intersect are known as *margins of transference.* The intensive margins for uses *A* and *B* intersect at *ab* (point *P* on the horizontal axis). At this point it is more profitable to shift to use *B* than to continue with use *A*. Other significant margins of transference occur at points *bc* or *R* where it becomes more profitable to shift to use *C* than to continue with use *B* and at *cd* or *S* where it becomes more profitable to shift to use *D* than to continue with use *C*. The operator in each of these cases can continue his use beyond the margin of transference as far as his extensive or no-rent margin and still make money. Those individuals who operate between their margins of transference and their no-rent margins (between *P* and *P'* in the case of use *A; R* and *R'* with use *B;* and *S* and *S'* with use *C*) are said to operate within their *zones of transference.* Operations carried on within these zones are not unprofitable; but they are never as profitable as they could be if the operator would shift to his highest and best use.

As this example suggests, the concepts of land rent and highest and best use can be used to explain both the competition between land uses and the resulting allocation of land resources between uses. This competition continues as a never-ending process and its effects are observable in the continual allocation and reallocation of land resources that takes place between various uses and users.

Naturally, the model set up in Figure 6-12 seldom operates in a perfect sense.[18] Numerous circumstances and considerations cause operators to

---

[18] Three general observations are in order concerning the model used in Figure 6-12. To begin with, this model assumes enough uniformity in the site requirements of the competing uses to permit a fairly uniform set of criteria regarding land use-capacity. Insofar as this uniformity fails to exist, some uses may be able to earn their

carry on some uses within their zones of transference (and occasionally beyond their no-rent margins). Nevertheless, general profiles of land use such as the near-curve *ET* in Figure 6-12 may be used to illustrate the relationship between land rent-producing capacity and decreasing land use-capacity. Profiles of this type indicate the effects of location with respect to the 100 ·percent spot, increasing distance from market, decreasing fertility, and other aspects of decreasing use-capacity·upon the competitive position of various types of land use.

Applications of the margin-of-transference approach. The margin-of-transference approach provides a meaningful technique for explaining the allocation of land areas between users with different rent-paying capacities. Diagrams such as Figure 6-12 can be used to illustrate the allocation process that takes place in and around typical cities. When cities are small the triangles for use *A* (commercial) and use *B* (urban residential) may be reasonably small. As cities grow in size, the triangles expand both in height and width with the result that some sites used for residential purposes shift to commercial uses while farm lands around the city shift to residential uses.

The land use allocation and shifting process does not always operate as smoothly as the margin-of-transference diagrams suggest. Various factors may keep lands from shifting as soon as they should, and the expectations of an imminent market for a higher use may cause operators to neglect their properties or use them for lower valued uses than they otherwise would.

Figure 6-13 depicts two problem situations involving the use of land in urban areas. The first situation concerns the margin of transference *ab* at

highest land rent at sites that have little value for other uses. This situation together with the dispersed location of our cities and markets makes it impractical to try to apply models of this type to whole countries. Except in a homogeneous isolated state such as that envisaged by von Thunen, we must usually think in terms of numerous overlapping margin of transference models.

A second observation concerns the amount of land rent earned by each use in Figure 6-12. If each operator used his land for its highest and best use only, the land rent earned by use *A* would represent only that portion of triangle *EOP'* that lies directly above the area *OP*. The land rent for use *B* would be limited to that portion of *FOR'* that lies above the area *PR*, and so on for uses *C* and *D*. Each of the uses requires only a limited land area; and each of the higher-priority uses would earn less land rent if it could be carried on alone on the land of highest use-capacity. With the competition between uses, however, the price and rent levels associated with the higher-priority uses rise while all of the lower-priority uses are pushed outward onto lands of lower use-capacity.

Finally, it should be noted that the land rent triangles associated with some land uses may never get high enough to give these uses preferential status as a highest and best use. Yet uses of this type may be carried on to advantage because of the manner in which they supplement or complement other use practices. In this sense, these uses may never be regarded as uses of high comparative advantage; but they may be carried on profitably in comparison with other uses operating within their zones of transference.

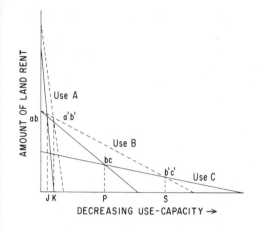

FIGURE 6-13. Example of applications of the margin of transference approach.

point *J*. This is the present margin between commercial and residential uses. Property owners just to the right of point *ab* frequently assume that urban growth will soon push the margin to *a'b'* at point *K*. Anticipating this emerging higher use, they neglect and hold back on plans to remodel, repair, or rebuild their residential properties in the transition zone between *J* and *K*. Should the expected emerging use develop, this decision may prove financially profitable from the standpoint of the individual owners.

Unfortunately, the demand for the expected higher uses does not always materialize, or, if it does, it may not come until years after it was first anticipated. Unless strong positive measures are taken in these situations, the usual result is a circle of spreading blight, slums, and urban decay around downtown commercial centers. Individual owners frequently sacrifice rental returns and satisfactions they could have had although they sometimes find ways of exploiting their situations by acting as slumlords. The real tragedy in these situations involves the transference of social costs to the public, for it is society and the urban community that usually bears the major losses.

A second land use problem centers around the margin of transference between residential and agricultural uses. In an earlier time period, when most urban residents lacked automobiles, the edge of the urban residential area occurred at point *P* in Figure 6-13. An increase in city size would have called for more intensive use of the areas already in residential use plus some additions of residential lands around the city's edge. With the relaxation of the transportation constraint that has come with the widespread ownership of automobiles and the building of improved streets and highways, urban workers can now commute to work from point *S* in less time and with less effort that their grandparents expended in traveling from sites located to the left of point *P*.

Relaxation of the transportation constraint has facilitated a suburbanization and residential scatteration trend. It has made it possible for urban families to enjoy the advantages and amenities of suburban and rural living; but it has also greatly complicated the continued agricultural use of lands located in the vicinity of large cities.

This problem is most serious when occasional tracts are acquired for residential purposes while large areas are expected to remain in agricultural and open space uses. The high land values and rent-bid prices of the residential users may involve only a small proportion of the total land area but they affect the pattern of land prices and tax assessed values for the entire area. Meanwhile, the new urban-oriented residents demand local governmental services not previously provided and add to the local population that must be educated and protected. Farmers and other rural land users feel that they are being squeezed out by rising property taxes and the larger investments required for any expansion of their business operating units; and speculators, attracted by the expectation of burgeoning subdivisions, acquire lands that often are allowed to lie idle. Society again suffers as large areas become blighted for agricultural and other rural uses before a genuine need develops for their use for residential or urban purposes.

Another pertinent application of the margin-of-transference approach can be visualized with public and private decisions concerning choices between single-purpose and multiple-use alternatives in resource management. A public forest management agency, for example, may identify several individual uses such as commercial forest production, public recreation, or game management that it could emphasize as dominant uses in its management programs. It may also want to pursue a multiple-use management program in which joint emphasis is given to two or possibly all three of these uses.

Comparison of the relative benefits associated with these management alternatives calls for examination of the economic and social costs and returns associated with each management approach. For multiple-use management to receive rational top emphasis, the sum of the economic and social land rents associated with this approach should exceed those attainable when dominant managerial emphasis is given to any single use. Once the economic and social land rents are determined, an agency may rationally decide, for example, that public recreation should be the dominant use of area A, multiple-use management should be applied to area B, and that commercial forest production and game production should be emphasized in areas C and D, respectively.

Relationship between land rent and intensity of use. Before leaving this discussion of the influence of land rent upon the allocation of land areas between different uses, a brief word should be said concerning the relationship between land rent and the intensity of land-resource use. These two concepts are often closely correlated with each other; but they are really quite different.[19] Land rent represents the economic return that

---

[19]Cf. Conrad Hammar, "Intensity and Land Rent," *Journal of Farm Economics,* Vol. 20, November, 1938, pp. 776-91.

land receives for its use in production. Intensity of use, on the other hand, refers to the relative amounts of human and capital resources used in connection with a given unit of land resources. These two concepts tend to parallel each other because intensive use practices are often associated with high land rents. It is a mistake, however, to assume that this situation always holds.

Intensive use practices are frequently used to overcome the inherent deficiencies of low-rent sites. Businessmen with poorly located sites sometimes use costly advertising programs to attract customers to their places of business. Farmers with soil of low natural fertility often use large inputs of fertilizer to increase the productivity of their lands. In similar fashion, peasant operators and workers in cottage industries often find it necessary to make lavish use of their family labor resources if they are to eke a livelihood from their limited land resources.

The fact that a site commands a high land rent does not always mean that it is subject to intensive use. Small family farms in low-rent areas are frequently used more intensively on an acre-to-acre basis than the larger commercial units found in areas of higher productive potential. Low-rent housing facilities are usually subject to more intensive human use than high-rent luxury apartments. And low-rent commercial and industrial sites are sometimes used just as intensively as the high-rent locations found in downtown areas.

—SELECTED READINGS

Alonso, William, *Location and Land Use* (Cambridge: Harvard University Press, 1964), chaps. III-V.

Bober, Mandell M., *Intermediate Price and Income Theory* (New York: W. W. North & Co., Inc., 1955), chap. XIV.

Bye, C. R., *Developments and Issues in the Theory of Rent* (New York: Columbia University Press, 1940).

Due, John F., *Intermediate Economic Analysis,* 3rd ed. (Homewood, Ill.: Richard D. Irwin, 1956), chap. XVIII.

Keiper, Joseph S., Ernest Kurnow, Clifford D. Clark, and Henry H. Segal, *Theory and Measurement of Rent* (New York: Chilton Company, 1961), Part I.

Ricardo, David, *The Principles of Political Economy and Taxation* (London, 1817), chap. II.

Whittaker, Edmund, *A History of Economic Ideas* (New York: Longmans, Green & Co., Inc., 1940), chap. XX.

7

Land Resource
Development Decisions

Man develops and uses land resources primarily because of the products and satisfactions they provide. His appetite for most of these products is increasing. It is not surprising therefore to find that there is widespread interest on the part of both public agencies and private operators in possible new resource developments.

Resource development decisions are characterized by a concern about economic productivity over time. Unlike many business decisions, the developer commits his capital, labor, and management resources for extended time periods. His decisions often freeze the uses made of the land areas with which he works for periods up to and beyond the expected economic life of the development. Moreover, the developer and his backers are concerned with the flow of returns, costs, and land rents that can be expected in the future. They try to maximize their investment returns and satisfactions over time by assuring themselves that there will be a continuing surplus of returns and satisfactions above costs.

Resource developers like to make certain that the time is ripe for their developments—that there is a ready market for their products. They have a natural interest in product prices and probable future levels of demand because these factors influence the total returns they can expect. They recognize the need to keep their costs within bounds so that their projects will pay off and so that they might expect reasonable returns both to the land factor and to their managerial inputs.

Emphasis is given in this chapter to some leading factors that influence the land and water resource development decision making process. Consideration is given first to the concept of succession in land use and to the economic rationale for resource development. This is followed with an examination of the principal costs associated with land resource development and finally with a discussion of the benefit-cost analysis techniques used in formal project evaluations.

SUCCESSION IN LAND USE

Land resources tend to move to those operators who bid the most for their control and to those uses that offer the highest return for their utilization. This concept operates with rural and urban lands alike. Its general operation suggests a phenomenon known as the principle of "succession in land use." According to this principle, whenever changes in the effective demand for different types of land use lead to changes in the use-capacities of the lands available for these uses, the land resources in question tend to shift to their highest and best economic uses unless prevented by institutional barriers, contrary goals, or individual inertia.

The history of man's use of land resources has been one long story of succession in land use. Man has been content to leave some land resources in their natural state. But most land resources—particularly those that are readily accessible and those with high capacities for economic use—have been modified and developed by human action. This development process has never been a once-for-all-time affair. Time after time, properties have been developed for particular uses only to be redeveloped within a few months or years for other uses that promise a higher net benefit or net return.

Examples of succession in land use appear all around us. Through the land development process, the forest primeval has given way to productive farms. Cutover brush lands have been developed for commercial forestry. Lands once written off as the Great American Desert have been utilized for irrigation, dry framing, and grazing purposes. Isolated wonders of nature have become summertime meccas for thousands of tourists.

This succession process finds its most vivid illustrations in the rise of our larger cities. The central business districts of most of the nation's cities were wilderness areas a scant two centuries ago. From this beginning, they became the sites of frontier trading posts and humble agricultural settlements, later the hubs of thriving business communities, and finally the commercial cores of expanding metropolitan centers.[1] In this succession process, the moccasined tread of the Indian and the frontiersman has yielded to the tumultuous traffic of downtown business areas. The rude shelters of the early settlers have given way to the great

[1] Cf. Earl S. Johnson, *The Natural History of the Central Business District with Particular Reference to Chicago* (Chicago: University of Chicago Press, 1944).

banks, stores, and skyscrapers that now occupy the 100 percent locations. Lands that the government sometimes found it difficult to sell at its initial charge of $1.25 an acre have come to support market values of thousands of dollars per front foot.

The succession process is a dynamic process. It calls for adjustments to changing demands and changing technology. As cities develop, houses and stores are built in the cow pastures and cornfields of yesteryear; private wells and primitive sanitation facilities give way to public water and sewerage systems; utilities are provided; new streets are built. As these cities prosper and expand, costly redevelopments become desirable. Streets that were suitable for horse and buggy traffic must be widened and relaid; sewers are dug up and enlarged; stores are rebuilt; houses are torn down to make way for new commercial developments; and occasional areas are redeveloped to provide parks and open spaces.

Succession in land use often requires far-reaching decisions. Most resource developments call for substantial cash outlays. They call for careful investment calculations—for a weighing of expected benefits against the various operating, production, time, supersession, and social costs that may arise with the new development. They frequently involve important choices between alternatives—choices between different plans for development, between comparable projects of differing size and scale, and between projects that promise to maximize personal profits and projects that accent community and social goals.

Emphasis is given in the discussion that follows to three important types of decisions that arise with land-resource developments. These include: (1) the basic reasons for land-resource development, (2) the rationale for resource development, and (3) the problem of private versus social priorities in resource development.

Reasons for Land-Resource Development

Man develops and uses land resources partly because he must in the process of making a living and partly because the products of resource developments can add substantially to the quality of his level of living. His basic motivation for resource development stems from his urge for survival and from his desire to secure something more out of life than the food and shelter needed for subsistence. Man develops resources so that he may better use them to maximize the utilities and satisfactions he secures from life.

These satisfactions are frequently measured in monetary terms, as when one clears farm land, lays out a subdivision, or builds an office building with the expectation of increasing his total income. At times, they are also nonmonetary in character. They may involve spiritual or aesthetic values, a desire for personal power or a feeling of accomplishment, or any of a variety of other individual or social goals. Thus a pyramid may be built as a resting place for one's soul, a formal garden as a thing of beauty, a public building as a monument to one's philanthropy, or a system of fortifications as a line of military defense.

Regardless of whether he emphasizes profits or nonmonetary goals, the rational operator will not proceed with a land-resource development unless he visualizes a gross benefit that equals or exceeds his expected costs. His evaluation techniques may be relatively precise or quite fuzzy. He may compare his expected costs and returns both in the immediate and the more distant future. He may try to rate the value of his expected future returns and discount some values back to the present. Overall, his calculation of benefits and costs may be inexact and often involves vague standards of measurement. Unexpected conditions may prevent his development from turning out as expected. But successful or not, almost all land-resource developments stem from some operator's attempt to maximize his satisfactions.

The rationale of the business-minded operator who starts out to develop a land resource may be illustrated by the three examples pictured in Figure 7-1. With each of these examples, the operator starts with a given land-resource base and some specific plan of development. His

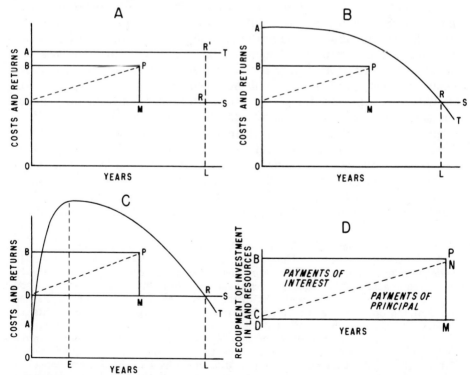

FIGURE 7-1. Effects of expectations concerning future costs and returns on investment decisions in land resource developments.

estimate of the gross receipts he can expect each succeeding year is depicted by the line *AT*. Figure 7-1A assumes a development for some use—such as farming—that justifies an assumption of relatively constant gross returns over time. Figure 7-1B assumes a building investment that will yield a high annual return at first but that will yield a lower and lower gross return in future years as the building depreciates and suffers from possible obsolescence. Figure 7-1C assumes the development of a commercial property that will not reach its highest earning capacity until *E* years after its establishment and that must also look forward to a period of decreasing gross returns as its value depreciates.

With each of these examples, the operator must calculate his expected annual cost of business operation. He can assume a constant average level of operating costs such as that indicated by the cost line *DS* in each of the three diagrams; or he might argue that these costs may increase (or possibly decrease) with passing years. Similarly, he must plan for the recoupment of his initial cost outlay for developing the farm, building, or commercial property.

If the operator owns his land, he will tend to think of his outlays for labor, materials, maintenance, taxes, insurance, interest on loans for production purposes, and so on, as operating costs. The surplus above these costs (*ADRR'* and *ADR* for *L* years) represents his returns of rent to land and profits for management. Of these two types of returns, the expected future flow of land rents can easily be quantified through use of a capitalization approach. Thus an operator may logically view land as a fixed cost factor in his future projection while the residual surplus above costs becomes a profit return to his management.

With this approach, the operator can visualize the investment value of his land resource as being represented by a rectangle such as *BDMP* in Figure 7-1.[2] He might logically plan for the recoupment of his capital investment over several years and assume repayment of its full value on an amortized basis with fixed periodic payments involving larger and larger credits to principal and steadily declining payments for interest. (Figure 7-1D.) The total time period assumed reflects his capitalization rate (a 5 percent rate corresponds with a 20-year period) and should not exceed the

---

[2] The decision planning models depicted in Figure 7-1 represent the expected costs and returns as the operator visualizes them at the time he decides whether or not to invest in a development. Operators do not live into these models. New models must be visualized whenever the situation is reevaluated. With this situation, the polygon *CDMN* in Figure 7-1D represents the periodic repayment of the present capitalized value of the operator's land resource investment while polygon *BCNP* represents the interest payments on this investment value. The interest may be paid to a mortgagee, or, if the land resource is held free of debt, it will go to the owner as interest on the full capitalized value of his land resource investment. In this process, the full expected future value of the land rental returns is discounted back to the present. Some discounting of other expected returns might also be argued. For the sake of simplicity in presentation, this issue is ignored in Figure 7-1.

expected number of years during which his gross returns are expected to exceed his operating and investment costs.

Once the operator has calculated his prospective gross receipts, development costs, and operating costs, he may feel free to proceed with his resource development plan if his expected receipts (*AOLR'* in 7-1A and *AOLR* in 7-1B and 7-1C) exceed his expected costs (*DOLR* and *BDMP*). He should give serious consideration at this point, however, to the alternative uses he could make of his investment inputs. If he decides in favor of his development plan, he will naturally plan to limit his operations to the number of years (*L* years in 7-1B and 7-1C) he expects his gross receipts to exceed his operating costs.

These examples illustrate the operator's normal tendency to maximize his land rents and profits. The same basic type of reasoning is involved every time a family builds a home, plants a garden, or landscapes a yard and every time a city develops a civic center, lays a new street, or creates a public park. The emphasis in these examples is often placed on non-monetary considerations—on personal, family, community, and social satisfactions and on general welfare. These values cannot always be translated into monetary terms, but they frequently play important roles in justifying individual examples of land-resource development.

Rationale for Redevelopment of Land Resources

Up to this point we have been concerned with the initial development of land resources—with the development of farms on what might otherwise be regarded as idle land and with the construction of buildings and other improvements on vacant lots. Developments of this type are important; but most land-resource development decisions now involve additions to or replacements of already existing developments. Shifts in land use can take place on existing developments, but the succession process ordinarily involves some redevelopment of the land resource base. For example, whenever forests are cleared for farming, farms are converted into building sites, single-family residences are converted into apartments, or existing structures are torn down to make room for newer developments, redevelopments take place.

Redevelopment decisions are responsive to market pressures; and, as was the case in Figure 7-1, reflect the business calculations of individual operators. The average operator "is constantly alert to the possibility that some new use for his land may yield a greater return than the continued operation of the present use."[3] When opportunities of this type present themselves, operators tend to shift to the higher and better uses. And insofar as several operators are able to undertake redevelopment projects, the market prices on individual properties are often bid up to levels

---

[3] Richard U. Ratcliff, *Urban Land Economics* (New York: McGraw-Hill Book Company, Inc., 1949), p. 403.

justified by the going estimates of their value for conversion to the new uses.

The rationale for the redevelopment of existing resource developments may be illustrated graphically as in Figure 7-2.[4] The two diagrams with solid lines correspond with the diagrams presented in Figures 7-1A and 7-1B. It is assumed, however, that changing market conditions support a demand for a new type of development in the year E. This proposed new development calls for higher annual operating costs ($D'S'$) than either of the existing developments and also significantly higher levels of total returns, at least in the immediate future. The expected surplus of returns above costs promises higher levels of land rents, which again can be quantified in the rectangles $B'D'M'P'$, plus higher returns to management.

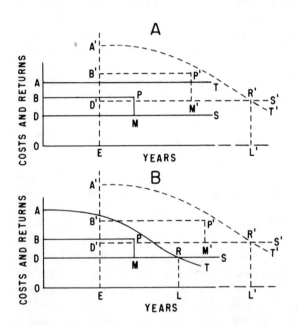

FIGURE 7-2. Effects of expectations concerning future costs and returns on investment decisions calling for the redevelopment of land resources.

Under these circumstances, most business-minded operators who enjoy adequate financing will soon shift to the new higher and better use. They will operate in terms of their future opportunities even though this calls for writing off part of their current capital investment. Many operators, however, will hesitate to shift to the new use. Some will hold back because of pessimistic appraisals of their future opportunities, some because of personal inertia, and some because of various considerations of supersession costs.

Should the new opportunity offer higher gross receipts with a net reduction of development and operating costs, only a foolish or overly

4Cf. *ibid.,* pp. 403-405.

conservative operator would refuse to shift. With the prospect of higher development and operating costs, many operators may find that they lack the financial backing they need to redevelop their properties. Some will hold back until they have paid off their existing capital investment costs. Still others may hesitate to write off the current market value of their existing developments.

The problem of shifting to a higher use can pose quite a different problem in 7-2A than in 7-2B. The operator in Figure 7-2A will definitely lose income he could otherwise have had if he refuses to redevelop his property. Yet the shape of his present gross return curve (AT) makes it possible for him to continue to operate on a profitable basis as long as he wishes. This expectation can be upset if higher property taxes and other rising operating costs (an upward tilt of his operating-cost curve) narrow his margin of profit.

A somewhat different prospect faces the operator in 7-2B. He may prefer the continued operation of his existing development even though he could secure a larger net return by redeveloping his property.[5] However, he cannot plan to continue his present operations beyond the year L. By then, his gross receipts will have declined to the level of his operating costs; and he must choose between losing money or redeveloping his property.

As was the case with Figure 7-1, the rationale for resource redevelopment has been viewed in terms of rent and profit maximization. But this rationale can again be broadened to include various psychic returns, personal satisfactions, and social values. The individual who remodels his house usually justifies his redevelopment more in terms of added family comfort and satisfactions than of a net increase in the market value of his property. In similar fashion, our cities are continually redeveloping their streets, water and sewerage systems, and other facilities with the avowed intent of increasing the social utility of these resources. Most slum clearance, urban redevelopment, and urban renewal projects also are undertaken to promote social and psychic as well as economic goals.

Abandonment and shifts to "lower" uses. Land-resource developers are perennially optimistic; and in their optimism, they sometimes overestimate their prospective returns, underestimate their costs, or both. Miscalculations of this type frequently prevent developments from paying off as expected. When this situation arises, the operator can continue to

[5] When the expected gross return curve for the new development follows a pattern similar to that in Figure 7-1C (*i.e.,* if it starts around B' and does not reach its peak until some years later) the operator may find it profitable to continue with his present use for several years. He should not shift until his current rate of return has declined sufficiently to make his prospect of higher returns with the redeveloped use—either immediately after redevelopment or after a reasonable waiting period—appear definitely desirable.

live with his development even though it provides less profit (or satisfactions) than expected. He can sell his development for whatever price he can get and write off his capital investment loss. He may abandon his development entirely if he can neither operate it at a profit nor sell it to someone else. Or he may shift his property to some "lower" use, which calls for fewer variable inputs but which is really a higher and better use for him because it promises a larger net return above its expected lower costs of operation.

What happens to the unprofitable resource development depends largely on the location of its gross-return, operating-cost, and capital-investment-cost curves. As long as gross returns exceed total costs, the operator will be inclined to continue his use of the development. If gross returns exceed operating costs but are insufficient to cover capital investment costs, the use can continue with the writing off of all or part of the capital investment cost. If gross returns drop below operating costs, the operator will usually be forced to discontinue his operations and abandon his development unless he can in some way subsidize his operations.

The history of land settlement and land-resource development in the United States is replete with examples of resource developments that have not turned out as expected. Thousands of settlers have tried valiantly to develop productive farms in areas not physically suited for this purpose. Some of these settlements thrived for a time but gave out because of fertility exhaustion or changed market conditions. Some have survived largely because their operators have subsidized them with large investments of capital and family labor. Many have been abandoned as unprofitable.

Much the same story applies with numerous other resource developments. Thousands of building projects undertaken during the 1920s remained in operation during the 1930s only because of the writing off of large portions of their capital investment costs. Similarly, many large reclamation, public housing, and urban redevelopment projects could not have been carried out without considerable public subsidy.

Like other operators, the resource developer or owner who has misjudged the expected cost and returns situation must concentrate on maximizing his returns and satisfactions from now on. He would naturally like to recoup his capital investments, but his chief concern is with the future, not with costs already sunk. He will actively seek and analyze alternatives he might follow to increase his net returns. He will consider the conversion of an underutilized commercial building into a warehouse or the shifting of cultivated fields to grass or forest crops if the expected relationship between his lower costs and returns promises a higher net return than he can secure from his existing development.

Land speculation. A few comments also are in order concerning the rationale for land speculation. This practice has been a common phenomenon in American history particularly along the frontier and more recently in fringe areas where rural lands are shifting to urban and recreation uses. As the term "speculation" implies, it involves the investment of monies at a risk with the hope of gain. Ventures in land speculation have brought moderate to substantial financial gains to some investors and losses to others.

From an economic point of view, land speculation may be defined as the holding of land resources, usually in something less than their highest and best use, with primary managerial emphasis on resale at a capital gain rather than on profitable use in current production.[6] Traditionally, the land speculator has shown little interest in the returns he could secure from the operation of his land resources. He tends instead to regard landed property as a commodity that he can buy and sell at a profit. He will sometimes invest in improvements that upgrade his properties. But his interests lie in quick sales, in a profitable and rapid turnover of his capital investment, not in the continued holding and operation of his properties. With this emphasis, he often leaves his frontier holding, his tract of farm land on the outskirts of the city, his vacant city lots, and sometimes even his buildings idle and unused while he looks to profits from the sale of land for his source of income.

Land speculation often flourishes during periods of rising prices. Under more stable market conditions, the speculator sometimes finds that he must hold his property several years before he can sell it at a profit. With this outlook, he may still hesitate to develop his rural lands or build upon his city lots if he feels that the profit he may secure by waiting for an anticipated higher use will more than pay for his accumulated holding costs.

A different situation exists when high interest charges for invested capital, increasing outlays for property taxes and insurance, or other pressures discourage the speculator from playing his waiting game. Under these conditions, the speculator may sell for whatever price he can get. He may give up his speculative dream and develop or redevelop his property for the highest use justified by existing market conditions. He also can compromise by shifting his resources to some extensive-type use, such as an urban parking lot, a golf course, or a private airfield, which promises sufficient returns to cover his current holding costs and still keep open his

---

[6] Various shades of meaning are associated with the term "land speculation." Horace Greeley is credited with describing the land speculator as "anyone who claimed or purchased raw land with no intent to farm it or who acquired more land than he could expect to develop." [Cf. Robert P. Swierenga, *Pioneers and Profits* (Ames: Iowa State University, 1968), p. 6.] This concept was generally accepted along the frontier, although the typical frontiersman usually distinguished between his own speculative land holdings and those of absentee owners. Owners who hold land with the hope of later selling it at a profit are sometimes called speculators. Practically all American landowners are speculators under this definition.

option for shifting to some anticipated higher and better use such as a shopping center or an industrial site at some later date.

Private Versus Social Priorities in
Land-Resource Development

Conflicts frequently arise between private goals in land-resource development and the social interests of the community. Whose interests should govern in these instances? The answers to this question depend upon the time and circumstances of each case. During some time periods and with some sets of circumstances, individuals are free to develop their land resources in almost any way they wish. On other occasions, they may find their opportunities definitely limited by various social controls and regulations.

In facing up to the conflicts that occasionally develop between private and social priorities in land-resource developments, it is important to note the reasons for these differences. The succession that takes place in private land-resource use often reflects the bidding and counterbidding that takes place in the market. No problems arise as long as the owner or top bidder puts the property to some socially acceptable use. Real conflicts may develop, however, if the operator decides to maximize his profits or other satisfactions by shifting to a use that damages or exploits the interest of his neighbors or the community at large.

These exploited interests are often extramarket in character. They may involve the continued right of the public to enjoy the scenery provided by the trees, lakes or streams, and geological formations found on private lands or their opportunities to make recreational use of these resources. They may also include the possible adverse impact of an operator's activities on the quality of the natural environment as when his operations result in unsightly land developments, air or water pollution, or the creation of excessive noise or glare. These impacts can involve important social costs. They are hard to quantify in the usual market sense, however, and accordingly may have but little impact upon the economic calculus of some individual operators. Group action involving the exercise of social controls over private land-use practices is often needed in these instances to defend and preserve community interests.[7]

Whether or not social controls should be used to guide, direct, and sometimes limit individuals in their land-development decisions depends both on the extent of the breach between the public and private interests involved and the prevailing philosophy regarding the desirability of social intervention. Planners frequently decry the wasteful and exploitive practices carried out on private lands in the name of free enterprise and private profit maximization. These practices can often be stopped by

[7]Cf. chapters 17 and 18 for more detailed discussions of these controls.

social action if the appropriate units of government are organized to act and if the necessary controls enjoy the sanction of public opinion. Social controls should not be employed without careful consideration and planning of the goals to be attained, and they should not be used unless the expected social benefits to be gained outweigh the personal and other losses associated with their use.

LAND DEVELOPMENT COSTS

Land resources are sometimes described as a free gift of nature. In their unconditioned natural state they are seldom ready for immediate use as productive or consumption goods. Before they acquire much economic value, they must usually be processed or developed. They must be made accessible for use and in most cases must be modified through applications of capital and labor.

Cost considerations play a significant role in resource development decisions. They guide operators in their choice of "what to produce, where and when to produce it, and by which of the available processes to produce it. Through a comparison of costs and prices with the productivity of the services hired, cost analysis coerces and lures the businessman into experimentation, into observation, into invention, with a view of finding out more economical ways of producing the things he is going to produce and more profitable things to produce."[8] Along with the prospect of benefits, cost considerations help to dictate the purposes for which land resources will be developed and the timing of these developments.

Several types of costs are ordinarily involved in the development of land resources. First and most important among these are the actual outlays of cash and human effort required to bring new land resources into use and to qualify partly developed resources for higher uses. Other significant costs include the social costs associated with individual and group sacrifices, the time costs, which arise because of the time it takes to bring resource developments into use, and the supersession costs associated with the frequent practice of scrapping existing developments to make way for new resource uses. A variety of reoccurring ownership and operating costs also become highly relevant once a development is brought into use.

Direct Outlays for Land Development

Almost every type of land development requires some direct outlays of

---

[8]Jacob Viner, "The Role of Costs in a System of Economic Liberalism," *Wage Determination and the Economics of Liberalism* (Washington: U. S. Chamber of Commerce, 1947), pp. 19-20.

capital and labor. The extent and nature of these outlay requirements vary both with the type of development undertaken and with the period during which it takes place. Virgin forests may be opened for economic use through the building of logging trails. Modern skyscraper developments, in contrast, call for tremendous expenditures of capital and labor.

Much of the farm-making that took place along the American western frontier was accomplished with relatively low cash outlays for initial developments. Settlers in Illinois in 1835, for example, could buy 320 acres of prairie or woodland from the government for $400 and were able to supply themselves with a cabin, corncrib, and stable and to hire others to break the prairie sod and fence 160 acres for cultivation for an additional outlay of $745.[9] Most of the settlers had little in the way of capital goods and suffered from a common tendency to spend most of what money they had in buying land. It is not surprising that large numbers of them regarded the cost of acquiring and developing farm land as high. Many minimized their cash outlays by clearing their own land, breaking the sod, and erecting their own buildings and fences. This process required long hours of hard work. It often took years for settlers in the forested areas to cut down and move the trees, remove stumps and stones, erect their buildings, put up rail fences, and expand their initial clearings into productive farms. Farms were developed more rapidly in the prairie and plains areas, but settlers on these lands often experienced problems in securing needed water and timber resources.

By 1970 the average purchase price of a developed 160 acre farm in Illinois had risen to $78,120. Land-clearing costs ranged from $30 to $200 per acre in many eastern states. The installation of tile drainage systems cost from $150 to $250 an acre, and the provision of supplemental irrigation systems called for investments ranging from $150 to $400 per acre irrigated (not counting the cost of the well).

High as these reclamation and land-development costs may appear, they are really quite low compared with the development costs reported for some mammoth power and irrigation projects undertaken in the western states. The Columbia Basin project, for example, was designed to provide irrigation for a gross area of 1,095,200 acres at an estimated construction cost of $697 million, approximately $491 million of which was charged to irrigation facilities. When the estimated cost of domestic water supplies, individual farm development, new roads, and local schools

[9]Cf. John Mason Peck, *A New Guide for Emigrants* (Boston: 1836), p. 313. Peck reports a contract charge of $2 per acre or $320 for breaking the prairie sod for 160 acres, an outlay of $175 for fencing four fields with an eight-rail fence with cross stakes, and a charge of $250 for cabins, corncribs, and other buildings. He added that: "In many instances, a single crop ot wheat will pay for the land, for fencing, breaking up, cultivating, harvesting, threshing, and taking to market." Also cf. Clarence H. Danhof, "Farm-Making Costs and the 'Safety Valve,' 1850-60," *Journal of Political Economy*, Vol. 49, June, 1941, pp. 317-56.

is added to this total, it appears that this land-development program cost approximately $834 per acre.[10]

Significantly higher land development costs are associated with the development of land for most nonagricultural uses. The process of platting and subdividing raw land for residential, recreation, and other urban-oriented uses usually involves substantial outlays for surveys, provision of roads, sewers, utilities, drainage facilities, and site improvements. A typical example is supplied by the experience of a Florida investor who produced 88 residential lots near Ft. Lauderdale in 1966 at a development cost of $178,181 or roughly $2,025 a lot.[11] Addition of this cost to the acquisition price of the land and the subdivider's marketing costs helps to explain why average residential building lots were priced in the $4,000 to $7,000 range in many American cities in 1970. New privately-owned single-family housing units had an average construction cost, excluding land and other nonconstruction items, of $18,325 in 1970.

Urban renewal projects are usually quite expensive both because of the high cost of acquiring already developed sites and demolishing the structures found thereon and because of the ambitious redevelopment programs that follow. The 12-acre Rockefeller Center project in New York City was completed during the 1930s at a total cost of $150 million. The 23 acres in Pittsburgh's Golden Triangle Gateway Center project were acquired and cleared for redevelopment during the late 1940s at a cost of $20 per square foot or approximately $870,000 per acre. Chicago's 100-story high John Hancock Center was built during the late 1960s at a cost of $95 million. Several office and commercial complexes with estimated costs of $100 million or more were on the drawing boards or under construction in 1970. Typical site acquisition costs of $500 per square foot and building construction costs of $40 per square foot were reported for new office buildings in downtown New York in 1969.[12]

---

[10]Costs cited by Rudolph Ulrich, "Relative Costs and Benefits of Land Reclamation in the Humid Southeast and the Semiarid West," *Journal of Farm Economics,* Vol. 35, February, 1953, p. 67.

[11]Cf. *House and Home,* Vol. 31, May, 1967, p. 5. The developer's cost outlays were reported as follows: land surveys $4,400, grading $9,900, paving of streets $19,200, sidewalks $13,000, provision of water $24,966, sewers $40,526, sewer hookup $4,400, storm drainage $5,500, landscaping $4,020, job overhead $3,768, contractor and engineer fees plus bond premium $18,600, carrying charges $9,084, taxes $3,000, insurance $50, FHA application fee $339, FHA commitment fee $678, FHA mortgage insurance $4,520, financing $4,520, title and legal fees $7,350, and organization cost $1,000. The raw land on this project had an FHA appraisal value of $146,461. For other examples, cf. A. Allan Schmid, *Converting Land from Rural to Urban Uses* (Baltimore: Resources for the Future, Inc. and the John Hopkins Press, 1968), p. 13, and Frank Miller, "Land—Its Potential," *The Appraisal Journal,* Vol. 38, April, 1970, p. 249.

[12]Cf. Eleanore Carruth, "Manhattan's Office Building Binge," *Fortune,* Vol. 80, October, 1969, p. 178.

New highways provide another example of high development costs. The Ohio turnpike was built during the 1950s at an average total cost, including financing, of $1,350,000 per mile. Construction was completed during the 1968 fiscal year on 11,871 miles of federal-aid rural primary and secondary roads and urban highways in the United States at a total cost of $4.13 billion or an average of $348,884 per mile.[13] These construction costs, which do not include site acquisition costs, vary over a wide range depending upon the type and width of the road, number of lanes, soil conditions, number of bridges and approaches that must be built, possible depression or elevation of the roads, and the necessity for providing sewers and drainage. Limited access expressway construction costs in Michigan ranged from a low of $348,746 per mile on one rural project to $12,600,000 per mile on an expressway built in an urbanized area in 1969.

Urban rapid transit systems and mining developments provide other examples of current development costs. Construction was completed on the San Francisco Bay Rapid Transit system (BART) with its network of 75 miles of track and tunnels in 1972 at a cost of $1.4 billion. The new Metro rapid transit system planned for the Washington metropolitan area will involve 98 miles of track and is expected to cost $2.8 billion by the time of its scheduled completion in 1980. Contracts were let in 1969 for the opening up of the iron deposits of Western Australia at an estimated development cost of $1.2 billion. A total of 43,486 oil and gas wells were drilled in the United States in 1964 at an average cost of $55,820 each.[14] This outlay, which does not include exploration and site acquisition costs, represents only part of the total costs. The total development cost is approximately double this amount as is indicated by the report that $4.9 billion was spent in finding and developing new reserves of oil and gas in the United States in 1968.[15]

Social Costs in Land Development

In addition to the cash outlays required for the improvement and processing of land resources, land development frequently results in social costs. These costs can be divided into two classes: social opportunity costs and social diseconomies or externalities. Social opportunity costs involve the returns and satisfactions foregone by society and its members because of the choices followed in resource developments.

---

[13]Cf. *Highway Statistics, 1968,* annual report of U. S. Department of Transportation, 1969, p. 180.

[14]Cf. *Petroleum Facts and Figures* (New York: American Petroleum Institute, 1967), p. 29. The average well was 4,340 feet in depth. Of the total number of wells, 21,012 were productive oil wells, 4,874 were gas wells, and 17,600 were dry holes. The 320 wells with depths of over 15,000 feet had average drilling costs of $715,261.

[15]Cf. *Petroleum Press Service,* February, 1970, p. 58.

Social diseconomies in turn involve the external cost and negative spill-over effects projects and developments can have on other individuals, communities, and society at large.[16]

High social opportunity costs were a common feature of frontier life. The early settlers on the American frontier had to clear, stump, fence, and prepare their lands for farming. They erected their own buildings and joined with their neighbors in providing schools, churches, roads, and other community facilities. They cheerfully accepted arduous labor and rugged living as the price they had to pay for the homes they carved out of the wilderness. They worked hard, invested their savings in capital developments, and went without comforts of life they could have enjoyed had they remained in older settled areas. When their developments bore fruit, they usually felt that their efforts were worthwhile and that their children and grandchildren could benefit from their sacrifices. Too often, however, their time and labor was wasted on poor and unproductive sites. Deserted cabins and shacks still stand on many abandoned clearings as monuments to some settler's broken hopes and as mute reminders of the social waste that results from misguided land developments.

Similar social opportunity costs can arise with developments of land resources for urban uses. Family sacrifices are often needed to finance the building or purchase of new houses and to provide businessmen with their necessary supplies of working capital. Urban redevelopment projects normally involve the social waste associated with the scrapping of earlier developments. As with rural lands, the promoters of urban developments can experience setbacks and heartaches. Their projects sometimes involve unwarranted expenditures and result in business losses or failures. The social costs and waste associated with these losses can be great, particularly when they imperil the savings and security of innocent investors.

Social diseconomies and externalities are a problem when public or private projects have adverse effects on others. A land clearing operation may disrupt the natural ecology and desecrate scenic and other values that have long been enjoyed by others; a smelter may pollute the air around a city; or an industrial plant may dump untreated wastes in a neighboring stream and destroy its value for many users. Costs in each of these instances are shifted from the operators to others in society. In

---

[16]Externalities can be positive and beneficial to others as well as negative and costly. A private development, for example, may provide landscaped open space or free recreation opportunities for the residents of an area or it may attract supporting industries that bring better business, credit, and transportation conditions for the entire community. For additional comments on externalities, cf. Ezra J. Misham, *The Costs of Economic Growth*, (New York: Frederick A. Praeger, 1967), Part II; Willis L. Peterson, *Principles of Economics Micro*, (Homewood, Ill.: Richard D. Irwin, Inc., 1971), pp. 134-139; and Robert H. Haveman and Julius Margolis (eds.), *Public Expenditures and Policy Analysis*, (Chicago: Markham Publishing Company, 1970), pp. 81-95.

times past, these costs were often overlooked or dismissed as parts of the necessary price of progress. With the emphasis now given to environmental concerns, the problem of identifying these diseconomies, minimizing their occurence, and more closely associating the cost and responsibility for coping with them with the parties who created them has become a key issue in environmental economics.

Time Costs

Land development always involves the passing of time. Weeks and sometimes years elapse before improvements are completed and developed resources are ready for productive or consumer use. Throughout this time interval, land developers ordinarily find that their investments are tied up in assets that are not as yet ready to yield an economic return. They also find that they must gauge their present plans and operations to their expectations concerning the market conditions that will prevail after their properties have been developed. This process involves elements of risk and speculation and sometimes results in extensions of the time intervals that elapse before developed properties can be sold or put to economic use. The costs associated with the holding of land developments under these conditions may be described as time costs. This cost concept includes two closely related types of costs—waiting costs and ripening costs.

Waiting costs may be defined as those costs that arise because of the waiting period that elapses between the time of the operator's first outlay of capital and labor and the time when he can either liquidate his investment or put it to actual use. The two principal types of waiting costs involve the allowances for interest on investment and for taxes that must be paid during the development and normal sales period.

Of these two items, the allowance for property tax payments represents a definite cash outlay the promoter cannot avoid without endangering his investment. Allowance of an interest payment on the operator's total capital investment throughout the period during which he must expect to hold his lots may or may not represent a cash outlay. Substantial portions of this allowance ordinarily go for interest payments when the promoter operates with borrowed capital, while an opportunity-cost return must be credited to whatever capital he advances from his own resources.

Significant examples of waiting costs are found with most types of land development and building activity. People who have their houses built to order always find that they must pay interest, and often taxes as well, on their land and building investments in the weeks or months that elapse before their houses are ready for occupancy. The only real differences between the waiting costs that arise in these cases and those associated with clearing a farm, planting an orchard, drilling an oil well, or building a

Rockefeller Center stem from differences in the size of the total investments involved and the duration of the time periods over which the waiting costs accrue.[17] Waiting costs arise even in the development of tax-exempt public properties such as schools and reclamation projects. In these examples, as in instances of private ownership, interest payments are required and should be calculated from the time construction funds are made available until the completed project is ready for use.

Before leaving the subject of waiting costs, it should be noted that they are by no means limited to cases of land development. The merchant who buys his stock of Christmas toys in August always has a portion of his capital tied up until he can turn over his investment. Similarly, the farmer who buys seed, fertilizer, and machinery in the spring must allow interest on these and other production costs until he sells his harvest in the fall. Reforestation projects provide another excellent example of waiting costs because interest and taxes must often be carried for 50 years or more before the planted seedlings are ready for harvest as commercial timber.

Closely related to and sometimes overlapping the concept of waiting costs is the parallel concept of *ripening costs.* This concept applies to those increases in the cost of holding property that stem from the ripening or imagined ripening of properties from lower to higher uses. Typical examples of ripening costs occur whenever tax assessors begin to treat cutover land in the same property value class as farm land, farm land in the same value class as residential sites, or residential lots in the same value class as industrial and commercial sites. With each of these examples, the increase in property taxes paid in the period that elapses before the land actually shifts to the higher use may be regarded as a ripening cost.

Ripening costs are usually associated with an actual or assumed increase in land rents and land values. Farm land, for example, is seldom assessed as potential residential land until the outward growth of urban communities and the residential development of adjacent sites indicates an obvious value for the higher use. In cases of this type, ripening costs in the form of higher tax assessments may be used as a lever to force the sale and settlement of speculative holdings along the frontier, the clearing and cultivation of wildlands, and the subdivision of rural lands located in or adjacent to urban and suburban communities.

The concept of ripening costs includes not only increases in tax charges associated with the shifting or potential shifting of properties to higher uses but also the costs sometimes incurred in holding developed properties for the anticipated higher values associated with their potential uses. A

[17] The *New York Times,* June 29, 1969, VIII, 1:1, reports that periods of from four to six years commonly elapse between the time that the developers of office buildings start to assemble their sites and the date when they can collect their first rents. Taxes and interest must be paid during this period. The fact that these costs have risen rapidly along with the site and construction costs is cited as a justification for the annual rental payments of up to $16 per square foot asked for prime office space in downtown New York in 1969.

land subdivider, for example, may assume that he can sell all of his lots in three years but find that his holding period actually lasts for five years. The additional carrying charges (interest and taxes) incurred during the extra two years represent ripening costs. They arise because of the promoter's premature development of the subdivision and because of the need for further "ripening" his project before his lots can be sold at his asking price.

Other comparable examples of ripening costs occur when new developments such as apartment houses or office buildings have additional capacity beyond that which can be immediately absorbed by the market. The ripening costs that arise during the months it may take for these projects to attain a normal occupancy level sometimes result from mistakes in judgment or from overoptimism concerning the potential market for the types of development undertaken. They may also result from production economies associated with large-scale developments and from the willingness of some operators to sponsor projects with temporary excess capacity they hope to later rent or sell at a profit.

The history of land development in the United States provides numerous examples of developments that have failed to fruit in the manner expected. Speculators frequently acquired lands along the frontier with the expectation of profits from their sale as soon as the advancing frontier made them more desirable for settlement. Land companies have cleared and drained potential farm lands; promoters have laid out extensive subdivisions; and builders have erected houses on speculation always in anticipation of early sales. As a rule, these investments have turned out to the investor's satisfaction. Sometimes, however, the anticipated demand has not materialized on schedule; and it has been necessary to carry the properties for later sale.

The ripening costs that occur when a land development or speculative holding must be held a few months or years can often be absorbed or passed on to the buyers, particularly if both market prices and demand hold high. Real problems arise, however, when investors find themselves caught in the onset of a recession. Under these conditions, some investors may find it possible to wait out the downswing of the business cycle. Many others, particularly those operating with credit, find their equities seriously reduced or wiped out by mounting ripening costs. With them, the alternative is often a choice between distress sales and bankruptcy, debt foreclosure, or tax reversion. Classic examples of these situations occurred along the frontier during every depression, with the collapse of the cutover land boom in the Lake States during the early 1920s, and with many of the ambitious but often premature residential subdivisions laid out during the late 1920s.

Unfortunately for many investors, numerous highly-touted land resource development projects in times past have been based upon wholly unwarranted concepts of property value and land-resource need. Projects of this type are often definitely premature. Once they are examined in the cold light of reality it is often obvious that they were "picked too green" to go through a normal ripening process. Instead of ripening to a higher use, these projects often deteriorate and "go down hill." Far from acquiring a higher value with more earning capacity, they often remain idle, become subject to misuse, or may even be abandoned. These developments frequently result in tax-reversion and land-title problems as well as in considerable social waste. The prohibitive ripening costs associated with these projects often assure their failure. At the same time, however, they illustrate the fact that it takes more than high hopes and high taxes to make land resources shift to higher uses.

Costs of Supersession

Much of the world's land area is utilized for a variety of uses that have continued with little change over long periods of time. Some sites found in and around growing urban centers, however, have experienced a frequent succession of uses. With these sites, changing value and use patterns often make new types of development economically desirable even though this may involve the writing off of investments in improvements already located on these sites. The costs involved in this process are known as *costs of supersession.*

Typical examples of supersession costs arise whenever city lots that have been used for residential purposes ripen for commercial use. This situation usually makes it profitable for property owners to redevelop their sites for some higher and better use. An owner with a house valued at $15,000 producing a land rent of $150 a month, for example, may feel that he can erect a $200,000 retail and office building that will provide him with a many-fold increase in his net rental returns. If his lot were vacant, there would be little question as to his line of action. But he has a $15,000 house on the lot. Before he can capitalize on his new opportunity he must either move or tear down his present building. Either approach involves the scrapping or writing off of a considerable portion of his present investment.

The problem of supersession costs thus boils down to a decision as to whether the owner is willing to sacrifice all or part of his present investment in improvements in order to capitalize on his opportunity to realize higher future returns. Should he decide to shift to the higher use, he must write off most of the value of his house and then proceed with the redevelopment of his site. On the other hand, if he fails to shift to the prospective higher use, he will suffer an opportunity cost equal to the difference between the net income he receives and that which he could receive by redeveloping the site.

Numerous other examples can be cited to illustrate the concept of supersession costs. A fruit farmer may feel that he can make more money by shifting to dairying. But he may logically hesitate before shifting to this new venture if the shift requires the destruction of the already developed orchards upon which he now depends for a livelihood plus the cost of supplying a productive dairy herd together with certain necessary dairy buildings. Supersession costs are also involved when workers refuse to shift to higher-paying jobs because of their fear of losing seniority and pension rights. They arise again when a businessman questions whether he should close down his business and scrap part of the value of his present quarters while he remodels or rebuilds with the hope of improving his future competitive and income status. In other instances, public and private agencies incur large supersession costs when they spend millions of dollars in buying properties in blighted neighborhoods and in relocating displaced families so they may have appropriate sites for new housing developments.

The promise of higher returns makes most land operators both willing and anxious to shift to higher uses. But this shift is often discouraged by man's limited foresight, inadequate financing, and the investor's understandable concern over the scrapping of structures and improvements that still retain considerable earning capacity. As long as operators definitely foresee a prospect of higher returns from redevelopments and as long as they have adequate financing to undertake their contemplated changes, they are usually willing to shift to new uses. When uncertainties exist concerning the earning capacity or duration of the new opportunities or when they lack adequate financing, they often continue with their existing use patterns.

Property owners who are either unwilling or unable to undertake complete redevelopment programs often work out piecemeal compromises. Generally speaking, these arrangements are designed to tap part of the operator's potentially higher earning capacity while minimizing his actual costs of supersession. Familiar examples of this are provided by the many houses that are converted into shops, restaurants, and office buildings; by the houses that have commercial structures built on in what once were their front yards; and by merchants who remodel their stores while carrying on business as usual. The results of this expedient are often less satisfactory and less sightly than those provided by complete redevelopment; but they do involve lower supersession costs.

BENEFIT-COST ANALYSIS

Few aspects of the land resource development process are more important than the marshalling and analysis of basic data that guides actual decisions to approve or reject development proposals. Developers and investors normally proceed on the assumption that their benefits will exceed their costs. To act otherwise would be irrational. This is as true with small purchases as with huge developments such as the construction of a Hoover Dam.

Simple observations show that a wide range of practices are associated with the weighing of benefits and costs. Individual consumers, private operators, and public officials frequently give little thought to precise evaluations of benefits and costs in their purchase decisions. This is particularly true with habitual transactions and purchases that can be justified on the basis of earlier precedents. More thought is given to benefit-cost considerations and to the justification of the buyer's decision when he buys something new or when a large consideration is involved, as when one buys a car or a house. The buyer in these cases may or may not consider the appropriate facts. He may be overly receptive to the claims made for a product. He may underestimate or ignore his probable costs. But attention is given to some weighing of expected benefits and costs, and the decision to buy can be interpreted as an expectation on the buyer's part that his purchase will provide him with an excess of benefits above his costs.

Project evaluation techniques of a more sophisticated nature are normally used with public and private land and water resource development projects. The decision making process in these cases is guided by public investment criteria and by private desires for the maximization of returns. Neither private operators nor public agencies have unlimited resources. They want to make certain that each of their projects has a potential for paying for itself. They would like to select that project design for any given development that promises the highest surplus of benefits above costs. Moreover, if they are free to invest in a choice of developments, they may apply the equi-marginal returns concept as a guide in their decisions concerning the allocation and investment of their resources. They may argue that each last input in a public or private resource development should provide marginal economic and/or social benefits at least as high as the returns, satisfactions, or benefits that could be attained through investments in alternative projects or programs.

Benefit-cost analysis provides a leading example of the techniques used in evaluating the economic prospects of resource development proposals. This approach is used by public agencies in the United States in the formal evaluation of all water resource development projects proposed for federal funding. The final decisions regarding appropriation of public monies for these projects are made in the political arena and are subject to various public and private pressures. Congress requires, however, that every water resource development proposal pass a test of economic feasibility as a prior condition for approval.[18]

---

[18]Cf. Mark M. Regan and Elco L. Greenshields, "Benefit-Cost Analysis of Resource Development Programs," *Journal of Farm Economics,* Vol. 33, November, 1951, pp. 866-78. A general requirement that project benefits exceed costs is stated in the Reclamation Act of 1902 and certain other early legislation. A more specific requirement for positive benefit-cost ratios appears in the Flood Control Act of 1936. Since the passage of that act, Congress has moved steadily in the direction of requiring an excess of economic benefits above cost with all public water resource developments.

Benefit-cost analysis can be applied to a wide variety of resource development and public investment programs.[19] It can be used to rate or establish priorities between comparable alternative proposals, but it is ordinarily used simply to determine whether or not single project proposals are economically justified in the sense that they promise a surplus of benefits above costs. Students of government have recognized the potential for using similar techniques to compare the productive potential of alternative public projects and programs. This broader approach is incorporated to some extent in the planning-programming-budgeting system (PPBS) initiated by the United States government in 1965.

Nature of Benefit-Cost Analysis

Benefit-cost analysis is designed "to provide a guide for effective use of the required economic resources, such as land, labor, and materials, in producing goods and services to satisfy human wants." It shows "whether economic resources are used more effectively than would be the case without the project."[20] Benefit-cost analysis emphasizes economic efficiency in resource use. It is not the only basis for approving or disapproving resource development projects. National defense, foreign policy, and other considerations often play a governing role. But insofar as economic considerations prevail, the benefit-cost approach points the way to the most beneficial use of public funds in land-resource developments. It assumes that (1) projects have economic value only to the extent that a need or desire exists for their services; (2) each project should be developed at that scale that provides the maximum excess of benefits above cost; (3) every project or separable segment thereof should be developed at the least practicable cost commensurate with the over-all objectives of the project; and (4) the development priorities assigned to various projects should follow the order of their economic desirability.

Concept of benefits and costs. Before one can proceed with a benefit-cost analysis it is first necessary to identify the meaning of the terms

[19] Benefit-cost analysis was initially applied to irrigation developments. Its use has been expanded to cover multiple-purpose, hydroelectric power, navigation, flood control, watershed development, recreation, fish and wildlife, drainage, reforestation, land clearing, and other similar projects. It has been recommended that this technique also be applied in the evaluation of public investments in highways, urban renewal, outdoor recreation, civil aviation, public health, and government research. [Cf. Robert Dorfman, ed., *Measuring Benefits of Government Investments* (Washington: Brookings Institution, 1965).]

[20] Federal Inter-Agency River Basin Committee, *Proposed Practices for Economic Analysis of River Basin Projects* (Washington: U. S. Government Printing Office, revised 1958), p. 5.

"benefits" and "costs." Prevailing practice now calls for recognition of two types of benefits and three types of costs.[21]

Primary benefits are defined as the value of the immediate projects and services—the value of the farm crops, electric power, flood protection, and so on—that result from a project. Emphasis is given to tangible material benefits that can be measured in marketplace terms, but values may also be assigned to intangible social values such as the provision of recreation opportunities, protection against floods, and national defense. Intangible benefits are defined as: "Those benefits which, although recognized as having real value in satisfying human needs or desires are not fully measurable in monetary terms, or are incapable of such expression in formal analysis."[22]

Secondary benefits involve those additional values that result from activities "stemming from" or "induced by" a project. These benefits may involve the value of bread, over and above the value of wheat, that is produced as a result of a project. In some instances, they may also be stretched to include the value of the progress or economic development "induced by" a project.[23] Secondary benefits should not be claimed,

[21] Up until 1950, several different definitions and practices were used by the various federal agencies. This situation caused the Federal Inter-Agency River Basin Committee to appoint a Subcommittee on Benefits and Costs in 1946 to formulate "mutually acceptable principles and procedures for determining benefits and costs for water-resource projects." These principles and procedures appear in the committee's 1950 report, *Proposed Practices for Economic Analysis of River Basin Projects.* Most of the discussion in this section is digested from the 1958 revision of this report. For other discussions, cf. Regan and Greenshields, *loc. cit.;* Mark M. Regan and John F. Timmons, "Current Concepts and Practices in Benefit-Cost Analysis of Natural Resource Developments," *Water Resources and Economic Development of the West,* Report No. 3 Western Agricultural Economics Research Council, 1954, pp. 1-15; President's Water Resources Council, *Policies, Standards, and Procedures in the Formulation, Evaluation, and Review of Plans for Use and Development of Water and Related Land Resources,* Senate Document 97, 87th Cong., 2nd Sess., 1962; Stephen C. Smith and Emory N. Castle, eds., *Economics and Public Policy in Water Resource Development* (Ames: Iowa State University Press, 1964), Part I; Otto Eckstein, *Water Resource Development: The Economics of Project Evaluation* (Cambridge: Harvard University Press, 1965); Robert Dorfman, "Basic Economic and Technologic Concepts" in Arthur Maass *et al., Design of Water Resource Systems* (Cambridge: Harvard University Press, 1966), pp. 88-158; Joe S. Bain, Richard E. Caves, and Julius Margolis, *Northern California's Water Industry* (Baltimore: Resources for the Future, Inc. and The Johns Hopkins Press, 1966), pp. 255-72, 363-418; and *Procedures for Evaluation of Water and Related Land Resource Projects,* Report of Special Task Force to the Water Resources Council, June, 1969, Washington: Water Resources Council, 1969.

[22] Senate Doc. 97, 87th Cong., 2nd Sess., 1962, pp. 8-9.

[23] Measurement of secondary benefits involves a complicated process. This factor, together with the possible double-counting of benefits in the measurement process, has caused some students of this problem to recommend that benefit-cost analyses be based only on primary benefits and costs. Cf. S. V. Ciriacy-Wantrup, "The Role of Benefit-Cost Analysis in Public Resource Development," *Water Resources and Economic Development of the West,* Report No. 3, pp. 17-28; William E. Folz, dis-

however, "unless it can be shown that there is an increase in net incomes as a result of the project as compared with conditions to be expected in absence of the project."[24]

Project costs include the full value of the land, labor, and materials used in establishing, maintaining, and operating the project plus an allowance for any adverse effects resulting from the project. Associated costs refer to the value of any additional goods and services needed to make the products or services of the project available for use or sale. With an irrigation project, all of a farmer's crop-production costs except his charge or project cost for water would be treated as associated costs.

Secondary costs involve the value of any goods or services in addition to project and associated costs that are used as a result of the project. They include the cost of any processing of immediate products or services the value of which is claimed as a secondary benefit. Thus, if the value of bread above the value of the wheat is claimed as a secondary benefit, the cost of transporting and storing the wheat, milling it into flour, operating the bakery, and distributing the bread to customers must be charged as a secondary cost.

Once the benefits and costs have been calculated, any surplus of primary benefits above project and associated costs can be called a net primary benefit. Any surplus of secondary benefits above secondary costs is a net secondary benefit. These two types of benefits and costs are treated together in the determination of benefit-cost ratios.

Measurement of benefits and costs. If benefit-cost analysis is to have any real meaning, special care must be taken to secure as accurate and realistic an estimate of the probable benefit-cost picture as is reasonably possible. Consistent standards should be used in the selection of price levels, interest rates, risk allowances, and determinations of economic life. It is recommended that benefits and costs be calculated in terms of the price levels expected at the times when the benefits and costs will occur. Project construction costs are usually calculated at current price levels if the project is to be started in the near future. Estimates of benefits and future operating, maintenance, and replacement costs ordinarily involve assumptions regarding future price levels. These estimates should be on the conservative side. Some agencies use long-term price and agricultural crop yield projections as a standard guide for their estimates.

Since project evaluations are concerned with all the benefits and costs associated with projects throughout their full period of use, consideration must be given to the fact that these benefits and costs "occur in diverse

---

cussion of Wantrup's paper, *ibid.*, pp. 29-34; and Maurice M. Kelso, "Evaluation of Secondary Benefits of Water-Use Projects," *Water Resources and Economic Development of the West*, Report No. 1, 1953, pp. 49-62.

[24]*Proposed Practices for Economic Analysis of River Basin Projects* (1958), p. 9.

physical forms, at different times, and over varying periods of time."[25] For analytical purposes, it is recommended that the benefits and costs associated with projects be viewed in terms of their present discounted values. This requires decisions on the appropriate discount interest rates and risk allowances that should apply, the probable economic life of each project, and the probable salvage value of each project at the end of this period. Other measurement problems "include the treatment of tangibles and intangibles, adjustments for levels of economic activity, costs of affected public facilities, acquisition of land and improvements, taxes, displaced facilities, extensions of useful life, and consequential damages."[26]

Interest and discount rates are used in the project evaluation process to adjust all estimates of future benefits and costs to a comparable present value basis. The Federal Inter-Agency River Basin Committee recommends that these rates reflect the average yield rate on long-term government bonds. These rates fluctuate from year to year. Under a formula established by the Water Resource Council in 1968, a rate of 5 1/2 percent applied in 1972.

The Committee recognized that some project risks are predictable and can be covered by insurance or appropriate allowances while others take the form of uncertainties that cannot be predicted on an actuarial basis. In dealing with this problem, it recommended that:

> ... net returns exclude all predictable risks, either by deducting them from benefits or adding them to project costs, usually on a present worth or annual equivalent basis. Allowance for uncertainties or unpredictable risks in benefit accrual should be made indirectly by use of conservative estimates of net benefits, requirement of safety margins in planning, or including a risk component in the discount rate.[27]

Wide variations exist between the economic life expectations of different projects. For benefit-cost analysis purposes, it is considered expedient to limit economic analyses to the expected life of a project, or 100 years, whichever is less.[28] All costs in excess of the probable salvage value of the project are amortized during this time period.

Formulation of the project. Determination of the probable benefits and costs represents only one aspect of the over-all problem of formu-

---

[25]*Ibid.*, p. 19.

[26]*Ibid.*, p. 17.

[27]*Ibid.*, p. 23.

[28]*Ibid.*, p. 25. The Committee suggested that 50 years should be considered the upper limit with projects when obsolescence is likely to become an important factor. A 50-year limit was recommended by the Bureau of the Budget in its Circular No. A-57, December 1952.

lating projects that are worthy of development. Emphasis must also be given to three other aspects of project formulation. These include: (1) the establishment of a need for the project; (2) determination of the best size or scale for the proposed development; and (3) ascertaining the most economic means for developing the project.

As a first step in the project-formulation process, care should always be taken to establish the fact that a need or demand exists for the products or services of the proposed project. Unless a real need exists, there is little point in trying to justify a project. If a definite need is found to exist, consideration should be given to the probable benefits and costs associated with projects of varying size. Information of this type is needed for decisions relative to the optimum scale of proposed developments.[29]

Projects are at optimum size when they produce more net benefits than can be secured at any larger- or any smaller-scale level. The determination of this scale level may be illustrated by the two diagrams presented in Figure 7-3. Both diagrams show the changing relationship between benefits and costs that occurs as projects increase in size. Point *B* indicates the scale of development that has the highest ratio of benefits to costs. Point *C* represents the scale level that produces the greatest excess of benefits above costs. As the lower diagram indicates, this is the scale level at which the marginal benefits associated with increasing size or scale of project equal the marginal costs—the point at which the ratio between marginal benefits and marginal costs becomes unity. Points *A* and *D* represent the levels at which total benefits equal total costs and the points at which a unity ratio exists between benefits and costs.

Under conditions of perfect competition, the optimum scale for a project is always found at scale level *C*—at the level at which the benefits added by the last increment of increased scale just equal its incremental cost. As is the general case in input-output relationships (cf. chapter 5), this situation holds only with the assumption of unlimited resources. With the more realistic assumption of limited development funds, the optimum scale level depends upon the location of the point of equi-marginal returns. It thus shifts to some scale level between *B* and *C*, to a point at which the marginal benefit-cost relationships of all the operating projects are in balance.

In practice, too little attention has been given to determinations of optimum scale. As Regan and Timmons have observed:

> Decisions concerning scale are sometimes based upon comparison of only a limited number of projects, which represent variations in scale. More frequently,

[29] Speaking on this point, Regan and Greenshields (*loc. cit.*, p. 871) observe: "In too many instances, projects are conceived and designed simply on the basis of their physical potentialities for utilizing to the limit available physical resources. Then, after the project is set up, the economist is invited to come in to show whether the plan is economically feasible. The amount of genuine guidance that economic analysis can provide in decisions affecting the public interest at this stage of project development is often quite limited."

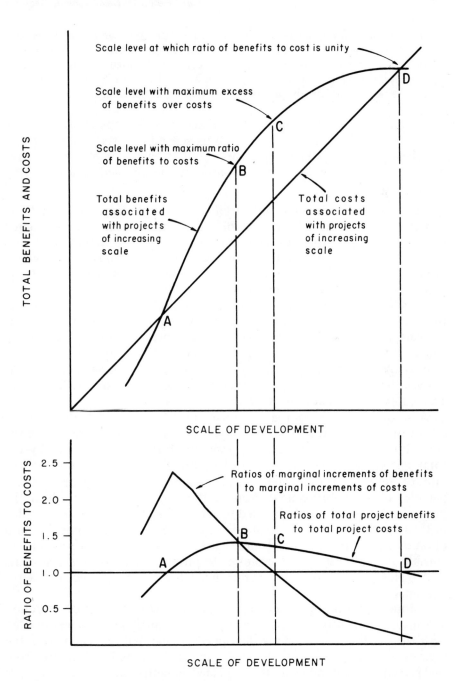

FIGURE 7-3. Relationship between benefits and costs with projects involving different scales of development.

formulation is based largely on the judgments of those designing the projects. Economic considerations often receive little attention unless those responsible for design are familiar with the economic concepts involved. In any case, the application of proper formulation procedures is extremely difficult because of the absence of sufficiently precise information on incremental relationships.[30]

Once the size of the project has been determined, steps should be taken to make sure that the project and all its separable parts have the lowest practicable cost. A project is poorly formulated when its objectives or the purposes of some of its separable parts can be attained at less cost by some other means.

Determination of economic feasibility. Once the appropriate data on benefits and costs have been assembled and analyzed and their estimated totals discounted to provide a measure of their present values, a determination can be made of the economic feasibility of individual projects. Four different approaches can be used to indicate the relative desirability of single or alternative projects.

As a first approach, one could subtract the total cost of each project from its benefits and rate projects according to their total excess of benefits above costs. This approach (B-C) measures the net economic benefit or return but gives no weight to the relative costs incurred in each case. It is unacceptable as a measure of benefit-cost relationships because it gives the same weight to a $1,000,000 project that costs $999,000 as to a $10,000 project that costs $9,000.

A second possible approach involves measurement of the rate of net return on the expected total cost outlay. Under this procedure, total costs are subtracted from total benefits, and the difference is divided by the total cost to get a percentage rate of return. This method (*B-C/C*) gives a rate of return on the total costs associated with the project. Comparable answers are secured from a third approach under which the present value of the total expected benefits is divided by the present value of the expected costs (*B/C*) to provide a benefit-cost ratio. A positive ratio (a ratio of more than 1.0) indicates that a project proposal is economically feasible in the sense that it promises to produce benefits in excess of its costs. This is the approach recommended and generally used in benefit-cost analysis.

A fourth possible approach differentiates between project construction and investment costs and the operation and maintenance costs associated with the productive use of the developed project. With this approach, the present annual value of the expected operating costs is subtracted from the present annual value of the expected benefits, and the difference is divided by the present annual value of the project investment costs (*B-OC/IC*) to provide a rate of return on project investment costs. This

[30] Regan and Timmons, *loc. cit.*, p. 5.

approach has been advanced as a better and more realistic measure of the comparative effectiveness of resource investments than the simple benefit-cost ratio.[31] It has the disadvantage, however, of having "limited usefulness . . . for determining the relative desirability of projects when construction funds are limited and when the relative cost of operation and maintenance is considered of secondary importance."[32]

As the example reported in Table 7-1 shows, the B/C ratio and the B-OC/IC rate of return on investment approaches can provide conflicting guidelines as to the comparative priorities that might be assigned to alternative project proposals. Project A has the highest benefit-cost ratio (1.6) and the lowest rate of return on investment costs (175 percent) while project D has the lowest benefit-cost ratio (1.3) and the highest comparative rate of return on investment costs (225 percent).

TABLE 7-1. **Example of the Rates of Return and Benefit-Cost Ratios for Four Alternative Projects**

	Alternative projects			
Item	A	B	C	D
	(values in millions)			
Annual value of benefits	$20	$24	$42	$65
Annual operating costs	2.5	6	18	38
Annual share of total investment cost	10	10	12	12
Measures of net benefits				
Benefits minus costs (B-C)	$ 7.5	$ 8	$12	$15
B-C / C	60%	50%	40%	30%
Benefit-cost ratio (B/C)	1.6	1.5	1.4	1.3
B-OC / IC	175%	180%	200%	225%

Critique of Benefit-Cost Analyses

Several observations both pro and con may be made by way of critique of the benefit-cost approach to project evaluations. On the positive side, it may be argued that some method of project evaluation is definitely needed to guide the allocation of public and private investments, that benefit-cost analysis provides a logical and useful technique for this

[31] Cf. Roland N. McKean, *Efficiency in Government Through Systems Analysis* (New York: John Wiley and Sons, 1958), pp. 108-13; and Richard J. Hammond, *Benefit-Cost Analysis and Water Pollution* (Stanford: Food Research Institute Misc. Publ. 13, 1960), pp. 17-21.

[32] *Proposed Practices for Economic Analysis of River Basin Projects* (1958), p. 16. Eckstein, *op. cit.,* pp. 53-65, compared the two approaches and concludes that the benefit-cost ratio is the better for the purposes for which it is used.

purpose, and that the resulting benefit-cost ratio is easily understood. Furthermore, the benefit-cost approach has been accepted for many years and numerous improvements have been incorporated in the techniques applied.

Critics of benefit-cost analysis have argued that it is at best a system of partial analysis, that the actual decision to proceed with projects is a political rather than an economic one, and that the data used in computations of benefits and costs are often inadequate and incomplete with the result that benefits are sometimes underestimated and on other occasions inflated. It is also charged that there is a lack of consistency in the standards used by different agencies in their evaluations, that the discount rates used with large public projects are unrealistically low, and that significant impacts such as the effect a project may have on the natural environment or on local prospects for economic growth are ignored.

In actual practice, the federal government has used benefit-cost analysis mostly as a means for determining the economic feasibility of individual project proposals. Congress requires project proposals to have a positive benefit-cost ratio as a condition for approval. This practice discourages absurd projects, but it still falls short of full maximization of investment returns. Individual projects are eligible for Congressional approval as long as they fall in the range between points A and D in Figure 7-3. Projects with positive benefit-cost ratios may or may not be planned at their optimum scale and in some instances may include separable features that could not be justified on a marginal value productivity basis.

Another problem with benefit-cost analysis stems from the frequent disassociation of benefits and costs. The principle that a project proposal is eligible for funding if it has a positive benefit-cost ratio may be wholly justified if the same party pays the costs as receives the benefits. Complications arise when different parties are involved. Property owners in a proposed small watershed project area, for example, may oppose a project that has a positive overall ratio because most of the benefits will be received by downstream residents while they are expected to bear most of the costs. Similar questions may arise when the government is expected to bear the cost of a harbor dredging project that will be of primary benefit to a few local industries. Another aspect of this problem may be discerned in the attitude of local groups concerning possible federal "pork-barrel" projects. As long as the local people are not asked to pay a portion of the costs, any positive benefits expected of a project may make it appear desirable simply because the decision by Congress to fund or not fund the project will have no appreciable effect on their total tax load.

Questions may be raised concerning the lack of consistency that exists between the benefit-cost analysis techniques used within and between agencies. A continuing examination and reappraisal of the techniques used in benefit-cost appraisal has resulted in some refinement and standardization of the approaches used. More progress is needed, however, in exploring the appropriate weights that should be associated with intangible and social benefits and costs and in standardizing the approaches used by different agencies. Present differences make it easier for projects of doubtful value to secure positive ratios from some reviewers than others.

One of the more critical issues associated with benefit-cost analysis involves the choice of the appropriate interest rates for discounting the value of future benefits and costs back to the present.[33] Higher present values are secured with low interest rates than with high rates. Proponents of public investments are often inclined to favor low rates such as the yield rate on long-term government bonds while supporters of private investments usually argue for acceptance of the higher interest rates associated with commercial credit.[34]

In practice, the federal agencies have used discount rates ranging from 3 to 12 percent and on some occasions have not discounted future benefits.[35] A discount rate of 6 7/8 percent, considered consistent with the government's cost of borrowing money, was specified by the Water Resources Council in 1973 with the provision that the rate could be raised or lowered by a maximum of one-half of a percent in any succeeding year.[36]

Benefit-cost analysis provides a general yardstick for evaluating the relative economic efficiency and feasibility of proposed projects. As such, it often provides an incomplete measure of the overall desirability of individual project proposals. Most projects involve a complex mix of goals, many of which cannot be measured adequately in exclusive economic terms.[37] This situation was highlighted in a series of recommendations submitted to the Water Resources Council in 1969 and 1970 which proposed that the framework for evaluating project proposals be broadened to give joint recognition to the need for enhancing national economic development, environmental quality, social well-being, and

[33] Cf. Eckstein, *op. cit.,* pp. 94-104; McKean, *op. cit.,* pp. 116-18; and Kenneth Arrow, "Discounting and Public Investment Criteria," in Allen V. Kneese and Stephen C. Smith, ed., *Water Research* (Baltimore: Resources for the Future, Inc. and The Johns Hopkins Press, 1965), pp. 13-32.

[34] For examples of the effects of the use of alternative interest rates on the benefit-cost ratios associated with selected projects, cf. John V. Krutilla and Otto Eckstein, *Multiple Purpose River Development* (Baltimore: Resources for the Future, Inc. and The Johns Hopkins Press, 1958).

[35] Cf. Report of Comptroller General in *Interest Rate Guidelines for Federal Decision-making,* Hearings of Subcommittee on Economy in Government, 90th Cong., 2nd Sess., 1968, p. 34.

[36] This rate, which narrows the prospect of individual projects receiving a positive benefit-cost ratio, can be compared with the rate of 5 1/8 percent recommended and applied by the Water Resources Council in 1940 and with the rates of 1 1/2 percent on public investments and 4 percent on private investments recommended by the Federal Inter-Agency River Basin Committee in 1950.

[37] Cf., for example, Arthur Maass, "Benefit-Cost Analysis: Its Relevance to Public Investment Decisions," in Kneese and Smith, *Water Research,* p. 312.

regional development.[38] These recommendations have considerable merit. Even with their adoption, however, significant problems would still exist in choosing and quantifying the appropriate weights that must be given to these separate evaluations in final decisions concerning the acceptability of individual project proposals.

Thus far the formal use of benefit-cost analysis has been limited for the most part to determinations of the economic feasibility of individual project proposals. Little effort has been made to use it to assign development priorities to alternative projects. Some have argued that it is not an appropriate measure and was never intended for this purpose.[39] This argument aside, there are strong reasons for using a benefit-cost analysis test of economic feasibility with other types of public investments. Program evaluation techniques such as those used in PPBS are needed to help guide agencies and officials in the allocation of public funds between alternative projects and programs.

—SUGGESTED READINGS

Dorau, Herbert B., and Albert G. Hinman, *Urban Land Economics* (New York: The Macmillan Company, 1928), chaps. XI, XIII, XIV.

Eckstein, Otto, *Water Resource Development* (Cambridge: Harvard University Press, 1965).

Ely, Richard T., and George S. Wehrwein *Land Economics* (Madison: The University of Wisconsin Press, 1964), chap. V. Originally published by The Macmillan Company, 1940.

Federal Inter-Agency River Basin Committee, *Proposed Practices for Economic Analysis of River Basin Projects* (Washington: U. S. Government Printing Office, revised 1958).

Johnson, V. Webster, and Raleigh Barlowe, *Land Problems and Policies* (New York: McGraw-Hill Book Company, Inc., 1954), chap. X.

Procedures for Evaluation of Water and Related Land Resource Projects, Report of Special Task Force to the Water Resources Council (Washington: Water Resources Council, 1969).

Ratcliff, Richard U., *Urban Land Economics* (New York: McGraw-Hill Book Company, Inc., 1949), chaps. XII, XIII.

Water Resources Council, "Water and Related Land Resources—Establishment of Principles and Standards for Planning," *Federal Register,* vol 38, No. 174, Pt. III, pp. 24777-24869.

---

[38]Cf. *Procedures for Evaluation of Water and Related Land Resource Projects,* pp. 20-25. This report was revised in 1970 and published under the same title as Senate Committee on Public Works, Committee Print Serial No. 92-20, 92nd Congress, 1st Session, 1971.

[39]Cf. Hammond, *op. cit.,* chap. II.

8

Conservation
of Land Resources

Conservation is a concept of many meanings. Some people visualize it as a moral issue tied up with man's responsibility to safeguard certain resources for the use of future generations. Technical workers sometimes identify it with the physical techniques they use to retard soil erosion, plant fish, or manage a deer herd. Sportsmen frequently think of it in terms of better fishing or hunting. Politicians often treat it as a political "sacred cow" closely allied with voter interests. Conservation evangelists regard it as the symbol of a better life, as an almost mystical means for securing "the greatest good to the greatest number— and that for the longest time."[1]

Our discussion here is only indirectly concerned with the moral, physical, recreational, political, and mystical aspects of conservation. It deals instead with the economic and social questions that frequently arise concerning the optimum use of land resources over time. Operators must often decide between policies that promise to maximize their returns during the short run but that may result in the depletion or exploitation of their land resources and other policies that emphasize the maintenance or saving of these resources for use over longer time periods.

Which of these approaches should the rational operator follow? What position should society take regarding these

[1] Charles R. Van Hise, *The Conservation of Natural Resources in the United States* (New York: The Macmillan Company, 1910), p. 379.

policy alternatives? These questions strike at the economic heart of the conservation problem and provide the basis for the following discussion of the economics of conservation as it applies to land resources. Emphasis is given in this discussion to the economic meaning of conservation and to some leading factors that affect conservation decisions.

THE ECONOMIC MEANING OF CONSERVATION

Conservation can be defined in several different ways. In a dictionary sense, it involves the preserving, guarding, protecting, or keeping of a thing in a safe or entire state. As applied to land resources, this strict and narrow definition calls for "the preservation in unimpaired efficiency of the resources of the earth, or in a condition so nearly unimpaired as the nature of the case or wise exhaustion will permit."[2]

The idea of preserving land resources intact for future use has never gained much popular acceptance. To be sure, many conservationists stress the need for saving certain resources for future use; and some have probably overemphasized this point. Most people, however, react negatively to policies of nonuse. They favor the maintenance and saving of land resources, but only to the extent to which conservation policies are consistent with programs of effective current use. Because of this rationale, much of the emphasis in conservation discussions is on the need for orderly and efficient resource use, the elimination of economic and social waste, and the maximization of social net returns over time.

From an economic and social point of view, conservation may be defined simply as the wise use of resources over time. This definition has the weakness of being both vague and confusing—vague because of differences of opinion concerning what constitutes "wise use" and confusing because conservation practices vary widely with different types of resources. Yet it should be recognized that conservation is basically concerned with choices in the timing of resource use. It deals with public and private decisions concerning the allocation of resources between the present and future and with policies and actions that are designed to increase the future usable supplies of particular resources. It involves the *when* of resource use.[3]

As we explore the economic meaning of conservation, it is important that we emphasize the goal of wise or optimum use of resources over time and its interrelationship with the concepts of orderly and efficient resource use, elimination of waste, and maximization of social net returns

[2] Richard T. Ely *et al., Foundations of National Prosperity* (New York: The Macmillan Company, 1917), p. 3.

[3] Cf. Siegfried V. Ciriacy-Wantrup, *Resource Conservation* (Berkeley: University of California Press, 1952), p. 51. Originally published by the University of California Press; reprinted by permission of the Regents of the University of California.

over time. These issues will be considered in some detail later in this section. Before turning to this discussion, consideration should first be given to two important facets of the conservation problem: (1) the classification of land resources for conservation purposes, and (2) the use of discount and compound interest rates in conservation decisions.

Classification of Land Resources for Conservation Purposes

Although one may speak generally of the conservation of land resources, it is much more meaningful to talk of the conservation of particular resources or classes of resources. Indeed, it makes little sense to discuss the specifics of conservation practices without focusing one's attention on some definite resource or class of resources. This situation stems from the fact that some classes of resources have a longer use-life, are more exhaustible, or can be more easily renewed than others and that different conservation goals accordingly apply to them.

Most classifications of land resources for conservation purposes are now based on the relative renewability of the resource. With this basic criterion, we can distinguish between three principal classes of land resources: fund resources, flow resources, and a composite group of resources that has some characteristics of both fund and flow resources. This composite group in turn can be subdivided into three important subclasses: biological resources, soil resources, and man-made improvements such as buildings.

Resources such as metals, mineral fuels, coal, stone, gravel, sand, and peat soils are properly classed as *fund* or *stock resources*. Our total physical supply of these resources is relatively fixed and nonrenewable. Coal, petroleum, natural gas, and peat soils can be replaced over long periods of time. But we cannot expect any significant increase in the total physical quantity of these resources during the time period in which we operate. Fund resources fall into two general subclasses: (1) resources such as coal and the mineral fuels, which are exhausted or chemically changed through use, and (2) resources such as metals and stone, which wear out very slowly and which are often capable of reuse.

The concept of *flow resources* applies to resources such as precipitation, the water in streams and lakes, sunlight, wind, tides, and climate. The flow of these resources comes in a continuous and predictable stream, which continues regardless of whether the resources are used or not. From a conservation standpoint, these resources are renewable. But they must be used as they become available; and failure to use them results in permanent loss of the value they could have had. Flow resources can sometimes be captured and stored for future use. Water can be retained in surface or underground reservoirs while the energy from the sun can be stored both in plants and in certain chemicals. When flow resources are stored in this manner, they take on some characteristics of fund resources.

Biological resources include crops, forests, range and pasture cover, livestock, wildlife, fish and even human beings. These resources have some flow characteristics in that they are replaceable over time, provided care is taken to safeguard and use the seed stock needed for each new generation. At any given time, however, they may also be treated as fund resources, which can be so used or exploited as to greatly reduce or even prevent their future flow or growth. Unlike fund and flow resources, the productivity of biological resources "may be decreased through exploitation, maintained at the present level, or increased by the actions of man."[4]

Soil resources represent a combination of fund, flow, and biological resources. A farmer may exploit or destroy a fund of fertility stored up over periods of several centuries. He may use his land in such a way as to draw only upon the annual flow of fertility created by the action of plant roots, soil solutions, and organisms in releasing various soil nutrients for possible plant use; or he may carry on a soil-building program (use of legumes, manure, and green manure crops), which emphasizes the action of plant roots and soil micro-organisms in building up the productive capacity of his soil. Soils lack the life-cycle characteristics of plants and animals. Except for peat soils, which are better treated as fund resources, they are comparable to biological resources in the sense that their productivity can be decreased, maintained, or increased by human action over time.

Man-made improvements represent a special classification of land resources in that they are not natural resources. Most buildings, streets, multipurpose dams, and other similar improvements have a predictable economic life. Aside from this characteristic, they may be treated for conservation purposes in much the same way as soil resources. Their productivity over any given time period can be adversely affected by abuse or destructive action. Yet with good management and the timely application of an appropriate flow of inputs for repairs and other improvements, their long-run productivity can be definitely enhanced.

Use of Interest Rates in Conservation Decisions

Conservation decisions call for deliberate choices between the present and future use of resources. In this decision making process, operators weigh the benefits expected from the holding of resources during some given planning period against the costs associated with their holding.

On the benefit side, the operator considers the expected value of his resource at the end of the time period for which he is willing to plan, together with the value of any expected flow of land rents he may secure from his resource during this period. His cost calculations in turn include

[4] Arthur C. Bunce, *The Economics of Soil Conservation* (Ames: Iowa State College Press, 1945), p. 4. Reprinted by permission from HETEROSIS, edited by John W. Gowen, ©1952 by The Iowa State University Press, Ames, Iowa.

the present value of his resource and any operating, holding, or resource-improvement costs that might arise during the planning period. Strong cases can be made for conservation practices when the expected future values and benefits exceed the present values and expected holding costs. When these expected benefits fall below their costs, conservation can usually be written off as economically impracticable.

This balancing of expected future benefits against present values and expected costs is complicated by the use of interest rates. Property owners and investors normally insist upon some definite rate of return on their investments. By the same token, they usually place a higher value on the present possession or receipt of a given income than on the promise of a comparable income in the future.

Interest-rate considerations have two important effects on conservation decisions. Operators ordinarily plan in terms of the discounted present values of their expected future net benefits, and they may logically charge compound interest on any outlays for conservation practices that they may have to hold for extended periods before they can recoup their investment costs. The choice of the interest rate used in these calculations is a matter of strategic consequence in conservation decisions. As Gray has observed: "The primary problem of conservation . . . is the determination of the proper rate of discount on the future with respect to the utilization of our natural resources."[5]

Under the conditions of perfect competition, private operators use the interest rate prevailing in the current money market in discounting their expected future values and in compounding their cost outlays. All individual operators could thus be expected to use a 5 percent rate if this were the current market rate of interest. They also would shift to a 4 percent rate (more favorable to conservation) or a 6 percent rate (less favorable to conservation) if the going market rate shifted to either of these levels. Large corporations and governments also could be expected to use their going market interest rates—both of which are usually lower and thus more favorable to conservation than the rates available to individual operators.

This assumption of uniform discount and compound interest rates breaks down in practice. Factors such as imperfect competition, lack of perfect knowledge and foresight, different institutional settings, capital rationing, and differences in individual goals contribute to the use of a wide range of interest rates in conservation decisions. Some operators tend to use the going market rates—often with adjustments for the relative certainty or uncertainty of the expected future income—in their calculations. Many others use higher or lower rates. Still others make little or no attempt to identify the specific interest rates they use. Far from making detailed calculations of their probable benefits and costs, these operators

[5] Lewis C. Gray, "The Economic Possibilities of Conservation," *Quarterly Journal of Economics*, Vol. 27, May, 1913, p. 515.

often act on the basis of hunches and subconsciously-determined interest rates, which may be high or low depending upon the operator's inclinations at the particular moment.

The interest rates operators use in their conservation calculations ordinarily depend upon two important factors: (1) the operator's time-preference rate, and (2) the adjustments he makes for uncertainties. Of the two, *time-preference*—the relative weight one gives to the receipt of a given quantity of income or satisfactions at some future date as compared with receipt of the same quantity of income or satisfactions at the present time—is usually more important.[6] Some people place high emphasis on the current use and exploitation of their resources—on a philosophy of "eat, drink, and be merry, for tomorrow we die." Some others go to the opposite extreme in following a miserly policy of setting aside all of their income and resources above that needed for subsistence living to provide for some future rainy day.

Individual time-preference rates vary widely between these two extremes. They vary from person to person, and from day to day in the examples of some operators, depending upon the operator's alternative opportunities, his immediate need for income, his desire to put something aside for his old age or his heirs, the extent to which he is imbued with a conservation or "stewardship of the land" philosophy, and his general feeling of optimism or pessimism at the moment. Individual operators may apply different rates over long as compared with short planning periods and they may use one interest rate in discounting the value of an expected income and quite a different rate in compounding the interest charged on current conservation-cost outlays.

As this discussion indicates, time-preference rates reflect individual differences; and these differences have a considerable effect upon the interest rates operators assume in their conservation decisions. The practical effect of these differences on an operator's basic willingness to carry out conservation practices may be illustrated as in Table 8-1. This

TABLE 8-1.   Present Value of an Income of $1,000 at Varying Numbers of Years in the Future when Discounted at Selected Rates of Interest

Discount interest rate	$1,000 income at end of:			
	30 years	40 years	50 years	80 years
None	$1,000.00	$1,000.00	$1,000.00	$1,000.00
1 per cent	741.92	671.65	608.04	451.12
2 per cent	552.07	452.89	371.53	205.11
3 per cent	411.97	306.56	228.11	93.98
4 per cent	308.32	208.29	140.71	43.38
5 per cent	231.38	142.05	87.20	20.18
6 per cent	174.11	97.22	54.29	9.45

[6] The "rate of individual time preference" may be defined more precisely "as a ratio between the present marginal utility of . . . money in more distant future intervals and the present marginal utility of the same amount of money in intervals nearer the

tabulation indicates the present value of a future income of $1,000 discounted at varying rates of interest. It shows that with a zero discount rate it would be immaterial whether the operator received his income now or 80 years in the future. With a 2 percent rate, however, his prospective income 80 years hence would have a current value of $205.11 and with a 6 percent rate it would have a current value of only $9.45.

Another illustration of this same principle is shown in Figure 8-1. This graph indicates the effects of different compound interest rates on calculations concerning the accumulated future cost of current conservation

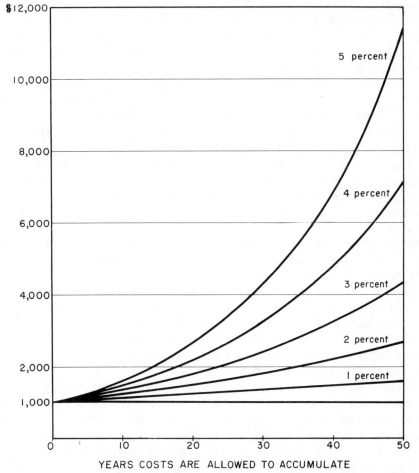

FIGURE 8-1. Illustration of the cumulative effect of using different compound interest rates in computing the cost of a current investment of $1,000 in conservation practices at different numbers of years in the future.

investments. With a zero interest rate, one would consider only the actual cost of the conservation practice. With a 5 percent interest charge compounded annually, the cost of a $1,000 investment at the present time would climb to $11,467 if one had to hold the resource 50 years before he could recoup his costs.

Wise Resource Use over Time

The question of what constitutes conservation and wise resource use over time differs with each type of resource. Conservation of fund resources calls for spreading the use of the relatively fixed supply of these resources over an extended time period. It "involves a reduction of the rate of disappearance or consumption, and a corresponding increase in the unused surplus left at the end of a given period."[7]

A very different situation exists with flow resources. Except for the storage of resources such as water, there is no practical way to save these resources for future use. Good conservation practices call instead for elimination of the economic and social waste that comes with the nonuse of these resources and for their maximum practicable economic use under existing circumstances. The wise use of biological, soil, and man-made resources calls for practices that yield the highest possible net return throughout each operator's planning period while at the same time maintaining or possibly even improving their expected productive capacity.

Important questions arise with each of these types of resources when one tries to determine the optimum rate or timing of resource use. Complications often develop because of the limited duration of the operator's planning period, his choice of interest rates, and his estimates of expected costs and returns. Major problems also stem from the two-stage nature of conservation decisions: (1) the initial choice between developing a resource now or holding it for future development; and (2) the determination now or later of the optimum rate or timing of the use that comes with the development of a resource.

Factors such as high expectations of economic and social gains, high time-reference rates, willingness to assume risks, high resource-holding costs, and uncertainties regarding future supply, demand, and price conditions often favor the early development and use of resources. Other factors such as imperfect knowledge, owner inertia, lack of financial backing, individual supersession costs, high development and processing costs, insufficient market demand for the product, or the expectation of higher future market prices or technological improvements that may reduce production costs can have a contrary effect in causing owners to postpone possible developments.

[7] Erich W. Zimmermann, *World Resources and Industries* (New York: Harper & Brothers, 1933), p. 790.

Fund resources are often conserved or saved (and flow resources are often lost or wasted) simply because the resource owner chooses a policy of nonuse. Some owners follow policies of this sort because of their social outlook—their desire to hold or preserve certain resources for future use. Some hold reserves for their own future business use. Some are specu-*is this* lators who hold resources in the hope that they can realize a significantly *a diff* higher return by postponing their development to a later date. Others hold *speculty* back because they doubt that their contemplated developments will pay off.

A second stage decision concerning the wise use of resources over time must be made when the operator decides to go ahead with the development of his resource. At this point, planning decisions must be made concerning the rate and timing of resource use. These decisions are always geared to the operator's expectations of the future, although they may be based on hunches and fairly indefinite assumptions. When operators spell out their interest rate and expected cost and return assumptions, they can gear their decisions to the probable optimum economic use of their resources over time. The calculation of what constitutes wise use of one's resources over time in these cases can logically be viewed in terms of those decisions and practices that will lead to maximization of the operator's economic returns and satisfactions. This rationale can best be illustrated with examples involving the various classes of land resources.

Flow resources. Operators who visualize current opportunities for the successful and profitable use of flow resources have a definite incentive to proceed with the early development of their plans. Examples include the possible use of oceans and streams for commercial navigation, the development of hydroelectric and solar power facilities, the use of windmills to capture power from the wind, and the development of recreation and resort facilities at sites that boast specific climatic attractions.

The development decisions associated with these situations parallel the resource development decisions described in chapter 7. As long as demand exists for the product or service visualized, and the cost of providing this product or service is expected to fall below its expected selling price, the development is economically feasible. Operators may postpone their developments for a variety of reasons including the prospect that emerging future demands may justify projects of larger scale. Postponement, however, involves the loss of land rents and profits that could otherwise be realized.

A planning model such as that shown in Figure 8-2 can be used to illustrate the nature of these decisions. As long as the continuing flow of expected annual returns exceeds the expected annual costs, early development of the flow resource should be encouraged. Postponement of a promising project for later development results only in a loss of net benefits (land rent and profits) that could otherwise be received.

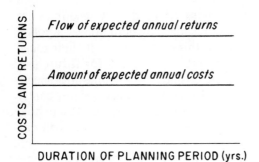

FIGURE 8-2. Relationship of expected annual returns and costs over an investor's planning period with a contemplated development of flow resources.

Conservation and wise use of resources in this instance calls for early development and utilization of the flow resource.

Fund resources. Developments that call for the exploitation, extraction, or mining of fund resources involve a different rationale. The operator who wishes to utilize a deposit of oil, coal, or iron ore, for example, must recognize the fixed and nonreplacable nature of his resource. He frequently lacks information concerning the exact quantity of his deposit as well as technical ability to extract and utilize all of his fund resource. He knows, however, that once the resource is removed from his land that it is no longer there and that the supply will not be replenished.

Once an operator decides to proceed with a mining operation, he may wish that he could remove and sell his entire deposit of fund resource at one time. This, of course, is not possible. Drilling and mining operations require installations and equipment and time is needed for removing the resources. Plans for the early capture of a resource can easily call for the drilling of several oil wells or the opening of several mine shafts and for other high investment costs of questionable economic feasibility. The operator who wants to maximize the present value of his possible future returns must plan for both the optimum scale and timing of his mining operations.

Much of the problem of optimum timing in mining operations centers in the choice of an optimum scale. In determining his optimum size of operations, the operator should seek that scale that will allow him to capture the greatest amount of fund resource that can be recovered at a profit and also the scale that will permit exploitation of the resource in an optimum time period. An operator's range of choices in selecting the scale that will permit maximum recovery of a typical buried deposit of fund resource can be visualized as in Figure 8-3. If the operator has a deposit of oil or mineral ore, he can drill a single oil well or sink a single mine shaft and plan to use these facilities to advantage for a substantial time period. He may find that the addition of one or more oil wells or mine shafts will facilitate the recovery of portions of his resource deposit that cannot be tapped effectively by a single well or shaft. An optimum scale measured in

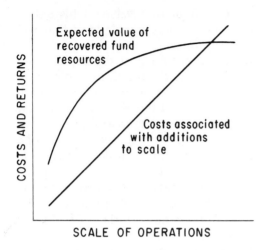

FIGURE 8-3. Relationship of expected value of recovered fund resources to costs associated with scale of operations needed to effect their recovery.

terms of number of oil wells or mining shafts can soon be reached, however, beyond which additional scale will add little if anything to the volume of the resource that is recovered. The addition of more wells, shafts, or other mining exploitation units beyond this optimum can speed the rate of total recovery but will involve less output per input unit together with fewer net returns.[8]

From a conservation point of view, operators should seek that scale level that will permit the highest rate of economic recovery and the least wastage of their fund resource. The operator's ability to attain this goal in practice is usually clouded by lack of knowledge concerning the extent and nature of his resource deposit. Decisions concerning optimum scale also are affected by factors such as government regulations affecting the spacing of oil wells, the relative control or lack of control one enjoys over the pumping of oil or the mining of ore from a given source, and the operator's ability to assemble needed installations, equipment, and work crews.

Choices as to scale of operations also affect conservation in the sense that they usually determine the timing of the operator's mining and resource exploitation practices. Operators with several oil wells, mining shafts, or units of mining equipment can exploit a given deposit of fund resources in far less time than operators with fewer mining units. Rapid exploitation allows the operator to realize the market value of his resource at an earlier date, but this approach entails higher investment and

[8] A general illustration of the diseconomies of excessive scale is suggested by comparative statistics on oil production in 1960. The Middle East had 1,300 oil wells in production in 1960 with an average production of 4,300 barrels per well per day [cf. J. E. Hartshorn, *Politics and World Oil Economics* (London: Faber and Faber, 1962), p. 52] while the United States had 591,158 oil wells in production with an average production of 12 barrels per well per day. (cf. U. S. Department of Interior, *1960 Minerals Yearbook*, Vol. 2, Fuels, p. 390.)

operation costs. To maximize the expected present value of his anticipated future net returns, an operator must choose a scale level that will
permit optimum timing of his mining operations.

The rationale associated with the optimum timing of the exploitation
of a deposit of a fund resource can be illustrated with an example of an
operator who controls a large surface deposit of some fund resource such
as sand, gravel, limestone, or a mineral ore. (Cf. Table 8-2.) Surveys show
that the deposit contains three million tons of the resource and that it can
be mined at an average cost of $4 per ton. The mining operation can be
handled by blasting-mining-loading-and-trucking units, which are capable
of handling 100 tons per day or 30,000 tons annually at an initial
investment cost of $250,000 each. These units have an assumed economic
life of 20 years and limited salvage value if used for shorter periods. The
operation also involves a general overhead investment outlay of $200,000
for an office building and office equipment.

With these assumptions, the operator can choose between a variety of
rates and scales. He can use a single blasting-mining-loading-and-trucking
unit and spread the operations of his firm over a 100-year period. He
might also use 5 units for 20 years of operations, 10 for ten years, 20 for
five years, or 50 for two years. The expected cost of his operations at his
various alternative scales and operation planning periods can be itemized
as in Table 8-2. These calculations show that when costs are limited to
recoupment of investment outlays plus variable operating costs that the
operator will realize his lowest average unit cost per ton (AUC_1 in Figure
8-4) by selecting a scale that will spread his operations out over 20 or
more years. Most operators, however, will allow themselves compound
interest on the amount of their investment outlay for the simple reason
that payments would be made for these funds if they operated with
borrowed money and payments could be received if they invested their
funds in alternative enterprises. Allowance of an interest charge of 6
percent compounded annually raises the average unit costs (AUC_2 in
Figure 8-4) associated with each alternative planning period. The lowest
average unit costs now come with operations scheduled over a 14.3-year
planning period.

The operator in Table 8-2 has a natural inclination to maximize his net
returns. This objective favors his selection of the planning period and scale
of operations that will yield the highest present values that he may
associate with his expected flow of future net returns. Using the cost
assumptions of Table 8-2 and assuming a uniform average unit return
(AUR) or market price of $8 per ton for his resource, he will find that he
can realize his highest average net return per ton ($2.507) by using 7
operations units and planning his mining operators over a 14.3 year
period. This calculation assumes no discounting of the values of his
expected future net returns. If he chooses to discount these returns at a 4
percent rate, his optimum planning period drops back to 9.1 years with 11
operations units. (Cf. Figure 8-4A.) Acceptance of an 8 percent discount
rate favors the use of 13 operations units over a 7.7-year period and use of

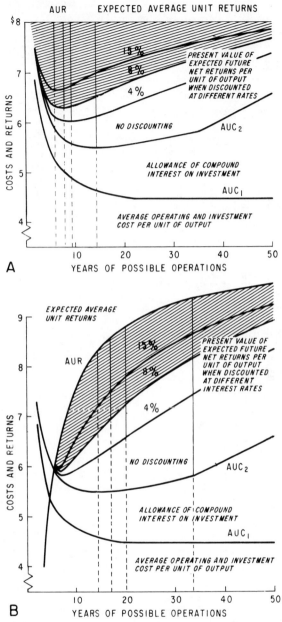

FIGURE 8-4. Use of planning models which assume expected average rates of returns, average costs, and the discounting to their present values of expected average net returns per unit of output for operations scheduled over alternative time periods to indicate optimum duration of extractive production periods.

a 15 percent discount rate favors use of 20 operations units over a 5-year period.

The operator may feel that the assumption of a uniform average unit return is unrealistic and that he can count on higher market prices if he plans to sell his resource gradually over a number of years rather than

TABLE 8-2. Illustration of Planning Model Used in Determining Optimum Timing Period for Exploitation of a Known Deposit of a Fund Resource

Number of blasting-mining-loading-and-trucking operation units used	Planning period (number of years over which mining operations are to be carried out)	Calculation of total and average unit production costs							
		Total operating cost with assumed average of $4 per ton (millions)	Investment in buildings and equipment (millions)	Allowance for salvage value of equipment (thousands)	Total costs (no allowance for interest on investment outlay) (millions)	Average unit cost per ton (no allowance for interest on investment)	Charge for compound interest at 6% on investment outlay (millions)	Total costs with allowance of compound interest on investment (millions)	Average unit cost per ton with allowance of compound interest on investment
1 + 4	100.0	$12.0	$1.45	—	$13.450	$4.483	$70.419	$83.869	$27.956
2 + 3	50.0	12.0	1.45	—	13.450	4.483	6.243	19.693	6.564
3 + 2	33.3	12.0	1.45	—	13.450	4.483	3.954	17.404	5.801
4 + 1	25.0	12.0	1.45	—	13.450	4.483	3.417	16.867	5.622
5	20.0	12.0	1.45	—	13.450	4.483	3.200	16.650	5.550
6	16.7	12.0	1.70	—	13.700	4.567	2.791	16.491	5.497
7	14.3	12.0	1.95	—	13.950	4.650	2.529	16.479	5.493
8	12.5	12.0	2.20	—	14.200	4.733	2.360	16.560	5.520
9	11.1	12.0	2.45	—	14.450	4.817	2.232	16.682	5.561
10	10.0	12.0	2.70	$125.0	14.575	4.858	2.132	16.710	5.570
11	9.1	12.0	2.95	275.0	14.675	4.892	2.061	16.736	5.579
12	8.3	12.0	3.20	333.3	14.867	4.956	2.002	16.869	5.623
13	7.7	12.0	3.45	406.25	15.044	5.015	1.953	16.997	5.666
14	7.1	12.0	3.70	437.5	15.263	5.088	1.911	17.174	5.725
15	6.7	12.0	3.95	535.7	15.414	5.138	1.877	17.292	5.764
16	6.25	12.0	4.20	571.4	15.629	5.219	1.847	17.476	5.825
17	5.90	12.0	4.45	708.3	15.742	5.247	1.820	17.562	5.854
20	5.00	12.0	5.20	833.3	16.367	5.456	1.759	18.125	6.042
25	4.00	12.0	6.45	1,250.0	17.200	5.733	1.693	18.893	6.298
34	3.00	12.0	8.70	2,125.0	18.575	6.192	1.662	20.237	6.746
50	2.00	12.0	12.70	4,166.7	20.533	6.844	1.570	22.103	7.368

Calculation of discounted present value of expected net returns

		Assumption of uniform market price of $8 per ton					Assumption of a sliding scale market price				
		Expected average unit return	Expected net return per ton	Present value of expected net return when discounted at:			Expected average unit return	Expected net return per ton	Present value of expected net return when discounted at:		
				4%	8%	15%			4%	8%	15%
1 + 4	100	$8.00	—	—	—	—	$10.000	—	—	—	—
2 + 3	50	8.00	$1.436	$.617	$.351	$.191	9.667	$3.103	$1.333	$.759	$.413
3 + 2	33.3	8.00	2.199	1.203	.761	.436	9.377	3.576	1.957	1.238	.709
4 + 1	25	8.00	2.378	1.486	1.015	.614	9.096	3.474	2.171	1.483	.898
5	20	8.00	2.450	1.665	1.203	.767	8.823	3.273	2.224	1.607	1.054
6	16.7	8.00	2.503	1.802	1.357	.904	8.558	3.061	2.204	1.660	1.105
7	14.3	8.00	2.507	1.882	1.463	1.011	8.301	2.808	2.108	1.639	1.133
8	12.5	8.00	2.480	1.921	1.533	1.093	8.052	2.532	1.961	1.565	1.116
9	11.1	8.00	2.439	1.939	1.576	1.154	7.810	2.249	1.788	1.455	1.064
10	10	8.00	2.430	1.971	1.631	1.220	7.576	2.006	1.627	1.346	1.007
11	9.1	8.00	2.421	1.997	1.676	1.278	7.349	1.770	1.460	1.225	.934
12	8.3	8.00	2.377	1.976	1.689	1.309	7.129	1.506	1.252	1.070	.830
13	7.7	8.00	2.334	1.974	1.696	1.334	6.915	1.249	1.058	.908	.714
14	7.1	8.00	2.275	1.958	1.685	1.342	6.708	.983	.846	.728	.580
15	6.7	8.00	2.236	1.937	1.684	1.350	6.507	.743	.643	.560	.451
16	6.25	8.00	2.175	1.892	1.663	1.353	6.312	.487	.424	.372	.303
17	5.9	8.00	2.146	1.866	1.659	1.363	6.123	.269	.234	.208	.171
20	5	8.00	1.958	1.743	1.564	1.313	5.607	—	—	—	—
25	4	8.00	1.702	1.545	1.409	1.215	4.904	—			
34	3	8.00	1.254	1.160	1.077	.954	3.632	—			
50	2	8.00	.632	.596	.564	.514	2.285	—			

Example assumes a known surface deposit of 3 million tons of a fund resource that can be mined at an average variable operating cost of $4 per ton. Overhead costs include an investment of $200,000 in office buildings and facilities plus an investment outlay of $250,000 for each blasting-mining-loading-and-trucking operation unit. Each operations unit is capable of handling 30,000 tons of ore annually, has an economic life of 20 years, and has limited salvage value if used for shorter periods. Salvage values are calculated at one-half of the initial value in the second year, one-third in the third year, and no value thereafter. No salvage value is assumed for the office headquarters or facilities. Compound interest at 6 percent is allowed on the operator's investment outlay for buildings and equipment. Discounted present values are computed for the expected net returns associated with each possible planning period for two assumed price levels: (1) a uniform price of $8 a ton, and (2) a sliding scale of prices, which assumes a price of $10 a ton if only 30,000 tons of ore are marketed annually with a three percent reduction in market price for each additional 30,000 tons marketed annually.

within a short time period. With an assumption of a sliding scale of market prices starting at $10 per ton if only 30,000 tons are marketed annually and dropping three percent for each additional 30,000 tons offered for sale (Table 8-2 and Figure 8-4B), the operator will find that his highest net return per unit comes when he plans his operations over a 33.3-year period. Application of a 4 percent discount rate favors shortening the planning period to 20 years. Use of the 8 and 15 percent discount rates favor shortening the planning periods to 16.7 and 14.3 years, respectively.

Operators seldom enjoy as much knowledge concerning the extent and value of their fund resources as that assumed in Table 8-2. Higher compound interest and discount rates are often used to compensate for the risks and uncertainties associated with lack of knowledge and foresight concerning the extent and quality of deposits, the ease or difficulties of capture, and future costs and prices. Regardless of the interest rates used, however, a rationale similar to that used in the above example should govern economic decisions concerning the optimum timing of fund resource mining operations. As in the example, the charging of compound interest on investment outlays and the discounting of expected future returns to obtain measures of the present values of these returns tend to favor shorter operation planning periods than would be the case if no interest rate assumptions were used. High operator time-preference rates prompt the use of high compound interest and discount rates and lead logically to a shortening of the time periods over which mining operations can be expected to occur.

Planning models such as those suggested by Figure 8-4 can provide helpful guides for operator decisions. They are never more accurate, however, than the assumptions upon which they are based. Adjustments must be made in the models whenever new or better planning data become available. The successful operator must always be ready to adjust to changing conditions. If market prices increase or if his operating costs decrease, he may extend his production period and attempt to recover oil, coal, or ore deposits that would appear uneconomic under less favorable conditions. On the other hand, if his prices drop or his costs increase, he may find it necessary to cut back or even abandon his production plans.

Biological resources. The conservation and wise use of biological resources calls for managerial practices that maximize the operator's net returns over time while at the same time maintaining or improving the future productive capacity of his resource. These practices vary widely according to the resource. Some operators deal with food crops that grow and mature in the space of a few months. Others deal with resources (grass, forage crops, livestock, fish, and wildlife) with life cycles running into several months or years; and some work with resources such as human beings and forests that have productive life periods covering several decades.

Some operators are mostly concerned with the products and services they can secure from resources such as bees, milk animals, draft animals, orchards, and scenery. Others deal with resources (crops, forests, fisheries, and meat animals) that involve the eventual harvesting and use of the resource itself. Some use managerial practices that call for complete harvesting of the resources found in given areas (field crops and rotation cutting of forests). Others maintain herds and forests with animals and trees of mixed ages from which selected animals are sold or trees are cut while other young stock is always coming along.

By and large, few questions are usually raised concerning the conservation of farm crops or animals. Individual operators are free to expand or contract the scale of their operations. Each operator is expected to follow the course that will help him maximize his returns, and each is expected to either grow and save his own seed and breeding stock or buy these resources from others.

More emphasis is given in conservation discussions to the practices used to maintain and improve biological resources such as forests, grass lands, fish, wildlife, and natural scenery. History shows that the operators of the "robber baron" era often tended to view these resources as an inexhaustible fund that they could exploit at will without need for practices to secure their regeneration and continued flow. This situation has changed. While there are still some operators who would like to operate on a "cut-out-and-get-out" basis, most forest owners, ranchers, and fishery operators are in business to stay. They can no longer exploit their present resource holdings and then move on to greener pastures. Most of them accept voluntary or public restrictions on their forest cutting, grazing, or fishing practices because they recognize the need for insuring the continued flow and growth of their basic resource.

A major economic consideration with the production of biological resources centers in the optimum timing of the harvest operations. Operators have little choice concerning the best time to harvest some biological resources. A wheat crop, for example, must be harvested when it is mature and ripe. As Figure 8-5 indicates, the crop has little value before the grain is ready for harvest; it can be harvested to advantage during a limited time period only; and, if it is not harvested during this

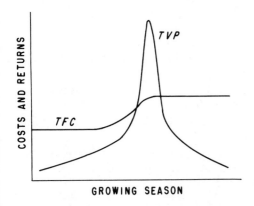

FIGURE 8-5. Typical interrelationship of total value of product and total factor costs associated with timing of harvest of a crop such as wheat.

period, most of its commercial value is lost. Fruit crops such as peaches and strawberries also must be harvested during the brief period when they can be picked and marketed before they are overripe.

Operators have a broader range of choices in their harvesting decisions with biological resources such as meat animals and forests. These resources can be harvested early or they can be stored "on the hoof" or "on the stump" for later use. Thus a rancher may choose between the sale of his animals as veal, baby beef, or mature beef and the forester between the holding of his product for sale as Christmas trees, posts, pulp logs, or sawlogs. Both operators will usually find it to their economic advantage to harvest their products before they reach a point of maximum growth and before they suffer from decadence or decay.

The problem of optimum timing is a matter of economic arithmetic and may be illustrated with a planning model for a forestry enterprise such as that depicted in Figure 8-6. It is assumed in this example that the operator starts with a tract of essentially bare land that he acquires and afforests at an initial investment cost of $100,000. His annual costs for taxes and management are $2,000. The forest has little commercial value for the first 20 years. Thereafter, its commercial value increases rapidly until it reaches its highest economic value of $855,000 in its 70th year. This expected increase in total value product is shown by the *TVP* curve in Figure 8-6.

If the operator limits his calculations to actual cash outlays for his initial investment plus his annual management and tax costs, he will visualize his costs as shown by the total factor cost curve *TFC*. He will then find that he can maximize his net returns—secure the highest possible spread between his *TVP* and *TFC* curves—by limiting his forest holding plan to 65 years. A decision to discount the value of his expected future returns back to the present calls for changes in his calculations. His expected net returns have discounted present values for the different years for which he can hold his forest equivalent to those shown in the shaded portion of the diagram when discounted at three percent. Lower discount rates would produce higher present values and higher discount rates lower values.[9] With the three percent discount rate, he can maximize the present value of his net returns by limiting his planned production period to 37 years.

The operator in this example can logically insist that compound interest be charged on the initial investment and annual charges that he must carry until his forest resource is ready for harvesting. TFC_2 in Figure 8-6B shows the effect of charging a two percent compound interest rate on these costs over the life of the project. With the addition of these costs, the optimum operating planning is 45 years when there is no discounting

---

[9] Low discount and compound interest rates are used in Figure 8-6 for the obvious reason that higher rates would so reduce the discounted value of the net returns that they would be hardly visible in the two diagrams.

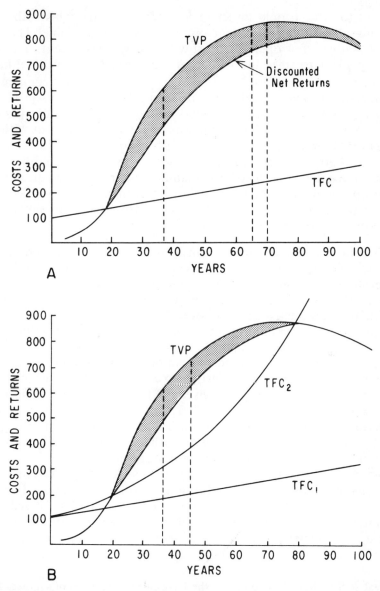

FIGURE 8-6. Use of planning models which assume rates of total value appreciation, total cost outlays, and discounting of expected future net returns to their current values to determine the optimum timing of a harvest of a forest of uniform age.

of net returns. When the net returns are discounted at three percent as shown by the shaded portion of Figure 8-6B, the optimum planning period drops back to 36 years.

With situations such as that assumed in Figure 8-6, questions can be raised as to why people invest in long-term forestry when other more promising alternative investment opportunities are available. The simple truth is that very few operators start with isolated investments in raw land that they plant to trees and hold over long periods for eventual harvest. When this happens, operators often receive much of their compensation from recreation and the pleasure of seeing land shift into production. Commercial operators ordinarily work either with forests of mixed ages where growth and harvesting take place alongside each other or with series of tracts with even-aged stands that can be harvested in a long-term cutting cycle. Carrying charges in both cases are usually covered by current receipts. Except for the need for maintaining growing stands and determining optimum times of harvest, the profit maximization objectives of the operators in these cases calls for conservation decisions similar to the flow-resource case described in Figure 8-2.

Soil resources. With proper management, most soil resources can be used and still retain their productive capacity over long periods of time. [10] The problem of conserving these resources is thus one of accepting practices that permit their effective use while at the same time safeguarding their productive capacity over time.

There is little unanimity concerning the precise meaning of soil conservation. In a strict economic sense, one might distinguish between those practices that can be used to maintain the productive capacity of a soil resource and those that go further to develop, build up, or improve its productivity. When emphasis is given to the maintenance concept, soil conservation may be defined as "prevention of diminution in future production on a given area of soil from a given input of labor or capital with the techniques of production otherwise constant" or as "the retention of a given production function over time."[11]

Most soil conservationists include provisions for the development and improvement of soils in their definitions of soil conservation. For them, soil conservation is "a system of using and managing land based on the capabilities of the land itself, involving the application of the best measures or practices known, and designed to result in the greatest

---

[10] Peat soils such as those found in the Lake Okeechobee area of southern Florida represent a definite exception. These soils deteriorate at a predictable rate once they are drained or opened up for use. The wise use of these soils calls for (1) measures to keep peat-soil areas from being drained until their owners are ready to put them to productive use, (2) development of techniques for extending the productive life of these soils and for slowing down their rate of deterioration, and (3) adoption of management practices that will bring the maximum use of these soils (up to the point at which the operator can secure equi-marginal returns from his inputs) during their productive life once they have been brought into use.

[11] Earl O. Heady, *Economics of Agricultural Production and Resource Use* (Englewood Cliffs, N.J.: Prentice-Hall, Inc., 1952), pp. 781-82.

production without damage to the land."[12] Or as the Soil Conservation Service has defined it:

> Soil conservation is the application on the land of all necessary measures in proper combinations to build up and maintain soil productivity for efficient, abundant production on a sustained basis. Soil conservation, therefore, means proper land uses, protecting the land against all forms of soil deterioration, rebuilding eroded and depleted soils, conserving moisture for plant use, proper agricultural drainage and irrigation where needed, and other measures which contribute to maximum practical yields and farm and ranch incomes—all at the same time.[13]

With this broad definition, soil conservation is mostly a matter of good land use and management. Operators can usually choose between a variety of managerial practices. In so doing, they ordinarily try to maximize their returns and satisfactions both in the present and during whatever number of years they consider in their planning period. Insofar as they understand the consequences of their actions, they can be expected to consider the costs and returns expected with different managerial practices, the probable distribution of these costs and returns throughout their expected operating periods, and the effects of these practices on the market value of their soil-resource base.

Two major managerial problems are involved in the conservation and wise use of soil resources. Operators must show care in selecting and timing their production practices so as to secure the maximum practicable return. They also must show comparable care in choosing and timing the conservation investments and practices they use to build up and maintain the productivity of their soils.

Whether or not an operator will accept and use soil conservation practices depends upon his understanding of the soil conservation problem, the urgency of his conservation needs, his calculations regarding the effects of the proposed conservation program on his income expectations both now and in the foreseeable future, his capital position, his time-preference rate, and his general willingness to accept a conservation philosophy. Some of the major problems that arise in this regard are illustrated by the four problem situations depicted in Figure 8-7.

Figure 8-7A involves a situation in which the operator can expect a gradual but steady decrease in the income and production he receives from his soil resources. He can remedy this situation and stabilize his expected crop yields and income by adopting conservation practices. Possible examples include the application of lime and fertilizer to his soil

[12] William R. Van Dersal, "What Do You Mean: 'Soil Conservation,'" *Journal of Soil and Water Conservation*, Vol. 8, September, 1953, p. 227.

[13] From a statement prepared by Robert M. Salter, Chief of the Soil Conservation Service for *USDA,* a house organ of the U.S. Department of Agriculture. *USDA,* December 17, 1952, p. 1.

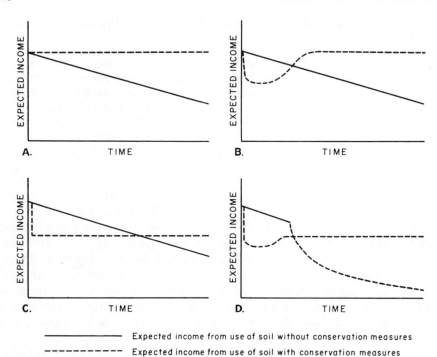

Expected income from use of soil without conservation measures
--------- Expected income from use of soil with conservation measures

FIGURE 8-7. Use of projection curves showing incomes expected from the use of soil resources over a period of years with and without conservation measures to illustrate four type-situations frequently encountered in conservation decisions.

and the adoption of strip-cropping or summer-fallowing practices. Under these conditions, those operators who understand their opportunities will shift to conservation practices with little prompting while educational programs may be needed to acquaint the uninformed of their opportunities. Both groups can begin to maximize the returns from their conservation investments almost immediately; and any reluctance to accept these practices may be regarded as a mark of poor or uninformed management.

A more perplexing situation arises with 8-7B. In this example, the operator who would use conservation practices to stabilize the income-producing capacity of his soil must first accept a period of reduced income while he invests in conservation practices or while he changes his cropping system to emphasize the use of soil-building rather than soil-depleting crops. He may find, for example, that he must sacrifice income from cash crops while he uses part of his land to grow crops that he plows under as green manure. He may reduce the income he has available for other purposes by spending several hundred dollars to build terraces and check dams or to provide a better drainage system for his land. He also may find that he must shift from primary dependence on row crops to the use of a forage crop and pasture program—a shift that often brings a period of reduced income while he builds up a livestock enterprise capable of replacing the income he could have secured from the sale of cash crops.

The big question here centers on the operator's willingness to forego income in the immediate future so as to maximize his expected returns over a longer future time period. The case for adopting conservation practices is not as clear-cut in 8-7B as in 8-7A. The line of action the operator will choose to follow in this case reflects the duration of his planning period, his current need for income, and his ability to get credit to tide him over until his expected period of higher returns.

An additional complication is introduced in 8-7C. This example assumes a situation in which the operator has small prospects for restoring the productive capacity of his soil to a level that will maintain his present income. Instead, he finds that the long-run sustained use of his soil calls for a permanent shift from soil-depleting crops to forage crops, grass, or trees. By delaying his shift to these uses, the operator can expect a higher annual return from continuation of his present use pattern up to the year when his alternative production curve would intersect his currently decreasing production curve. But by waiting, he would also suffer a continued loss of top soil from sheet erosion, which would further reduce the productive capacity of his soil resources for lower alternative uses.

The operator in 8-7C may be reluctant to shift to his lower income-producing alternative for undestandable reasons. His willingness to shift, however, might be heightened if he faced a situation such as that pictured in 8-7D. The operator in this example is conscious of the declining productivity of his soil and also of the fact that sheet erosion has now taken all but a few inches of his topsoil or that gullies are now threatening to ruin his most productive fields. He recognizes that he is fast approaching a *critical danger point* after which his soil resources will be almost worthless for their present use. With this prospect, he may be quite willing to employ conservation measures (terraces, check dams, sodded waterways) and shift his land to a lower use because this may be the only practicable way of keeping his land in use.

These four examples illustrate some of the circumstances that complicate soil conservation decisions. No emphasis has been given thus far in this discussion to the effect the operator's discounting of net returns may have on his willingness to accept soil conservation practices. This is not an important problem with the example presented in Figure 8-7A because the operator in that example can expect an early return from his conservation investments. It becomes a problem, however, whenever the operator must plan to forego some of his immediate expected income while he invests in conservation measures that promise to increase his total income expectations during a later time period.

This problem may be illustrated by the example pictured in Figure 8-8. This example assumes a farm with a cropping program that now produces a net return of $20,000 but that is associated with soil losses that will

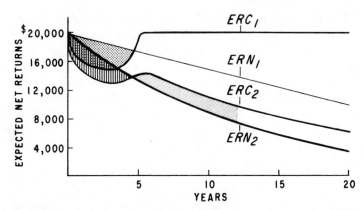

FIGURE 8-8. Illustration of the effect the discounting of the expected net returns to be secured from the use of a soil conservation program as compared with continued use of an exploitive soil use program may have on an operator's decisions concerning the possible adoption of soil conservation practices.

reduce the expected annual net return (ERC_1) by a predicted $500 each year over the next 20 years. The operator understands that he can stabilize his net returns at their approximate present level (ERC_1) if he is willing to forego current income and make conservation investments with a value of $20,000 over the next five years. If the operator makes no attempt to discount his expected future net returns, the prospect of shifting to the conservation program will appeal to him as being economically feasible if his planning horizon extends five or more years beyond the fifth year or for a long enough time period for him to recoup his $20,000 investment.

If the operator reacts as most investors do, he will place a somewhat higher value on the $20,000 he is asked to forego in the next five years than upon the $20,000 of added net returns he can expect in the second five years. Time preference considerations will cause him to discount his expected net returns both with conservation and no conservation (ERC_2 and ERN_2) and may cause him to use a higher discount rate with the conservation investment than with the no investment alternative.

As ERC_2 and ERN_2 show, the discounting of the expected returns with the conservation investment at six percent and the net returns associated with the no conservation option at five percent complicates the conservation planning decision. The operator must now have a planning horizon that extends at least seven years beyond the fifth year if he is to visualize a present value of future net returns adequate to compensate for the present value of his investment outlay for the conservation program. Should he borrow money to finance his conservation investment or to replace the income foregone during the first five years, the cost of carrying his loan could be charged as an additional cost against his expected returns with conservation and would further prolong his break-even period.

Man-made resources.   Most man-made land resources such as houses, office buildings, farm service buildings, highways, and multipurpose dams have economic lives of some predictable length. Under some circumstances, operators find it wise policy to exploit these resources. This may be the situation when the site occupied by a building has ripened for some higher use. In this event, the owner may try to get all the use he can from his resource during a relatively short time period with a minimum outlay for maintenance and operating costs so he can shift to his higher use with a minimum of loss from the writing off of his present investment. Cases of this type are more the exception than the rule. Far from wanting to exploit or abuse their properties, most owners find it advisable to carry on property-use programs designed to prolong the economic life of their structures.

The conservation of man-made resources is concerned for the most part with the use of techniques designed to extend the economic usefulness and life of these developments. The rationale involved in the conservation of this type of resource usually parallels that pictured in Figure 8-7A, B, and D for soil conservation projects. Changes in current use practices can sometimes stabilize development values. More often, some current income must be foregone as funds are invested in renovation, remodeling, or improvement programs. A conservation program with buildings calls for their continuous upkeep and repair. It may also require some occasional remodeling or adding of new features if these changes are needed to forestall obsolescence. Highways can be conserved through proper use, the replacement or repair of defective areas, and improvements where needed. Conservation of multipurpose dams calls for continuous upkeep, measures to slow down or prevent reservoir silting, and the replacement of worn-out or outmoded installations. Whether these conservation measures also qualify as wise resource use depends upon the extent to which the expected returns or satisfactions exceed their cost.

A special problem in the conservation of man-made resources arises with the conservation of urban neighborhoods. The desirability of a neighborhood as a place to live usually depends upon the separate actions of its various residents. By exploiting or abusing their properties, a minority of the families living in a neighborhood can often lessen its desirability and create the cancerous conditions that lead to area blight. Group action is often needed to prevent developments of this type. This action takes two principal forms: (1) joint effort of the neighborhood property owners to maintain or improve the appearance, utility, and value of their properties, and (2) use of area improvement or redevelopment programs to improve the physical layout and environment of the neighborhood area.

SOME CONSERVATION ISSUES

Consideration has been given in the above discussion to some of the more important economic and social factors that affect conservation decisions. In supplementing this discussion, emphasis is given here to three additional aspects of the land-resource conservation problem. These include (1) the question of whether conservation pays, (2) the nature of society's interests in conservation, and (3) the problem of overcoming obstacles to conservation.

Does Conservation Pay?

One of the first questions the practical businessman asks concerning conservation is: Does it pay? As an average citizen, he may approve of conservation in principle and endorse its general objectives. As a businessman, he is profit-conscious; and he has little interest in investing in conservation measures or foregoing present income for conservation reasons unless he is reasonably convinced that these investments will pay off.

Experience shows that conservation measures can and frequently do pay off, particularly when they represent wise resource use over time. There also are frequent instances in which a policy of safeguarding or saving land resources is not profitable to individual operators and may not even be desirable from the standpoint of society. Whether or not a conservation program will prove profitable depends primarily on the costs of the program, the volume of expected benefits, the time period that will elapse before these benefits can be realized, and the discount rate used in their present valuation. Beyond these factors, the question of whether conservation really pays depends upon a miscellaneous group of factors. Important among these are (1) the duration of the operator's planning period, (2) the investment and disinvestment aspects of the conservation plan, (3) the operator's ability to choose between alternative conservation measures, and (4) the over-all impact of the program on the conservation of other resources.

Operator's planning period. Historical and statistical studies often emphasize the *ex post* or already accomplished aspects of conservation and nonconservation programs. In practice, conservation decisions must be *ex ante* and forward-looking.[14] They are made in advance or at the time of resource use, and almost always assume some expected planning period. They involve actions and uses that are expected to take place in time periods that may range from a few hours to many decades in length.

When an operator decides to carry on or not carry on a conservation

[14]Cf. Wantrup, *op. cit.,* pp. 30-33, 54.

program, he commits himself, at least temporarily, to a given line of action. His decision is not necessarily binding for all time. He is usually free to adjust his program to changing conditions. A forest owner who plans to hold his resource for 25 years, for example, can amend his plan to harvest it in 15 years or in 35 years if he so desires. But his program must usually be geared to a plan of operations that appears feasible within the time interval for which he is willing to plan. If his planning horizon is short, he will often use the short-run nature of his calculations to justify the early cutting of his forest, the mining of his soil, or other types of resource exploitation.

The relationship between an operator's decisions regarding conservation and the duration of his planning period may be illustrated by the example of a soil conservation program that promises to pay off in eight years. An operator in this instance may be willing to adopt conservation measures if his planning period covers eight or more years of continuous operations or if he feels that he can operate his land until near the end of this period and then sell it for a sum sufficient to more than compensate him for his conservation investments. His attitude may be much different, however, if his planning period is limited by a one-year lease, if he has a year-to-year leasing arrangement with no provision for compensation for unexhausted improvements, if he plans to move to another community within five years, or if other factors make him unable or unwilling to plan ahead for as much as eight years of continuous operations.

As this example indicates, the question of whether conservation pays depends in many instances upon the operator's ability or willingness to use a long enough time period in his calculations to permit recoupment of his conservation costs. Wise resource use over time calls for planning horizons of sufficient duration to permit resource harvesting and use programs that will return a maximum of economic and social net returns. Operations involving shorter planning periods can be both exploitive and wasteful in the sense that they may favor either the underuse or overuse of resources.

Planning periods are frequently influenced by factors other than the operator's tenure status or his willingness to plan ahead. Operators with long lives ahead of them sometimes have short planning periods simply because their present scale or pattern of operations calls for a rapid rate of resource use. A mine owner, for example, may find that he could have maximized his return over time from a given coal or ore deposit if he had operated on a smaller scale. Once he has sunk his mine shaft and purchased his mining equipment, however, he finds it best to continue with his present scale of operations. A forest owner with a substantial investment in a large sawmill may find it unprofitable to shift to an otherwise desirable sustained-yield production program if this adjustment makes it impossible for him to operate his present mill on an efficient basis. In similar fashion, a farmer with a large inventory of relatively new equipment may decide to continue his exploitive soil-use program rather than write off part of the value of his machinery investment.

Investment and disinvestment considerations. The businessman who practices conservation is not interested in simply saving or storing resources for some vague future use. He expects his investments to pay off within his planning period. Thus if he postpones his mining or oil drilling operations or if he pumps his oil at a conservative rate, he expects a positive economic return for his conservation efforts. This return may come in the form of higher prices, a larger quantity of product taken, or both. The forest owner, hunter, or fisherman who postpones the harvesting or taking of his resource expects larger and possibly more trees, animals, or fish in the future. The farmer who invests in soil-building practices expects to build up a reserve of fertility that he can use and replace gradually over time or that he might draw upon in much the same way as a bank account when he needs additional capital. Building owners invest in structures and improvements with the idea that they can gradually reap the full benefit of their investments.

Wise use with most land resources—particularly those with characteristics of both fund and flow resources—involves a continual process of investments and disinvestments. During periods of peace and plenty, we often use the soil-bank principle to invest in soil improvements, enlarge and improve our forests, and increase our inventory of buildings and improvements. Under wartime and emergency conditions, this process can be reversed as emphasis is placed on increasing food production, larger timber harvests, and the restriction of private construction activities.

Important conservation considerations are involved in the timing of operator investments and disinvestments. Ordinarily, it is assumed that the operator should make a series of investments in conservation practices before he can disinvest. In practice, however, operators often find it both economically and socially expedient to capitalize on the investments made by nature or by previous operators. Individuals thus can use disinvestments at times to secure needed capital for desired improvements. Nations, such as the United States during the 1800s, can also use widespread resource disinvestment policies to provide the capital and resources needed for economic growth.

The American frontiersmen started with the accumulated natural-resource investments of many centuries. In developing and exploiting these resources, they tended to follow a disinvestment policy. This policy had its regrettable aspects. All things considered, however, it was desirable from the standpoint of both the average individual operator and the society of his day. A disinvestment policy was favored because it provided the quickest means operators could use to maximize their individual returns and because it facilitated the economic development of the frontier and the nation.

Conservation investment policies were scorned on the frontier largely because the plentiful nature and low monetary value of the available forest, wildlife, and soil resources made conservation practices unprofitable. Once these conditions changed—as soon as it became obvious that the supply of these resources was definitely limited relative to the potential demand for them—the American people became conservation-conscious. Conservation policies were then developed to protect and safeguard our oil, mineral, forest, wildlife, and soil resources. But exclusive emphasis was not given to the idea of saving these resources for future generations. A reasonable amount of disinvestment is expected every year; and disinvestments somewhat in excess of the amounts justified by current investments are expected during wartime and emergency periods.

This concept also applies with private conservation investments. Some operators carry on forestry or soil-improvement practices with the idea of maintaining a continuous level of future productivity. Some plan to lay aside a reserve of productivity that they can draw upon in periods of unusual income need. Others—particularly those operators with a high debt load and a real need for additional operating capital—borrow from their resources with the intent of repaying their loans with future conservation investments. This disinvestment practice can result in exploitation in the short run. Over time, however, it can represent a good management practice if the operator follows through with his planned reinvestment program. This situation exists because a certain amount of resource disinvestment is permissible and may be actually desirable if the operator uses it to provide himself with additional operating capital, which he uses to improve his over-all position as an operator.

Choices between alternative conservation programs. Another important factor affecting operator attitudes and decisions concerning the profitability of conservation centers in the operator's ability to choose a conservation program that meets his particular needs or inclinations. In this respect, operators are seldom faced with the need for choosing between conservation and no conservation. They can usually choose from a variety of practices, some of which are more exploitive than others. A mine owner, for example, can take only the richest or most accessible ores, discard the less desirable ore brought to the surface along with his slag, and abandon his mine as soon as it begins to play out. But he may also follow a more conservational policy by stockpiling his less desirable ore for possible future use or by keeping his mine open and available for use when a change in demand so warrants.

Some of the best examples of conservation alternatives apply to forestry and the use of soil resources. A forest owner may follow an inactive management program under which he leaves the growth of his forest entirely to nature; or he may use various combinations of management practices ranging from preoccupation with fire-control and disease-prevention measures to an intensive management program, which also involves tree planting, selective thinning, and other comparable measures. He can choose between rotation clear-cutting and a sustained-yield program in which he occasionally cuts selected trees but always leaves a good stand of young trees for future growth. He may cut most of his stand but leave a few trees to reseed the area; or he may plan to clear-cut his forest and then either reseed it or regenerate it by transplanting young seedlings.

Farmers also choose between a variety of goals and practices when they decide on conservation measures. They decide in a general way as to whether they want a program that will build up their soil, merely maintain it at its present productive level, or permit some acceptable amount of soil depletion or erosion. Once this decision is made, they can usually decide between alternative means for achieving the goal they have in mind.

This range of choices is illustrated by the indifference curves shown in Figure 8-9.[15] Three goals are assumed: (1) a farming program that will build up the soil and result in an annual loss of only two tons of top soil per acre, (2) a program that will result in an annual loss of four tons of

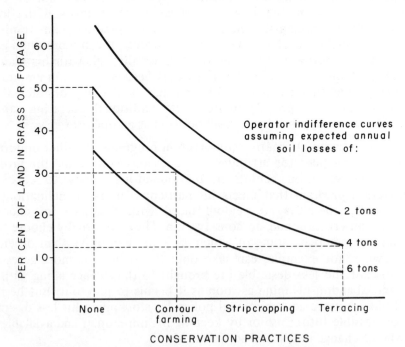

FIGURE 8-9. Use of indifference curves to illustrate the range of choices between alternative management programs available to individual operators.

[15] This example is suggested by data assembled by William H. Heneberry and Elmer L. Sauer in a study of net returns from alternative soil conservation practices on two types of soil found in Illinois.

soil per acre—the maximum loss consistent with the goal of maintaining yields at their current level with present technology, and (3) a program that will lead to an annual loss of six tons of soil per acre. It is further assumed that attainment of each of these goals calls for a crop rotation program that will put part of the farmer's land in grass or forage crops and require some combination of conservation practices on his remaining cropland.

If the operator in this example can identify his soil-conservation goals and has specific knowledge concerning the effects of his alternative practices on the productivity of his soils, he can then choose between the possible combinations found along his two-ton, four-ton, or six-ton indifference curves. For example, he may attain his four-ton goal by using a crop rotation that puts 50 percent of his land in grass or forage crops and that calls for no other conservation practices, or by using a rotation that puts 30 percent of his land in grass or forage crops and requires his use of contour-farming measures on the remaining land, or by using a rotation that puts 12 percent of his land in grass and forage crops and requires contour-farming, strip-cropping, and terracing practices on his remaining land.

As this example suggests, the operator with several conservation alternatives can often find some programs that appeal more to him and that have greater prospects of paying off under his operating conditions than others. With the above example, an operator living in a cash-grain area and another operator living in a dairy region (assuming comparable indifference curves) might each work out a profitable conservation program. A smaller range of choices may reduce or even eliminate each operator's opportunity to work out a profitable conservation program.

Effects on other resources. The question of whether conservation practices really pay cannot be answered in an ultimate sense until consideration is given to the impact of these practices on other resources. Operators frequently find it practicable to substitute one type of resource for another in their production programs. These adjustments normally result in the conservation or reduced use of the displaced factor. The overall effect of this substitution also involves its impact on the supply of the new factor. Substitution of one scarce resource for another may save the operator money or lead to higher production or a better product and thus make substitution economically desirable. It may also contribute, however, to depletion of the supply of the new factor and thus have a negative or neutral over-all effect.

Whether resource substitution complicates or simplifies the conservation problem depends upon the circumstances and one's tendency to view conservation in physical or economic terms. Physical conservation calls for limiting the use of exhaustible and nonrenewable resources, for the substitution of flow resources for fund resources. This practice is often unprofitable in the short run. Individual operators seldom substitute resources for each other unless they can save money or reap a higher benefit. Quite the opposite, they frequently substitute fund resources for flow resources—even though this process leads to physical depletion—if they find it pays.

Numerous examples may be cited to illustrate the frequent tendency of accepted business practices to lead to physical-resource depletion. The American frontiersman substituted land resources for capital and labor in his production combinations because he had a plentiful supply of land resources while his supplies of capital and labor were scarce. Steam turbines (using coal or mineral fuels) are used in many areas to produce electric power because they provide a more efficient and less expensive source of power than hydroelectric plants. Natural gas and oil are substituted for coal in more and more heating systems even though they involve resources that are considered more limited in supply. Commercial fertilizers are used on many farms as a partial substitute for the fertility that might otherwise be gained or retained by soil-building practices. Gasoline-powered automobiles and tractors have replaced the hay-and-oats-fed horse as our principal source of transportation power.

As these examples suggest, our system of price allocation often contributes to the physical depletion of some types of resources. A policy of physical conservation is practicable in our economic system only when the costs and values associated with different resources are such that operators find it profitable to substitute renewable or plentiful resources for resources that are either nonrenewable or in scarce supply. As matters stand, we tend to use those resources that promise the highest economic return. With continued use, the prices of the more critical of these resources can be expected to rise. This will favor more intensive mining or production practices and the treatment of these resources as a limiting factor in production. It will also prompt a search for additional substitutes—a process that must eventually lead to the increased development and use of renewable and reusable resources.

Society's Interest in Conservation

Mention is frequently made in conservation discussions of differences between the interests that individuals and society have in conservation. Individuals are usually assumed to have high time-preference rates and short planning periods. Society, on the other hand, is supposed to use a longer planning period and use a lower discount rate because of its interest in the welfare of future generations and its ability to borrow money at a lower interest rate.

A realistic view of this supposed dichotomy of interests shows that the interests of society are not necessarily contrary to those of individual operators. Society is made up of individuals: and its interests necessarily reflect those of its members. The real division comes between each individual's desire to maximize his personal satisfactions and his desire to stress his social and community interests. Businessmen emphasize personal and firm goals and often find that they must pit their personal interests against those of the other operators who make up their economic order. One's social goals, in contrast, are best expressed through collective action—through public opinion, the joint action of individuals in groups and organizations, and the action of the state.

Rational individuals are always concerned with their personal survival and the returns and satisfactions they can secure for themselves and their families. At the same time, they are also interested to a greater or less degree in the future of the race, the welfare of their heirs, and the well-being of their fellow men. Every person has some combination of these sometimes complementary, sometimes conflicting interests. These combinations make for a wide range of attitudes regarding conservation, varying from extreme conservation-mindedness to almost exclusive emphasis on policies of resource depletion or exploitation.

This range of interests in conservation also applies to business organizations and public agencies. Corporations, which are ordinarily assumed to have longer planning periods and lower interest rates than individuals, sometimes stress the conservation and sometimes the rapid depletion of particular resources. Governments also vary in their conservation practices. They frequently live up to Pigou's admonition that:

> It is the clear duty of Government, which is the trustee for unborn generations as well as for its present citizens, to watch over, and if need be, by legislative enactment, to defend the exhaustible natural resources of the country from rash and reckless exploitation.[16]

On certain other occasions, as during a war when the continued life of the nation is at stake, they may engage in resource-disinvestment policies that are every bit as exploitive as those of the self-seeking businessman.

Society's interests in conservation can be described and illustrated in terms of the effects of social interest rates or social planning periods on what constitutes wise resource use. However, the concept of social interest in conservation has little meaning unless it is related to group action, unless some effort is made to cause social interests to prevail.

Important questions can be raised concerning the proper criteria for social action to secure conservation goals. With our prevailing political philosophy in the United States, we frequently argue that it is desirable to limit social intervention and allow individuals considerable free-agency in the management of their personal affairs. But no land owner or land user lives on an island unto himself. His land-use practices frequently affect his neighbors and the whole community. His practices become a matter of group and public concern anytime they have an adverse effect upon the productivity, value, or cost of maintaining an area's resource base.

[16] A. C. Pigou, *The Economics of Welfare*, 4th ed. (New York: St. Martin's Press, Inc., and London: Macmillan & Co., Ltd., 1946), pp. 29-30.

A clear case can be made for social action to promote conservation anytime an operator's practices are regarded as detrimental to the nation's security and anytime public programs are needed to facilitate desired resource developments. Social controls are justified when they are used to prevent individual property-use practices that contribute to neighborhood blight or that cause drainage, erosion, fire, siltation, or soil-drifting problems on other properties. Comparable action may also be needed at times to help individuals help themselves. As Bunce has indicated:

> ... social action to achieve conservation is desirable: (1) when it would be economic for the individual entrepreneur to conserve but he does not; (2) when conservation is not economic for the individual but is economic for society; and (3) when intangible ends desired by the majority of individuals in a democracy can be attained only by collective action.[17]

Public agencies use much the same tools in promoting society's interests in conservation as in other examples of the social direction of land use.[18] Educational measures and possible subsidies for the acceptance of conservation measures are used in those instances in which lack of knowledge is considered the chief obstacle to conservation. Credit facilities and technical assistance are provided with soil and neighborhood conservation programs to help operators finance and adjust their conservation practices.

Favorable taxation measures are used with forest resources to encourage conservation practices. The police power is used with forest cutting restrictions, oil well spacing regulations, and area zoning measures for conservation purposes. The power of eminent domain may be used to acquire park, wildlife, and other conservation holdings. The public spending power and power of public ownership are also used quite extensively to foster conservation objectives.

Overcoming Obstacles to Conservation

One of our chief problems with conservation is that of overcoming obstacles to the acceptance of conservation practices. Some of these obstacles, such as the hidden nature of most mineral resources and the tendency of some soils to erode faster than others, are primarily physical in nature. Others involve economic, institutional, and technological barriers.

With physical obstacles, we usually accept the layout of our resources as we find it and proceed to use resources when and where they occur. In this process we often sink mine shafts, build dams, plant forests, use

[17]Bunce, *op. cit.*, p. 105. Reprinted by permission from HETEROSIS, edited by John W. Gowen,©1952 by The Iowa State University Press, Ames, Iowa.
[18]Cf. discussion in chapters 17 and 18.

terraces and sodded waterways, and employ other techniques to modify the natural situation and overcome the physical obstacles to what we consider wise resource use. Social action of quite a different type is ordinarily needed to overcome economic, institutional, and technological obstacles.[19]

Economic obstacles. Lack of knowledge and foresight constitutes a ← major obstacle to the wise use of resources over time. Operators frequently fail to accept conservation practices simply because they do not realize that they might maximize their returns through their use. This problem can be handled in part by educational programs designed to make operators conservation-conscious. Beyond this awareness of the merits of conservation, rational conservation decisions also call for considerable knowledge concerning the extent of one's fund or other resources, one's market and cost expectations, and the possible benefits and costs associated with alternative conservation practices.

A second major economic obstacle to conservation stems from the ← average operator's lack of capital. Most operators have some capital resources; but very few have all the capital they need to operate in the manner they wish. This factor frequently causes them to disinvest their resources or use a high time-preference rate simply because they feel that they must increase the current incomes they have available for living and operating purposes.

Special credit facilities are needed in many instances to help operators finance conservation practices. Credit and outright income grants can be used to help tide operators over the periods of reduced income that sometimes elapse before they can capitalize on the longer-run benefits of their conservation programs. Compensation arrangements can be worked out to encourage individuals to carry on conservation practices that are desired by society but that might not be profitable to individual operators.

Economic instability provides a third major economic barrier to ← conservation practices. Many operators use short planning periods and high discount rates because they find themselves unable to predict future cost, price, and market conditions. This situation can be improved by measures to reduce uncertainties, stabilize the economic system and minimize the fluctuations in net returns that come with periods of inflation and depression. In the absence of these measures, a system of guaranteed markets or a system under which society shares the costs and

[19]For other discussions of these obstacles cf. Wantrup, *op. cit.,* pp. 111-219; Anthony Scott, *Natural Resources: The Economics of Conservation* (Toronto: University of Toronto Press, 1955), pp. 99-152; John C. Frey, *Some Obstacles to Soil Erosion Control in Western Iowa,* Iowa Agricultural Experiment Station Research Bulletin 391, 1952; and John F. Timmons, "Institutional Obstacles to Land Improvement," *Journal of Land and Public Utility Economics,* Vol. 22, May, 1946, pp. 140-50.

returns of conservation along with individual operators may be necessary to prompt some types of conservation.

Institutional obstacles. Like other types of human behavior, conservation decisions are often influenced by institutional factors. Many people practice conservation as a matter of habit or custom or because they are imbued with "a stewardship concept of the land" philosophy. Many others find that their conservation plans are favored by the relative stability of their governments, the clear titles they have to their lands, their eligibility for public conservation payments, their expectations regarding public price supports, or the guarantees they have against exploitive taxation.

On the other side, it should be recognized that institutional arrangements can and frequently do discourage conservation. Customary practices, inertia, and ignorance of the principles of wise land use can lead to resource exploitation. Operators with limited tenure rights, a mortgage that may soon be foreclosed, a clouded real estate title, or a vacillating government have little incentive for using low discount rates or long planning periods. Customary rental arrangements frequently give neither the landlord nor the tenant much reason for practicing conservation. High property or severance taxes, operating units of inadequate size, and a lack of suitable credit facilities provide other important causes of resource exploitation.

Society can play an important role in overcoming these obstacles. Educational, demonstration, and subsidy measures can be used to acquaint people with their opportunities under conservation and to persuade them to try conservation practices. Positive action can be taken to stabilize political institutions and to clarify titles and the various use rights people have in property. Programs can be developed to promote leasing and tenure arrangements that encourage investments in conservation practices, to devise tax systems that favor private construction practices, and to subsidize the introduction and private acceptance of conservation measures. Steps may also be taken to promote public resource developments and the public ownership and administration of particular resource holdings.

Technological obstacles. Man's use of resources is always conditioned by the existing state of the arts. Primitive man often practiced conservation unknowingly because he lacked the motivation and know-how for exploiting land resources. As he acquired this motivation and know-how, he often wrecked his resource base, not so much because he wanted to but rather because of his inability to discipline himself in his use of new technology.

Many people still endorse an undisciplined policy of resource exploitation on the assumption that technology will solve all our resource-scarcity problems. They argue that "necessity is the mother of invention" and that science will come to the rescue with improved extraction and production processes and with new substitutes as the prospect of resource exhaustion approaches.

Whether technology can supply all the needed answers to our future resource-use problems is a question beyond immediate answer. It is obvious, however, that wise resource use calls for some thought of the future and that technology can and will play a significant role in helping man expand his economic supplies of most land resources.

The task of technology in this instance is simple but challenging. Technology can help us discover more fund resources, facilitate the easier and more complete extraction and use of these resources, and extend their useful life over time. It can promote the economic development and more extensive productive use of flow resources. It can lead to the development of improved breeds and species of biological resources that will yield better products at lower cost. It can point the way for improved soil conservation techniques and for construction and repair practices that will extend the economic life of man-made improvements. Society has definite responsibilities to help promote the development and use of new and improved techniques for each of these purposes.

—SELECTED READINGS

Bunce, Arthur F., *The Economics of Soil Conservation* (Ames: Iowa State College Press, 1945).

Ciriacy-Wantrup, Siegfried V., *Resource Conservation,* rev. ed. (Berkeley: University of California Press, 1963).

Gray, Lewis C., "The Economic Possibilities of Conservation," *Quarterly Journal of Economics,* Vol. 27, May, 1913, pp. 497-519.

Heady, Earl O., *Economics of Agricultural Production and Resource Use* (Englewood Cliffs, N. J.: Prentice-Hall, Inc., 1952), chap. XXVI.

Johnson, V. Webster, and Raleigh Barlowe, *Land Problems and Policies* (New York: McGraw-Hill Book Company, Inc., 1954), chap. VII.

Scott, Anthony, *Natural Resources: The Economics of Conservation* (Toronto: University of Toronto Press, 1955).

Timmons, John F. *et al.,* (Committee on Soil and Water Conservation), *Principles of Resource Conservation Policy,* National Academy of Sciences, National Research Council Publication 885 (Washington: 1961).

9

Location Factors
Affecting Land Use

In the world of economic theory, it is common practice to ignore differences in spatial location. With the frequently used concept of perfect competition, for example, it is ordinarily assumed that all buyers, sellers, and products in the market have perfect mobility—that they are either located at the market or can be moved instantaneously and without cost to that point.[1] This assumption has its place and value in theoretical analysis; but it does not meet the conditions of reality. Land resources in particular are fixed in their location. They are always found at varying distances from the centers of economic activity, and costs are involved in moving land products to market and in bringing capital and labor to the land. Locational differences play a highly significant role both in determining the economic uses that can be made of land and in affecting the rent and value levels associated with its use.

Most people prefer to live in areas that boast a pleasant climate, low living costs, and opportunities for the satisfaction of their various wants and desires. In deciding where they and their families will live, individuals often are torn between the counterpull of their wants as consumers and their wants as producers. As consumers they "seek to settle where living is secure, cheap, and agreeable. As producers, they seek to locate

---

[1] Cf. Walter Isard, *Location and Space-Economy* (New York: John Wiley and Sons, 1956), pp. 42 and 53.

256

where earnings will be large and assured and the working conditions pleasant."[2]

Despite their frequent complaints about the weather, a high proportion of the people in most areas are reasonably content with their present locations. This is particularly true if they have lived there all their lives or if they have come to regard these locations as home. Yet numerous conflicts do exist between consumer and producer wants and goals. Where these conflicts exist the more ambitious, energetic, and productive individuals often move to areas of greater economic opportunity. This willingness to move encourages successful operators to seek out those locations at which they can maximize their economic returns. Their activities in turn often attract workmen and others to the same locations. In this way the lure of higher returns causes many people to live and work in areas that may appear less than ideal from a strictly consumer point of view.

All things considered, operators and areas ordinarily concentrate on the production of those goods or services for which they have the highest comparative advantage—the greatest opportunity for realizing a profit in their trade with others. Our discussion of the economics of this situation and its effects on enterprise location logically begins with a brief examination of the concepts of economic specialization and comparative advantage. Consideration is then given to the impact of location factors on the allocation of land areas between particular uses, to the factors that influence the location of cities and the determination of their internal land-use structures, and to factors affecting the location of industrial, commercial, and residential areas.

ECONOMIC SPECIALIZATION
AND COMPARATIVE ADVANTAGE

Economic specialization is a common phenomenon in the present world. An exceptionally good example of this is provided by the separation, specialization, and sometimes routinization of labor in modern industry. Other examples are easy to find. Individuals starting out in business for themselves often perform a wide variety of tasks. They may do their own buying and selling, bookkeeping, decorating, and janitorial work. Once their business expands and prospers, however, new employees are usually hired, a division of labor takes place, and each employee tends to do that type of work that he can do best in comparison with his fellow employees.

This does not always mean that the most qualified person is found at every position or that every person works at the job he can do best. An

---

[2] Edgar M. Hoover, *The Location of Economic Activity* (New York: McGraw-Hill Book Company, 1948), pp. 4-5.

office executive may be able to type faster than his secretary or do a
better job of bookkeeping than his accountant; but he works as an
executive because of the higher value of his services in this position.
Similarly, a salesman may have talents that make his services worth $200 a
week as an ad writer as compared with $175 a week as a salesman. But if
the firm needs only one ad writer and this position is filled by an individual whose services are worth $225 a week, it is most economic for the
firm to keep the salesman at his present position.

Many of the principles that apply to individual specialization also apply
to area specialization in production. Each area could attempt to provide
all the products needed by man. The Midwest, for example, could try to
provide its needs for cotton, coffee, and bananas. But even if it were
possible to produce a sufficient supply of these products, this process
would prove both expensive and wasteful. It makes much more sense for
areas to concentrate on the production of those products for which they
have a natural or economic advantage and to trade their surplus of these
products for goods they need that can best be produced in other areas. By
permitting and encouraging land areas to specialize in those types of
production for which they have high comparative advantage, man has
been able to increase his total supply of goods and with it his average
standard of life.

Principle of Comparative Advantage

Generally speaking, each area tends to produce those products for which
it has the greatest ratio of advantage or the least ratio of disadvantage as
compared with other areas. This concept is known as the "principle of
comparative advantage." In practice, it helps to explain why some areas
tend to concentrate on the production of a limited number of products
while they look to other areas for many of the products they use.

The operation of the principle of comparative advantage can best be
described in terms of a few simple examples involving two areas and two
products. In our first comparison, we may assume that areas A and B each
produce all of the shirts and shoe products they need, that each area is
capable of producing enough of either product to supply the needs of
both areas, and that each area receives the net output per unit of input
indicated in Case I. Under these circumstances neither area possesses a
production advantage for either product. Consequently, neither area has
an incentive to specialize or trade its production with the other. This same

CASE I

Land use	Area A	Area B
Shirts	40	40
Shoes	60	60

situation would hold true if the production in area B dropped to 30 and 45 units or increased to 50 and 75 units, respectively, for the shirts and shoes. In each of these cases, both areas would have identical ratios between the units of shirts and shoes they could produce, and neither would find it to its advantage to specialize.

If the production situation is changed in area B as in Case II, it immediately becomes profitable for each area to specialize. Area A finds its ratio of advantage highest when it concentrates on shoe products, while area B finds it most profitable to concentrate on shirt production. In this case, each area has an absolute advantage in the production of one product.

CASE II

Land use	Area A	Area B
Shirts	40	50
Shoes	60	40

Under the conditions of real life, some areas occasionally have an absolute advantage for more than one use while most areas fail to enjoy an absolute advantage for any use. The disadvantaged areas in these instances do not go unused. Instead, they are ordinarily used for those purposes for which they have the least comparative disadvantage. In Case III, for example, area B has an absolute advantage for the production of both

CASE III

Land use	Area A	Area B
Shirts	40	70
Shoes	60	65

shirts and shoe products. Yet since it lacks sufficient productive capacity to supply the needs of both areas for both products, it will concentrate mostly on shirt production—the use for which it has the highest comparative advantage—while area A will concentrate on shoe products—the use for which it has the least comparative disadvantage.

To push this analysis further, it must be recognized that areas sometimes find it advantageous to concentrate on their second or third rather than their most productive use. In Case IV, for example, area B again has an absolute advantage in the production of both shirts and shoes, but it

CASE IV

Land use	Area A	Area B
Shirts	40	45
Shoes	60	90

concentrates upon shoes because this use involves its highest comparative advantage.

Area B in this instance can produce two units of shoes for every unit of shirts while area A can produce only three units of shoes for every two units of shirts. In terms of trade, B would be willing to give up two units of shoes for one unit of shirts as compared with three units of shoes for every two units of shirts in the case of A. At the same time, A would be willing to give up two units of shirts for every three units of shoes while B would give up only one unit of shirts for every two units of shoes. These conditions make it advantageous for A to concentrate on the production of shirts while B concentrates on shoes. Area A concentrates on the production of the less productive of its two products because B has a definite competitive advantage in the production of shoes and because the shoe market is left to A more or less by default.

The joint operation of these principles may be illustrated by the hypothetical situation outlined in Case V. This example assumes four separate producing areas and predictable estimates of the average amounts

CASE V

Land use	Area A	Area B	Area C	Area D
Wheat	$10	$12	$11	$8
Corn-hogs	8	20	10	1
Potatoes	14	12	13	–
Dairying	18	18	10	–

of land rent associated with four alternative uses. For illustrative purposes, area A may be considered as representative of parts of the Northeastern or Lake States region, area B of parts of the Midwest, area C of some irrigated sections of the West, and area D of the nonirrigated dry farming areas of the western Great Plains.

Examination of the data in Case V indicates that area B has an absolute advantage in the production of wheat and corn and that it can earn as high a net return in dairying as any other area. Its highest comparative advantage lies in corn-hog production and a high proportion of its resources accordingly are used for this purpose. Area A has an absolute advantage in potato production, but its highest comparative advantage lies in dairying. Areas C and D do not enjoy an absolute advantage in any of the four enterprises. Area C could diversify and engage in any of the enterprises but would probably find its least comparative disadvantage in potato production. Area D has the lowest wheat yields of any of the areas but would concentrate on wheat production because of the extremely limited nature of its alternatives.

Scope of Comparative Advantage

Comparative advantage is frequently thought of in terms of natural advantages such as favorable climate, soils, and topography. With this approach, it is easy to assume a static situation in which some areas are destined for particular uses and in which their successful use for these purposes is more or less guaranteed. In practice, the concept of comparative advantage is both more dynamic and more all-inclusive. It is affected to a considerable extent by human judgment and man-made decisions and policies as well as by physical conditions. In the final analysis, comparative advantage is measured by the economic ability of an area to compete with other areas in the production of particular goods or services. Certain comparative advantages may stem from the natural endowment. Others may involve favorable combinations of production inputs, favorable location and transportation costs, favorable institutional arrangements, or desired amenity factors.

Natural endowment. Numerous examples may be used to illustrate the contribution of the natural endowment to comparative advantage. Minerals must be available in economically-attractive concentrations if commercial mining is to take place. Favorable climatic conditions and specific natural resources such as sand beaches, good fishing waters, or ski slopes are a "must" for many types of recreation developments. Good natural harbors coupled with productive hinterland areas have usually favored urban developments. The relatively frost-free climates of Florida and southern California have encouraged the use of these areas for the production of citrus fruits and other semitropical crops. The long growing season enjoyed by the South has given it an advantage for cotton production. Rich soils have favored corn production in the Midwest. Level and rolling fields provide distinct advantages for mechanized farming. Areas with favorable air drainage located near large bodies of water often enjoy natural advantages for the production of orchard crops. Mountain valleys frequently provide excellent sites for reservoirs and power dams.

Favorable production combinations. Comparative advantage implies ability to produce goods or services at a profit. It calls for favorable combinations of the inputs needed for production and also for satisfactory markets. A shortage of capital or skilled management or a lack of adequate marketing or credit facilities may easily outweigh any natural advantages associated with an area. Skilled labor often is an important factor; and low labor costs per unit of production give an area a distinct production advantage. With industrial production, consideration must also be given to the availability and cost of such factors as raw materials, water, power, and other utilities.

Those operators who find it possible to work out low-cost combinations of their factors of production often find that they have a comparative advantage in production over other producers. Their low-cost combinations may result from favorable raw material, climatic, and other natural advantages. They may also be the result of superior management, the application of special skills or ingenuity, or utilization of the agglomeration economies associated with locations next to other established industries. Comparative advantage may stem from existing situations, but it may also be created. With dynamic leadership, areas of limited natural advantage can often develop their own supplies of skilled labor and management, capital, water and utilities, and even build up market areas that will tend to give them high comparative advantage.

Transportation considerations. Location and transportation considerations are a third group of factors that significantly affect comparative advantage. Businessmen are always concerned about the distances from which they must import raw materials and the market points to which they must ship their finished products. Local producers often benefit from their ability to move products to market at lower cost, in less time, and in fresher condition than their outlying competitors. Savings in transportation costs frequently make it possible for local producers to compete on favorable terms with producers who live in areas that boast strong natural advantages and good production combinations for particular products. Local operators, for example, are often able to supply manufactured goods, farm products, and recreation opportunities at lower cost than they can be secured from prime production points in other parts of the country.

Changes in the transportation cost situation have provided a major boost for the economic development of many areas during the past two centuries. As late as 1816, the market price of flour in the United States did not justify its transportation for distances of over 150 miles overland and bulky and heavy articles could be shipped 3,000 miles across the Atlantic Ocean at about the same cost as 30 miles over land.[3] The cost of shipping wheat from Buffalo to New York City was approximately $100 per ton in 1817 or roughly three times its delivered value in New York City. With the opening of the Erie Canal in 1825, this shipping cost dropped to $8.81 a ton, and it suddenly became economically feasible for farmers in western New York and along the Great Lakes to ship their excess produce to the eastern market.[4]

As late as the middle 1800s, limited transportation facilities and high transportation costs favored concentrations of land settlements along navigable streams. Distant overland transportation was limited primarily to objects with high value-to-weight ratios, and cities were usually dependent upon their immediate hinterland areas for much of their food as well as other products with low value-to-weight ratios. The building of canals, railroads, highways, airports, and pipelines, and the introduction of

---

[3] Cf. letter of Robert Fulton to Secretary of the Treasury Albert Gallatin, December 8, 1807, *American State Papers—Miscellaneous,* Vol. 1, p. 919; and Caroline E. MacGill *et al., History of Transportation in the United States Before 1860* (Washington: Carnegie Institution, 1917), p. 78.

[4] Cf. MacGill *et al., op. cit.,* p. 84.

new and improved modes of transportation since 1850 have provided most areas with a wide variety of transportation opportunities while at the same time reducing transportation costs, times, and perishability hazards. These developments have greatly relaxed the transportation constraints of the past and have made it possible for producers to consider far-off places both as potential sources of raw materials and as market areas. As long as transportation involves costs and time, however, it will influence location and production decisions and accordingly will influence the comparative advantages associated with various production sites.

Institutional advantages. Comparative advantage may also arise from the operation of particular institutional arrangements. Nations with histories of political stability offer greater attractions for investors than nations threatened with frequent revolutions. Tariff barriers and trade restrictions have long been used to shut off outside competition and to enhance the production advantages enjoyed by local or domestic producers. Protective tariffs often give definite market advantages to agricultural and industrial enterprises that might otherwise be hard pressed for survival. Comparable situations exist when other institutional controls such as quarantine restrictions or city milk inspection requirements protect local producers against outside competition.

Other examples of institutional factors affecting comparative advantage include the use of two-price systems to help domestic producers, public subsidies for certain types of production, and special tax concessions to new industries. The actions of public agencies in adjusting and regulating freight rates also have a far-reaching effect in enlarging or restricting the area within which particular industries can compete. The potash industry at Carlsbad, New Mexico, for example, found that it could not compete with the French and German producers in the eastern market as long as its freight rate to the Texas seaports stood at $14.90 a ton. A reduction of this rate to $5.50 a ton in 1931 made it profitable for this industry to compete not only in the eastern market but also in some foreign markets.[5]

Amenity factors. The cultural and aesthetic attractions associated with various local amenities provide a fifth facet of comparative advantage. Amenity considerations can be and often are ignored when significant economic advantages are associated with particular sites. Producers, workers, and consumers are far more conscious of amenity factors now, however, than was the usual case in the past. Moreover, decisions as to prospective operating sites can often be narrowed to several sites that offer quite comparable economic opportunities. When this situation exists, final decisions are frequently influenced by the general attractive-

---

[5] Cf. Louis H. Kurrelmeyer, *The Potash Industry* (Albuquerque: Department of Government, University of New Mexico, 1951), p. 23.

ness of a community and the climatic, cultural, education, recreation, and other opportunities it offers for potential residents.

   Interrelation of comparative advantage factors. Operators must consider all of the above sets of factors in their calculations of comparative advantage. Marked advantages associated with any one group of factors can be and often are neutralized by others. The interrelationship of the various factors may be illustrated by a hypothetical example of a Detroit industrialist who seeks a plentiful supply of a particular item that he plans to market in combination with his own product. Suppliers at five different locations can produce and deliver the needed item at the prices reported in Table 9-1.

TABLE 9-1. Hypothetical Example of Costs Associated with Delivered Prices Quoted for A Product Needed by a Detroit Industrialist

| Site of production | Costs per unit of product for: | | | | Delivered price per unit |
	Raw materials	Production costs	Shipment to Detroit	Customs duty	
Windsor	$1.00	$2.35	$ .15	$ .50	$4.00
Tokyo	.95	1.55	.90	.50	3.90
Los Angeles	.85	2.20	.65		3.70
St. Louis	.95	2.40	.40		3.75
Cleveland	1.00	2.45	.25		3.70

   Examination of these costs shows that the prospective supplier in Los Angeles enjoys a natural endowment advantage with the lowest unit cost for raw materials and the prospective supplier in Tokyo has the lowest production costs, while the prospective supplier from across the Detroit River in Windsor, Ontario has the lowest transportation costs. The three domestic suppliers enjoy an institutional advantage with their freedom from the need to pay customs duties. When all of these costs are considered, it appears that the suppliers in Cleveland and Los Angeles can deliver the needed item at the same lowest price. At this point, personal considerations and amenity factors may become the deciding factors in determining which supplier gets the contract. If the industrialist wants a supplier close at hand, he may prefer the Cleveland producer. Should he seek opportunities to visit friends in southern California or to spend occasional winter weekends golfing at Palm Springs, he may favor the Los Angeles supplier.

   Comparative advantage involves ability to compete on highly favorable terms with alternative production sites in the production of goods or services for a given market. High comparative advantage for particular uses, however, does not necessarily mean that the sites will be used for these purposes. Sites near metropolitan centers often enjoy high comparative advantages for many competing uses. Selection of the highest and best use in these cases involves the counter-bidding of the market-place. Individual sites tend to move to their highest and best or most profitable uses. The outbid uses move to less favorable sites where they can become highest and best uses even though these may involve uses of least comparative disadvantage.

Choices of the highest and best uses of particular sites sometimes involve a weighing of social values against commercial values. Individual sites such as a block in a commercial district that has a high potential for commercial development or a waterfall that could provide an ideal site for a hydroelectric power plant can be reserved for public park and scenic purposes if appropriate governmental action is taken to acquire and designate these sites for this purpose.

SPATIAL RELATIONSHIPS AFFECTING LAND USE

Land-utilization patterns frequently reflect geographic differences in location with respect to market. This is particularly true when one deals with land areas of like productive capacity located at different distances from market. Transportation cost is the key factor in these cases. Since these costs ordinarily increase with distance, sites near a market usually enjoy an element of comparative advantage over sites located farther away. This means that areas close to market receive a higher net price for their products and thus yield more land rent and have higher capitalized values than areas located at greater distance.

Most of our theory regarding the effect of spatial location on land-utilization patterns stems from von Thunen's concept.[6] As was pointed out in chapter 2, this concept starts with a simple model involving a series of concentric land-use zones surrounding a central city. Presented in its simplest form, this model assumes (1) rational behavior, (2) an isolated state, (3) one central city, (4) a village type of settlement, (5) uniform topography, (6) uniform fertility and climate, and (7) relatively primitive transportation facilities with all products being carried by man, hauled by horses or oxen, or transported under their own power. In our discussion of the effects of location on land use, we will start with von Thunen's model and then indicate the adjustments that come with the progressive relaxation of his various assumptions.

Importance of Transportation Costs

Von Thunen's model is concerned primarily with the role that trans-

[6] Cf. Peter Hall, ed., *Von Thunen's Isolated State* (London: Pergamon Press, 1966.) For other discussions of this subject, cf. August Lösch, *The Economics of Location* (English translation by William H. Woglom and Wolfgang F. Stolper; New Haven: Yale University Press, 1954); Edgar S. Dunn, Jr., *The Location of Agricultural Production* (Gainesville: University of Florida Press, 1954); and Isard, *op. cit.*

portation costs play in allocating the land resources found at varying distances from market between different agricultural uses. The basic assumptions that underlie the model, however, have widespread applications to all types of land use including urban and nonfarm uses. Von Thunen recognized that transportation costs involve not only the transfer of produce to market but also the time, effort, and inconvenience associated with moving workers and supplies to and from various production sites. With this reasoning, he indicated that the first zone around his central city would be employed for intensive uses that involve considerable care and travel to and from the zone on the part of the villagers. The second and third zones were allocated to uses involving heavy, bulky, and hard-to-transport commodities, while those uses involving more easily transported products were located at greater distances from the city.

The arrangement of the concentric land-use zones in this model strongly reflects the influence of transportation costs and convenience considerations. Von Thunen's villagers try to minimize the total effort, inconvenience, and loss of time associated with their use of various sites and the movement of their products to market. Their location decisions may be quantified in economic terms as in Table 9-2. Basic land rent levels may be assumed for each land use at the market. Average transportation costs per mile can be determined by dividing the total transportation costs associated with particular uses at different locations for specific production periods by distance from market. Distance from the central market to the extensive or no-rent margin for individual uses can be computed by dividing the level of land rent at the market by the transportation cost per mile. Zones of highest and best use occur between the transference margins of the most profitable uses.

Four types of land use are identified in Table 9-2. The land rent triangle for use *A* starts with $10 of land rent on its vertical axis and stretches horizontally for 4 miles. Use *B* is depicted by a land rent triangle that has a vertical apex at $7 and stretches out for 10 miles. The rent

TABLE 9-2. **Illustration of the Joint Effect Transportation Costs and the Rent-Producing Capacity Associated with Various Types of Land Use Have in Allocating the Land Areas Around a Central Market Between Alternative Uses**

Types of land use	Land rent type of use could earn if carried on at market	Transportation cost per mile of distance from market	Distance from market to extensive or no-rent margin	Range of distance from the market within which this use has first choice
A	$10.00	2.50	4 miles	0.0-1.7 miles
B	7.00	.70	10 miles	1.7-5.0 miles
C	4.50	.18	25 miles	5.0-19 miles
D	2.00	.05	40 miles	19.0-40 miles

triangles for uses *C* and *D* start with land rent values of $4.50 and $2 and extend horizontally for 25 and 40 miles, respectively.

When the four rent triangles are brought together in a margin of transference diagram as in Figure 9-1, it appears that use *D* alone will be carried on to its extensive margin. Use *A* promises the highest land rent for the sites immediately adjacent to the city. It accordingly is the highest and best use for the concentric zone that extends out to the transference margin *ab,* which occurs 1.7 miles from the city. Use *B* is most profitable in the zone that extends from *ab* to *bc* or from 1.7 to 5 miles from the central market. Use *C* is the highest and best use between *bc* and the transference margin *cd,* which is located 17 miles from the city. The margin of transference points for the overlapping rent triangles correspond with the respective boundaries of the concentric zones in the von Thunen model.

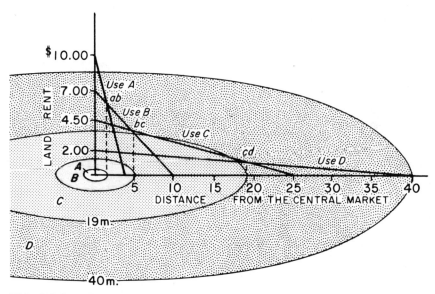

FIGURE 9-1. Example illustrating allocation of land around a central city market between four competing types of land use.

Figure 9-1 illustrates the relationship between the land rent triangles employed in margin of transference diagrams and von Thunen's concentric zones of land use. A third dimension also can be added to von Thunen's concentric zones as in Figure 9-2. Land rent cones now rise above the concentric land use zones and find their highest points at the central market. The surface of each overlapping cone depicts both the amount of land rent and the slope of the land rent function associated with a particular use at increasing distances from the central market. The height of the highest cone surface for each site around the central market indicates the amount of land rent it can produce when utilized for its

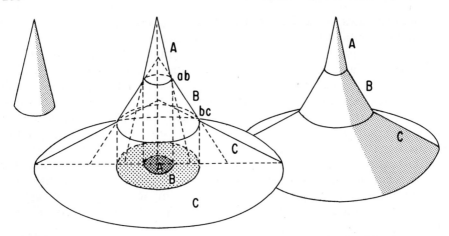

FIGURE 9-2. Use of land rent cones to illustrate relative levels of land rents or land values associated with highest and best uses of sites located at different distances from central markets.

highest and best use. Viewed in this way, it is obvious that the overlapping land rent triangles used in the margin of transference diagram represent a cross-section of the portion of the land rent cones found on a single side of the central city.

Von Thunen's basic concept, as depicted in Table 9-2 and Figure 9-1, illustrates the relationship of land rents to the cost of overcoming "the friction of space."[7] Transportation costs arise from the need to move products varying distances to market. These costs explain the higher land rents associated with sites near the market; and, as offsets to land rent, they set the outer limits within which specific uses can be carried on to advantage. Numerous location phenomena can be explained simply in terms of the relation of land rent to nearness to market.[8] In practice, however, this formulation often oversimplifies the situations found in real life.

[7] Cf. Robert Murray Haig, "Towards an Understanding of the Metropolis," *Quarterly Journal of Economics*, Vol. 40, pp. 421-22 (May, 1926). Haig observed:

Site rents and transportation costs are vitally connected through their relationship to the friction of space. Transportation is a means of reducing that friction, at the cost of time and money. Site rentals are charges which can be made for sites where accessibility may be had with comparatively low transportation costs. While transportation overcomes friction, site rentals plus transportation costs represent the cost of what friction remains. . . . The two elements, transportation costs and site rentals, are thus seen to be complementary. Together they may be termed the "cost of friction."

[8] Haig, *ibid*, p. 423, advanced the hypothesis that land-use patterns in metropolitan centers should "be determined by a principle which may be termed the minimizing of the costs of friction." See also Richard M. Hurd, *Principles of City Land Values* (New York: The Record and Guide, 1903), p. 78; Lowdon Wingo, Jr., *Transportation and Urban Land* (Washington: Resources for the Future, Inc., 1961), pp. 63-80; and William Alonso, *Location and Land Use* (Cambridge: Harvard University Press, 1968).

Realism can be introduced through the successive relaxation of von Thunen's various assumptions. If one assumes that a navigable stream flows through the central city, it immediately becomes less expensive to ship some products by boat or raft than by wagon. Forest products, which von Thunen located in his second zone, can now be produced to advantage at greater distance from the city as long as they are grown near the navigable stream. (Cf. Figure 2-3, p. 35.) Other transportation developments such as the construction of canals, railroads, and modern highways have had comparable effects in favoring elongated and star-shaped utilization patterns. Widespread private use of the automobile, in particular, has had a marked effect in reducing site rents in central business districts and in pushing out the distances from these centers at which specified land uses can be carried on to advantage.

Numerous examples of the effect of new transportation developments upon land values and land-utilization practices are found in the history of American land settlement. Transportation costs were a real problem to the early planters in the southern colonies. Most planters tended to locate along navigable streams; and even then they found it practicable to market their tobacco—their leading commercial crop—in hogsheads, which could be rolled rather than hauled to the water's edge. For a long time, the principal commercial products on the western frontier were furs, livestock, and whiskey. Furs had the advantage of being relatively light and portable. Cattle and hogs were frequently driven to market; and whiskey production provided a means by which frontiersmen could convert their grain into a high-value, less bulky product.

The development of highways, canals, and railroads facilitated the development and use of many frontier areas. New railroad construction between 1840 and 1890, for example, opened up several inland empire areas for settlement and development. Railroad construction made it economically feasible for farmers in the South and West to sell their products in the industrial centers of the East, for wheat growers on the Great Plains to produce for a European market, and for lumbermen to exploit forest resources which previously had lacked commercial value.

Land-utilization practices that could not be profitably carried on more than a few miles from the city in von Thunen's time are now carried on thousands of miles away. Lumber from the Pacific Northwest is used in eastern building operations; truck crops are shipped from the Imperial Valley of California to the kitchens of New England; Australian grain and New Zealand butter are standard commodities in the British market.

These developments have greatly extended the extensive margins of land use. But they have not wiped out the transportation advantages held by lands located close to market. Bulky and perishable products with a low value–weight ratio are still produced either near the market or at sites that enjoy favorable transportation costs. Sites with high transportation costs, on the other hand, usually find it necessary to concentrate on export commodities such as gold, copper, coffee, cocoa, spices, or palm oil that have high value-to-weight ratios.

Transportation facilities frequently favor some areas at the expense of others. Central points served by many highways, railroads, or other transportation facilities generally boast advantages for commercial and industrial developments. By-passed areas around cities that are not served with highway or railroad facilities in turn have often suffered because of their lack of accessibility. These extremes have fostered the development of star-shaped and spotty land-utilization patterns. Other developments such as the widespread operation of privately owned automobiles, the construction of roads, and the paving of streets have had a counter-effect in opening areas for use and in encouraging the shifting of activities once regarded as central place functions to outlying locations.

Differences in Land Quality

Variations in land quality associated with von Thunen's assumptions of uniform climate, fertility, and topography also have had a significant effect upon land-use patterns. If one assumes that the land west of a city is fertile, level, and easy to work, while the areas to the east are handicapped by low fertility or rough terrain, it is logical to expect some expansion of the concentric land-use zones to the west and a contraction of the zones to the east. (Figure 9-3A.) This situation results because the higher productivity and lower unit production costs associated with the better lands provide a larger economic surplus that can be applied toward paying shipping costs. The actual shipping cost per mile traveled might also be slightly lower than in the areas of rough terrain.

The importance of fertility and topography may also be illustrated as in Figures 9-3B and C. In the first of these two models, it is assumed that a central city is located at the apex of four evenly divided areas of different productive capacities. The first area is well suited for the uses carried on in zones 1 through 4. Area II, however, is primarily suited for the intensive cropping practices carried on in zone 1 but poorly suited for uses 2, 3, and 4. Area III is primarily suited for uses 3 and 4 but less well suited for uses 1 and 2, and area IV represents an area of low productive value for all uses. When these areas lie side-by-side, sharp breaks may be visualized in the land-use pattern as one moves from one area to the next. When the areas of varying fertility and productive capacity are scattered throughout the region the resulting land-use pattern may take a complex crazy-quilt form such as that suggested by Figure 9-3C.

Another variation of the von Thunen model occurs when the climatic and other natural productive advantages enjoyed by areas located at some distance from the city permit them to produce and ship certain products at a lower cost than they could be supplied near the city. In Figure 9-3D, for example, it may be possible for favorably endowed areas located away from the city to produce and ship some products at less cost than they can be produced in zone 1 or 2.

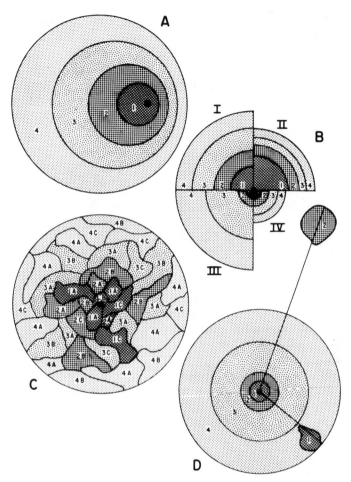

FIGURE 9-3. Examples of the effects of varying fertility and topographic conditions on land utilization.

The overall impact of differences in land quality along with improved transportation facilities can be visualized by assuming the example of an isolated state with a major city located in a valley at the foot of a mountain. With urban growth, the city can be expected to sprawl outward but primarily in the direction of lands of level terrain. The new commercial and industrial lands will usually call for flat lands and for highly accessible sites that offer good transportation facilities. Residential developments will come adjacent to the city and mostly on sites of gentle terrain, although some of the mountainous areas near the city undoubtedly will boast attractions for residential and recreation uses if they can be developed at reasonable cost. Bottomlands near the city will become logical sites for intensive agricultural uses. The remaining bottomlands together with some of the more accessible uplands will be used for less intensive crops. Some grain and hay crops may be produced on the uplands but the higher and rougher lands will likely be used for grazing and forestry purposes. The surrounding mountainous areas will be reserved mostly for forest recreation and wildlife uses. If there is a need for additional production and the city is connected by a pass to a second mountain valley, it may be economic to use the fertile bottomlands of this valley for crop or grazing purposes rather than attempt to reclaim additional lands for these uses in the first valley.

Impact of Satellites and Other Markets

Most urban market centers compete with other cities for the use of the land resources found in their hinterland areas. This means that land-utilization patterns are frequently affected by the pull of more than one market.

The importance of the pull of additional markets depends upon the size and needs of these markets together with their location and transportation ties to the lands in question. When two cities of comparable size and function are located next to each other, it is logical for them to divide their outlying areas with each city drawing upon and servicing those areas closest to it. Complications often arise, however, because of differences in transportation facilities and urban functions. A highway or railroad connecting one city with the natural hinterland of a second city will often claim much of the area served by these facilities for the first city. Similarly, if one has the only furniture factory while the other has the only flour mill, considerable overlapping of supply and market areas will occur.

When one or more smaller cities are located within the natural hinterland of a central city, the central city must compete with these satellites for the use of certain areas. The central city under these circumstances is still surrounded by a series of generalized land-use zones—zones that take the form of irregular bands rather than concentric circles because of differences in transportation facilities, topography, and land productivity. Each of the smaller cities also has need for surrounding land areas and can ordinarily outbid the central city for particular sites as long as its uses have a higher economic or social priority than those of the central city. (Figure 9-3.) When the central city's uses have highest priority, the satellite cities must seek alternative use sites—usually at greater distance from the central city—where they can better compete with the prices offered by the central city.

Product prices in satellite cities often reflect the cost of transporting goods to the larger market of the central city. As long as a surplus supply of a product is produced in the immediate area, its local price floor will represent the price offered in the larger city less the cost of transportation. For example, if milk is priced at $5 a cwt. in the larger city and can be shipped from the satellite city area for 60 cents per cwt., the minimum local cost will be $4.40 per cwt. If local producers are offered a lower price, they have the option of shipping to the larger market. In actual practice, satellite cities often pay more than this minimum. This situation may exist because of less desirable or less stable local market conditions or because of a need to attract supplies from areas lying between the satellite cities and the central market.

Occasionally, the prices in satellite city markets may actually be higher than in the central market. This is particularly true when a satellite area does not produce all of its own supplies or when the products grown in the area must go to the central market for processing. In meat-producing areas, for example, local livestock and meat prices may reflect the major packing house center price less freight. If an area is dependent upon Omaha packers for part of its meat supply, however, local prices are more apt to represent Omaha prices plus shipping costs.

Figure 9-4 illustrates the effect of satellite cities and variations in transportation facilities along with differences in land quality on the

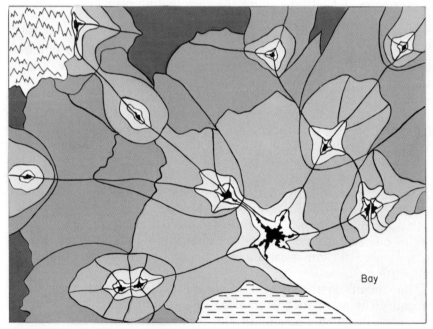

FIGURE 9-4. Illustration of the effect of satellite cities and variations in highway facilities and topographic conditions upon land utilization patterns around a central city.

generalized land use zones found around a central city. The impact of the same land use patterns on land rents and property values can be depicted by the value profile shown in Figure 9-5. One might also envisage a three-

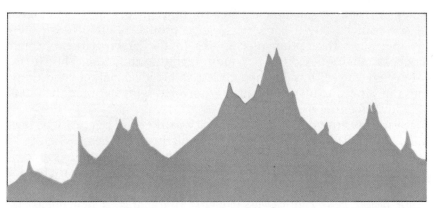

FIGURE 9-5. Profiles of land rents (or land values) associated with the example depicted in Figure 9-4.

dimensional topographic map of rent and value levels on which the land rents associated with the higher-and-better uses rise like mountain peaks, ridges, and hilltops above the surrounding plains and valleys.

Competition for market areas. Cities compete not only for the raw materials and supplies they secure from their hinterland areas but also for markets for the goods they produce. When two or more producers compete for the same market, price competition and even price wars sometimes develop. But cut-throat competition of this type is not likely to develop as long as producers refuse to sell at less than their actual cost of production plus transportation. When producers residing in different areas quote standard f.o.b. prices to their customers, their actions can have an automatic effect in dividing and allocating market areas.

This situation is illustrated in Figure 9-6, which assumes three producers of comparable products who are located in different cities and who market their goods at f.o.b. prices of $45, $35, and $50 respectively. As this figure indicates, as long as the producers hold to these prices and as long as one can assume uniform transportation costs, it is relatively easy to determine the areas within which each producer can undersell his competition.

Adjustments in the pattern of concentric circles must be made when recognition is given to the presence of different transportation facilities and to the fact that sites equidistant from a given city seldom enjoy equal transportation advantages. Complications also arise when some producers enjoy more favorable transportation rates than others, absorb their freight charges, or adhere to a "basing point system." Manufacturers of many standardized, much-advertised products absorb transportation costs so that their products may be sold at a uniform price all over the country. This practice naturally favors buyers in distant locations in comparison with those who reside near the point of production. A contrary situation

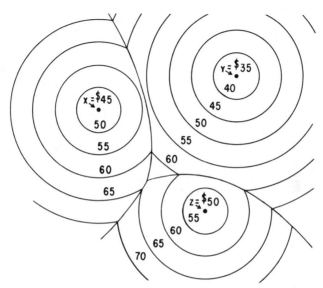

FIGURE 9-6. Division of market areas between three producers with different F.O.B. prices (assuming uniform transportation facilities and costs).

may exist when producers use geographic price discriminatory practices such as those involved under the basing point system.[9]

Other Modifications of von Thunen's Model

Additional adjustments are needed in the von Thunen model if it is to describe real-life conditions. Modifications are needed for his assumptions of a village-type settlement and an isolated state. Other adjustments also are needed when it is applied to industrial and commercial location decisions.

Rural people tend to live in central villages in many European farming communities. Typically, their fields are not laid out in compact farm units. Individual ownership holdings are frequently made up of several separate tracts. Because of the small size and isolated nature of these tracts, they ordinarily are used for the same purposes as the adjoining

[9] Cf. Fritz Machlup, *The Basing Point System* (Philadelphia: The Blakiston Company, 1949); also Vernon A. Mund, *Government and Business* (New York: Harper & Brothers, 1950), pp. 352-401. Under the basing point system all producers agree to quote delivery prices based upon the prices assigned to some basing point or points plus freight. The basing points usually represent important production or distribution centers. Outlying producers may be able to produce at as low a cost as the producers located at the basing points but unless a new point is created they are required to adhere to the basing point pricing formula. This method of pricing has been used with a number of products such as steel, cement, gasoline, and lumber but was declared unlawful by the U.S. Supreme Court in 1948.

tracts owned by other villagers. Each family may thus own parcels of land in each of von Thunen's land-use zones, and a policy of using lands at various distances from the village for different purposes can be worked out rather easily.

This system breaks down when one considers the usual farm pattern found in countries such as the United States. Most farm families in these areas live on their farms rather than in villages; and they usually farm solid blocks of land rather than scattered strips and parcels. As a result, they often find all of their acreage within a single land-use zone rather than scattered throughout the full range of zones.

These operators ordinarily let location and comparative advantage determine their major enterprises. The problem of complementarity in farm organization, however, usually favors a mixture and often a rotation of land uses. Farmers in one type of farming area may use a high proportion of their land for truck crops but also some of it for pasture and grazing purposes. Those living in wheat or ranching areas in turn will use most of their land for these purposes but still have their own gardens and possibly a small dairy herd.

Von Thunen used the concept of an isolated state to reduce the number of variable factors that affected his model. In so doing, he found it possible to disregard the effects that interarea trade, distant markets, tariff barriers, and public price and production programs have on the land-use practices of local producers. Von Thunen's approach facilitated his analysis. Under real-life conditions, it is difficult to identify an isolated state. Local land-use decisions frequently reflect the integration of local areas in the operations of regional and national economies. Also, with each new development in transportation facilities, local areas come into closer contact with each other, and local producers find themselves in competition with producers from other areas.

With these factors at work, producers often find that they must gear their operating decisions to national and international conditions. Instead of worrying about the local market demand for their products, operators often find their markets in distant cities. Instead of calculating their prospects for profit in terms of local competition, they often find that their market prices are influenced to a considerable extent by industrial employment, public price policies, and changes in the international supply-and-demand picture.

Von Thunen's simple model provides a meaningful basis for explaining the principal relationships between spatial location and land utilization.[10] Its focus on the land-use patterns associated with a single central market city, however, ignores the effects that diverse locations of sources of materials and markets can have on location decisions. An important

---

[10] Cf. Michael Chisholm, *Rural Settlement and Land Use* (London: Hutchinson University Library, 1962), for a discussion of current applications of von Thunen's concept in different parts of the world.

contribution dealing with this facet of location theory stems from the work of Alfred Weber.[11]

Weber's approach. Like von Thunen, Weber started his analysis with basic assumptions as to climate, topography, and the location of basic resources. He visualized several cities scattered over the region. He recognized that some inputs in the manufacturing process are "ubiquitous"—available almost anywhere—while others are found only in particular places and that cities can have both agglomerating attractions that draw industries to them and deglomerating features that have an opposite effect. With these factors in mind, he asked where an industry should locate if deposits of its chief raw material are found at a single site (point *A* in Figure 9-7), needed ingredients for the processing of the raw material occur at a second site (point *B*), and the principal market for the product is found at a third location (point *C*). His analysis highlights transportation considerations and the pulling and counter-pulling of various factors on location decisions and helps explain why the optimum location for a processing plant may be at some intermediate site such as point *D*.

A dynamic dimension is added to the Weberian model when one considers the impact that changing supply and market conditions over time can have on location decisions. One might start, for example, with an assumption that point *A* in Figure 9-8 is a market town and trade center located in the midst of a fertile plain or valley. At an initial stage, the economy of *A* and its surrounding area resembles that of von Thunen's isolated state. A trade route is established, however, across an unsettled forested region to site *B*. *B* is located along the ocean and is two days travel from *A*. Travel from *A* to *B* is inconvenient but is accepted because

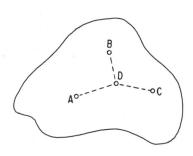

FIGURE 9-7. Illustration of Weber's location of industry model.

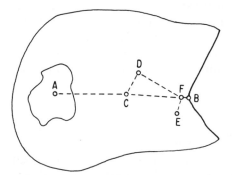

FIGURE 9-8. Illustration of changing conditions over time on locations of urban and industrial developments.

[11] Cf. Alfred Weber, *Über den Standort der Industrien* (Tubingen: 1909); also Carl J. Friedrich, *Alfred Weber's Theory of the Location of Industries* (Chicago: University of Chicago Press, 1929).

it provides *A* with a source of salt supplies. A village is established at *B* to produce salt. Later the villagers engage in fishing and ocean trade and find that they can provide *A* with supplies of salted fish along with spices and other imported luxuries. Grain and livestock are transported from *A* to *B* to pay for these products.

A settlement gradually develops at site *C*. At first it is simply an overnight camping spot. As trade increases between *A* and *B,* inns are built with barns and corrals to care for travelers and their animals. Iron ore is discovered in a treeless area at site *D* and is transported at first to *C* where the surrounding forests are cut to provide charcoal for smelting purposes.

Valuable coal deposits are found at *E*, and once the process of making coke is discovered, the iron and steel smelting industry moves to *F*. The proximity of this site to *B* adds to *B*'s position as an international trade and transshipment center. Imported raw materials are processed at *B* and then shipped inland or reshipped abroad. A metropolitan production and trading center develops around *B* and *F* while *D* and *E* continue to operate primarily as mining centers, *A* as a trading center serving an agricultural hinterland, and *C* as a transportation and minor industrial and trading center.

LOCATION OF PARTICULAR LAND USES

Some of the most relevant and most significant issues in location economics involve decisions concerning the location of particular land uses and the uses that can or should be made of particular sites. Some sites have far greater use-capacities and market potentials for selected uses than others. A basic problem in location decision making focuses on the identification of these optimum sites.

Five specific issues in location economics have been selected for discussion here. They include the location of cities, urban land-use patterns, industrial locations, location of commercial establishments, and location of residential developments.

Location of Cities

Cities have existed almost since the dawn of civilization. Much of their basis is found in the gregarious nature of man, but their rise also is associated with the cultural, economic, and political advantages that stem from the agglomeration or clustering together of people. Opportunities for trade and labor specialization have usually provided a strong urbanizing force. Without commerce and industry, few cities would have passed beyond the village stage. Many early cities started as religious centers, as political capitals, as the home of some royal court, or as fortified sites, which offered defense and military advantages in the event of war. In practically every case, however, the rise of these cities was associated with their development as centers of trade and commerce.[12]

Throughout the modern era, the presence or potential development of a strong economic base has always been a prime requisite for urban growth.[13] The urban growth prospects of urban sites now depend largely upon their location with respect to (1) a tributary or hinterland area, (2) transportation facilities and trade routes, and (3) supplies of materials and resources that can be used to advantage by local industries. In this sense, cities can be classified into four functional groups: trade centers, transportation centers, specialized function centers, and cities representing combinations of these types.[14]

Most cities and villages exist primarily as trade and commercial centers. They provide goods and services for a surrounding hinterland area and in return draw sustenance from the products of these tributary areas. The spacing of these centers reflects the nature of the population and land-resource base. In an ideal model, which assumes an even distribution of population and land resources of uniform quality, the local trade centers would be evenly distributed. Each trade and service center would be surrounded by a service area, which would have been small enough in the days of horse-and-buggy travel to permit easy commuting from the outskirts of the area to the trade center. With uniform transportation facilities, each trade center would normally be surrounded by a circular

---

[12] For a more detailed discussion of the rise of cities and the functional basis of the urban economy, cf. Richard U. Ratcliff, *Urban Land Economics* (New York: McGraw-Hill Book Company, Inc., 1949), chap. II.

[13] Viewed from another angle, it may also be observed that the rise of cities has had a marked impact upon the economic development of the areas around them. Experience shows that there is a distinct tendency for economic development to center at particular locations and for the developments taking place at these locations to push forward at a faster rate than in other areas. These growth centers or "locational matrices" are increasingly of industrial-urban composition. They provide the centers from which economic development spreads into surrounding areas. Because of this situation, the highest levels of economic development are usually found at or near industrial urban centers while lower levels of economic development and less satisfactory types of economic organization are usually found (as von Thunen's concentric-zone hypothesis suggests) towards the periphery of the areas that surround these centers. Cf. T. W. Schultz, *The Economic Organization of Agriculture* (New York: McGraw-Hill Book Company, Inc., 1953), chap. IX; and John R. P. Friedmann, "Locational Aspects of Economic Development," *Land Economics*, Vol. 32, August, 1956, pp. 213-37.

[14] Cf. Chauncey D. Harris and Edward L. Ullman, "The Nature of Cities," *Building the Future City, Annals of the American Academy of Political and Social Science*, November, 1945, No. 242, pp. 7-17. For other more detailed functional classifications, cf. Chauncey D. Harris, "A Functional Classification of Cities in the United States," *The Geographical Review*, Vol. 33, January, 1943, p. 86; and Arthur Weimer and Homer Hoyt, *Principles of Urban Real Estate*, 5th ed. (New York: The Ronald Press Company, 1966), pp. 236-37.

hinterland trade area; but the pressing together of trade areas to encompass all possible locations brings an overlapping of area boundaries. Definition of the outer boundaries of the various primary trade areas forces a squaring off of boundaries, a process that causes each idealized trade area to take the form of a hexagon—the form that most nearly approaches that of a circle and still permits division of the entire territory into trade areas of comparable shape and size. Viewed together, these hexagonal areas suggest a huge honeycomb, each cell representing a separate neighborhood or community center with its surrounding area. (Figure 9-9A.)

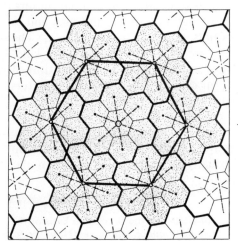

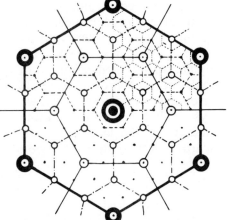

FIGURE 9-9A. Idealized distribution of cities (assuming uniform distribution of population and land resources, tendencies for small trading centers to develop at fairly equal distances throughout the countryside, and a tendency for these centers to form hexagonal patterns in their patronage of larger service centers, which in turn fit into hexagonal patterns around still larger commercial and service centers).

FIGURE 9-9B. Illustration (after Christaller, Central Places in Southern Germany, p. 66) of hierarchies of service centers with idealized distribution of cities in which

.   represents the center and
∽   the boundary of a A-level region,

○   and ---- the B-level region,
⊙   and –·– the C-level region,
◉   and —— the D-level region,

and

◎   and ▬ the E-level region.

This honeycomb pattern supports several hierarchial levels of trade and service centers. A cluster of six hexagons (A-level regions) around a seventh hexagonal area might logically look to the B-level trade center of the enclosed hexagonal cluster for services not normally provided in the other six. Groupings of six B-level regions located around a seventh cluster, in turn, may look to the C-level city of the central cluster for higher levels of services. The regions represented by these groupings in turn may look as in Figure 9-9B to still larger metropolitan centers (D- and E-level centers) for more specialized levels of service.[15]

This model is more suggestive of the spatial relationships that should exist under idealized conditions than of those found in practice. Even so, examples approximating this model have been observed in parts of Europe and also in some parts of the United States. Residents of rural areas generally look to a local village or town for selected commercial, educational, postal, and social services. For certain other classes of services such as banking, medical, hospital, legal, department store, and supermarket services, they frequently look to their county seat or to some other center that has grown faster than its neighbors and taken on the function of providing specialized trade and service functions for the surrounding communities. Groups of counties often look to state capitals and regional metropolitan centers for higher levels of services such as wholesaling, regional office headquarters, larger department and specialty stores, and opportunities for particular types of entertainment. Residents of the areas served by these centers may look in turn to large metropolitan centers for special services such as face-to-face contacts with corporation and financial leaders, ideal convention sites, better selections of specialty goods, and opportunities to see first-run Broadway shows. At each of these levels, the central city or village plays a hierarchal service role for its hinterland area and also supplies all of the services provided by lower level centers for its immediate area.

Location with respect to hinterland areas and to other cities is only one of the factors that affect urban growth. Complications ordinarily arise because of the uneven distribution of population, land resources, and local trade centers. Significant factors such as location along favored transportation routes, development of local industries, and far-sighted local leadership have often caused some villages to become cities when they might have remained as hamlets under the hexagonal approach. At the same time, the growing competitive power of these urban centers has often discouraged the parallel rise of neighboring trade centers, which may have boasted an initial advantage in location.

Since the beginnings of recorded history, locations along ocean and lake harbors, near the mouths of navigable streams, at intersections of land trade routes, and at transshipment or break-in-bulk points along water and land trade routes have usually favored urban growth. The

[15] For other discussions of this theory, cf. *ibid.;* Walter Christaller, *Die Zentralen Orte in Suddeutschland* (Jena: Gustav Fischer, 1933) translated by Carlisle W. Baskin as *Central Places in Southern Germany* (Englewood Cliffs, N.J.: Prentice-Hall, Inc. 1966); Richard T. Ely and George S. Wehrwein, *Land Economics* (New York: The Macmillan Company, 1940), pp. 432-33; Edward L. Ullman, "A Theory of Location for Cities," *American Journal of Sociology*, Vol. 46, May, 1941, pp. 853-64; and August Lösch, *The Economics of Location*, pp. 109-37.

development of railroads, highways, and air travel have brought the advantages of good transportation facilities to many new areas. At the same time, these developments have enhanced the advantages enjoyed by cities with good locations. The growth of port cities such as Montreal, Boston, New York, New Orleans, and San Francisco can be attributed both to their world trade advantages and to the industries and commercial establishments that have found it advantageous to locate in these cities because of the transshipment of goods and materials that takes place at these points. Inland cities such as Chicago, St. Paul, Kansas City, and Dallas enjoy comparable advantages because of their location as railroad and highway centers. In contrast, many once-thriving villages by-passed by railroads and early highways have virtually disappeared.

Just as the location pattern of cities is complicated by transportation factors, so also is it affected by the location of particular types of resources. The presence of valuable forests or mineral deposits, or of special recreation and resort attractions, often favors the rise of cities in out-of-the-way locations. Many industrial cities are located where they are because they specialize in the production or processing of goods that require local supplies of raw materials. Other types of specialized function cities such as political capitals and educational centers often owe their locations to historical accident or design.

Most large cities function as trade centers and also as transportation and specialized manufacturing or service centers. Their development can seldom be attributed exclusively to any one locational advantage. The joint impact of trade, transportation, and specialized production or service factors on the growth of urban centers is suggested by Figures 9-9 and 9-10. Figure 9-9 shows an idealized hexagonal arrangement of trade centers while Figure 9-10A depicts the effects of transportation facilities and particular resources on the rise of cities. When these patterns are

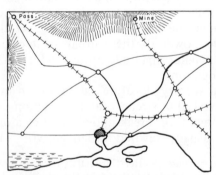

FIGURE 9-10A. Illustration of the impact of differences in the land resource pattern and differences in transportation facilities upon the location and distribution of cities.

FIGURE 9-10B. Composite effect of the hexagonal approach, differences in resource patterns, and differences in transportation facilities upon urban locations.

combined, one gets a complicated distribution pattern such as that shown in Figure 9-10B. At first view, this figure suggests a real-life situation in which cities appear to be located more or less at random without much respect to any set of principles. When considered in light of the factors discussed above and the effect of human decisions in modifying these factor relationships, however, it appears that some logical relationship does exist between the location of cities and the comparative advantages associated with particular sites.

Urban Land-Use Patterns

Cities come in many different sizes and shapes and vary in the functions they perform. Regardless of their size, shape, or function, however, they invariably include a variety of land-use districts. Sites located at and around the 100 percent points are normally used for central business district purposes. Other sites may be used primarily for business and commercial uses. Important areas are frequently used for light and heavy industries. Significantly large areas are used for residential developments and uses. Other areas are used for streets and parking areas, parks and playgrounds, public and private service areas, and transitional districts that are gradually shifting from one use to another. Residential suburbs may also be treated as a special urban land use even though they frequently are located outside city boundaries.

Very few cities start as planned developments. Instead, the average city usually begins as a village and gradually expands. Experience shows that this growth process is often haphazard, poorly planned, and frequently expensive. As cities grow, they usually sprawl outward. Business districts spill over into the surrounding residential areas. Sometimes this expansion has a relatively uniform effect on all the blocks surrounding the original 100 percent spot. Sometimes the expansion is all in one direction or it may follow a single street; and in some instances, business districts migrate with their 100 percent spots to new locations. Industrial areas also are affected by this growth process. The original industrial sites—ordinarily located around the outskirts of small cities—are soon engulfed by the growing city and frequently cut off from contiguous areas that could be used for plant expansion purposes.

Of the various land uses affected by the squeeze of urban growth, the residential area located around the commercial core of the original city is usually the first to give way. With the encroachment of commercial establishments and light industries upon this area, the prime residential districts usually shift in the direction of the city's outskirts. This movement often brings a succession of lower-valued residential uses in the transitional zone surrounding the heart of the city and frequently results in blighted neighborhoods. Timely redevelopment or redesigning of the transitional areas can contribute to the vigor and vitality of the urban economy. When the succession process brings lower uses faster than properties are redeveloped, however, blight often heralds the emergence of slums.

The great variety of growth and changing land-use patterns found in different cities complicates the process of identifying simple principles that govern the allocation of urban land uses. Various explanations of urban land-use patterns have been advanced. Three of the most important of these involve the concentric-zone, sector, and multiple nuclei theories.

Concentric zones in urban land use. One of the first theories designed to explain the internal land-use structure of cities was presented by Ernest W. Burgess in 1925.[16] Burgess developed a concentric-zone approach, which in many ways parallels von Thunen's explanation of rural land uses.

As Figure 9-11 indicates, Burgess designated his central zone as the loop area. This zone is oriented around the 100 percent spot and includes the principal stores, office buildings, banks, theaters, and hotels. It is the business center of the city—the focal point of its commercial, social, and civic life. The concentric zone surrounding the loop area is designated as a transitional zone. This area is made up, for the most part, of older homes and tenement houses. Factories and business establishments are encroaching on the inner portion of this zone and most of the remaining area is blighted. Many of the single-family homes are converted to rooming houses or small apartments, and some properties may be boarded

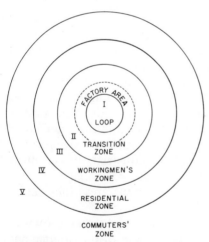

FIGURE 9-11. Burgess' concentric zones in urban land use.

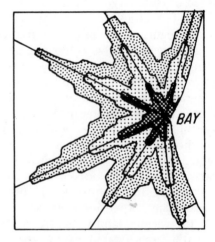

FIGURE 9-12. Illustration of a radial pattern of urban development.

[16]Cf. Ernest W. Burgess, "The Growth of the City," chap. II in Robert E. Park *et al., The City* (Chicago: University of Chicago Press, 1925). Burgess' use of the concentric-circle approach in connection with urban land uses was by no means new. Variations of this approach had been used by several earlier writers including Plato and Aristotle.

up. This area is often characterized by poverty, ill-kept properties, and slum or near-slum conditions.

Beyond the transitional zone lies the working class housing area. The people who reside in this area live in modest single-family homes, row houses, and two- or three-decker dwellings. They prefer to live here because of the lower rents and values and because they are within easy commuting distance of the central business district and their places of work. The higher-cost and more sumptuous residential districts are located near the city's outskirts in zone IV, while a suburban or commuters' zone is found still farther out in zone V.

Burgess used Chicago as an example of his theory; and while he recognized that this example did not exactly fit into his idealized scheme, he assumed that the concentric-zone pattern was more or less typical. In practice, this theory is subject to the same weaknesses as the von Thunen approach. Numerous allowances and modifications are needed to explain the roles played by important streets and transportation routes, by physical barriers such as lakes and rivers, by changing social preferences in land use, by the impact of satellite cities and shopping centers, and by changing land use-capacities.

Some of the principal weaknesses of the concentric-zone formulation can be remedied by shifting to a radial zone concept such as that depicted in Figure 9-12 in which the major land-use zones are aligned along the leading transportation routes. This approach is closer to reality, but allowances must still be made for the not infrequent failure of some classes of people and land uses to gravitate to their predestined zones. In other words, allowances must be made for the failure of the self-regulating aspects of this theory to operate as envisaged.

Sector theory. An important alternative to the concentric-zone hypothesis is provided by the sector theory of urban growth. This theory was developed by Homer Hoyt during the late 1930s and resulted from his analysis of residential neighborhood trends in a study involving more than 200,000 blocks in approximately 70 American cities.[17]

Hoyt assumes a pie-shaped city with a central business district and with numerous sectors or slices extending out from this central district to the city's outskirts. He then argues a theory of axial development in which the particular land uses found in various sectors tend to expand outward along principal transportation routes and along the lines of least resistance. (Figure 9-13.) This theory provides a logical explanation for string-street developments and for the tendency of commercial districts to expand along important streets and to sometimes jump several blocks and then reappear along the same streets. Where possible, factory and industrial districts also tend to continue their expansion along railroads, waterways, and sometimes principal streets.

[17]Cf. Homer Hoyt, *The Structure and Growth of Residential Neighborhoods in American Cities* (Washington: U. S. Government Printing Office, 1939).

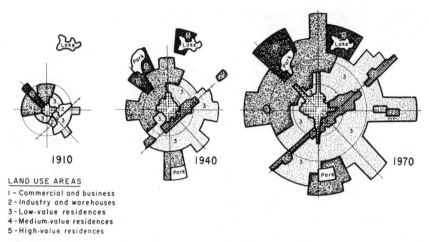

LAND USE AREAS
1 - Commercial and business
2 - Industry and warehouses
3 - Low-value residences
4 - Medium-value residences
5 - High-value residences

FIGURE 9-13. Illustration of Hoyt's sector theory showing generalized urban land-use patterns found in an expanding city at three different time periods.

The sector theory assumes urban growth with succession in land uses in already developed areas and in new developments around the fringe of the city. Commercial areas are usually contained by surrounding areas devoted to other uses and can be expanded only through the acquisition and redevelopment of neighboring uses. Properties in high-value residential areas filter down to lower-rent residential uses as their occupants shift to newer high-prestige locations. Some intermediate- and low-rent housing results from the filtering down process, but a high proportion of the housing occupied by low- and intermediate-income groups is built on new ground as urban growth causes the sectors used for these purposes to expand outward toward and beyond the city's outskirts.

The trend toward outward growth is particularly apparent in the case of the high-rent and high-grade neighborhoods. As Hoyt observed:

> The wealthy seldom reverse their steps and move backward into the obsolete houses which they are giving up. On each side of them is usually an intermediate rental area, so they cannot move sideways. As they represent the highest income group, there are no houses above them abandoned by another group. They must build new houses on vacant land. Usually this vacant land lies available just ahead of the line of march of the area because, anticipating the trend of fashionable growth, land promoters have either restricted it to high-grade use or speculators have placed a value on the land that is too high for the low-rent or intermediate-rental group. Hence the natural trend of the high-rent area is outward, toward the periphery of the city in the very sector in which the high-rent area started.[18]

The sector theory provides a reasonably realistic explanation of the

[18]*Ibid.*, p. 116.

basic structure of land uses found in many North American cities.[19] It must be recognized, however, that the process of urban growth is not entirely mechanistic. The land-use patterns of many cities vary from the model suggested by this theory, and occasional modifications and adjustments again are needed to make the theory fit the facts.

Critics of the sector theory argue that urban land development patterns are "too variable to be conceived in terms of two-dimensional cartographic generalizations."[20] They point out that urban growth structures are affected by numerous economic, social, and cultural factors. Historical accidents, changes in family incomes, aspirations for better housing, and the cultural associations of particular neighborhoods may have important effects upon urban land uses. In similar fashion, the direction and nature of neighborhood growth may be affected by street layouts, changes in transportation facilities, the location of parks and educational institutions, individual deed restrictions, zoning ordinances and city plans, and by public housing and redevelopment programs.

It may also be observed that the sector pattern is the product of a *laissez-faire* society. Most of the land-use sectors now found in our cities have evolved from an accumulation of individual decisions. Only occasionally have they resulted from deliberate city planning. As cities

[19]The sector theory has been most operative in modern industrial cities where sites have gone to the highest bidders and where the process of urban development has not been constrained by cultural and institutional controls. In contrast to the cities that fit this pattern, most of the older cities of Latin America have developed according to a "plaza plan." An open square or plaza provides the civic and social center of these cities. The cathedral, city hall, and state government buildings are located around this plaza, while the municipal market and the business and commercial district are usually concentrated in an adjacent area. Upper-class dwellings occupy most of the blocks immediately surrounding the central plaza while the homes of the lower classes tend to be farther out toward the periphery of the community. This urban development pattern represents the reverse of the "gradients of status" ordinarily found in North American cities and stems in part from regulations issued by Spain's Council of the Indies during the 1500s, which limited the subdivision of residential lots near the urban centers and thus prevented a filtering down of the higher-cost residential sites. Cf. Peter W. Amato, "Population Densities, Land Values, and Socioeconomic Class in Bogota, Colombia," *Land Economics,* Vol. 45, February, 1969, pp. 66-73.

Gideon Sjoberg's research [*The Preindustrial City* (New York: The Free Press, 1960), pp. 95-103] indicates that the "plaza plan" is typical of the land-use patterns found in most preindustrial cities and is directly related to the class system that existed in these cities. As these cities have become more industrial society-oriented and as they have experienced growth and urban redevelopment, they have tended to follow growth patterns more in keeping with those suggested by the sector theory. Cf. Arthur D. Jeffery, "Economic Development in Rhode Island in the Year 1975," *Rhode Island in the Year 1975* (Kingston: University of Rhode Island Bureau of Government Research, 1970), for an interesting comparison of the land use structures of cities of the preindustrial, industrial, and postindustrial periods.

[20]Walter Firey, *Land Use in Central Boston* (Cambridge: Harvard University Press, 1947), pp. 84-85. Also cf. Lloyd Rodwin, "The Theory of Residential Growth and Structure," *The Appraisal Journal,* Vol. 18, July, 1950, pp. 295-317.

develop master plans for the future and then take the necessary steps for the realization of these plans, they will often reshape their urban land-use patterns in the interest of particular social goals. In this respect, institutional factors and government action can have extremely important effects upon the structure and growth of cities.

Adjustments for multiple nuclei. A significant weakness in the concentric zone and sector theories is highlighted by Harris and Ullman's concept of *multiple nuclei.*[21] This concept envisages cities and metropolitan areas with more than one business district. (Figure 9-14.) These urban areas have a principal or downtown business district that provides a central core, but they also have one or more additional business districts located along major streets at some distance from downtown. Each of these districts becomes a nucleus for a competing hierarchy of land uses comparable to those shown for all land uses in Figures 9-4 and 9-5.

Several reasons may be advanced for the growth of the additional nuclei. Some cities in their outward growth have encompassed already existing commercial centers, which have continued to operate as small commercial nuclei within the land-use pattern of the larger cities. Population increase and expansion have posed distance and time-savings problems in many cities that have prompted the shifting and location of many commercial functions to neighborhood centers. Widespread acceptance of the automobile and the construction of new streets and freeways also have freed urban residents from transportation constraints that once made the urban core the transportation hub for the entire city. This situation together with the greater availability of free parking facilities in outlying shopping centers has prompted migration of some of the 100 percent advantage once held by central business district sites to neighborhood shopping centers.[22]

Variations in urban land-use patterns. The sector theory in combination with the multiple nuclei concept provides a meaningful approach for explaining most of the land-use patterns found in modern cities. Important variations occur, however, because of differences in historical backgrounds, the exercise of human choice, the activities of individual developers, and public planning programs. Variations also occur because of differences in urban function and size. The land-use patterns expected

---

[21] For a more detailed discussion of this problem cf. Harris and Ullman, "The Nature of Cities," *loc. cit.*, pp. 13-15.

[22] Richard M. Hurd's early analysis of urban property values (Hurd, *op. cit.*, chap. X) shows that the land-rent triangles and profiles of urban land values associated with central business districts in the nation's major cities rose like sharp needles above the surrounding areas in the early 1900s. These values have remained high, but the relaxation of transportation constraints has greatly broadened the base of the rent triangles with the result that commercial uses are carried on to advantage in far larger areas than was once the case. Cf. Homer Hoyt, "Changing Patterns of Land Values," *Land Economics*, Vol. 36, May, 1960, pp. 487-95.

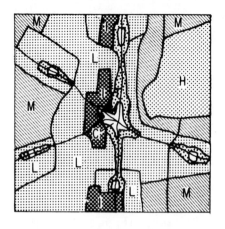

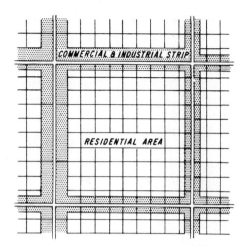

C ☐ COMMERCIAL CENTERS
I ▨ INDUSTRIAL AREAS
T ▨ TRANSITIONAL AREAS
L ▨ LOW-COST HOUSING
M ▨ MEDIUM-COST HOUSING
H ▨ HIGH-COST HOUSING

FIGURE 9-14. Illustration of a multi-nucleated urban land use pattern.

FIGURE 9-15. Example of a grid pattern of suburban development.

in a mining town or in a city with considerable heavy industry, for example, differ substantially from those expected in a college community, a resort area, or a residential suburb.

Explanations of emerging land-use patterns can benefit from classifications of cities by size and function. Nelson, for example, envisages four urban models: (1) the metropolitan commercial center, which he calls Commerce City, (2) cities of medium size, which he calls Centertown, (3) rural trading areas (Countyville), and (4) dormitory suburbs for larger cities (Forest Lake).[23] With this classification, a radial zone theory of growth may be sufficient to explain the urban land-use patterns in Countyville. The sector theory may prove adequate to describe the changing use patterns found in many Centertowns while the sector theory in combination with the multiple nuclei concept best describes the developments in Commerce City. Unlike the other centers, Forest Lake is a satellite community, which has some local shopping facilities but which looks to a central city both for employment opportunities and for many of the commercial goods and services its residents require.

Increasing urbanization and the outward sprawl of metropolitan areas has complicated the land-use patterns associated with smaller as well as larger cities. Aerial observations of typical cities show that central business

[23]Cf. Richard Lawrence Nelson, *The Selection of Retail Locations* (New York: F. W. Dodge Corporation, 1958), pp. 14-18.

districts still attract multistoried buildings and intensive uses; factory sites and industrial uses are frequently located nearby but are moving with increasing frequency to outlying locations; commercial uses tend to follow the major arterial streets that flow out from the central business districts, and neighborhood shopping centers often are developed along these streets; and areas between the major streets are used primarily for residential purposes.

Land-use patterns may or may not follow similar designs in the expanse of suburbs that surround large cities. Aerial views show that hierarchies of uses similar to those found in the cities radiate from many local shopping centers. Quite often, however, the hub designs are replaced by grid-like patterns in which the major avenues and cross-streets are lined with commercial and industrial uses or sites zoned for these uses while the enclosed blocks are reserved for residential uses. (Figure 9-15.) The residential streets found in these superblocks may intersect with the commercial avenues or may connect with feeder streets that insulate the residential areas from commercial traffic.

Industrial Locations

Decisions affecting the location and expansion of industries have a highly significant impact upon the prospects of different sites for urban development and growth. Like other businessmen, the industrialists who make these decisions try to maximize their returns. For them the key economic problem in industrial location is that of securing sites that provide optimum conditions for profit maximization. This means that the sites selected should meet the physical requirements of the industry and at the same time facilitate high productivity, low costs, and a large volume of sales.

Experience shows that most industrial enterprises start with small plants that may or may not expand. These plants frequently owe their location more to historical accident than to economic design. When industrialists deliberately seek an optimum site, however, their problem is often complicated by the simultaneous operation of numerous variables. Some of these involve the supply, cost, and general availability of the raw materials and land resources needed by the industry. Others deal with marketing problems, the size and characteristics of the labor supply, and a host of secondary issues.

Two principal types of costs—processing costs and transfer costs—affect the optimum location of industrial plants.[24] Processing costs include the

[24]Much of the basic thinking in industrial location theory is rooted in the pioneer work of Alfred Weber (cf. Friedrich, op. cit.). For other discussions of this subject cf. Edgar M. Hoover, The Location of Economic Activity; August Lösch, The Economics of Location; Walter Isard, Location and Space-Economy; Coleman Woodbury, The Future of Cities and Urban Redevelopment (Chicago: University of Chicago Press, 1953), pp. 105-43; and Glen E. McLaughlin, "Criteria in the Selection of Cities for Industrial Location," The Appraisal Journal, Vol. 17, April, 1949, pp. 168-72.

many expenses that arise in the industrial production process as labor and other factors are used to transform raw and semifinished materials into manufactured goods. Transfer costs, in turn, deal with the expense of moving materials to processing plants and finished goods to their points of sale or use. Industrialists naturally attempt to minimize both types of costs. In their search for optimum industrial locations, they recognize that transportation cost considerations cause some industries to be material-oriented and some to be market-oriented. Others are less affected by transportation costs and may be attracted by the agglomeration economies of particular cities or regions where the presence of other industries provides pools of skilled labor and management, capital availability, services of complementary industries, public utilities, and public services.

Material-oriented industries. Extractive industries such as mining, lumbering, and agriculture always locate near the source of their principal product. Quite naturally, the location of these industries is determined by the absolute need for operating at specific sites where coal, minerals, or timber may be found or where agricultural products can be and are produced.

Once raw materials of this type have been produced, questions frequently arise concerning where they should be processed. They can be shipped to other locations but this involves transfer costs. On the other hand, their processing at a local site usually entails the bringing in of some materials from other areas and the later shipment of the processed goods to market. In many cases, both sets of transportation costs are about equal; and there is no particular transportation-cost advantage in locating the processing industry near the source of material as compared with a location near the final market. Many processing activities, however, involve weight-reduction operations or other changes that result in transportation economies. It is usually to the advantage of the industry in these cases to locate its initial processing activities near the source of its raw materials.

Material-oriented industries may be divided into four principal groups. The first of these involves industries such as agriculture, fishing, lumbering, mining, and outdoor recreation, which are bound to the location of the basic natural resources upon which they depend.

A second group includes those processing activities that involve elimination of waste materials and excess weight. Minerals such as copper and iron are often found in combination with large quantities of rock and slag. These mineral ores are usually either smelted or subjected to flotation, beneficiation, or other weight-reduction processes near their sources. In this manner, most of the waste material is eliminated before the metal is shipped to other processing points. Except in those instances in which timber can be floated to a mill, most sawmill operations tend to be material-oriented. This situation results mostly from the reduction of bulk and weight that comes with the processing of logs into rough or finished lumber. Numerous agricultural processing operations also fall into this class. Farmers who sell butterfat usually separate their cream from the skim milk and thereby reduce the bulk of their marketable product. The high transport costs associated with bulky products such as sugar beets and sugar cane favor the location of sugar factories within reasonably short distances of their supply. Other products such as cheese, dried and condensed milk, vegetable oils, maple and cane syrup, turpentine, and rosin also are processed near their sources of supply.

A third group of material-oriented industries involves processes that require large quantities of fuels, power, or water that do not appear in the final product. The large quantities of coal and coke required for iron and steel production in times past often favored the location of steel mills near the sources of coal supply.[25] High electrical power requirements favor the location of synthetic nitrate, aluminum, and electrometallurgical plants near hydroelectric power sites. Similarly, the high water requirements of some industries together with the economies of water transportation favor industrial locations along navigable waterways.

A final group of material-oriented industries benefit from processing changes that make their product less bulky, easier to handle, less perishable, or more susceptible to bulk handling. These changes lead to transportation economies and thus favor material orientation. Cotton gins and compresses reduce the bulk of the raw cotton by forcing it into compact bales. Metals are often processed into ingots or sheets to facilitate their handling and reuse. Canning and preserving operations reduce the perishability of fruits and vegetables and thus lower their transportation and storage costs. Another type of material-oriented service is provided by local grain elevators, commission agents, junk dealers, and others who assemble carload lots of materials for shipment to other points.

Material-oriented and market-oriented industries are both concerned with processing as well as with transfer costs. Before an industry can be classified as truly material-oriented, its savings in transfer costs must outweigh the possible cost advantages of other sites. This problem is frequently complicated by the tendency of industries to use a variety of raw materials and to participate in the joint production of many products. It can also be affected by technological change. The coke industry, for

---

[25] The first large iron works in this country used several tons of coal or coke for each ton of finished product. Under these circumstances producers found it definitely to their advantage to locate their mills at sites such as Pittsburgh and Birmingham near their sources of coal supply. Technological developments have permitted large savings in fuel, and many steel mills now use a lower tonnage of coal than of iron ore. This development has favored the location of steel mills at transshipment points such as Cleveland, Buffalo, and Baltimore—and with coal secured by ballast-backhauling in ore boats at Duluth and at Volta Redonda in Brazil. It has also favored the development of steel mills at market-oriented sites such as Detroit, Gary, and Los Angeles. Cf. Hoover, *op. cit.*, pp. 42-44; also Erich Zimmermann, *World Resources and Industries*, rev. ed. (New York: Harper & Brothers, 1951), pp. 660-69.

example, started out as a material-oriented enterprise. Coke ovens were located near the mines because it took 2,000 pounds of coal to produce 1,200 pounds of coke. However, as soon as a commercial market developed for the coal gas produced in the coking process, it became more profitable to locate the coke ovens near industry.

Market-oriented industries. While some products benefit from weight-and-bulk reduction operations in the early stages of their production, many others experience a reversal of this process as they approach the final stages of their production-distribution process. As these products "approach by stages the form in which they will be delivered to the final consumer, they become progressively more fragile, more cumbersome to pack and handle, more valuable in relation to their weight, and differentiated into more separate types and sizes."[26] Developments of this type favor the market-orientation of many industrial operations.

Bottled-beverage plants provide an ideal example of a market-oriented industry because their operations normally involve the addition of carbonated water to a concentrated syrup—a process that adds considerable weight and bulk to the product. Bakeries fall into this class because of the bulk and weight they add to their product and because of the premium most customers place on freshness of product. The building construction industry is market-oriented as are the activities of most local plumbers, electricians, and service workers. Much the same situation applies with milk bottling, ice making, potato chip, popular priced brewery, and other similar establishments.

Most large industrial and mercantile concerns seriously consider the problem of market orientation when they locate new plants and stores. Several mail-order houses operate with both regional and local outlets. The automobile industry centers in the populous North Central region but operates branch production and assembly plants in other regions and countries. Even the famous Milwaukee beers are now produced in branch plants located in different sections of the country.

Foot-loose and other attraction-oriented industries. Many industries are neither material- nor market-oriented. From a transport cost standpoint, these industries may be regarded as relatively foot-lose and free to locate where they will. Transportation cost considerations often make it advisable for them to locate at points between their principal sources of raw materials and their major markets. Locations away from this area have the disadvantage of double transfer costs—shipment of raw materials to the factory and then backshipment of goods to market. Within the zone of optimum transfer costs, the so-called foot-loose industries usually find it best to locate at transshipment points or at locations that favor low processing costs.

Labor is the most important and most expensive ingredient in the

[26]Hoover, *op. cit.*, p. 36.

manufacturing process for many industries. These industries find it natural to seek factory sites in areas that offer adequate supplies of labor. Frequently, they share in the agglomeration economies of other firms by locating in populous centers where they can draw upon the large supply of skilled and semiskilled workers used by other industries. Location in these areas makes it possible for these industries to suddenly increase or decrease their labor force if such a need arises with a minimum of social repercussion. Industrialists frequently hesitate to relocate or open branch establishments in areas where they will be the leading industry until they have had years of management experience, feel competent to develop their own skilled labor force, and feel confident that they can offer employment stability in the new plant area.

Labor-oriented industries often seek particular types of employees. Textile mills frequently locate in heavy-industry towns so as to take advantage of the large potential supply of women employees found in these areas. Plants requiring highly skilled workers often avoid expensive recruiting operations by locating in cities with comparable plants. Many industrialists try to locate their new plants in low-wage areas, areas that offer facilities that contribute to low living costs, and, in some cases, areas where labor has not as yet been unionized.

Many industries not normally classified as material-oriented, market-oriented, or labor-oriented are attracted to particular locations by the availability of special attractions. Some "clean" industries, for example, have been attracted to industrial parks located near large universities by the prospects of professional consulting services and staff participation in the cultural advantages of university communities. Other industries find it logical to locate among similar or complementary industries in metropolitan regions where they can share in the local pools of managerial and consultant talent, the availability of banking and other needed industrial services, and the prospect of providing goods or services for complementary establishments.

Importance of the land factor. Business decisions regarding new industrial locations often hinge upon secondary issues. Operators may be primarily interested in finding favorable raw-material, market, transportation, and labor situations. But they are also interested in locating at sites that offer good living conditions for employees; adequate space for parking and plant expansion; good supplies of water, power, and other utilities; and moderately low land values and tax levies. In this respect, they are interested in the land factor, and their decisions are often influenced by considerations involving this factor.

Throughout the horse-and-buggy period, those sites that provided water power, favorable water or railroad transportation facilities, and a good labor supply ordinarily had first choice for industrial use. The proximity of these sites to central business areas often resulted in adjacent developments and some bidding up of land values. With the development of new power and transportation facilities, there has been a trend toward industrial decentralization. New industries—particularly the heavy industries—still tend to locate near water, railroad, or highway transportation routes; but there has been a distinct tendency for them to locate around the periphery of cities where land is less expensive, taxes are lower, and where large areas are available for use.

Past experience shows that many industries have reserved too little space for future expansion. Modern technology frequently favors a shift from multistory to single-floor factories. At the same time, good worker relations often call for the provision of large parking areas. Both of these situations call for more space. Yet many industries originally established on the outskirts of cities now find themselves hemmed in with only limited opportunities for expansion in contiguous areas. Urban redevelopment offers a high-cost answer to this problem. Plant relocation suggests another somewhat costly answer. Knowledge of these situations has caused many industrialists to place high emphasis upon space considerations in their choice of new plant locations.

Industries often occupy high-value sites and occasionally invest large sums in building- and site-improvement programs. As a general rule, their land costs are small compared with their cash outlays for raw materials, marketing, and labor. This situation sometimes causes people to dismiss land-cost factors as relatively unimportant. However, one should not downgrade the importance of this factor. An industrialist who pays $1,000 a month in rent or ownership costs on his place of operations has a definite advantage, other things being equal, over a competitor who pays $2,000 a month. Factory owners sometimes find that their properties have higher market and rental values for other uses than for their current uses. It is often good business in these cases for owners to sell or rent their properties and move their industries to new sites where they can benefit from lower land costs.

Personal and noneconomic considerations. Industrial location decisions often involve noneconomic considerations. Most industrial plants start as small businesses. As such, they are usually started in the operator's home community at a site that is both available and convenient to him. The plant owners who choose these locations are often motivated by personal conditions and preferences. Many of the sites they select enjoy considerable comparative advantage. With good management and the smile of fortune, businesses located at these locations often prosper and expand while businesses founded in less favorable locations frequently fail.

One cannot assume, however, that all industries that start at unfavorable locations are doomed to mediocrity or failure. An investor with a new idea, a new industry with exceptional business management, an ambitious city with strong leadership, or some historical accident such as a large government investment in a defense industry can often compensate for an initial lack of locational comparative advantage.

Following this line of thought, one might argue that many of our leading industries could have found more profitable sites than those at which they have developed. The automobile industry of Detroit and the rubber industry of Akron, for example, might have found it more profitable to locate at sites closer to their sources of material supply. Once these industries were established, however, they attracted skilled labor forces and developed industrial economies that gave these cities a relative advantage over potential competitive sites. Much of the success enjoyed by these industries can be attributed to these man-made advantages and to their favorable location with respect to their major markets.

Institutional arrangements such as favorable public regulations and tax policies, far-sighted planning for the provision of needed utilities and local services, and programs that contribute to civic pride and enhancement of local amenity values also can add to comparative advantage.

Shifts in industrial locations. History shows that industries frequently migrate to new locations and that this shift often has an important impact upon property values and the economic life of communities. Industrial migration sometimes results in stranded communities and ghost towns. This has often been the situation in mining, lumbering, and other one-industry towns. On other occasions, the effects of shifting industrial locations are sometimes cushioned by the growth of new industries.

Industries differ a great deal in their ability to shift to new locations. Light industries that depend on rented equipment and buildings can often move for relatively minor reasons. Heavy industries with huge investments in existing plants in turn are often bound to their present sites. Other industries may be more able to move, but find the process expensive.

Decisions to move are ordinarily prompted by factors such as: (1) exhaustion of a raw material base such as occurs when a forest is cut over or an ore deposit is mined out. (2) changes in material requirements such as the location of power-using plants away from water power sites once alternative sources of power become available, (3) changes in transportation costs made possible by the construction of new facilities, (4) adjustments in individual processing costs, which cause particular sites to either gain or lose low-cost production advantages, (5) increasing tax loads, (6) site restrictions, which prevent desired plant expansions at existing locations, (7) technological developments, which permit new products and call for new industrial plants, and (8) changing market tastes, such as the substitution of automobiles for buggies, which create new markets for some products and the phasing out of production for others.

Location of Commercial Establishments[27]

Compared with other types of land use, the total area used for business

[27]For more detailed discussions of this subject cf. Richard U. Ratcliff, "The Problem of Retail Site Selection," *Michigan Business Studies* (University of Michigan, 1939), Vol. 9, No. 1; Ratcliff, *Urban Land Economics*, chap. XIII; and Nelson, *op. cit.*

and commercial sites is usually small. From the standpoint of intensity of use, rent-paying capacity, and land values, however, the areas occupied by commercial business districts represent some of our most valuable lands.

Most businessmen recognize that their success or failure frequently depends upon their choice of a suitable business location. Accordingly, they have a definite incentive to seek locations that promise them the greatest opportunities for profit. Their actual decisions in this regard are affected by a variety of factors. Naturally, most businessmen prefer sites that promise a high volume of business activity. These locations are usually found in the central business district at or near the spot most accessible to the greatest number of potential customers. But before an operator decides on a site, he must weigh the costs associated with its use against its business advantages. If the added volume of business expected at the 100 percent site does not exceed the additional cost of this site, the operator will usually find it advisable to locate at the outskirts of the central business district, on an upper floor of a downtown office building, or in some outlying sector of the city.

Other factors may also favor locations away from the downtown area. A neighborhood grocer or druggist locates away from the central district so that he may better supply the needs of the people living in his particular neighborhood. Interior decorators and exclusive millinery or ladies wear shops usually cater to the tastes of upper-income groups and often find it desirable to locate near the homes of this group. Furniture stores, laundries, and dry cleaning establishments frequently locate on the outskirts of the business district or in the suburbs because of their space requirements and their need for lower rents and more adequate parking facilities than are often available in central shopping districts. Other establishments such as lumber and coal yards, warehouses, and freight depots have large space requirements and must usually locate along railroads or waterways.

In the idealized urban land-use pattern, most business, professional, and commercial activity takes place in the central business district around the 100 percent spot. This general situation holds in most small cities. Significant concentrations of commercial activity also are found in the central business districts of larger cities, but these cities typically have experienced considerable decentralization of their retail activities. Several factors including the flight of numerous upper- and middle-income families to the suburbs, increasing urban area size, shopper convenience, the acceptance of standard brands that can be purchased just as easily at outlying locations as at 100 percent sites, widespread ownership and use of automobiles, concern over parking problems in congested downtown areas, and decreasing reliance upon the urban mass transportation facilities that radiate from central business districts have favored local shopping center developments that cater to neighborhood and multi-neighborhood needs.

Central business districts grow and expand in response to demand for the services they provide. These districts are not always found at the exact geographic center of the city. However, they are almost always found near the hub of the city's traffic and transportation system and at sites both accessible and convenient to large numbers of people. Considerable concentrations of people are attracted to these districts during business hours. This contributes to high volumes of retail and other business activity, which in turn result in intensive land-use practices, high rents, and high land values.

Street sites around 100 percent spots ordinarily are used for retailing purposes. Large office buildings, banks, hotels, and first-run theaters also tend to congregate around this point. Among the retailing establishments, the central shopping district is a focal point for large department stores, apparel shops, variety stores, restaurants, drugstores, and the various specialty shops that serve the many shoppers who flock to this district. Surrounding the area of most intensive retail activity—and often inter-penetrating it—are a number of less intensive retail uses. Furniture, music, radio and television, sporting goods, and army surplus stores often appear in this class. The high demand for parking space favors the use of consid-erable areas within and around the central shopping district for parking lots.

> As the central business area merges into the wholesale and light-manufacturing district or into the slum and rooming-house area, there appear the lowest grade of central business uses—pawnshop, food store, pool hall and beer garden, burlesque house, automotive supply shop, shoe repairer, cheap photographer, and cheap restaurant. In the direction of the better residential areas, the retail area tapers off in specialty shops, food stores, restaurants, gift shops, small men's and women's apparel stores, and automotive showrooms.[28]

Sites near the 100 percent spot supposedly offer the greatest oppor-tunities for profitable use. They tend to have the highest site values and command the highest rents. The use-capacity and profit opportunities associated with the surrounding areas often decline rather rapidly. Sites located a few blocks away on a main street, a block away on a back street, or only a few floors above the street may have only a fraction of the income-producing value of a ground-floor location near a strategic business corner.

The scarcity factor in this situation causes considerable bidding and counterbidding between firms and operators for the choice locations. This process often results in land-use patterns in which retail space is allocated in accordance with the rent-paying capacities of the various operators. This pattern is seldom stable. New adjustments are always taking place. Operators are often tempted by the opportunities suggested by site vacancies in the 100 percent district. Very few of them, however, can

[28]*Ibid.,* p. 387.

estimate the exact effect a move may have upon their volume of business. As a result, most site bids involve an element of trial and error. Some blind bids turn out very favorably. Others sometimes involve higher rental commitments than the operators can pay and eventually result in bankruptcy, closing-out, and removal sales, and in the vacating of sites for use by new operators.

Successful location factors.   Many commercial firms—particularly those with chain operations—make a science of their selection of success-ful commercial locations. Before they choose any particular site, they analyze the advantages, disadvantages, and income-producing prospects of several alternative sites. They consider the space, parking, and other facilities associated with each site. Studies are made to determine the potential number of customers in the area, their levels of income, and their buying habits and tastes. Pedestrian traffic counts are made of the number of people who pass the various store sites during shopping hours. Consideration also is given to the problem of competition with other commercial establishments.

In their search for good commercial locations, individual businessmen must consider the characteristics and buying habits of their potential customers together with the nature of the various goods or services they provide. Men and women frequently vary in their buying habits. Except for their purchase of articles such as automobiles and hobby goods, men usually tend to be more hurried and impatient in their shopping than women. They are often "prone to buy the first article that approaches their requirements or taste. Convenience is more important in their minds, and the opportunity for comparison is less important."[29] Most women, on the other hand, seem to enjoy shopping, and attack their shopping problems with an enthusiastic thoroughness that often leads them to compare numerous articles both within and between stores before they make a purchase. "They are more observant, more susceptible to display, and hence indulge more generally in impulse buying."[30]

Differences in buying habits, tastes, and levels of consumer incomes often have an important effect upon retail locations, the types and volume of goods sold, and the manner in which the goods are displayed. Stores in low-income neighborhoods seldom stock luxury items. Some commercial establishments cater to men and thrive because of the convenience of their locations. Ladies' apparel shops, on the other hand, usually find it profitable to prepare attractive eye-catching displays, to afford their customers every opportunity to compare their products, and to facilitate milady's comparison process by locating near clusters of similar shops that deal in comparable and complementary products.

Another important consideration involves the type of goods or services

[29]*Ibid.*, p. 378.
[30]*Ibid.*

supplied and the relative frequency with which they are purchased. Frequently purchased products often are described as convenience or shopper goods. With small and relatively inexpensive convenience goods such as cigarettes, chewing gum, or newspapers, most customers tend to patronize the closest and most conveniently located vendor. Food stores can depend upon a wider range of patronage. Their usual space requirements, need for parking space, the bulk of their products, and the frequency with which they are purchased favor their location at points convenient to customers. Accordingly, they are often found in the central shopping districts of small cities but usually appear around these districts and in the community and neighborhood shopping centers of larger cities.

In contrast to convenience goods, articles such as pianos, TV sets, automobiles, and diamond rings represent sizable purchases that can easily be postponed until the buyer has made comparisons in other stores and "thought it over." Because of the tendency of buyers to shop around for these types of specialty goods, it is often economic to locate automobile showrooms, furniture stores, and other comparable establishments outside the central retail districts. Stores that feature specialty products such as jewelry find it to their advantage, however, to locate in central shopping districts where they can use glittering window displays to attract additional customers.

As the above discussion suggests, stores that feature convenience and shopper goods ordinarily find it advantageous to locate along the principal paths of pedestrian traffic. Similar locations are advantageous for service workers such as barbers and shoe repairmen. Locations near 100 percent spots are less important in the sale of postponable specialty goods such as automobiles or furniture. When dealers in these products have large space or parking area requirements, they ordinarily find it advisable to locate outside the high-rent district. It often is profitable for them to substitute larger advertising expenditures for the sums they could have paid in higher rents. Electricians, plumbers, and other service workers who depend largely upon telephone contacts find it just as well to locate outside the central business district.

Rise of shopping centers. Almost every city has neighborhood shops and stores that exist and sometimes thrive because of their ability to fulfill the convenience needs of nearby residents. As in the hexagonal concept of urban locations, these shops provide a low hierarchial level of services while the customers served look to higher hierarchial levels (central business districts and shopping centers) for the filling of more specialized needs.

Most older cities of the past typically offered only two levels of commercial services—neighborhood stores and the central business district. Rapid urban growth and the outward expansion of cities in combination with the advent of widespread ownership and use of automobiles and the acceptance of standard brands has favored the emergence of shopping centers as an intermediary hierarchial commercial service level.[31] These centers customarily provide a clustering of retail shops that specialize in the provision of convenience and shopper goods and services. Ordinarily, they are located at sites convenient to large numbers of shoppers and offer abundant parking facilities.

Several factors including ease of accessibility, the attraction of new facilities, the wide variety of convenience goods offered, and special shopping services such as free parking and opportunities to shop under one roof in air-conditioned comfort have contributed to the prosperity of shopping centers. These advantages have made it possible for these centers to siphon off much of the trade advantage once enjoyed by central business district establishments and by neighborhood shops. Not all shopping centers, however, are a commercial success. Some are poorly designed, lack a desirable mix of shops, have inadequate parking facilities, or already have lost the luster of newness. Some also are overbuilt or suffer from competition with other centers better located to serve the same market area.

From the standpoint of over-all successful location, shopping centers should be located at strategic sites that enable them to handle the convenience and shopper goods needs of large numbers of potential customers. An idealized location model for commercial establishments in the typical American metropolitan region calls for three (and sometimes four) hierarchial levels of service centers. Neighborhood shops, where they exist, provide the lowest level of service. Shopping centers should provide the next level of service and should be so located as to service the shopping needs of several contiguous neighborhoods. Two levels of shopping centers can be envisaged in some areas, with small centers serving several neighborhoods and larger shopping centers often duplicating these services but offering additional attractions for larger areas. Central business districts should provide the highest level of services. In so doing, they duplicate the lower orders of services for nearby residents and for those who choose to use their facilities while at the same time offering many specialty goods and services not provided at the shopping centers.[32]

In addition to selecting a site of adequate size, which is readily accessible to large numbers of potential customers, successful operation of a shopping center calls for careful selection of the shops and services found at the center. The final mix of shops and services should provide for

[31] Nelson, *op. cit.*, pp. 26-34, suggests a concept of interceptor rings, which places shopping centers at predictable distances from the downtown center along the major streets that radiate from the urban core.

[32] As is the case with the idealized location of villages and cities, this pattern of hierarchical levels of commercial establishments is more indicative of what ought to be than of what is. The particular talents, interests, and clientele of operators at even the neighborhood store level can cause them to provide specialized services normally available only at higher hierarchical levels.

a wide gamut of shopper needs and at the same time have definite drawing power. Success almost invariably calls for the presence of one or more *generative* businesses such as branches of department stores or large food markets, which use active advertising programs to attract customers to their sites of business.[33] Several *sharing* businesses (e.g. clothing, shoe, book, bakery, and liquor stores), which are usually smaller and do less advertising than the self-generators but which benefit from location near them, should be included in the mix. Some *suscipient* establishments such as barber, magazine, and tobacco shops, which benefit from locations near concentrations of people, also may be included.

Location of Residential Developments

Location decisions affecting residential developments can be influenced by economic considerations in much the same way as those involving commercial and industrial establishments. The typical householder wants convenience as well as space and a pleasing environment. He prefers to live near his place of employment, near market and service centers, and at the same time minimize his housing costs. Yet while the problem of house- hold location is similar in many ways to that of commercial and industrial locations, it is also different. Consumer satisfactions and personal prefer- ences play a bigger role and economic considerations a lesser role with residential location decisions. The commercial operator or industrialist who fails to heed the economic implications of his location decisions courts business failure. Householders who choose inconveniently located or overly expensive residential properties, in contrast, can often justify their choices on noneconomic grounds even though they may have to subsidize them with considerable outlays of time and money.

What people want and what they finally get in residential locations is a product of time and circumstances. Farm families in the United States tend to live on the farm tracts they operate. Urban workers in contrast live at other sites and commute to work. Before the advent of modern transportation facilities, these sites were almost always found near the worker's place of employment. Today they can be located almost any- where within a large commuting zone depending upon the worker's per- sonal choices and his willingness and ability to pay the costs associated with his location decision. Convenience of access is still an important factor for many people. The relative emphasis given to it, however, involves other considerations, several of which are associated with the workings of the succession process.

Succession in residential developments. Single-family homes often line the streets of towns and small cities to sites within a block or two of the 100 percent spot. The most pretentious and highest-cost homes are

---

[33]Cf. Nelson, *op. cit.,* pp. 52-53.

usually located on one or two streets near the center of town. Lower-cost housing is ordinarily found at less favored locations on the main streets, on back streets, near the local industries, and sometimes across the railroad tracks.

With urban growth, this pattern gradually changes. Expansion of the commercial district calls for the acquisition and redevelopment of adjacent residential sites and automatically brings nearby sites into a transitional use zone. New high-cost housing is built in open areas, usually as an extension of the existing high-cost housing district. New medium- and low-cost housing also is built around the fringe of the city. Meanwhile, occupants of the higher-cost older houses consider the prospect of modernizing and rebuilding their houses but frequently decide instead to sell and move to more prestigous new locations. In selling their houses, they start a "filtering down" process in which the high-cost and medium-cost houses of yesteryear gradually decline in market value, are occupied by a succession of lower-incomed owners and tenants, and eventually are converted into apartment houses, rooming houses, or are acquired for other purposes.

Virtually every American city has experienced growth patterns that demonstrate the ability of commercial and industrial establishments to outbid housing for the use of particular sites. With urban growth, new residential developments normally occur farther and farther from the downtown centers while residential properties located close to commercial sites often are allowed to deteriorate both in function and appearance. These properties could be refurbished or replaced with new housing developments, but their basic site values for possible commercial use often appear too high to justify new long-term commitments to residential development.

Meanwhile, new housing is constructed along the principal streets and highways that radiate from the city and in the back-street areas that lie between these streets. High-cost, medium-cost, and low-cost residential units normally are constructed in neighborhoods with properties of similar values. Frequently, new housing in each of these value classes is built farther out in a continuation of the same sectors in which similar developments already exist. Hoyt has observed that when no restraints are present, high-cost residential neighborhoods "do not skip about at random" but rather "follow a definite path in one or more sectors of the city." They gravitate to sites easily accessible to fast transportation lines, "grow toward the homes of the leaders of the community," "progress toward high ground which is free from floods," "spread along lake, bay, river and ocean fronts, where such waterfronts are not used for industry," and "grow towards the section of the city which has free, open country beyond the edges."[34]

[34] Hoyt, *op. cit.*, pp. 114-19.

High-cost residential neighborhoods frequently have first choice of the available sites for new residential subdivisions and developments. It must be recognized, however, that real estate developers and promoters ordinarily play strategic roles in determining the value-class levels of new sites. They may not be able to make poor sites attractive for high-cost developments, but through their decisions concerning lot sizes and prices, building restrictions, the preservation and enhancement of amenity features, and the construction of model houses, they can bend the direction of residential growth and make their sites attractive for high-, medium-, or low-cost developments.

Exceptions to the normal outward pattern of high-cost residential growth can be found in many cities particularly when factors such as sentiment, the presence of particular amenities, or private or public redevelopment programs are involved. Urban renewal programs have created unique opportunities for a reversal of the usual tendency of high-cost units to locate near the city's edge or in the suburbs, while lower-cost units occupy the sites closer to the urban core. Deluxe high-rent high-rise residential properties are frequently built in redeveloped, highly accessible, once down-trodden areas. The location of these developments at sites adjacent or near to low–income housing suggests some income-level integration in housing. This integration is largely illusory, however, because the high-income residents of the modern high-rise apartments tend to live apart from their lower-incomed neighbors. Their numbers are made up mostly of professional people who have decided to trade the privacy and open space offered by suburban living for the convenience and easy accessibility of downtown locations.

Explanations of residential locations.   Personal and family choices play a major role in residential site location decisions. A husband may want to live close to work. His wife wants to be reasonably close to commercial and social service centers. Both want to live in a "good" and prestigious neighborhood and, yet, secure housing at what they consider a reasonable price. They want indoor living space plus outdoor play areas for their children and easy access to schools and parks. They may want to live near particular friends or relatives or be near public transportation facilities. They may desire a spot away from the city and close to nature and perhaps a site where they can build their dream house. These objectives are seldom filled by any one location. Some goals must be emphasized at the expense of others in the decision-making process, and final decisions are often hard to explain.

In an early discussion of the economics of residential site locations, Robert Murray Haig observed:

> In choosing a residence purely as a consumption proposition, one buys accessibility precisely as one buys clothes or food. He considers how much he wants the contacts furnished by the central location, weighing the "costs of friction" involved—the various possible combinations of site rent, time value,

and transportation costs; he compares this want with his other desires and his resources, and he fits it into his scale of consumption, and buys.[35]

Haig emphasized two factors—the effect of nearness to central locations on site rents, and personal choice considerations.

If one assumes a single central market, standardized units of residential space, and exclusive concern with Haig's "costs of friction," it would make little difference where a person lived in a city. At all locations, his "costs of friction"—the sum of his site rent and costs of transportation—would be the same. These assumptions do not hold true in the real world. Residents are oriented to many different employment, shopping, social, and other service nodes; some residential sites are larger, more prestigious, of higher quality, and involve access to more amenities than others; and individual assumptions as to transportation costs vary with choices in transportation methods and time-cost considerations.

Haig's prospective resident obviously exercises personal choices in his selection of a residence site. Low-income constraints may cause him to sacrifice space, privacy, and housing services by locating in a congested, low-rent ghetto area. With more income or stronger desire for good housing, he could logically seek higher quality housing at a downtown location or pay the additional transportation costs required if he is to have access to the more spacious and better quality housing that is available at other locations.

Spatial and environmental considerations—the amounts of space and the relative access to a safer, more esthetic, more congenial or pleasing environment that can be secured per dollar of housing expenditure in combination with the average householder's desire to maximize the amount and quality of the living space he can secure for his housing outlays—are the important determinants of residential location decisions. Many urban families move to suburban locations as their circumstances permit because they feel that they can acquire more and better quality space there than they can afford at the more intensively used, higher-cost downtown sites. These decisions often involve higher joint costs for site rents and for commuting to work than would have been paid had the family remained closer to the urban core. Transportation costs aside, these families sometimes occupy lower-cost space on a family-unit basis in the suburbs than they would downtown, frequently pay about the same amount for housing at one location as the other, and on some occasions choose to occupy large lots that cost them more on a family-unit basis than the smaller lots with higher square-footage values they might other-wise occupy at more central locations.

Housing expenditures represent a consumptive expenditure for most families, and family goals are often weighted heavier in residential location decisions than are more strictly economic considerations. The family's

---

[35] Haig, *loc. cit.*, p. 423.

choice of the site where it will live involves its image of itself and the spatial and off-work-hours' environment it desires. High-income families tend to place more emphasis and value on amenities than lower-income families.[36] They tend to locate in neighborhoods where they can enjoy above average homes, more open space, and more privacy because they can afford to do so. Many medium- and lower-income families also aspire to these housing amenities and move to suburban and rural surroundings where they can enjoy these advantages even though their "costs of friction" may require subsidizing their housing expenditures with family income that could very well be used for other purposes.

The typical high-income family that selects a suburban residential location may give only secondary emphasis to the fact that the husband must travel a considerable distance to his office four or five times a week. A house in the suburbs may represent an inseparable part of their picture of the successful executive. The entire family may associate a wide spectrum of values with their opportunity to live in a suburban environment. The wife's life may be built around daily visits to stores, friends, and social functions in the area. The children will be close to "their" school and "their" friends. The husband may see professional, social, and recreation advantages in living near the country club or near the homes of his business associates.[37] Similarities of interests as well as incomes also tie large numbers of middle- and low-income families to neighborhoods composed mostly of individuals and families with comparable incomes.

—SELECTED READINGS

Alonso, William, *Location and Land Use* (Cambridge: Harvard University Press, 1968).

Hall, Peter, ed., *Von Thunen's Isolated State* (London: Pergamon Press, 1966).

Hoover, Edgar M., *The Location of Economic Activity* (New York: McGraw-Hill Book Company, Inc., 1948).

——, *An Introduction to Regional Economics* (New York: Alfred A. Knopf, 1971).

[36] Cf. R. N. S. Harris, G. S. Tolley, and C. Harrell, "The Residence Site Choice," *Review of Economics and Statistics*, Vol. 50, May, 1968, pp. 50-155.

[37] Cf. Alonso, *op. cit.;* and Lowdon Wingo, Jr., *Transportation and Urban Land* (Washington: Resources for the Future, Inc., 1961). Alonso argues that the "bid-price surfaces" represented by the slope of the urban residential rent cones or rent triangles should favor the location of high-cost housing at sites close to urban centers rather than farther out on cheaper land. In explaining this paradox, he indicates: "The locational pull of residences amounts to the price times the marginal rate of transportation costs. However, the bid-price gradient or pull per acre is the total pull divided by the substitution between land and travel times minus marginal quantity of land. Therefore, in many cases, where price and income elasticities of land are high, the slope of the bid-price surfaces of those with higher incomes will be less steep." (Alonso, "A Reformulation of Classical Location Theory and Its Relation to Rent Theory," *Regional Science Association Papers*, Vol. 19, 1966, p. 42).

Hoyt, Homer, *The Structure and Growth of Residential Neighborhoods in American Cities* (Washington: U. S. Government Printing Office, 1939).

Isard, Walter, *Location and Space-Economy* (New York: John Wiley & Sons, Inc., 1956).

Nelson, Richard I., *The Selection of Retail Locations* (New York: F. W. Dodge Corporation, 1958).

Nourse, Hugh O., *Regional Economics* (New York: McGraw-Hill Book Company, 1968).

Ratcliff, Richard U., *Urban Land Economics* (New York: McGraw-Hill Book Company, Inc., 1949), chaps. II, XIII.

10

Land Resource Values and the Real Estate Market

Land resources are frequently viewed primarily as economic commodities that can be bought and sold. Their possession involves rights people want for various reasons and for which they often are willing to pay substantial sums of money. The sale, mortgaging, and taxation of these resources requires special value appraisal techniques. The fact that they are wanted and have values that extend into the future gives them an attractive investment potential, and their frequent purchase and sale has brought the rise of real estate markets.

THE NATURE OF PROPERTY VALUE

Justice Brandeis once observed that "value is a word of many meanings."[1] The truth of this dictum is demonstrated by the dozens of different meanings we apply to this term in popular usage. In a broad sense, "value implies capacity to satisfy wants"; and "there are as many kinds of value as there are classes of wants."[2] Thus we may deal with aesthetic values, political values, psychic values, social values, spiritual values,

[1] Southwestern Bell Telephone Company v. Public Service Commission, 262 U. S. 276, 310 (1923)

[2] Edwin R. A. Seligman, *Principles of Economics* (New York: Longmans, Green & Co., Inc., 1905), p. 174.

and the like. Economists and appraisers are primarily concerned with economic and market values, but they too use the term "value" in many different contexts and with different adjectives to mean different things.[3]

Some of the more important concepts of economic value as it applies to land resources may be illustrated by the example of an operator who buys a building site for $50,000 and then spends an additional $200,000 to construct an office building. At this point, he has $250,000 invested in his property—a sum that may be taken as a measure of its investment cost. When he has his property appraised for a mortgage loan, he finds that it has a total loan value of only $210,000. The tax assessor assesses it for property-taxation purposes at $130,000. The owner decides to sell his property, and after discussing the matter with a real estate broker decides to list it for $300,000. Before he actually lists it, however, he discovers that his property is needed for some public project and that it has a condemnation value of $275,000.

Each of these five figures represents a measure of economic value; and each has its explanation and justification. Taken together, they indicate the aura of confusion often associated with the term "value" and the need for a more explicit understanding of what is meant by the "economic value of property."

Economic value has three important components.[4] The property in question must have use-value or *utility* to its owner or user. Otherwise, no one would want it. Coupled with the idea of utility are the assumptions that properties such as land resources promise expected future flows of returns and satisfactions and that effective demand exists for these flows of products or services. A second necessary component is *scarcity* in supply. Regardless of its utility, a product must be scarce if it is to command a price. Otherwise, it would be a free good. To have economic value, an object must also be *appropriable.* It must be something that can be possessed and be transferable from one owner to another.

Most economists identify the economic value of property with the going exchange value or market price of property objects. In this sense, economic value always depends upon the interaction of the forces of supply and demand. It represents the worth of given properties in given markets at a given time and place. Far from being something that is fixed for each type of property, economic value is really a subjective concept that is dependent on the desires of people to possess and use property objects and upon their ability and willingness to offer money or other considerations in exchange for the privilege of ownership or possession.

[3]McMichael lists some 73 types of value that appraisers deal with in their work. Cf. Stanley L. McMichael, *How to Operate a Real Estate Business,* rev. ed., (Englewood Cliffs, N.J.: Prentice-Hall, Inc., 1967), p. 132.

[4]Cf. Alfred A. Ring, *The Valuation of Real Estate* (Englewood Cliffs, N. J.: Prentice-Hall, Inc., 1963), p. 8.

Various writers in the past have confused the meaning of economic value by identifying it with other concepts such as utility, production cost, and "fair price."[5] Care should be taken to distinguish between economic value and each of these concepts. It may be noted with the concept of utility, for example, that property objects must have some type of usefulness or utility to someone if they are to have economic value. Mere possession of utility does not give an object economic value. As Adam Smith pointed out in his classic distinction between value and utility:

> The things which have the greatest value in use have frequently little or no value in exchange; and on the contrary, those which have the greatest value in exchange have frequently little or no value in use. Nothing is more useful than water: but it will purchase scarce anything; scarce anything can be had in exchange for it. A diamond, on the contrary, has scarce any value in use; but a very great quantity of other goods may frequently be had in exchange for it.[6]

Smith and several other early economists associated economic value with the cost of producing economic objects. This concept has some validity since the market price of a product must equal or exceed its production cost over time if producers are to have an incentive to continue production. During the typical short-run period, however, supply and demand conditions often cause the economic values and market prices of products to either rise above or drop below their production cost. Land-resource developments provide a common example of this discrepancy between economic values and costs. Desirable building lots frequently command market prices far in excess of their production or developmental costs. The market value of a 10-story hotel built in a desert, a ghost town, or some other area where little or no demand exists for its services, on the other hand, would fall far below its actual production cost.

The association of economic value with the concept of fair price can be traced back to the writings of the Greek philosophers and several medieval churchmen. This assumption that economic value corresponds with "some notion of a fair or ethical price higher or lower than the price at which the commodity or service in question is being sold or can be sold" is also used by the courts at times in their determination of reasonable values.[7] Under active market conditions, this fair-price concept of value is often rejected as unrealistic—as a measure of someone's idea of what ought to be rather than the actual exchange prices found in the market. It may have

---

[5]Cf. James C. Bonbright, *The Valuation of Property* (New York: McGraw-Hill Book Company, Inc., 1937), chap. II; and Edmund Whittaker, *A History of Economic Ideas* (New York: Longmans, Green and Co., 1940), chap. IX.

[6]Adam Smith, *The Wealth of Nations* (London, 1776: Modern Library edition; New York: Random House, Inc., 1937), p. 28.

[7]Bonbright, *op. cit.*, p. 23.

considerable judicial or political significance, however, in those instances in which there are no established guidelines for determining market values, value figures are not available for comparable properties, a court must determine reasonable values, or in which public action is needed to fix prices.

Many leading appraisers still argue a distinction between the concepts of economic value and market price.[8] They agree that the determination of market value is the end product of the appraisal process. Yet they often speak of the "justified" or "warranted" price of property as the normal price a property should sell for as compared with possible actual sales at higher or lower price levels. The American Institute of Real Estate Appraisers has defined its concept of market value as follows:

> Market Value: (1) As defined by the courts, is the highest price estimated in terms of money which a property will bring if exposed for sale in the open market allowing a reasonable time to find a purchaser who buys with knowledge of all the uses to which it is adapted and for which it is capable of being used. (2) Frequently, it is referred to as the price at which a willing-seller would sell and a willing-buyer would buy, neither being under abnormal pressure. (3) It is the price expectable if a reasonable time is allowed to find a purchaser and if both seller and prospective buyer are fully informed.[9]

Property values seldom remain constant for very long time periods. They fluctuate up and down with changing supply and demand conditions and even more important, with shifts in business and group psychology. Theoretically, every buyer should calculate the worth of an object in terms of his expectations regarding the flow of utilities and satisfactions he may receive through its possession and use. In practice, however, most of us judge the future in terms of our knowledge of the present and recent past. As Lord Keynes has observed:

> (1) We assume that the present is a much more serviceable guide to the future than a candid examination of past experience would show it to have been hitherto. In other words we largely ignore the prospect of future changes about the actual character of which we know nothing.
>
> (2) We assume that the *existing* state of opinion as expressed in prices and the character of existing output is based on a *correct* summing up of future

---

[8] For comments of this general order, cf. Frederick M. Babcock, *The Valuation of Real Estate* (New York: McGraw-Hill Book Co., Inc., 1932), pp. 12-16; and Earl F. Crouse and Charles H. Everett, *Farm Appraisals* (Englewood Cliffs, N. J.: Prentice-Hall, Inc., 1956), pp. 19-20. Also cf. Paul F. Wendt, *Real Estate Appraisal* (New York: Henry Holt and Company, Inc., 1956), pp. 4-11, for a general discussion of these views.

[9] American Institute of Real Estate Appraisers, *Appraisal Terminology and Handbook* (Chicago: American Institute of Real Estate Appraisers, 1954), p. 163. Cf. also Ralph Turvey, *The Economics of Real Property* (London: George Allen & Unwin Ltd., 1957), chap. II.

prospects, so that we can accept it as such unless and until something new and relevant comes into the picture.

(3) Knowing that our own individual judgment is worthless, we endeavor to fall back on the judgment of the rest of the world which is perhaps better informed. That is, we endeavor to conform with the behavior of the majority or the average. The psychology of a society of individuals each of whom is endeavoring to copy the others leads to what we may strictly term a *conventional* judgment.[10]

Our acceptance of this conventional judgment of society causes us to adjust our ideas and expectations concerning the economic value of property to the shifting tides of the business cycle. During periods of business prosperity, we are ordinarily optimistic about the future and frequently add fire to the business boom by expanding our activities and bidding property values up to new heights. Let something happen to shake this mass faith in the soundness of the economy,. however, and we frequently make an abrupt about-face. "The practice of calmness and immobility, of certainty and security, suddenly breaks down. New fears and hopes will, without warning, take charge of human conduct. The forces of dissillusion may suddenly impose a new conventional basis for valuation."[11] Panic and economic fear become the order of the day with some operators. Others are slower to change. But they too are frequently engulfed in a tide of conventional pessimism, which leads to sometimes short, sometimes extended, periods of depressed business conditions and reduced property values.

VALUATION AND APPRAISAL OF REAL ESTATE

Property owners, prospective buyers, real estate credit agencies, tax assessors, and others have frequent need for value figures indicating the worth of individual properties for various purposes. The determination of these value figures is usually accomplished through a property appraisal process. Thousands of these appraisals are made each day. Many are made by owners who seek the highest sale price at which their properties can be expected to clear the market and by individual buyers who try to determine the maximum prices they should consider paying for properties. Many others are made by loan appraisers, tax assessors, and professional appraisers who make a regular business of appraising properties.

Conscious efforts have been made in recent decades to improve and formalize the techniques used in appraisal work. As a result, most professional appraisers proceed on a more scientific basis now than in

[10]John M. Keynes, "The General Theory of Employment," *Quarterly Journal of Economics*, Vol. 51, February, 1937, p. 214.

[11]*Ibid.*, p. 215.

times past. Even with these improvements, property appraisal is still more an art than a science. Appraisers usually start with a given property and try to determine a property-value figure that reflects "the current attitude of typically informed users and investors as to the probable future utility of that property."[12] They try to discover the market price at which given properties would probably exchange in a willing buyer-willing seller market.

The leading principles and techniques of sound appraisal can often be learned from textbooks. Success in appraisal work, however, calls for more than booklearning. An appraiser's success is highly dependent upon his ability to assemble pertinent information concerning individual properties and to provide a realistic interpretation of these data in light of present market conditions and the probable future productivity of these properties. "The appraiser is not a fortune teller and he does not attempt to foretell the future." Yet "he must be a keen observer of known facts and of the current attitude of informed persons toward future probabilities as reflected by current market action."[13] He should be thoroughly familiar with current local market conditions and display both skill and judgment in his assembly and interpretation of the value data for individual properties.

Much of the appraisal work done by untrained individuals is conducted in a haphazard and often confused manner. With trained appraisers, however, the appraisal process follows a fairly well defined course.[14] The appraiser first determines the exact location and legal description of the property he is to appraise; the nature of the property rights (ownership, lease, mineral, or other rights) being appraised; the purpose of the appraisal; the type of value (sales value, rental value, loan value, insurable value, or whatever) desired; and the specific date for which the appraisal is to apply.

After the appraiser has determined the nature and purpose of the appraisal, he examines the property and its surroundings and assembles whatever relevant information he can concerning the various physical, economic, and institutional factors that affect its value. He interprets these data and employs one or more of the standard valuation approaches in computing the value of the property. He then reconciles any differences

[12]American Institute of Real Estate Appraisers, *The Appraisal of Real Estate,* 2nd ed. (Chicago: American Institute of Real Estate Appraisers, 1951), p. 28.

[13]*Ibid.*

[14]For more detailed discussions of the steps involved in the appraisal process, cf. American Institute of Real Estate Appraisers, *The Appraisal of Real Estate,* 5th ed. (Chicago, 1967, hereinafter referred to as AIREA), chap. IV; Sanders A. Kahn, Frederick E. Case, and Alfred Schimmel, *Real Estate Appraisal and Investment* (New York: The Ronald Press, 1963), pp. 14-19; and Arthur A. May, *The Valuation of Residential Real Estate,* 2nd ed. (Englewood Cliffs, N.J.: Prentice-Hall Inc., 1953), chaps. III and XIX.

that may result from his use of alternative valuation techniques; and he submits an appraisal report in which he indicates his opinion as to the value of the property appraised.

Three principal methods of determining real property values are now in use in the United States. These include: (1) the market-comparison or market approach, (2) the net income-capitalization or income approach, and (3) the replacement-cost or cost approach.

Market-Comparison Approach

The market-comparison, sales-comparison, or market approach provides a basic and highly realistic method for determining the market value of land resources. With this approach, the appraiser studies the conditions and prices associated with the sale of comparable properties and values the property he is appraising in terms of the price he feels it would bring in the current market. This approach has particular merit and validity when one is seeking the current market value of a property, because it relates appraised values to current supply and demand conditions. It recognizes the fact that current market prices frequently rise above or drop below the averages suggested by longer run trends and that market price levels may vary from one community to the next. Its close association with fluctuating local market trends, however, makes it less useful for determining what some appraisers regard as the longer-term justified or warranted value of properties.[15]

Emphasis is given with the market approach to the association of property values with the actual sales values of comparable properties at the date of the appraisal. This approach finds its rationale in the economic principle of substitution. Informed buyers and renters will not pay more for given properties than it costs them to buy or rent comparable substitute properties. It is only natural, therefore, that appraisers should look to the current real estate market for some indication of the actual going market values of the properties they appraise.

This valuation technique works quite well with properties such as urban and suburban residences, apartment houses, and farms that can be considered as somewhat standardized and that are exchanged in sufficient numbers to provide sales data on comparable properties in the existing market. The approach is less applicable to commercial, industrial and other properties that are seldom sold. Problems also can arise in its application to residences and farms when few properties are sold or when those that are sold are too dissimilar to provide a reasonable basis for sales comparisons.

In their use of the market-comparison approach, appraisers frequently encounter wide variations in market prices. They find that most buyers

---

[15] Cf. Wendt, *op. cit.*, pp. 253 and 255-60.

and sellers operate with incomplete knowledge of their market opportunities, that their properties have a wide variety of characteristics, and that some properties sell for more than they probably should while others sell for less. This lack of standardization between properties and this general fluctuation in actual market prices for comparable properties complicates the appraiser's problem. As long as he deals with samples of several comparable properties that have sold at prices agreeable to willing buyers and willing sellers, however, he can use market data as an indicator of the range of prices accepted by typical users and investors under actual market conditions.

A major problem with the market-comparison approach stems from the appraiser's need for bonafide sales data for comparable properties sold under comparable market conditions. This information may be non-existent for those types of properties that are rarely sold. A seasonal dearth of sales or the small size of the local market area may cause it to be scarce even with frequently sold types of properties. Even when considerable sales are on record, questions sometimes arise concerning the comparable nature of the properties and their sales conditions.

No appraiser expects to find properties that are exactly alike. Even when two houses have identical floor plans or when two farms are of the same size and general layout, they are always found at different locations and often in different neighborhoods. The most an appraiser can hope for is general comparability. In his search for comparable examples, he usually finds it necessary to study the characteristics of numerous properties listed or sold in the market along with the conditions and circumstances of their sale.

Most local appraisers have an up-to-date working knowledge of the listing and sales prices of almost every type of property found and sold in their areas. In selecting the properties they use in their comparisons, they give first emphasis to physical factors—type of property, size and layout, age and styling of buildings, and the like. Six-room frame-construction houses are compared with other six-room frame dwellings while farms are compared with similar farms. They try to choose properties in the same neighborhood or in neighborhoods with like characteristics.

Special emphasis is usually given to the time, circumstances, and conditions of sale. Sales examples from the current market are desired because market conditions can change so rapidly that a sales example of even a few months earlier must often be adjusted to be meaningful in the current market. Care should also be taken to check the conditions of these benchmark sales to make sure that they involve bonafide willing buyer-willing seller transactions and that they do not involve unduly long sales periods, heavy advertising costs, or special sales-financing arrangements.

Once the appraiser has assembled the relevant sales data on comparable properties, he should carefully compare these examples with the property he is appraising. With residential properties, for example, he should compare his benchmark properties with

> the property under appraisal in accordance with the following plan:
> 1. *Comparison of the physical aspects*—the lot's size, shape, area, frontage, soil, topography, and location within the block; the building's architecture, interior and exterior construction, size, floor plan, equipment, livability, functional adequacy and future life expectancy.
> 2. *Comparison of the social aspects*—the environing features, social and physical; comparative desirability of the neighborhood; and expected future life of the present social stratum resident therein.
> 3. *Comparison of market data*—present and future rental levels; present and future anticipated sales price; present offering prices and the duration of exposure to the market; and present and future anticipated listing price of the subject property.[16]

In this comparison process, the appraiser looks for similarities and dissimilarities between properties. He notes the plus and minus features associated with the property he is appraising. He considers the property from the standpoint of market trends and his knowledge of the preferences and desires of buyers regarding architectural styling, floor plans, building materials, and other relevant items. With these facts in mind, he estimates the probable market value of the property at the date of its appraisal.

Income-Capitalization Approach

Theoretically, the market value of a property should always equal the present worth of all its future incomes. It should equal the discounted present value of the expected future flow of its land rents. The logic of this reasoning has prompted widespread use of an income-capitalization approach in property appraisal work. As was indicated in chapter 6, this valuation approach involves the simple formula $V = a/r$ in which V represents the value of the property, a represents the estimated average annual land rent or net return to land expected in the future, and r represents the rate of interest used in the capitalization process. With this formula, a property with an expected average annual net return of $1,000 is worth $20,000 when this income is capitalized at 5 per cent ($1,000 ÷ .05 = $20,000).

This formula is designed for use with farms and other properties that are expected to produce an even flow of land rents year after year into the distant future. Where this situation exists, the appraiser is concerned with only two variables. He must determine the average annual land rent

[16]May, *op. cit.*, p. 166. Also cf. Wendt, *op. cit.*, pp. 267-90; AIREA, *op. cit.*, chaps. XX and XXI; and William G. Murray, *Farm Appraisal and Valuation*, 5th ed. (Ames: Iowa State University Press, 1969), chaps. V-X.

attributable to the property; and he must choose an appropriate capitalization rate.

Complications arise when the property being appraised will not provide an even flow of land rent in the future. Typical examples of this situation arise with the appraisal of apartment buildings, mines, and other properties with limited economic lives. (Cf. Figure 10-1.) With these properties the standard capitalization formula may be used to compute

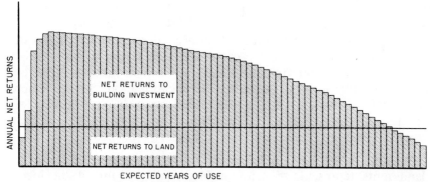

FIGURE 10-1. Illustration of expected pattern of future land rents associated with a typical investment in a new building.

the market value of the site; but adjustments are needed to correct the total value estimate for the declining rate and limited duration of the returns associated with the building improvements.[17]

Other modifications are needed when the land rents are expected to either increase or decrease in the future and when they are expected to continue for only a limited number of years. With the first of these situations, the appraiser may either adjust his estimate of the average annual land rent to take these expected changes into account; or he may shift to use of a modified capitalization formula $V = \dfrac{a}{r} + \dfrac{i}{r^2}$ [18]   In this

[17]Cf. AIREA, *op. cit.*, chaps. XVIII and XIX. Appraisers use two general approaches in dealing with this problem. Some appraisers use compound interest tables (either the Hoskold annuity or Inwood tables) to determine the present discounted value of the expected returns attributable to the building improvements. Others use the present net return attributable to the building as their *a* factor in the capitalization formula and add either a straight-line or a sinking-fund depreciation correction factor to their capitalization rate. This correction factor results in a market-value estimate for the building that equals the present discounted value of its expected flow of net returns less a depreciation allowance sufficient to cover its investment cost.

[18] Cf. Clyde R. Chambers, *Relation of Land Income to Land Value*, U.S. Department of Agriculture Bulletin 1224, 1924, pp. 28-29. When this expected increase or decrease is expected to continue for a specific number of years and then be followed

modified formula, *a* represents the average annual land rent currently received by the property while *i* represents the average increment of increased or decreased return that is expected to result from more intensive use of sites now used as parking lots or as golf courses, from a proposed land-drainage program, continued soil erosion, or some other factor. With the second situation, as when one appraises a mine that is being liquidated at a steady rate that will reduce its value to zero in *x* years, use should be made of the formula

$$V = \frac{a}{r} \left[1 - \frac{1}{(1+r)^x} \right].$$

Another type of adjustment is often needed when the appraiser deals only with monetary income factors in the calculation of his *a* variable. The appraiser's final determination of value in these instances frequently calls for the addition of allowances for locational advantages, amenity factors, and other items that add to property value and the possible subtraction of varying sums for detriments or hazards that may reduce the value of the property.

Estimating future land rents. Computation of the average annual level of land rents represents a major problem with the use of the income-capitalization approach. In theory, the appraiser should try to determine the average annual flow of land rent that a property can be reasonably expected to earn in the future. Most appraisers give serious attention to this problem. In practice, however, their estimates of future net returns are usually weighted quite heavily by their knowledge of the returns received by properties in the present and recent past.

Appraisers have a relatively simple problem in estimating an appropriate level of future land rents when a property is leased on a long-term basis at a mutually satisfactory rental rate to a tenant who is using it for its current highest and best use. The appraiser in these instances can use the landlord's current net rent (his contract rent less his outlays for taxes, insurance, cost of managing and operating buildings, and so forth) as a measure of the expected future land rents. Situations of this order tend to be more the exception than the rule. Appraisers usually find that they must compute land rental rates for properties that are owner-operated or that are leased at rates somewhat out of line with their present or future income-producing potential.

In determining the net incomes or land rents associated with urban properties, appraisers usually give first attention to the character of the neighborhood, the economic base of the city, and various trends evident

---

by a period of relatively constant returns, the appraiser should use the formula

$$V = \frac{a}{r} \pm \frac{i}{r^2} \left[1 - \frac{1}{(1+r)^n} \right].$$

Cf. Ernst H. Wiecking, "Farm Real Estate Values and Farm Income," *Annals of the American Academy of Political and Social Science,* No. 237, March, 1930, pp. 240-41.

in the national economy.[19] They then use operating income and expense statements for the property and such other information as may be available to determine its income productivity, estimate its expected average gross income, and calculate its expected operating costs. These costs may then be subtracted from the expected gross income to provide the estimated annual net return or land rent of the property before depreciation.[20]

Farm appraisers usually start their rent-determination process by considering the physical resource base of the farm, the productivity of the soil, and the average crop yields reported for the farm during the preceding 5- to 10-year period. These data are used along with information concerning the typical or most likely cropping system to provide a picture of the over-all productivity of the farm. Average farm-product price levels are determined and used to compute the average expected gross income. The appraiser then subtracts the estimated operating expenses (including an allowance for the operator's labor and management) from the estimated gross income to get the net return or land rent attributable to land and buildings.[21]

Both the urban appraiser and his rural counterpart now use fairly well defined procedures in estimating the future income flow of properties. Skill and judgment are needed in most instances, however, if the appraiser is to arrive at an approximately correct answer. Even under ideal conditions, the process of estimating future production, business conditions, price levels, and net returns is fraught with hazards. Small errors frequently have a pronounced effect on the final value determination. Minor errors in the assumptions regarding future contract rental rates, office or apartment vacancy rates, or the effective economic life of a building can have far-reaching effects on the values of urban properties. Similarly with farm appraisals, a mistake of 2 bushels per acre in the appraiser's crop-yield calculations or 5 cents a bushel in his long-run price estimates may make a $40 to $60 difference in the acreage value of farm land.

Choice of a capitalization rate. The capitalization rate is the second

---

[19]Cf. AIREA, *op. cit.*, chaps. XV-XVI; also May, *op. cit.*, chaps. IV-IX.

[20]Many urban appraisers split the net rental return between the site and the building improvements so that the value of these two items may be computed separately. Land and building residual techniques have been developed to guide appraisers in this income-splitting process. (Cf. AIREA, *op. cit.*, chap. XVIII, and Wendt, *op. cit.*, pp. 172-85.) Urban appraisers are not unanimous in their acceptance of this practice and most rural appraisers regard it as nonapplicable to farm properties. (Cf. Richard U. Ratcliff, "Net Income Can't Be Split," *Appraisal Journal*, Vol. 18, April, 1950, pp. 168-72; Kahn *et al.*, *op. cit.*, pp. 151-53; Murray, *op. cit.*, chap. XV; and Crouse and Everett, *op. cit.*. p. 17.)

[21]Cf. Murray, *op. cit.*, chaps. XI-XII; and Crouse and Everett, *op. cit.*, chaps. VII-VIII.

important variable in the capitalization formula. Here again, the validity of the appraiser's value estimate depends upon the discretion and judgment he shows in his choice of an appropriate capitalization factor. This situation is easily illustrated by the variations in value estimates that come with the use of different capitalization rates. A property with an average expected land rent of $1,000 has a value of $20,000 when capitalized at 5 percent. Its value rises to $25,000 when it is capitalized at 4 percent and drops to $16,667 when capitalized at 6 percent.

The appraiser's problem is that of determining the appropriate capitalization rates that should properly apply with individual properties. [22] If all properties were held without income risk or uncertainty under the conditions of perfect competition, owners could be expected to capitalize their property incomes at a low safe rate of interest comparable to that used with government bonds. But this situation does not exist in practice. Investors take a certain amount of risk when they invest in property; they often suffer from illiquidity when they tie their capital up in particular investments; and they frequently assume considerable burdens of management. Each of these factors contributes to the use of capitalization rates that are higher than the relatively safe, nonrisk rate used with government bonds.

In the past, the simplest problem in determining capitalization rates has usually occurred with farm properties. A high proportion of the farm appraisals have been made by representatives of mortgage credit agencies; and these appraisers have tended to accept the going farm mortgage interest rate as an appropriate capitalization rate. Many rural appraisal authorities are critical of this identity of farm capitalization rates with mortgage interest rates and argue "that farm ownership carries more risk than mortgage lending and therefore is entitled to a higher rate of return." [23] The Americal Society of Farm Managers and Rural Appraisers suggests that appraisers consider (1) the physical and economic risk factors that affect the regularity of the owner's net return from his land

---

[22] It should be noted that the capitalization rate is the reciprocal of the number of years of expected income it takes to equal the property's present value. A property with an annual land rent of $1,000 capitalized at 5 percent to give a $20,000 value has a reciprocal of 20 and may thus be described as a 20 years' purchase property. This years' purchase concept is widely used in Great Britain and some other European countries. Farm land values in England are often expressed in terms of 20, 25, or in recent years even 30 years' purchase of their annual rents. The value of residential and other urban properties ranges from as little as three years' purchase if the buildings are old, in a poor state of repair, or prevented by rent control regulations from charging more than a low nominal rent, to many times this number of years' purchase with more desirable properties. This approach to urban and rural land resource valuation is particularly applicable in areas where large numbers of properties are held under leaseholds.

[23] Crouse and Everett, *op. cit.,* p. 35. Also cf. Roland R. Renne, *Land Economics,* 2nd ed. (New York: Harper & Brothers, 1958), p. 236.

and building investment, (2) the effect of the relative marketability of farms in the area on the liquidity of farm property investments, and (3) competition with other forms of investment along with the prevailing interest rate on farm mortgages and bank loans in the area in their determination of capitalization rates.[24]

It is usually recommended that rural appraisers apply uniform capitalization rates to all their appraisals in given areas. This recommendation does not apply, however, with urban appraisals. Differences in the risk, capital liquidity, and burden of management factors with different types of properties and sometimes with properties of the same type have brought the use of a wide range of capitalization rates. Three principal approaches are used in the determination of these rates. These include: (1) the summation method, (2) the band-of-investment theory, and (3) selection by comparison.[25]

With the *summation* method, the appraiser builds up his capitalization rate by assuming a series of independent rates for the various factors he considers in the capitalization process. Thus he may start with a safe nonrisk rate of 3.25 percent, add 1.5 percent as a rate for the income risks associated with the property, add 1.25 percent as a penalty for nonliquidity of capital, and add 1.0 percent as an allowance for burden of management. By totaling these separate rates he arrives at a total capitalization rate of 7.0 percent.

Different combinations are frequently used in this summation approach. In one prominent example of this summation method (Table 10-1), the Federal Housing Administration uses a range of rates for five

TABLE 10-1. Summation Method Used by the Federal Housing Administration in Determining Capitalization Rates for Residential Income Properties

Risk features	Rates for 5 grades of properties ranging from poor to excellent risks					Rating for property
	1	2	3	4	5	
Safety of principal	3.50	3.25	3.00	2.75	2.50	—
Certainty of return	2.00	1.75	1.50	1.25	1.00	—
Regularity of return	1.75	1.50	1.25	1.00	0.75	—
Liquidity	1.50	1.25	1.00	0.75	0.50	—
Burden of management	1.25	1.00	0.75	0.50	0.25	—
Total capitalization rate						—

Source: Federal Housing Administration, *Capitalization Rates and Rent Multipliers.*

[24]Cf. "The American Rural Appraisal System," *Journal of the American Society of Farm Managers and Rural Appraisers,* Vol. 10, October, 1946, p. 93. Many appraisers tend to use capitalization rates of around 5 or 5.5 percent with farm appraisals.

[25]Ring, *op. cit.,* pp. 225-27, suggests a fourth approach, which he calls the "banker's rate selection method." This rate involves consideration of mortgage interest payment rates and loan-to-value ratios for different properties.

risk features: safety of principal, certainty of return, regularity of return, liquidity, and burden of management. The appraiser must determine the appropriate rate that applies with each risk feature in building up his capitalization rate. If he assigns the lowest suggested rate to each of the five risk features (column 5), he will end up with a 5 percent capitalization rate. If he uses the highest suggested rate in each instance (column 1), his capitalization rate will go up to 10 percent.

With the *band-of-investment* theory approach, the capitalization rate is computed as the weighted average of the gross market interest rates that apply to various portions or "bands" of one's investment. As an example, one may assume a case in which 50 percent of the value of a property can be covered by a first mortgage bearing 6 percent interest, 25 percent by a second mortgage bearing 7 percent interest, and in which buyers expect a 9 percent return on their equity funds, which make up the remaining 25 percent. With these basic data, a 7 percent capitalization rate may be computed as follows:

	Percent of Value	Interest rate	Fractional rate
First mortgage	50	6	3.00
Second mortgage	25	7	1.75
Owner's equity	25	9	2.25
Total capitalization rate			7.00

Most urban appraisers use a *comparison approach* in selecting their capitalization rates. With this approach, they tend to base their capitalization rates on the percentage relationship that exists between the annual net returns and going market values of comparable properties.[26] In this comparison process, consideration may be given to the income quality of the property, to the risk associated with the receipt of future incomes, and to such other factors as the reliability of the appraiser's income and expense predictions, the income-expense ratio of the enterprise, the likelihood of serious competition arising from the development of comparable enterprises, the marketability of the property, the stability of the property's value, and the burden of management. Rating sheets covering these items are used by some appraisers in their selection of an appropriate capitalization rate.

A property depreciation factor is frequently added to the capitalization rates derived by use of the summation and band-of-investment methods.

[26]Cf. AIREA, *op. cit.* pp. 274-75; Wendt, *op. cit.,* pp. 155-62, and May, *op. cit.,* p. 177. This approach is somewhat less precise than the other two; but it may be noted that all three approaches call for subjective choices. After his review of these three approaches, Wendt (*op. cit.,* pp. 300-301) concludes that none of them "provides a scientific and objective method for establishing the capitalization rate for a given property" and that the choice of a capitalization rate "is essentially one of subjective estimation."

The size of this correction factor depends upon the method of its calculation and the estimated remaining economic life of the building improvements. It should be large enough to enable the owner to recoup the investment cost of his improvements but not so large as to rob the property of its fair present value. With a typical example involving a building that has an estimated remaining economic life of 25 years, a 4 percent depreciation rate may be added to a 7 percent capitalization rate to provide an over-all rate of 11 percent. This correction may already be included in rates selected through the comparison approach.

Use of gross-rent multipliers. Gross-rent multipliers have been used frequently since the 1920s as a simple short-cut to the income-capitalization method of estimating the market values of rented residential and commercial properties. The multipliers used with this valuation technique assume a somewhat fixed relationship between annual or monthly gross contract rental rates and the market values of the rented properties.

A gross-rent multiplier was used in the popular rule-of-thumb of the 1920s and 1930s that a house was worth 100 times its monthly rent. Other accepted multipliers at the same time assumed that elevator apartment houses were worth four to six times their gross annual rentals and that office buildings were worth from four to five times their gross annual rentals.[27]

Several appraisal authorities have roundly denounced the use of gross-rental multipliers as an appraisal technique because of their exclusive concern with gross rather than net rents and their failure to deal with variations in operating expenses. Babcock warns that this "method should not be used even for quick estimating except for very typical properties."[28] May describes it as "the most fallacious rule-of-thumb ever devised for the estimation of value based on income."[29] Wendt and others have found wide variations between the gross and net rents associated with comparable properties in the same cities.[30] Winnick's studies show considerable variations between the gross-rent multipliers applicable to residential properties at various benchmark years between 1890 and 1949.[31] Even with these criticisms, the use of gross-rent multipliers has

[27]Cf. Philip A. Benson and Nelson L. North, *Real Estate Principles* (Englewood Cliffs, N.J.: Prentice-Hall, Inc., 1924), pp. 170-71.

[28]Babcock, *op. cit.,* p. 180.

[29]May, *op. cit.,* pp. 178-79.

[30]Wendt, *op. cit.,* pp. 200-204.

[31]Louis Winnick, "Long-Run Changes in the Valuation of Real Estate by Gross Rents," *Appraisal Journal,* Vol. 20, October, 1952, pp. 484-98. Winnick reports gross rent multipliers ranging from 7.4 to 14.1 years' annual rent with single-family dwellings, 3.2 to 10.5 years' annual rent with tenement houses, and 4.1 to 10.6 years' annual rent with apartment houses during the 60 years between 1890 and 1949.

persisted in many areas, largely because of the relative ease with which this approach can be used.

Replacement-Cost Approach

A third-important method of determining property values is provided by the replacement-cost approach.[32] This approach is rooted in the early classical assumption of a close relationship between production costs and value. It assumes that properties should be worth their present replacement cost (or the cost of providing an acceptable substitute property) less an allowance for accrued depreciation and possible obsolescence.

Like the market-comparison and income-capitalization approaches, this method has both advantages and disadvantages. As a rule, replacement costs tend to set an upper limit on property values. Just as the well-informed rational buyer will refuse to pay more for a property than he must pay for a comparable substitute, so also will he refuse to pay more than it would cost to reproduce the property new or replace it with another property capable of providing comparable utilities and satisfactions.

The general truth of this statement provides much of the rationale for the replacement-cost-less-depreciation approach. Yet although this statement is generally true, it must be recognized that there are occasions when imperfect competition and inadequate or faulty knowledge result in sales prices above this level. Time considerations and a demand for the immediate use of a property are also important in that they frequently cause buyers to bid up prices rather than wait the usual number of months it takes to construct new buildings.

On the other extreme, it may also be noted that the replacement-cost approach can easily result in property values somewhat in excess of those justified by current market conditions. This is particularly true when this approach is used to appraise overdeveloped properties such as the large mansions and other "white elephant" structures found at various locations. These properties have often been developed for the personal satisfaction of their owners with little thought of future resale value. In many instances, they could not have been sold at their original production cost when they were new. Large portions of this initial production cost (and current replacement cost) must often be written off in the valuation process.[33] Even then the prospect of continued high operating costs often reduces the number of potential buyers.

[32]This method is also described at times as the reproduction-cost approach. (Cf. AIREA, p. 180.) Some appraisers think in terms of the cost of reproducing an improvement with the same or similar materials. Others prefer to think of the cost of replacing an improvement with one of similar utility.

[33]This problem is handled by deducting an allowance for economic obsolescence along with other depreciation from the estimated replacement cost of the property.

The replacement-cost approach is best used with properties that fit between these two extremes. As Babcock noted: "A building is worth its cost of replacement provided it is new, represents the highest and best use of the site, and provided its construction is·justified by the expected returns which it will produce."[34] With the passing of time, the related concept of replacement-cost less an allowance for accrued depreciation can be used as a continuing measure of the value of most buildings. This is especially true "when the appraiser is justified in thinking that, if the property were lost or destroyed, the owner would rationally replace it."[35]

Widescale use is made of this valuation method in appraisal work, particularly in the appraisal of residential and other urban-oriented properties. This broad acceptance can be attributed to five principal factors: (1) the need for a standardized technique that can be applied to mass appraisals, (2) the general acceptance of replacement costs as a ceiling on value estimates, (3) the relative simplicity of this approach and ease with which it may be applied, (4) the tendency of many appraisers to reject market sales as a measure of justified or warranted value,[36] and (5) the difficulties encountered in use of the income-capitalization approach.

Three major problems arise in the use of this approach. The appraiser must determine the cost of providing a site of comparable value. He must determine the cost of replacing the present building improvements or of providing a suitable substitute. And he must compute the allowance he expects to make for the accrued depreciation and obsolescence of the present improvements.

The first problem—that of placing a value on the site—ordinarily calls for use of a market-comparison approach.[37] Lots and building sites are normally valued in terms of the going prices of other sites of comparable size, location, and use-capacity. More difficult problems usually arise in the determination of the replacement costs and depreciation allowances associated with building improvements.

Estimating replacement costs. When an appraiser computes the cost of replacing a building, he is seldom concerned with the cost of constructing an exact replica. Changes in materials and building techniques usually make this an impractical approach. But he does try to determine the cost

---

[34]Babcock, *op. cit.,* p. 477.

[35]Wendt, *op. cit.,* pp. 219-20.

[36]Cf. *ibid.,* pp. 213-18.

[37]Three other possible methods may be used. They include (1) a distribution, abstraction, or allocation method, which can be used to allocate value between land and improvements when a price that corresponds to value is known, (2) an anticipated use or development method, which assumes a value for a developed property and subtracts the probable development costs to secure a measure of the value of the undeveloped land, and (3) a land residual method, which capitalizes the imputed rent of land with a hypothetical improvement to secure its value. (Cf. AIREA, pp. 119-30.)

of replacing the present building with a structure of comparable size, design, and use-capacity.

Important decisions must be made at this point concerning the quality of the construction and the level of building costs the appraiser is to assume in his calculations. He must decide whether he will think in terms of the costs associated with the highest standards of workmanship, average quality standards, or those that may apply with more slipshod construction. He must choose whether he will "seek the costs of the most efficient builder, the marginal builder, or some imaginary 'typical' builder."[38]

Once these decisions are made, the appraiser's next problem is that of choosing the specific method he will use in calculating his estimate of building replacement costs. Three principal methods are used for this purpose. These include: (1) the quantity survey method, (2) the inplace unit-cost method, and (3) the square-foot and cubic-foot methods.

With the *quantity survey* method, the appraiser duplicates the contractor's original procedure in determining the actual construction cost of the building improvements. He may work with the blueprints and floor plans of the present building to determine the amount and quality of materials needed and the probable labor costs required for its replacement. Along with these materials and labor costs, allowances must also be made for the contractor's profit, his overhead costs, the architect's fee, insurance, and any other costs one might encounter in replacing the structure at the appraisal date.

This quantity survey method provides the most accurate measure of building replacement costs. It is time-consuming and costly, however, and accordingly is seldom used. A substitute approach known as the *repeat case* method is occasionally used with residential appraisals. With this approach, the appraiser uses the lump-sum cost of constructing comparable dwellings along with lump-sum additions or subtractions for variations between properties as a basis for his building-cost estimates.

The *inplace unit-cost* method short-cuts some of the detail required with quantity surveys. With this approach, the appraiser breaks the building down into its component parts and applies appropriate unit prices in calculating the cost of putting each of these parts in place. Thus he will apply some calculated cost for each square or lineal foot of exterior and interior wall space, each square foot of roof area, plumbing installations, the heating system, electric wiring and fixtures, tile work, concrete driveways, and other component parts of the structure.

The *square-foot* and *cubic-foot* methods provide another commonly used short-cut for computing replacement costs. The appraiser calculates the total square feet of floor space or cubic feet of interior space in the building and applies the current square- or cubic-foot cost figures quoted by local builders for comparable structures to determine its replacement

---

[38]Cf. Wendt, *op. cit.,* p. 225.

cost. At $12 a square foot, a house with 1,500 square feet of floor space would thus have a replacement cost of $18,000. In similar fashion, a structure that cubes at 20,000 cubic feet has a replacement cost of $15,000 when one assumes a building cost of 75 cents per cubic foot.

Allowances for depreciation. After the appraiser has estimated the cost of replacing the building and other land improvements, he calculates the deduction from this replacement cost that he will make for accrued depreciation and obsolescence. Three general methods are used in calculating depreciation.[39] Of the three, the breakdown-observed-depreciation method is ordinarily favored in land-resource appraisals. On some occasions, particularly in determinations of book value, use is made of one of the theoretical approaches (straight line, years digit, equal percentage, sinking fund, annuity, or liability to replace methods) to calculate depreciation. Use also may be made of an engineering-observed-depreciation approach under which percentage deductions from value are estimated.

With the breakdown-observed-depreciation approach, the appraiser starts by considering the loss in value that the property has suffered because of physical deterioration and possible functional obsolescence.[40] The items that contribute to these two types of depreciation are usually classified as either curable or incurable. Curable items such as a faulty roof, a worn-out heating system, an outmoded kitchen, or inadequate electric wiring can be replaced. Incurable items such as the advancing age of the structure or a generally outmoded layout, on the other hand, must be accepted for appraisal purposes as they are.

For depreciation-cost computing purposes, the cost of the curable items is ordinarily measured in terms of their cost of replacement or repair. Three alternatives are used in measuring the cost of incurable items. The appraiser may use the observed-condition method by observing the property and expressing an opinion as to the monetary or percentage loss of value it has suffered in comparison with its new replacement value. He may use age-life tables to compute the depreciation he should allow for structures of varying types, ages, and economic life expectancies. He also may capitalize the difference between the assumed rental value of the property with all the curable items replaced or repaired and the rental value of a new replacement property to determine the amount of depreciation he should allow.

As a final step, appraisers frequently make allowances for possible economic obsolescence. Allowances for this type of value loss apply when

[39]Cf. AIREA, pp. 195-213; and Ring, *op. cit.*, pp. 151-61.

[40]A distinction is usually made in appraisal literature between these two concepts. Physical deterioration comes as a result of wear and tear, cracks, decay, and the like, while functional obsolescence is attributed to outmoded floor plans and functional inadequacy owing to the size, style, or age of the structure. Cf. AIREA, *op. cit.*, p. 195.

building improvements are overdeveloped for their use, when their value suffers because they are located in areas of declining property values, or when they do not represent the highest and best use of the site. The depreciation allowance for this factor may be computed by capitalizing the difference between the assumed rental value of a building with all its physical and functional deficiencies corrected at its present site and the rental value of this same building at some ideal location where it would represent the highest and best use of the site.[41]

Once the appraiser has calculated his various allowances for depreciation he totals them to get his total accrued depreciation. This figure is then subtracted from his estimated replacement cost (site plus building improvements) to provide his estimate of value. For example, a property may have an estimated replacement cost of $10,500 for the site and $76,500 for the building giving a total of $87,000. Its depreciation allowances may include a charge of $5,400 for curable deterioration and functional obsolescence items, $15,500 for incurable items, and $13,500 for economic obsolescence—a total of $34,400. Subtraction of this total from the estimated total replacement cost leaves $52,600 as the estimated value of the property.

Choice of a Valuation Method

Most appraisers find it desirable to use at least two and sometimes all three property valuation methods in their appraisal work.[42] As one might expect, this practice frequently results in more than one answer. Questions then arise as to which value estimate the appraiser should use in his final determination of value. When the appraiser finds himself in this position, he should recheck his calculations and try to narrow the difference between his high and low estimates. He should re-examine the purpose of the appraisal, the adequacy of the data used with each appraisal method, and the applicability of his various appraisal assumptions. In this correlation process, appraisers ordinarily give maximum weight to the appraisal approach they consider as most reliable. They use the other methods as checks to guide them in the determination of a reasonable value figure.[43]

---

[41]In this process, the appraiser treats the difference between the current market value of a property and his depreciated cost-of-replacement value as economic obsolescence. As Kahn, Case, and Schimmel (*op. cit.*, p. 180) observed, at this point the "significant measure of depreciation can only be found in the market place, which leads the appraiser back to the sales-comparison approach."

[42]The American Society of Farm Managers and Rural Appraisers recommends that its members use the income-capitalization and market-comparison methods in farm appraisals. Several government agencies require their appraisers to use all three approaches. This practice is also recommended by the American Institute of Real Estate Appraisers.

[43]Cf. AIREA, *op. cit.*, pp. 84-85.

Individual appraisers naturally differ in the emphasis they give to different appraisal methods. Some appraisers feel that the market-comparison approach provides the only practicable means for estimating market values. Others reject this approach because of its acceptance of fluctuating market values and its tendency to deviate from their concepts of justifiable market values that "ought-to-be." In similar fashion, many appraisers argue that income capitalization provides the only sound basis for estimating value. Others reject this approach because of the difficulties that complicate the calculation of average expected net returns and the selection of a proper capitalization rate. Many appraisers like the sense of certainty they get with the replacement-cost approach; others argue that this approach has little practical use until its depreciation allowances are adjusted to bring its value determinations in line with those found by market comparisons.

As the old adage "the worth of a thing is the price it will bring" suggests, the market-comparison method provides a logical and direct approach to the determination of property values. This method provides a definite bridge between the theory of economic value and the actual exchange values of the market. It is accordingly given considerable weight in most appraisals made for purchase or sale reasons. It is also used to a considerable extent as a check on other methods with other kinds of appraisals.

The income-capitalization approach is usually emphasized with the appraisal of income properties. Emphasis is given to this approach in most appraisals involving commercial farms, industrial and commercial properties, and rental housing. Loan agencies give major weight to this approach in their appraisals for mortgage lending purposes because of its emphasis on the future income-producing capacities of individual properties. Emphasis is also given to this approach in the appraisal of such miscellaneous things as the value of a tenant's interests under a long-term lease and the value of the severance damages that result from condemnation of some portion of an owner's property holdings.

The replacement-cost approach is widely used along with the market-comparison method in the valuation of residential and certain other urban properties. Its ease of application, its frequent dependence on standardized cost and depreciation allowance tables, and its tendency to treat all properties on a comparable basis have brought its widespread acceptance in tax assessment work. It is also favored by many courts as an appropriate method for use with condemnation appraisals.

LAND AS AN AREA OF INVESTMENT

Land resources and real estate have long been regarded as a prime area of investment. Ownership and investment conditions vary considerably, however, between different cultures and areas. Most of the land area is held by the crown, the state, or by a few leading families in some societies, while widespread opportunities for private ownership are available to most individuals in others. Custom and family status considerations discourage sales of land holdings in some countries, while nearly every tract of land is viewed as potentially for sale in areas such as the United States.

Opportunities for land ownership have always rated high among the average American's goals. The prospect of easy access to ownership provided a major incentive for the migration of thousands of Europeans to the United States and Canada during the 1800s. The relative freedom with which landed properties can be bought and sold has made the average citizen of these two nations more willing to move and less land-hungry than his ancestors, but has done little to lessen his desire for land ownership.

Several factors help explain the high regard usually associated with investments in land. These include (1) the traditional tendency of people to rate property ownership as desirable, (2) the characteristic durability and long life of land investments, (3) the investor's feeling that he understands land and real estate, (4) the realization that investors can often manage their own investments, and (5) the belief that ownership of real estate and land resources provides an excellent hedge against inflation.

Much of the prestige associated with land resource investments may be attributed to the advantages and privileges associated with land ownership in the past. Under feudalism, those individuals who held rights in land almost invariably enjoyed special economic, social, and political status. Most of these advantages have been greatly diluted by various reforms, but their vestiges still clothe land owners with special status in many communities.

Real estate investments are frequently looked upon with favor because of their durability and relative immobility. Most land-resource developments have the advantage of long life. They can be used now but they will still have considerable use value many years hence. Their values may deteriorate because of exploitation, depletion, or depreciation, but losses of this type can be minimized.

Compared with other types of investments now available, land resources enjoy several distinctive advantages. Individual investors usually find it possible to acquire complete ownership control rather than just a share of the total ownership rights. This type of investment involves physical assets investors can see and easily inspect. Furthermore, their management involves familiar types of operations that many investors feel that they can take over and handle without the help of hired management.

Land-resource investments usually compare favorably with other investment alternatives during periods of stable or rising prices, although they may show up somewhat less advantageously during deflationary periods. As the comparison of increases in market values of alternative investments reported in Table 10-2 indicates, investments in farm real

TABLE 10-2. Comparison of Relative Market Values of Selected Alternative
Investments, 1950 to 1960 and 1970

Type of investment	Initial investment in 1950	Average market value if held to:		Value in constant 1950 dollars in:*	
		1960	1970	1960	1970
Cash held in a safety deposit box	$1,000	$1,000	$1,000	$ 795	$ 611
Savings account at 4 to 5 percent interest**	1,000	1,480	2,311	1,176	1,412
Investment in an average common stock†	1,000	3,158	5,089	2,509	3,110
Investment in an average farm††	1,000	1,708	2,862	1,357	1,749
Investment in an average urban residential building lot§	1,000	2,386	4,785	1,896	2,924
Investment in a typical, well-kept urban single-family residence§§	1,000	1,297	1,440	1,030	880

*Deflation factor used in calculation of constant 1950 dollar values is based on the Bureau of Labor Statistics' consumers price indices for the month of March in each of the three years.

**Compound interest is computed at 4 percent during the 1950s and at 5 percent for the 1960s. These were common rates in use during the two decades.

†Trend data are based upon Standard and Poor's index of the average market prices for 500 common stocks during the month of March for each year.

††Price trend data are based upon the U. S. Department of Agriculture's index for farm real estate market prices. Data are reported as of March 1 of each year.

§Price trends are based upon the Federal Housing Administration's report on average appraised values of new building sites upon which houses covered by FHA loans were built for each year.

§§Trends are based upon the Wenzlich index of residential real estate values for March of each year and apply to typical well-kept single family urban residences in stable neighborhoods that have experienced average growth. (Courtesy of Roy Wenzlich Research Corporation.)

estate and in urban residential building sites provided good hedges against inflation between 1950 and 1970. Average farm properties in the United States increased 2.9 times and average house lots 4.8 times in value during this 20-year period. Measured in constant 1950 dollars, average farm real estate market prices increased 75 percent and average new residential lot values 192 percent as compared with increases of 41 percent for investments held in typical savings accounts and 211 percent for investments in average common stocks. Typical single-family urban residences increased approximately 44 percent in value between 1950 and 1970 but lost 12 percent of their value when viewed in 1950 constant value terms.[44] Of

[44]The percentage of increase reported for housing values suffers because of the choice of base years for comparison. A comparison of the increases in value for the 1940-1950 period show that average common stock values increased 67 percent during the decade as compared with increases of 112 percent for farm real estate and 142 percent for typical well-kept single-family urban residences. Valued in constant March 1950 dollars, the investments with market values of $1,000 in 1950 would have had 1940 values of $1,005 with common stocks, $790 with farm real estate, and $692 with typical well-kept single-family urban residences.

the six investment alternatives listed, it may be noted that investments in housing, farm real estate, and common stocks provided their owners with continuing flows of returns and services while their market values were increasing.

Goals in land investment. Investments in land, along with holdings of stocks and bonds, savings, and insurance, are often cited as the component parts of a rational investment program. This does not mean that all investments in land resources are equally good. Some investment opportunities offer higher prospects of profit or of capital gain than others, and some offer special advantages that appeal to particular investors, while others involve risks and undesirable features that make them opportunities of questionable value.

Potential investors should ask themselves what they want of their investments. Their economic goals may well include the following:[45]

(1) safety of investment—assurance that the investment will produce sufficient yield or increase enough in value to permit its resale at a price that will justify the initial investment;

(2) certainty of yield—ability of a property to provide periodic returns or increments of additional capital value that will give the investor an acceptable return on his investment;

(3) liquidity of investment—relative ability of the investor to sell his interests at their market value within a short period of time;

(4) capital appreciation—the hope that an investment will increase in capital value, that there will be little or no depreciation in values, and that the investment will provide a good hedge against inflation;

(5) taxation advantages—expectations that the investment will qualify for special tax treatment advantages that will leave the investor with a lower total tax load than would his investment alternatives;

(6) managerial responsibilities—opportunities, as the investor wishes, to participate in or to be free from managerial responsibilities and the possible liabilities associated therewith;

(7) reinvestment of net returns—opportunities to reinvest periodic land rents and profits in the investment; and

(8) opportunities for leverage—ability to use one's equity funds along with borrowed capital to spread one's realm of economic control over larger amounts of property.

In addition to the economic goals listed above, investors may also have goals associated with personal satisfactions and desired amenities. An investor may acquire a tract of forest land, for example, as much for its open space and recreation advantages as for its economic potential for timber production. Others may acquire land resources because of the satisfactions they attribute to ownership.

Alternative methods for land investment. Most investments in land

[45] Cf. Kahn, Case, and Schimmel, *op. cit.*, pp. 307-16.

resources involve either the purchase of residential lots and houses for family use or the acquisition and development of properties for business purposes. These are the land investments commonly recommended for people who need land for residential and business reasons. Once one goes beyond these basic investments, a variety of alternatives are available for potential investors who want additional investments in land resources.

One possibility involves the sometimes questionable activities of certain real estate promoters who specialize in the development and sale of home sites for recreation and retirement purposes. These promoters frequently use effective selling tactics involving complimentary dinners and free trips to view the sites along with arguments that stress the upward trend in land values, opportunities for speculative profits, and the obvious clincher that "God doesn't make land anymore" to sell their lots. Most other investment arrangements leave more of the responsibility for initiating interest in particular properties and for deciding what is or is not a good investment to the potential investor.

If an operator has money to invest and is willing to assume the risks, he can acquire real estate that he can lease out to others or that he can turn over to a management agency to handle. He may also acquire prospective building sites that he can hold for later resale or later development. With speculative investments of this type, the operator can realize a capital gain if he picks the right sites. His expectations may go unfulfilled, however, if his property is zoned for a lower use than he planned, undesirable developments are located in the area, the city does not grow in his direction, or the expected ripening of the site fails to materialize.

Investors frequently find that they can operate on a bigger scale by combining their investment funds with those of others. Operating in this way, an investor may pool his funds with those of friends to acquire an apartment house, an office building, or a shopping center, which they manage for their mutual benefit. Partnerships of this order involve joint responsibilities for the actions of others. Investors can avoid these responsibilities along with the direct responsibilities of management by investing in the shares offered by incorporated real estate syndicates.

Investments in syndicate shares provide many of the advantages of direct investments in land resources.[46] These organizations are frequently large enough to spread their investments over a wide spectrum of properties, a situation that reduces the risks associated with investments in single properties. They also assume responsibility for management. As corporations, however, they are subject to the corporation income tax.

This problem has been handled by legislation that exempts incor-

[46]Cf. Robert Kevin Brown, *Real Estate Economics*, (Boston: Houghton Mifflin Co., 1965), pp. 231-34; Kahn *et al., op. cit.*, pp. 319-21; Hugo Rothschild (revised by Daniel S. Berman), *How to Invest and Protect Your Profits in Real Estate Syndicates* (New York: Doubleday & Company, 1964); and Bertram Lewis, *Profits in Real Estate Syndication* (New York: Harper & Brothers, 1962).

porated real estate trusts from this tax as long as they pay out at least 90
percent of their current net earnings to their stock holders. Several real
estate trusts are now in operation. They provide unique opportunities to
operators who wish to invest in a variety of real estate holdings without
assuming managerial responsibilities. Additional liquidity has been
provided for some of these investments through the listing of real estate
trusts on stock exchanges.

Residual nature of investments in land resources. Investments in land
resources are far from infallible. While it is true that land values tend to
rise during inflationary periods, history also shows that real estate values
have often suffered from drastic declines during depression periods.

The actual returns that can be realized on land-resource investments
vary over a wide range. Sometimes they are high, sometimes low,
depending both upon individual cases and the relationships between costs
and prices. Under typical operating conditions, land resources have only a
residual claim upon the gross returns received from their use in combination with other productive factors. In the actual allocation of the
receipts received from the operation of an office building or from farming,
first consideration must be given to the payments made for wages,
supplies, and utilities. Without the payment of these operating costs,
businesses soon lose whatever earning power they have. Office managers
give top priority to operating outlays because they realize that they must
provide elevator and janitorial service, heat, and electric power if they are
to retain their present tenants and attract new occupants for their vacant
office suites. Farmers also frequently minimize their operating-cost
outlays when their incomes are low; but they must still arrange for seed,
supplies, hired labor, and their own living expenses if they plan to stay in
business.

Second priority is usually claimed by taxes and insurance. These costs
can go unpaid when business incomes are low; but the risk of losses from
insurable items, penalties for late payment of taxes, and the threat of
property-tax reversion ordinarily favor their prompt payment. More
leeway is usually possible with payments covering long-term capital costs.
Operators can often postpone maintenance and repair operations for
several months; they can forego the setting aside of depreciation reserves;
and they can default on their mortgage and bond interest payments. When
the choice is between the payment of these costs during short-run periods,
operators ordinarily prefer to keep up their interest payments while they
postpone their outlays for repairs and depreciation. When this problem
continues for longer periods, these payment priorities are often reversed.
Mortgagees and bondholders may then have to wait for their interest
because it is necessary to replace worn-out equipment and to carry on
certain maintenance and repair operations if plant deterioration and losses
in production capacity are to be avoided.

Any income that remains after payment is made for the above

operating costs can be treated as land rent or as interest on the operator's equity. The size of this residual return is affected by all of those factors that bear upon the relationship between costs, prices, and volume of business. Between 1940 and 1970, commodity market prices tended to increase faster than costs, and substantial profits were realized by most productive enterprises. This net return was often capitalized into higher property values; and thus contributed to the upward trend in real estate and stock values reported in Table 10-1. When prices falter and cost-price squeezes develop, the residual return attributable to land resources almost always declines and may disappear entirely.

One of the most important factors affecting the returns to land-resource developments is the problem of "sunk costs." While projects are being planned and developed, careful consideration is usually given to the relationship between costs of development and potential receipts. At this stage, every project must be justified by its favorable prospects for producing a surplus of returns above costs. Once a project is completed, however, the actual cost of production or development loses significance as far as its further effect upon operations is concerned. The production outlays already made in the development process become "sunk costs" at this point because they can no longer be withdrawn or recovered. The total investment is then more or less committed to the use for which the project was designed. Instead of enjoying a guaranteed income, the owner must now accept whatever return he can secure in the market. Naturally, he still wants to break even on his over-all investment. But he will take a higher return if he can get it, and he will accept less if he must.

As the above discussion suggests, property owners can never plan to price their products in terms of production costs. In each successive short-run period, they must accept whatever return the market offers. Sometimes this means profits, sometimes it involves operating at a loss. Yet over the long run, most well-planned and well-managed properties can count on a surplus of returns above production and operating costs. This situation prevails because of the recurring need for new resource developments that comes with the wearing out of old properties and with changes in supply and demand conditions. The entrance of new developments into the market is always prompted and guided by the prospects of profits above production costs. Before new capital will be invested, profits must usually be realized on the developments already in existence.

OPERATION OF THE REAL ESTATE MARKET

What is often referred to as the "real estate market" is really a conglomerate concept made up of thousands of smaller markets that operate in different areas and deal with different types of properties. Separate markets exist for every type of property that involves different groups of buyers and sellers. Distinctions ordinarily are made between the markets for farm, residential, commercial, industrial, mining, forest, and recreation properties; and at times distinctions also are made between the markets associated with various subtypes of properties.

Emphasis in this discussion is centered primarily on the characteristics and general operation of two types of aggregate markets—the farm real estate market and the market for urban and suburban residential properties. These are the largest and best-organized land-resource markets. Neither of these markets involves enough sales of closely comparable properties to permit day-to-day market quotations, but both have sufficient sales in most communities to permit the use of market-comparison valuation techniques and to facilitate a certain continuity in market-price relationships.

Characteristics of the Real Estate Market

The real estate market deals for the most part with the buying and selling of land resources that have already been developed and brought into use. New developments can result when market transactions lead to new construction or the shifting of land areas to higher uses. But most of the productive properties offered for sale have already benefited from development work on the part of previous owners and have been used for crop production, grazing, forest, mining, industrial, or commercial purposes. Similarly, the average residential property placed on the market also represents a used second-, third-, or fourth-hand structure that has been occupied and used by earlier owners. Unlike many commodity markets, new products are the exception rather than the rule in the real estate market.

Real estate markets are characterized by (1) the fixed location of the product around which they center, (2) the nonstandardized and frequently heterogeneous nature of their product, (3) special legal requirements that affect the transfer of real estate, (4) dependence on local supply and demand conditions, (5) the large considerations involved in most transactions, (6) a customary use of credit arrangements to supplement the limited equity interests held by many sellers and most buyers, (7) infrequent participation in the market by the average buyer and seller, and (8) the common use of a broker's services.

Like the properties and legal descriptions with which it deals, the real estate market is definitely site- or location-oriented. Real estate brokers frequently find it possible to sell comparable lots, houses, or farms, but they can never standardize their product in the same sense that they could provide duplicate models of an automobile, typewriter, or can-opener. They cannot quote real estate prices f.o.b. Detroit. Landed property must always be sold where it is.

The fixed-location factor makes the real estate market primarily a local market. Florida real estate may find a market among northern investors, but this is the exceptional case. Once a prospective buyer has decided where he wants to acquire property, he must look to local property owners to supply the market listings. Similarly, local property owners who wish to sell ordinarily expect to find buyers among the people who live or who expect to live in the area. Local market conditions often buoy up property values and the level of real estate market activity in the immediate area without having any appreciable effect on property values outside of the local commuting zone.

Sales and other transactions that involve the holding or sharing of rights in real estate are subject to a number of legal requirements not ordinarily applied to other sales commodities. Every tract of land has its legal description. All claims against land titles must be registered to have legal standing. Titles are carefully checked for flaws and possible claims against them. These procedures, which are designed to protect ownership rights, highlight the fact that land resources and real estate are legally different than other market commodities.

Unlike most markets in which average buyers and sellers participate on a day-to-day basis, real estate market transactions usually involve substantial considerations. Property sale agreements ordinarily involve cash outlays of several hundred if not several thousands of dollars. Buyers quite often spend their entire life savings plus all the money they can borrow on the properties they buy in one market transaction.

The average seller is a private owner with only a single property to sell. His property is ordinarily a used property and is frequently encumbered by a mortgage that has not as yet been paid off. This means that he can sell only his equity interest and that he must plan to either transfer the mortgage to the buyer or use part of the proceeds from the sale to satisfy this claim against the property. As a general rule, he is not in the business of selling and trading real estate, and his experience in the marketing of real properties is definitely limited. Usually, his decision to sell is associated with outside circumstances such as desire to move to a larger or smaller house or farm, plans to retire or transfer to a job in another area, or need to liquidate his investment.

In addition to his other characteristics, the average seller frequently cherishes a somewhat erroneous notion regarding the value of his property. During inflationary periods, owners sometimes fail to realize how much the market value of their properties has climbed. More often, the owner's failing lies in the direction of overvaluing rather than undervaluing the product he expects to market.

Like the average seller, the average buyer may come from any walk of life. In most cases he, too, has had little experience in the buying or selling of real estate. His supply of capital is ordinarily limited, and he usually plans to mortgage the property he buys to secure a substantial part of its purchase price. If he is in the market to buy a house or a farm, he has probably shopped around for awhile and may have a fairly good idea concerning the amount and quality of the property he might expect for the price he is able to pay. If he has not checked market prices and listings, his first reaction will often be one or surprise or astonishment when he is informed of the prices asked for real estate.

The inexperience and infrequent participation of the average buyer and seller in the real estate market is often compensated through use of a broker's services. Most real estate brokers have considerable knowledge concerning the operation of the market and the transfer of properties. Through their office contacts, advertising, and joint listing arrangements with other brokers, they have facilities for bringing buyers and sellers together. Their day-to-day contact with market conditions provides them with a knowledge of real estate price trends and often qualifies them as property appraisers.[47]

All of these factors make it possible for brokers to provide a valuable service to both the average buyer and the average seller. They can advise the prospective buyer regarding both the types of properties available and the prices he can expect to pay. At the same time, as supposedly neutral parties to the transaction, they can often do a better job of pointing out the advantages of and actually selling a property than can the seller.

There is probably no market in the American economy where as much haggling and "horse trading" over price terms takes place as in the real estate market. Offers and counteroffers are common, even expected in most cases. Far from the usual approach with many commodities in which the buyer expects to pay the amount listed on the price tag, most buyers of real estate expect to start their bargaining with an initial offer somewhat below the price asked by the seller. In consequence, many sellers list their properties at prices somewhat in excess of the amounts they expect to get. The broker often plays the important intermediary role in this bargaining process. He not only carries offers and counteroffers back and forth between the buyer and seller but also frequently finds himself in the position of advisor to both parties on questions concerning the adequacy or fairness of the offer, the buyer's prospects for getting the property at less than the list price, and the seller's prospects for securing a higher price than that offered.

Farm Real Estate Market

Factors such as size of holdings, extent of improvements, quality of

---

[47]Real estate brokerage started in the United States around 1800 and became an established business during the 1840s and 1850s. Cf. Pearl J. Davies, *Real Estate in American History* (Washington: Public Affairs Press, 1958), pp. 18-27. Brokers' offices range from small one-man operations to large firms with several departments and numerous personnel. Some brokers limit their activities to the listing and selling of properties. Others act as buying and leasing agents, manage properties for investors, appraise real estate, sell property insurance, act as real estate mortgage credit agents, and plan and supervise real estate developments. Brokers are expected to follow a professional code of ethics and are licensed to operate by the state. The term "realtor" is a coined title used to describe those brokers who are members of local real estate boards associated with the National Association of Real Estate Boards.

production resources, and location cause farm properties to vary over a wide range in market values. It is not uncommon for properties in the same community to differ considerably in average acreage values. Wider variations frequently stem from regional differences as farming areas vary greatly in their climates, soil and water resources, and locations with respect to major markets. Farms located near metropolitan centers usually sell for higher prices than farms in more rural areas, and farms in the Corn Belt for more than ranch land. Average farm land values by states ranged from highs of $1,028 per acre in New Jersey, $795 in Connecticut, and $710 in Rhode Island in 1970 to lows of $36 in Wyoming, $42 in New Mexico, and $44 in Nevada.

Thanks to the services of the United States Department of Agriculture, considerable data have been collected and reported concerning the situation and trends in the farm real estate market.[48] Since 1912, the first year for which annual trend data are reported, this market has witnessed two important periods of rising prices plus an intervening period of falling and depressed farm property values.

During the World War I period

> ... few people questioned the soundness of farm real estate as an investment. Land values had been rising for more than 50 years and further increases were generally expected. Most of the public lands suitable for farming had been settled, and population was increasing much faster than was the supply of land. Technological developments capable of greatly increasing agricultural production from existing land resources were not foreseen. The favorable market for agricultural exports was expected to continue. Moreover, considerable prestige was attached to ownership of land. In this general setting, an ever-increasing demand for land was assumed as well as a reluctance of owners to sell. Consequently, a high proportion of the current farm income was capitalized into land values in the expectation that the long-time upward trend in values would more than make up for any temporary decline that might occur in the postwar period.[49]

With this feeling of optimism at work, the average index of farm real estate values (1957-59 = 100) climbed from 36 in 1912 to 48 in 1918 and then shot up to 64 in 1920. (Cf. Figure 10-2.) This boom condition was accompanied by a wave of speculative buying in many areas, buying that in many cases was financed on a shoe-string basis by overoptimistic lending agencies.

The decline in farm-product prices between 1918 and 1920 and the sharp drop in farm-product prices in the fall of 1920 brought an abrupt end to this land boom. Farm real estate values dropped to an index level

---

[48]The U.S. Department of Agriculture publishes a situation report entitled *Current Developments in the Farm Real Estate Market* twice each year. These reports provide current and up-to-date information on farm real estate values and market trends by states, regions, and for the nation.

[49]W. H. Scofield and R. D. Davidson, *The Farm Real Estate Situation: 1947-48 and 1948-49,* U.S. Department of Agriculture Circular No. 823, 1949, p. 38.

FIGURE 10-2. Trend in farm real estate market prices, United States, 1912-1970.

of 52 in 1922 and then gradually declined to 42.5 in 1930. With the onset of the depression, the index sank to a low of 26 in 1933, and then gradually rallied. Between 1936 and 1941 the market was relatively stable with the average index of value ranging around 30 and 31.

World War II brought higher farm prices and a gradually increasing demand for farm properties. Vivid memories of the disastrous effects of the 1920 land boom and the wave of property foreclosures that followed throughout the 1920s and 1930s helped to keep prices down. Even so, farm land values increased at a rate of approximately 1 percent per month throughout most of the war and early postwar period. The big increase in land values again came in the postwar period. The index of farm real estate values, which had increased from 31 in 1941 to 46 in 1945, shot up to 58.5 in 1947 and 66 in 1949. This trend was favored by many factors including national prosperity, a tremendous demand for farm products for domestic and foreign use, decontrol of farm prices, and the public credit and veterans' loan-guarantee programs.

This upward trend was stalled and temporarily reversed during the business recession of 1949. Then an upswing in general economic conditions and the inflationary pressures associated with the Korean crisis joined to push the index up to 75 in 1951 and 82 in 1952. The end of the Korean War and declining farm prices caused the index to level off in 1954, after which it started a long steady upward swing that brought the index up to 85.5 in 1955, 111 in 1960, 139 in 1965, and 186 in 1970.[50]

[50] For more detailed information on the year by year indices of average farm real estate values per acre for the 48 states, cf. *Farm Real Estate Market Developments*, CD-64, August 1963, p. 40, and subsequent issues.

Much of the trend toward higher farm land prices since 1940 can be credited to inflationary pressures. The nation's consumers' price index rose from 48.8 in 1940 to 135.3 in 1970 (1957-59 = 100) in the same time period that the farm real estate price index was rising from 30.5 to 186. As this comparison suggests, farm land prices have been rising approximately twice as fast as the general price level. Viewed over a longer period as in Figure 10-2, it appears that farm land prices, measured in 1957-59 constant dollars, declined from 1917 to 1933 after which they increased. The rate of increase was both steady and rapid between 1954 and 1970.

Number of voluntary transfers. Market listings and the number of voluntary transfers provide a second important facet of the real estate market. The number of farms offered for sale in any given community is always limited by the ownership pattern and the trend toward parcellation of units or combination of fields into larger farms. It also depends to a considerable extent on cultural attitudes. In many parts of the world, the ties between man and land are such that owners are extremely reluctant to sell or trade any of their land. Farm properties in these areas usually pass mostly by inheritance; and it is an unusual event when farms are offered for sale in an open market. This is not the situation throughout most of the United States. Since colonial times, most American farmers have been willing to move to new opportunities and have been willing to sell their holdings when the price was right. Almost every farm may be considered as being potentially for sale, although only a fraction of the total number are ever listed at one time.

Analysis of the available data on voluntary farm transfers (Figure 10-3) shows that the volume of transfers reached peaks in the early months of the 1916-20 and post-1941 land booms. The prospect of high selling prices—high in comparison with those of the recent past—brought a

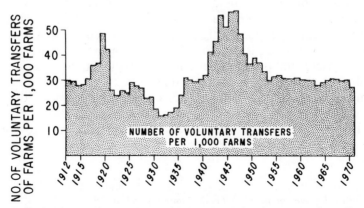

FIGURE 10-3. Trend in annual number of voluntary sales and transfers of farms, United States, 1912-1970.

considerable flow of properties into the market after both World War I and World War II. More than 5 percent of the farms (57.7 farms per 1,000 in both 1945 and 1946) were sold in voluntary transfers in each of the years between 1944 and 1947. Once this backlog of properties (many of which would have been offered earlier had prices been higher) was sold, the number of willing sellers declined and the number of voluntary sales dropped to the 28 to 32 farms per 1,000 level, which has applied since the middle 1950s.

High land prices have provided sales opportunities for those farm owners who were approaching retirement or who planned to sell anyway. They have also encouraged some operators located in the path of urban growth to sell out and relocate in more rural areas. Generally though, they have had little direct impact, other than raising the costs of farm enlargement, for the large number of operators who have planned to stay in farming or who have seen no particular advantages in seeking replacement properties.

Market conditions in 1970. Farm land prices presented a perplexing picture in 1970. For three decades they had been rising faster than the general price level. This situation could easily be explained if farm incomes had been high. But this was not the case. Farm incomes had generally lagged behind those secured in the rest of the economy. Net returns to farm real estate (land rents) had dropped from an annual average of $4.5 billion in the 1945-49 period to $3.9 billion in 1950-54 and $2.7 billion in 1955-59, and then risen to $4.3 billion in 1960-64 and $6.9 billion in 1965-69. Stated as a rate of return on the current market value of farm land, these returns dropped from 8.0 percent in 1945-49 to 5.3 percent in 1950-54, 2.8 percent in 1955-59, 3.6 percent in 1960-64, and 4.2 percent in 1965-69.[51]

In the absence of high farm incomes, other factors obviously contributed to the doubling of farm land values between 1955 and 1970 and to the 60 percent increase in average values between 1960 and 1970. Five sets of factors may be identified. These include: (1) land speculation and purchases in anticipation of higher prices, (2) acquisitions for nonagricultural uses, (3) acquisitions for the enlargement of farms, (4) capitalization of agricultural program benefits into higher land values, and (5) the availability of credit for farm land purchases.[52]

In many respects, the general aura of optimism associated with land investments during the 1960s was the most important cause of rising land prices. Investments in land were regarded as safe and almost foolproof. As with some of the more glamorous stock issues, many investors gave far

[51]Cf. Bruce B. Johnson, "An Active Land Market in Perspective," *Farm Real Estate Market Developments,* CD-71, December 1968, p. 29.

[52]Cf. William H. Scofield, "Land Returns and Farm Income," *Farm Real Estate Market Developments,* CD-67, August 1965, p. 44.

more emphasis to expectations of capital gains than to their immediate prospects for net returns. The attraction of farm land investments to nonfarmers is shown by the fact that nonfarmers accounted for a third of the farm purchases between 1959 and 1967, for 39 percent in 1968, and 38 percent in 1969 and 1970.

Average price levels were influenced by the sale of considerable acreages near expanding cities at suburban prices ranging up to several thousands of dollars per acre. The sellers of these farms frequently moved to other farming areas where they were willing to pay above average prices to secure the farms they wanted. Farmers in nonurban areas also found good markets in many cases for small acreages of often rough and marginal lands with recreation possibilities.

Most of the land sold was purchased by active farmers. Many of these operators saw opportunities to increase production efficiencies by expanding their scale of operations and accordingly were willing to pay reasonably high prices for additional tracts that they could add to their operating units. Transfers for farm enlargement purposes rose from 26 percent of the total in 1950-54 to 37 percent in 1955-59, 49 percent in 1960-64, to 57 percent in 1968.[53] Farm buyers and sellers also recognized that some types of lands such as those with historical rights to tobacco allotments or to grazing permits on public lands enjoyed economic advantages that gave them higher market values.

Farm land purchases were encouraged throughout the 1960s by the general availability of credit both to farmer and nonfarmer purchasers. As interest rates rose and the supply of credit tightened near the end of the decade, the number of voluntary transfers declined to 27.8 per 1,000 in 1970. Considerable emphasis was still given, however, to the sale of small tracts, usually for farm enlargement purposes, and many sellers financed buyers in the purchase of their lands. Land prices rose rapidly during the 1960s but started to level off in 1970 largely because of credit and financing problems and the cooling off of the business economy.

Market for Residential Properties

Unlike the farm real estate market, the federal government has not assembled data on urban residential real estate trends until recent years. The Departments of Commerce and of Housing and Urban Development report that the median sales price of new single-family homes sold in the United States rose from $18,000 in 1963 to $18,900 in 1964, $20,000 in 1965, $21,400 in 1966, $22,700 in 1967, $24,700 in 1968, $25,600 in 1969, and $23,500 in 1970.[54] The median prices by regions in 1970 were

[53]Cf. *Farm Real Estate Market Developments*, CD-72, March 1969, p. 14.

[54]Data on housing production and cost trends are reported monthly and annually in *Housing and Urban Development Trends*. Data on house sales prices are reported in the annual summaries of this publication and in the *HUD Statistical Yearbook*.

$20,400 in the South, $24,000 in the West, $25,000 in the North Central states, and $30,400 in the Northeast. Median prices for the same year by types of financing ranged from $19,300 for Federal Housing Administration-insured and $23,700 for Veterans' Administration-guaranteed mortgages to $24,800 for cash and related sales and $30,000 for houses with conventional mortgages.

A longer term look at the price and volume of sales trends in the real estate market is provided by the indices computed by the Roy Wenzlick Research Corporation of St. Louis, Missouri. One of these indices measures residential real estate market activity and shows that there have been three boom periods in activity since 1900. A boom period extending from 1903 to 1910 reached its peak in sales activity in 1906. A second boom extending from 1919 to 1929 peaked in 1925, while a third boom period between 1944 and 1949 had its peak volume of sales activity in 1946. Low periods of sales activity came in 1900, 1918, and 1934. Residential real estate sales activity has fluctuated around normal since 1949 but was 15 percent below normal at the beginning of 1970.

Two other indices measure the price trends for the typical new house and lot and the selling prices of typical well-kept single-family houses. The major trends indicated by these two indices for the 1913-70 period are summarized in Figure 10-4. As this figure shows, the trends in residential property values have followed much the same pattern as farm land values except that they have not increased as rapidly since 1950 in constant value dollar terms.

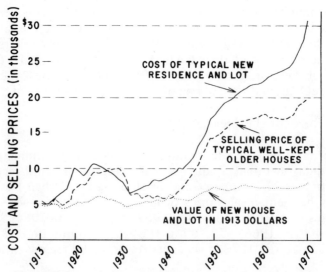

FIGURE 10-4. Trends in new and existing residential property values expressed in current dollars and in constant 1913 dollars, United States, 1913-1970. (Courtesy of Roy Wenzlick Research Corporation.)

Residential property values were relatively low between 1913 and the end of World War I. The cost of a typical newly constructed residence and lot then rose from $5,400 in 1914 to $10,000 in 1920. Prices declined slightly in 1921 and 1922 but were up to a high of $10,500 in 1925 after which they declined to a low of $6,700 in 1932. Since 1932, the trend has been almost steadily upward to $8,500 in 1940, $10,000 in 1945, $17,600 in 1950, $20,400 in 1955, $22,200 in 1960, $23,500 in 1965, and $30,600 in 1970. Prices for typical well-kept older single-family residences followed the same general trend except that they usually rose later and then to lower levels than the new residences. The typical house and lot used as a benchmark in this trend series experienced a market value increase from $4,800 in 1917 to $10,100 in 1929. Resale prices then dropped to $5,950 in 1932 and $5,800 in 1938 after which they rose to averages of $8,000 in 1945, $13,900 in 1950, $16,300 in 1955, $17,400 in 1960, $17,200 in 1965, and $19,690 in early 1970.

Trends with new construction. The nonfarm residential real estate market is concerned primarily with two types of properties—used dwellings and new construction. Of the two, new construction often has a dominant effect on market price trends both in providing new additions to the supply and in setting the replacement cost of existing dwellings. The trends in new residential construction and in residential building costs for the 1910-70 period are summarized in Figure 10-5.

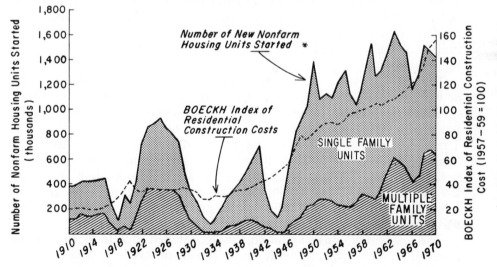

* The data series on numbers of nonfarm housing starts was revised in 1959 to make the total correspond more closely with the definition of housing used in the 1960 Census of Housing. Under the old series, the totals were limited to an incomplete count of new permanent housing starts in the 48 contiguous states. The new series involves somewhat higher totals than those reported earlier and provides more complete coverage of the number of temporary and permanent housing units started in the 50 states.

FIGURE 10-5. Trends in construction of new nonfarm housing units and average residential construction costs, United States, 1910-1970.

A pre-World War I peak in new residential construction came in 1909 when 573,000 new nonfarm dwelling units were started. Residential construction then remained at a fairly constant level of around 400,000 new units a year until 1916. New construction was limited during World War I and got off to a slow recovery in 1919 and 1920. After 1921, however, the number of new starts rose to a high of 937,000 units in 1925. This building boom gradually subsided after 1925 and dropped rapidly after 1928 to a depression low of 93,000 units in 1933. The volume of new construction then gradually increased to 706,000 new units in 1941.

Residential construction was again limited throughout World War II; and another building boom started immediately after the war in 1946 and 1947. This boom brought 1,396,000 new permanent nonfarm dwelling starts in 1950. Mortgage credit restrictions were imposed by the government in late 1950 to hold back the inflationary pressures generated by the beginning of the Korean crisis. These restrictions brought a reduction in the total number of new nonfarm housing starts to 1.09 million in 1950. New construction of permanent nonfarm housing units remained at the 1.04 to 1.34 million level throughout the 1950s. A more complete method of counting new housing units was introduced in 1959.[55] This approach, which includes Alaska and Hawaii and counts temporary as well as permanent structures, shows construction highs of 1.53 million units in 1959 and 1.62 and 1.54 million in 1963 and 1964, respectively, and lows of 1.27 and 1.17 million in 1960 and 1966. Of the 1.44 million new nonfarm housing units provided in 1970, 5.67 percent were single family units, 5.9 percent were 2-, 3- or 4-family units, and 37.3 involved 5 or more family units.

Despite the wide fluctuations reported in residential construction activity, building costs have been quite sticky in those periods when they have not been rising to new levels. Between 1910 and 1915 the Boeckh index of residential construction costs (1957-59 = 100) stood around 19. This index rose to 29 in 1918 and 44 in 1920. It dropped following the business recession of 1920 and then rallied and remained fairly stable at between 36 and 37 from 1923 through 1930. It dropped to a depression low of 18 in 1932 and 1933. This was only 20 percent below the cost level that had prevailed during the construction boom of the 1920s and was higher than the costs reported for any year prior to 1918.

The residential construction cost index climbed back to its 1928 index level of 36 by 1938; and with the outbreak of war in Europe in 1939, building costs started a steady upward trend, which continued until 1948 when the index stood at 78.2. This level dropped to 76.2 following the

---

[55]Extension of the new series back to 1945 shows that the number of new housing starts was undercounted by 4.66 million units in the 1945-58 period. This series shows that a record number of 1,952,000 new units were constructed in 1950 and a second highest total of 1,646,000 in 1955.

business recession of 1949. The downward trend was reversed in 1950 when the index rose to 80.3. From then on it rose steadily to 92.4 in 1955, 104.2 in 1960, 115.2 in 1965, and 155.9 in 1970. Meanwhile, the construction cost index for apartments, hotels, and office buildings rose from 49.4 in 1945 and 75.9 in 1950 to 162.7 in 1970.

Trend in urban lot values. Higher residential site values have contributed significantly to the upward trend in housing costs since 1950. The National Association of Home Builders found in a survey of its membership in 1965 that the costs associated with the raw land used for residential building had increased 15 percent annually between 1960 and 1964 while finished lot prices had risen at a 16 percent annual rate.[56]

A general indication of the upward trend in urban residential lot values is provided by the reports of the Federal Housing Administration on the estimated site values associated with new and existing houses covered by new FHA-insured mortgages. (Cf. Table 10-3.) These reports, which involve properties of less than average value for the nation, show that the average market value of the building sites with new housing units rose

TABLE 10-3. Trends in Estimated Market Values and Estimated Values of Equivalent Building Sites for New and Existing Single-Family Houses, FHA Sample of Properties, 1950-1969

Year	Average FHA estimates of market value of single-family houses		Average estimated market values of equivalent building sites		Average ratio of site value to total value	
	New units	Existing units	New units	Existing units	New units	Existing units
1950	$ 8,594	$ 9,298	$1,035	$1,150	12.0%	12.4%
1955	12,118	12,047	1,626	1,707	13.4	14.2
1960	14,899	13,304	2,470	2,356	16.6	17.7
1965	17,190	15,394	3,427	3,219	19.9	20.9
1967	18,970	16,286	3,766	3,504	19.9	21.5
1969	21,036	17,165	4,277	3,717	20.3	21.7
1970	23,559	18,519	4,952	3,973	21.0	21.5

Source: U. S. Department of Housing and Urban Development, *1970 HUD Statistical Yearbook,* p. 198.

from $1,035 in 1950 to $2,715 in 1960, and to $4,952 in 1970. With this five-fold increase in lot prices, the ratio of site values to total values rose from 12.0 percent in 1950 to 16.6 percent in 1960 and to 21.0 percent in 1970.

Residential lot prices have increased in market value with the increasing impact of demand upon the supply of available lots. Most of the increase in average prices reflects the rising prices associated with the acquisition and development of raw land for building site purposes. Some of the

---

[56]National Association of Home Builders, Economics Department, Special Report 65-8, "How Land and Lot Costs Went Up in Four Years" (Washington: 1965).

increase also stems from the fact that the average lot now tends to be somewhat larger than was the case in 1940 and 1950, and lots are often more developed now than they once were.

Residential market trends since World War I. The conglomerate effect of the many factors that have affected residential market values in recent decades can best be described through a recounting of recent market history. World War I gave rise to a housing shortage, a general increase in rental rates, and a considerable increase in real estate market activity and residential property values between 1918 and 1920. But this early postwar period did not witness a market boom comparable to that experienced in the farm real estate market.

The business recession that started in late 1920 brought a downward adjustment in building costs, a reduction in real estate sales activity, and a temporary leveling off of market prices. Rental rates continued to rise, however; and after a short period of adjustment, the volume of residential construction started to climb. By 1922 a building boom was definitely under way and the volume of real estate sales and market prices again increased. Except for agriculture, business conditions were booming; and considerable mortgage credit was available for prospective home builders and buyers. Hundreds of new subdivisions were laid out. Considerable subdividing, home building, and home buying was financed on a shoe-string basis with high-percentage loans and second and third mortgages. The peak of the building and buying boom was reached in 1925. Yet even though the amount of sales activity and new building dropped off after 1925, market prices on residential properties remained strong until after the stock market crash in late 1929.

With the onset of the Great Depression in 1930, residential rents declined, new building activity dropped to a low level, and a definite buyers' market developed for existing properties. The supply of real estate mortgage credit all but disappeared; and home owners, pressed by reduced incomes and high mortgage indebtedness, frequently offered their properties at distress prices. Residential property values declined to their pre-World War I level; and even then many properties went unsold because of the relative lack of buyers who were both willing and financially able to take properties out of the market.

Mortgage foreclosures, which had started to increase after 1925, became a common occurrence. In 1933, a peak of 252,400 nonfarm home mortgages were foreclosed and more than 100,000 foreclosures were reported in every year from 1928 to 1939. Tax delinquency also became a problem as lot owners, particularly those with holdings in premature subdivisions, and even some homeowners began to lose their properties through tax reversion.

The low point in the housing market was reached in 1932 and 1933. Property sales, market prices, new construction, building costs, and rental rates were all at their lowest ebb. Incomes were low, and many families doubled up in overcrowded quarters while many rental facilities stood vacant. Recovery from this point was gradual, but was facilitated to a large measure by government help. The Home Owners Loan Corporation was established in 1933 and gave valuable assistance to distressed owners in refinancing home mortgages. Further help was provided the next year when the Federal Housing Administration was set up to foster a freer flow of credit into the housing market.

Conditions in the housing market gradually improved after 1933. Property values remained low; but the amount of market activity increased. Rental rates climbed slightly, and building costs began to go up as the amount of residential construction increased with each new year. By 1939, 1940, and 1941, a new building boom was in the making. Employment was up; average incomes were increasing; and real estate market activity was getting back to normal. These conditions gave rise to a slight increase in property values and set the scene for an even greater increase after the nation became involved in World War II in December, 1941.

World War II brought numerous complications for the housing market. Rental rates and property values started to climb in many defense areas in 1940 and 1941. Rent controls were applied to these areas in early 1942. Private construction was restricted and placed under a priority system which channeled most new private and public housing construction to military areas and cities with defense industries. Insufficient housing, increased employment, and higher incomes favored property price increases in many cities. Nationwide, however, the war prompted a general feeling of uncertainty, which led to a decline in sales activity until late 1943 when an increasing volume of sales and rising property values heralded the beginning of another market boom.

With the end of the war in 1945 and the demobilization of the armed forces in the months that followed, it soon became apparent that the nation suffered from a critical housing shortage. Rental quarters were difficult to find and often commanded black market prices. New families had been created at a rapid rate during the war; and population, particularly in urban areas, was rising rapidly. This natural demand for housing was intensified by full employment, higher incomes, a backlog of wartime savings, and by veterans' assistance and credit programs. In the face of this sudden increase in effective demand, real estate sales activity increased and prices began to spiral upward. Sales activity reached its peak in 1946 and then dropped off until 1950; but market prices remained high and kept on rising with the continued existence of a sellers' market. Building costs increased rapidly, and the volume of new construction, which at first had been held down by material shortages and construction management problems, climbed to a new high level.

By 1950, the market value of old as well as new homes in many areas stood at double and sometimes three times their prewar level. This upward price trend leveled off for some months in 1949 and early 1950 and then rose again with the inflationary spiral and building restrictions that came with the outbreak of war in Korea in 1950. The cost of new single-family houses then rose steadily at a rate of roughly 2 percent annually until 1966 after which the rate of increase accelerated. Older house values also increased but at a slower rate until 1961, dropped slightly until 1966, and then experienced an upward surge.

Several factors contributed to the rising price trends of the 1950s and 1960s. Family incomes were rising along with the general cost of living. Average house rental rates increased gradually after the dropping of rent controls in most areas in the early 1950s. Higher rents and new construction permitted the housing vacancy rate in cities to rise to the 7 percent level in 1961 and then to almost 8 percent in 1965. Housing credit was readily available throughout most of this period even though average interest rates rose from 4.5 and 5 percent in the late 1940s to 6 percent by 1960. Foreclosure rates also rose, particularly with properties purchased on a minimal down payment basis. Overall, foreclosures increased from a low of less than 2 percent in the early 1950s to over 5 percent in 1967 (6.7 percent with VA-guaranteed loans in 1964 and 12 percent with FHA-insured loans in 1965 and 1966).

By the late 1960s, it was obvious that residential housing was in trouble. The Vietnam war was draining the nation's resources. Real estate credit was becoming scarce. Average interest rates had risen to 7 percent in early 1968, 8 percent in 1969, and were at the 8.5 and 9 percent level in 1970. Construction and building site costs had continued to rise. Vacancies were down to 4.3 percent in the metropolitan centers in 1969, and older house values started to rise in price. Financing problems caused the rate of new construction to fall below the nation's needs at a time when large numbers of children born in the post-1945 period were beginning to move into their household-formation years. In the absence of other low-cost housing opportunities, many people turned to the use of mobile homes. The number of these shipped to dealers in the United States increased from 90,200 in 1961 to 412,690 in 1969 and 401,200 in 1970.

Other Real Estate Markets

Little attempt has been made to systematically record the trends with other real estate markets. Their price trends have generally followed those of the farm and urban residential real estate markets.

Land areas with recreation and second-home residential potential have increased substantially in demand and in price since 1950. Much the same situation has applied to urban commercial and industrial sites in the more active cities. Office rents have risen to new highs in most metropolitan areas, and the demand for more offices, modern commercial developments, and new industrial properties has triggered considerable public and private urban renewal in the cities as well as the development of new sities in suburban areas. A significant measure of the investments associated with these developments is indicated by the construction trends data reported in Table 10-4. These data show that nonresidential building construction provided approximately two-thirds as much new floor space

TABLE 10-4. **Value of New Construction and New Floor Space Provided,** United States, 1960 to 1970

Class of construction	Value of construction			Floor space of buildings		
	1960	1965	1970	1960	1965	1970
	(millions of dollars)			(millions of square feet)		
Nonresidential buildings						
Commercial	3,725	9,090	9,724	283	415	536
Industrial	2,114	3,614	3,887	178	265	210
Education and science	3,005	5,234	5,480	196	225	195
Hospitals	832	2,823	2,780	36	60	75
Public buildings	679	1,017	1,141	33	36	29
Religious	789	581	669	53	45	27
Social and recreational	631	1,137	1,100	44	47	47
Miscellaneous	464	940	886	31	38	42
Total	12,239	24,436	25,667	854	1,131	1,161
Residential	15,105	24,792	25,219	1,300	1,711	1,779
Nonbuilding construction	8,972	18,706	16,539	–	–	–

Source: *Statistical Abstract of the United States, 1971*, p. 665.

in 1960, 1965 and 1969 as residential construction and that it involved investment costs of $12.2 billion in 1960, $17.2 billion in 1965, and $25.2 billion in 1969.

Land Booms and Their Control

Land booms have been a familiar feature in the past history of the real estate market. Many of these booms such as the Chicago canal boom of the 1830s, the Southern California land boom of the 1880s, and the Florida land boom of the 1920s have been more or less localized.[57]

[57]Cf. Homer Hoyt, *100 Years of Land Values in Chicago* (Chicago: University of Chicago Press, 1933); Glen M. Dumke, *The Boom of the Eighties in Southern California* (San Marino, California: Huntington Library, 1944); Homer B. Vanderblue, "The Florida Land Boom," *Journal of Land and Public Utility Economics*, Vol. 3, May and August, 1927, pp. 111-31 and 252-69; and Philip H. Cornick, *Premature Subdivision and Its Consequences* (New York: Institute of Public Administration, Columbia University, 1938).

Others such as the land booms of 1815-18, 1832-36, 1854-57, and the market booms after World Wars I and II were nation-wide in scope.

Most of these booms have been associated with periods of high demand for local products, rapid population growth, public improvements such as canals and railroads, discoveries of oil or valuable minerals, and inflationary movements. Most of them have been carried along on waves of optimism and overconfidence—conditions that often favored considerable speculation with loose financing and an upward spiraling of market prices to levels that were unreasonably high in light of the immediate income-producing potentialities of the properties involved. Some of these booms were fostered and fed by the promotional activities of particular groups; some gradually petered out; and some blossomed into full-sized bubbles only to bring substantial losses to many investors at the time they burst.

The collapse of some of the leading land booms of the past led to depressed business conditions for the nation as a whole. Examples include the panics of 1819, 1837, and 1857. The agricultural depression of the 1920s was seriously aggravated by the high debt loads many farmers carried over from the land boom collapse of 1920. The debt problems of numerous urban property owners during the 1930s also stemmed from the widescale use of loose financing arrangements during the housing and subdivision boom of the 1920s.

The distressing after-effects of these land booms has prompted considerable interest in ways and means of keeping real estate markets from getting out of hand. Among the more important control measures, mention should be made of the possible use of market education, credit restrictions, taxation of capital gains, price ceilings, sales restrictions, and inflationary control measures.

Land-boom psychology can often be dampened through the judicious and effective use of educational measures. Newspaper and radio publicity, speeches by public officials and others, and editorial comment may be used to advise prospective buyers of the market facts and of the unfortunate consequences of unfettered boom conditions. Public credit restrictions also provide an effective control measure that governments can use to limit the number of potential buyers. The housing credit restrictions applied in the United States during the Korean War, for example, had a restraining effect both in holding down the amount of new residential construction and in forestalling a threat of rapidly rising housing prices.

Higher taxes on capital gains can be used to discourage speculation and the ready transfer of properties during boom periods. This approach is naturally unpopular with sellers. Yet a tax approaching 100 percent of the seller's capital gain can provide a very effective means for discouraging speculation. Price ceilings might also be used to freeze real estate market values during emergency periods. This approach would undoubtedly lead to administrative difficulties and would probably invite black market operations. Direct controls of this type have their place, however, in those times when similar controls are applied to wages and salaries, rents, and most market commodities.

These control measures can be used alone or in various combinations to discourage land booms. In their application, however, it should be remembered that there is nothing basically wrong with rising land values as long as the increase reflects higher expectations regarding productive capacity. The need for controls arises when land values go up to unreasonable levels.

Land values frequently tend to spiral upward during inflationary periods, partly because of the rising money value of real estate and partly because of counterbidding between investors who hope to use real estate as an inflationary hedge. Effective market control under these circumstances calls for measures that strike at the heart of inflation. Either the supply of goods and services should be increased to satisfy the available purchasing power; or monetary and fiscal measures such as price, rent, and wage (and other income) controls, higher taxes, or forced savings plans should be used to reduce purchasing power to the available supply of goods and services.

—SUGGESTED READINGS

American Institute of Real Estate Appraisers, *The Appraisal of Real Estate,* 5th ed. (Chicago: American Institute of Real Estate Appraisers, 1967).

Kahn, Sanders A., Frederick E. Case, and Alfred Schimmel, *Real Estate Appraisal and Investment* (New York: The Ronald Press, 1963).

Murray, William G., *Farm Valuation and Appraisal,* 5th ed. (Ames: Iowa State University Press, 1969).

Ring, Alfred A., *The Valuation of Real Estate* (Englewood Cliffs, N.J.: Prentice-Hall, Inc., 1963).

Ratcliff, Richard J., *Urban Land Economics* (New York: McGraw-Hill Book Company, Inc., 1949), chaps. X-XII.

Weimer, Arthur M., and Homer Hoyt, *Real Estate,* 5th ed. (New York: The Ronald Press, 1966), chaps. XIII-XIV, XX-XXV.

Wendt, Paul F., *Real Estate Appraisal* (New York: Henry Holt & Company, Inc., 1956).

11

Impact of
Institutional Factors
on Land Use

Man's use of land resources always takes place within a broad institutional framework. This framework involves the role that our cultural environment and the forces of social and collective action play in influencing our behavior as individuals and as members of families, groups, communities and society. It is concerned with the impact of cultural attitudes, custom and tradition, habitual ways of thinking and doing things, legal arrangements, government programs, religious beliefs, household considerations, and other similar factors on man-to-man and man-to-land behavior.

The various factors that make up this institutional framework can be and often are classified as cultural, economic, political, religious, and social phenomena. Some of these factors have more economic significance than others. But economic or not, each factor usually plays an important role—sometimes strategic, though more often routine—in directing the course of human behavior. In this respect, each factor represents a part of the social organization into which man is born, which he is always modifying, and which in turn directs and controls him in his various activities.

Institutional factors are important to us because of the continuing influence they exert upon our economic behavior. They help make economic behavior more stable; and at the same time they help make it changeable, dynamic, and nonpredictable. Their significance is often overlooked or taken for granted in economic discussions. Their over-all impact is such that they can never be assumed away once economic theory is taken out of its academic vacuum and applied in the arena of real life.

NATURE OF INSTITUTIONAL FACTORS

To understand economic behavior, one must start with man himself. As Ernest S. Griffith has observed, anyone "who would really understand the changes in government or economics must start a long way from his ultimate goal by asking himself what sort of a creature man really is; for changes in man's group or institutional behavior are generated ultimately by his individual nature and must not do too great violence to this nature."[1]

No attempt will be made here to analyze the basic appetites, drives, desires, and other forces that provide the basis for human motivation; nor will an effort be made to explain the effects that the biochemical composition of the body or that man's glandular secretions, nervous system, or social nature have upon his individual outlook and behavior.[2] Suffice it to say that most human beings have wide potentials for development; that their capacities, personalities, and attitudes develop in different ways; that they are invariably conditioned in their development by different experiences and environments; and that they react differently to situations because of these and other differences.

While each individual stands at the center of his own world, it is important to note that most individual activity involves operations in a larger universe. Man is a social animal. He is born into the stream of society; and from the moment of his birth he shares in a social heritage that both conditions and controls his attitudes and reactions. Unlike Robinson Crusoe, he is seldom in a position to make his own rules. Instead he tends to accept and conform to the rules, social organization, and institutions that surround him during his formative years. He usually accepts the system of "discipline and obedience" into which he is born because experience tells him that "conformity to repeated and duplicated practices . . . is the only way to obtain life, liberty, and property with ease, safety, and consent."[3]

The various rules and institutions incorporated in our social heritage

[1] Ernest S. Griffith, *The Impasse of Democracy* (New York: Harrison-Hilton Books, Inc., 1939), p. 344.

[2] For a detailed discussion of this approach to economic behavior, see C. Reinold Noyes, *Economic Man in Relation to His Natural Environment* (New York: Columbia University Press, 1948).

[3] John R. Commons, *Institutional Economics: Its Place in Political Economy* (Madison: The University of Wisconsin Press, 1959), p. 45. Originally published by The Macmillan Company, 1934.

often change with time. At all stages, however, they tend to dictate what is and what is not considered acceptable behavior. In this respect, it is well to remember that:

> Human behavior is made up of two separate and distinct elements, the one biological, the other cultural. . . . On the one hand is the organism, composed of bones, muscles, nerves, glands, and sense organs. This organism is a single coherent unit, a system, with definite properties of its own. On the other hand is the cultural tradition into which the organism is born. It could have been born into one cultural tradition as well as another, into Tibetan as well as American or Eskimoan culture. But from the standpoint of subsequent behavior, everything depends upon the type of culture into which the baby is introduced by birth. If he is born into one culture he will think, feel, and act in one way; if he is born into another, his behavior will be correspondingly different. Human behavior is, therefore, always and everywhere, made up of these two ingredients: the dynamic organization of nerves, glands, muscles, and sense organs, that is *man,* and the extrasomatic cultural tradition.[4]

Definition and Scope of Meaning

The various aspects of group, collective, or social action that influence and control individual behavior may be described as *institutions* or as institutional factors. This concept is conveyed by Commons' well-known definition of an institution as "collective action in control, liberation, and expansion of individual action."[5] It is also suggested by Griffith's definition of an of an institution as "purposeful cooperative behavior,"[6] and by Barnes' treatment of institutions as "the social structure and machinery through which human society organizes, directs, and executes the multifarious activities required to satisfy human needs."[7]

It is often desirable to classify the many different types of institutions found in our society into two general groups—primary and secondary institutions.[8] The first of these groups is made up of the more fundamental or elemental institutions such as government, property, industry,

[4] From *The Science of Culture* by Leslie A. White. Copyright 1949 by Leslie White. Used by permission of the publishers, Farrar, Straus and Cudahy, Inc., pp. 121-23.

[5] Commons, *op. cit.,* p. 5.

[6] Griffith, *op. cit.,* p. 20.

[7] Harry Elmer Barnes, *Social Institutions* (Englewood Cliffs, N.J.: Prentice-Hall, Inc., 1942), p. 29.

[8] Institutions are sometimes classified in other ways. Some sociologists, for example, differentiate between "nucleated" institutions such as churches, schools, or local welfare agencies and "symbolic-diffused" institutions such as law, language, or ethics. Cf. F. Stuart Chapin, *Contemporary American Institutions* (New York: Harper & Brothers, 1935). Others distinguish between associations such as the family or the state and other types of institutions. Cf. Robert M. MacIver, *Society* (New York: Farrar and Rinehart, Inc., 1937).

education, religion, and the family. Each of these primary institutions is composed of or associated with a subordinate group of secondary institutions. The institution of government, for example, involves a legion of subordinate institutions including such separate factors as constitutions, legislatures, political parties, civil service systems, tax regulations, tariffs, social security, and local zoning ordinances. In similar fashion, religions involve many secondary institutions such as beliefs, creeds, rituals, sacraments, symbols and taboos.

As these examples suggest, many widely different factors in our society may be classified as institutions or institutional factors. The broad scope of this coverage was emphasized by Walton H. Hamilton when he wrote:

> Institution is a verbal symbol which, for want of a better, describes a cluster of social usages. It connotes a way of thought or action of some prevalence and permanence, which is embedded in the habits of a group or the customs of a people. . . . Institutions fix the confines of and impose form upon the activities of human beings. The world of use and wont, to which we imperfectly accommodate our lives, is a tangled and unbroken web of institutions. The range of institutions is as wide as the interests of mankind. . . . Arrangements as diverse as the money economy, classical education, the chain store, fundamentalism and democracy are institutions. They may be rigid or flexible in their structures, exacting or lenient in their demands; but alike they constitute standards of conformity from which an individual may depart only at his peril. About every urge of mankind an institution grows up; the expression of every taste and capacity is crowded into an institutional mold.[9]

Generally speaking, institutions represent established arrangements in society and established ways of doing things. They involve the working rules of society. And in many instances—as with such primary institutions as our economic, educational, family, legal, and political systems—they provide systems of control that point the way to what is considered acceptable individual and group behavior. As Steiner observes:

> . . . these systems are neither contiguous nor mutually exclusive. Rather, they are inextricably interwoven and interdependent. Clusters of institutional arrangements and methods of doing things exist in each system. These set the pattern of operation of the system of control. Some of these institutions and methods of doing things are merely formalized codes of human conduct. As such, they tie directly into cultural values. At this point, systems of control and cultural values get rather well tied together and become almost indistinguishable.[10]

[9]Walton H. Hamilton, "Institution," *Encyclopedia of the Social Sciences* (New York: The Macmillan Company, 1932), Vol. 8, p. 84.
[10]George A. Steiner, *Government's Role in Economic Life* (New York: McGraw-Hill Book Company, Inc., 1953), p. 23.

Economic Institutions

Economic activity often involves the close functioning and interplay of economic and institutional factors. In this process, institutional factors often take on an economic cast and become forces of economic significance. Our concepts of private property and the sanctity of contracts, for example, are really institutions of legal origin. Yet they are often regarded as economic institutions because of the essential role they play in the operation of the economic system. Other institutions such as public fiscal policy, taxes, and price control measures also have a tremendous impact upon economic life even though they may be classed as governmental controls.

Those institutional factors that are intertwined and identified with economic activity may be regarded as economic institutions. As one writer has observed: "Economic institutions are social arrangements . . . by means of which business and economic life are organized, directed, conducted, and regulated."[11]

Hundreds of economic institutions are found in modern society. In an early discussion of this subject, Ely listed public and private property, inheritance, contract and its conditions, vested rights, personal conditions, custom, competition, monopoly, authority, and benevolence as fundamental economic institutions.[12] This list may be supplemented with numerous additions varying from fundamental institutions such as the free enterprise system and the profit motive to more specific items such as labor unions, unemployment compensation, anti-trust regulations, security markets, and credit facilities.

IMPORTANCE OF SPECIFIC INSTITUTIONS

Those institutional factors that affect the ownership and use of land resources are sometimes described as *landed institutions.* Of these factors, the concept of property rights is by far the most important and most fundamental.[13] Several other institutions—some of them economic and some of them primarily noneconomic—also have important impacts upon the ownership and use of land resources. Special consideration is given here to the general impact of the family system and education, government, law, custom, and religion, on the ownership and use of land resources.

[11] Vernon A. Mund, *Government and Business* (New York: Harper & Brothers, 1950), p. 4.
[12] Cf. Richard T. Ely, *Property and Contract in Their Relation to the Distribution of Wealth* (New York: The Macmillan Company, 1914), pp. 52-53.
[13] This institution is considered in more detail in the next chapter.

The Family System and Education

The family system and education represent two basic institutions that underlie many of the concepts and attitudes people have concerning land resources and their use. Like many institutions, attitudes concerning these two institutions have changed over time. It is still normal, however, for young couples to marry, to have and raise children, and to consider education as a means of preparing themselves and their children for participation in and enjoyment of modern life.

Families involve social systems of privileges, joys, and responsibilities. They provide basic incentives for land use and development. Workers who are concerned with the support, comfort, and future security of their families are inclined to develop and use land resources somewhat differently than those who think only of their own personal welfare at the moment.

The family represents a planning and resource-using unit. Under adverse circumstances, support and protection of the family can necessitate disinvestment and exploitive practices. Ordinarily, however, the family system favors the planning and development of land resources for uses that extend far beyond current needs. Husbands and wives look to direct and indirect uses of the land for their livelihood. They seek a house and home and often a spot of earth they can call their own. They plan for the future welfare and security of the family and its members; and, once a basic level of affluence is attained, they become increasingly conscious of amenity and recreation values and of the qualitative as well as the more strictly quantitative aspects of their lives.

Education has become a stepping stone to participation in the opportunities of modern life. People go to school to enhance their income-producing abilities and also to develop understanding and appreciation of how the physical world and human society operate. Education teaches one how to make a living and also how to live and appreciate life. Education has affected land use by raising individual aspirations, by facilitating the development of new technologies, and by pointing the way for better resource management.

Considerable emphasis has been given to public education programs in all of the more developed nations. Education permits most adults in these countries to function as skilled workers. It has helped them to make improved uses of land resources that have led to higher incomes. Higher incomes have brought improvements in living standards, more emphasis on education, and aspirations for better things to come. Education is helping man to realize his own potential and also the potential that can be attained through intelligent and knowledgeable use of his land-resource base.

Government and Political Institutions

Most of the rugged individualists who settled and developed the American frontier placed high personal value upon their economic and political freedom. Many of them felt that "that government governs best which governs least." This emphasis upon individual freedom from governmental restraint has permeated much of our political thought and has caused many people to view every extension of governmental influence with alarm.

Despite this point of view, recent decades have brought a gradual expansion of the scope of government in the United States and in most other countries. Much of this expansion has come with the exercise of public power in the resolution of conflicts of interest, in the advancement of the public welfare, and in the pursuit of new social goals. Far from resulting in losses of individual freedom, these actions have often enhanced the economic opportunities and freedoms enjoyed by average citizens. They have also contributed to the rise of a "great leviathan," which now plays a dominant role in our lives. As Steiner observes:

> The influence of government . . . is felt today in every home, every manu-facturing plant, and every farm. It circumscribes, channels, directs, and controls actions of every description. Economic institutions operate on the basis of government action or the conscious lack of government interference. No corner of economic life escapes the hand of government. The touch is sometimes light and sometimes heavy, at times helpful and at other times restraining; it may be agreeable or arbitrary, and beneficient or greedy. But whatever may be its character at any one point, the power of government affects our economic lives intimately and often irrevocably. Government regulation is a silent partner in all economic activity and an active partner in most economic activity.[14]

Government and political institutions have long exerted an extremely important impact upon the ownership and use of land resources. The effects of these institutions are manifold. For our purposes, however, it is sufficient that we view their importance from two principal angles: (1) the over-all effect of government policies and restrictions on public and private decisions regarding land resources, and (2) the impact of the organization and framework of government on the development and administration of public land-resource policies.

Effects of government policies and restrictions. Almost every decision regarding the ownership or use of land resources is in some way affected by public policies or restrictions. Real property taxes represent an annual levy against land ownership and can be used to force lands into more intensive uses. Inheritance taxes—or "death duties" as they are known in Great Britain—can force the breaking up of landed estates. The power of eminent domain can be used in the public acquisition of properties from owners who are unwilling to sell. Various aspects of the government's sovereign or police power may be used to protect property rights, prevent

---

[14] Steiner, *op. cit.*, p. 2.

fraud, and force individual compliance with public health standards, building codes, or local land-use zoning ordinances.

The over-all impact of government policies and restrictions on the development and use of land resources can be illustrated by the wide variety of land policies that have been and are now being used in the United States.[15] During the early years of the nation, the federal government played an essential role in acquiring additions to the public domain and in prescribing a liberal public land disposal program, which prompted the rapid settlement of most public lands. More recently it has reserved large areas of public lands as public park, forest, mineral, grazing, and wildlife reserves. It has used public funds to reacquire certain lands from private owners for forestry, military, and other uses. It has undertaken numerous large-scale multipurpose resource-development programs such as the construction of the Hoover, Grand Coulee, and Shasta dams in the West and the development of the Tennessee Valley Authority in the East. It has engaged in numerous public works such as building highways, digging canals, and providing locks and other navigation improvements.

The federal government has established several agencies to increase the credit facilities available to farmers, home owners, and businessmen. It has used its tariffs to protect and favor domestic industries. It has used subsidies to encourage conservation practices, dispose of farm surpluses, construct factories for defense industries, and promote the construction of low-rent public housing. It has used a system of price supports to bring stability to the agricultural sector of the economy and rent controls to prevent tenant-gouging during periods of severe housing shortages. And it has developed an elaborate system of cost-sharing arrangements with state and local governments to promote new highway construction, the improvement of small watershed areas, metropolitan planning, and the redevelopment and renewal of blighted urban communities.

In addition to these federal policies, the state and local governments have also developed several important policies that affect us in our use of land resources. Some of the most significant of these involve use of the state police power to develop land-use zoning ordinances, subdivision regulations, building codes, forest-cutting restrictions, and other similar measures for the direction of private land-use practices in the public interest. Other important programs include the provision and administration of parks and recreation areas, the location and building of streets and highways, and the provision of public parking areas in urban areas. State and local action are needed with area planning, urban renewal, and public housing projects. State legislation also governs the rights we hold in

[15]Cf. V. Webster Johnson and Raleigh Barlowe, *Land Problems and Policies* (New York: McGraw-Hill Book Company, Inc., 1954), chap. IV; and John F. Timmons and William G. Murray, *Land Problems and Policies* (Ames: Iowa State College Press, 1950); Land Economics Institute, *Modern Land Policy* (Urbana: University of Illinois Press, 1960); and Howard W. Ottoson, ed., *Land Use Policy and Problems in the United States* (Lincoln: University of Nebraska Press, 1963).

land and water resources and the ways in which we can allocate these rights between landlords and tenants and between mortgagors and mortgagees.

Framework of government. Governments vary considerably in their organization and in the scope of the powers assigned to their various levels. They range from the absolute monarchies of the past under which all political power stemmed from the pharaoh, emperor, or king to theoretical, unorganized, anarchistic socities under which no individual is subject to the political control of others. Most nations now operate under constitutional forms of government. This means that their organization and the scope and distribution of their powers are spelled out either in a written constitution or in legislation and recognized precedents.

Some constitutional governments, such as France before World War II, have been highly centralized with most of the sovereign power concentrated in the central government. Others such as the American States under the Articles of Confederation may be loosely organized and have practically all of their political power centered in their state governments. Still others such as the United States and Canada operate as federal systems in which political power is divided between the national government and the several states or provinces.

Patterns of government organization affect land-resource use through their effects upon the development and administration of land policies. Under constitutional systems of government, the scope of these policies must fall within the legitimate powers assigned to government and must not conflict with the rights and privileges guaranteed to individuals. Furthermore, policies must be developed and administered by those branches and levels of government duly authorized to exercise such powers. In the United States, this means that some policies can be instituted on a national basis while other require state or local action.

The federal government of the United States operates with delegated powers. Its *express* powers are limited to those enumerated and conferred by the federal Constitution. Those powers not delegated to the federal government are known as *residual* powers and are reserved to the states or to the people. Strictly construed, this framework of government leaves the states with all those powers not delegated to the federal government and not prohibited to them by either the federal constitution or the constitutions of the several states.[16] Counties, cities, townships, and other local units of government operate with powers delegated to them by the states.

This organization pattern makes the federal government a government with limited powers. The scope of its power, however, has been definitely broadened by liberal interpretation. The courts have accepted a doctrine of *implied* powers, which makes it possible for the federal government to

---

[16]In contrast to this division of power, the federal government of Canada holds residual powers while the provinces operate with delegated authority.

do many things not specifically authorized by the Constitution.[17] In its exercise of its implied powers, however, it must respect the prohibitions of the Constitution, the guarantees of individual liberties and privileges covered by the Bill of Rights, and the general reservation of residual powers to the states and to the people. To infringe upon any of these areas would be to act in an unconstitutional manner. In the *Hoosac Mills* case, for example, the majority of the Supreme Court held the Agricultural Adjustment Act of 1933 invalid because its program for regulating agricultural production invaded "the reserved rights of the states" and involved statutory action "beyond the powers delegated to the federal government."[18]

Because of the division of powers between the federal and state government, different units of government are invariably involved in the development and administration of policies affecting land resources. The federal government can operate and administer its own lands, set up land disposal policies, and acquire private properties for public use. It can provide funds for land-use research, housing and reclamation projects, agricultural conservation payments, price supports, highway and canal construction, and the administration of government-insured mortgage credit programs. It can also exert a direct or indirect influence on the ownership and use of land resources through the exercise of its many other powers. But in actual practice, except for its powers in areas such as the District of Columbia, the federal government lacks many of the sovereign powers involved in familiar day-to-day cases of land-resource control. It must act for the states, however, in all matters that call for treaty negotiations with other nations.

Most public powers over the ownership and use of land resources are vested in the several states. This means that virtually all legislation dealing with problems such as police protection, landlord-tenant relations, water rights, property taxation procedures, plat restrictions, and state land administration must be drafted on a state basis. Local units of government in turn operate as agencies of the states. It is essential that the states establish them as political entities, clothe them with powers and responsibilities, and provide them with the appropriate enabling legislation. Legislation of this type is required before local governments can proceed with the enactment of zoning ordinances or building codes, the

---

[17] The doctrine of implied powers was suggested by Alexander Hamilton in 1791. Twenty-eight years later in the famous case of *McCulloch v. Maryland,* 4 Wheaton 315 (1819), this doctrine was enunciated by the United States Supreme Court. In the reasoning of Chief Justice Marshall, the federal government has an implied power to use such measures as are necessary in the exercise of the powers bestowed upon it. "Let the end be legitimate, let it be within the scope of the constitution, and all means which are appropriate, which are plainly adapted to that end, which are not prohibited, but consist with the letter and spirit of the constitution, are constitutional."

[18] *United States v. Butler et al.,* 297 U.S. 1 (1936).

creation of planning commissions, and the establishment of soil conservation, grazing, irrigation, drainage, or levee districts.

Counties, cities, villages, townships, and various other local districts occupy a bottom rung of the hierarchy of political power. Despite this position they often exert a far greater influence upon land-resource use than either the states or the federal government. These are the units of government that levy and collect property taxes, enact and enforce zoning ordinances, and provide the officials who actually protect individuals and their property from violence, theft, fraud, and fire. They enforce the public police power regulations that affect public health, safety, morals, and general welfare. Through their educational, planning, and other activities they have considerable opportunity and power to affect individual attitudes and actions regarding land-resource use.

Public land policies sometimes call for international agreements such as those that govern the development of power and water storage facilities on the Rio Grande and the control of pollution in the waters of the Great Lakes. Interstate compacts such as the Colorado River compact are occasionally needed to deal with interstate problems. Regional watershed approaches such as that used by TVA are also used at times. Within the states, counties and other minor civil divisions sometimes work together on drainage and water management problems or in planning the coordinated development of metropolitan areas. *Ad hoc* units of government are also set up at times for administrative and tax purposes to deal with the particular problems that arise in the establishment of grazing, conservation, drainage, irrigation, flood control, and levee districts. These special districts normally disregard political boundaries and include only those areas affected by the land problem in question.

Law and the Legal System

Law has been defined as that body of rules and regulations recognized as binding by man or nations. These rules and regulations represent an easily visualized type of collective action in control of individual behavior. They are important to us because they set the legal boundaries within which accepted individual and group behavior takes place. Because of its scope, "law is an all-pervading part of our social structure" and "there is no moment in our lives when our actions or inactions are not in some way subject to legal valuation."[19] As Barnes observes:

> Laws and lawyers are today the most important directive element in our civilization. Our technique of production, transportation, and communication may be determined and controlled by science and machinery, but our

[19] J. H. Beuscher, *Farm Law in Wisconsin* (Appleton, Wisc.: C. C. Nelson Publishing Co., 1951), p. 1.

institutional life is dominated by law and lawyers. . . . Ours is as much a lawyer-made civilization, on its institutional side, as the civilization of Assyria and Rome was a military one, and that of the Middle Ages a religious one.[20]

What we ordinarily recognize as law really comes from three sources: (1) from statutes, ordinances, and administrative regulations; (2) from established customs that have gained the sanction of legal authority; and (3) from judicial interpretations and decisions. It has been estimated that we have over 2½ million statutes on the law books. Many of these were passed by Congress and the state legislatures. Many have been enacted by city councils, county boards, and by the voters themselves. Still others represent administrative rules laid down by agencies such as the Department of Interior or the Interstate Commerce Commission. Important as statutory legislation is, however, one must not lose sight of the fact that a high proportion of our law is court-made.

From a historical standpoint, the beginnings of law are found in the social customs accepted and enforced by primitive peoples. As civilization developed, these social usages often became the basis for written law. Sometimes their substance was enacted into statutes. More often they were accepted as a type of precedent and became part of the law because of their recognition and acceptance in judicial decisions. Eventually, many judicially sanctioned customs found their way into various codifications of law such as the Code of Hammurabi (2,000 B.C.), the Justinian Code (529 A.D.), and the Code Napoleon (1804 A.D.). But even when codified, the real meaning of these laws has usually depended upon judicial interpretations.

This evolutionary pattern describes the development of the legal system accepted in most English-speaking countries. Units of government within these countries have their constitutions, statutes, ordinances, and regulations—many provisions of which are based upon custom. Some of them have codified portions of the prevailing legal theory advanced in judicial decisions. But most of them still look to the English common law for a significant portion of their ruling law. This is particularly true of laws relating to land resources. As Beuscher indicates:

Almost all of the law of contracts; practically all of the law of torts (intentional or unintentional injury to person or property); much of the law of real estate and most of the law of agency is based, not on statutes, or administrative legislation or municipal ordinances but on court opinions.[21]

The English common law upon which much of our legal system is based is court-made law. It is found not in the statute books but rather in leading court opinions and in legal commentaries and compendiums. Many

[20]Barnes, *op. cit.*, p. 354.
[21]Beuscher, *op. cit.*, p. 14.

common-law principles go back to the customary practices of medieval England. But while the common law places heavy emphasis upon precedents established in times past, it nevertheless represents a dynamic, flexible body of legal doctrine. Its framework is such that it can easily adjust to new situations and changing conditions.

The common-law approach, under which individual decisions are accepted as precedents for future action and thereby become rules of the game, is widely used in our society. It is frequently applied in individual households and firms as well as in the formulation of public law. It provides a workable means of resolving conflicts of interests. In their use of this approach courts often make far-reaching decisions that have a telling impact upon various aspects of economic and social life as well as upon legal institutions. In its decisions concerning subjects such as racial segregation, anti-trust regulations, and agricultural marketing quotas, the Supreme Court really acts as "an authoritative faculty of political economy for the United States."[22]

It should be noted in passing that the legal system accepted in English-speaking countries is not the only system of law that prevails in the world today.[23] Eight important systems of law are now in use.[24] These systems have developed from different customs, circumstances, and attitudes. They differ in content and coverage, in their philosophy and points of view. Some, such as the English system, emphasize individual rights while others exalt the state and stress an absolutist approach. With these differences, it is only natural that the legal concepts of rights and responsibilities accepted in some countries should appear quite foreign to the thinking in others.

Effects of law upon land resources. Hundreds of examples can be cited to illustrate the imprint of law and legal institutions upon land resources. Constitutions involve laws that control government. They allocate various powers concerning the use of land resources between units of government. They also contain protective clauses, such as the "due process" and "equal protection of the law" clauses of the Constitution of the United States, which safeguard personal and property rights against arbitrary actions.

[22]Commons, *op. cit.*, p. 712.

[23]The English common law is accepted in all of the United States except Louisiana, which follows the Code Napoléon. Various aspects of Spanish law are accepted in some of the Southwestern States.

[24]Sixteen important systems of law have been developed during recorded history. Of these the Egyptian, Mesopotamian, Hebrew, Greek, Roman, Celtic, Maritime, and Canon systems no longer operate as separate systems. Wigmore classifies the present systems as Anglican, Romanesque, Germanic, Slavic, Chinese, Hindu, Japanese, and Mohammedan. In addition to these classifications, tribal customs still rule in many areas where no organized system of law has developed. Cf. John H. Wigmore, "A Map of the World's Law," *Geographic Review,* Vol. 19, 1929, pp. 114-20; also Wigmore, *A Panorama of the World's Legal Systems* (St. Paul, Minnesota: West Publishing Company, 1928).

Our various governments have laws and ordinances concerning the acquisition of real property, the registration of land titles, and the leasing and mortgaging of properties. The inheritance and transfer of properties between generations is carefully regulated by legal procedures. Land owners are both protected and controlled by laws relating to property boundaries, trespass, and adverse possession. Operators are directly affected by taxation measures, police power restrictions, laws setting up drainage or conservation districts, and by many other measures such as those requiring produce grading or fair trade practices.

Most present laws affecting land resources involve the distribution or control of the rights and responsibilities individuals and groups have in property. This is true of all laws of real property. It applies to our recognition of the individual's right to personal liberty—freedom to own property and freedom from the slavery or peonage rights that others could hold in his person. It also applies in varying degrees to the laws of torts, agency, and contract. The right of individuals to claim damages for injuries, for example, often has a tempering effect upon the manner in which land resources are used. In similar manner, the use of land resources is often affected by laws that define the powers of agency that can be delegated to others to act in one's behalf and by the emphasis given to fulfillment of contracts.

Custom and Habit

Law and government represent organized forms of collective action. As such they have considerable effect upon individual behavior. The importance of their influence, however, is often matched, if not exceeded, by the less formal controls exerted by custom and habit. Reference has been made to the continuing role custom plays in the development of law. Like law, custom represents an accepted way of doing things. Yet it differs from law in the extent to which it has been formalized and to which it can be enforced. The areas of collective action covered by custom and law overlap in many respects; but they are by no means contiguous. Laws cover many matters not affected by custom; and customs in turn involve many practices not as yet covered by law.

Most customs start as rational decisions. Perhaps a farmer finds that a certain cultural practice fits his conditions. He accepts it; others follow him; and soon this precedent for action becomes a working rule of his society. Others coming later may accept this and other customary practices without question because of the prestige they have acquired with age. Even when people are inclined to question the authority ascribed to the "dead hand of the past," they often accept customs because they represent part of the system of collective controls into which man is born. As Commons has observed:

> Individuals begin as babies. They learn the custom of language, of cooperation
> with other individuals, of working towards common ends, of negotiations to

eliminate conflicts of interest, of subordination to the working rules of the many concerns of which they are members. They meet each other, not as physiological bodies moved by glands, nor as "globules of desire" moved by pain and pleasure, . . . but as prepared more or less by habit, induced by the pressure of custom, to engage in those highly artificial transactions created by the collective human will. They are . . . found where conflict, interdependence, and order among human beings are preliminary to getting a living. Instead of individuals the participants are citizens of a going concern. Instead of forces of nature they are forces of human nature. Instead of mechanical uniformities of desires . . . , they are highly variable personalities. Instead of isolated individuals in a state of nature they are always participants in transactions, members of a concern in which they come and go, citizens of an institution that lived before them and will live after them.[25]

Man is a rational being. His ability to reason and plan separates him from lower forms of life. Yet even though he is capable of deep thought, much of his activity is rooted in habits of thought and habits of action. When he must, he can compute his marginal rates of substitution for different goods and he can determine the approximate value of the marginal utilities he receives from various expenditures. In countless cases, however, he avoids the need for these calculations by following routine patterns of action already established by custom or habit. Most of his routine activities are rooted in earlier deliberate decisions. On a day-to-day basis, however, he often brushes his teeth in the morning, drives on the right side of the road, goes to work at eight o'clock and quits at five, and does a host of other things mostly as a matter of habit.

Custom and habit affect land resources in many different ways. Most Americans have developed a customary preference for varied diets, which are rich in animal products. As a result, large areas of agricultural land are used to produce pasture and feed for livestock and poultry while smaller areas are needed to grow food crops such as cereals and potatoes. Customary use of products such as tobacco, coffee, tea, coke, and alcoholic beverages has favored the diversion of considerable areas to particular uses. Without our acceptance and habitual use of these products, the two million acres planted to tobacco in the United States could be used for other purposes, Brazil and Ceylon would lose their leading exports, and Milwaukee would no longer produce the beverage that made it famous. Important urban land uses would also be affected because the processing plants that handle these products would no longer be needed while the sites now used for tobacco shops, tea rooms, coffee houses, taverns, and cocktail lounges would be used for other purposes.

Tastes in clothing also have important effects upon land-resource use. In times past, the average citizen usually accepted a simple wardrobe— perhaps a bearskin, loin cloth, the simple tunic of ancient Rome, or the warmer homespuns of the early American settler. With the opportunities

[25]Commons, *op. cit.*, pp. 73-74.

provided by modern society, we have turned to the customary acceptance and use of colorful and elaborate wardrobes. As a result, large areas must be used for the production and processing of cotton, wool, and flax. Natural resources such as pulpwood and coal are utilized in the manufacture of rayon, nylon, and other synthetic fibers. Fur farms are required to fill the demand for the furs used on articles of adornment. New markets also have emerged for leather products, bird feathers, coral, and semiprecious stones.

Many other examples can be used to illustrate the effect of now habitual modes of life upon the demand for land products. The customary use of the daily newspaper, for example, requires the production of tremendous quantities of wood pulp. Long-accepted attitudes concerning housing facilities call for the use of billions of tons of building materials. Great quantities of coal, oil, and natural gas are used each year in the customary heating of homes. The customary use of the areas around homes for lawns and grounds requires the use of substantial acreages for this purpose.

Customs frequently have a direct as well as an indirect effect upon the ownership and use of land resources. Many farmers both here and abroad cling to customary cultural and crop-rotation practices even when improved practices are brought to their attention. Sometimes they refuse to change because of the proven value of their practices and because "what was good enough for my father is good enough for me." On other occasions, particularly in those areas where human life is supported by a slender thread and where people are motivated mostly by hope for survival, operators may hesitate to risk the uncertainties associated with their suggested shift to new and (for them) untried methods.[26] Rigid adherence to custom can lead to inefficiency in production and the loss of potential income not only for farmers but also for builders, craftsmen, merchants, miners, woodsmen, and other users of land resources.

Property inheritance, rental, and ownership arrangements also are affected by custom. Our emphasis upon the equal division of estates among heirs of equal relationship, for example, is based as much upon custom as is the system of primogeniture used in some other countries. Similarly, our acceptance of particular rental and purchase financing arrangements involves the acceptance of custom. All things considered, even the emphasis we place upon the goal of home ownership has much of its basis in traditional habits of thought.

Religious Institutions

Although religious institutions are primarily concerned with spiritual

[26]For an illuminating discussion of this problem, cf. Herrell DeGraff, "Some Problems Involved in Transferring Technology to Underdeveloped Areas," *Journal of Farm Economics*, Vol. 33, November, 1957, p. 700.

matters, they nevertheless do have important effects upon both economic life and man's use of land resources. With land resources, this influence usually takes one of three forms: (1) ownership or operation of land by religious bodies, (2) claims of the church or religious body to the income of land, or (3) religious beliefs affecting land-use practices.

Church and religious bodies have owned or controlled substantial property holdings throughout most of the world's history. One of the most extreme examples existed in ancient Egypt, where the land belonged to the pharaoh, a quasi-divine ruler, who administered it with the aid of his priests and nobles. Church ownership of property and domination of temporal affairs was also important in Western Europe throughout the Middle Ages. During this period, the Catholic Church acquired numerous properties by gift and will and became the principal landowner in many countries. It is estimated that almost a third of the landed property in England was held by the church during the thirteenth century.

Churches and religious bodies own considerable real property in the United States. But their share of the total is small, and the problem of church ownership is not considered serious. Important land-use problems do stem, however, from the location of churches and synagogues at sites of high commercial value near the 100 percent spots of downtown business districts. The preemption of these sites for religious uses, together with the tax-exempt status of these properties, naturally discourages their development and redevelopment for what many people regard as their highest and best economic use. Viewed from a different angle, it may be noted that churches, cathedrals, and other religious centers have some-times provided the focal points around which cities have developed.

The extent of the claim that religious bodies have to the income derived from land resources varies over a wide range. When a church owns a house or an office building it naturally has first claim on the income or rent derived from the use of its property. With other types of property, the church may claim tithes, or its claim for support may be limited to the voluntary contributions of its members. During Biblical times and begin-ning again during the Middle Ages, tithes equal to one-tenth of the returns from land were often collected by governments for the support of the state church. These collections have for the most part been discontinued. Several European governments, however, still support their official churches with funds collected from taxes that affect church members and nonmembers alike. Tithes also are contributed voluntarily by the members of some religious groups.

Numerous examples can be cited to illustrate the impact religious beliefs have upon the ownership and use of land resources. Many possible practices are discouraged in tribal societies because they are regarded as taboo. Some of these taboos, such as those against eating certain kinds of food or working on certain days of the week, have carried over into our present society and still have an indirect effect upon land-resource use. Another type of taboo is accepted in India, where the Hindu belief in the transmigration of souls has resulted in the toleration of large local populations of cattle and monkeys. The refusal of local people to keep the numbers of these animals in check has resulted both in crop losses and in a lowering of the country's agricultural carrying capacity.

Even in ancient times particular sites were often regarded as holy spots. With the passing of time some of these sites such as Rome, Jerusalem, Mecca, and the Ganges River have become the focal points of great pilgrimages. Burial grounds also have been maintained for religious reasons; and significant areas of potentially productive land are retained for this purpose in many countries. Another example involving the sanctity of earth is suggested by the religious objections that for many years discouraged mining in Tibet. These objections were based upon a belief that the removal of minerals would disturb the spirits of the earth and result in losses of soil fertility.

Among the ancient Hebrews land was considered a sacred possession of Yahweh (God). Property sales to foreigners were frowned upon because land was not to be alienated from Yahweh's chosen people. Another Hebrew belief called for periodic years of complete rest. During the jubilee years, all cropland was supposedly left fallow.

Most of the early civilizations had agrarian deities. Sacrifices were offered and special rituals held to insure favorable crop planting and growing conditions. Special rituals and festivals also were celebrated at harvest time, and feast days were held throughout the year. Agricultural operations in ancient Rome were complicated and delayed by 45 different festival days each year.[27] This picture has changed somewhat in many countries. But priests are still asked to bless the fields or the fishing grounds; and a variety of religious festivals still punctuate the lives of many people. The adornments of some of these festivals, such as the popular use of Christmas trees, have even given rise to new land uses.

Many of the religious beliefs that have influenced man's use of land resources in times past have been discarded. Yet beliefs such as the golden rule, respect for authority, and faith in the future still have a strong impact upon human behavior. Two other important land-resource concepts—the stewardship concept of land use and the goal of family farm and urban home ownership—also have religious roots. The stewardship concept—the idea that man should turn his resource base over to the next owner in as good or better condition than he received it—has positive implications for the development of a sound conservation philosophy. Home ownership—the idea that everyone should have an opportunity to enjoy life "under his vine and under his fig tree"—on the other hand, is already accepted as a popular goal of land policy in many countries.

PERSONAL AND HOUSEHOLD CONSIDERATIONS

In addition to the institutional factors listed above, economic behavior

[27]Cf. Barnes, *op. cit.*, p. 74.

is often affected to a considerable extent by personal and household considerations. These considerations include several factors—such as an individual's attitudes and goals, his ability to work, and his family obligations—that cause him to differ from the prototype of the economic man. Some of these factors bear the imprint of important institutions such as the family, our educational and religious systems, and our cultural heritage from the past, while others are tied more to the life cycle of man. Regardless of how they are classified, however, these factors are usually closely associated with institutional factors in the sense that they help to provide the man-made conditions under which economic activity takes place.

The importance of personal and household considerations can best be illustrated if we start with the concept of the economic man. As an operator, this remarkable character is blessed with perfect foresight and knowledge. As a worker, he is ageless, immune to sickness and worry, and always in possession of his fullest physical and mental powers. As an individual, he is not troubled by family or group obligations; he has a single-minded devotion to the principle of profit maximization; and he always strives to attain the highest possible level of economic efficiency in his operations.

This idealized assumption has its rightful place in economic analysis. Under real-life conditions, however, it is just as foolish to assume that the average operator will act like the economic man as it is to assume that our institutional environment matches the void so often assumed in economic models. Personal attitudes, choices, and goals always have an important effect upon individual economic behavior. And personal factors can make programs that pass the test of economic practicability unacceptable on an individual level in much the same way that institutional barriers sometimes prevent their successful operation on a larger scale.

Most people are motivated by nonmonetary as well as by monetary goals. Naturally, wide differences exist in the extent to which different people emphasize these two sets of goals. Some businessmen approach the concept of the economic man, particularly during business hours. But it is the rare individual who gives full allegiance to the profit-maximization goal. Somewhere along the scale of their potential income possibilities, most operators tend to substitute welfare and nonmonetary goals for at least part of their interest in additional economic returns. This substitution process often causes them to forego opportunities to make more money so that they will have more time to relax, go fishing, or play golf. In similar fashion, it often prompts them to take time and money they could use to advantage in their businesses to indulge in charitable, civic, cultural, political, religious, and other activities.

An operator's success or failure as a businessman can often be explained in terms of his attitude toward his work, his willingness to adapt himself to change, and his ability to get along with other people. To a considerable extent, his success is also determined by his capacity and ability to perform those tasks he undertakes. Many operators fail because they are not "cut out" for their particular jobs or enterprises. Others fail to realize their potentialities because of sickness, ill health, or sometimes sheer laziness. Man's changing life cycle with his tendency to reach his physical peak in his early twenties and his tendency to slow down after forty also has important implications that affect his capacity for physical labor.

Individual economic behavior is often conditioned in a very significant way by various types of group obligations. Family responsibilities and community ties frequently discourage operators from migrating to areas of greater economic opportunity. At times, they also call for a large portion of an operator's time—as when he personally cares for disabled members of his family or when he gives considerable time to service organizations—and thus leave him with a minimum of time for his normal economic pursuits.

These obligations often have a severe effect upon the operator's ability to accumulate and reinvest capital. Young businessmen and farmers usually have far less working capital than they could use to best advantage. Yet their heaviest family obligations ordinarily come at the very time when they are most in need of additional money for land, equipment, and other input factors. As operators, they are usually conscious of their capital needs and of the fact that it "takes money to make money." Many of them skimp on personal and family expenditures so that they may use a maximum portion of their earnings as production and working capital. Yet when their disposable incomes are low—as they frequently are—they usually give first priority to shoes for their children or medicine for their wives even though this choice may keep them from operating in the so-called rational zone of economic action.

—SELECTED READINGS

Barnes, Harry E., *Social Institutions* (Englewood Cliffs, N.J.: Prentice-Hall, Inc., 1942).

Commons, John R., *The Economics of Collective Action* (New York: The Macmillan Company, 1950).

Ely, Richard T., *Property and Contract in Their Relation to the Distribution of Property* (New York: The Macmillan Company, 1914), Book I, chaps. I and II.

Gruchy, Allen G., *Modern Economic Thought* (Englewood Cliffs, N.J.: Prentice-Hall, Inc., 1947).

Steiner, George A., *Government's Role in Economic Life* (New York: McGraw-Hill Book Company, Inc., 1953), Part I.

Wehrwein, George S., "Institutional Economics in Land Economic Theory," *Journal of Farm Economics*, Vol. 23, February, 1941, pp. 161-70.

12

Property
in Land Resources

Land resources are something more than a strictly physical factor of production. From a cultural, economic, and social point of view, they have become "an element of nature inextricably interwoven with man's institutions."[1] They are objects that man covets and wants for his personal use and satisfaction and for which he has devised institutions that permit people to acquire, own, possess, and utilize them to the exclusion of others. The systems of rights embraced by these institutions form the basis for the concept of property.

Property rights play a major and omnipresent role in determining what people can or cannot do with land resources. Their importance is such that some understanding of the rights individuals and groups hold in land resources is essential if one is to fully comprehend man's behavior and conduct with respect to land. The discussion that follows focuses on the rights people hold in land. It starts with a general commentary on the nature, characteristics, and scope of property rights and then proceeds to more detailed examinations of the various types of interests individuals and society have in real property, in water, and in air and subsurface resources.

[1] Karl Polanyi, *The Great Transformation* (New York: Farrar and Rinehart, 1944), p. 178.

NATURE AND SCOPE OF PROPERTY RIGHTS

Property is a complicated legal concept. Many people think of it in terms of objects that can be owned or possessed. In a legal sense, however, property consists not of objects but rather of "man's rights with respect to material objects."[2] As one court has held:

> The term "property" may be defined to be the interest which can be acquired in external objects or things. The things themselves are not, in a true sense property, but they constitute its foundation and material, and the idea of property springs out of the connection, or control, or interest which according to law, may be acquired in them, or over them. This interest may be absolute when a thing is objectively and lawfully appropriated by one to his own use in exclusion of all others. It is limited or qualified when the control acquired falls short of the absolute.[3]

Generalizing from these definitions, one might describe property as "the exclusive right of possessing, enjoying, and disposing of a thing"[4] or as "the exclusive right to control an economic good."[5] Our concept of property rights is both broad and diverse. It ranges from the complete ownership one may enjoy in his house to the more limited rights he may hold under a lease or under an inheritance arrangement that grants a fractional interest in a farm once an existing life estate has ended. In more eloquent terms, it may be noted that:

> Property is a euphonious collocation of letters which serves as a general term for the miscellany of equities that persons hold in the commonwealth. A coin, a lance, a tapestry, a monastic vow, a yoke of oxen, a female slave, an award of alimony, a homestead, a first mortgage, a railroad system, a preferred list and a right of contract are all to be discovered within the catholic category. Each of these terms, meaningless in itself, is a token or focus of a scheme of relationships; each has its support in sanction and repute; each is an aspect of an enveloping culture. A Maori claiming his share of the potato crop, a Semitic patriarch tending his flock, a devout abbot lording it vicariously over fertile acres, a Yankee captain homeward bound with black cargo, an amateur general swaggering a commission he has bought, an adventurous speculator selling futures in a grain he has never seen and a commissar clothed with high office in a communistic state are all men of property. In fact, property is as heterogeneous as the societies within which it is found, in idea, it is as cosmopolitan as the systems of thought by which it is explained.[6]

---

[2] C. Reinold Noyes, *The Institution of Property* (New York: Longmans, Green & Co., Inc., 1936), p. 353.

[3] *Griffith v. Charlotte et al.,* 23 S.C. 25, 38 (1884).

[4] *McKeon v. Bisbee,* 9 Calif. 137 (1858).

[5] Richard T. Ely, *Property and Contract in Their Relation to the Distribution of Wealth* (New York: The Macmillan Company, 1914), p. 101.

[6] Walton H. Hamilton and Irene Till, "Property," *Encyclopedia of the Social Sciences* (New York: The Macmillan Company, 1932), Vol. 12, pp. 528-29.

Attributes and Characteristics of Property

Property has many important characteristics.[7] First of all, it is an attribute of human beings, not of chattels.[8] It involves rights to the use of material things, not personal rights or liberties. It differs from free goods in the sense that it involves only appropriable objects of value over which man can and does exert possession. Furthermore, it is an *exclusive* not an *absolute* right. Individuals can hold property rights alone or share them with certain others to the exclusion of all other persons. But these rights are always subject to the controls and limitations vested in the sovereign power. In our society, the existence of property rights presupposes the presence of (1) an owner together with other persons who can be excluded from the exercise of ownership rights; (2) property objects that can be held as private or public possessions; and (3) a sovereign power that will sanction, and if necessary protect, the property rights vested in individuals or groups.

Property involves exclusive rights. These rights obviously cannot exist until there is both an owner to possess and use the object in question and other interested persons who can be excluded from possession and use. Property, as we know it, simply does not exist in areas where there is no population and no outside claimants. Nor does it exist in those isolated instances in which a single user, such as Robinson Crusoe, may be present. Property rights come into existence only when two or more people compete for the possession and use of some object and need develops for the allocation of recognized rights between them. In this sense, it may be noted that the concept of property involves more than a simple relationship between persons and things. It also involves relationships between

---

[7] For other descriptions of these characteristics cf. Noyes, *op. cit.,* chaps. IV-VI; and Ely, *op. cit.,* Book I, chap. V.

[8] People frequently speak of a bird's cage, a dog's bone, a horse's saddle, or a slave's clothes. These suggestions of ownership are merely descriptive terms because the property in each case belongs to the master, not to the chattel. Sentiment often causes people to treat chattels and physical objects as though they had human rights. Thus one occasionally reads of an estate being left to a pet parrot or a favorite cat. Actually these estates are only held in trust for the support of these creatures and they naturally exercise no true ownership rights. Ripley's "Believe It Or Not" has featured stories of a facelike rock formation at Ploumanach, France, which was legally conveyed to itself and of the bridge of Pre-St.-Didier in Italy which was made the legal property of two trees that stand like sentinels at one end of the bridge. These examples, together with that of a tree in Athens, Georgia, which received an unrecorded deed to the land upon which it grew (cf. Ely, *op. cit.,* p. 96, 109-10), represent cases in which ownerships without legal foundation are tolerated as long as society respects the grantor's sentiment and withholds its power of taxation. The position of society in cases of this type is illustrated by the Pennsylvania example of a 600-acre forest, which was deeded to God but which reverted to the state for nonpayment of taxes. (Cf. *American Forests,* February, 1931, p. 112.)

individuals and other persons regarding their rights to use and to exclude others from the use of particular objects.

Before property can exist there must always be a property object. These objects usually involve material things though they may also involve quasi-material items such as franchises, patents, copyrights, industrial good will, or the rights to given radio wave lengths or telecast channels.

Two of the most important attributes of property objects are their appropriability and value. Before anything can be classed as a property object, it must be capable of appropriation. The lands beneath the deeper portions of the ocean and beneath the polar ice caps are not property because they have not as yet been appropriated for human use. Free goods such as air and ocean water can be appropriated. In their natural state, however, they are not regarded as property objects because man cannot enforce exclusive rights over their use.

Our supply of property objects has come from two sources—from the capture of free goods and from the creation of new goods through the processing of existing resources. Man ordinarily tries to capture, develop, or produce things that have value. By accident, or as a by-product of his activities, he sometimes produces things of negative value such as the slag from mines; and he sometimes continues to hold objects that have lost their value. As a general rule, however, property objects have value. Otherwise, owners have little incentive for the continued maintenance of their property rights.

As a final requirement, the rights of property imply the assent or sanction of a sovereign power vested with both authority and ability to protect the rights of its subjects. Man has been able on various occasions to acquire and hold objects of his desire through cunningness or sheer force. By these means, he has acquired possession; but he has not acquired property rights. Possession may be defended by strategy or force over long periods of time. But property rights, and with them the right of protection against those one would exclude from the holding or use of a property object, arise only when a soverign authority—the family, clan, tribe, or the state—recognizes and enforces one's exclusive right of possession.

The dependence of the concept of property rights upon the protection afforded by sovereign powers is best illustrated by examples of what happens when this power is weakened or destroyed. Children often appropriate the toys or possessions of others. Gangsterism and lawlessness sometimes breaks out when the enforcement powers of government appear weak or ineffective. Similarly, the breakdown of authority that comes with armed conquest often results in some appropriation, "liberation," or pillaging of private possessions by the personnel of the conquering armies.

Bundle of rights. Property involves several distinct interests or rights, which can be held separately and which when taken together represent a "bundle of rights." The largest bundle of rights a private owner can hold in landed property in our society is known as complete ownership or as ownership in *fee simple*.[9] The fee simple owner has the right to possess, use, and within reason to exploit, abuse, and even destroy his land resource. He can sell his land with or without deed restrictions that affect its future use. He can give it away, trade it for other things, or devise it in any of a number of ways to his heirs.[10] He can lease his use rights to others. He can mortgage his property or permit liens to be established against it. He can subdivide his land holding or grant easements for particular uses. He can enter into contractual arrangements involving the use or disposition of his resource holdings. And he exercises these rights, as long as he has not disposed of them, to the exclusion of all other persons.

Fee simple ownership is one of the broadest and most complete concepts of property ownership yet developed. Yet the fee simple owner holds exclusive, not absolute rights. His ownership rights are always limited and conditioned by the over-all interests of society administered by the state. The most important of these limitations involve the government's exercise of its taxation, eminent domain, and police powers.

Some imperial rulers in times past have claimed and exercised absolute rights of property ownership. The nearest approach to absolute rights of ownership in our system is found in the land holdings of the state and federal governments. Since these owners exercise the powers of government, it may be argued that they hold all the rights of property and thus possess absolute ownership. The rights they hold, however, are definitely limited by public opinion and by various reservations of public economic and social policy.

Qualified property. Property rights can be asserted only over those objects that man can appropriate to his exclusive possession. This means that most objects can be classified as either free goods or property. An intermediate classification is often applied to those free goods that can under certain circumstances be reduced to private ownership. These objects, often described as "qualified property," include such items as wild game and fish, wild fur-bearing animals, dogs, and water.

Wild creatures such as deer, rabbits, pheasants, and fish ordinarily have the status of free goods. Most states now have laws declaring these

---

[9] The term "fee" is used in English law to signify an estate of inheritance (interests in property that can be passed on to one's heirs) as contrasted with an estate that can be held only for life. There are three major types of fee estates: estates in fee simple or fee simple absolute, which connote the most complete possession of private ownership rights permitted in our society, and the conditional fee and fee tail estates, which are described later.

[10] In legal parlance, a property owner can *bequeath* personal property but he *devises* real property.

creatures the property of the state.[11] This public proprietary interest, however, is asserted for the purpose of regulating and controlling the administration and private taking of these resources, not for their exploitation or use as public property. Individuals can acquire property rights in these creatures if they kill, catch, or capture them in compliance with the licensing provisions and other regulations set up by individual states.

Wild animals valued for their fur are usually treated in much the same way as game and fish. They exist as free goods in nature but can be trapped or captured subject to public regulations. Dogs have a comparable status in many jurisdictions where they are not legally treated as property until they are licensed or listed on the tax rolls.[12] In its natural state, the water found in streams, lakes, and the ocean might also be treated as a free good. As a New York court has observed: "Water, when reduced to possession, is property, and may be bought and sold and have market value, but it must be in actual possession, subject to control and management. Running water in natural streams is not property, and never was."[13]

Basis of the Concept of Property

Most authorities agree that our concept of property rights is really the outgrowth of a long period of evolutionary development.[14] Among the

[11] In two key decisions, the U.S. Supreme Court has indicated that these creatures are free goods even when claimed in state ownership. The question of state title to migratory waterfowl was raised in *Missouri v. Holland,* 252 U.S. 416 (1920). Justice Holmes observed on this occasion: "No doubt it is true that, as between a state and its inhabitants, the state may regulate the killing and sale of such birds, but it does not follow that its authority is exclusive of paramount powers. To put the claim of the state upon title is to lean upon a slender reed. Wild birds are not in the possession of anyone; and possession is the beginning of ownership. The whole foundation of the state's rights is the presence within their jurisdiction of birds that yesterday had not arrived, tomorrow may be in another state, and in a week a thousand miles away." In *Toomer v. Witsell,* 334 U.S. 384 (1948) Chief Justice Vinson observed that: "The whole ownership theory, in fact, is now generally regarded as but a fiction expressive in legal shorthand of the importance to its people that a State have power to preserve and regulate the exploitation of an important resource." According to some observers, this decision delivered "a death-dealing blow . . . to the doctrine of state ownership of fish. The states were stripped of their proprietary rights in game and fish and were told that all they had was merely the police power to regulate their taking." Cf. Nicholas V. Olds and Harold W. Glassen, "Do States Still Own Their Game and Fish?" *Michigan State Bar Journal,* Vol. 30, April, 1951, pp. 16-23.

[12] Cf. Ely, *op. cit.,* pp. 103-4.

[13] *City of Syracuse v. Stacey,* 169 N.Y. 231, 245 (1901).

[14] Several theories have been expounded at various times regarding the origins of and justification for property rights. Important among these are the legal, occupancy

primitive and nomadic societies from which our culture sprang, land resources were at first regarded as free goods to be used at will. Group ownership rights were later extended to particular types of land—such as burial grounds, watering areas, and sites of religious significance—and finally to favored grazing and tillage areas. Even then, these lands were usually held in common under a communal or tribal type of ownership. The transition from these early concepts of common use rights to the present systems of private property rights has often involved a slow evolutionary process.

Development of fee simple ownership. The concept of fee simple ownership now accepted in most English-speaking areas evolved from the village and feudal tenure systems found in Western Europe during the Middle Ages.[15] Most of the nomadic native tribes in these areas settled down to a village economy during Roman times.[16] The early residents of these villages were primarily dependent upon agricultural pursuits. Ordinarily they used an open field system in the operation of the lands around the villages. Under this system, all the land was usually held in common ownership—at least at first—and each family shared a portion of each field.

With the rise of feudalism, most of the villages came under the political control of various overlords who frequently converted them into manorial or feudal estates. The actual ownership of the land in these estates was vested in the overlord or king while various types of usufructary rights were held by the villagers, serfs, and villeins. These rights varied considerably. Some land occupants enjoyed relatively free tenure. Most of the

---

and possession, gift of God, natural right, social contract, human nature, labor, and general welfare theories of property. Cf. Ely, *op. cit.,* Vol. 2, pp. 531-51; and Edmund Whittaker, *A History of Economic Ideas* (New York: Longmans, Green & Co., Inc., 1940), pp. 175-241.

The more relevant aspects of the first seven of these theories may be combined in a general welfare or social theory of property. With this approach, one may argue that society is the true fount of property rights. Society allows individuals (or those who count in the eyes of the ruling group) to acquire, exercise, and maintain property rights and thereby maximize their personal satisfactions because this procedure usually enhances the prevailing concept of "social welfare." In an ultimate sense, however, society always retains its right to regulate the allocation and distribution of property rights; and as the interests and goals of society change, the institution of property also changes.

[15]For more detailed discussion of this subject, cf. Marshall Harris, *Origin of the Land Tenure System in the United States* (Ames: Iowa State College Press, 1953); Donald R. Denman, *Origins of Ownership* (London: George Allen & Unwin, Ltd., 1958); V. Webster Johnson and Raleigh Barlowe, *Land Problems and Policies* (New York: McGraw-Hill Book Co., Inc., 1954), chap. II; and Roland R. Renne, *Land Economics,* 2nd ed. (New York: Harper & Brothers, 1958), pp. 315-39.

[16]Private property rights were recognized in the ancient world, and a relatively full concept of property rights was developed under the Roman law. Much of the fullness of this concept was lost, however, with the breakdown of the Roman Empire and the rise of the feudal system.

land, however, was operated by villeins, who were born to their status and who exercised tillage rights subject both to certain customary obligations to the lord and to his arbitrary will.

A general trend in the direction of freer tenure conditions in England began with the gradual weakening of the feudal system during the thirteenth and fourteenth centuries. This movement was implemented by the rise of royal power and the consequent lessening of the military and administrative roles played by local noblemen. It was also speeded by the improved bargaining position held by those peasants who survived the Black Death and by the attempts of many land owners to consolidate their holdings during the "enclosure movement." These events brought the end of villeinage tenure throughout much of England during the fifteenth century and the virtual extinction of this type of tenure by the seventeenth century. With this change, the average land operator became either an owner or a tenant.

Development of property rights in other areas. England gave up the feudal system gradually and at an early date. The English pattern in this respect was quite different from that experienced in other areas. France retained its feudal system until the French Revolution; and vestiges of feudalism remained in many parts of Central and Eastern Europe until the uprisings of 1848, the Czarist emancipation of the Russian serfs in 1862, and the Armistice of 1918. Feudalistic and semifeudalistic practices persisted in many other parts of the world until they were ended by the land reform programs that followed World War II.

As one might expect, wide variations exist between the property right concepts developed in different areas. Many countries have developed relatively full concepts of private property rights comparable to those enjoyed under fee simple ownership. The average citizens in many other countries, however, have never really experienced full ownership rights in land. Some of these areas have held to semifeudalistic practices under which most of the land has been held by a limited number of often absentee landlords. Others have emphasized village communal ownership, while those within the communistic orbit have shifted to state and collective ownership.

TYPES OF INTERESTS IN LANDED PROPERTY

Property can be classified in many different ways. From a physical standpoint, property objects may be regarded as mobile or immobile, tangible or intangible, or they may be treated as types of objects such as a student's clothes, furniture, books, and car. In an economic sense, they can be divided into production goods and consumer goods, into land resources and other types of resources. They may also be classified as real property (land, realty, or real estate) and personal property (personalty), as public and private property, or as properties held by individuals, partnerships, and corporations.

Some of the most important classifications of property interests involve the distribution and sharing of the bundle of rights people can hold in land. With this approach, emphasis may be focused upon (1) the types of estates or interests held in land, (2) layers of rights, (3) number of owners, (4) conditions of holding, (5) duration of interests, and (6) time of enjoyment. First emphasis is given in the discussion that follows to the leading types of estates people hold in land, after which brief attention is given to the other five classifications and to the general nature of the interests society has in landed property.

Leading Types of Estates in Landed Property

The rights and interests one holds in the ownership, possession, or control of property are often described as one's *estate*. Estates vary in scope from fee simple ownership to estates of remote or negligible importance. The most important estates in landed property involve the interests held by owner-operators, holders of life and remainder estates, landlords and tenants, mortgagors and mortgagees, and the givers and holders of land contracts. Lawyers ordinarily give detailed consideration to the nature, characteristics, rights, and responsibilities associated with each of these estates. It is sufficient here, however, to briefly identify each of the leading types of property interests.[17]

Complete or *fee simple ownership* represents the highest combination of rights a person can hold in landed property. Most owner-operated properties are held in fee simple. Many properties nominally regarded as estates in fee simple, however, actually involve some legal limitations of the owner's rights. These limitations ordinarily arise because of easements against the property or because of deed reservations, restrictions, or covenants.

Easements involve rights held by others to use one's land for special purposes. A utility company, for example, may hold an easement that

[17]The following discussion is limited to the presentation of a thumbnail over-all picture of the principal rights people hold in landed property under the American and English system of law. For more detailed popular treatments of this subject, cf. Robert Kratovil, *Real Estate Law,* 5th ed. (Englewood Cliffs, N.J.: Prentice-Hall, Inc., 1969), or the appropriate chapters in most standard textbooks dealing with real estate principles. Readers who want a working knowledge of real property law will also find it desirable to study some of the standard legal sources in this field. For examples of these cf. Curtis J. Berger, *Land Ownership and Use: Cases, Statutes, and Other Materials* (Boston: Little, Brown and Company, 1968); Richard R. Powell, *The Law of Real Property,* 7 volumes (New York: Matthew Bender and Company, 1954); George W. Thompson, *Commentaries on the Modern Law of Real Property,* 12 volumes (Indianapolis: Bobbs-Merrill Co., Inc., 1940); Herbert T. Tiffany, *The Law of Real Property,* 6 volumes (Chicago: Callaghan and Company, 1939); or A. James Casner *et al., American Law of Property,* 7 volumes (Boston: Little Brown & Company, 1952).

permits it to run its utility lines either above or beneath the surface of one's property and that gives its workmen a right of access for the servicing of these lines. Easements can involve a wide variety of privileges such as the right to encroach upon one's airspace, the right to cross and transport goods across one's property, the right to drain water across one's land, or the right to compel a property owner to maintain his share of a common driveway. Easements can be created by oral or written agreement or sometimes by implication. They can be acquired by purchase, deed reservation, gift, condemnation, or adverse use and possession throughout the prescriptive period recognized by law. They "run with the land" when property is transferred to new owners. And they cannot be revoked except by sale, release, abandonment, or condemnation.

Property owners are frequently affected by specific provisions in their deeds which limit the scope of their ownership rights. Sometimes these provisions involve *deed reservations* that reserve mineral rights, timber-cutting rights, rights-of-way, or other comparable privileges to the grantor. Reservations of this type often create easements against the property. On numerous other occasions, *deed restrictions* and *covenants* are used to impose private controls over the future use of land. Building lots in most residential subdivisions, for example, are now sold with the stipulation that the sites must be used for single-family residential purposes and that the buildings be located and constructed in conformance with certain prescribed specifications. Deed restrictions may also be used to limit or forbid the future use of the premises for particular purposes such as the sale of alcoholic beverages.

Deed restrictions and covenants are used to secure specific ends desired by grantors or grantees. They may run indefinitely, for definite periods, or they may be limited by statute. Ordinarily, they are legally enforceable as long as they do not run counter to public policy.[18] Restrictive covenants can be enforced by court orders or injunctions issued against persons who would violate the covenants or by personal actions for damages against violators. Unlike covenants, deed restrictions usually contain forfeiture or reverter clauses that provide for the forfeiture of properties and their reversion to the original grantors whenever restrictive conditions are broken. Thus an owner may grant a site for a church, donate a tract of forest land to the state, or sell commercial property for specified noncompetitive uses with the stipulation that the ownership rights will revert to him, his heirs, or assignees should the land ever be used for other purposes. The ownership rights held by the grantees in these cases are called *determinable, base,* or *qualified fee* estates.

---

[18] Some older deeds to residential properties contain restrictive covenants against occupancy or ownership by persons not of the Caucasian race. Racial covenants of this type are not enforceable in the United States because they run counter to public policy. Cf. *Shelley v. Kraemer,* 334 U.S. 1 (1948); and *Barrows v. Jackson,* 346 U.S. 249 (1953).

Another type of limitation upon the rights of ownership occurs with the entailment of estates. This practice has been largely discontinued. Yet in some of the American colonies and for a long period in England, it was a common practice for property owners to entail their estates by specifying that they could be handed down only to "heirs of the body." Under this system of *fee tail* estates, the owner in each succeeding generation (usually the oldest son of the previous owner) had the right to possess and enjoy the property but could not sell nor dispose of it to persons other than the heir next in line of succession.

In contrast to estates held in fee, many properties are held as *life estates.* Under this arrangement, the life tenant can enjoy, possess, and use the property throughout his own lifetime. He can lease it to others; and assuming he can find someone willing to risk such a venture, he can even mortgage or sell his interests for the duration of his lifetime. But these rights exist only for the period of his life. At his death, the estate either reverts to the grantor, his heirs or assignees, or passes to some designated remainderman. A comparable but somewhat uncommon arrangement known as an estate *pur autre vie* exists when an owner's rights are limited to the lifetime of some other person or persons. A son-in-law, for example, may hold an estate of this type during the lifetime of his wife.

Life estates ordinarily fall into two classes: (1) conventional life estates created by deeds, wills, and other contracts; and (2) legal life estates authorized by law.[19] Some life estates are set up during the lifetime of the donor with the donor holding a *reversion* interest. Most conventional life estates, however, are established by will, as when a man leaves his widow a life estate in his property with the provision that their children hold a *remainder* interest, which will vest them with the estate at her death. The principal legal life estates involve the rights of dower, curtesy, and homestead.

Most states recognize the *dower* right of a wife to a life estate in one-third of a husband's property at the time of his death.[20] This share may be more or less than the widow receives under the husband's will or as her statutory share under the laws of descent. Since she cannot take both shares, she is ordinarily required to choose between her dower right and the shares she would otherwise receive.

[19]Closely analogous to life estates are the rights involved in *trusts.* Trusts involve contractual arrangements under which properties are held and administered by trustees for the benefit of specific beneficiaries. As is the case with life estates, a *living trust* can be established during a property owner's lifetime while a *testamentary trust* can be provided by will. *Business trusts* are sometimes established and operated for investment and other business purposes, while *land trusts* are occasionally used by some operators as a means of concealing property ownership while they benefit from the acquisition or control of properties.

[20]A few states allow larger dower interests in the husband's property. Several others have abolished dower and substituted a widow's share (usually one-third or one-half) of the deceased husband's real property to be held in fee simple ownership. Dower is not recognized in community-property states.

Some states recognize a dower right of the husband to the property of his deceased wife. A few others give a husband a *curtesy* right to a life estate in the real property owned by the deceased wife during the marriage. This right is analogous to the right of dower except that it usually applies to all rather than merely a third of the wife's property. Another arrangement similar to dower and curtesy exists in the community-property states of the West and Southwest. Husbands and wives in these states can hold property separately or together as community property. Whenever a husband or wife dies, the community property is divided into halves and the survivor receives his own share plus one-half of the deceased spouse's share. This share, however, passes in fee simple rather than as a life estate.

Most states recognize a real property concept known as the *homestead,* to which particular homestead rights apply. Homesteads are usually defined as a portion of the holding, limited both as to total area and value, owned and occupied by families as their home. In the rural areas of Michigan, for example, property owners hold homestead rights to their dwelling and not more than 40 adjoining acres of farm land with an exempt property value of not more than $2,500. Homesteads of this type are exempt from forced sale for debt; and they cannot be mortgaged or sold during the lifetime of the husband and wife without the consent of both parties. After a husband's death, the widow and children can continue to occupy the homestead for the duration of the widow's life or so long as the children are minors without regard to the provisions of the husband's will or the claims of his creditors. Homestead rights cannot be sold, but they can be lost through the remarriage of the widow or by abandonment.

Most people are familiar with the general division of rights that takes place with the leasing of properties. A *lease* is the relationship created by a contract that gives a tenant or lessee the right to possess and use property held or owned by a landlord or lessor. Leases can run for given periods of time or continue indefinitely by mutual consent. Rent or some other consideration is normally paid by the tenant to the landlord or his agent as a condition of the lease. At the expiration of the lease, it is ordinarily expected that the tenant will return the premises to the landlord in approximately the same condition as he received them less normal wear and tear or any damage caused by the elements. Throughout the period of the lease, the landlord normally has no right to enter upon the property without the tenant's permission and no right to interfere with the tenant's use of the property unless these rights are reserved to him in the lease. Under a leasing arrangement, a tenant is said to have a *leasehold* estate while the landlord retains a reversion interest.

A *mortgage* represents a conveyance of landed property by a borrower (mortgagor) to a lender (mortgagee) as security for the payment of a debt, with the provision that the conveyance is to be void if the debt is paid in the manner and period prescribed. In early England, the term *mort gage* meant dead pledge. Mortgagors actually turned their properties over to their mortgagees; and the latter not only enjoyed the use and the income from these properties during the mortgage period but also acquired full ownership rights if the mortgagor failed to repay his debt on the due date.

This distribution of rights has been modified in several respects. Mortgagors now retain their properties during the mortgage period; and if they default in their payments, they can remain in possession during redemption periods which range up to 18 months in length while the mortgagee initiates foreclosure proceedings. Also, if a property is foreclosed, the mortgagee has a valid claim only to the outstanding value of his loan plus interest, not to the entire property.

The exact distribution of property rights between the mortgagor and mortgagee depends upon the details of the mortgage agreement and the laws under which the mortgage is prepared and filed. In "title-theory" states such as Arkansas "legal title passes, at law, directly to the mortgagee, subject to be defeated by the performance of the conditions of the mortgagee." In contrast, "lien-theory" states such as Oklahoma hold that "a mortgage does not vest any estate in the mortgagee, but is merely a security operating as a lien or incumbrance on the property." Still other states accept variations of these two theories. Mississippi, for example, treats the mortgagor as "owner of the legal title of the property conveyed" except that "upon a breach of the conditions of a mortgage, the legal title becomes absolute in the mortgagee."[21]

Land or *purchase contract* arrangements are accepted in some areas as a popular means by which buyers with limited capital may acquire rights to property. These contracts bear some resemblance to mortgage transactions but they differ in the types of estates created. The giver of a land contract can gradually build up his equity in the property he is buying to the point at which he can convert his contract into a mortgage or possibly assume complete ownership. However, as long as he continues to operate under a land contract, the title of the property remains with the holder of the contract. The buyer under these conditions has the right to possess and use the property. These rights together with his equity in the property can easily be forfeited without need for foreclosure proceedings if he defaults in his payments.

Another rights-sharing arrangement that bears some resemblance to mortgage transactions involves the use of liens. A *lien* is a right enjoyed by certain classes of creditors (including mortgagees) to require, if necessary, the sale of a debtor's property to satsify some debt or charge. The principal types of liens that affect the average property owner are mechanic's liens for charges associated with the use of labor and building materials; tax liens for the payment of delinquent property, inheritance, gift, or income taxes; and judgment liens, which result from court actions.

---

[21] Leonard A. Jones, *A Treatise of the Law of Mortgages of Real Property,* 8th ed. (Indianapolis: Bobbs-Merrill Co., Inc., 1928), Vol. 1, secs. 21, 40, 52.

As long as a lien is properly filed, it constitutes a threat to the owner's right to the continued use of his property; and it places a cloud upon his title, which may affect his ability to sell his property or secure mortgage financing. Liens can be discharged by payment of the debts or charges for which they are made. They also can lapse at the end of statutory periods—usually one year with mechanic's liens and ten years with judgment liens—unless they are renewed by court action. As long as a lien stands, legal action can always be taken to force the foreclosure of an owner's property to pay the claims against it.

Other Classifications of Property Interests

It is often convenient to classify property rights into layers of rights—surface, suprasurface or air rights, and subsurface rights. Most discussions of property deal primarily with rights to surface land. The rights one may hold in surface waters, in the air and space above one's surface holding, and in the minerals and other resources below the surface represent significant aspects of the concept of property. These rights, which are discussed in some detail later in this chapter, can be and often are separated from the bundle of surface rights held in land.

Other criteria also are used in the classification of the legal interests individuals hold in landed property. Important among these are the classification of estates by number of owners, conditions of holding, duration, and time of enjoyment.

Number of owners. Estates held in landed property can be classified by number of owners into three general groups: (1) resources held as the common property of all the members of a community or society, (2) properties held as undivided interests by two or more co-owners, and (3) properties held in severalty by single owners.

Many primitive societies have treated land resources as the *common property* of the village or group. Each individual or family in these societies has enjoyed use rights in these resources but no single individual has had a recognized ownership right that he could lease, mortgage, sell, or devise to others. This system of ownership has for the most part broken down; and most properties are now held *in severalty*—that is, in separate individually controlled ownerships. Vestiges of the common-property concept still remain, however, in the Mexican ejidos, in the common holdings of some American Indian tribes, and in some of the mountain pastures found in Switzerland and other parts of Europe. Common grazing lands were used in many early American village settlements.

Properties held by two or more persons in *undivided ownerships* are normally held under one of three arrangements: tenancy-in-common, joint tenancy, or tenancy-by-the-entireties. An additional classification of community property applies in those states that accept the community-property system.

When ownership interests are held under *tenancy-in-common,* each party owns an undivided share in the property. He may sell this undivided interest or dispose of it by will; otherwise it becomes part of his estate upon his death and passes to his heirs at law. Under *joint tenancy,* two or more persons may hold joint or co-ownership in a property, each with rights of survivorship to the interests of the others. This means that if one of the owners dies, his ownership rights go automatically to the survivor(s) rather than to his heirs or devisees as would be the case under tenancy-in-common.

Joint tenancies cannot be created without the inclusion of an express statement to this effect in the deed that confers title. Whenever deeds are made out to two or more persons, not husband and wife, without stipulations concerning the type of tenancy created, the grantees acquire title as tenants-in-common. Some states have even gone so far as to deprive joint tenants of their rights of survivorship in those instances in which their deeds fail to specify that the title has passed to "joint tenants with the right of survivorship." Joint tenancies can be dissolved by the mutual consent of the owners or by the action of one tenant should he request a court to partition the property. They also are broken up and become tenancies-in-common when one tenant sells his undivided interest. This situation results because of a legal rule that requires that joint tenants share the same interest, acquired at the same time and in the same deed, and held throughout in the same undivided possession.

Some states treat husbands and wives as legally the same person in matters involving the co-ownership of property. A husband and wife in these cases cannot hold property as tenants-in-common or as joint tenants. Instead they hold their ownership rights as *tenants-by-the-entireties.* This co-ownership arrangement is very similar to joint tenancy, except that neither the husband nor the wife can break it without the other's consent once it has been established. Also when the husband or wife dies, the surviving spouse takes the entire ownership, not by right of survivorship, but under the terms of the original title. In some states, any deed or will of real property to a husband and wife creates a tenancy-by-the-entireties. Some others do not recognize this type of ownership unless it is expressly provided for in the deed. Still other states have acted to abolish tenancies-by-the-entireties, usually by converting them into tenancies-in-common.

In the community-property states, husbands and wives can hold any property they owned at the time of their marriage or that they acquired by gift, will, or inheritance during marriage as separate property. All other property acquired during marriage is shared equally as community property. Under this doctrine, both parties share in the ownership of real property acquired during marriage regardless of whether the deed is made out to the husband, wife, or both.

Conditions of holding an estate. Except for those estates held in fee simple absolute, most estates in real property are subject to particular conditions. These conditions may be classified into two groups: (1) conditions *precedent,* which involve requirements that must be met or events that must occur before an estate will vest, and (2) conditions *subsequent,* which involve events or types of action the nonperformance of which will defeat estates already vested. Conditions precedent are involved whenever a will provides that property shall vest with a given heir on a specified birthday, when he marries, or on the death of a life tenant. Other examples may involve the promise of a father to set his son up in business when he graduates from college, or the agreement of a holder of a land contract to exchange the contract for a mortgage once the buyer builds his equity up to the 25 percent level.

Estates granted subject to conditions subsequent continue only until the happening of certain events or "during," "while," or "so long as" the grantee complies with certain conditions. A will may provide that an heir shall enjoy an estate for life, or perhaps only until "John becomes of age," or only so long as he cares for an invalid relative. Similarly, a father may grant property to a son-in-law to be held only so long as he remains married to the grantor's daughter. In other examples, a tenant may retain his leasehold so long as he pays rent, maintains the landlord's property, and does not sublease it to others; while a mortgagee will surrender the mortgage once the debt is paid, and the mortgagor can forestall foreclosure by keeping up his payments.

Numerous conditions can be attached to the holding of estates. Courts usually insist, however, that provisions must be made for the grantor's reentry into the rights of the estate if actual reversion is to take place. Also, the conditions attached to the vesting of ownership must be possible of fulfillment. Most courts, for example, would not accept a condition that an heir must marry a certain person before an estate vests if this person died before the marriage could take place. Generally speaking, the courts do not favor restrictions or conditions that may defeat estates that have already vested in fee.

Duration of estates. From the standpoint of duration, estates can be classified into six groups: estates in fee, for life, for years, from year to year, at will, and at sufferance. Estates held in fee simple are not limited as to duration. Each owner has the right to select his successor in ownership and to use deed or other restrictions to qualify the interests he sells, devises, or otherwise conveys to the next owner. Life estates involve a period of shorter duration because they are limited to the holder's lifetime. Both of these types of interests involve freehold estates.

The classification of estates for years, from year to year, at will, and at sufferance involves leasehold estates. A *tenancy for years* is created whenever a lease specifies the time period during which a tenant is to possess and use a landlord's property. When a tenant originally rents a property for a year and at the end of the year holds over and remains in possession of the premises, the landlord can either evict him or hold him for another year's rent.[22] If the landlord chooses the second course or if he accepts rent from the tenant, *a tenancy from year to year* (or *from month to month* with most residential properties) is created. Once this type of tenancy has been established, advance notice is usually required for its termination.

Whenever a tenancy continues for an indefinite period subject to termination by either the landlord or the tenant on short notice, a *tenancy at will* exists. Some states require minimum periods of notice for termination. But subject to this restriction, this type of leasehold involves leases for indefinite periods, which can be terminated at the will of either party, at the sale or conveyance of the landlord's interests to others, or at the death of the landlord or tenant.

Holdover tenants who continue to occupy the landlord's premises after the expiration of their leases become *tenants at sufferance.* As long as the landlord does not consent to their continued occupancy of his premises and does not accept rent from them, he can terminate the tenancy at any time and treat the occupants as trespassers. Tenants who hold over in this fashion can be held liable for penalty rent.

Time of enjoyment of estate. Estates can be enjoyed either now or in the future. Those that are enjoyed at the present time must be held in current possession. The principal examples of these are estates in fee, life estates, and the leaseholds held by tenants. In contrast to these types of estates, reversion, remainder, and executory interests cannot be enjoyed until some future date.

Whenever a holder of property rights grants some of his interests to others with the provision that they shall come back or revert to him at the expiration of the grant, he retains an *estate in reversion.* Landlords retain this interest when they lease their premises to tenants. Persons who give life estates to others during their lifetimes may also retain a reversion interest. Much the same situation exists with the grantors of determinable fee estates, though the uncertainty of reversion in cases of this type gives the grantor only a possibility of reversion.

Estates in remainder are created when interests are conveyed to a person or persons to take effect after the termination of some prior estate. This type of estate with its promise of future rights of enjoyment usually accompanies grants of life estates. Thus a property owner may leave his wife a life estate in his property while he vests his nephew with a remainder interest, which entitles him to the property upon her death. In times past, owners sometimes used their right to name remaindermen as a means of entailing their estates in perpetuity. Most jurisdictions now limit this possibility with rules against perpetuities.

[22]Some states have abolished or modified the rule that makes a tenant liable for another year's rent if he voluntarily holds over beyond the expiration of his lease. In some of these states, the holdover tenant is treated as a tenant from month to month or as a tenant at will.

Future interests that vest after a given period of time or after the happening of some particular event are known as *executory interests.* These interests are similar to remainder rights except that they need not follow the termination of some prior estate.

Social Controls over Landed Property

Society has an inherent interest in all arrangements involving the ownership and use of landed property. This interest exists because of (1) the original role society plays in granting, recognizing, and protecting property rights; (2) the economic and social significance of property in our daily lives; and (3) the over-all responsibility society has for maximizing social returns both now and in the future.

Except for the countries behind the Iron Curtain, most nations now favor the private ownership of most types of land resources. This private ownership involves exclusive rights of possession. But these rights are exclusive, not absolute. They are always held subject to certain social controls. Some of this social control is informal and occurs in the form of customs, tradition, religious practices, education, codes of ethics, moral restraints, and public opinion. On the more formal side, private property rights are also conditioned and limited by various actions of the sovereign powers, which interpret and implement the will of society.

Definite limits can seldom be assigned to the powers governments claim and exercise over landed property. Some nations such as ancient Egypt and the Soviet Union have exercised almost complete control over their land resources. Others have used constitutional and legislative measures to limit their powers over private property, but in so doing have often modified their stand to fit changing conditions. The development of the concept of fee simple ownership in England, for example, brought a gradual strengthening of the position of the average individual owner until around 1800. Since that high point in the exercise of individual ownership rights, the pendulum has swung more in the direction of greater social controls over property.

At the present time, the governments of Canada and the United States have five important formal powers they can use in their direction and control of land resources. Three of these powers—the police, eminent domain, and taxation powers—involve social controls over landed property, while the spending and proprietary powers represent auxiliary powers that governments can use to achieve particular objectives in land use.[23]

The first of these powers—the police power—involves the sovereign

[23]The use of these powers is discussed in more detail in chapters 17 and 18. Donald R. Denman, *Land in the Market* (London: Institute of Economic Affairs, 1964), pp. 35-43, lists the public means for controlling property as sanctions, levies, prescribed maxima, forced sale, land nationalization, and compulsory reallocation.

power of governments to limit personal liberties and property rights in the interest of public health, safety, morals, and the general welfare. As one writer has observed, this power involves "the inherent right of people through organized government to protect their health, life, limb, individual liberty of action, property, and to provide for public order, peace, safety, and welfare."[24]

As long as they are utilized in a legal manner for a reasonable purpose, police power measures can be used to attain a wide variety of social goals. They are used to provide police protection; to set up and enforce fire, health, and traffic regulations; to control air and water pollution, to prohibit billboards at particular locations, to eliminate and prevent public nuisances, to enforce quarantines, and to require the slaughter of diseased animals.

The police power may be used in rural areas to zone land uses; to set up wind-erosion, weed-control, soil-conservation, grazing, and other districts; and to enforce forest-cutting restrictions. It is used in urban and suburban areas to provide land-use zoning regulations, to establish and enforce building and sanitary codes, to set up subdivision regulations, and to provide for public planning agencies and commissions. On other occasions, the police power can be used for such purposes as the regulation of oil production, the maintenance of acreage controls and marketing quotas for farm products, and the enactment of rent- and price-control measures.

Governments have always maintained their right to take private properties for public uses. Sometimes they have interpreted this right broadly and used it to strip owners of their wealth and possessions or to expropriate whole classes of owners with little or no compensation. Most constitutional governments, including Canada and the United States, limit this right of expropriation to what is known as the power of eminent domain. This power enables governments to appropriate private property for public uses without the consent of the owner as long as the property is taken under due process of law with the payment of just compensation.

Taxation represents a third important power of government over landed property. Most of the taxes levied by the federal, state, and local levels of government are levied for the express purpose of collecting revenue. Uniformity clauses are used in most jurisdictions to keep these taxes from being arbitrary, discriminatory, or unreasonable. Yet as Chief Justice Marshall's famous observation that "the power to tax is the power to destroy" suggests, the taxing power can be used to attain particular ends. Taxes can be used to force the redistribution of property holdings; exemptions can be used to favor particular classes of owners; and tax policies can be used to encourage either conservation or the more intensive use of particular land resources.

[24]Eugene McQuillan, *The Law of Municipal Corporations,* 3rd ed. (Chicago: Callaghan and Company, 1949), Vol. 6, p. 464.

Governments ordinarily possess an almost unlimited right to spend money as long as funds are available for this purpose. In times past, most government expenditures have gone for routine administration or for military and defense purposes. More recently large amounts have been spent for education, public works, and for a variety of informational and promotional activities. With this shift, governments have found that they can use public funds to foster such varied land-use goals as the building of new highways, the development of huge reclamation and power projects, the provision of better farm and housing credit facilities, and the redevelopment and renewal of blighted urban areas.

In addition to their controls over privately owned lands, governments also have the right to acquire and administer land resources for their own use. This power can be used to establish public forests, parks, highways, and military reserves. It can be used to set up experimental areas for demonstration and research purposes, and to develop or reclaim resources that may later be sold to private owners. It can be used to nationalize industries in the public interest. The threat of nationalization may also be used at times to force a greater measure of social control over particular industries or resource uses.

RIGHTS IN WATER

The rights people enjoy in the use of water differ in many respects from the interests they may hold in surface land. Whenever a society enjoys a plentiful supply of water, this resource is usually treated as a free good that individuals can take or use as they wish. Once the demand for water resources approaches the available supply, however, conflicts of interest develop and working rules become necessary.

Several different legal doctrines now apply regarding the rights individuals have in the use of water from different sources. For discussion purposes, these sources can be classified into four principal groups: (1) ocean waters; (2) *diffused surface waters* (from rain, melting snow; or possible waste water from irrigation works) found either standing in natural depressions, bogs or marshes, or flowing vagrantly over land while enroute to some watercourse, lake, or pond; (3) *surface waters* found in lakes, ponds, rivers, streams, and springs; and (4) subsurface or *ground waters,* which occur either as flowing water in defined subterranean channels or as diffused percolating waters.

Ocean waters are generally regarded as a more or less free good that individuals can use for navigation, fishing, recreation, and other purposes subject to certain national and international regulations. Among the countries and states that accept the English system of law, diffused surface waters, together with the water in the soil, are normally regarded as the property of the land owner. The principal water-rights problem with this resource concerns the drainage of unwanted waters. More complicated water-rights issues are associated with the use of surface and ground waters. Surface water rights are governed by the riparian rights doctrine in most of the more humid areas of the United States. Among the more arid states of the West, however, constitutional and statutory provisions require the application of either an appropriation or a modified riparian doctrine. Comparable differences occur in the doctrines that govern the allocation and use of ground waters.

Riparian Doctrine [25]

Under the common-law riparian doctrine, all land owners whose properties are bounded or traversed by a river, stream, spring, or natural body of water have riparian rights. These owners have a right to use those waters to which they are riparian for domestic and household purposes, for watering their livestock, for navigation, for the generation of power, for fishing and recreation purposes, and for certain other uses.

Strictly interpreted, the riparian doctrine grants riparian owners a right to have water flow by or through their lands undiminished in quantity, undisturbed in time of flow, and unchanged in quality except for its use by upper riparian owners for domestic purposes and for the watering of livestock. As this statement suggests, riparian owners have usufructuary but not proprietary rights in the water that flows by their land. They can use the water for a variety of purposes. But except for domestic and stock watering purposes, they have no right to divert or take more water from a stream or lake than they expect to return to it.

Few state courts now hold to this strict "natural flow" doctrine with its limitation of riparian rights to "ordinary and natural" uses. Most of them have substituted a reasonable-use doctrine, which permits the diversion or taking of some waters for "extraordinary and artificial" uses. These uses may involve the consumption of all or part of the water taken and thus preclude its complete return to the stream. With this modification, riparian waters can be used for municipal, industrial, irrigation, and other "extraordinary" uses as long as an adequate supply of water remains available to meet the "natural" needs of other riparian owners.

It should be noted that the right to take water for "extraordinary" purposes is a limited right, which can be exercised only with reasonable regard for the equal rights of other riparian owners. An upper riparian owner can take the entire flow of a stream for "natural" riparian uses such as the watering of his cattle. He can take water for industrial or irrigation uses, however, only as long as sufficient water remains to care for the "natural" uses of lower riparian owners. Whenever lower riparian

[25] For other discussions of this subject, cf. Wells A. Hutchins, *Selected Problems in the Law of Water Rights in the West,* U.S. Department of Agriculture Misc. Publ. No. 418, 1942, pp. 38-64; and Roy E. Huffman, *Irrigation Development and Public Water Policy* (New York: The Ronald Press, 1953), pp. 37-39.

owners suffer material injury because of upper diversions for "extraordinary" purposes, they can request court action to enforce their right to a continued flow of a stream.

Riparian rights are not dependent upon an owner's use of water and under ordinary circumstances they cannot be lost through disuse or nonuse. However, upper riparian owners can acquire prescriptive rights to the use of certain volumes of water for municipal, industrial, and irrigation purposes, which they can later exercise despite the complaints of lower riparian owners. To be valid, these prescriptive rights must be secured through the owner's continuous, uninterrupted, notorious, and adverse use of the said quantity of water throughout the prescriptive period recognized in his state. Even when rights of this type are secured by adverse use, they can be exercised only in relation to the rights of lower owners on the stream. No riparian owner who acquires a prescriptive right to the full flow of a stream can prevent upstream riparian owners from making lawful use of the water before it reaches his land.

Riparian rights are limited to riparian land. This means that nonriparian owners have no rights to the use of riparian waters—except for their rights as citizens to use public waters, public beaches, and public fishing sites. All riparian owners enjoy the same use rights regardless of the extent of their property frontages along streams or lakes. When riparian waters are used in connection with land (as in the case of irrigation), the right of use applies only to those holdings that lie within the watershed of the stream, lake, or pond and which are contiguous to or abut upon these waters. In many jurisdictions the riparian right "extends only to the smallest tract held under one title in the chain of title leading to the present owner."[26] This means that riparian rights do not always apply to lands added to a riparian owner's holdings if the lands added have at some time been parts of nonriparian holdings.

Riparian owners ordinarily have the right to change their points of use and diversion and also the right to use dams to retain water if their exercise of these rights does not cause injury to others. They also can reserve or separate the riparian rights from land when it is granted or conveyed to others. As a rule, however, riparian rights pass with conveyances of riparian land unless the grantor specifically reserves or excepts the right from the conveyance. An owner of water frontage who sells a right-of-way for a highway between his home and a lake, for example, may reserve his riparian rights and thus retain his right of access to the lake.

Appropriation Doctrine

With the settlement of the arid lands of the American West, it soon became apparent that water is a strategic resource and that its most

[26]Hutchins, *op. cit.,* p. 46.

beneficial use sometimes calls for outright appropriation. This situation was clearly recognized by the Mormon pioneers who appropriated surface waters without regard for riparian rights when they started their irrigation of the Great Salt Lake valley in 1847. Similar practices were soon applied on a larger scale by the early gold miners in California. An appropriation doctrine was accepted in both of these areas as a matter of expediency, primarily because the riparian doctrine did not serve the best interests of the settlers.[27]

Under the appropriation doctrine, both riparian and nonriparian owners can file claims to take or divert water from streams or other bodies of water as long as their claims do not conflict with prior claims on water from the same source. As each successive claim is filed on the water from a particular source, a system of priorities develops. This system vests each claimant with a recognized exclusive right to take water up to the amount of his claim for beneficial use provided there is sufficient water to satisfy all claims of higher priority.

The principal features of the appropriation doctrine may be summarized as follows:

1. It gives an exclusive right to the first appropriator; and, in accordance with the doctrine of priority, the rights of later appropriators are conditional upon the prior rights of those who have proceeded.
2. It makes all rights conditional upon beneficial use—as the doctrine of priority was adopted for the protection of the first settlers in time of scarcity, so the doctrine of beneficial use became a protection to later appropriators against wasteful use by those with earlier rights.
3. It permits water to be used on nonriparian lands as well as on riparian lands.
4. It permits diversion of water regardless of the diminution of the stream.
5. Continuation of the right depends upon beneficial use. The right may be lost by nonuse.[28]

The essence of the prior-appropriation doctrine is aptly summarized by the catch-phrase "first in time, first in right." As this maxim suggests, the

[27]From a legalistic standpoint, the beginnings of the appropriation doctrine are often traced to the Spanish and Mexican law applied in the Southwest prior to the Mexican cession of this area to the United States in 1848. However, as Hutchins points out: "the appropriation principle in the form in which it is now recognized throughout the West—embodying the essential element of priority—is not traceable to Mexican laws and customs, but sprang from the requirements of a mining region for protection in the use of water supplies needed to work the mining claims. . . . The miner's customs became law, adaptable to diversions of water for irrigation as well as for mining purposes; and it is the specific principles there developed under the exigencies of that environment, rather than the less widely known principles of Mexican appropriation law and custom, that have been adopted by legislation and court decisions and are now a part of the water codes throughout the West." Hutchins, *op. cit.*, pp. 67-68.

[28] Roy E. Huffman, *Irrigation Development and Public Water Policy*, Copyright 1953, The Ronald Press Co. (New York: The Ronald Press, 1953), p. 43.

key feature of the appropriation doctrine involves its recognition of priorities in appropriative rights. The operation of these priorities can best be illustrated by an example of a stream, such as that depicted in Figure 12-1, upon which several claims for water have been filed.

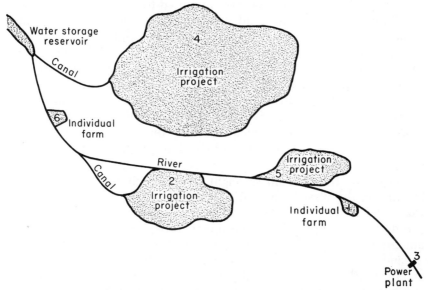

FIGURE 12-1. Example showing priorities in appropriative rights under the appropriation doctrine.

Let us assume that the first and sixth claims involve riparian users who take water to irrigate relatively small acreages, that the second and fifth priorities are held by irrigation projects along the stream, that the fourth priority involves a large irrigation project located several miles away from the stream, and that the third priority is held by a downstream hydroelectric plant which claims a definite minimum flow of the stream at all times.

Regardless of their location along the stream, each of these claimants enjoys water rights only in accordance with the priority of his (or its) claim. The first and second claimants may expect to take water up to the full amount of their claims at any time. After them, the power company can insist upon a minimum natural flow of the stream, which may take all of the flow during drought periods. Since the priorities of the first three claimants may entitle them to the full flow of the stream during the drier months of the year, the remaining claimants can find their rights cut off at the very time they feel the greatest need for irrigation water. They can remedy this situation by building an upstream storage reservoir that will hold seasonal flood water for later use.

A seventh claimant located at some site above the reservoir or on some tributary stream would also find it necessary to relate his claims to the reservoir storage project. Since the normal summer flow past his land would be covered by prior claims, he would be able to get water only by helping to finance the storage of seasonal surplus waters, which he could use as a trade-off for the natural flow he needs during the drier summer months.

The appropriation doctrine is now accepted to a greater or lesser degree in 18 Western States. The eight intermountain states—Montana, Idaho, Wyoming, Colorado, Utah, Nevada, Arizona, and New Mexico—and Alaska have completely abrogated the riparian doctrine in favor of the appropriation doctrine. Oregon also might be listed with these states because it too has abandoned the riparian doctrine except for its application in a few early cases in which riparian rights were established for beneficial uses. These states are sometimes said to adhere to the "Colorado doctrine," so named because the exclusive appropriation doctrine was prescribed in the constitution of that state when it was admitted to the union in 1876.

Throughout the remaining eight Western States—Washington and California on the West Coast and North Dakota, South Dakota, Nebraska, Kansas, Oklahoma, and Texas on the eastern fringe of the arid and semiarid West—the appropriation principle is used in combination with the riparian-rights doctrine. Each of these states has some humid or subhumid areas and most of them have superimposed the appropriation doctrine upon an underlying riparian doctrine. Variations exist between these states; but in general they have all tended to modify the riparian doctrine by restricting the claims of riparian owners while at the same time recognizing appropriation rights to reasonable amounts of water used for beneficial purposes.[29] California was the first of these states to spell out this *modified riparian doctrine.* For this reason, this approach is often referred to as the "California doctrine."

Unlike the riparian doctrine, the operation of the appropriation doctrine calls for a certain amount of administration. Administration is involved in the filing and recording of claims, in the checking of water gauges to make sure that appropriators do not exceed their rights, and in the action of courts and administrative boards in defining and adjudicating water rights. Some of the most notable administrative differences involve methods of filing claims. In Wyoming, for example, the state claims

[29]For more detailed discussion of the water-rights doctrines accepted in these states cf. Hutchins, *op. cit.;* and *Water Resources Law,* Vol. 3 of the Report of the President's Water Resources Policy Commission, 1950; Frank J. Trelease, Harold S. Bloomenthal, and Joseph H. Geraud, *Cases and Materials on Natural Resources Law* (St. Paul: West Publishing Co., 1965), Part I; and Jacob H. Beuscher, *Water Rights* (Madison: College Printing & Typing Co., Inc., 1967). Several humid-area states have modified the riparian doctrine in various respects. Mississippi enacted legislation that accepts aspects of the appropriation doctrine in 1956. Iowa adopted a ten-year permit law in 1957. Hawaii, Maryland, Minnesota, North Carolina, and Wisconsin also have laws that limit the riparian doctrine.

ownership of the water found in streams, and all water rights must be filed with and granted by the state. Some of the other states in times past have permitted water users to file their claims simply by posting a notice at their point of diversion and then filing copies of this notice with the appropriate county officers. This approach has resulted in considerable confusion and in the filing of more claims on some streams than can possibly be filled. Nearly all of the states now require the filing of appropriation claims with some state agency.

Use of Ground Waters

Wells have been used as a source of domestic water supplies almost since the beginning of history. Throughout this period, the use of ground waters has often been taken for granted with little consideration being given to the matter of water rights. The increased taking of this resource in recent decades for domestic, municipal, industrial, irrigation, and other uses, however, has heralded the rise of a ground water conservation problem.

From a legal standpoint, ground waters are often divided into two groups: underground streams and percolating waters. Most courts apply the same water-rights doctrine to underground streams that they apply to surface waters. Thus if a definite underground stream is found in a riparian-doctrine state, its waters are normally subject to the riparian rights recognized in that state. Likewise, if the underground stream is located in an appropriation or modified riparian doctrine state, its waters in most cases are available for appropriation.

Percolating waters—those waters below the surface that are not confined to any channel—are affected by four different legal doctrines: (1) the doctrine of absolute ownership, (2) the doctrine of reasonable use, (3) the doctrine of correlative rights, and (4) the prior appropriation doctrine. The first of these doctrines, the English or common-law rule of absolute ownership, was originally accepted in most areas that accept English law. This doctrine recognizes the land owner's right to all of the water on or under the surface of his land as long as it is not part of a definite stream. As one court has complained, this doctrine "affirms the right of the owner of land to sink wells thereon, and use the water therefrom, supplied by percolation, in any way he chooses to use it, to allow it to flow away, even though he thereby diminishes the water in his neighbor's wells or dries them entirely, and even though in so doing he is actuated by malice." [30]

The obvious lack of justice associated with unreasonable withdrawals of ground water under the absolute ownership rule has caused the courts in most states to qualify this rule. Out of these actions has come the American doctrine of reasonable use. This doctrine recognizes that land owners hold joint rights in the use of common ground waters. Individual

[30] *Schenk v. City of Ann Arbor*, 196 Michigan 75, 82 (1917).

owners are permitted considerable freedom in their use of percolating ground waters on overlying lands. But the rule of reasonable use may be interpreted to prevent wasteful, malicious, or other unreasonable uses of water, particularly if these uses have a harmful or injurious effect upon others. Owners who suffer injuries from ground water depletion can in some cases secure legal action to prevent the pumping of ground waters for sale or for use on nonoverlying lands. Under some circumstances, they may also seek and secure damages from persons whose pumping activities cause them injury.

The doctrine of correlative rights is applied in California and some other Western States and represents an outgrowth of the rule of reasonable use. According to this doctrine, landowners share coequal rights in the use of percolating waters from a common ground-water supply for reasonable purposes on or in connection with their overlying lands. These rights can be limited to a reasonable or equitable proportion of the total supply any time the supply appears inadequate to meet the needs of all the owners. Where surplus waters over and above the amounts required to provide for the reasonable needs of the overlying land exist, provisions can be made to appropriate them for use either in or outside of the ground water area.

A few Western States apply the prior-appropriation doctrine to percolating ground waters. The application of this doctrine permits the use of ground waters on a first-come, first-served basis. It also permits the appropriation of ground waters from overlying lands not owned by the appropriator for use on lands that do not overlie the source of the water supply. As Hutchins observes:

> One of the main reasons for the slow growth of the appropriation principle, with regard to percolating waters, has been the practical difficulty in identifying such waters and proving their characteristics. To protect an appropriator adequately, it is not sufficient to establish the existence of the ground-water supply, but the origin, destination, boundaries, and quantity and rate of flow must also be ascertained within reason. This is a very different matter from making proof of right on a surface watercourse.[31]

With the growing use of ground waters for municipal, industrial, and irrigation purposes, the problem of ground water conservation and use is becoming increasingly critical in many localities. As these problems are recognized and publicized, more and more attention will be given to the development of regulations affecting ground waters. In some Eastern States these problems may call merely for a greater exercise of the police powers of these states in regulating the taking or use of ground waters. In other areas, they may call for the enactment of comprehensive ground water codes. Several Western States have already faced up to this problem. New Mexico, for example, has a highly regarded ground water code, which

[31] Hutchins, *op. cit.,* p. 161.

asserts public ownership of the ground waters of the state and provides for their apportionment in the public interest.

Most observers agree that the optimum development of both surface and ground water resources calls for a framework of law that will permit the wise use of these resources. One of the thorniest problems that arises in connection with the attainment of this goal involves the often inadequate factual basis for the development of sound policies. As Thomas has indicated, a good bit of our

> existing water law is unsound, chiefly because it has been developed on the basis of meager hydrological facts and in some cases incorrect assumptions. As a result, some statutes and court decisions are so written as to preclude effective development and maximum utilization of water. A body of workable water law is needed for effective control of development and to protect water rights. But first there must be adequate reliable information upon which to base determinations as to questions of fact and questions of law.[32]

Rights Affecting Drainage

Thus far in this discussion we have been concerned with the rights individuals and groups have to take and use water for various purposes. A different type of problem arises when one considers the rights land owners have to drain surplus waters from their lands or to construct levees that will prevent unwanted waters from encroaching upon their properties.

Most states have constitutional or statutory provisions that authorize the establishment of drainage or levee districts together with the construction and maintenance of drainage and levee works. In addition to these provisions, most of the more humid states have enacted laws covering drainage problems. These laws tend to follow one or the other of two alternative doctrines. They either accept the common-law or so-called "common-enemy" rule or they follow the civil-law rule.[33]

The common-law rule treats both flood waters and unwanted runoff waters as a common enemy against which a landowner has a recognized right to protect his lands. Some courts have modified this rule to permit the drainage of upper lands upon lower lands provided no appreciable damage is done. As a general rule, however, the owners of upper lands

---

[32]Harold E. Thomas, *The Conservation of Ground Water* (New York: McGraw-Hill Book Co., Inc., 1951), p. 13.

[33]Cf. Bernard A. Etcheverry, *Land Drainage and Flood Protection* (Stanford University, Calif.: Stanford University Press, 1940), pp. 282-84. This author indicates that the common-law rule has been adopted in Arkansas, Connecticut, Indiana, Kansas, Maine, Massachusetts, Minnesota, Missouri, Nebraska, New Hampshire, New Jersey, New Mexico, New York, Oklahoma, South Carolina, Virginia, Washington, and Wisconsin. The civil-law rule applies in Alabama, California, Georgia, Illinois, Iowa, Kentucky, Louisiana, Maryland, Michigan, North Carolina, Ohio, Pennsylvania, and Texas.

have no lawful right to drain their unwanted waters onto lower lands or to use tile, drainage ditches, or other man-made means to discharge drainage waters into a natural stream if their actions in any way cause injury to lower owners.

Unlike the common-enemy rule, the civil-law rule recognizes the right of upper land owners to have their flood and runoff waters flow naturally to lower lands. Lower owners cannot obstruct or refuse to receive the natural runoff from upper lands. But they can object whenever an upper landowner holds back water for later release, uses terraces or dikes to concentrate the runoff in given locations, or uses ditches or furrows to implement and speed up his runoff.

The courts in several civil-law-rule states have held that land owners have a right to natural drainage but that they have no right to increase the flow of water from their lands to those of lower owners. In some of these states, however, upper owners are allowed to speed up the drainage of their lands by artificial means as long as they have an outlet in a watercourse or natural depression and as long as they do not change the natural direction of water flow.

Both rules allow upper owners to acquire drainage rights over the lands of lower owners through the use of easements or by maintaining adverse uses over the authorized prescriptive period. They also recognize that different situations exist whenever drainage or levee districts are created. Land owners living within drainage districts, for example, have a lawful right to use tile, ditches, and other man-made devices when they discharge drainage waters into artificial watercourses—that is, into public drains or into natural watercourses that have been improved for drainage purposes.

Property owners living within drainage and levee districts are usually subject to special assessments for drainage and levee works even when they receive few, if any, benefits from these works. In the absence of these districts, upper land owners covered by the common-law rule can often be assessed for downstream improvements necessitated by their use of artificial drainage methods. Upper owners treated under the civil-law rule, however, are often exempt from special assessments of this type. Owners of lower lands can usually claim damages from upper owners for just cause. In many jurisdictions, they can also secure injunctions against the future use of artificial drainage measures by upper owners if the additional water flow caused by these measures threatens injury or damage to the lower owners.

Public Interests in Water

In addition to the rights individual land owners hold in water, important powers concerning water also are vested in various units of government to be exercised in the public interest. Some of these powers in the United States are held by the federal government while others are exercised by the states.

The federal Constitution clothes Congress with the power "to regulate commerce with foreign nations and among the several states" and with the power "to dispose of and make needful regulations respecting government property." These two grants of power—commonly referred to as the "commerce power" and the "property clause"—underlie most of the interest the federal government has in water resources. But important powers involving the administration, use, and development of water resources may also be implied from the authority vested in Congress "to provide for the common defense," "to provide for the general welfare," and to pass upon interstate compacts. Still other federal powers over water are associated with the federal treaty-making power and with the original and exclusive jurisdiction the Supreme Court has over all controversies between states.

Under the commerce power, Congress is responsible for the control of navigation and has full jurisdiction over the navigable rivers of the United States. Because of the scope of this power, considerable importance attaches to the meaning of "navigable waters." The English common law limits the legal concept of navigability to ocean waters and to inland waters affected by the ebb and flow of tides. This doctrine was accepted for awhile in the United States and then expanded to cover those inland waters that are navigable in fact. The concept of legal navigability has been further expanded to include all those rivers and lakes that are used, are susceptible of being used, or with reasonable improvements can be used in interstate commerce.[34] Moreover, it appears that "the commerce jurisdiction of Congress may be appropriately invoked both as to the upper nonnavigable reaches of a navigable waterway and as to its nonnavigable tributaries, if the navigable capacity of the navigable waterway is affected or if interstate commerce is otherwise affected."[35]

In the exercise of its power over commerce and navigation, "Congress has enacted legislation governing erection of dams, bridges, dikes, causeways, piers, wharves, and other structures; the removal of sunken vessels; the deposit of refuse materials; the operation of drawbridges; the use, administration, and navigation of waterways; the deposit of oil in coastal waters, and other protective measures."[36] Beyond this, the federal

---

[34]In the *Daniel Ball* case, the Supreme Court held: "Those rivers must be regarded as public navigable rivers in law which are navigable in fact. And they are navigable in fact when they are used, or are susceptible of being used, in their ordinary conditions, as highways for commerce, over which trade and travel are or may be conducted in the customary modes of trade and travel on water." *The Daniel Ball,* 10 Wallace 557, 563 (1870). Later in the *New River* case, it held further that: "The power of Congress over commerce is not to be hampered because of the necessity for reasonable improvements to make an interstate waterway available for traffic." *United States v. Appalachian Electric Power Co.,* 311 U.S. 377 (1940).

[35]President's Water Resources Policy Commission, *A Water Policy for the American People* (Washington: U.S. Government Printing Office, 1950), p. 278.

[36]*Ibid.,* p. 283.

government has provided numerous navigation aids and has specified rules for navigation. It has licensed private power plants on "navigable" waters and at times has required the removal of unauthorized structures regarded as obstacles to navigation. It has conducted navigation research, built storage dams and locks, deepened channels, improved harbors, acquired private canals for public use, and developed its own water transportation facilities. It also has interpreted the "commerce power" to permit its active participation in flood-control and various water-resource development programs.

In addition to its commerce power, the federal government has used its proprietary power under the "property clause" to undertake resource development programs such as those carried on under the Reclamation Act of 1902. Under this power, the federal government can acquire and condemn such property rights as it needs. It can build irrigation, flood-control, and multipurpose dams and generate and sell electrical power as an incident of ownership.

Broad powers concerning water are also exercised by the states. Each state has the power, within constitutional limits, to prescribe the rules that govern the use of surface and ground waters within its jurisdiction; and a few states have asserted proprietary interests in water by declaring their ownership of the surface or ground waters found within their boundaries. States can engage in water-resource developments; and they can use their police powers to control water pollution, to prescribe measures affecting the supply and treatment of municipal water supplies, to regulate the pumping of ground waters, to authorize flood-control measures and drainage works, and for other comparable purposes.

One of the most important interests states have in water involves the perpetual and inalienable trust each state holds to safeguard the rights of its citizens in the use of public waters. The full nature of these rights is subject to court interpretation, but most courts agree that these public rights include the privilege of individuals to use public waters for such purposes as navigation, fishing, fowling, bathing, skating, and the enjoyment of scenic beauty. Also, even though each state has its own definition of "public waters," the courts generally agree that all navigable waters are public waters.[37]

---

[37] "Navigability" is treated in many states as the criteria for determining whether or not a lake or stream is "public water." Some of the Atlantic Coast states hold to a salt-water test of navigability, which treats only those waters affected by the ebb and flow of tides as navigable. In contrast, many states have used a sawlog test, which holds that streams that can or have floated a log or boat are navigable. Between these two extremes, states such as Texas hold that a stream is navigable only as far as it retains an average width of 30 feet while Mississippi specifies that a navigable stream must be deep enough for any 30 consecutive days to float a steamboat large enough to carry 200 bales of cotton.

Some of the most important differences in definitions concerning "public waters" relate to the distinction between public and private lakes or ponds. Lakes or ponds

Two problems occasionally arise concerning the exercise of public rights to public waters. The first of these involves the ownership of the ground underlying the public waters; the second concerns rights of access. Most of the states have retained public ownership of the land beneath their public waters. Some, however, have surrendered the ownership of these lands to the riparian owners. Questions sometimes arise in these states concerning the rights fishermen and others have in the use of waters that flow over privately owned land. In a leading case on this point, one state court has held that a fisherman can wade upstream, angling as he goes and contrary to the posted warnings of the riparian owner who owns the bottom of the stream, without being guilty of trespass as long as he does not go upon the owner's upland.[38]

Lack of access rights keeps many people from exercising their rights to the use of public waters. Several states have recognized this situation and have taken specific steps to acquire riparian sites that give citizens access to public waters for fishing, bathing, boating, and other recreation uses.

Another major problem of emerging concern for the states and the federal government centers in the need for controlling water-pollution. The discharge of untreated sewerage and other wastes into lakes, streams, and the ocean was accepted for a long period as a convenient and inexpensive way of disposing of unwanted materials. This practice, which appeared both logical and relatively harmless in an earlier time when few people lived along the public waters, became unacceptable from a health standpoint once modern medicine discovered its impact upon the spread of disease. It also became esthetically objectionable as thousands of people turned to this means for disposing of their wastes, as the volume of wastes began to tax the dilution and purifying capacities of the available water supplies, and as problems of deteriorating quality made many public waters unattractive or unacceptable for recreation uses.

Treatment of public water supplies and of municipal wastes was pushed for many years as the most practical way to cope with the water pollution problem. More recently, and since the enactment of the Water Quality Act of 1965 in particular, the public has become very much aware of the relationship of water pollution to the quality of the human and natural environment. Water quality standards have been established for different water uses in all of the states, and steps have been taken to initiate strong public and private programs for the control and elimination of significant sources of water pollution.

---

connected with navigable streams are ordinarily regarded as public waters. They may also be so regarded if they cover more than a prescribed area, if they were meandered in the original public survey, or if the owner has consented to the public planting of fish in what was his private water. Cf. Leighton L. Leighty, "The Source and Scope of Public and Private Rights in Navigable Waters," *University of Wyoming Land and Water Law Review,* Vol. 5, 1970, pp. 391-440, and Vol. 6, 1971, pp. 459-90.

[38]Cf. *Collins v. Gerhardt,* 237 Michigan 38, 211 N.W. 115 (1926).

AIR AND SUBSURFACE RIGHTS

The property rights individual owners hold in land are sometimes visualized as an inverted pyramid which starts at the center of the earth and extends upward through the surface boundaries of the owner's holding to the highest heavens. As this concept suggests, landed property rights can be divided into layers of rights—into air rights, surface rights, and subsurface rights. From a legal standpoint, each of these layers can be held separately from the others and each has its particular characteristics.

Air Rights

Up until recent years, the courts have almost universally accepted the principle that surface owners hold all of the rights to the column of airspace above their surface holdings. This doctrine has been modified to permit public use of the air for air travel. But it is still recognized that individual owners have a right to all of the airspace above their land they can occupy and use. As one court has held:

> The air, like the sea, is by its nature incapable of private ownership, except insofar as one may actually use it. . . . We own so much of the space above the ground as we can occupy or make use of, in connection with the enjoyment of our land. This right is not fixed. It varies with our varying needs and is coextensive with them. The owner of land owns as much of the space above him as he uses, but only so long as he uses it. All that lies beyond belongs to the world.
>
> When it is said that man owns, or may own, to the heavens, that merely means that no one can acquire a right to the space above him that will limit him in whatever use he can make of it as a part of his enjoyment of the land. To this extent his title to the air is paramount. No other person can acquire any title or exclusive right to any space above him.
>
> Any use of such air or space by others which is injurious to his land, or which constitutes an actual interference with his possession or his beneficial use thereof, would be a trespass for which he would have remedy. But any claim of the land owner beyond this cannot find a precedent in law, nor support in reason.[39]

Under our accepted concept of air rights, land owners can claim trespass whenever telephone wires, limbs of trees, or overhanging parts of buildings based on adjacent properties project into their columns of airspace. Easements affecting air rights are often purchased by utility companies and others. These rights may also be secured by deed reservations or by adverse possession. In exceptional cases, they are sometimes

[39]*Hinman v. Pacific Air Transport,* Ninth Circuit Court of Appeals, 84 F.2d 755 (1936).

sold or leased to others. The airspace above some of the railroad tracks in downtown Chicago and New York, for example, has been sold together with rights of support for commercial developments such as the Chicago Merchandise Mart.

Surface land ownership carries with it the right of access and exposure to sunlight, air, and rain. Every land owner holds these rights within his own column of airspace. His rights may be limited, however, by structures placed on adjacent lands. Under the doctrine of "ancient lights" accepted in Great Britain, building owners who have enjoyed access to light and air from their windows for a 20-year period have a prescriptive right to retain this access even though it involves an easement against the adjacent owner's air rights. This doctrine is not accepted by the American courts. Property owners in the United States can put up buildings that completely shut off the air and light received by abutting windows on adjacent properties. Problems of this type are often averted by easements, deed restrictions, zoning ordinances, and building setback regulations.

Some of the most important problems involving air rights arise because of the movement of undesirable odors, smoke and chemical substances, rain clouds, and aircraft across property lines. Individuals and communities that suffer because of offensive odors caused by slaughter houses, glue factories, or other comparable property uses can ordinarily take legal action to have these uses modified or stopped. The courts have often held, however, for the offending users—particularly when their prospective losses have outweighed the promised social gain—when the offensive uses have continued for a long period, and when the individuals who have protested have acquired their properties since the beginning of the offensive use.

Many large cities together with numerous rural areas are now plagued with smog and air pollution problems. These are old problems; but we have complicated and aggravated them by adding the exhaust fumes from automobiles and the smoke and chemical wastes belched forth from our many manufacturing and smelting plants to the smoke emitted from incinerators and home heating systems.[40] The seriousness of the air-pollution problem has prompted the initiation of public programs that deal with both the esthetic and the physically harmful aspects of air pollution.

Air pollution standards have been enacted to reduce the magnitude of the pollution problem. The enforcement of these standards limits the rights of individuals and others to discharge undesired wastes into the atmosphere. Prior to the enactment of these regulations, legal action could

---

[40] Attempts to control these problems go back to the smoke-abatement law enacted by Edward I of England in 1273. Cf. *Air Pollution Control: A Symposium, Law & Contemporary Problems,* Vol. 33, Spring 1968; and Orlando E. Delogu, "Legal Aspects of Air Pollution Control and Proposed State Legislation for Such Control," *Wisconsin Law Review,* 1969, pp. 884-907.

be taken against polluters when it was found that their actions interfered with the legitimate rights of others.[41] Before granting damages or issuing injunctions against pollution practices, however, the courts usually weighed the equities on each side and gave the offending parties an opportunity to install pollution abatement facilities.

No definite customs or legal rules have as yet been developed concerning ownership rights to atmospheric moisture. The development of artificial rain-making techniques, however, has focused considerable attention on the problem of atmospheric water rights.[42] At present, it appears that land owners have no more of a property right in the clouds that cross their land than they have in the birds that fly overhead. Until specific rules are developed, rain-makers will probably continue to treat atmospheric moisture as a free good. As the techniques used to cause rain to fall in specific areas become more exact, however, possible legal grievances will rise both from (1) those persons deprived of the benefits of rainfall, and (2) those land owners who suffer damage from unwanted rainfall.[43]

Under the Air Commerce Act of 1926, Congress declared that the United States has "complete and exclusive national sovereignty" over the nation's airspace. This modification of the common-law doctrine of air rights was necessary to permit commercial air navigation without countless trespass suits. "Navigable airspace" is defined by law as that airspace above the minimum safe altitudes of flight prescribed by the Civil Aeronautics Authority. This agency has prescribed minimums of 500 feet during the day and 1,000 feet at night for air carriers together with definite patterns of glide near airports.

The problem of air rights around airfields often gives rise to serious complaints. Zoning regulations and easements can be used to keep individual property owners from erecting high structures that may impede

---

[41] Some of the worst damage from chemical substances has been caused by the sulphur dioxide fumes given off by smelting plants. In a prominent case involving damage from this type of air pollution (*Georgia v. Tennessee Copper Company and Ducktown Sulphur, Copper and Iron Co., Ltd.,* 206 U.S. 230, 1907) the State of Georgia secured an injunction "to enjoin the defendant copper companies from discharging noxious gases, from their works in Tennessee over the plaintiff's territory." The smelter fumes in this case were reported to have injured vegetation as much as 30 miles from the plant. This injunction was vacated by the court in 1937. In a somewhat similar case, damages were collected by property owners in Washington through the International Joint Boundary Commission both in 1932 and 1938 for injuries to crops and forests caused by fumes from a smelter located 9 miles from the international boundary at Trail, British Columbia.

[42] Cf. Huffman, *op. cit.,* pp. 33, 52-53; also Marion Clawson, "Land Use Potentialities of Artificially Induced Precipitation in the Western United States," *Land Economics,* Vol. 28, February, 1952, pp. 54-62.

[43] Cf. Stanley Brooks, "Legal Aspects of Rain Making," *California Law Review,* Vol. 37, March, 1949, pp. 114-21; also Everett J. Olinder and Vincent A. Pepper, "Rain and the Law," *Georgetown Law Journal,* Vol. 39, March, 1951, pp. 466-81.

safe air travel. But what of the property owner's rights? Low-flying planes, an increasing volume of air traffic, ear-splitting take-offs, and the nerve-racking effects of sonic booms are not conducive to the enjoyment of property and may lead to losses in property values. The Supreme Court has recognized this problem and held that property owners can claim damages for actual losses caused by low-flying planes. In a leading case involving a claim for damages on a chicken farm located near an air base, the Court observed that:

> The path of glide for airplanes might reduce a valuable factory site to grazing land, an orchard to a vegetable patch, a residential section to a wheat field. Some value would remain. But the use of the airspace immediately above the land would limit the utility of the land and cause a diminution of its value.
>
> We have said that the airspace is a public highway. Yet it is obvious that if the land owner is to have full enjoyment of the land, he must have exclusive control of the immediate reaches of the enveloping atmosphere. Otherwise buildings could not be erected, trees could not be planted, and even fences cound not be run. The principal is recognized when the law gives a remedy in case overhanging structures are erected on adjoining land. The land owner owns at least as much of the space above the ground as he can occupy or use in connection with the land. . . . The fact that he does not occupy it in a physical sense—by the erection of buildings and the like—is not material. As we have said, the flight of airplanes, which skim the surface but do not touch it, is as much an appropriation of the use of land as a more conventional entry upon it.[44]

Subsurface Rights

Land owners hold rights to the minerals and other materials found beneath the surface of their land as well as to the land surface itself. These surface and subsurface rights are usually held and conveyed together. They can be divided and held separately, however, either by the sale, devising, or leasing of mineral or oil and gas rights to others or by deed reservations that permit owners to sell their surface resources but still retain their subsurface rights. Although complete or partial separation of these rights is a common practice in many areas, it often complicates both the ownership and mortgage credit status of the surface owner. Some states now provide for the separate taxation of subsurface rights when these rights have known economic value.

Most of the problems involving subsurface rights concern either mineral or oil and gas rights. Before passing to these subjects, however, it may be observed that the rights property owners hold in the use of subsurface resources are often conditioned by the rights of other property owners. An owner who plans to excavate his lot, for example, must observe the subjacent rights of adjacent property owners to have such side support as is necessary to keep their properties from caving into the excavated area.

[44]*United States v. Causby,* 328 U.S. 256 (1946).

Mineral rights. Land owners in the United States have a recognized right to mine the minerals found on or under their surface holdings. When mineral rights are held separate from surface rights, the owner of the mineral rights has certain recognized rights or easements over the surface. He can make mineral explorations, sink shafts, and build such roads and railroad tracks over the surface as may be needed to transport supplies to the mine and carry minerals to market. At the same time, the holder of the surface ordinarily has a right to continued support. This means that the mining operations must be carried on in such a way as to prevent the land surface from sinking or collapsing.

Unlike the United States, the governments of many nations reserve mining rights to themselves. This situation prevails in continental Europe, in Mexico, and in South America.[45] Even among the English-speaking countries, royalties representing specified percentage shares of certain minerals were long reserved to the Crown. This practice was carried over in the early land legislation of the United States. The Ordinance of 1785, for example, provided that the federal government should receive one-third of the gold, silver, lead, and copper found in the lands granted from the public domain.

This federal royalty system was not repealed until 1866. It was applied in the Missouri and Upper Mississippi lead regions where it broke down because of lackadaisical enforcement during the 1840's.[46] No effort was made to collect royalties from the gold miners in California. These miners were free to prospect all over the public domain and frequently rushed to new "strikes" in unsettled areas where the public lands had not yet been surveyed for sale. Lacking enforced government regulations, they proceeded to stake out and operate individual claims in accordance with their miners' rules. These rules spread from community to community and usually recognized "that discovery and development of a mine were the foundation of a property right in it."[47] Congress finally legitimized these local mining rules, abolished the royalty system, and opened the public domain for free mining in its mining act of 1866.

At the present time, individuals are free to prospect on the public domain. If they make a strike, they can obtain rights of possession and protection by staking out their claim and reporting it to the proper authorities. Full ownership is granted later after the prospector begins the actual development of his claim.

[45]Cf. Rudolf Isay, "Mining Rights," *Encyclopedia of the Social Sciences* (New York: The Macmillan Company, 1932), Vol. 10, pp. 513-17.

[46]Cf. James E. Wright, *The Galena Lead District: Federal Policy and Practice, 1824-1847* (Madison: State Historical Society of Wisconsin, 1966), and Robert W. Swenson, "Legal Aspects of Mineral Resources Exploitation" in Paul W. Gates, *History of Public Land Law Development* (Washington: U.S. Government Printing Office, 1968), pp. 701-16.

[47]Isay, *loc. cit.,* p. 517.

The scope of the private rights one can hold in minerals has been modified in two important respects by federal legislation. The federal mining law of 1866 gives the owner of a vein or lode of ore extralateral rights—the right to follow his claim beyond the boundaries of his surface ownership—if the vein or lode has its top or apex within the owner's holding. A second modification of far-reaching consequence is contained in the Atomic Energy Act of 1946. This law declares all fissionable material, now or hereafter produced, to be the property of the Atomic Energy Commission. Individuals are encouraged to discover and develop uranium deposits; but the ores discovered and mined must be sold to the Atomic Energy Commission.

Oil and natural gas rights. Rights to oil and natural gas are often treated in much the same way as mineral rights.[48] Like ground waters, oil and natural gas are migratory resources. They ordinarily occur in underground basins that cover substantial areas and underlie numerous ownership holdings. No land owner can be sure how much oil or natural gas underlies his land. And none can prevent these resources from flowing to the ownership of others, particularly when others have drilled deep wells for their capture.

Because of the migratory nature of these deposits, owners of oil and natural gas rights do not acquire title to these resources until they actually capture them. This situation has often put a definite premium on the early tapping and capture of these resources. Land owners who have struck oil have often drilled several offset wells around the borders of their property to insure a maximum take on their part. This practice forces the owners of adjacent properties to either join in the mad scramble for oil or risk the loss of their share of the possible profits. As one might expect, the acceptance of the "rule of capture" has resulted in considerable wasteful competition. Many unneeded wells have been drilled; and these wells in turn have reduced oil reservoir pressures and have contributed to the too-rapid depletion of many petroleum deposits.

All of the leading oil producing states now have conservation laws that prohibit avoidable wastes. These states fix and regulate production quotas for individual wells and thus reduce the underground waste that often results from overly rapid depletion. They can also require 10-, 20-, or 40-acre units as the minimum spacing for new wells. Unitization—the development of a complete oil field by one management under a unified

---

[48]For more detailed discussions of the nature of oil and gas rights cf. L. A. Parcher, John H. Southern, and S. W. Voelker, *Mineral Rights Management by Private Land Owners,* Great Plains Agricultural Council Publication No. 13, Oklahoma Agricultural Experiment Station, 1956; Stanley W. Voelker, *Mineral Rights and Oil Developments in Williams County, North Dakota,* North Dakota Agricultural Experiment Station Bulletin 395, 1954; Howard R. Williams, Richard C. Maxwell, and Charles J. Myers, *Cases and Materials on the Law of Oil and Gas* (Brooklyn: The Foundation Press, Inc., 1956); and Frank J. Trelease *et al., Cases and Materials on Natural Resources Law,* (St. Paul: West Publishing Co., 1965), Parts II and III.

drilling and production program—also has been suggested as a conservation measure. This approach is easily applied only in those cases in which an entire oil field is controlled by one company.

The widescale leasing of oil rights in areas believed to overlay petroleum deposits provides another means by which wasteful competition in the drilling of oil wells can be and often is prevented. Under the leasing approach, the various surface owners who lease their oil rights receive nominal rental payments together with the promise of royalties if petroleum is discovered and pumped on their land. Since the lease rights are usually held by a limited number of oil companies, this system often results in the drilling of fewer wells.

—SELECTED READINGS

Berger, Curtis J., *Land Ownership and Use: Cases, Statutes, and Other Materials* (Boston: Little, Brown and Company, 1968), pp. 113-244.

Ely, Richard T., and George S. Wehrwein, *Land Economics* (Madison: The University of Wisconsin Press, 1964), chap. V. Originally published by The Macmillan Company, 1940.

Fisher, Ernest M., and Robert M. Fisher, *Urban Real Estate* (New York: Henry Holt & Company, Inc., 1954), chap. IV.

Hutchins, Wells A., *Selected Problems in the Law of Water Rights in the West,* U.S. Department of Agriculture Miscellaneous Publication No. 418, 1942.

Kratovil, Robert, *Real Estate Law*, 5th ed. (Englewood Cliffs, N.J.: Prentice-Hall, Inc., 1969).

Ratcliff, Richard U., *Urban Land Economics* (New York: McGraw-Hill Book Company, Inc., 1949), chap. I.

Renne, Roland R., *Land Economics,* 2nd ed. (New York: Harper & Brothers, 1958), chaps. XV-XVI.

13

Acquisition and Transfer of Ownership Rights

Some of our most important land-resource problems stem directly from the arrangements under which people hold and share property rights. These problems provide the subject-matter of *land tenure*—a concept that involves the many relationships established among men that determine their varying rights to control, occupy, and use landed property. Land tenure concerns all of the ways in which people, corporate bodies, and governments share in the bundle of property rights. It is concerned also with the time periods during which these rights are held.

Emphasis is given in this chapter and in the three chapters that follow to four major aspects of land tenure. This chapter deals with the principal problems associated with the acquisition and transfer of ownership rights. Chapter 14 deals with leasing arrangements, chapter 15 with real estate credit problems, and consideration is given in chapter 16 to the techniques of land tenure improvement and land reform. The content of the first three of these chapters relates mostly to the tenure conditions found in the United States and Canada.

ACQUISITION AND MAINTENANCE OF OWNERSHIP

Most people have a strong desire for property ownership, particularly for home ownership. This desire has some basis in human nature. It also is magnified and stimulated by (1) traditional attitudes and sentiments favoring ownership, (2) the cultural approval of society, and (3) the promotional efforts of groups that develop and sell properties.

There is nothing new about this desire for ownership. It was a recognized factor in ancient times. And it has been nutured down through the centuries both by the average man's limited opportunities to own land and by the social status, economic and political power, and other privileges so often identified with the ownership of property.

Much of our strong emotional sentiment favoring farm and home ownership in the United States and Canada can be traced to the attitudes of the land-hungry settlers who helped develop these countries. These settlers agreed with Arthur Young that "the magic of property turns sand to gold" and with Thomas Jefferson that "the small landholders are the most precious part of the state."[1] Their belief in a public policy favoring farm and home ownership was expressed most forceably by Thomas Hart Benton when he declared on the Senate floor that:

> Tenantry is unfavorable to freedom. It lays the foundation for separate orders in society, annihilates the love of country, and weakens the spirit of independence. The tenant has, in fact, no country, no hearth, no domestic altar, no household god. The freeholder, on the contrary, is the natural supporter of a free government, and it should be the policy of republics to multiply their freeholders as it is the policy of monarchies to multiply tenants.[2]

This sentiment favoring farm and home ownership has had a marked effect upon the nation's land policies, and it has become a part of our accepted political philosophy. Land ownership has long since lost much of its identity with social, economic, and political privilege; and in many cases it must now be justified on sentimental rather than economic grounds. Yet we still endorse the ideas of home ownership, family owner-operatorship of farms, and a wide dispersion of ownership rights as high-priority goals in public policy. And we still look somewhat askance at anyone who dares to question the desirability of the ownership ideal.

With the ownership goal playing the important role it does, the strategic question in many minds is not so much "should I become an owner" as rather "how can I become an owner" and "what problems will I encounter in maintaining my ownership rights once I acquire them." Emphasis will be given here to four land ownership issues: (1) acquisition of land titles, (2) roads to ownership, (3) costs of land ownership, and (4) risks to successful ownership.

[1] Thomas Jefferson, *Writings* (Monticello edition; Washington, 1904), Vol. 9, p. 18.

[2] Congressional Debates, May, 1926. Reported in *Abridgment of the Debates of Congress from 1789 to 1856* (New York: D. Appleton and Company, 1858), Vol. 8, p. 568.

Acquisition of Land Titles

Two distinctly different types of problems usually arise in the ownership acquisition process. Prospective owners must take the steps necessary to acquire legal titles of ownership; and, in most instances, they must also concern themselves with the age-old problem of securing sufficient capital and financial backing to establish themselves as owners. The first of these problems ordinarily begins with one's choice of a method of acquisition and thereafter concerns his problem in getting a clear and merchantable title to the property whose ownership he claims.

Methods of acquisition. Land ownership can be acquired in any of several different ways. Among these alternative methods one might list: (1) patents or grants from the government, (2) private grants by deed, (3) grants by devise, (4) acquisition under the laws of descent, (5) dedication, (6) eminent domain, (7) forfeiture, (8) adverse possession, (9) accretion, and (10) escheat.

Very little land ownership is now acquired by *government patent.* This method of acquisition has been very important in times past, however, because every land title in the United States and Canada can supposedly be traced back through an unbroken chain of ownerships to an official grant of title from the government or the Crown. Most of these patents were originally acquired through grants to royal favorites; through purchase at a public sale; or through homestead, military bounty, or railroad and other public-improvement grants. This initial public ownership can in turn be traced back through various purchase and treaty arrangements to the ownership claims various European sovereigns asserted to portions of the New World by right of discovery and to the actions of the American and Canadian governments in extinguishing the claims of the original Indian population.

Most landed properties now pass from owner to owner by the private grant of a deed. The *deed* in this case represents a properly drafted written statement by which an owner conveys or transfers the rights he has in a given tract of land to someone else. Deeds are usually granted because of the sale of properties. They may also be granted as a gift or as part of a trade.

Real property is often acquired through inheritance. This process usually takes one of two forms. If the deceased leaves a valid and effective will, he is said to die *testate,* and his real property passes by *devise* to his designated heirs. When no valid will is known to exist, the deceased is said to die *intestate* and his estate is divided according to the *laws of descent.* The over-all importance of inheritance as a method of ownership acquisition in the United States is suggested by a recent report on methods of farm real estate transfers.[3] Between 19.8 and 34.6 farms per 1,000 (16 to

[3] *Farm Real Estate Market Developments* (Washington: Economic Research Service, U. S. Department of Agriculture CD-73, August, 1969), p. 21.

22 percent of the total number of transfers) were transferred each year through estate settlement procedures in the 1960-69 decade while numerous additional properties were transferred by gift and other inheritance arrangements.

The process of *dedication* represents one of the less frequently used methods of ownership acquisition. This process takes place when a private land owner makes specified areas available for public use. Dedication may result from an owner's unrecorded offer and the public acceptance and use of a tract for a park, street, or some similar use; or it may result from an official statement dedicating the area to public use. Official statements dedicating specified areas for streets, alleys, and other public uses are found in most subdivision plat recordings. These dedications do not become final until they are officially accepted by the units of government that must bear the responsibility of administering and maintaining these uses.

Lands needed for public purposes can also be acquired under the power of *eminent domain.* This power to acquire needed sites by condemnation is limited to public, quasi-public, and certain specified private agencies and groups. Its use is limited to the acquisition of lands for public purposes; and reasonable compensation must ordinarily be paid for the lands taken.

Landed property is occasionally acquired by *forfeiture,* either through mortgage foreclosure proceedings or through reversion to some unit of government for nonpayment of taxes. Most of the properties lost through forfeiture are offered for purchase at a public mortgage foreclosure or tax sale. The highest bidders at these sales usually receive either a deed for the properties they buy or a certificate of deed, which can be converted into a deed if the forfeiting owner does not redeem his ownership within a specified redemption period. Some states, however, have mortgage foreclosure arrangements that permit mortgagees to take title to delinquent properties without public sale. Several also have legislation that permits the automatic bidding off of tax titles to the state or county at the time of tax sale.

In spite of our great faith in recorded titles, rights can be transferred through an important though seldom-used property acquisition method known as *prescription* or *adverse possession.* This method permits one to acquire specific rights in a property or even the title itself if he makes continuous use of the property in an open and visible manner, without the owner's expressed permission, while always claiming his right of use or ownership throughout the prescriptive period set by law. Many instances of acquisition by adverse possession involve specific interests such as the right to drain water or use a road across some other person's land. But this method also permits one to acquire title to unused or abandoned lands and to clear possible clouds against one's title. Most states require that a use continue for periods of 15 or 20 years before one can acquire title by adverse possession. Periods of as little as 5 or 7 years are permitted in some states when this process is used to remove color of title.

Ownership rights can be acquired by *accretion* in two different ways. A common example occurs when a property bounded by a watercourse has surface land added to it by action of the stream. A second type of accretion occurs when a house or some other improvement is added to one's land without his consent. If a house is built on one's lot by mistake, the land owner acquires title by accretion and is under no obligation to pay its cost of construction. A final method of property acquisition known as *escheat* involves the reversion of estates to the state whenever a person dies intestate without any known heirs who are eligible to receive the property under the laws of descent.

Need for a clear title. Regardless of how one acquires ownership rights, he naturally wants and expects security in his continued possession and exercise of these rights. To secure this end, the new owner should always make sure that he secures clear title to his property and that he follows the proper procedures in registering his evidence of ownership. Since deeds are used in most property transfers, this means that the average owner should make certain that he receives a valid deed, that the deed is duly recorded, and that the grantor is able to convey all the expected rights and privileges of ownership.[4]

The requirements of a valid deed vary somewhat from state to state. As a rule, a valid deed contains the name of the grantor (who must be a competent person), the name of the grantee, a recital of the consideration given for the property, a legal description of the property, a statement of conveyance, and the signature of the grantor.[5] In addition, it may also contain the date of transfer, the addresses or some other identification of the grantor and grantee, a warranty of title, statements concerning outstanding mortgages and other encumbrances, a statement of possible restrictions and conditions, a waiver of dower and homestead rights,

---

[4]In this respect, it should be noted that deeds can be classified into four different types according to the rights they convey. A *warranty deed* contains covenants of title guaranteeing the conveyance of a clear title that is unencumbered except for those claims specifically stated in the deed. Should any of these covenants be violated by the later discovery of claims against the title, the grantor can be held liable for damages. Under a *special warranty deed,* the grantor assumes less risk because he covenants the title only against the lawful claims of persons who have claims arising during his period of ownership. A third type of deed known as a *bargain and sale deed* conveys land without any warranty of title. Still another type, known as a *quitclaim deed,* is used to convey whatever interest a grantor may have in land rather than the land itself. Quitclaim deeds are frequently used to clear up possible claims against titles.

[5]Cf. Robert Kratovil, *Real Estate Law,* 5th ed. (Englewood Cliffs, N.J.: Prentice-Hall, Inc., 1969), chap. VII. The recital of consideration ordinarily lists the actual sales price when the property is conveyed by a corporation, trustee, or executor. In cases of transfers between individuals, the amount of the sales price is usually cloaked by some phrase such as "one dollar and other valuable considerations." The requirement that there be a recital of consideration does not prevent an owner from giving his property to another. A gift or sale for a nominal consideration can be invalidated, however, if it can be shown that this means of disposal was used to prevent satisfaction of the claims of a grantor's creditors.

signatures of witnesses, an official acknowledgement by the grantor before a notary public or other public official, the grantor's official seal, and revenue stamps.

Once a deed is prepared, it must be delivered to the grantee (usually during the lifetime of the grantor) and be accepted by him before it becomes valid. This action makes the transfer of ownership effective as far as the two parties to the deed are concerned. The deed remains ineffective, in several states, insofar as it may involve subsequent purchasers and mortgagees of the same land, until it is recorded and becomes a matter of official record. The new owner can accomplish this process simply by depositing his deed with the public recorder or register of deeds. This official makes a copy of the deed for his record books, indexes it, and returns the original deed to the grantee or his agent.

Possession of a valid deed or other legal instruments showing conveyance of ownership gives an owner evidence of title.[6] Yet this does not necessarily mean that the owner has a clear or merchantable title. For one to have a clear or merchantable title, he must acquire and still possess all the property rights he claims; and he must be able to support these claims with legal evidence of the extinction or severance of the interests previous owners and others have held in the property.

One is said to have a perfect title when he can show that each item in the chain of legal actions involving his property going back to the time of its original patent from the government has been properly handled and recorded without error. Titles of this type are a rarity in most older settled areas. Somewhere in its history, almost every title involves some minor errors or defects such as a faulty or incomplete property description, a wife's failure to waive her dower interest, or an owner's failure to register the release of a mortgage. These defects can usually be cleared by reasonable interpretation or by use of affidavits and quitclaim deeds to provide a merchantable title. Titles involving minor errors or omissions are usually regarded as imperfect and should be cleared before they are transferred even though they can often be accepted with little risk to the grantee.

Titles with major errors or omissions are usually described as

---

[6] Official evidences of ownership are also needed with most properties acquired by methods other than the granting of a deed. A homesteader on the public domain needs his patent of ownership from the government before he can fully exercise the rights of ownership. The rights of heirs operating an unsettled estate are often in doubt until the estate is probated and an official determination of heirs is made. Specified procedures and official records are necessary when a unit of government acquires land ownership by eminent domain, tax reversion, or escheat or when a mortgagee acquires property by foreclosure. Rights acquired by adverse possession must be legally recognized and recorded in the owner's name before they can be transferred to others. Private dedications of land areas for public use should be made a matter of public record even though this is not strictly necessary. No legal action or recording is needed for properties acquired by accretion because the property objects acquired are always within one's property boundaries.

incomplete, defective, or bad. These titles can usually be redeemed with some time, expense, and litigation. The cost of this process and the possible claims others may have against the title, however, make it prudent policy for buyers to refuse to accept these titles until the necessary steps have been taken to make them merchantable.

Title examinations. Since very few buyers or sellers have the training needed to examine and vouch for the merchantable nature of their land titles, it is usual practice to enlist the services of an attorney for this purpose. In his title examination, the attorney reviews all the legal entries of record involving the property and renders an opinion as to validity of title.

The title examination process ordinarily involves the preparation of an *abstract of title* by the lawyer, some public official, or a private abstracting company. This abstract represents a chronological summary of all the recorded legal actions—data on deeds, wills, mortgages, liens, judgments, foreclosure proceedings, tax sales, and so on—that affect one's title to property. An abstract provides no guarantee of title. But it does provide a condensed history of the legal actions affecting a property, which will usually disclose any errors or omissions in the official records that could cloud the title.

In his examination of an abstract (or of the various legal entries of record covered by abstracts), a lawyer will sometimes check every item back to the original patent from the government.[7] On other occasions, he may limit his study to those entries of record made since some prior title examination. Following this examination, the lawyer prepares a statement known as a *title opinion* (or in some states as a certificate of title) in which he indicates that he has examined the title and that he believes it to be merchantable or not merchantable. In the latter event, the opinion often goes on to list specific errors, omissions, or other factors that cloud the title.

Even under ideal conditions, a title search will sometimes fail to disclose hidden defects such as a forged signature on a deed or a grantor's minority, possible insanity, or his failure to indicate that he was married. This means that one often assumes some risks even when he has a title examination. This situation, together with the normal costs of clearing title and the tendency of some attorneys to indulge in a practice known as "flyspecking" (the raising of numerous technical objections to details that would ordinarily pass as merchantable), has caused many buyers to look to other means for guaranteeing their titles. The two most important of these involve the use of title insurance and registration under the Torrens system.

[7] Some states have simplified this process by enacting marketable title statutes, which invalidate old claims after a specified time period. These laws make it unnecessary for the title examiner to go back more than the specified number of years (40 years under the Michigan law).

Title insurance. Title insurance is now available in most cities and in many rural areas. The companies that offer this insurance naturally refuse to insure bad titles; but they will often disregard many of the technical objections that could be raised by an attorney examining an abstract. Before giving a title policy, these companies always make a title check; and if they find no serious defects in the title, they will usually issue insurance, which guarantees the owner's title against possible defects or claims up to some specified policy value. Under these policies, the insurance company agrees to defend at its own expense any lawsuits attacking the validity of the title and to reimburse the owner up to the amount of his policy if he should be ejected from his ownership.

Unlike most other insurance, a title insurance policy involves a flat fee that protects the owner for his full period of ownership. Title insurance policies vary in their details depending upon the issuing company. Policies are not ordinarily transferable. They apply only to defects of title that exist on or prior to the date of the policy. And they usually involve exceptions and conditions that limit the company's liability. Title insurance is widely used in many cities—partly because of the protection it gives and partly because it is required by numerous real estate credit lending agencies.

The Torrens System of Title Registration. As an alternative to our usual system of land titles, several jurisdictions use the so-called Torrens system of title registration. This system calls for the updating of land titles, the creation of indefeasible titles warranted and guaranteed by the state, the official registration of land titles rather than the registration of mere evidences of title, and the eventual elimination of the time-consuming and frequently expensive practice of clearing land titles. To get his title registered, a land owner must first file an application for this purpose together with a complete abstract of title for his property with the proper public official. An examination is made of his title, and official notices are sent to all persons who appear to have any interest in the property, advising them of the owner's action and of their right to contest the owner's claim to title. Special court proceedings are then conducted to establish the validity of title.

If the court finds the title defective, it naturally refuses to take further action until the title is cleared. If it finds that the owner has an acceptable title, it issues him a certificate of title and orders his title registered in an official record. This registered title is warranted by the state and is considered indefeasible in the sense that it cannot be nullified by possible past claims against the title. For this service, the owner must pay a fee that covers the cost of establishing his title plus a contribution to an indemnity fund, which is set up to pay off possible future claims for damages.

Once the title has been registered, all future deeds, mortgages, and other legal actions involving the property must be noted on an official registration sheet maintained for the property; and changes in title can come only with the issuance of new certificates of ownership. With this procedure, a search of title becomes unnecessary, and future transfers can be made speedily at a nominal cost.

The Torrens system was first used in South Australia in 1858 and has since been accepted in many countries throughout the world. Nineteen states have authorized its use on a permissive basis. Between the high initial cost of title registration and the provision for permissive or voluntary use, however, this system has never been used on more than a limited scale in the United States. Most proponents of the Torrens system argue that it has never been given a fair trial in this country and that its full benefits can be realized only with a mandatory system of title registration. The chief arguments against its acceptance stem from the cumbersome and expensive nature of the initial registration process, the vested interests some individuals and groups have in the present system, and the general reluctance of people to change to a new way of doing things.[8]

Roads to Ownership

While prospective owners are always concerned with the problem of acquiring a good title, they must also consider their individual problems in securing the necessary capital they need to acquire ownership. Some people acquire ownership or the money they need to establish themselves as owners through gifts, inheritance, or marriage. These roads to ownership have obvious advantages for their beneficiaries. Unfortunately, however, these routes are not open to most prospective owners. Instead of pursuing this route, most would-be owners find that they must follow a more arduous path as they save and accumulate the capital they need for their later purchase of homes and other properties.

Except for those individuals who enjoy the help and financial assistance of others, most would-be owners start at the bottom of the economic heap with little more than their education and their ability and willingness to work. Yet as long as they apply themselves in their work, they can usually start their capital accumulation process simply by saving and investing part of their income. With a prudent investment policy, these savings will gradually increase so that they will eventually provide the capital resources needed for ownership.

Many operators use the savings they have accumulated, together with the experience and know-how they have picked up, to branch out into

[8]For more detailed discussions of the Torrens system, cf. *Urban Planning and Land Policies,* Vol. 2 of the Supplementary Report of the Urbanism Committee to the National Resources Committee, Washington, 1939, pp. 245-47; Henry E. Hoagland, *Real Estate Principles* (New York: McGraw-Hill Book Company, 1940), pp. 55-57; and Arnold G. Cameron, *The Torrens System* (New York: Houghton Mifflin Company, 1915).

business for themselves. By showing wisdom and skill in the management of their own resources as well as with the resources that they rent, borrow, and hire from others, these operators often find that they can increase their productivity and with it their supplies of capital. With this improvement in their economic status, they then find it possible to go on to ownership and to even larger business undertakings.

This concept of a young person starting at the bottom and gradually working his way to the attainment of his goal has its roots deep in American tradition. As a road to ownership, it smacks of Horatio Alger and suggests opportunities for economic advancement unknown in many parts of the world. Yet it represents the time-honored approach used by millions of farm and home owners in the United States and Canada.

The agricultural ladder. Our traditional ownership acquisition process is typified in the concept of the *agricultural ladder*. This ladder has four basic rungs representing time spent as (1) a youth or unpaid laborer on the parent's home farm, (2) a hired man working on a farm, (3) a renter or tenant operating a farm, and (4) an owner-operator of a farm. Two additional rungs may also be listed for time spent as a worker in nonfarm employment and for those operators who retire or "retreat" from owner-operatorship to a landlord status. For discussion purposes, these rungs can be represented by the symbols P, H, R, O, N, and L, respectively. As visualized by the writers who first used this concept, any farmer who had P-H-R-O experience was said to have climbed the full agricultural ladder, and any owner with experience on at least two of these four rungs qualified as a ladder climber.

It was a common observation during the first two decades of the present century that almost every farm owner had climbed the agricultural ladder. A study of a large sample of Midwestern farm owners at the end of World War I, for example, indicated that 21 percent of the owners had climbed a P-H-R-O ladder while 13 percent had P-H-O, 32 percent P-R-O, and 34 percent P-O experience.[9]

Depressed agricultural business conditions during the 1920s and 1930s slowed down most of the operators who were climbing the ladder and in many instances caused them to slip back down the ladder rather than continue their upward climb. This situation caused many people to raise questions concerning the possible breakdown of the ladder concept. Analysis of the tenure experiences reported in the national farm land ownership survey in the United States in 1946, however, shows that 86 percent of the farm owners had climbed the agricultural ladder—31 percent by using at least three of the P-H-R-O rungs, 10 percent by working as hired men or renters before becoming owners, and 45 percent with P-O or P-N-O records.[10]

[9] Cf. W. J. Spillman, "The Agricultural Ladder," *American Economic Review, Supplement*, Vol. 9, March, 1919, pp. 170-79.

[10] Cf. Buis T. Inman and W. H. Fippen, *Farm Land Ownership in the United States,*

As these survey findings suggest, many farm operators still use an agricultural ladder in their climb to ownership. Numerous prospective farm owners now look, however, to a period of nonfarm employment for some of the capital they need to get themselves established in farming. Many also are climbing a new ladder, which operates within the framework of the farm family.[11] This ladder usually starts with a 4-H Club or Future Farmer project on the home farm and then progresses through a father-son partnership arrangement to an intrafamily transfer of the farm from father to son.

A road-to-ownership concept comparable to the agricultural ladder can also be visualized in cases of nonfarm home and business ownership. With home ownership, for example, the average young worker starts as a member of his parent's household. When he starts to work he often pays room rent at home or moves to a rented room. With marriage or an increase in income, he ordinarily moves to an apartment or possibly a rented house. Then as he becomes better established in his job or in the business world and as he acquires a family, he usually follows most of his fellow citizens in the common practice of buying a home. Years later after his children have grown up and left home, he and his wife often rent out their extra rooms; or they may even sell or rent their house while they retreat back to an apartment where they can shift the problems of upkeep and maintenance to someone else.

Public policies to implement ownership. Although would-be owners must usually take the initiative if they are to acquire ownership, public policies often play an important role in implementing their attainment of this goal. The United States and Canada have both used a variety of public land disposal policies involving low sale prices and the granting of preemption, homesteading, and other rights to facilitate the shifting of land from public to private owner-operatorship. With the disposal of their better lands, these nations have turned to other programs, including the reclamation of new lands, encouragement of residential construction, and the provision of additional credit facilities for prospective home owners, farmers, and businessmen, that further facilitate the attainment of private ownership.[12] They have also used mortgage moratoria, mortgage refinancing arrangements, submarginal land purchase measures, rehabilitation grants, and resettlement programs to help disadvantaged operators establish or reestablish themselves.

U.S. Department of Agriculture Miscellaneous Publication 699, Washington, 1949, Appendix Table 40; also Raleigh Barlowe and John F. Timmons, "What Has Happened to the Agricultural Ladder?" *Journal of Farm Economics*, Vol. 32, February, 1950, p. 40.

[11] Cf. Marshall Harris, "A New Agricultural Ladder," *Land Economics*, Vol. 26, August, 1950, pp. 258-67.

[12] These policies are discussed in Chapter 16 along with several other measures designed to implement better land use and land reform.

Costs of Land Ownership

When one discusses the costs of land ownership, it is natural to think in terms of the purchase cost of acquiring property. This cost represents only one element in the over-all cost picture. Yet it frequently constitutes the most important single hurdle in the ownership acquisition process.

The purchase price or market value associated with any given piece of property always depends upon the characteristics of the property, its location, and the supply and demand situation at the time of sale. Other things being equal, an eight-room house will cost more than a five-room house; and a 200-acre farm will cost more than a farm of 120 acres. In like manner, a house located in or near a large city will ordinarily have a higher sales value than a house of the same design in a small village; and farm land located near a good market will sell for more than comparable land at a more remote location.

Time of purchase is also important because properties normally command somewhat higher prices during periods of business prosperity than during depressions. The nature and significance of these shifts in market value can best be illustrated by examples based on the national indices of farm and residential real estate prices. (*cf.* Figures, 10-2 and 10-4, pp. 340 and 344.) An average farm valued at $10,000 in 1912 was worth $17,520 in 1920 but only $7,520 in 1933 and then increased to a value of $8,720 in 1940, $17,780 in 1950, $30,381 in 1960, and $50,908 in 1970. Meanwhile, a residence that could have been built for $5,400 in 1914, would have cost $10,000 in 1920, $6,700 in 1932, $8,500 in 1940, $17,600 in 1950, $22,200 in 1960, and $30,600 in 1970.

Fortunately for the average buyer, it is not necessary for one to save or otherwise accumulate the entire purchase price of a property before he can become an owner. Credit arrangements make it possible for buyers to acquire ownership with minimum down payments ranging from practically nothing with some veteran housing loans up to 50 percent or more of the purchase price of many properties. This use of credit definitely opens the door of ownership to many people who could not otherwise afford to buy properties of their own. At the same time, it merely shifts a portion of the buyer's cost problem from the present to the future. In this sense, it complicates the new owner's problem of maintaining his property rights by adding a debt servicing cost to his normal maintenance and operating costs.

In addition to the capital investment outlay—the buyer's down payment plus his periodic payments of principal under his credit arrangement—needed for property ownership, owners also bear a number of direct ownership costs. The buyer who uses real estate credit can itemize these costs as follows: (1) fees for securing mortgage credit; (2) debt servicing costs; (3) allowance of interest on his equity in the total value of the property; (4) taxes and special assessments; (5) fire and other property insurance; (6) repair and maintenance costs; (7) allowances for depreciation and obsolescence; and (8) a charge for other items such as utilities, fuel, and yard work, which the buyer may or may not have paid as a tenant.

These costs vary considerably depending upon individual circumstances. If the buyer can secure mortgage credit from a private lender or local lending agency, his cost of obtaining credit may be limited to a nominal charge for the preparation and filing of the mortgage. On the other hand, if he deals through a mortgage broker, he will normally pay a fee—often paid in the form of a discount of "points" from the face value of his mortgage—for the broker's service in placing his mortgage. In addition, the lending agency will usually require a series of charges for a property appraisal and survey, a title examination, title insurance, and the preparation and filing of the mortgage. Taken together, these charges for securing credit often add between 2 and 15 percent to the actual purchase cost of ownership.[13]

Debt service charges vary according to the size of one's mortgage, the interest rate, the length of the repayment period, and the amortization provisions. Most real estate loans in 1970 were financed at interest rates ranging from 8 to 9 percent and were amortized over periods ranging from 10 to 30 years with the requirement of monthly payments on residential loans and annual or semiannual payments on farm loans.[14] Even with lower interest rates, debt service charges can represent a substantial cost of ownership. With a standard amortization plan and a 6 percent interest rate, a borrower pays $1,719.36 in principal and interest for every $1,000 borrowed and repaid over a 20-year period and $2,158.56 for every $1,000 borrowed and repaid over a 30-year period. With a 7½

---

[13] Mortgage placement fees vary over a wide range depending upon one's choice of a broker, the supply and demand situation with mortgage money, and the difficulties the broker may encounter in placing a mortgage. Typical placement fees in 1970 ranged from 3 to 12 percent of the amount of the mortgage with most home buyers paying in the 4 to 7 percent range. The Federal Housing Administration reported average incidental costs of $428 and an average purchase price of $19,568 with the new housing units covered with its mortgage insurance in 1968 and an average incidental cost of $370 and purchase price of $16,106 with existing units.

[14] With the typical amortized loan, the borrower commits himself to the periodic payment of a series of set sums, a portion of each payment is used to pay current interest charges, and steadily increasing portions of the periodic payments are credited as payments on the principal of the loan. The mortgage interest rates applied with these loans vary with the lending agency, the locality, and the time when the loan is granted. Typical house and farm purchase loans called for interest payments in the 4 to 5 percent range around 1950. A general shortage of real estate mortgage investment funds relative to current demands prompted an increase in average rates to the 8 and 9 percent level for housing and 10 or more percent for some commercial loans in 1970. Mortgage interest rates started to decline from these high levels in late 1970 when several leading banks announced reductions in their prime interest rates.

percent rate, these payments rise to $1,934.44 over a 20-year period and $2,517.12 over a 30-year period.

Owners frequently fail to consider the opportunity costs associated with the equity values they hold in the properties they own. From an economic standpoint, however, one should always assign an ownership cost to the income he could receive if he had his money invested in some alternative enterprise. The interest rate applied in calculating this cost varies with one's alternative investment opportunities. As a bare minimum, one should allow himself a rate of return at least equal to the interest rate he could receive if his funds were invested in a savings account or in government bonds.

Property taxes and special assessments vary from year to year and from community to community. On an annual basis, these costs ordinarily range between 1 and 3½ percent of the property's value. Fire and other property insurance costs also vary somewhat but ordinarily range from one-eighth to one-half of 1 percent of the insured value of the property each year.

Wide variations also apply with repair and maintenance costs. These costs are usually lower with new sets of buildings than with older structures; and they are always higher in some years when one installs a new furnace or puts on a new roof than in years when no major repairs are made. Year in and year out, an owner of a relatively new property should allow around 1 to 1½ percent of the value of his buildings and improvements for repairs and maintenance costs. Owners of older properties should raise this annual cost outlay to sums representing 2 to 2½ percent of the value of their buildings.[15]

Since the buildings and improvements associated with land ownership tend to deteriorate with passing time, allowances must also be made for their depreciation and eventual replacement. This charge varies somewhat with the quality of the original structure, the wear and tear it receives, and the owner's policy in caring for his property. A depreciation charge of from 1½ to 3 percent of the value of buildings and other improvements should be allowed each year unless offset by expenditures for improvements and property renewal. In many instances, a charge for obsolescence should also be listed among the costs of ownership. This cost is particularly important whenever a property's value declines because of neighborhood blight or because of the effect of changing tastes and new technology in outdating older structures.

A final group of ownership costs involves a miscellaneous assortment of expenditures that a prospective owner may or may not have paid as a tenant. Tenants living in urban apartments often find their charges for electricity, gas, heat, water, and garbage and trash disposal included in their rents. They also benefit from the yard work and janitorial services

---

[15] Cf. John P. Dean, *Home Ownership: Is It Sound?* (New York: Harper & Brothers, 1945), p. 112.

normally provided by the management. The costs associated with these services represent a significant item in most household budgets. Buyers who fail to reckon with the importance of these costs at the time they make their ownership commitment often end up with unbalanced household budgets and with a more healthy regard for the costs of ownership.

Investment alternatives. Once an operator visualizes the costs of property ownership, he will often ask himself: Is it really wise for me to become an owner? His answer to this question is often influenced by sentimental considerations—by his desire to own, to please his family, to free himself from dependence upon a landlord, and by the extent to which he views property ownership as a consumption expenditure rather than as a production investment. When the operator is production-minded and thinks in economic terms, he will carefully evaluate his investment alternatives and weigh his expected costs of ownership against the costs he would encounter as a nonowner.

When he considers his alternative investment opportunities, the operator often finds that he can realize a higher economic return by using his available capital for some purpose other than the acquisition of ownership. Farm tenants in areas of high land values, for example, often find that it is more profitable for them to invest their savings in machinery and livestock than to invest in land.[16] Operators of grocery stores, ready-to-wear shops, and other businesses often covet their mobility as tenants and argue that it is far better for them to use their capital to expand their scales of operation than it would be to purchase their sites of business. Businessmen with limited capital resources frequently find that they can use their capital savings to better advantage in their business operations than to purchase a home. In a similar vein, many wage and salary workers have found that they would rather live as tenants and invest their capital resources in other enterprises than use them to acquire ownership.

In contrast to this situation, property ownership often represents a wise investment for the prospective owner. If the buyer expects to become an owner anyway, he can often benefit by acquiring the rights of ownership now rather than later. With liberal use of credit, he can acquire ownership with a relatively small down payment and build up his equity with payments not greatly different from rent. If he finds it hard to save money, he will sometimes benefit from the system of forced savings dictated by his mortgage or land contract payment schedule. By investing in his own home or business, he can pamper his investment along. And he

---

[16]These operators feel that they can make more money as well equipped renters on highly productive farms than as the owner-operators of the smaller or less productive units they could afford to buy. Many tenants and part-owners in areas of extensive farming operations also prefer to invest in machinery and sometimes in livestock they can use and move over large rented areas rather than operate as full owners on smaller farms. Cf. T. W. Schultz, "Capital Rationing, Uncertainty, and Farm Tenancy Reform," *Journal of Political Economy*, Vol. 48, June, 1940, pp. 309-24.

can treat it as a personal "savings bank," which he can convert into cash at some future date through the mortgaging, sale, or leasing of his interests.

To buy or not to buy. Prospective buyers usually find it wise policy to carefully evaluate and compare the costs and advantages associated with their ownership and renting alternatives. Like the prospective investor who weighs the estimated benefits and costs associated with his alternative investment opportunities, business operators should compare the economic opportunities available to them as owners and as tenants. An operator should not plan to buy his site of business operations unless it offers him economic opportunities at least as good as those he could enjoy as a tenant. In similar fashion, prospective buyers of residential properties should carefully evaluate and compare the expected economic benefits and costs as well as the consumer satisfactions associated with their opportunities for buying and renting.

To illustrate the economic cost portion of this evaluation process, one might assume the cost comparisons of a prospective home owner who now rents an unfurnished apartment for $225 a month, no utilities included. He has an income of $12,000 a year, anticipates no marked increase or decrease in his income in the near future, and has $10,400 in a Building and Loan Association savings account drawing 5½ percent interest. His present apartment is adequate for his present needs and he enjoys security of tenure; but he feels that he would like to own his own home. He finds a house he likes, which he can buy for $25,000 plus an estimated $400 for closing costs. He can borrow the additional money he needs at 7 percent interest. The house he is interested in is 15 years old and is in good condition; but it will need repairs in the future.

With this combination of circumstances, the operator will find that his initial costs of ownership include his outlay of $400 for closing costs plus any payments he makes for repairs or changes in the house before he moves into it. His probable future costs of ownership can be visualized as in Table 13-1. When his expected future annual costs of ownership are compared with his current annual charge of $2,700 for apartment rent, it appears that the prospective buyer may save money by remaining as a tenant. A stronger case for buying can be made when consideration is given to the incentives for ownership provided by the federal system of income taxation. An even better case exists if one assumes continued inflation with appreciation of property values at rates such as those experienced between 1950 and 1970 (cf. Table 10-2) along with rising contract rental rates. Should the operator not like his landlord, want to move to the suburbs or to a more prestigious address, feel that the house offers more living space or satisfactions than his apartment, or contemplate an increase in residential property values, he will have other good reasons for favoring ownership. On the other hand, if his job makes him subject to transfer at any time, if the decision to buy entails a longer ride to work or requires the purchase and operation of an additional automobile, if he contemplates a decline in housing prices, if he wants a 7 percent return on

TABLE 13-1. Hypothetical Example Illustrating Costs of Owning a Residential Property in the First and Twenty-First Year after Purchase*

Cost item and rate of charge	1st year after purchase	21st year after purchase
Debt service (decreasing from one-twelfth of 7 percent of $15,000 in first month to nothing in 21st year)	$1,039	None
Property taxes (decreasing from 2.5 percent of $25,000 in first year to $20,000 assumed assessed value in 21st year)	625	$500
Property insurance (0.2 percent of $21,000)	42	42
Repairs and maintenance (rising from 2.0 percent of $21,000 in first year to 2.5 percent in 21st year)	420	525
Total cash outlay for ownership	$2,126	$1,067
Depreciation (computed at a straight 2 percent of $21,000 annually)	420	420
Interest on owner's equity in total investment (increasing from 5.5 percent of $10,400 in first year to 5.5 percent of $25,400 in 21st year)	572	1,397
	$3,118	$2,884
Federal income tax benefits**		
Savings from owner's option of itemizing portion of his property taxes and interest payments that exceed his standard deduction limit of $1,800 (19 percent of itemized deductions)	0 - 316	0 - 95
Savings from exemption of interest on equity in property from income taxation (19 percent of 5.5 percent of $10,400 in first year and 5.5 percent of $25,400 in 21st year)	105	261
Total income tax benefits	$105 - 421	$261 - 356
Net cost of home ownership	$2,697 - $3,013	$2,528 - $2,623

*Example assumes a husband and wife and two children with a family income of $12,000 annually, $10,400 in savings invested at 5.5 percent interest, and living as tenants in a house that rents for $240 a month. The house they are considering is 15 years old, is generally comparable with their present house, and can be purchased for $25,000 plus $400 in closing and incidental costs. They can borrow $15,000 at 7 percent interest on a 20 year amortized loan. Their payments will come to $116.30 a month and will total $27,911 in 20 years.

**Income tax example assumes the personal exemptions of $750 per person and the standard deduction limit of 15 percent of the total family income (maximum of $2,000) which become effective in 1973 under the Tax Reform Act of 1969. Under the tax rate scheduled in effect in 1970, the family is in the 19 percent tax bracket (pays 19 percent of the last increments of its income as federal income taxes).

his equity funds or charges 3 percent for depreciation and obsolescence, or if he had only $2,000 in savings, he might logically consider it best to remain as a tenant.

No blanket conclusions can be drawn from this example because the costs of ownership and renting vary widely from case to case and from area to area. But this cost-comparison approach does provide a means that would-be owners can use to maximize their interests. Before one takes these calculations too seriously, however, it should be noted that they are far from infallible. Their failure to fathom the uncertainties of future price, cost, and income trends often leads to plausible but still inaccurate conclusions. In this sense, one must agree with Ratcliff that:

> Whether or not the purchase of a home in a given case is or is not a "good investment" cannot finally be determined until the investment is liquidated or shifted by sale. Not until the end of the ownership is it possible to make a full accounting. If the home were purchased when prices were depressed and sold during inflation or even in a normal market, the result would be favorable. If conditions were reversed, so would be the result.[17]

At the same time it must also be recognized that most people are prone to accept less space and fewer facilities in the properties they rent than they look for in the houses they buy. Buyers frequently upgrade their housing standards when they acquire ownership. They tend to buy homes more for the community status, feeling of independence, and other satisfactions they expect to secure than for strictly economic investment purposes. Viewed in this context, one can justify an extra expenditure on a home in much the same way that he justifies the sums he spends for other consumer goods such as theater tickets, a television set, a flashy sports car, or a mink coat for his wife.

Risks to Successful Ownership

Once one has acquired ownership, he has the problem of maintaining his ownership rights. His success in this regard is conditioned by the supply of capital and human resources he has at his command, by the ability he shows in managing these resources, and by his exposure to various risk factors.

No attempt will be made here to discuss the problems of business management. It may be noted in passing though that those operators who have the resources and managerial skill they need to make productive use of their business sites ordinarily have little trouble in maintaining their ownership status. Similarly, those owners who have adequate sources of outside income to pay for their homes also experience little difficulty in this regard. Serious problems often arise, however, when an owner tries to operate on a "shoestring" basis with too little capital, when his income is inadequate to meet his costs of ownership, when his ownership equity is reduced or wiped out by an unexpected decline in property values, or when his operations are adversely affected by personal or family factors.

---

[17]Richard U. Ratcliff, *Urban Land Economics* (New York: McGraw-Hill Book Company, Inc., 1949), p. 109.

Risks involving overcommitments. Some of the chief risks to successful ownership stem from the tendency of many buyers to overcommit themselves. This situation arises whenever a prospective home owner commits himself to a higher schedule of housing costs than he can rightly afford. It also arises every time a businessman agrees to pay more for a property than its future productivity can justify. Serious problems seldom develop in these cases if the buyer is able to pay cash or mostly cash for his property. But pitiful situations often result when the buyer commits himself to a heavy mortgage debt and later finds that he has taken on a heavier load than he can carry.

No buyer rationally decides that he should overcommit himself. He stumbles into this situation—usually through bad judgment or over-optimism. Buyers who allow themselves to be pressured into unfavorable ownership situations or who blindly agree to a higher schedule of ownership costs than they can afford must usually charge their decisions to bad judgment. Misfortune sometimes strikes even those buyers who carefully consider their prospective costs and returns as owners. This is particularly true when an optimistic buyer acquires ownership only to be victimized by his unfortunate time of purchase, unfavorable conditions of purchase, unpredictable property deterioration, or unstable neighborhood change.[18]

As this statement suggests, overoptimism can lead to overcommitments when one buys a property and assumes a mortgage under boomtime conditions and later experiences a decline in both his income and his property value. It occurs again when one amortizes his mortgage debt over too short a time period and thus takes on a heavier debt load than he can conveniently carry. It occurs when one buys a building in good faith only to find that it is a jerry-built structure or that it has hidden defects that result in rapid deterioration. Overoptimism can also lead to problems when the value of one's property suddenly declines because of the devastating effects of a drought or an earthquake, because of the loss of its chief market, or because of the sudden blighting of a neighborhood.

Most people are guilty of occasional decisions involving bad judgment or overoptimism. Common sense, careful consideration of one's alternatives, refusal to be stampeded into rushed decisions, and a willingness to seek and take impartial advice provide the best deterrents to bad judgments. These factors can temper overoptimism and at the same time provide a rational basis for the average investor's faith and hope in the future.

A major problem with the overoptimistic buyer is that of getting him to recognize the limits within which he can operate. With productive properties, a buyer should never offer a higher price than that justified by the property's productive potential. He should protect his future equity in the property by making a substantial down payment and by making sure

[18] Cf. Dean, *op. cit.,* p. 75.

that he has or can borrow sufficient capital to cover his normal operating expenses.

Three rules-of-thumb have been used at various times to guide home buyers in their ownership-acquisition decisions. A study of family expenditures in the United States during the middle 1930s indicated that the average family spent approximately one-fourth of its income for housing and household operations.[19] This proportion is often cited as a good index of the portion of one's disposable income that should go for housing purposes. Families with no children and families with high incomes can naturally afford to spend higher portions of their income on housing.

A second rule-of-thumb proclaims that families should spend no more than 2 to 2½ times their annual disposable income on housing. This rule is also flexible. Families with considerable savings can naturally feel safe in spending more for a home than families with limited savings. Similarly, childless couples can usually justify higher expenditures than large families; and families that get a great deal of enjoyment out of their homes can often pay more than families that want to be on the go. Buyers have probably ignored this rule more than they have honored it since World War II. Yet it still provides a conservative index of how far one can safely commit himself in acquiring home ownership.

A third rule-of-thumb asserts that residential properties should have market values equal to approximately 100 times their monthly rental rates. This rule fell into disuse during World War II when property values were allowed to increase while contract rental rates were subject to public rent controls. Rental rates have since tended to rise toward the 100 to 1 ratio level, largely because owners of residential rental properties must receive gross rental returns of approximately 12 percent of the value of their properties annually if they are to realize fair returns on their investments.[20]

Influence of personal and family factors. Experience shows that property owners themselves often constitute the chief risk to successful ownership. A person's prospects for success as an owner frequently reflects (1) his personal and family attitudes regarding the obligations of ownership, (2) his relative youth or maturity, (3) changing family needs, (4) size and fluctuations in the family income, and (5) family mobility.

---

[19] Cf. National Resources Committee, *Consumer Expenditures in the United States* (Washington, 1939), p. 78. This study indicated that families with annual incomes of less than $750 in 1935-36 spent more than a third of their income, on the average, for housing and household operations, while the average family with an income of $15,000 or more spent less than a sixth of its income for this purpose.

[20] When allowances of 2.5 percent of a rental apartment or house's market value are made annually for property taxes and insurance payments, 2.0 percent for repairs and maintenance, and 2.0 percent for depreciation and obsolescence, an owner must receive 12 percent of the value of his property as contract rent if he is to realize a 5.5 percent return on the investment value of his property.

An unhappy or discontented owner often ends up as an unsuccessful owner. Insufficient housing space and farm or business holdings of inadequate size are common causes of dissatisfaction.[21] Beyond this, discontent finds its seeds in many places. Sometimes it springs from a buyer's underestimation of his costs and obligations as an owner or from his overestimation of the satisfactions to be derived from ownership. Sometimes it has its roots in the buyer's feeling that he was pressured into buying by his wife's insistence, by a salesman's slick talk, or possibly by the seller's misrepresentation of certain facts. At times, it also results from factors such as envy of one's neighbors, ill health, family discord, a death in the family, unemployment, alcoholism, or the buyer's disdain for work.

Considerable significance can often be attached to the buyer's age and the stage of his family cycle at the time he takes on his ownership obligations. A buyer who is in his forties usually has certain definite advantages over a younger buyer. He should have more money saved for a substantial down payment on his home or business property. His ideas on what he wants are ordinarily more set. And since the size of his family has already been determined in most cases, he knows how large a house he needs or, in the case of a farm, how much family labor he can count on in the future.

Unlike the older buyer, a young owner has a longer period of productive work ahead of him. Yet his ideas as to what he wants in a home or a business property are often more subject to change. He also finds it difficult to plan for the future because he always has the problem of trying to match the size of his house to the estimated future size of his family. In this process, he sometimes ends up with a larger and presumably more expensive home than he needs while at other times he may find that he must choose between either adding additional bedrooms to his house or selling his property so that he may move to a larger house.

The problem of income and job security also looms large as a risk factor, particularly during depression periods. Most buyers look forward to long periods of steady employment and steady or rising incomes at the time they acquire ownership. Past experience with layoffs and depressions show that this hope is not always justified. The thousands of ownerships sacrificed through mortgage foreclosures and tax forfeitures during the depression of the 1930s bear mute evidence of the need for steady incomes to support continued ownership.

---

[21] A 1955 study indicates that insufficient space was the leading reason given by owners and renters for dissatisfaction with their present housing arrangements. Cf. "1955 Survey of Consumer Finances: Housing Arrangements of Consumers," *Federal Reserve Bulletin,* August, 1955, pp. 856-68. According to this survey, 15 percent of the owners and 32 percent of the renters were dissatisfied. Thirty percent of the owners with homes of four rooms or less indicated dissatisfaction as compared with 10 percent of those with larger houses. The study indicated that tenants usually had one room less than owners of similar age, income, and family size, and that rented quarters usually had less space devoted to garages, basements, and storage facilities.

Family mobility represents still another risk to successful ownership. This factor often takes the form of frequent moving from one apartment, house, or farm to another—usually because of dissatisfaction with one's present quarters or holding and a continuing search for "greener pastures." Many owners as well as tenants indulge in this moving practice, often with considerable wastage of resources. A reverse phase of the mobility problem can operate during depression periods when owners feel that they are tied to their present jobs and their present locations because their life savings are sunk in a home that they can sell only at considerable discount.[22]

As these risk factors suggest, the ownership ideal should not be held out as a boon to all people. Business and home ownership have their satisfactions for those people who can afford it and for those who can maintain their ownership rights once they have acquired them. But for many people, the risks of successful ownership outweigh the advantages. For these people, it may be wise policy to discourage ownership and thereby prevent the heartaches and waste of resources that so often accompany cases of unsuccessful ownership.

TRANSFERRING OWNERSHIP RIGHTS

Sooner or later every privately owned property changes hands. Sometimes these transfers occur only once in a generation; sometimes on a far more frequent basis. Year in and year out, however, they always account for a substantial number of properties. In 1965, for example, approximately 3.6 million residential properties were sold in the United States.[23]

Most ownerships of residential properties in the United States have been acquired by purchase. Some of these have involved funds received by gift or inheritance, but only a small minority have been acquired entirely by this means. Figure 13-1 provides a more detailed picture of the changing importance of the farm property transfer methods used since

[22] Commenting on this situation, Charles Abrams [*Revolution in Land* (New York: Harper & Row, 1939), pp. 48-49] has observed that: "Universal home ownership fits ideally into the industrial scheme, for once fixed to his investment, the home owner makes a most satisfactory and reasonable worker, quick to yield in industrial disputes, anxious to maintain the status quo by doing almost anything to preserve his nominal ownership of the 'equity' into which he has placed his savings, even where prodigious sacrifices of food, clothing, or comfort are required."

[23] George Katona *et al.*, *1967 Survey of Consumer Finances* (Ann Arbor: University of Michigan Survey Research Center, 1968), p. 48, report that 6.3 percent of the nation's nonfarm families bought houses in 1965. Of this total, 1.8 percent bought new houses and 3.9 percent used houses. The percentage of families buying houses between 1959 and 1966 ranged from a low of 4.1 percent in 1966 to a high of 6.3 percent in 1965. Three percent of the farms of the United States were transferred in 1965.

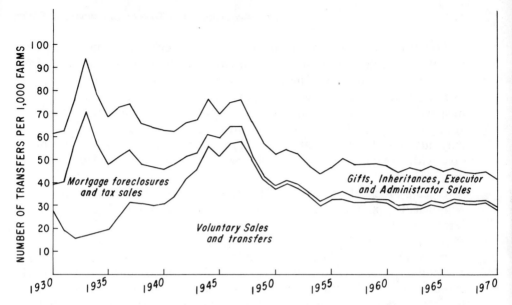

FIGURE 13-1. Estimated number of farms changing ownership each year by major transfer methods, United States, 1920-1970.

1926. This chart indicates wide variations in the year-to-year importance of the three principal transfer methods. Approximately 3 percent of the total number of farms in the United States were transferred by voluntary sale in most years between 1926 and 1970. The importance of this method ranged from a low of 16.2 transfers per 1,000 farms in the depression year of 1932 to a high of 57.7 transfers per 1,000 farms in 1946 and 1947. Forced sales and forfeitures of ownership accounted for the largest number of transfers during the 1931-36 depression period and reached a peak of 54.1 transfers per 1,000 farms in 1933. This method has been relatively unimportant in the post-World War II period. Between 12 and 17 farms per 1,000 or approximately a fourth of the total were transferred in most years by gift, inheritance, or related methods.

Emphasis is placed in this discussion on two major methods for transferring ownership rights. Consideration is given to the leading problems that arise when deeds are used to transfer properties. This is followed with a discussion of inheritance goals and the procedures owners can use to transfer their properties to their heirs.

Transfers by Deed

Two important problems usually arise when a property ownership is transferred by deed. The first of these concerns the working out of a suitable transfer arrangement and the second involves the procedure of transferring title to the new owner.

Some transfers by deed involve outright gifts; but the usual case involves a purchase-and-sale arrangement. Before an owner can enter into this type of arrangement, he must first find a prospective buyer. In some instances, the buyer seeks out the owner and offers to purchase his property. More often, the owner must take the initiative. He may approach an acquaintance with the proposal that he buy the property. He may advertise the fact that his property is for sale. He may list his property with a real estate broker, or he may even offer his property for sale at public auction.

Once a prospective buyer and the seller are brought together, the buyer will usually examine the premises and inquire concerning the owner's terms of sale. The prospective buyer can then decide whether or not he should buy the property. If he is interested in buying but does not like the owner's terms, he will often bargain for more favorable conditions. In this bargaining process, he usually tries to get the property at a lower price. He can also bargain for the inclusion of certain "extras" in the sales price, for the provision of specific improvements, for an earlier possession date than the seller has specified, or, if the seller is financing the sale, for a lower down payment or more favorable credit terms. With each of these items, the seller can accept or reject the buyer's offer; or if he wishes to bargain further, he may make a counter offer, which may lead to a compromise price.

As soon as the buyer and seller definitely agree on the terms of sale, both parties are committed to the fulfillment of their portion of the sales agreement.[24] There is no formal requirement that the details of these agreements be committed to writing. Whenever a purchase agreement involves a substantial consideration or is made through a broker, however, it is normal procedure for the buyer and seller to sign a purchase-and-sale contract.[25] This contract provides legal evidence of the fact that a

[24] For a more detailed discussion of the land sale and title transfer process, cf. Kratovil, *op. cit.,* chaps. XI-XIII.

[25] Three other types of agreements—usually made in writing—may also be used in the selling process. When a seller lists his property with a broker, he ordinarily signs a *listing contract.* This contract lists the names of the seller and the broker, a description of the property to be sold, the owner's sale price and other terms of sale, the duration of the broker's agency to sell the property, the broker's commission, and usually an agreement as to whether or not the broker has exclusive sales rights.

When a buyer deals directly through a broker rather than with the seller, his "offer to buy" is usually written up in a document known as a *binder.* This document specifies the terms under which the buyer will purchase the property. If the seller accepts these terms by signing the binder, the sales agreement is then formalized by a purchase-and-sale contract. Buyers often limit their offers by making them subject to their ability to secure adequate financing.

A third type of agreement known as an *option* may be used if a buyer wants to hold a purchase opportunity open while he analyzes his alternative opportunities, secures adequate financing, or sells another property. Under this arrangement, a seller receives a consideration for which he agrees to sell his property to the optionee at a

purchase agreement has been made; it itemizes the terms of sale so that there will be no future misunderstandings owing to faulty memories; and it protects both the buyer and the seller from a possible change of intentions on the other's part.[26]

No definite form is required in purchase-and-sale contracts. But a well drafted contract will always (1) identify the buyer and seller, (2) provide a reasonably accurate description of the property being sold, (3) list the actual sales price and any other conditions of sale, and (4) bear the signatures of the various parties to the sale. In addition, it may specify the approximate "closing date" when the ownership title is to be transferred to the new owner and the date when the seller is to vacate the property so that the buyer can take actual possession.

At the time a purchase-and-sale contract is signed, the buyer is normally expected to deposit a sum of money with the broker or a third party to indicate his good faith in going through with his purchase offer. This deposit—usually between 5 and 10 percent of the purchase price—is known as *earnest money*. If the buyer follows through with his plans, this sum is applied toward the purchase price. Should he fail to carry out his purchase agreement, this money can be used to compensate the seller and his broker for any losses they may incur because of the buyer's failure to take title.

Since buyers are always interested in securing good titles to the properties they buy, it is normally assumed that the seller will provide the buyer with a merchantable and unencumbered title. Purchase-and-sale contracts often specify that the buyer will take the property subject to existing easements and restrictions, that he will recognize the rights of tenants under existing leases, or that he will take over an existing mortgage. In the absence of provisions of this type, the seller must be ready to grant a warranty deed and to clear his title of any easements, restrictions, mortgages, liens, tenancies, or other claims that might limit his ability to convey a merchantable and unencumbered title. If the seller fails in this regard, the buyer is under no obligation to accept the title.

Buyers ordinarily insist upon an examination of title before the "closing date." As a part of this process, the seller usually makes his documents regarding the property—his deed, abstract of title, opinion as to title, title insurance policy, and property surveys—available to the buyer or his agents for their examination. Any omissions in the record or

---

fixed price any time during a specified period of time. If the optionee does not buy the property during this period, the option expires, and the owner is again free to sell to anyone.

[26] Occasional problems arise when a buyer or seller fails or refuses to comply with his obligations under a purchase-and-sale contract. Under these conditions, the offending buyer or seller can usually be sued either for specific performance of the contract or for breach of contract and damages.

any clouds against the title that might be detected at this point are ordinarily cleared up at the seller's expense.

Some contracts specify a definite closing date when the deed will be granted and the title will actually pass to the new owner. When not mentioned in the contract, the closing transaction is usually scheduled within a reasonable period after the buyer has had an opportunity to check the validity of the land title he is to receive. This transaction quite often involves the simple exchange of a buyer's personal or certified check for the seller's deed. On numerous occasions, however, this transaction is complicated by a settlement process, which involves the prorating of certain costs—property insurance premiums paid by the seller, property taxes for the year, value of fuel on hand, and so on—between the buyer and seller. And it is frequently complicated further by the presence of a large number of interested parties and by a grouping of several near-simultaneous transactions.

A closing transaction involving a mortgaged property will often call for a meeting of seven different parties: the seller and his wife, the buyer and his wife, the listing broker, the broker through whom the buyer made his offer to buy, the seller's mortgagee, the buyer's mortgagee, and a lawyer. The seller and his wife must be present to accept payment for the property and to sign the deed in which they convey all their rights—including dower and homestead rights—to the grantee. The buyer and his wife are present to pay for the property, accept the deed, and to mortgage the property as soon as they acquire title. The two brokers are present to represent their clients and to collect their commission. The seller's mortgagee (or his agent) is present to accept full payment of his mortgage and to sign a mortgage release. The buyer's mortgagee (or his agent) is present to advance the funds the buyer needs for the transaction and to receive the new mortgage. A lawyer is present because of his role in preparing the sale documents.

Properties are frequently transferred in *escrow.* Under this arrangement, the buyer and seller designate a third person who acts as an escrow agent. These three parties then sign an escrow agreement, which specifies the conditions each party must fulfill to close the sale. The seller can then deliver his deed to the escrow agent to be delivered to the seller as soon as he provides a merchantable and unencumbered title to the property. As soon as both parties have met the terms of the escrow agreement, the seller receives his payment and the buyer receives a deed, which he can then have registered in his own name.

Goals in Property Inheritance

Talk about property inheritance and almost everyone perks up his ears. Property owners wonder how they might best handle their estates; prospective heirs wonder how they will make out; even neutral bystanders are interested in who will get what and when. From almost every angle, inheritance makes an interesting and intriguing subject. Part of this situation arises because of the variety of differences between individual cases and because of the atmosphere of uncertainty regarding future developments. A flavor of intrigue also is added by occasional rumors of underhanded dealings, and by the general hush-hush treatment that surrounds many inheritance plans.

Most people agree that the question of how property is transferred and who receives it deserves careful consideration. Unfortunately, however, this subject is not one that we discuss freely at the breakfast table. As long as parents are not under pressure, they ordinarily prefer to leave their plans fluid and unjelled so that they can be adjusted to changing situations. As a result, most property owners tend to postpone their decisions relative to inheritance arrangements. Even when they have made definite plans, they frequently hesitate to discuss the details with their prospective heirs.

Children and other heirs, on the other hand, are usually just as hesitant in asking questions about the details of future inheritance arrangements. Rather than give the appearance of being vulturous or "grabby," many prospective heirs seem content to operate on faith and hope, with no definite assurances concerning their future position as heirs. This atmosphere of uncertainty is sometimes sobering and wholesome. But just as often—and particularly when one of the prospective heirs has assumed responsibility for operating the family business or for looking after his parents—this situation may involve injustices and present a barrier to the efficient management and operation of a family farm or business.

Four important goals should be stressed in planning inheritance arrangements. These goals call for: (1) minimizing the cost, time, and trouble involved in estate settlements: (2) maintaining productive properties as going operating units; (3) safeguarding the security of the parents; and (4) securing fair treatment of the heirs.

Most families want to hold their property inheritance costs to a minimum. At the same time, they want to avoid time-consuming delays in estate settlements; and they would like to forestall misunderstandings and quarrels between heirs. Attainment of these objectives cannot always be assured in advance. It should be recognized, however, that many family quarrels could be avoided if parents would discuss inheritance arrangements with their children and join with them in coming to some mutual agreement concerning the shares each heir should expect.

From the standpoint of the heirs, local communities and society at large, it is usually desirable to discourage the breaking up of economic operating units. Divisions of the physical assets of going businesses between two or more heirs often result in production inefficiencies and sometimes in their demise as economic going concerns. Good reasons sometimes exist for breaking up large business holdings, particularly holdings that involve sizable acreages or more than one operating unit. Except when holdings involve readily separable units, however, attempts should be made to work out inheritance arrangements that will permit complete economic units to pass as going concerns. The entire inheritance need not go to one person. Joint ownership arrangements may be considered; some heirs may receive cash or other properties; or arrangements may be worked out to have the recipient of a farm or other business pay off the interests of the other heirs over a suitable period of time.

Property owners who work out inheritance arrangements usually give considerable attention to the welfare and well-being of their prospective heirs. They recognize that an heir who has reached the age when he can operate on his own can often benefit from the productive use of his expected inheritance, and that the value of this opportunity can decline with the years that may pass before its receipt. As long as parents can afford to do so, they usually provide their children with various types of help in getting started. Some children are sent to college; some receive money to start their businesses or to provide an initial payment on their home. Children may be taken into the family business, and parents can work out intrafamily business transfer arrangements to permit an heir to take over the family business while he is still in his physical prime. Yet despite their good intentions regarding their children, parents must also consider their own future welfare. Before they transfer their properties, they should consider the satisfactions they associate with retention of the managerial control over their properties, the effects of their actions should they outlive their children, and their need for maintaining financial reserves to offset the eventualities that may arise with inflation, high medical expenses, or depressed business conditions.

As a final goal, serious consideration should be given to the equitable treatment of heirs. Our inheritance laws favor equal treatment of children. "Equal treatment," however, can result in inequitable treatment. Almost every community has instances of sons or daughters who have operated the family business for their parents, or who have cared for their parents during their declining years, while brothers and sisters have been free from this responsibility. In cases of this type, it is only fair that the heirs who have stayed at home or those who have cared for their parents should receive special consideration. When some heirs have received special financial help for their education, for the launching of their businesses, or for other purposes, these grants should also be considered in the determination of what is and what is not equitable treatment.

Alternative Inheritance Arrangements

Property owners can use any of several alternative arrangements in transferring their ownership rights to their normal heirs. If the owner so desires, he can give his property away. Quite frequently he will arrange to sell it to one of his heirs at the prevailing market price or possibly at a specially reduced price. Sometimes he will use a contractual arrangement to turn his ownership rights over to another party during his lifetime or at the time of his death in return for special services or support. The owner can hold his ownership rights in joint tenancy with his wife or another person, each with rights of survivorship. He may draw up a will, which designates the portions of his estate that are to pass to various individuals or organizations at his death. And if he takes no action governing the transfer of his estate, his property will be distributed among his legal heirs after his death in accordance with the laws of descent and distribution.[27]

Transfers by gift. Parents frequently give property, money, and other assistance to their children and other heirs. As long as the parent can afford to give away part of his property, the decision to do so often results from a simple choice between giving the property now or letting the recipient wait until the parent's death. With this choice of alternatives, property owners frequently choose to give because (1) gifts usually provide the donee with an opportunity to make an earlier and faster start in his business;[28] (2) this method of transferring property avoids some of the taxes, lawyer fees, and other costs normally associated with estate settlements; and (3) most donors gain considerable satisfaction from the act of giving and from seeing their children prosper.

Gifts provide a highly satisfactory method of property transfer as long as the donor reserves sufficient property or other resources to provide for his future comfort and support. But the property owner must always remember that he loses his control over the property at the moment he gives up his ownership rights and that he should retain at least partial control if his gift will in any way endanger his future security.

Some owners try to meet this situation by giving a joint tenancy

[27] For more detailed discussion of these property transfer arrangements as they apply in different areas, cf. J. H. Beuscher and Louise A. Young, *Your Property—Plan Its Transfer,* University of Wisconsin Extension Circular 407, 1951; Robert Brosterman, *The Complete Estate Planning Guide* (New York: McGraw-Hill Book Company, 1964), Part II; George E. Cleary, *Estate Planning* (Philadelphia: American Law Institute and American Bar Association, 1949); W. L. Gibson, Jr. and H. H. Ellis, *Inheritance—Your Farm and Family,* Southern Farm Management Extension Publication 5, Clemson College, 1953; Marshall Harris and E. B. Hill, *Family Farm Transfer Arrangements,* University of Illinois Extension Circular 680, 1951; Mayo A. Shattuck, *Estate Planner's Handbook* (Boston: Little, Brown and Co., 1948); John F. Timmons and John C. O'Byrne, *Transferring Farm Property Within Families in Iowa,* Iowa Agricultural Experiment Station Research Bulletin 394, 1953; and Arthur J. Walrath and W. L. Gibson, Jr., *Farm Inheritance and Settlement of Estates,* Virginia Agricultural Experiment Station Bulletin 413, 1948.

[28] Gifts and inheritances usually prove of economic benefit to their recipients. It may be noted, however, that financial coddling and continual "dependence upon dad" often has its adverse effects. A child who squanders his inheritance or who never learns the value of money is often worse off than the operator who starts out with no promise of family assistance.

interest in the property or by giving a deed with the reservation of a life estate to the present owner. These arrangements can prove satisfactory under certain conditions. They may complicate possible management, leasing, mortgaging, or sale arrangements, however, and definite problems can arise if the donor outlives the donee. Arrangements of this type should be used only when they fit the owner's circumstances and needs.

Sales arrangements. Property owners often find it advantageous to use sales arrangements in the disposition of their properties. If an owner wishes to retire, he can sell his business to one of his heirs at the going market price or at a reduced price, which involves an element of gift; or he might sell to a nonrelative—usually at the highest price he can get.

In selling his property, the owner usually transfers a going business to the buyer. The buyer ordinarily acquires ownership and control of the property during his most productive years. The seller receives money from the sale that he can use to purchase an annuity, to invest in another enterprise, or to support himself and his wife during their declining years. Any residue left at the time of the seller's death can be passed on as part of his estate.

Contractual arrangements. Contracts can be used to cover a wide variety of property transfer arrangements. Sons and other heirs frequently operate a family business with verbal promises or understandings that the ownership is to pass to them in the future. Oral agreements of this type are usually undesirable because of the difficulties attendant to their enforcement. When these agreements are formalized in a written contract, however, they often provide a satisfactory method of intrafamily property transfer.

Several types of contractual arrangements may be used to transfer landed properties. Owners frequently use land contracts in the sale of farms, businesses, and residential properties. Potential heirs and even nonrelatives sometimes operate family businesses or care for a property owner with the agreement that they can buy the property at a specified price or that they will acquire it at the owner's death. Contracts are also used in many areas to transfer ownership rights to a son or other heir and at the same time reserve certain rights, perquisites, and support for the parents. These arrangements are sometimes described as "bonds of maintenance" or "bonds of support."[29]

Joint tenancies. Joint tenancies (described in chapter 12) are fre-

[29] Bonds of maintenance have been used in some farming communities to provide a type of retirement annuity for retiring parents. The bonds are often written in considerable detail and provide the parents with specified perquisites such as use of a separate house on the property, free or exclusive use of certain rooms in the family dwelling, food and care, spending money, transportation, medicine and medical care, funeral and burial expenses, and sometimes cash grants to other heirs. Cf. Kenneth H. Parsons and Eliot O. Waples, *Keeping the Farm in the Family,* Wisconsin Agricultural Experiment Station Research Bulletin 157, p. 608, 1945.

quently used by husbands and wives, widowed mothers and sons, or other combinations of two or more persons as a means of holding property in joint ownership. Under this arrangement, the entire ownership is transferred at one's death to the surviving owner or owners. This method of transfer has obvious advantages in some cases. A husband, for example, may want his ownership rights to pass to his wife at his death or he may want his wife's rights to come to him by right of survivorship if she dies before him. Similarly, a widowed mother may find it desirable to give her only child joint tenancy rights in her property if she feels that this arrangement will not interfere with her future management and operation plans.

If an owner holds all his property in joint tenancy, his ownership rights automatically pass to the survivor at his death and there is no need to probate his estate. This feature reduces the time, cost, and trouble associated with estate settlements. Yet this system of ownership and transfer has certain drawbacks. An owner who enters into a joint tenancy always gives up the exclusive rights of control over the management of his property, which he could exercise as sole owner. In this respect, joint tenancy works all right as long as the joint tenants agree. It can become a burdensome arrangement when they disagree. It provides an unsatisfactory inheritance arrangement when one has several deserving heirs, and it is hard to apply to most types of personal property. The possibility of unexpected death seldom makes it wise for a son or other prospective heir to put all of his own property under joint tenancy with a parent. In doing so, he would risk the chance of having his property go to his parent (or other joint tenant) rather than to his wife and children.

Use of a will. A property owner who wishes to hold all or part of his property throughout his lifetime can use a will to stipulate how his estate shall be divided after his death. Wills are used in the transfer of approximately one-half of the properties subject to estate settlement. Many wills, however, may be classified as deathbed wills because they are prepared within a few days or weeks of the testator's death.

A *will* may be defined as a gift of property that takes effect on the giver's or testator's death unless revoked before that time.[30] To be valid, a will should be written in ink or be typed, though oral wills are accepted in some cases. It must be made by a testator of legal age and sound mind; and it should be signed by the testator and witnessed by two or more disinterested persons. Once a will has been made, the testator is free to revoke it at any time, replace it with a more recent will, or add a codicil that supplements or alters certain of its provisions.

Testators can "give, devise, and bequeath" any property they own, subject to legal claims, to any person or organization of their choice. Ordinarily, they provide that their property should pass to their normal

[30] For a more detailed discussion of wills and estate settlements, cf. Kratovil, *op. cit.,* chap. XVIII.

heirs. But they are free to establish eccentric trusts and inheritance arrangements, such as the famous Toronto baby derby of the 1920s, which started when a wealthy Canadian left the bulk of his estate to the family that would have the most children in the ten years following his death. A testator's freedom in this regard is always limited, however, by the legal requirement that he recognize all his children, that he cannot defeat the dower rights of the wife or the homestead rights of the family, that he cannot avoid the claims of rightful creditors, and that he cannot transfer property rights he no longer owns.

Following the testator's death, his will must be filed in the proper court and be admitted to probate. An executor named in the will or an administrator appointed by the court will then administer the estate until it has been settled. This settlement process ordinarily involves periods ranging from four months to a year, though it sometimes extends over periods of several years. During this settlement period, the various claims of the heirs, creditors of the deceased and his estate, tax officials, and others are aired and settled so that the residual estate can be divided according to the terms of the will.

Wills are often regarded as a highly desirable method for transferring property to one's heirs. They permit the owner to hold and control his property throughout his lifetime and give him an opportunity to apportion his estate among his heirs in what he regards as an equitable manner. But they have the disadvantage of calling for a settlement period, which necessitates a certain amount of cost, time, and trouble. They may also delay the actual transfer of property until sometime after the period when the prospective heir could realize the greatest benefit from its receipt and use.

Even when a property owner uses some other method to transfer most of his property, he often finds it desirable to use a will to direct the distribution of the residual portion of his estate. Wills can also be used along with other transfer arrangements to handle the problem of contingent beneficiaries (as when a husband and wife holding property in joint tenancy die in the same fire or accident), to designate a guardian for one's minor heirs, and for other similar purposes.

Settlements under the laws of descent. When a property owner dies intestate—without a will—his estate is settled under the laws of descent and distribution in much the same way that it would be settled under a will. The details of these laws vary from state to state. As a general rule, however, between a third and a half of the estate passes to the surviving husband or wife while the balance is divided equally between the children. The share that would have gone to any child who has died ordinarily goes to his heirs, if he has any, by right of representation. When there is no surviving spouse, the entire estate goes to the direct heirs. When there are no direct heirs, the estate passes to the parents of the deceased and after them to his brothers, sisters, and their legal heirs.

Laws of descent usually call for an equal division of the estate among heirs of equal relationship. This system provides a logical average way of distributing estates. In this respect, it parallels the practices used in many wills. But it completely ignores the fact that equal division may result in inequitable sharing arrangements, with some deserving heirs receiving smaller shares than they actually deserve.

When a property owner is satisfied with the distribution arrangement provided by law, he may find it just as well not to prepare a will. A will should be prepared and used, however, if he plans to favor particular heirs, wants his wife to enjoy complete control of his estate until after his minor children are grown, or wishes to attain some other specific goal.

Choice of an inheritance arrangement. Every family should give careful thought to its choice of an adequate and appropriate property inheritance plan. These plans are just as important to young families and operators who are still getting themselves established as they are to older people who have already acquired considerable property. No hard and fast rules can be made regarding one's choice of an inheritance arrangement. There is usually a best arrangement for every property owner; but the choice of this arrangement depends upon his goals and his particular circumstances.

A property owner who is working out an inheritance arrangement should always start by considering the amount of property he owns, its value, the manner in which he holds or shares rights in the property, and the validity of his title. He should then ask himself what goals he wishes to attain in the inheritance process; how his property rights might best be distributed among his heirs in the event of his death; and what inheritance arrangement or combination of arrangements can best be used to attain these ends. He should seek competent advice from his attorney, his banker, or some other person before he finally decides on an inheritance arrangement. The plan he chooses should facilitate the smooth transfer of his estate to his intended heirs while minimizing possible troubles, time delays, estate and inheritance taxes, and other estate settlement costs.[31]

Once he has decided on a plan, he will ordinarily find it desirable to have an attorney draw up the proper papers, if any are needed. Then as time goes on, he should review his plans from time to time to make sure that they keep up with changes in his family and ownership situation. As Beuscher and Young have observed, "Plans carefully worked out may save money, will give peace of mind to the family, and will save long drawn out settlement proceedings."[32]

---

[31] Cf. William J. Bowe, *Tax Savings Through Estate Planning* (Nashville: Vanderbilt University Press, 1963); John A. Clark, *How to Save Time and Taxes in Handling Estates* (New York: M. Bender, 1966); Normal F. Dacey, *How to Avoid Probate* (New York: Crown Publishers, Inc., 1965); and J. K. Lasser and Ralph Wallace, *How to Save Estate and Gift Taxes* (Larchmont, N. Y.: American Research Council, 1965).

[32] Beuscher and Young, *op. cit.,* p. 15.

——SELECTED READINGS

Brosterman, Robert, *The Complete Estate Planning Guide* (New York: McGraw-Hill Book Company, 1964), Part II.

Dean, John P., *Home Ownership: Is It Sound?* (New York: Harper & Brothers, 1945).

Fisher, Ernest M., and Robert M. Fisher, *Urban Real Estate* (New York: Henry Holt & Company, Inc., 1954) chaps. V, VI, VIII.

Harris, Marshall, and Elton B. Hill, *Family Farm Transfer Arrangements,* University of Illinois Extension Circular 680, 1951.

Kratovil, Robert, *Real Estate Law,* 5th ed. (Englewood Cliffs, N.J.: Prentice-Hall, Inc., 1969), chaps. VI-VII, XI-XIV, XVIII.

Ratcliff, Richard U., *Real Estate Analysis* (New York: McGraw-Hill Book Company, 1961), chap. VIII.

14

Leasing Arrangements

Unencumbered owner-operatorship has long been viewed as a foremost goal in American land-tenure policy. Yet a brief look at the present tenure situation in the United States shows that 63 percent of the residential units are tenant-occupied and that tenants operate approximately one out of every eight farms. Furthermore, a high proportion of the people who do own property hold their ownership rights subject to a real estate mortgage.

To some ways of thinking, these statistics suggest an unhealthy tenure situation—a compromise that falls far short of unencumbered owner-operatorship. It must be remembered though that the property ownership goal represents the end product of a dynamic process. Millions of families find it both expedient and wise to use leasing and credit arrangements as a means to the ultimate attainment of their ownership goals. Viewed in this light, the present tenure situation may be regarded as definitely favorable—favorable both from the standpoint of past experience and because of its proximity to our concept of what the tenure system ought to be.

As the above comments suggest, some highly important land-tenure problems are associated with the leasing arrangements that bind the interests of landlords and tenants and with the credit arrangements worked out between mortgagors and mortgagees. The first of these two tenure arrangements constitutes the subject-matter of this chapter.

TENANCY AND LEASING ARRANGEMENTS

Every time a property is leased or rented, there is a transfer of rights from the landlord to the tenant. As the *lessor,* the landlord retains his ownership rights while he grants most of his rights of use and possession to the tenant (or *lessee*) for some given period of time. In return for this delegation of rights, the tenant agrees to a schedule of periodic rental payments and to certain other responsibilities associated with his use and possession of the landlord's property.

Widescale tenancy is often regarded as undesirable in modern society. This does not mean that leasing arrangements are undesirable *per se.* Far from this, they provide a valuable and serviceable function in enhancing the interests of both landlords and tenants. They provide a means by which prospective landlords can lease their surplus land resources to others and thus receive a monetary return from properties they do not wish to occupy or operate. At the same time, they make it possible for prospective tenants to acquire use and possession rights to the properties held by others.

Tenancy encourages landlords to invest in and develop properties for the large number of businesses, office users, urban residents and others who prefer to rent the quarters where they work and live. It also helps numerous property owners to secure a supplemental or retirement income from their properties while at the same time providing timely assistance to others who want or need rental properties.

Viewed in the aggregate, numerous objections undoubtedly would be raised if most land resources were owned by a small group of people and if price and social barriers prevented much movement from tenancy to ownership. But as long as these conditions do not exist, a certain amount of tenancy is needed in the tenure system to facilitate the operation of the agricultural and residential ownership ladders, to permit an orderly retreat from owner-operatorship on the part of older owners, and to fill the continuing demand for commercial and residential rental properties in urban areas.

Most of the criticisms heard of tenancy are related to various abuses or undesirable phenomena that sometimes creep into the tenancy system. Problems often arise when the landlord's bargaining power makes it possible for him to foist a one-sided leasing arrangement on the tenant, when the landlord claims a disproportionate share of the economic returns of a property as rent, or when a tenant regards rented property as a resource to be exploited for his personal benefit. These problems are most acute when the income produced by a property is too low to provide the landlord with the rental return he desires and still leave sufficient income to insure decent living standards for the tenant. Problems also arise in many instances because of the vagaries of human nature and because of the failure of many vague leasing agreements to represent an actual meeting of minds regarding the details of the rental arrangement.

The discussion of tenancy problems and leasing arrangements that follows begins with an over-all look at the importance of tenancy in the American economy. Attention is focused on the characteristics of a lease, the principal types of rental arrangements now in use, and on some economic considerations that affect the determination of rental rates.

Importance of Tenancy

Attitudes regarding the desirability of tenancy as compared with owner-ship vary widely from community to community and from one type of land use to another. Some residential and farming communities are composed almost entirely of home owners; some involve a considerable intermixture of owners and tenants; and some, such as the multistoried apartment areas of our larger cities, are inhabited almost entirely by tenants.

Comparable variations occur with different types of land use. Leasing arrangements are a common phenomenon with commercial estab-lishments, light industries, urban residences, farms, grazing land, and mineral rights. Yet they are used only on rare occasions with heavy industrial properties, forests, developed mines, and the lands used for highway and railroad transportation purposes.

Trends in nonfarm residential tenancy. Census findings on the resi-dential and farm tenure situations have been reported in the United States since the late 1800s. As Table 14-1 indicates, 52.2 percent of the nation's occupied dwelling units and 63.1 percent of the occupied nonfarm dwellings were tenant-occupied in 1890. The proportion of tenant-occupied nonfarm units increased to 63.5 percent in 1900 and

TABLE 14-1. Tenure Status of Occupied Dwelling Units, United States, 1890-1970

Census year	All occupied dwelling units (000s omitted)	Percentage of tenant occupancy	Occupied nonfarm dwelling units (000s omitted)	Percentage of tenant occupancy
1890	12,690	52.2	7,923	63.1
1900	15,964	53.3	10,274	63.5
1910	20,256	54.1	14,132	61.6
1920	24,352	54.4	17,600	59.1
1930	29,905	52.2	23,300	54.0
1940	34,855	56.4	27,748	58.9
1950	42,826	45.0	37,105	46.6
1960	53,024	38.1	49,458	39.0
1970	63,450	37.1	60,354	36.7

Source: *Statistical Abstract of the United States*, 1971, p. 673.

then slowly declined to 54.0 percent in 1930. Depression conditions during the 1930s brought a reversal of this downward trend and helped push the proportion of residential nonfarm tenancy up to 58.9 percent in 1940.

Between 1940 and 1950, the total number of occupied nonfarm dwellings increased from 27.7 to 37.1 million units and the proportion of residential tenancy dropped to 46.6 percent. This marked decrease in nonfarm residential tenancy can be credited primarily to three factors: (1) the effect of wartime and postwar prosperity in fostering home purchases, (2) the availability of real estate credit for the acquisition of home ownership, and (3) the impact of the wartime and early postwar rent control programs on landlord decisions to sell properties they might otherwise have kept as rental investments.

Nonfarm residential home ownership continued to increase after 1950 as the number of dwelling units climbed to 49.5 million in 1960 and to over 60 million in 1970. Most of the new units were owner-occupied. The proportion of tenancy-occupancy dropped to 39.0 in 1960 and to 36.7 percent in 1970.

The 1970 Census of Housing showed that 46.8 million of the nation's 67.7 million year-round housing units were single family dwellings. Three-fourths of these were owner-occupied as compared with 31.4 percent of the 5.4 million 2-family units, 6.7 percent of the 3-or-more family units, and 86.6 percent of the 2.1 million mobile home units.[1] Some 4.25 million units were unoccupied for various reasons

Farm-tenure situation. Farm-tenure data have been reported for every census enumeration since 1880. As the tabulation of tenure trends reported in Table 14-2 indicates, the first census report in 1880 showed that slightly more than a fourth of the nation's farms were tenant-operated. This proportion gradually increased during the next few decades until 1930, when 42.4 percent of the farm operating units were reported in this tenure class. Following 1935 and more particularly following World War II, the proportion of tenancy dropped until it reached a record low of 12.9 percent in 1969. Acreagewise, the proportion of farm land under lease decreased from 44.7 percent of the total in 1935 to 33.2 percent in 1950 and then rose to 34.0 percent in 1960 and 38.0 percent in 1969.

Table 14-2 deals with numbers of farm operating units and presents a picture of decreasing tenancy since 1930. It does not follow, however, that there has been an increase in the number of full owner-operators or of the acreage they operate. As the total number of farms dropped from a high of 6.8 million in 1935 to 3.9 million in 1959 and 2.7 million in 1969, the number of full owners dropped from 3.2 million to 2.1 million and 1.7 million and the number of tenants from 2.9 million to 0.7 million and 0.35 million, respectively. Meanwhile, the number of part owners—

---

[1] *1970 Census of Housing, Detailed Housing Characteristics, United States Summary,* Table 22, pp. 1-242.

TABLE 14-2. Number of Farm Operating Units, and Proportion of Farm Land Operated by Tenants, United States and Major Regions, 1880-1969

Census year	Number of farm operating units	Proportion of farm units operated by tenants			
		United States	North	South	West
1880	4,008,907	25.6	19.2	36.2	14.0
1890	4,564,641	28.4	22.1	38.5	12.1
1900	5,739,657	35.3	26.2	47.0	17.0
1910	6,366,044	37.0	26.5	49.6	14.0
1920	6,453,991	38.1	28.2	49.6	18.2
1925*	6,371,640	38.6	28.0	51.1	18.7
1930	6,295,103	42.4	30.0	55.5	21.5
1935*	6,812,350	42.1	31.8	53.5	23.8
1940	6,102,417	38.8	31.1	48.2	21.8
1945*	5,859,169	31.7	25.0	40.4	14.5
1950	5,388,437	26.9	21.1	34.1	13.4
1954*	4,782,416	24.4	20.5	30.0	12.2
1959	3,710,503	20.5	19.6	23.1	12.3
1964	3,157,857	17.1	17.0	18.5	11.5
1969	2,730,250	12.9	14.2	11.7	11.8

*Alaska and Hawaii not included

Source: *1964 Census of Agriculture,* Vol. II, p. 756; and *1969 Census of Agriculture,* Vol. II, Ch. 3, p. 14.

operators who own some land and rent in additional acreage—increased from 688,867 in 1935 to 868,180 in 1954 and then declined to 671,607 in 1969.

As Table 14-3 indicates, full owners gained somewhat as a percentage

TABLE 14-3. Percentage Distribution of Operator Units and Land Area in Farms Operated by Different Tenure Groups, United States, 1920-1969

Item	1920	1930	1940	1950	1959	1964	1969
	(percentages of total number)						
Number of operating units							
Full owners	52.2	46.3	50.6	57.4	57.1	57.6	
Part owners	8.7	10.4	10.1	15.3	22.5	24.8	
Managers	1.1	0.9	0.6	0.4	0.6	0.6	
Tenants	38.1	42.4	38.8	26.8	19.8	17.1	
Area in farms							
Full owners	48.3	37.6	35.9	36.1	30.8	28.7	
Part owners	18.4	24.9	28.2	36.4	44.8	48.0	
Managers	5.7	6.4	6.5	9.2	9.8	10.2	
Tenants	27.7	31.0	29.4	18.3	14.5	13.1	

Source: *1964 Census of Agriculture,* Vol. II, pp. 763 and 765; and *1969 Census of Agriculture,* Vol. II, Ch. 3, pp. 16, 25-27.

of all farm operators between 1920 and 1964, but accounted for a steadily decreasing proportion of the total land area in farms until 1969. Their rate of decline in this respect was exceeded only by that of the tenant group. Part owners became steadily more important as a tenure class and controlled 48.0 percent of the farm land in 1964 as compared with 18.4 percent in 1920. Managers, though few in number and no longer enumerated after 1964, also became more significant as their holdings rose from 5.7 percent of the total area in 1920 to 10.2 percent in 1964.

Most of the nation's farm tenants have operated in the cotton-producing states of the South and in the corn and wheat belt portions of the Middle West and the Great Plains region. When farm tenancy was at its peak during the 1930s, more than 60 percent of the farm units in the eight cotton belt states—Alabama, Arkansas, Georgia, Louisiana, Mississippi, Oklahoma, South Carolina, and Texas—were operated by tenants, mostly by sharecroppers and "third and fourth" share tenants who operated tracts within larger plantation holdings. During the same period, more than half of the farm land in Georgia, Illinois, Iowa, Kansas, Nebraska, Oklahoma, North Dakota, and South Dakota was operated under lease. Much of the overall change in the national farm-tenancy picture since 1935 can be credited to a marked reduction in the proportion of tenancy in these two regions.

Some 994,456 or 36.5 percent of the farm operators for 1969 counted in Tables 14-2 and 14-3 were part-time, semi-retired, or other low-income operators who sold $2,500 or less of farm products in 1969. Table 14-4

TABLE 14-4.   Percentage Distribution of Major Farm Tenure Groups and Type-of-Owner Groups by Four Measures of Comparative Importance, Commercial Farms in the United States, 1969*

Group	Farm operating units	Acres of farm land	Reported value of farm land and buildings	Receipts from sales of farm products in 1969
Tenure groups:				
Full owners	50.8	28.7	33.3	40.7
Part owners	33.5	57.5	49.4	43.8
Tenants	15.6	13.8	17.3	15.5
Owner groups:				
Individuals	85.4	72.5	75.2	49.0
Partnerships	12.8	17.8	17.3	19.2
Corporations	1.2	8.8	6.6	31.4
Others	0.6	0.9	0.9	0.4

*Commercial farms (Economic Classes 1-5 that reported farm product sales of $2,500 or more) accounted for 63.5 percent of the total number of farms and for 97.6 percent of the total value of farm products sold in 1969. The Class 1 units with sales of $40,000 or more accounted for 8.1 percent of the farm units and 56.8 percent of the farm product sales while the Class 1a units with $100,000 or more in sales accounted for 1.9 percent of the farm units and 33.6 percent of the product sales.

Source: *1969 Census of Agriculture,* Vol. II, Ch. 3, pp. 16, 25-27, 128, and 152-53.

indicates the comparative importance of the major tenure and type-of-owner for the most productive commercial operators.

Full owners accounted for half of the commercial operators but for smaller shares of the farm area, value of land and buildings, and value of farm sales. Part owners accounted for a third of the total operators, 57.5 percent of the land (much of it grazing land in the West), and above average shares of the value of land and buildings and farm sales receipts while tenants accounted for 14 to 17 percent of each category. Among the type-of-owner groups, it is interesting to note that partnerships and corporations accounted for 14 percent of the operating units but for significantly larger portions of the farm area and value of land and buildings and for more than half of the value of farm sales. Many of these units involve family farm operations but a significant number are controlled by absentee investors who operate as partners with active farmers or as shareholders in corporations rather than as simple landlords. Partnerships and corporations accounted for 26.4 percent of the farms with sales of $40,000 or more and for 40.6 percent of the large scale units with farm product sales of $100,000 or more in 1969.

Characteristics of Leasing Arrangements

The key feature in the landlord-tenant relationship is the leasing arrangement. This arrangement ordinarily involves a contract known as a *lease* by which the landlord conveys his rights of use and possession in a given property to a tenant for a definite period of time in return for a specified rental payment.

A lease may be oral or written; but all leases covering periods of more than one year in some states, and more than three years in others, must be written to be legal. Leases can be limited to short periods of time such as a month or a year or may cover periods of 99 years or more.[2] Their terms may be the end product of detailed negotiations; they may be dictated entirely by the landlord or in some instances by the tenant; or they may be implied by a general understanding that the landlord and tenant will accept a customary rental arrangement.

Regardless of how the landlord-tenant relationship is established, it vests the tenant with a leasehold estate, which he can enjoy as long as he fulfills his obligations as a tenant. These obligations ordinarily involve payment of rent in the amount and at the time agreed upon together with some responsibility for making repairs and maintaining the property

---

[2] Some states such as California and Nevada have laws limiting the duration of agricultural leases to periods of 10 or 15 years and other leases to periods of 99 years. Where no time limits are prescribed by law, valid leases may be written for periods of 1,000 years or more. Cf. Stanley M. McMichael and Paul T. O'Keefe, *Leases: Percentage, Short and Long Term,* 5th ed. (Englewood Cliffs, N.J.: Prentice-Hall, Inc., 1959), chap. XIII.

against undue deterioration. The landlord in turn must protect the tenant's exclusive rights of use and possession throughout the lease period unless specific arrangements to the contrary are included in the leasing arrangement.[3]

Legal requirements of a lease. Inasmuch as a lease involves a temporary transfer of property rights, it follows a legal form quite similar to that of a deed. It should always identify the landlord and the tenant by name, contain an accurate and complete description of the property being leased, indicate the time duration of the leasehold, and specify the amount of contract rent and the time when it shall be paid. Most written leases also contain a granting clause in which the lessor "demises and leases" or "grants, demises, and lets" the specified property to the lessee.

Written leases are ordinarily prepared in duplicate with signed copies going to both the landlord and the tenant. Like a deed, a lease does not take effect until it is delivered by the lessor to the lessee. Before this delivery takes place, it is necessary in some states to have written leases sealed, witnessed, and acknowledged in the same manner as deeds. Leases involving periods of more than a year are often recorded. This practice is not always required by law; but it does provide a desirable service in protecting tenants from complications that could result from the sale or mortgaging of their properties.

The creation of a landlord-tenant relationship always assumes certain covenants on the part of the landlord and tenant. Under the "covenant of possession," the landlord is obligated to convey possession of the property specified in the lease to the tenant. And under the "covenant of quiet possession" implied by use of the word "demise" in the lease, the landlord warrants the tenant's use and possession of the property against disturbance by persons having legal claims against his title as lessor.

Tenants are bound by covenant to pay rent in the amount and manner prescribed and to care for their rented properties "in a tenantlike manner." Except when they are prevented from doing so by the express wording of the lease, their implied "covenant regarding use of the premises" gives them a right to use their leased property for any legal purpose, to assign their tenancy rights to others, and to hold some of their rights while subleasing others.

Under the "covenant of fitness for intended use," the tenant takes

---

[3] Many leases are vague and inexplicit regarding the duties and privileges of the landlord and tenant. When legal questions arise regarding these leases, they are ordinarily interpreted according to the provisions of statutory and common law. Care should be taken in the drafting of a written lease if the landlord or tenant wishes to deviate from these usual legal interpretations. For more detailed discussion of the legal aspect of leasing arrangements, cf. Robert Kratovil, *Real Estate Law*, 5th ed. (Englewood Cliffs, N. J.: Prentice-Hall, Inc., 1969, chap. XXX and XXXIV; Curtis J. Berger, *Land Ownership and Use: Cases, Statutes, and Other Mateirals* (Boston: Little, Brown and Company, 1968), pp. 290-391; and Ernest M. and Robert M. Fisher, *Urban Real Estate* (New York: Henry Holt & Company, Inc., 1954), chap. VII.

possession of the property as it is at the time it is leased and assumes full responsibility for its condition and for its fitness or lack of fitness for his intended use. This covenant makes it unnecessary for landlords to maintain the premises, pay for repairs made by their tenants, or provide heat, electricity, water, and other services unless they have specifically agreed to do so.

The following exceptions apply to this rule: (1) landlords who rent furnished quarters for short periods of time have an implied obligation to provide premises that are both safe and habitable; (2) landlords can be held liable for injuries suffered by tenants from concealed defects in rented properties of which the landlords had knowledge; (3) a landlord who makes repairs, but who is negligent in doing so, is liable for any injuries resulting from his negligence; and (4) landlords who retain control over the halls, exits, elevators, and heating systems of their apartment or office buildings are obligated to maintain these facilities and provide their tenants with the associated services and utilities. Additional exceptions are also found in some states where legislation has been passed to require landlords to keep their rented housing accommodations in repair and to hold them liable for injuries suffered by tenants because of the landlord's failure to make repairs.

Termination of leases. Most leasehold estates are terminated automatically at the end of the lease period. At this time, the lease may be renewed; the tenant may stay on with the permission of the landlord; or the tenant may move away. Many leases, however, are terminated earlier by mutual consent, by the action of the landlord or tenant, or by termination of the landlord's estate.

A landlord-tenant relationship can be ended at any time if the tenant voluntarily surrenders his leasehold and if the landlord accepts this action. Many leases contain cancellation clauses, which authorize the landlord to terminate the lease—usually with proper notice—if he feels his property is not put to its best use or if he decides to sell it to someone else. Landlords also have an implied right to (1) terminate a lease if the property is abandoned by the tenant, and (2) seek legal eviction of the tenant if he fails to pay his rent or otherwise violates the terms of the lease. In either instance, the tenant can often be held liable for any loss of rent suffered by the landlord during the remainder of the lease period.

A tenant has an implied right to terminate the lease whenever the landlord evicts him from all or part of the property by occupying and using it contrary to the tenant's wishes. He also has this right when the landlord acts in such a way as to make the premises uninhabitable. For example, when a landlord agrees to provide heat, electricity, and water but fails to do so or when he fails to provide certain agreed-upon repairs, the tenant can terminate the lease on the ground that he has been subject to "constructive eviction." In addition to terminating the lease in these instances, tenants can also sue their landlords for damages.

A lease is always terminated when a tenant buys the property from the landlord. It is also terminated when the property is acquired for some public purpose by eminent domain or if some third party proves that the title belongs to him rather than to the lessor.

Security deposits. Unless other provisions are included in the lease, rent is payable at the end of the use period—*i.e.,* at the end of the month or at the end of the year. It is not an uncommon practice, however, for the lessors of residential and commercial properties to specify that rent be paid in advance. When there is some chance that the tenant may abandon or damage the property, go bankrupt, or default on his rental payments, landlords may also insist that their tenants make a security deposit.

Security deposits take several forms. The owner of a commercial site may require his tenant to deposit money or securities of a certain value with him with the provision that they will be returned with interest at the end of the leasehold period. The lessor of a furnished house or apartment may require a cash deposit, which will later be returned to the tenant with deductions for any damage to the owner's property.

Some leases call for a bonus payment to the landlord at the time the lease is signed. This bonus becomes the property of the landlord although arrangements may be made for rebating some portion of the bonus during the last month or year of the lease. Still another arrangement involves the advance payment of rent. At the time the lease is signed, the tenant makes an advance payment of all or almost all of the rent required for the last month or last few months covered by his lease.

Periodic tenancies. Although most landlord-tenant relationships start with the mutual acceptance of an oral or written lease, this relationship often continues as a tenancy-from-month-to-month or from-year-to-year. Periodic tenancies of this type result when no definite time period is specified at the time the leasing arrangement is made or when a tenant is allowed to hold over at the end of his lease.

The rights and duties of the landlord and tenant in these cases are governed by rules of law. These rules include the covenants described above and require certain minimum periods of notice for termination of the tenancy. A tenant-from-month-to-month—one without a valid lease who pays monthly rent—cannot be evicted unless he has received proper notice. This period of notice—usually between 7 and 15 days—is also required when the tenant wishes to move and thus end his liability for rent.

A tenancy involving the annual payment of rent but no lease for a definite time period is usually regarded as a tenancy-from-year-to-year. This type of tenancy is usually established when a tenant holds over or remains in possession of the landlord's property at the end of his lease year. A tenant-from-year-to-year who holds over for even one day (except when he holds over against his will as when he and his family are quarantined) can be held for another year's rent. The tenant who holds over, however, cannot force the landlord to extend the tenancy.

A landlord can evict a tenant who holds over without his expressed approval. But a tenancy-from-year-to-year is established if the landlord accepts rent from the tenant or if he allows him to remain until the middle of the year or until he has planted his crops. Several states have passed laws requiring periods of notice varying from 30 days to six months for the termination of a year-to-year tenancy. Some have abolished the rule that a hold-over tenant is automatically liable for another year's rent to make him a tenant-at-will or a tenant-from-month-to-month.

Types of Rental Arrangements

Many different types of rental arrangements are used in the leasing of landed properties. Some leases involve an elaborate array of provisions; others are limited to a minimum of detail. Some run for periods of less than a year while others run for periods of from one to ten years or for longer periods of up to 99 years or more. Some involve all of a landlord's property while others are limited to a few acres, square feet, or rooms out of a larger holding. And some involve all the use and possession rights associated with a given property while others are limited to specific interests such as the owner's mineral rights or certain rights in the use of surface land.

Many leases call for a flat cash rental while others specify definite sharing arrangements. Some give the tenant full responsibility for managing the property; others provide for varying amounts of landlord supervision or domination. Some give the tenant little incentive to improve the property while others provide considerable security for the tenant with compensation arrangements for unexhausted improvements and with options for the possible future purchase of the property.

These differences will be touched upon in the discussion that follows. Primary emphasis, however, will be given to five important types of arrangements. These include the fixed-cash, agricultural-share, and percentage-sharing arrangements used with most leases; long-term leases; and oil and gas leases.

Cash rent. Most property leases call simply for a specified cash payment every month or every year. This arrangement is used with almost all rentals of residential properties and with most leases involving commercial and industrial properties. It is somewhat less popular in agriculture, where less than one lease in every five called for a fixed cash rent in 1964, but is used extensively in the renting of pasture and grazing land.

Whenever a lease calls for a fixed cash rental payment, it is ordinarily assumed that the landlord's return is or should be adequate to cover his costs of property ownership (taxes, insurance, upkeep, and depreciation) plus a fair return on his investment. This arrangement protects the landlord's interests. But it leaves the commercial, industrial, and farm tenant subject to all the risks and uncertainties associated with his business activities. Since the cash tenant is committed to pay a fixed rent regardless of his success or failure as a business operator, he is ordinarily entrusted with full responsibility for managing his rented property. In addition, he is usually free to allocate his fixed and variable inputs as he wishes, and he receives the full return from his marginal inputs.

Any time a lease calls for a flat rental rate, the rate usually remains fixed for the duration of the lease or, in case of a tenancy from month-to-month or from year-to-year, until the landlord notifies the tenant of a change in the rental rate. Graded rental arrangements are used with some commercial leases to specify that the rental rate will be stepped up or down at some future date. Arrangements of this type are sometimes used when the landlord and tenant anticipate a future increase or decrease in the rental value of the property. They may also be used if the landlord is willing to accept a lower rental return at first with the promise of a higher return later on after the tenant has established his business and built up his earning power.

Agricultural-share renting arrangements. Most farm leases in the United States involve some type of share rental arrangement.[4] These arrangements frequently stem from customary practices and thus vary from region to region and from one type of farming area to another. Sometimes they involve a straight share of all the crops or all the livestock products produced, sometimes shares of specific crop and livestock enterprises, and sometimes a combination of crop and livestock sharing arrangements or the use of sharing arrangements with some enterprises and the payment of cash rent for others. Regardless of the combinations used, these sharing arrangements ordinarily shift some of the risks of farming along with some of the responsibilities of management to the landlord.

Two of the most publicized sharing arrangements—the "third and fourth" and the sharecropping systems—have been used for many years in the South. Both of these systems have been closely tied to the plantation economy even though they have also been used on a customary basis on many smaller farms. In both instances, the landlord ordinarily provides

---

[4]For other discussions of this subject see Alvin L. Bertrand and Floyd L. Corty, eds., *Rural Land Tenure in the United States* (Baton Rouge: Louisiana State University Press, 1962), chap. VII; Virgil L. Hurlburt, *Farm Rental Practices and Problems in the Midwest,* Iowa Agricultural Experiment Station Research Bulletin 416, 1954; Harold Hoffsommer *et al., The Social and Economic Significance of Land Tenure in the Southwestern States* (Chapel Hill: University of North Carolina Press, 1950); and Max M. Tharp, *The Farm Tenure Situation in the Southeast,* South Carolina Agricultural Experiment Station Bulletin 370, 1948.

the tenant with a house, a tract of land suitable for raising a cash crop, and frequently with sufficient credit to cover family living expenses during the crop year.

Sharecropping has declined considerably in importance since World War II and is no longer reported separately by the Census.[5] Under the customary cropping arrangement, the cropper worked a portion of the landlord's holding—an average of 35 acres per cropper family in 1954—subject to the landlord's supervision. He and his family provided the field labor needed to make a crop, and he also shared (usually on a credit basis) in certain production expenses such as the cost of fertilizer, insecticides, and ginning. At harvest, he then received a specified share of the crop—usually one-half—as payment for his services. From both a legal and a practical point of view, the sharecropper has often been regarded more as a laborer paid in kind than as a tenant who pays rent.

The "third and fourth" tenant has usually enjoyed a higher economic and legal status and frequently a higher social status than the cropper. In addition to his own and his family labor, he ordinarily supplies his farm power, equipment, tools, seed, and his portion (depending upon his share of the crop) of the other production expenses. Within the plantation system he has often operated under the close supervision of the landlord. Outside this system he has usually enjoyed considerable opportunity to display his talents as a manager. In both cases, custom has favored the payment of one-third of the corn crop and one-fourth of the cotton and other specialty crops as rent.

Three important types of sharing arrangements—the crop-share, live-stock-share, and share-cash systems—are used in the northern and western states. A crop-share arrangement quite similar to the "third and fourth" system is used in many areas, particularly in the Middle West and the Great Plains States. This leasing system is favored in the high-risk grain-farming area of the western Great Plains where a bonanza crop in one year may be followed by one or more years of crop failure. It is also widely used in many general farming areas such as the eastern Corn Belt.

Under the crop-share system, the landlord shares the risks and some of the management with his tenant and usually receives as rent between one-fourth and one-half of the crops produced. His exact share varies somewhat depending upon local custom and the landlord's contributions to the total inputs needed for production. In North Dakota, for example, the landlord receives either one-fourth or one-third of the grain crop, as local custom may dictate, when his inputs are limited to provision of the

[5] Cf. D. David Moyer, Marshall Harris, and Marie B. Harmon, *Land Tenure in the United States: Development and Status,* Agriculture Information Bulletin No. 338, (Washington: U. S. Department of Agriculture, 1969), p. 15. The number of share-croppers in the South dropped from 776,000 in 1930 to 121,000 in 1959 and probably did not exceed 40,000 in 1964. Most of those who still operated as sharecroppers were old people. The others shifted out of agriculture, to other agricultural tenures, or became employees on mechanized farms.

land and buildings.[6] His share increases to one-half of the crop when he increases his inputs to include the seed plus one-half of the harvesting costs.

Livestock-sharing arrangements are used extensively in the dairying and corn-hog producing areas of the Middle West. Under this arrangement, the landlord and tenant usually share equally in the livestock inventory, in the cost of producing feed crops and caring for the livestock, and in the division of the farm income. The landlord and the tenant both have an important stake in the managerial decisions made under this type of lease. Their mutual success usually depends upon their ability to work closely together, to work out their differences amicably, and to so balance or share their inputs that each party will find it to his interest to work for the maximization of their combined return.

Crop- and livestock-share arrangements are sometimes combined when the farm produces both cash crops and livestock products. Both rental arrangements are frequently used in combination with cash rent—particularly in the western Corn Belt area—to provide a share-cash system. Under this arrangement, the tenant gives a share of some crop or livestock enterprises as rent while he pays cash rent for his pasture and hay land or for the land used for certain other enterprises. A tenant may also pay share rent on most of his enterprises and pay additional cash rent as a bonus for an above-average house or for some other special advantages or perquisites.

Percentage leases. Leases for commercial sites have almost always called for a stipulated cash rent in times past. During recent decades, however, more and more retail establishments have shifted to the use of sharing arrangements under which the landlord receives a specified percentage of the business receipts as rent.

This use of percentage leases started around 1915 but did not come into prominence until the early 1930s. Percentage arrangements were accepted then as an expedient measure by many tenants who wanted long-term leases but who could not pay much rent under existing business conditions and by many landlords who expected "the depression to pass quickly [and who] did not want to be saddled with long-term, low-rental agreements."[7] With the return of prosperity and the inflationary trend of the 1940s, many landlords turned to this approach as a means of securing a higher rental return from their properties.

Percentage leases take four principal forms. Some leases specify that the tenant pay a straight percentage of his gross sales receipts as rent. Some require a straight percentage payment but also specify a minimum rent. Some accept the percentage principle but specify both a minimum

[6]Cf. Baldur H. Kristjanson and Ernest Solberg, *Farm Rental Bargaining in North Dakota*, North Dakota Agricultural Experiment Station Bulletin 372, 1952.

[7]"The Percentage Lease—Its Functions and Drafting Problems," *Harvard Law Review*, Vol. 61, January, 1948, p. 317.

and a maximum rent. And some provide that the landlord's share be based on a percentage of the net profits rather than the gross receipts.

The second arrangement with its minimum rent requirement is used with most percentage leases. Under this arrangement, a minimum rent is usually fixed at between 70 and 80 percent of the estimated fair cash rental value of the property or at a level at least sufficient to cover the landlord's costs for holding and maintaining his property. Landlords generally favor this provision for a minimum rental payment; and by the same token, they ordinarily refuse to specify a maximum rent.

Some percentage leases contain no provisions on minimum rent. In these cases and in many instances in which a minimum rent is specified, landlords frequently protect their interests by inserting a recapture clause into the lease. This clause makes it possible for the landlord to cancel the lease after reasonable notice if the tenant's business volume falls below expectations. Comparable provisions are also used in many leases to protect the tenant by making it possible for him to cancel the lease if his business proves unprofitable.

Little use is made of the percentage-of-net-profits approach. Landlords are usually advised against this arrangement—partly because of the difficulties that arise in the definition of net profits and partly because some lawyers feel that this arrangement creates a legal partnership between landlord and tenant.

The sharing rates used in percentage leases vary a great deal depending upon the bargaining power of the landlord and tenant, the general use-capacity of the site, and the tenant's type of business. A 1 or 2 percent rate may be quite adequate with a chain grocery that uses a low price mark-up to gain a high volume of business, while a 50 or 60 percent rate may be justified with downtown garages and parking lots.[8] Community experience often provides a guide to the proper percentage rate. But the actual determination of the rate is normally left to the bargaining process. In this process, each site and each prospective tenant use is treated as an individual case; and the percentage rate decided upon frequently represents an approximation of the proportion that the landlord's desired rent is of the anticipated business receipts.

Questions sometimes arise concerning the use of fixed or variable percentage rates. Some percentage leases include provisions for a sliding scale under which the percentage rate may rise or fall with changes in business volume. These provisions can be used to maximize the landlord's interests or to safeguard the tenant's interests during periods of slack business activity. A downward graduated rate, which provides a reduced rate of return on all gross receipts over a given level can often be justified on the ground that the additional business results from the tenant's decision to (1) concentrate on a high-volume low-mark-up selling program;

[8]Cf. McMichael and O'Keefe, *op. cit.*, pp. 43-47; and National Institute of Real Estate Brokers, *Percentage Leases*, 10th ed. (Chicago: National Association of Real Estate Boards, 1961).

or (2) use a large outlay of inputs for advertising or for services designed to attract additional customers.

Percentage leases are often favored on the ground that they help the landlord secure the true rental value of his property and provide him with incentive to find the tenant who will make the best use of his property. They also have a leveling effect in reducing the tenant's costs during periods of reduced income and in gearing the landlord's return to general business conditions. In this respect, percentage leases provide a hedge against both inflation and the fixed-rent problems that develop under possible public rent controls.[9]

Several disadvantages are associated with percentage leases. They make it possible for landlords to benefit from additional productivity prompted by the tenant's inputs or his managerial ability rather than the site. They can call for additional bookkeeping by the tenant, landlord inspection of the tenant's books, and landlord supervision of some tenant business practices. In this last respect, the landlord may require certain book-keeping practices, insist that certain minimum sums be spent for adver-tising, demand that the establishment be kept open during normal business hours, prevent transfer of the leasehold to another party, or prohibit the tenant from investing in competitive establishments to which he might divert business.

Percentage leases are most applicable at or near the 100 percent spots found in central business districts and in some community shopping centers. They are best used when the tenant's gross receipts are directly related to his business location and when these receipts come primarily from the sale of goods rather than services.

Long-term leases. Leases that run for periods of 15 years or more are ordinarily described as long-term leases. This type of lease is used occasionally in the operation of public utilities and in the administration and private use of certain public lands. Its most spectacular use, however, is associated with the development of commercial sites.

Many valuable sites in some large cities—sites such as those now occupied by Rockefeller Center and the Waldorf-Astoria Hotel in New York City—have been developed by tenants operating under 99-year leases. The owners of these sites often prefer to retain their ownership for investment or other purposes rather than sell, while the tenants often prefer long-term leases to the alternative of actually buying their sites. In this respect, long-term leases frequently represent a method of real estate financing in which the tenant enjoys a 100 percent loan of the value of the landlord's property.

With most long-term leases involving business sites, the tenant starts

---

[9]Under the state and federal rent control regulations used in the United States during the 1940s, the percentage rates used in percentage leases were frozen, but actual rent collections usually increased with the growing volume of business receipts experienced by most tenant establishments.

with an unimproved lot or with a site covered with structures that do not fit his use. Once the lease is signed, he is expected to clear the site, erect the structures he desires, and administer the property throughout the duration of his leasehold. He is expected to pay all real estate taxes and all the operating costs associated with his use of the property.

Long-term leases must be carefully written to cover many contingencies. Some of the most important of these involve the determination of the rental rate, protection of the landlord's interests, and termination of the lease.

Many long-term leases granted prior to the 1930s provided for a low initial rent with step-ups at five- and ten-year intervals. Others specified a cash rental rate for the first ten years with the rental rate in each succeeding decade being based on a fixed percentage—usually between 4 and 6 percent—of the reappraised base land value. These arrangements were often designed for the tenant's welfare; but in practice, they frequently resulted in rental rates somewhat in excess of the tenant's ability to pay. In light of this experience it is now recommended that future long-term leases use a flat annual cash rental rate equal to from 5 to 6 percent of the market value of the land at the time the lease is executed.[10]

The buildings erected by the tenant ordinarily provide the landlord with adequate security for future payment of his rent. Security deposits of various types, however, are often used during the time period that elapses before the buildings are erected; and some type of security may be required once the tenant's improvements become obsolete.

When no provisions to the contrary are in force, the tenant's improvements pass to the landlord at the end of the leasehold. This eventuality could have a deteriorative effect upon the tenant's property-management practices during the later years of the lease. Arrangements are accordingly included in most leases for automatic renewal of the lease if the tenant so desires and for the tenant's possible purchase of the site at some designated price. If the tenant, his heirs, or assigns accept neither of these options, the lease may provide that the landlord will purchase the tenant's improvements at their appraised value. Since the interests of both the landlord and the tenant can be terminated by condemnation proceedings, provisions are also included in most leases relative to the division of any possible indemnity award.

A long-term leasing arrangement known as *ground rent* is commonly used as a real estate financing measure in parts of Maryland and eastern Pennsylvania.[11] Considerable areas used for residential, commercial, industrial, and other purposes are leased under this arrangement for 99-year periods, with provisions for perpetual renewal. All property taxes

[10] Cf. McMichael and O'Keefe, *op. cit.*, p. 100.

[11] Cf. *ibid.*, pp. 95-104; and National Institute of Real Estate Brokers, *Ground Leases* (Chicago: National Association of Real Estate Boards, 1965).

on these sites are assessed to the tenant operators; and these operators are bound to the periodic—usually semiannual—payment of a specified ground rent to their landlords. If a tenant defaults in his payments, the landlord can cancel the lease and evict the tenant.

Many of the ground-rent arrangements found in these two states date back to colonial times. Problems have arisen in some instances because of the refusal of some landlords to sell and because of the failure of the original leases to include a tenant purchase option. Legislation has been passed in both states since 1884 making it possible for tenants to purchase the land at the capitalized value of the ground rent.

Oil and gas leases. Much of the land area of the United States is underlaid with oil and natural gas deposits. Every time drilling operations reveal, or even suggest, the presence of commercial quantities of these products in a new area, there is usually a flurry of interest in the leasing of oil and gas rights. Owners are seldom able to develop their own properties; and they are usually inclined to lease their rights to agents of various oil producing companies. Leases are frequently taken for speculative purposes. They are also used by many oil and gas companies to forestall the possible overdevelopment or overexploitation of an oil or natural gas field. An estimated 424 million acres in the United States were covered by oil and gas leases in 1960 and 336 million acres in 1967. Payments for royalties, bonuses, and rentals under these leases amounted to $12.8 million in 1960 and $7.9 million in 1967.

Oil and gas leases vary somewhat in details.[12] As a rule, they run for limited periods ranging up to ten years and for as much longer as oil or natural gas "are produced in paying quantities." Most leases provide for a fixed annual cash rental rate per acre plus a one-eighth share or royalty on any oil or natural gas that may be produced. The lessee normally secures the right to take his equipment onto the lessor's surface land to drill for oil or natural gas. Fees are sometimes paid for this privilege; and provisions are often inserted in the lease concerning the location of wells, the burying of pipes, and the lessee's use of the surface land.

Mineral-rights owners must often choose between selling or keeping their rights and between leasing their rights for a relatively low rental on the strength of a "wildcat" development or waiting for a possible higher rental. Lease management problems also arise when a development company decides to drill wells on some of the lands to which it holds lease rights but not others. Under this arrangement, some surface owners may

[12] Cf. L. A. Parcher, John H. Southern, and S. W. Voelker, *Mineral Rights Management by Private Landowners,* Great Plains Agricultural Council Publication 13, Oklahoma Agricultural Experiment Station, 1956. For other discussions of this subject, cf. Howard R. Williams, Richard C. Maxwell, and Charles J. Meyers, *Cases and Materials on the Law of Oil and Gas* (Brooklyn: The Foundation Press, Inc., 1956); and the annual *Proceedings of the National Institute of Petroleum Landmen* (New York: Mathew Bender, 1960 and later years).

enjoy considerable income from royalties while others receive none. Mineral-rights owners seldom have enough bargaining power to require their lessees to drill wells on their properties if other wells are drilled in the area. Arrangements have been worked out in many communities, however, for the pooling of royalty interests. This arrangement makes it possible for every participating owner to share in any royalties received from oil or natural gas production on the lands of any member of the pool.

ECONOMIC CONSIDERATIONS AFFECTING RENTAL RATES

Landlords and tenants have various goals in mind at the time they strike their rental bargain. Under adverse circumstances, a landlord may be mostly interested in just finding a reliable tenant; or a prospective tenant's primary goal may be simply that of securing suitable rental quarters at a price he can afford. Occasionally, one party may deliberately plan to exploit the interests of the other; a landlord may grant a favorable lease to a tenant he wishes to help along; or a tenant may cheerfully pay abnormally high rent with the knowledge that he is helping to support a needy landlord. As a general rule, however, both parties are motivated by the hope that they can maximize their economic returns and general satisfactions and at the same time participate in an arrangement that is fair to the other party.

The attainment of these goals is invariably complicated by the fact that rental bargains are made prior to the period of property use and possession. Since neither party can predict the future, both must act on faith. In this process, many operators are inclined to the optimistic acceptance of customary, unilateral, or vague rental arrangements without too much thought concerning their ultimate consequences. Some dictate the terms they want and offer them to prospective tenants (or landlords) on a take-it-or-leave-it basis. Others analyze the over-all rental proposal and bargain for the terms they desire.

With this conglomerate situation, it is not at all surprising that custom, the going rental rates supported by current supply and demand conditions, and hit-and-miss arrangements play major roles in the determination of most rental rates. Many landlords and tenants, however, give considerable thought to the development of workable rental arrangements that are both equitable and fair. This reasoning process causes some people to argue for a straight cash rental payment, which is equivalent to the current market rate of return on the landlord's investment. Some favor sharing arrangements that relate the landlord's return to the marginal productivity of his inputs; and some endorse combinations of the cash- and share-rent approaches.

Two major sets of goals—(1) maximizing of economic efficiency in resource use, and (2) attainment of distributive justice in the allocation of returns between landlords and tenants—have far-reaching effects upon the determination of ideal and workable leasing systems. Economic efficiency is often heralded as one of the principal objectives to be attained under leasing arrangements.[13]   This objective is secured when profits are maximized for the entire firm representing the combined interests of the landlord and tenant. Deviations from this maximum occur whenever the provisions of the rental arrangement make it more profitable for the tenant to combine his resources in some manner other than that which spells maximum profit for the over-all firm, and whenever the rental arrangement fosters a transfer of income from one resource owner to the other. Distributive justice in turn involves ethical, moral, and political values. It involves man's sense of fairness in his dealings with others and goes beyond the realm of economics.

Among the leading issues that arise in the development of mutually acceptable and advantageous leasing arrangements are the concerns over (1) equitable sharing arrangements covering costs and returns, (2) comparable rental arrangements with all products, (3) opportunities for a fair return from all investment inputs, (4) flexibility, which permits adjustments for changing costs, prices, and production, and (5) arrangements that recognize social justice and welfare objectives. The first three of these issues have an economic efficiency-orientation while the last two are concerned mostly with social justice.

Equitable Sharing of Costs and Returns

Share and percentage leases are often advocated because they relate the landlord's return to the marginal productivity of his inputs. They are frequently criticized, however, on efficiency grounds. This criticism stems from differences between the income incentives of share tenants and those of owner-operators and cash tenants. An owner-operator or cash tenant ordinarily has every incentive to apply his variable inputs to the point at which MFC = MVP because he knows he will receive the entire economic surplus from each of his marginal inputs. But when the share tenant "has to give his landlord half of the returns to each dose of capital and labor that he applies to the land, it will not be to his interest to apply any doses the total return to which is less than twice enough to reward him."[14]

---

[13] For more detailed discussions of this criterion as it relates to leasing arrangements, cf. Earl O. Heady, *Economics of Agricultural Production and Resource Use* (Englewood Cliffs, N.J.: Prentice-Hall, Inc., 1951), chap. XX; Hurlburt, *op. cit.;* Walter E. Chryst, "A Framework for Orienting Research in Land Tenure Within the Efficiency Concept," *Journal of Farm Economics,* Vol. 37, December, 1955, pp. 1333-40; and Howard W. Ottoson, "The Application of Efficiency to Farm Tenure Arrangements," *Journal of Farm Economics,* Vol. 37, December, 1955, pp. 1341-53.

[14] Alfred Marshall, *Principles of Economics,* 8th ed. (London: Macmillan and Company, 1938), p. 644. For an early discussion of this problem, cf. Adam Smith,

This concept may be illustrated by the two examples depicted in Figure 14-1. The first graph represents the situation that exists under an agricultural-share lease in which the landlord supplies a fixed input of land and improvements in return for a one-half share of the crop while the tenant supplies all of the variable inputs. Under these conditions the tenant pays the full marginal factor cost of each successive variable input unit but receives only half of the marginal value product.

If the operator in this example were an owner-operator or a cash tenant he would find it profitable to apply S inputs (the number of inputs at which MFC = MVP). A share tenant operator would find it more profitable to stop with R inputs because this is the point at which his marginal factor cost equals his one-half share of the marginal value product. The landlord would benefit if the tenant applied up to T inputs (the point at which he would receive his highest possible return); but a rational tenant would not go this far because any application of inputs beyond R would involve a transfer of income from the tenant to the landlord.

This same type of analysis may be applied to the percentage leases used by many commercial establishments. The example pictured in the second part of Figure 14-1 assumes a retail firm that uses a low-mark-up policy to encourage a large volume of business. The landlord's inputs are limited to the provision of a desirable commercial site in a central business district, for which he receives a 10 percent share of the tenant's gross receipts. Here again the tenant pays the full cost of each successive variable input while his returns are limited to 90 percent of the marginal value product, a fact that makes it uneconomic for him to apply more than R inputs in his business.

The tenant in this example may recognize the opportunities an owner-operator or cash tenant would have to increase the volume of business and total profits of the firm by using additional inputs—up to S input units—for advertising, delivery service, or other items. Yet as a tenant operating on a percentage lease, he would find it best to stop with R inputs because any additional inputs would call for a higher contract rent payment which he would have to supply from his normal returns as a tenant.

These two examples show that from a theoretical point of view the use of share and percentage leasing arrangements can result in less intensive

---

The Wealth of Nations (1776) (New York: Modern Library edition, 1937), p. 367. For more recent and more elaborate discussions cf. Rainer Schickele, "Effects of Tenure Systems on Agricultural Efficiency," *Journal of Farm Economics,* Vol. 23, February, 1941, pp. 185-207; Earl O. Heady, "Economics of Farm Leasing Systems," *Journal of Farm Economics,* Vol. 29, August, 1947, pp. 659-78; D. Gale Johnson, "Resource Allocation Under Share Contract," *Journal of Political Economy,* Vol. 58, April, 1950, pp. 111-23; and Louis S. Drake, "Comparative Productivity of Share- and Cash-Rent Systems of Tenure," *Journal of Farm Economics,* Vol. 34, November, 1952, pp. 535-50.

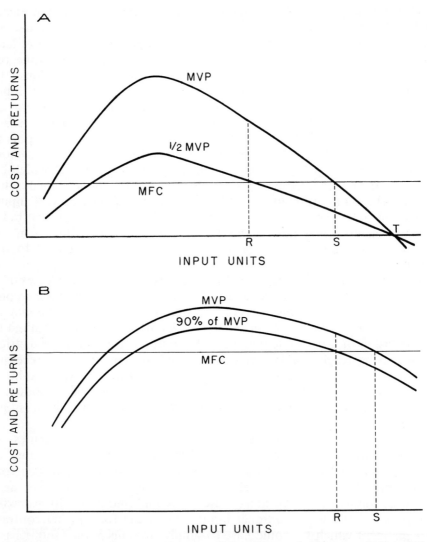

FIGURE 14-1. Illustration of the possible effects of (A) a one-half rental arrangement and (B) a 10 percent percentage leasing arrangement upon the tenant's willingness to apply additional inputs in the production process.

and less efficient resource use than one might expect under owner-operatorship or cash tenancy. It is surprising, therefore, to note that little consideration has been given to this problem in the case of percentage leases, that sharing arrangements are used by the great majority of farm tenants in the United States, and that the average share tenant tends to combine his input factors and operate with approximately the same intensity as most owner-operators and cash tenants.

Several reasons can be given for the share tenant's failure to act in the manner suggested above. Like other operators, he has difficulty in predicting in advance the exact combination of inputs that will give him his maximum return. At times, he may be unaware of the fact that he can maximize his short-run interests by operating differently than owner-operators. His calculations as to the optimum number of variable inputs he should use also are complicated in numerous instances by the tendency of landlords to use relatively short-term leases and restrictive leasing arrangements. Commercial landlords, for example, ordinarily specify certain managerial practices in their percentage leases while farm landlords frequently provide portions of the variable inputs such as shares of the seed, fertilizer, pesticides, and harvesting costs. Tenants also realize that they are evaluated as tenants and as credit risks in terms of their overall performance. Percentage and share tenants who want to retain their leaseholds or who hope to move on to the operation of more productive enterprises accordingly find it to their advantage to manage their inputs in much the same way as owner-operators or cash tenants.

Another explanation of the tendency of many share and percentage tenants to operate at the same level of overall efficiency as owner-operators involves factors assumed away in the theoretical model. Figure 14-1 assumes that the labor and managerial inputs supplied by the tenant are priced at going market levels and that alternative opportunities exist for the profitable utilization of any surplus variable inputs. With these assumptions, it is logical to argue that tenants will maximize their positions as producers by adding variable inputs only to the point at which their share of the marginal value product equals their share of the marginal factor costs. Under real life conditions, however, tenants find their maximization opportunities constrained by the terms of their leases, by the fact that the supplies of land resources available for their use are often definitely limited, and frequently by an absence of opportunities for the profitable utilization of their surplus inputs of labor and management in other enterprises. The typical tenant operating under these conditions often finds it to his advantage to apply his inputs of labor and management somewhat beyond the point at which his share of the marginal value product is equal to the market price of his marginal factor costs. He receives less than the full average market value of the additional inputs used, but his surplus inputs have a supply price of near zero and, with no alternative opportunities for their productive use, some return is better than no return at all.[15]

---

[15] Cf. Steven N. S. Cheung, *The Theory of Share Tenancy* (Chicago: University of Chicago Press, 1969), pp. 51-55, for an elaboration of this theme. Cheung indicates that some tenants may be inclined to apply inputs to points beyond the most profitable point for owner-operators and cash tenants but that competition between tenants and between landlords will tend to bring the optimum point for share tenants as well as for owner operators and cash tenants to the point at which MVP = MFC.

Comparable Rental Arrangements
with All Products

A second situation affecting the efficiency of resource use frequently arises when two or more rental or tenure arrangements affect a single set of operations. A simple example of this occurs when a tenant who produces two competing crops with comparable production costs and product values finds that he is expected to pay a larger share rent with one crop than with the other. Under these conditions, the tenant has an income incentive to shift resources to the crop that offers him the largest return, while the landlord has a comparable incentive for favoring production of the crop with the highest share rent.

This same situation applies when the tenant produces

> ... two or more crops with different unit costs, different yields and different prices with a given quantity of resources. ... Because of the opportunity to obtain a higher income, the operator will want to shift resources into production of that crop which gives the highest income on the factors he contributes. This will not necessarily be the one on which the lower share rental is paid because differences in unit costs may more than compensate differences in shares, and some minimum acreage of a crop like clover may be essential in the rotation to maintain the yield and income from corn. The inclination usually will be to shift more resources into production of the crop with the lower rental share.[16]

Similar situations occur when the tenant pays a share rent on some enterprises or fields and cash rent or no rent at all on others, or when a retailer operates two adjacent properties, one under a cash lease and one under a percentage lease. Operators under these conditions can find it advantageous to concentrate their most remunerative activities on their cash-rent or rent-free land. In so doing, they can maximize their returns at the sites where rent is a fixed cost while they can carry on necessary but less productive activities at those sites where rent is treated as a variable cost.

Comparable examples often occur with cases of part-ownership. As Ottoson has observed, farm owners who rent additional land usually tend

> ... toward greater intensity of production on the land owned by the operator. The productivity per input of operator's resources is higher on owned land than on a tract rented under a share lease. The notion is commonly suggested that part-owners tend to spread on their owned tracts the manure resulting from feed grown on their rented tracts, thus effecting a transfer of fertility. Operators will likely give priority to the owned tracts with respect to expenditure of working capital where capital is rationed. They may also favor the owned tracts in time of crop operations during crucial periods. This tendency toward less intensity would be less true where the rented part is under cash lease, although even here

[16]Hurlburt, *op. cit.*, p. 89.

the operator will have little or no incentive to make expenditures for inputs that become associated with the landlord's resources and that do not produce returns in the same year. [17]

As these examples suggest, mixed rental arrangements frequently provide the tenant with an opportunity to maximize his returns at the landlord's expense. This situation can result in a certain amount of inefficiency in total resource use together with considerable ill-will between landlord and tenant. These consequences are usually averted when the same sharing arrangement is applied to all products. When this practice is not followed, it is best to evaluate the different rental arrangements and make such adjustments as are necessary to insure efficient use of the combined resources of the landlord and tenant.

Most landlords recognize that the tenant's opportunity to maximize his personal interests is largely dependent upon his power to make important production decisions. This opportunity is definitely limited when the landlord makes most of these decisions or when he participates jointly with the tenant in the decision-making process. Provisions are often included in farm leases specifying the acreage or scope of the principal enterprises and sometimes even the field layout and cropping practices the tenant will use. Comparable limitations are also used with commercial property leases when the landlord requires a minimum cash rent in connection with his percentage lease, uses a recapture clause to cancel the lease if the tenant's business falls short of the anticipated level, or acts to prevent his tenant from acquiring interests in adjacent properties.

Opportunities for a Fair Investment Return

Another important leasing problem arises when the most efficient or most desirable pattern of operations calls for certain types of investment inputs without providing any assurance of a fair return to the party who makes the investment. This is a frequent problem when farm, residential, and commercial tenants operate under short-term leases. It also provides a deterrent to possible landlord action in the improvement of farm and urban housing facilities.

Landlords and tenants frequently find that they can use investments in certain types of improvements to increase both the productivity and the satisfactions they secure from their combined resources. With commercial

---

[17] Ottoson, *loc. cit.*, pp. 1350-51. George Washington recognized this problem in a letter of February 25, 1784 in which he wrote: "From the first I laid it down as a maxim, that no person who possessed Lands adjoining, should hold any of mine as a Lease, and for this obvious reason, that the weight of their labour, and burden of their crops, whilst it was in a condition to bear them, would fall upon my Land, and the improvement upon his own, in spite of all the covenants which could be inserted to prevent it." *Writings of George Washington* (Washington: U. S. Government Printing Office, Vol. 27, 1938, p. 344).

business properties, these improvements may involve the shifting of wall partitions, the installation of air conditioning facilities, or the erection of a new store front. With a rented house or apartment, they may call for modernizing the kitchen, installing built-in cabinets, or updating the architectural styling. With farm properties they may involve applications of lime or commercial fertilizer, land-clearing practices, or installation of drainage tile or an irrigation system. A shift to a longer crop-rotation program or to more livestock enterprises may also call for investments in green manure and soil-building crops and for construction of new or better farm service buildings.

The real problem in these cases often boils down to one of who is to pay for the cost of the improvement. Since these improvements ordinarily add to the use-capacity and value of the landlord's property, it is often assumed that the landlord should bear the cost. Landlords often object to this reasoning, however, on the ground that all or most of the benefits will accrue to the tenant. This is particularly true when the landlord makes an improvement without adjusting his cash or share rental terms.

As long as the tenant is regarded as the major beneficiary, it may be argued that he should bear the cost of the desired improvements. Experience shows, however, that the average tenant is usually quite hesitant to contribute time or money to the improvement of the landlord's property. When the improvement promises to pay for itself within the time period of the lease, the tenant ordinarily finds it good business to go ahead with his investment in much the same way as an owner-operator. The tenant who operates under a short-term lease, however, can offer three important reasons for not making the desired improvements. "First, he is uncertain that he will remain on the property long enough to get full benefit from the improvements. Second, he has no assurance he would be compensated for his unused value of the improvement in case he moves. . . . Third, since improvements make the landlord's property more valuable and attractive to other tenants, an increased rent may result."[18]

As these reasons suggest, the problems of tenure instability and insecurity of expectations may cause landlords and tenants to operate on a lower and less productive plane than their potentialities warrant. Several alternative approaches can be used by landlords and tenants to avoid this situation.[19] Intermediate- and long-term leases are frequently used, particularly in urban commercial districts, to protect and strengthen the income incentives tenants have for investing in property and other business improvements. Tenant improvements can be encouraged by arrangements that provide that the tenant be compensated for the value of his unexhausted improvements at the time he gives up his leasehold.

---

[18] John F. Timmons, *Improving Farm Rental Arrangements in Iowa*, Iowa Agricultural Experiment Station Research Bulletin 393, p. 86, 1953.

[19] Cf. *ibid.*, pp. 89-95.

Landlords are often willing to make property improvements if their tenants will agree to the payment of improvement rents. And joint action can be secured with programs that call for landlord-tenant sharing of improvement costs and returns, landlord provision of the materials while the tenant supplies the labor, or compensating arrangements under which the landlord makes one type of improvement while the tenant makes another.

A tenant's unwillingness to invest in property improvements when he has no assurance of security in his expected ability to profit from his investment has its counterpart in some situations involving landlords. When an urban landlord finds himself subject to rent controls or when he has leased his property for a long period at a fixed rental rate, he often has little incentive to provide more than the necessary repairs and upkeep for his property. A farm landlord may feel that the accepted rental market in his community will provide him with no more return if he provides a new modern home for his tenant than if he provides a less desirable but still habitable tenant house. Under these circumstances, the landlord may resist pressure for housing improvements—unless they are necessary to attract or keep desirable tenants—simply because he has no assurance of a fair return on his improvement investment. Additional cash rent for housing improvements is sometimes recommended as an answer to this problem.

Adjustments for Changing Conditions

Even when a landlord and tenant accept what appears to be an ideal rental arrangement, distribution problems often arise because of unexpected changes in cost, price, and production assumptions. These changes frequently bring a somewhat different distribution of the income associated with the rented property than that contemplated in the original leasing agreement.

Problems of this order are a frequent occurrence in agriculture; and they are not at all unusual with urban properties. Many urban tenants found during the depression years of the early 1930s that they had agreed to fixed commercial or residential rental rates that far exceeded their reduced ability to pay. These tenants frequently found it necessary to demand rent reductions as a condition of continued business operations or residential occupancy. The changed conditions encountered a decade later during the 1940s found many landlords bound to contract rent commitments that were definitely low relative to the rising business and personal incomes of their tenants. Some of these landlords were able to raise their rents; but many were prevented from doing so until after the end of rent controls.

The impact of wide fluctuations in farm incomes on rental payments is vividly illustrated by the rental payment situation on Iowa farms during the 1920s and early 1930s. Cash-rent tenants paid an average of 59 percent of their estimated net returns from farming before payment of rent as rent in 1921, 19 percent in 1922, 64 percent in 1923, and between 20 and 37 percent from then until the early 1930s, when average net returns fell below the amounts needed to pay the specified cash rent. Rental payments for crop-share tenants ranged from averages of 18 percent of the net returns in 1925 to 227 percent in 1931 while livestock-share tenants experienced comparable wide ranges in their rental payments.

Numerous arrangements can be used to keep the landlord's return somewhat proportionate to the marginal productivity of his inputs and to keep actual rental payments somewhat in line with the distribution plan envisaged in the initial rental arrangement. Since these arrangements must be agreed upon prior to the tenant's use of the landlord's property, they must always be sufficiently flexible to allow for adjustments to changing cost, price, and production conditions. Beyond this, they should also favor maximum efficiency in resource use together with some protection to the landlord against inferior management by the tenant.[20]

No rental system has yet been devised that has the advantage of always appearing as equitable to both parties at the time rent is paid as at the time when the rental agreement is made. Percentage leases, however, are often favored with commercial properties because of their characteristic of relating the landlord's return to the tenant's level of business activity. Sharing arrangements are used to this same end in agriculture.

Much less progress has been made in working out flexible cash rents. Proposals have been advanced for relating residential rents to a cost-of-living index during periods of rent control. Several somewhat similar proposals have been made in agriculture. One of these proposals—the Iowa flexible cash rent plan—calls for a landlord-tenant agreement on a cash base rental figure, which is adjusted at the end of the year for general price and production changes in the area to determine the actual rental payment. A second proposal—the Missouri multiple commodity plan—calls for a base rent associated with a mutual landlord-tenant estimate of the expected gross income of the farm. At the end of the year, this base rent is used to compute an actual rental rate, which bears the same percentage relationship to the base rate as the annual gross income bears to the estimated gross.[21]

Social-Justice and Welfare Considerations

No discussion of the conditions needed for an ideal rental system would

[20]Cf. Walter E. Chryst and John F. Timmons, *Adjusting Farm Rents to Changes in Prices, Costs, and Production,* Iowa Agricultural Experiment Station Special Report No. 9, 1955.

[21]Cf. *ibid.,* pp. 29-44; and John F. Timmons, *Landlord-Tenant Relationships in Renting Missouri Farms,* Missouri Agricultural Experiment Station Bulletin 409, 1946 (2nd ed.).

be complete without some mention of the overlying importance of the concepts of social justice and welfare. Most people adhere to an ethical or moral code, which causes them to regard some types of leasing arrangements and some lines of action as more right or just than others. They feel some responsibility for the welfare of their associates. They are both conscious of and responsive to the attitudes of their community; and they are more inclined to do those things regarded as acceptable and praiseworthy by their group than to follow lines of action generally frowned upon by society.

These factors play a highly significant role in limiting the extent to which landlords and tenants deliberately maximize their own interests at the expense of others. They help to make the landlord-tenant relationship a cooperative arrangement under which both parties benefit rather than a tooth-and-claw struggle for economic dominance. They explain the tendency of most landlords and tenants to work together, particularly when they are members of the same community. By the same token, they also explain why the leading examples of inequitable and exorbitant rental arrangements on the world front involve instances of absentee ownership in which the landlord group has isolated itself from immediate personal contact with the tenants.

Yet important as the concepts of equity, social justice, and welfare are in the determination of rental arrangements, they are often neglected and underemphasized in comparison with economic efficiency criteria. Production-oriented observers frequently equate equitability in the division of income between landlord and tenant with the marginal value productivity of the resource inputs each party contributes in production. This marginal-productivity concept of equity in rental arrangements has some justification when the landlord and tenant enjoy relatively equal bargaining power, when both possess alternative opportunities, and when both can command an adequate return from their resource inputs. It provides a superficial and meaningless measure of equity, however, when the cards are stacked in favor of either party.

History shows that tenant groups have often suffered from a lack of equal bargaining power with their landlords. When this condition has been combined with lack of alternative opportunities for the tenant, tenants have frequently bid up the rent they were willing to pay while at the same time bidding the returns for their own inputs down to a subsistence level. By imputing the going rates of return to the tenant's variable inputs, one could easily use the marginal-value-productivity approach to justify the "rack rents" of nineteenth-century Ireland and the exorbitant rents of pre-1950 Egypt or India as "an equitable division of the product." Conclusions of this order run definitely counter to our prevailing concepts of equity, justice, and social welfare.

In addition to their use as an informal individual and group control over rental arrangements, social-justice and welfare considerations often become the subject of public policy. Many countries have used agricultural and residential rent controls to secure distributive justice for tenants. Special credit programs, resettlement arrangements, and public housing programs are often used to improve the tenant's alternatives and his bargaining position. Antipeonage legislation has been used in countries such as the United States to protect tenants against undesirable rental conditions. Land reform measures of various types also have been used in many nations to provide a larger measure of social justice and welfare for tenant-operators and other would-be owners.

—SELECTED READINGS

Bertrand, Alvin L., and Floyd L. Corty (eds.), *Rural Land Tenure in the United States* (Baton Rouge: Louisiana State University Press, 1962).

Fisher, Ernest M., and Robert M. Fisher, *Urban Real Estate* (New York: Henry Holt & Company, Inc., 1954), chap. VII.

Heady, Earl O., *Economics of Agricultural Production and Resource Use* (Englewood Cliffs, N.J.: Prentice-Hall, Inc., 1952), chaps. XX, XXI.

Johnson, V. Webster, and Raleigh Barlowe, *Land Problems and Policies* (New York: McGraw-Hill Book Company, Inc., 1954), chap. XI.

Kratovil, Robert, *Real Estate Law*, 5th ed. (Englewood Cliffs, N.J.: Prentice-Hall, Inc., 1969), chaps. XXX, XXXIV.

Moyer, D. David, Marshall Harris, and Marie B. Harmon, *Land Tenure in the United States*, Agriculture Information Bulletin No. 338 (Washington: U. S. Department of Agriculture, 1969).

Renne, Roland R., *Land Economics*, 2nd ed. (New York: Harper & Brothers, 1958), chap. XVII-XVIII.

Timmons, John F., *Improving Farm Rental Arrangements in Iowa*, Iowa Agricultural Experiment Station Research Bulletin 393 (Ames: Iowa State College, 1953).

15

Use
of Real Estate Credit

Credit is frequently described as the "life blood" of the real estate business. The reasons for this characterization are easy to find. Real estate credit is used in the acquisition of a great majority of the homes, farms, and other real properties purchased in the United States. Credit arrangements have provided a shortcut to property ownership for millions of farm, business, and home owners. Credit has made ownership possible for thousands of individuals who would otherwise have found their personal roads to ownership closed or filled with time-consuming detours. At the same time, it has undoubtedly contributed to a different type of real estate market than would exist if less credit were available.

The discussion of real estate credit that follows is divided into four principal parts. Emphasis is first given to an over-all view of the importance of real estate credit in the American economy. Attention is then focused on the chief characteristics of mortgage and land contract arrangements. These discussions are followed with a brief analysis of the problems lenders and borrowers face in their administration of real estate credit.

IMPORTANCE OF REAL ESTATE CREDIT

Credit arrangements go back to the dawn of private ownership. Almost from the first recognition of exclusive private property rights in land, owners and prospective owners have found it good business to borrow and use the capital resources of others. This use of credit has persisted because it has usually provided a mutually advantageous arrangement for both the lender and the borrower. Lenders have secured interest payments from the use of their surplus funds. Most borrowers in turn have sought credit with the expectation that they could use it to maximize their own returns or satisfactions.

Real estate credit has been much more popular and more widely used during some periods of history than others. Throughout the Middle Ages, lending practices calling for payments of interest were generally frowned upon and sometimes denounced by the church. Credit contracts were ordinarily tolerated and enforced by the state, but moral considerations kept most people from borrowing money. Mortgaged properties were frequently transferred to the lender to be held and used for his benefit until the loan was repaid, and money lenders were often scorned for their practice of usury.

Most of this stigma against the use of credit gradually disappeared with the rise of modern capitalism. With this development, more and more people sensed the significance of the role borrowed capital can play in implementing increased productivity and economic development. Governments instituted legal controls to prevent the chief abuses associated with the earlier uses of credit. People were encouraged to put their savings to work by loaning them to others. Emphasis was given to the development and provision of credit facilities; and the credit system emerged as a dominant force in the economy.

Impact of Credit on Land Resources

Since the rise of capitalism, and during the last century in particular, the use of credit has come as a boon to many operators. Along with leasing arrangements, the use of savings to acquire property, and the acquisition of property by gift or inheritance, real estate credit now provides one of the four major means that operators can use to acquire possession and control over land resources. The widescale use of real estate credit facilities also has three other important effects upon the manner in which we hold and use land resources.

The use of credit frequently makes it possible for operators to expand the scale of their operations, step up the efficiency of their operations, and increase their over-all productivity. When the supply of credit is short—as it usually is in frontier and other underdeveloped areas—operators often fail to make the most effective or highest and best use of their land resources simply because they lack the necessary capital to do so. With more adequate supplies of credit, they find it possible to work out more productive combinations of their various input factors. These combinations result in higher returns to land, labor, and management—

returns that are often plowed back into additional land improvements. This increased productivity helps to stimulate economic activity and frequently gives rise to new demands and new markets which prompt additional resource developments and the shifting of many land areas to new higher and better uses.

Real estate credit arrangements ordinarily have an important impact on the distribution and holding of property rights in land resources. Property rights are transferred every time a borrower gives a mortgage as security for a grant of credit and every time a seller gives a land contract to the purchaser of a given property. These rights-sharing arrangements seldom constitute much of a problem as long as the mortgagor or the buyer keeps up his payments. Should he become delinquent, however, the mortgagee or holder of the land contract may press for payment; and if the debt is not repaid as provided, the lending party may start legal proceedings to divest the mortgagor or buyer of the rights he holds in the property affected by the credit arrangement.

Still another effect of credit on land resources occurs when lenders prescribe particular management practices or a certain amount of managerial control as a condition of the loan. Frequent examples of this are found both in agriculture and in industry. The agricultural credit merchants once found in many Southern communities usually insisted that their clients grow specified acreages of cotton or certain other cash crops. The Farmers Home Administration provides managerial supervision along with the loans it makes to its borrowers. Bankers often participate in certain managerial decisions of their borrowers, and large financial institutions frequently claim representation on the boards of large corporations.

Real Estate Credit Situation

The term "real estate credit" is ordinarily limited to those types of loans in which real property is pledged as security for a credit grant. These loans are usually made for the purchase or improvement of property, but may be used for other purposes as well. Real estate credit arrangements ordinarily involve the granting of mortgages; and most of the interest in and statistics concerning real estate credit center on this type of credit. Other methods of real estate financing, however, are in use. Land contracts provide an important type of real estate credit for property buyers in many areas; ground rents and long-term leases are used as a real estate financing device in some localities; and a variety of real estate bond, stock, and land trust arrangements can be used to provide real estate credit.

The importance of real estate credit in the American economy can best be illustrated by a brief review of recent credit trends. At the end of 1970, property owners in the United States owed $451.1 billion in outstanding debt on real estate mortgages and land contracts. This total included $279.7 billion of debt outstanding on one- to four-family residences, $140.2 billion on multifamily residential and commercial properties, and $31.2 billion on farm properties. (Table 15-1.) Altogether, the real estate debt load for 1970 represented a 13-fold increase over that for 1945.

TABLE 15-1. **Outstanding Real Estate Debt in the United States, 1930-1970**
(billions of dollars)

Year	Total real estate debt*	Nonfarm one- to four-family residences	Total outstanding debt on: Multifamily residences and commercial properties	Farm properties
1930	47.8	18.8	9.4	9.4
1935	37.3	13.1	4.4	7.4
1940	36.5	17.4	12.6	6.5
1945	35.5	18.6	12.2	4.8
1950	72.8	45.2	21.6	6.1
1955	129.9	88.2	32.6	9.0
1960	206.8	141.3	52.7	12.8
1965	325.8	212.9	91.6	21.2
1970	451.1	279.7	140.2	31.2

*Data represent year-end totals and include mortgages, purchase-money mortgages, and land contracts but do not include corporate bonds or real estate debt on multifamily residential and commercial properties that corporate owners may owe to other nonfinancial corporations. Totals do not always add up because of rounding.

Source: Data for 1930-40 from *Survey of Current Business,* October 1949 (Washington: U. S. Department of Commerce, 1949), p. 11; data for 1945-65 from *Statistical Abstract of the United States, 1968* (Washington: U. S. Department of Commerce, 1968), p. 459; 1970 data from *Federal Reserve Bulletin,* May 1971, p. A-50.

Examination of the nonfarm residential real estate market in the United States indicates that the total outstanding mortgage debt for this type of property increased from $2.7 billion in 1896 to $4.4 billion in 1910 and $27.6 billion in 1930.[1] This debt load dropped to $22.2 billion in 1935 and then gradually increased to $24.6 billion in 1945, after which it skyrocketed to totals of $55.3 billion in 1959, $161.6 billion in 1960, and $337.6 billion in 1970. (Cf. Figure 15-1.)

Comparable studies of the farm mortgage debt situation show that the total outstanding farm real estate debt increased from $3.2 billion in 1910 to a peak of $10.8 billion in 1923. (Figure 15.2.) This total was gradually pared down to a low of $4.8 billion at the end of 1945. Following World War II, however, it increased at a rapid pace, which brought the total past the $30 billion mark in 1970. But as Table 15-1 shows, the farm real

[1] Cf. L. Grebler, D. M. Blank, and L. Winnick, *Capital Formation in Residential Real Estate: Trends and Prospects* (Princeton: Princeton University Press, 1954), appendix N. The data on nonfarm residential mortgages in this study include those reported for one- to four-family residences in Table 15-1 plus the mortgages on multifamily residential properties.

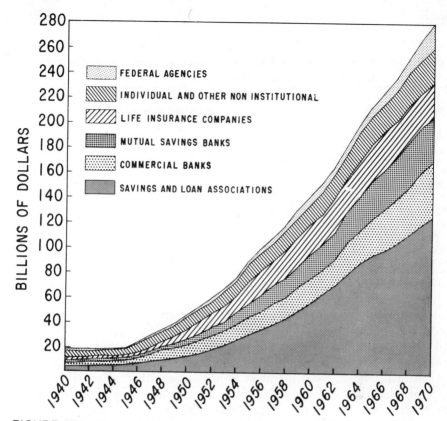

FIGURE 15-1. Farm mortgage debt held by major classes of lenders, United States, 1910-1970.

estate debt load increased some 6.5 times between 1945 and 1970 as compared with an 11.5-fold increase in the outstanding mortgage debt on multifamily and commercial properties and a 15-fold increase in the debt on one- to four-family residences.

Census findings indicate that 28 percent of the farms and nonfarm residential properties were mortgaged in 1890. (Table 15-2.) These proportions increased to a high of 44.6 percent of the farm properties in 1930 and 45.3 percent of the nonfarm dwellings in 1940. By 1960 some 38.3 percent of the farm owners had mortgages while mortgages were reported by 56.8 percent of the rapidly increasing number of residential property owners. Outstanding mortgage debt accounted for 41.5 percent of the estimated value of the mortgaged farms in 1940, for only 25.3 percent in 1950, and 26.4 percent in 1960. The median outstanding first mortgage on owner-occupied residential properties in 1960 amounted to 49.3 percent of the value of the mortgaged property.

Major Sources of Credit

Prospective borrowers can usually turn to several sources for real estate credit. Individual investors have always provided an important source of

TABLE 15-2. **Mortgage Status of Farm and Home Owners as Reported by the United States Census, 1890-1960**

Census year	Percentage of owner-occupied properties with reported mortgage debt	
	Farms (percent)	Nonfarm residences (percent)
1890	28.2	27.7
1900	31.1	32.0
1910	33.6	33.3
1920	41.1	39.8
1930	44.6	*
1940	38.8	45.3
1950	27.5	44.0
1960	38.3	56.8

*Data not reported.

mortgage funds and ordinarily account for most of the land contract credit. Other important sources of mortgage credit are provided by savings and loan associations, life insurance companies, commercial banks, savings banks, and various public credit agencies.[2] Individuals and other non-institutional lenders were the most important suppliers of mortgage credit for farm mortgage loans in 1970 while savings and loan associations were the leading single source of mortgage credit for one- to four-family residences and life insurance companies for multiple-family residential units. (Cf. Table 15-3.)

Figure 15-1 presents a graphic picture of the changing importance of the major sources of home mortgage credit between 1940 and 1970. During this time period the total volume of outstanding mortgage credit increased almost 15-fold from $18 to $267 billion. Individual and other noninstitutional lenders provided the largest single source of mortgage funds in 1940 when they accounted for more than a third of the home mortgage debt. The volume of credit from this source more than quadrupled in the next three decades but accounted for less than 10 percent of the outstanding indebtedness in 1970.

Savings and loan associations, which had accounted for a third of the volume of mortgage credit in the late 1920s, held less than a fifth of the total in 1940 and then surged ahead to account for 44 percent of the total in 1970. Commercial banks held slightly over 10 percent of the loan

[2]For more detailed discussions of the facilities provided by these agencies, cf. Stanley L. McMichael and Paul T. O'Keefe, *How to Finance Real Estate,* 3rd ed. (Englewood Cliffs, N. J.: Prentice-Hall, Inc., 1967), chaps. III-VII; Sherman J. Maisel, *Financing Real Estate: Principles and Practices* (New York: McGraw-Hill Book Company, 1965), chaps. III-V; Aaron G. Nelson and William G. Murray, *Agricultural Finance,* 5th ed. (Ames: Iowa State University Press, 1967), chaps. XVI-XXII; and Arthur M. Weimer and Homer Hoyt, *Principles of Urban Real Estate,* 5th ed. (New York: Ronald Press, 1966), chaps. XIX-XXI.

TABLE 15-3. Outstanding Real Estate Mortgage Debt in the United States Held by Major Lending Groups, January 1, 1970

Lending agencies	Nonfarm one- to four-family residences	Multiple-family residential properties	Farm properties
Total outstanding debt (in billions of dollars)	$266.9	$51.8	$28.4
Proportion of debt held by:		(percentage distribution)	
Savings and loan associations	44.3	22.4	—
Life insurance companies	10.5	27.0	20.2
Commercial banks	13.6	6.0	14.5
Mutual savings banks	15.6	23.6	—
Federal land banks	—	—	23.5
Federal agencies*	6.4	5.0	1.6
Individuals and others	9.6	16.0	40.2

*Includes Federal National Mortgage Association, Government National Mortgage Association, Federal Housing Administration, Veterans Administration, and Farmers Home Administration.

Source: Data on residential property mortgages from U.S. Department of Housing and Urban Development, *Housing and Urban Development Trends, Annual Summary,* May, 1970, p. 51. Data for farm mortgages from U. S. Department of Agriculture, *Agricultural Finance Review,* December, 1970, Vol. 31 Supplement, p. 2.

volume in 1940, around 20 percent between 1945 and 1955, and then dropped back to around 15 percent during the 1960s. Meanwhile, the mutual savings banks, which had accounted for less than 10 percent of the loans prior to the 1950s, boosted their share to more than 15 percent in 1970. Life insurance companies held less than 10 percent of the loan volume in 1940, around 20 percent in the early 1950s, and then saw their share of the total drop to around 10 percent again in 1970.

Two important additional sources of funds are provided by the Federal National Mortgage Association (popularly known as "Fannie Mae") and the Government National Mortgage Association. FNMA was established in 1938 to buy and sell Federal Housing Administration-insured mortgages and later Veterans Administration-guaranteed loans. GNMA plays a comparable special assistance function in buying and holding mortgages.

Trend data showing the changing importance of the leading sources of farm credit since 1910 are presented in Figure 15-2. Individual and noninstitutional investors accounted for more than half of the total outstanding farm mortgage credit in all the years prior to 1933 and for approximately two-fifths of the credit throughout most of the 1933-70 period. Commercial banks and life insurance companies provided practically all of the institutional credit up to 1921, a major portion of this credit between 1921 and 1933, and a somewhat smaller proportion after 1933. Together, they have accounted for around a third of the outstanding farm mortgage debt in most years since 1945.

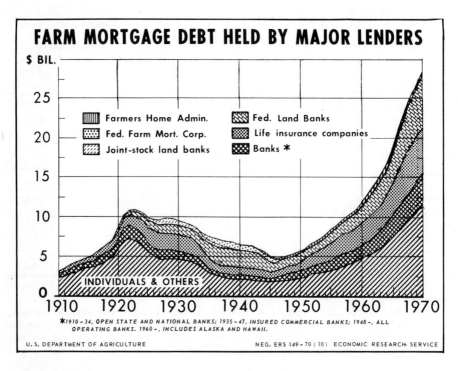

FIGURE 15-2. Outstanding real estate mortgage debt on nonfarm one- to four-family residential units by major lender groups, United States, 1940-1970.

The federal land banks, created under the Federal Farm Loan Act of 1916, became an important source of credit in the 1920s, provided the principal source of new farm credit during the 1930s, accounted for roughly a fourth of the farm mortgage debt at the end of World War II, held less than a fifth of this total between 1948 and 1965, after which their share rose to almost a fourth of the total in 1970. The joint stock land banks, also created under the Federal Farm Loan Act of 1916, played a far less important role in supplying new credit and were discontinued in 1933. The Federal Farm Mortgage Corporation—set up in 1933 to administer the Land Bank Commissioner loans, which were used as second mortgages in association with land bank loans and as first mortgages on properties on which the land banks would not make loans—provided an important secondary source of funds during the 1930s and 1940s. The Farm Security Administration, now the Farmers Home Administration, has provided an additional source of farm real estate credit since 1937.

Public credit since 1932. Some of the most significant developments involving sources of credit came during the 1930s when both the farm and residential mortgage credit markets suffered from the paralyzing grip of the depression. With the onset of the depression, the credit situation tightened; thousands of mortgagors started defaulting on their payments; most of the conventional credit sources, which might have helped, found major portions of their assets immobilized; and owner after owner faced the prospect of losing his property through mortgage foreclosure.

In the midst of this situation, debt conciliation committees were established in numerous counties and states to facilitate voluntary debt adjustments, which would put borrowers on a sounder footing and help forestall foreclosure proceedings. The Federal Home Loan Bank Board was created in 1932 and the Farm Credit Administration in 1933 to promote better credit arrangements. Debt moratoria and farm mortgage relief laws were passed by most state legislatures and by Congress.

Federal funds were poured into the farm and residential mortgage markets through the federal land banks and the Home Owners Loan Corporation. Federal Land Bank and Land Bank Commissioner loans accounted for two-thirds of the farm loans made in 1934; and the portion of the total farm mortgage debt held in these two types of Federal Land Bank loans increased from 13 percent of the total in January, 1932, to 34 percent in January, 1935. At the same time, the Home Owners Loan Corporation used funds advanced by the Reconstruction Finance Corporation to refinance more than a million home-mortgage distress cases within a three-year period. These loans were refinanced mostly on a 15-year basis at 5 percent interest. In its refinancing operations, this agency scaled the principal indebtedness of its borrowers down by an average of 7 percent.

The operations of the HOLC, the Federal Land Banks, and the Federal Farm Mortgage Corporation came too late to help many distressed borrowers. Some one and a half million home mortgages and around a third of a million farm mortgages found their way through the foreclosure wringer before the decade was out. These federal programs, however, did much to stabilize the real estate credit market and to instill renewed confidence in the mortgage credit system. In this sense, they forestalled a complete collapse of the real estate market and set important precedents for possible future federal action under emergency conditions.

Following up on its earlier action, Congress passed the National Housing Act in 1934. This act created the Federal Housing Administration and charged it with the responsibility of providing mortgage insurance on several types of home loans. Comparable responsibility for guaranteeing certain loans to World War II veterans was later given to the Veterans Administration under the Servicemen's Readjustment Act of 1944. This provision of FHA-mortgage insurance and VA-loan guarantees has made it possible for federal credit agencies to more or less dominate the operations of the home mortgage market. Thirty-four percent of the outstanding mortgage debt on nonfarm one- to four-family residences in 1970 was underwritten by the federal government—$56 billion by the Federal Housing Administration and $36 billion by the Veterans Administration.

Federal assistance has also been continued with farm loans. The Federal Land Banks have continued their loan program even though the use of Land Bank Commissioner loans was discontinued in 1947. The Farm Security Administration (now the Farmers Home Administration) was created in 1937 to make rehabilitation loans to disadvantaged farm people and to underwrite an ownership-acquisition (tenant-purchase) program. And VA guarantees were extended to cover certain farm real estate loans made to veterans.

MORTGAGE ARRANGEMENTS

Most people who contemplate the use of mortgage credit have a variety of questions regarding the nature and characteristics of a mortgage, the amount of money they can borrow, the probable interest and repayment terms of their mortgage, and possible foreclosure procedures.

Characteristics of a Mortgage

A mortgage may be defined as "a conveyance of land given as security for the payment of a debt."[3] Like a deed, a mortgage provides for the conveyance of certain property rights to a second party. But unlike a deed, these rights are conveyed only for the purpose of providing security for the payment of a debt; and the mortgage becomes void once the debt is paid in accordance with the terms specified in the mortgage agreement.[4]

From a legal standpoint, mortgages fall into three general classes: regular mortgages, deeds of trust, and equitable mortgages. Regular mortgages call for the conveyance of a property from the borrower to the

[3] Robert Kratovil, *Real Estate Law,* 5th ed. (Englewood Cliffs, N. J.: Prentice-Hall, Inc., 1969), p. 203.

[4] As indicated in chapter 12, some states hold to a *title theory* approach, which assumes that a mortgage actually vests the mortgagee with a legal title to the mortgaged property. Others hold to a *lien theory* approach, which treats a mortgage as a mere lien to secure the loan made to the mortgagor; while several states take intermediate positions between these two approaches. The legal concept of a mortgage accepted in a state has an important effect on the rights a mortgagee has to possess or take rent from a property once it has been mortgaged and once the mortgagor has defaulted on his payments. Even in the title-theory states, the courts have limited the rights once exercised by mortgagees to a shadow of their pre-seventeenth century importance. Mortgagees in these states still enjoy greater rights to the possession and rents of mortgaged properties than is the case in the lien-theory states. Cf. *ibid.,* pp. 206, 223-26.

lender and for the voiding of the mortgage once the debt is paid in full. Deeds of trust provide that the conveyance be made to a third party who holds the mortgage rights in trust for the benefit of the lender or lenders until the debt is paid.[5] Certain other arrangements such as faulty or incomplete mortgages, the giving of a deed as security for a loan, or the conditional sale of land are treated by the courts as equitable mortgages if there is written evidence that the parties intend that real estate be held as security for the payment of a debt.

When two or more mortgages affect the same property, the first mortgage filed is known as a *first mortgage.* First mortgages have top priority in their claim against the property offered as security in the event of possible foreclosure proceedings and thus rate as a better security risk than second, third, or other junior mortgages. A first mortgage can usually be refinanced without losing its priority; and the rights of a first mortgagee can be safeguarded by the terms of a junior mortgage. A mortgage may be described as a *purchase-money mortgage* if it is taken by a seller as part of the consideration in a property sale. It may also be described as a *packaged mortgage* if it is used to finance the purchase of household or other equipment along with real property.

Mortgages represent important legal documents; and they should be executed with considerable care. Every mortgage provides either specifically or by implication for the conveyance of the mortgagor's property to the lender and the voiding of this conveyance once the debt is paid. In addition, it should carry the date of agreement, identify the parties to the mortgage, describe the property covered by the mortgage, indicate the amount of the debt and any arrangements for future advances of credit, specify the interest rate and the time and amount of payments, provide for the mortgagor's payment of taxes and property insurance, and itemize such other conditions as circumstances may dictate. Like a deed, the mortgage must bear the signature of the mortgagor and his wife. In some states, it must also carry their official seal, the signatures of witnesses, or an acknowledgement made before a notary public or other official. Also like a deed, a mortgage must be delivered to the mortgagee before it becomes effective.

At the time he signs his mortgage, the borrower may also be required to give the lender a promissory note, known as a mortgage note or mortgage bond, which is secured by the mortgage. The requirement of this note has been dispensed with in several states on the assumption that the mortgage provides sufficient security for the credit granted. Where mortgage notes are used, they make the mortgagor personally liable for the payment of his mortgage debt. This liability follows the mortgagor; and if his mortgage is ever foreclosed, the mortgagee can secure a

---

[5] Deeds of trust, also called trust deeds and trust indentures, are used extensively in California, Colorado, Illinois, Mississippi, Missouri, New Mexico, Tennessee, Virginia, West Virginia, and some other states.

deficiency judgment holding him liable for any deficiency between the foreclosure sale price and the amount of the mortgage.[6]

Lending agencies are naturally interested in the merchantable character of the land titles held by their borrowers. As a minimum, the potential borrower must usually turn his abstract of title over to the lender for examination before a loan is granted and for holding throughout the loan period. Many lenders also require credit reports, a title examination, a property survey, and title insurance. The costs of these services are normally charged to the mortgagor along with the cost of preparing and filing the mortgage and a possible broker's commission for placing the mortgage. These closing costs are sometimes nominal, particularly when a lender's knowledge of the circumstances makes some of these costs unnecessary or when the lender absorbs part of the costs. Yet they can and sometimes do add up to a substantial charge, which reduces the net amount of the loan the borrower receives without adding anything "to the borrower's equity, the seller's receipts, or to the lender's net income."[7]

Once a mortgage is signed and delivered, it should be filed with the local register of deeds in the same manner as a deed. Early filing is desirable to prevent other possible mortgages from acquiring a prior claim status. When the mortgage is paid off, the lender normally issues a mortgage *release,* which should also be filed as legal evidence that the mortgage has been extinguished. Most states have legislation making promissory notes and mortgages nonenforceable some specified number of years (20 or 30 years in most states) after their maturity date. When a mortgage has not been extended and no payments have been made beyond the maturity date, it can be *barred by limitations* in this manner; and its cloud against a land title can be removed even though no mortgage release has been filed.

Borrowers are free to sell or otherwise dispose of their rights in mortgages properties. In most instances, the borrower pays off his mortgage at the time the title is transferred to the new owner and the new owner handles his own financing. Sometimes arrangements are made for the new owner to assume the existing mortgage. Borrowers are free to secure

---

[6]Deficiency judgments were sought by numerous lenders who foreclosed mortgages during the 1930s. These judgments were the subject of considerable bitterness in many instances, particularly when the mortgagee, as the only bidder at the foreclosure sale, bid the property to himself at a price considerably below the amount of the unpaid mortgage debt. Several states abolished deficiency judgments as a result of this experience. Several others have limited judgments to the difference between the mortgage debt and the fair market value of the property established by the court or its appraisers.

[7]Ernest M. Fisher and Robert M. Fisher, *Urban Real Estate* (New York: Henry Holt & Co., Inc., 1954), p. 386. The Federal Housing Administration reported average incidental (closing) costs of $428 with the new houses covered by its mortgage insurance in 1968. This total does not include possible brokers' fees for placing the mortgages.

junior mortgages, which are always subject to the prior claims of the first mortgage. Lenders can also sell or otherwise assign their mortgage rights to other parties. Notice of such assignments, however, should always be given to the borrower so that he will make his payments to the rightful holder of the mortgage.

Size of Mortgage Loans

Most borrowers are interested in securing loans of maximum size on their properties. Most private lenders in turn are interested in a relatively conservative loan policy that promises them a reasonably safe margin of security on their loan investments. The conservative leanings of these lenders is usually balanced, however, by a desire for a loan policy liberal enough to insure them what they consider their fair share of the mortgage market.

Private noninstitutional lenders are free to loan any sum they wish on mortgages. Institutional lenders, on the other hand, are usually bound by definite house rules, government regulations, or legislative authorizations, which specify the maximum loan-value ratios they can use in granting long-term real estate credit.

Throughout the 1920s it was common policy for many lending agencies to limit their loans to a maximum of 40 to 50 percent of their appraised loan value of the borrower's property. A property with a current market value of $9,500, for example, might have had an appraised loan value of $8,000—a conservative estimate of its safe market value throughout the loan repayment period—and thus have qualified for a 50 percent loan of $4,000. This arrangement often provided borrowers with far less credit than they needed and invited the use of junior mortgages as supplemental sources of credit.

Since the late 1930s most loan agencies have adjusted their loan-value ratios upward. Savings and loan associations can loan up to 80 percent of the appraised value of their mortgaged properties. National banks are limited to maximum loan-value ratios of 50 and 60 percent depending upon the type of loan. State regulations specify maximum loan-value ratios varying from 50 to 66 2/3 percent for life insurance companies and from 50 to 80 percent for mutual savings banks. Federal land banks can loan up to 65 percent of the normal agricultural value of a farm property.

The concept of high loan-value ratios on home mortgage loans was pioneered by the Federal Housing Administration. This agency provides FHA-mortgage insurance for loans of up to 97 percent of the appraised value of low-cost single-family dwellings. Following this same approach, the Veterans Administration can give 100 percent VA-loan guarantees on some types of properties and the Farmers Home Administration has made 100 percent plus loans to those owner-operators who used its supervised credit to acquire farm ownership plus the ownership of needed equipment, livestock, or supplies.[8]

Most loan agencies are free to limit their loan-value ratios to some level below the maximums permitted by law. And each is free to adjust its loan policies somewhat by either relaxing or liberalizing its property appraisals. The Federal Housing Administration uses a graduated loan-value ratio schedule, which allows higher ratios on low-valued than on high-valued properties.[9] And its ratios are often adjusted up or down depending upon whether its immediate policy objective calls for curtailing or stimulating activity in the home construction and real estate markets.

With the raising of loan-value ratios, much of the need for second mortgages has disappeared. The Land Bank Commissioner loans authorized between 1933 and 1947, for example, made it possible for farmers with federal land bank loans to get a second mortgage that would raise their total debt to 75 percent of the normal agricultural value of their farms. Extensive use was made of these loans during the 1930s. When the maximum loan-value ratio for the federal land banks was raised from 50 to 65 percent in 1944, much of the need for these supplemental loans vanished and their authorization was discontinued.

Interest Rates and Repayment Terms

Every borrower has a vital interest in the repayment terms of his mortgage. If the interest rate is low and the repayment provisions fit his convenience, he naturally has a more desirable arrangement than if a reverse situation applies.

Interest rates. Mortgage interest rates tend to reflect market supply and demand conditions. When the supply of mortgage investment funds is high relative to demand, mortgage interest rates usually decline. This situation prevailed in the United States from the middle 1930s until 1950. When the supply is short relative to demand, a tight money market frequently develops; and mortgage interest rates rise as they did between 1950 and 1970.

Mortgages almost invariably provide for a fixed interest rate. These rates vary with different lending agencies, with the borrower's location with respect to the major sources of mortgage capital, and with the

[8]Cf. W. Keith Burkett and Kenneth H. Parsons, "Buying Farms with Hundred-Percent Loans," *Land Economics,* Vol. 27, May, 1951, pp. 151-68.

[9]FHA regulations permitted mortgage insurance on home loans of up to a maximum of $33,000 on single family dwellings in 1970. Loans of up to 97 percent of the first $15,000 of appraised value, 90 percent of the next $10,000 of value, and 80 percent of the insurable excess above $25,000 were authorized and could be made for 30-year periods or for three-fourths of the remaining economic life of the property, whichever was less. These loans carried an annual interest rate charge of 8.5 percent (reduced to 8.0 percent late in the year) plus 0.5 percent for loan insurance.

lender's risk. Most mortgages made in 1970 were financed at interest rates ranging between 8 and 9 percent.[10] Borrowers depending upon local credit sources often find that they must pay higher interest rates when they live a considerable distance from the major money markets than when they live close to these markets. Junior mortgages ordinarily call for higher interest rates than first mortgages because of the added risk they involve to the lender. Borrowers dealing in high-risk enterprises such as farming in potential drought areas also frequently find that they must pay higher interest rates than borrowers who represent lower risks.

Repayment provisions. From the standpoint of repayment provisions, mortgages can be classified into four groups: (1) straight-term mortgages, (2) fully amortized mortgages, (3) partial-payment mortgages, and (4) past-due mortgages. Straight-term mortgages provide for the complete payment of the mortgage in one lump sum at the end of the mortgage period. Interest is usually paid periodically on these mortgages but can be accumulated for payment at the end of the mortgage period.

A mortgage is fully amortized when provisions are made for a schedule of periodic payments of principal and interest that lead to complete repayment of the loan by the end of the mortgage term. Under the standard amortization plan, uniform payments are required on each payment date; and each successive payment involves a gradually declining charge for current interest and larger and larger payments of principal. A second amortization arrangement known as the Springfield plan calls for uniform periodic payments on the principal of the loan plus the current charge for interest.

Partial-payment mortgages involve some amortization with the payment of the remaining principal as a lump sum at the end of the mortgage term. Past-due mortgages exist whenever a mortgage continues past its due date, usually with the lender's permission, but always subject to his demand for payment.

The typical mortgage with farm and home properties in many parts of the United States during the 1920s called for a five-year straight-term loan arrangement. At the end of this term, the borrower could pay off his mortgage; but in many instances, he simply extended, renewed, or refinanced it for another five-year period. This policy worked as long as there was a plentiful supply of mortgage credit. But it led to near disaster when the credit market tightened during the early 1930s. This experience favored a general shift to the use of amortized mortgage payment plans.[11]

---

[10] Cf. footnote 14 in chapter 13, p. 425.

[11] Raymond J. Saulnier, *Urban Mortgage Lending by Life Insurance Companies* (New York: National Bureau of Economic Research, 1950), pp. 130-31, indicates that only a fifth of the mortgage loans the 24 leading life insurance companies made on one- to four-family dwellings in the 1920s were fully amortized. By the middle 1940s more than 95 percent were fully amortized. During this same period, the proportion of straight-term loans made by these companies dropped from around 20 percent to less

The data on nonfarm residential mortgages reported in the 1960 Census of Housing show that approximately 98 percent of the outstanding mortgages on nonfarm residential properties were amortized and that almost two-thirds of the remaining mortgages were straight-term mortgages. Most farm mortgages are also either fully or partially amortized.

Mortgages are always made for a specified time period, which may range from one to 40 years. The usual straight-term or partial-payment mortgage is made for shorter periods, ranging from one to ten years, often with a verbal assurance that the loan can be renewed if no unforeseen circumstances arise. Most conventional amortized mortgages run for periods of ten to 30 years. FHA-insured loans can be written for periods of 25, 30, 32, and 40 years depending upon the type of property; VA-guaranteed loans can be written for periods of up to 30 years; and Farmers Home Administration mortgages run for 40-year periods.

Prepayment privileges. In addition to the repayment terms already described, most mortgages allow the borrower to pay off all or part of his debt in advance of the payment dates specified. Some mortgages give the borrower a maximum of freedom in this regard by providing that the mortgage be paid "on or before" a given due date and that the borrower pay some specified sum "or more" each pay period. Some lenders require that all advance or surplus payments be made in specified amounts that fit in with their bookkeeping procedures. Most mortgages that authorize prepayment privileges also provide that the borrower pay a specified penalty if he pays the entire debt off in less than a given time period. This provision safeguards the lender's interests by guaranteeing him a minimum return for his initial trouble in granting and servicing the loan.

Flexible payment arrangements are sometimes recommended as a means for adapting mortgage repayment schedules to the changing fortunes of farmers and other borrowers.[12] These proposals relate the size of the borrower's payments to his current income. Under this arrangement, a borrower's payments are high when his income is high; but may drop to nothing when his income is low. Only limited progress has been made thus far in the application of this approach. The federal land banks and a few other major lending agencies, however, have developed reserve payment plans allowing borrowers to make advance payments, which are

---

than 1 percent of the total. A comparable study of the urban residential mortgage lending practices of 116 commercial banks indicates that straight-term mortgages accounted for 41 percent of their loans during the early 1920s but only 4 percent during the middle 1940s, while the proportion of fully amortized loans increased from 15 to 68 percent of the total during this period. Cf. C. F. Behrens, *Commercial Bank Activities in Urban Mortgage Financing* (New York: National Bureau of Economic Research, 1950), p. 50.

[12]Cf. Nelson and Murray, *op. cit.,* pp. 170-73, 184; *Improving Land Credit Arrangements in the Midwest,* Purdue Agricultural Experiment Station Bulletin 551, 1950; and Virgil L. Hurlburt, "Economic Effects of Flexible Land Credit Arrangements," *Journal of Farm Economics,* Vol. 35, February, 1953, pp. 110-21.

held in reserve for application during possible later hardship periods when borrowers may find it difficult to meet their mortgage commitments.

Foreclosure Procedures

Every mortgage is considered a good mortgage at the time it is made. Yet adverse circumstances are always possible and some borrowers default on their mortgage obligations even in prosperous times. When a mortgagor defaults on his payments, the lender who wishes to realize on his security often finds it necessary to take legal steps to extinguish the borrower's rights by foreclosing the mortgage.[13]

Mortgage foreclosure procedures differ from state to state. In every state, however, the borrower has an *equitable right of redemption,* which makes it possible for him to redeem his land by paying off his mortgage after the due date fixed in the mortgage. This equitable right of redemption continues until the mortgage is legally foreclosed.

A common foreclosure procedure starts with the mortgagee filing a foreclosure suit in the local courts against the borrower and all persons having junior liens or claims against the mortgaged property. This suit is heard by the court; and if decided in the mortgagee's favor, a decree or judgment of foreclosure is issued. This decree verifies the borrower's right to foreclose, indicates the amount due on the mortgage, describes the property that is to be sold, and names the person who is to sell the property. Public sale of the mortgaged property—usually at public auction—is then advertised together with information regarding the time, place, and terms of sale. The mortgagee is permitted to bid at the sale and, in so doing, can bid all or part of the amount of the outstanding mortgage debt without putting up any money. This arrangement makes it possible for mortgagees to bid the foreclosed properties to themselves.

Following a court review and confirmation of the sale, the highest bidder receives a deed to the mortgaged property in some states. In others, he receives a certificate of sale, which ripens into ownership if the mortgagor and other persons interested in the property fail to redeem their rights by paying off the debt within the *statutory period of redemption.*[14] This statutory period of redemption ranges from two months in some states to as much as two years in others.

[13] Most mortgages contain acceleration clauses, which provide that the entire principal becomes immediately due and payable if the borrower defaults on any one payment. Without this provision, a mortgagee could seek foreclosure action only on the successive payments as they became due. Cf. Kratovil, *op. cit.,* p. 222.

[14] Care should be taken to distinguish between the concepts of equitable redemption and statutory redemption. The borrower's equitable right of redemption—his right to redeem mortgaged property by paying the mortgage debt in full with interest after the due date when it supposedly forfeited to the mortgagee—was recognized by the English courts at an early date and became a general rule after 1625. The foreclosure process was established as a means of formally extinguishing this right. The statutory

As an alternative to the usual procedure used in foreclosing mortgages, some states permit foreclosure of mortgages by exercise of the power of sale without resort to court proceedings. Where this procedure is used, mortgages and trust deeds often spell out the conditions of default under which the mortgagee or trustee—or a public official in some states—has the right to sell the mortgaged property. The sale must usually be advertised, and notice of the sale must be given to the mortgagor. Unless permission is granted by the terms of the mortgage, the mortgagee (or trustee) is normally barred from purchasing the property. This permission is usually given, however, and the mortgagee (or trustee) is thus eligible to make the highest bid and have the deed executed to himself.

Connecticut and Vermont use a somewhat different procedure known as *strict foreclosure,* under which a mortgagee files a foreclosure suit to secure a court decree or judgment of foreclosure. This decree gives the mortgagor a specified period of time (usually six months or less) in which he can redeem his property. If it is not redeemed within this period, the title vests in the mortgagee without the formality of a public sale. Two other arrangements known as *foreclosure by writ of entry* and *foreclosure by peaceful entry and possession* are used in some New England states to vest title in the mortgagee without a formal sale.

Foreclosure proceedings ordinarily take several months and usually involve considerable time, cost and trouble for both parties. In some instances, they afford the borrower an opportunity to exploit or "milk" the property before he relinquishes his possession rights. During the 1930s, many borrowers voluntarily signed their rights over to their mortgagees rather than go through the foreclosure process. Many others worked out arrangements with their lenders for a scaling down of their debt loads and for refinancing their loans on a sound payment basis.

Debt moratoria legislation. The flood of mortgage defaults and foreclosure proceedings experienced during the early 1930s prompted many states to enact debt moratoria legislation. Approximately two-thirds of the states passed mortgage relief laws, which provided for temporary moratoria on foreclosure proceedings, extensions of the normal mortgage redemption periods, or both. In Iowa, for example, the legislature authorized farm mortgage debtors to petition the courts for relief from foreclosure proceedings "when and where the default or inability of such party . . . to pay or perform is mostly due to . . . drought, flood, heat, hail, storm, or other climatic conditions or by reason of the infestation of pests . . . , or when the governor . . . by reason of a depression shall have . . . declared a state of emergency to exist." [15]

---

right of redemption is a concept of more recent vintage. This right stems from the legislative action of several states during the past century and provides an additional redemption period (usually a year) after the actual sale of the property at a foreclosure sale during which the borrower can still redeem his ownership. Cf. Kratovil, *op. cit.,* chaps. XX and XXIII.

[15] *Iowa Code* (Reichmann, 1939), par. 12383.3.

Most of these laws were limited in their application to periods of one to two years; but many were renewed and extended several times. Provisions were included in most of them requiring those debtors who took advantage of the moratorium provisions to pay their creditors a sum equal to the fair rental value of their properties. The constitutionality of these laws was upheld in the *Minnesota Moratorium Act* case in 1934.[16] In its decision in this case,

> The United States Supreme Court emphasized the restriction of the relief to the period of economic emergency, the requirement of the debtor to apply for relief, the discretion on the part of the court to grant it, and the necessity of fair compensation to the creditor in the form of a rental payment.[17]

Comparable action for the nation as a whole was taken by Congress— first by amending the Federal Bankruptcy Act in 1933 and then by passing the Frazier-Lemke Act in 1934. This law, which declared a five-year moratorium on farm mortgage foreclosures, was declared unconstitutional in 1935. A modified version of this law calling for a three-year moratorium was passed a few months later. This modified version, which continued under various extensions until 1949, outlined a procedure under which a farmer-debtor could file a petition of bankruptcy and either get an extension of time for paying his debts or forestall the foreclosure of his mortgaged property for three years.[18]

LAND CONTRACT ARRANGEMENTS

As mentioned earlier, mortgages do not provide the only source of real estate credit. Land contracts, or installment or purchase contracts as they are sometimes called, provide an important source of real estate credit in many areas. Ground rents and long-term leasing arrangements are used for real estate financing purposes in some communities.[19] Financing arrangements involving real estate bonds, stock issues, and the setting up of land trusts also are used at times for this purpose.

Land contracts usually arise because of the willingness of property owners to help finance the sale of their properties. Under the usual land contract arrangement, the buyer makes a down payment on the property and agrees to pay the balance of the purchase price in periodic payments.[20] Once the contract goes into effect, the buyer takes

---

[16] *Home Building and Loan Association v. Blaisdell,* 290 U.S. 398 (1934).

[17] *Improving Land Credit Arrangements in the Midwest,* p. 21.

[18] Cf. *ibid.,* pp. 22-25.

[19] Cf. discussion of long-term leases and ground rents in chapter 14.

[20] For other discussions of land contracts, cf. Marshall Harris and N. William Hines, *Installment Land Contracts in Iowa,* Agricultural Law Center Monograph No. 5 (Iowa City: University of Iowa College of Law, 1965); R. Vern Elefson and Philip M. Raup, *Financing Farm Transfers with Land Contracts,* Minnesota Agricultural Experiment Station Bulletin 454, (1961); and Wilfred H. Pine and Ronald K. Badger, *Buying and Selling Farms by Contract in Kansas,* Kansas State University Circular No. 390 (1963).

possession of the property and operates it in much the same manner as a mortgaged owner. The seller or his assigns, however, retain legal title to the property until all the payments are made or until the buyer's equity permits him to refinance his purchase with a mortgage.

Contractual arrangements of this type are used quite extensively in many sections of the United States in the sale of rural, suburban, and urban properties. Their use is somewhat spotty, however, with some communities making very little use of land contracts while others employ them as a principal means for financing property sales.

Two categories of land contracts should be recognized: (1) contracts that involve a strictly commercial credit arrangement, and (2) contracts between relatives or close friends. With commercial land contracts, buyers are ordinarily expected to make a down payment equal to at least 10 percent of the purchase price of their properties. They usually pay a higher rate of interest than would apply with a mortgage. They are often expected to pay a somewhat higher purchase price for their property than would apply if they could pay cash or if they could use a purchase mortgage arrangement. The seller or his assigns also tend to take prompt legal action to void the contract and repossess the property if the buyer defaults on any of his commitments.[21]

Buyers use this type of credit arrangement because it enables them to acquire property with a smaller down payment than that required by conventional mortgage lenders. But this advantage is balanced by the higher interest rate the buyer usually pays and by the prospect that his rights will be cut off if he defaults on any of his payments. These conditions make it advantageous for buyers to shift from land contracts to mortgage arrangements as soon as they can build their equities up to the levels required by mortgage lenders. Many land contracts either provide or are made with the understanding that the seller or his assigns will convey legal title to the buyer and take a mortgage in exchange for the contract once the buyer has built up his equity to some given level.

Some sellers hold their land contracts for investment purposes; but many sell or assign them to others. In this respect, land contracts are bought and sold in many communities in much the same way as mortgages. Depending upon the nature of this market, the seller can sometimes command a premium for his contract, or more often finds that he must discount it by selling at some figure below the face value of the contract. This discounting process lends justification to the higher purchase prices often associated with properties sold under land contracts.

Many of the characteristics associated with commercial land contracts

---

[21] From the creditor's standpoint, it is usually argued that land contracts have an advantage over mortgages in that the title holder can dispossess a defaulting buyer immediately after he defaults in his payments without any lengthy mortgage fore-closure proceedings. Several courts, however, have acted to protect the buyer's interests, to give him a second chance, and to narrow the difference between these two types of foreclosure.

do not apply with the land contracts used by relatives and close friends. Parents sometimes use contract arrangements to transfer properties to their children; and property owners occasionally use them to help a neighbor or a friend. Under these conditions, the down payment may range from practically nothing to a high percentage of the purchase price. Interest rates are often below the going mortgage rate and may be purely nominal. Defaults are handled on a mutually favorable basis; and buyers usually enjoy as much security as they would have with mortgages.

Like mortgages and deeds, land contracts should be registered and care should be taken to check the validity of the seller's title at the time the contract is made. Surprisingly enough, both of these procedures are frequently ignored. The legal search of title is frequently postponed until the actual transfer of title takes place. This delay can give rise to legal problems, particularly if the seller finds himself unable to convey a merchantable title. In like fashion, most buyers make no effort to register their contracts. Their attitudes in this regard are explained by factors such as their feelings of reasonable security, a general lack of pressure for registration, and the fear that the possible sale of their contract may lead to registration complications.

ADMINISTRATION OF REAL ESTATE CREDIT

Some of our most important real estate credit problems center on the administration and management of credit. Many of these problems are of primary concern to the lender; others are of immediate interest to the borrower. Considerable attention has been given by lenders to the various standards they should use in their lending operations; and numerous rules have been expounded for a borrower's wise use of credit.[22] Emphasis is given in this brief discussion to some of the leading factors lenders and borrowers should consider in their use of mortgage credit.

Considerations Affecting Lending Policies

Mortgage investors are primarily interested in their prospects for receiving a safe and adequate return on their investments. They seldom have any real interest in acquiring property ownership via the foreclosure route. For them, real estate credit provides a means for securing a reasonable and reliable return on their investment funds. With this basic concern, they are inclined to emphasize the three C's of credit—capacity, collateral, and character—or the three R's—returns, repayment capacity, and risk-bearing ability.[23]

---

[22]Cf. McMichael and O'Keefe, *op. cit.*, chaps. XVIII-XIX; Maisel, *op. cit.*, chaps. VI-VIII and Nelson and Murray, *op. cit.*, Part I.

[23] Cf. Nelson and Murray, *op. cit.*, pp. 505-10; and William H. Husband and Frank R. Anderson, *Real Estate*, 3rd ed. (Homewood, Ill.: Richard D. Irwin, 1960), p. 354.

Security-minded lenders find it desirable to give careful consideration to the ability and capacity of both the borrower and the mortgaged property to repay the loan. The careful lender makes inquiries regarding the borrower's personal character, employment status, credit history, and his rating as a credit risk. With mortgages on residential properties, he will always seek information concerning the borrower's income, the security of his employment, his age, his family responsibilities, and often the state of his health. Comparable information may also be required with loans on commercial and farm properties.

The borrower's personal capacity-to-pay is frequently affected by factors such as advancing age, ill health, accidents, and death. Lenders accordingly find that they must look beyond the borrower to the debt-paying capacity of the mortgaged property. In this respect, they are very much concerned with the earning-capacity and productivity of farm and business properties, with their current market value and their probable future values. They are also concerned with the repayment capacity of residential properties, the desirability of their layouts, the neighborhoods and communities in which they are located, and their probable future rental and market values.

Since the lender is always concerned with the risk factor, it is common practice for him to limit his loan to some portion of his estimate of the probable future market or security value of the mortgaged property. He will often insist that the borrower follow a repayment schedule that insures full payment of the loan by the end of the mortgage term.

Lenders are always concerned with their alternative investment opportunities and with the risk factor. The amount of money available for real estate loans reflects the ability of people to set aside earnings for investment purposes. It also reflects the confidence prospective investors have in real estate mortgages and the manner in which they rate them relative to other investment opportunities. Plentiful supplies of mortgage money are usually forthcoming when the economy is healthy, most workers are employed, and people enjoy a sense of economic security. Low incomes, high taxes, or high living costs can have a depressing effect on the supply of money available for real estate mortgages. Opportunities for high returns from investments in business and other alternative ventures or expectations of runaway inflation can have similar effects in siphoning off funds that could be available for real estate loans.[24]

Lenders are naturally interested in securing as much net return as they can get from their investments commensurate with what they consider sound investment planning. In choosing his investments, the investor or

[24] The threat of inflation provides a logical deterrent to long-term commitments of funds for real estate loans that provide fixed rates of return. A solution to this problem has been used in Chile since 1957. The unpaid balances on mortgages and mortgage payments are adjusted each year in accordance with cost-of-living and wage indices so as to provide lending agencies with a relatively constant level of real income return. (Cf. *Wall Street Journal,* October 25, 1967, pp. 1:1 and 19:2.)

lender always encounters the problems of risk and uncertainty. Higher rates of return are generally associated with the more risky alternatives. An investor can seldom enjoy a high rate of return with maximum security. Instead, he must choose between the prospect of a higher return with more risk or receiving nothing or less return with more security. Regardless of which way his inclinations take him, he will ordinarily insist upon receipt of the prevailing market rate of return as a minimum; and, if he is operating in a lender's market, he may bargain for additional advantages in the form of higher interest rates, bonuses, or some discounting of the loan.[25]

Lending agencies are keenly aware of the many servicing costs associated with loan administration. They recognize that a high interest rate has little appeal when it is associated with high servicing costs or with a high element of risk. Accordingly, they often insist upon some given differential between their gross interest rate and their cost of servicing loans. With second mortgages and high-risk loans, they frequently require a higher-than-normal interest rate as a premium for their willingness to assume a higher risk.

Savings and loan associations, commercial banks, and several other lending agencies ordinarily place and service their own loans. Many investors, however, operate through mortgage companies or brokers who make a business of placing loans for prospective borrowers. A middleman of this sort acts as an intermediary between the borrower and lender and does much of the initial paper work for the lender. A commission, placement fee, or finder's fee is usually charged for this service. Fees of 4 to 7 percent were paid on typical housing loans for this service in 1970. Some mortgage companies also service mortgages for their investors.[26]

Factors Borrowers Should Consider

Real estate credit can be a great asset to borrowers if they use it wisely to acquire property or to improve their productivity and earning capacity. But it can also prove a detriment when it is poorly managed. As Thomas Nixon Carver once observed: "There is no magic about credit. It is a powerful agency for good in the hands of those who know how to use it. So is a buzz saw. They are about equally dangerous in the hands of those who do not understand them."[27]

There is no simple test of wisdom in the use of credit. From a

[25] A mortgage is discounted when the borrower receives a smaller sum than that listed in the mortgage. With a 2 percent discount, for example, a mortgage may list a debt of $10,000 but the borrower would receive only $9,800 from the lender.

[26] Cf. McMichael and O'Keefe, *op. cit.,* pp. 58-60; and Nelson and Murray, *op. cit.,* pp. 149-50.

[27] T. N. Carver, *How to Use Farm Credit,* U.S. Department of Agriculture Farmers' Bulletin 593, 1914, p. 1.

production point of view, real estate credit is put to its best use when it is used (1) to provide operators with access to land resources they can use to advantage in their business operations, (2) to supply needed inputs that add to the over-all efficiency and productivity of the borrower's enterprise, or (3) to provide capital for alternative uses that will add to the operator's income and overall productivity. Credit plays a second significant role in providing for consumer satisfactions and for the fulfillment of consumer goals. The use of credit to provide family housing is a common example. With some individuals, credit also has a negative value in the sense that they derive important satisfactions from its nonuse. The joint impact of these three sets of considerations on individual decisions suggests that one should use that credit which is available to him to the point at which the marginal utilities associated with its use in production equal the marginal utilities associated with its use for consumption purposes and the marginal utilities or satisfactions associated with its nonuse.

Each person must decide for himself how much credit he wishes or should use. Conservative operators of the old school often made sparing use of credit and were pleased with the satisfactions that came with freedom from debt. Present day operators tend to view credit as a legitimate and often desirable means to an end. For most of them, real estate credit plays a proper role in helping one to acquire access to property and in providing needed operating funds, but it should not be used to finance vacations, new wardrobes, or excursions into speculative ventures.

Some individuals hold a more liberal view. Families with high time preference rates are frequently tempted to use credit to improve or upgrade their present living standards even though this may prove costly over time. Others, who are willing to take risks and who seek capital leverage, use real estate credit to magnify the scale of their investments or operations. With these people in particular, it is well to remember that every time a property owner uses real estate credit, he pledges his property as security for his loan. His equity in the property is always held in the balance. If by good management or good luck he succeeds in increasing his income, he can use his added income to protect his equity. If the reverse situation holds, he may find his equity wiped out.

Good credit management usually resolves itself into a problem of good business, farm, or home management. The operator or property owner must learn to recognize when credit is needed, when it can be used to advantage, and when it should not be used. In this process, the operator must always allow for certain risks and uncertainties. Many home, farm, and business owners feel justifiably safe in their use of credit so long as they are able to provide for their families. But they have no guarantees against accidents, ill health, or untimely death. This factor makes it desirable for most operators to use various types of term, life and health, or mortgage insurance programs to protect their families against possible mortgage default or foreclosure problems in the event of their death or incapacity.

Comparable insurance is not available to protect families against possible business reverses. Here the borrower finds that he must take definite chances. If he is willing to take risks and if his period of credit use coincides with a period of general prosperity, he can often carry a substantial mortgage debt to advantage. A comparable mortgage loan under less favorable conditions, however, could easily lead to disaster both for the borrower and his family. Many borrowers find it advisable to follow a safer middle course by limiting their debt commitments at all times to the maximum loads they can reasonably carry under adverse conditions.

—SELECTED READINGS

Bryant, Willis R., *Mortgage Lending: Fundamentals and Practices,* 2nd ed. (New York: McGraw-Hill Book Company, 1962).

Fisher, Ernest M., and Robert M. Fisher, *Urban Real Estate* (New York: Henry Holt & Company, Inc., 1954), chap. XV.

Kratovil, Robert, *Real Estate Law,* 5th ed. (Englewood Cliffs, N.J.: Prentice-Hall, Inc., 1969), chap. XX.

McMichael, Stanley L., and Paul T. O'Keefe, *How to Finance Real Estate,* 2nd ed. (Englewood Cliffs, N.J.: Prentice-Hall, Inc., 1953).

Maisel, Sherman J., *Financing Real Estate: Principles and Practices* (New York: McGraw-Hill Book Company, 1965).

Nelson, Aaron G., and William G. Murray, *Agricultural Finance,* 5th ed. (Ames: Iowa State University Press, 1967).

Ratcliff, Richard U., *Real Estate Analysis* (New York: McGraw-Hill Book Company, 1961), chap. VII.

Renne, Roland R., *Land Economics,* 2nd ed. (New York: Harper & Brothers, 1958), chap. XII.

16

Planning
for Better Land Use

The twentieth century has blossomed forth as the age of the common man. It has unfolded as an era of wondrous technological advance and rising material standards of life. Its benefits have been extended to people of all classes and have helped to free millions of individuals from much of the drugery and servile status of their earlier life. It has helped the average man to emerge as a political force with power to demand the rights of first-class citizenship.

But the twentieth century has also been a time of increasing economic interdependence. With the growing complexity of modern economic life, new tensions and conflicts of interest have evolved. Group and collective action have been widely substituted for the individual *laissez faire*-type action that characterized the eighteenth and nineteenth centuries. Popular opinion has made it expedient for governments to expand their functions and to coordinate, direct, and plan many activities once reserved to the private sector of the economy. Along with its other characteristics, the twentieth century has become a plan age, an era of expanded social action.

The next three chapters are concerned primarily with the role society can and should play in directing and controlling the use of land resources. Emphasis is given in this chapter to the nature of land-resource planning and to the uses made of land reform and other planning measures for securing better land use. Chapter 17 examines the principal powers governments use in directing land use, while chapter 18 is concerned with the taxation of land resources and the use of the taxing power as a means for directing land-use practices.

NATURE OF LAND-RESOURCE PLANNING

Planning may be defined as the conscious direction of effort toward the attainment of a rationally desirable goal.[1] The ability to reason and plan ahead is an attribute of human beings. We all plan our day's work, our vacations, and the houses and other structures we build. Businessmen plan when they combine resources in various ways with the intent of maximizing their returns. Corporation executives plan when they devise production and sales programs to increase their shares of a market. Families plan when they budget their incomes to permit home ownership, retirement for the parents, or college educations for the children. Military leaders plan when they devise strategies for attack or defense. Governments plan every time they develop policies to achieve particular ends.

Private and public planning play a necessary role in modern society. Our present economy and high material standards of life have not just happened. They have come as the end product of the plans of millions of individuals, groups, and government bodies. Most of our planning has been and probably will continue as private planning. Yet varying amounts of over-all planning and coordination are needed if people are to work peacefully together with some thought of maximizing the social welfare.

Arguments are seldom heard concerning the desirability or need for private planning. The importance of private ownership and private planning is normally taken for granted. But wide differences of opinion are associated with almost every mention of public planning. These differences have had an unfortunate impact upon the concepts many people have of the planning process. Instead of viewing planning as an essential aspect of our way of life, these people sometimes regard it as the ugly symbol of something that should be avoided at any cost.[2] In this respect, it is important to note that:

> The word "planning" has been widely and loosely used. It has meant different things to different people. To crusaders it has been a Holy Grail leading to the

[1] Webster's dictionary defines a plan as "a method or scheme of action, procedure, or arrangement." With this definition, planning may be described simply as the devising or projection of a course of action.

[2] Cf. Friedrich A. Hayek, *The Road to Serfdom* (Chicago: University of Chicago Press, 1944). Hayek identifies planning with the "central direction of all economic activity according to a simple plan, laying down how the resources of society should be 'consciously directed' to serve particular ends in a definite way." This definition is rejected here for the simple reason that it concerns only one type of planning—the type that applies in a controlled economy.

sunlit hills of a better day. To conservatives it has been a red flag of regimentation heralding the dawn of collectivism and the twilight of the old order of free private enterprise and the democratic way of life. But to the humble practitioners of the art, viewing the matter with the cold eye of engineering rationality and a matter-of-fact indifference either to crusades, Red hunts, the class struggle, or the omnipotent state, it has been merely a process of coordination, a technique of adapting means to ends, a method of bridging the gap between fact-finding and policy-making.

Planning is the opposite of improvising. In simple terms it is organized foresight plus corrective hindsight.[3]

In the discussion that follows, consideration is first given to the case for public planning, the nature of the planning process, and some examples of land-resource planning. Emphasis is then focused on the uses that may be made of land reform and other similar programs to secure better land use.

The Case for Public Planning

No one can deny the need for some government planning. Like their counterparts in private business, governments must plan their functions and the uses they make of resources if they are to make order out of what might otherwise be chaos. But granting the fact that governments must plan when they provide for the national defense, for the maintenance of civil order, and for the balancing of their expenditures against prospective revenues, why must the modern state engage in economic and social planning? Why shouldn't we return to the relatively planless conditions of the early 1800s?

Several factors have contributed to our present interest in economic and social planning. With an increase in population numbers and the development of an industrial society, people have been brought into closer contact with each other. The subsistence operator and the self-sufficient community have become things of the past. Our health, safety, and welfare as individuals often depend upon the activities and decisions of people we never see, of people who may live hundreds of miles away from us. This dependence upon others has multiplied the prospect for individual and group conflicts of interests—conflicts that could easily upset our normal working and living arrangements were it not for our use of planned group action to designate and enforce certain minimum rules of the game.

Economic and social planning is not an innovation of the twentieth century. Governments have used various types of public planning almost since the dawn of history. Ancient Egypt had its grain-storage and

[3]George B. Galloway, *Planning for America* (New York: Holt, Rinehart and Winston, Inc., 1941), p. 5.

pyramid-building projects. Rome had its public works and its policy of "bread and circuses." Even at the peak of the *laissez faire* period, the United States had its protective tariff, its public land disposal programs, and its experiments with monetary and credit policy. But while public planning is not new, much of the emphasis now given to economic and social planning can be credited to changing attitudes concerning the rightful functions of government.

The prevailing attitude regarding the function of government in planning economic and social matters has changed considerably in the United States during the past century. Up until the end of the nineteenth century, most Americans held religiously to a philosophy of rugged individualism. They believed that "that government governs best which governs least." They espoused a *laissez faire* doctrine, which assumed that an "unseen guiding hand" would operate to coordinate individual actions and cause them to total up to the optimum social welfare.

During the late 1800s, many average people began to doubt and reorient their attitudes regarding the desirability of unchecked free enterprise. Abuses associated with the rise of big business and the exploitive business practices of certain operators provided convincing evidence of the failure of unbridled individualism to maximize social welfare. Instead of the basic harmony of interests assumed by the *laissez faire* doctrine, the uncoordinated self-seeking of millions of individuals frequently led to frustrating conflicts of interests, to human exploitation and misery, and to something far less than the optimum social welfare.

At this stage, people began to turn more and more to collective and group action as a means for minimizing conflicts and maximizing their joint interests. Businessmen joined together in corporations and trade associations; laborers organized unions; farmers formed cooperatives and political pressure groups; and large blocs of citizens looked to the government for action programs that would enhance their economic and social interests. Whereas most individuals had once looked to government primarily for protection, justice, and the preservation of civil order, the realization spread that group action can and should be used to promote the social welfare and material well-being of the great mass of the citizenry. With this change in attitudes, it was easy to justify public economic and social planning, particularly when it contributed to the well-being of large portions of the citizenry either by expanding the opportunities and liberties available to people or by minimizing the risks and uncertainties that would otherwise afflict them.

The demand for public action that followed has brought new social controls such as the government's supervision of interstate freight rates, its pure food and drug regulations, and its requirements for minimum safety standards in factories and mines. It has prompted social welfare measures such as urban redevelopment, the provision of public credit facilities, the sponsorship of public multipurpose resource developments, social security, and the public use of fiscal and monetary measures to stabilize the nation's economy. The first of these two types of social action has expanded the rights and liberties of large groups of people by limiting the opportunities some groups formerly had to exploit the interests of others. The second has sometimes brought the government into active competition with certain of its citizens; but it has gained popular support by assisting people to attain economic and social objectives that could not be attained as easily, as fast, or as well through strictly private action.

Rationale for land-resource planning. Some of our most important economic and social planning needs involve land resources. The total physical supply of these resources is fixed both in quantity and geographic location. Under our system of property rights, we have given private owners considerable freedom to decide how they might use or abuse their land resources. But the property rights held by these owners are exclusive, not absolute. Society still has a strong vested interest in the manner in which the various portions of its over-all resource base are used and maintained. And group action is needed from time to time to discourage unwise and wasteful practices, which may prove injurious to the owner himself, to his neighbors and community, and to society at large.

Demand for public action to direct land-use practices seldom arises as long as there is a sufficient supply of land resources at the right locations to care for the needs of prospective users. With the growing competition for land resources that comes with increasing population numbers and with rising per capita demands for land products, however, the case for social action takes on considerable meaning. Individual operators and community groups discover that the operation of the free-enterprise price system does not lead inevitably to the best use or allocation of land resources. They find that unguided individual action often results in resource exploitation, social waste, and a shifting of costs to other members of society. They discover that social goals in land-resource use frequently involve extramarket considerations that cannot be achieved without social action and that public action can often be used to attain a higher or more nearly optimum level of resource development than would be feasible with purely private developments.

Once these facts are realized, several types of land-resource planning may come into being. Some plans use building codes, weed-control, forest-cutting, and other similar regulations to enforce performance standards that protect the best interests of both the property owner and the public. Some use master plans and zoning regulations to establish orderly patterns for future area developments. Some call for the public acquisition and management of forest, recreation, and other lands or in some instances for special measures to retain areas in agricultural, forest, or other uses. Still others call for sizable public expenditures for urban redevelopment, agricultural crop acreage controls, large multiple-purpose dams, and other similar projects.

Land-resource plans always find their justification or rationale in the objectives they seek. These objectives range from the picayune to the grandiose. Most of public land-resource planning in the United States has been designed to promote the orderly development of the nation's land resources, minimize certain problems and conflicts associated with private land use, foster the optimum development of the land-resource base, and maximize the public welfare. Our record in attaining these objectives has thus far been good. Yet some mistakes have been made. Plans have been abandoned or revised at times because they were considered overly ambitious or overly restrictive; and we have frequently fallen into the error of planning for too little rather than too much.

To plan or not to plan. Land-resource planning is one of the most essential and one of the more easily defended types of economic and social planning. Like other types of public planning, it is often subject to varying amounts of criticism and fearful speculation. Many observers have expressed the fear that public planning logically leads to more planning and that the planning road leads inevitably to a controlled economy, a police state, or something akin to George Orwell's *1984*. They question the motives of our planners and ask whether we can really trust political leaders to stop with planning measures designed to enhance the public welfare. Going further, they question the willingness of the average citizens who make up the "mass mind" of our democratic society to resist the lure of public planning when it offers them "bread and circuses," security, and other benefits in exchange for segments of their individual liberties.

In commenting on this fear of economic and social planning, it should first be observed that there is no inevitable conflict between the use of planning measures and personal freedom. Whether planning will mean more or less freedom for the individual always depends upon the objectives and techniques of the planning process, the people who devise and administer the plan, and the individual's definition of freedom.

The term "freedom" means different things to different people. When it is defined broadly as "the absence of obstacles to the realization of desires,"[4] almost any type of public action may be regarded as a threat to the freedom of some individual. Public action can limit one's license to steal the property of others or to engage in socially undesirable practices; it can restrict personal privileges that one may regard as vested rights; or it may limit the realization of one's desires by cutting off the opportunities he could have had to supply unemployment insurance or some other

[4] Robert A. Dahl and Charles E. Lindblom, *Politics, Economics, and Welfare* (New York: Harper & Brothers, 1953), p. 29. This definition is also used by Barbara Wootton, *Freedom Under Planning* (Chapel Hill: University of North Carolina Press, 1945), p. 4; and by Bertrand Russell, "Freedom and Government," in Ruth Nanda Anshen, ed., *Freedom, Its Meaning* (New York: Harcourt, Brace & Company, 1940), p. 251.

service were he equipped to provide it as well or on as large a scale as the government. By the same token, public planning can also be used to remove the obstacles that prevent millions of people from realizing their desires. From this point of view, one might say that planning contributes to individual freedom and that the failure of a government to push social welfare measures often represents a major obstacle to personal freedom.

The concept of freedom has little meaning when treated in an abstract sense. As Erven Long has observed:

> It becomes meaningful only in specific terms which must include *a structure of opportunities* which makes the realization of the freedom possible. Any freedom enjoyed by any individual consists in a set of securities of expectations concerning the behavior of other individuals and groups. These secure expectations of an individual result from a system of rules—rights, duties, restraints—developed by processes of public action and enforceable at law—which determine what others may and may not do.
>
> ... Any individual freedom exists in consequence of the public organization which defines this freedom and secures it for the individual against the adverse action of others. The slave became a free man, not in virtue of anything new put to him, but in consequence of a set of restraints imposed upon others. . . . By himself, an individual is anything but free—because only by joining efforts with others can he create a structure of opportunities for translating his "wishes" into realities.[5]

Viewed in this context, it appears that the concept of individual freedom is rooted in group action. Public planning measures may be used to deprive criminals, draftees, and common citizens of their so-called "inalienable rights" or to limit the license or vested rights of various individuals or groups. They may also be used to greatly expand the freedom and opportunities available to large portions of the citizenry.

With the basic question of whether or not it is safe to plan, it should be remembered that every society is the custodian of its own future. The planning process is neutral. A nation can plan to destroy its individual liberties; or it can use the planning process to maintain, strengthen, and expand these liberties. Democratic governments use planning techniques to enhance the public welfare and to attain socially desirable ends. Some police states, on the other hand, use planning as a technique of control—as a means for repressing freedom, stifling criticism, and subjugating individuals to the will of the state. Public planning does not lead automatically to either end. If we cannot trust ourselves or our leaders, it is possible that planning will lead to certain abuses. But no nation can save itself from authoritarianism simply by refusing to plan.

There is no more reason for social planning to lead to a controlled economy than there is for the average dinner guest to stuff himself to the point of indigestion. Self-restraint is necessary in both instances. Planned

[5] Erven J. Long, "Freedom and Security as Policy Objectives," *Journal of Farm Economics,* Vol. 35, August, 1953, pp. 318-19.

economies of the police-state type have developed in many countries with authoritarian traditions. This consequence is hardly probable in countries such as Canada, Great Britain, and the United States as long as the leaders in these nations preserve their traditional respect for the dictates of the ballot box.[6]

Our past use of public planning in the United States has often led to more planning, particularly when the majority of the people and their representatives have felt that planning provided them with the means to attain desired economic and social goals. But we have always weighed each new benefit against its cost in individual liberty; and except for certain public security and defense measures, we have not hesitated to reject those types of planning we do not like. We have placed the trust a democratic society must place in the actions of its leaders and in the majority will of its citizens; but we have not forgotten that eternal vigilance is always the price of liberty. As a nation, we have recognized that the willingness of a liberty-conscious people to use forward-looking planning as an instrument of public policy provides the best guarantee of continued freedom.

The Planning Process

Plans do not just happen. All planning, be it public or private, involves a process. As such, it embraces a series of important steps. These steps can be classified in different ways but normally involve: (1) an assumption or determination of the objectives to be sought, (2) formulation of the plan or policy to be followed, and (3) execution of the plan.

Goals and objectives in planning. Every plan starts with some concept of a goal or objective, with some motive or purpose for the act of planning. This goal may be rooted in the individual's customary way of thinking and may be accepted without rational examination or thought; it may be the end product of the conscious thinking of an individual or a group of people; or it may be specified in the legislation that establishes a planning agency. Planning goals may be wise or foolish. They may be regarded as fixed for all time or be accepted as temporary objectives subject to future re-evaluation and possible revision. Yet regardless of their nature or origin, planning goals always play a vital role in giving direction to the planning process.

People engaging in the public planning and policy-formation process should always start with the question: "Planning for what?" They should think through their objectives and reasons for planned action. If they have time, they should formalize their goals by writing them down. They should examine them in detail and discuss them with others.

In this examination process, the planner will often find that he has

[6]Cf. E. F. M. Durbin, *Problems of Economic Planning* (London: Routledge and Kegan Paul Ltd., 1949), pp. 91-106.

several goals to consider, that some of his goals operate at cross-purposes with others, and that he must temper or compromise some of his objectives if he is to attain others. The author of a housing improvement program may find that he must limit his goal of securing larger and more luxurious housing units if he is to pay more than lip service to his goal of reducing housing costs. The proponent of a farm tenure improvement program may find it necessary to compromise between his objectives of securing maximum efficiency in production and a wide distribution of ownership rights among many operators.

The planner who starts by recognizing and thinking through his planning goals can often avoid considerable wasted effort. By rationalizing the possible conflicts between his goals at this stage, he can proceed better in his preparation of a workable plan. He can use the sense of direction he acquires in this process to avoid embarrassing inconsistencies that might otherwise affect his plan.

Formulation of the plan. Once the objectives are established, the next major step in the planning process concerns the actual development or formulation of the plan. The approach used at this stage varies somewhat with individual cases. Most land-resource planning involves four substeps: (1) research or study concerning the nature of the problem situation, the resource base, and other factors that may be affected by the plan; (2) discovery and analysis of the various alternative solutions or approaches that can be used; (3) choice of the alternative or combination of alternatives—including the possible choice of doing nothing—to be used; and (4) the formal drafting of the plan in written or graphic form.[7]

Planning efforts frequently go astray because they are based more upon wishful thinking than upon a sound understanding of the facts. By accident or happenstance, some plans do succeed even though they are made in ignorance of the facts. The weight of planning experience, however, shows that a good working knowledge of the problem situation is a necessary prerequisite to successful planning. This is particularly true with land-resource planning. Area planners always find it desirable to assemble as much information as possible concerning their problems and the nature and potentialities of the resource bases with which they work. They often devote major portions of their time to objective research and to the accumulation and analysis of factual data.

It is sometimes impossible for planners to assemble and analyze all of the information that should be considered in their decisions. Policy decisions are frequently needed on short notice; and the processes of government and business cannot always wait for the final word in scholastic research. Planners and policy-makers often find that they must make spot decisions without a full knowledge of the facts. Insofar as it is practicable, however, they should always base their decisions on findings that represent a reasonably accurate picture of the situation at hand.

[7]Cf. Galloway, *op. cit.,* p. 6.

This responsibility creates problems in planning administration. Most successful planning directors recognize that every individual has his "blind spots." Regardless of how well-balanced his education has been, every person is the product of the "roundaboutness" of his training. His thinking and the points he tends to emphasize reflect his personal interests and background. In recognition of this situation, planning officials frequently utilize the services and advice of people with quite different backgrounds in the hope that their combined judgment will provide a balanced and reasonably realistic analysis of the action problems at hand.

Going beyond the problem of securing a balanced view of the facts, planners have a definite responsibility to seek out, analyze, and consider the various alternative approaches that may be used in the attainment of their objectives. In this process they must avoid panaceas. They should consider the legality and constitutionality of each proposal. They should reject those formulae that appear economically, politically, or socially unacceptable or unsound.[8] Where possible, they should seek workable solutions that can be dramatized for popular acceptance; and they should always ask themselves: "Is this proposal workable from an administrative standpoint?"

The planning process reaches its climax when the planner chooses between his alternatives and definitely commits himself to a given course of action or to a given set of recommendations. Up to this point, the planning process consists of preparation for planning, not planning itself. Real planning calls for more than the collection of factual data and the analysis of situations and trends. It calls for formulation of a course of action, for decisions between alternatives, for definite recommendations concerning what should or should not be done. These decisions involve the substance of planning and provide the real test of a planner. Plans are sometimes ambitious or visionary, sometimes inconsequential or faulty. But good or bad, they stand as monuments to the planner's ability or lack of ability to fulfill his function.

A key problem in the planning process centers on the question of who makes the planning decision. Planning officials and consultants are often called upon to formulate and recommend plans for action.[9] Emphasis is placed in these instances on specific planning recommendations, and little or nothing may be said of the alternatives that were considered but

---

[8] Cf. *ibid.,* pp. 44-46.

[9] Legislative bodies usually look to planners for competent advice on programs that should be implemented. On some occasions, however, planners are used in what might be described as a "scapegoat alternative" strategy. Land-use plans are prepared and recommended with the blessing of governmental legislative bodies and are then endorsed, modified, rejected, or ignored once their political popularity and acceptability is determined. Far-reaching planning proposals may be commissioned with the expectation that they will have an educational or shock impact that will pave the way for compromise programs. When a plan is politically popular, it can be accepted; when it stirs up controversy and opposition, both the plan and the planner can be castigated.

rejected. Plans of this nature are sometimes accepted and carried out. Unfortunately, they often bask in the limelight for a brief day of glory after which they are shelved, filed away, and forgotten. An alternative to this approach is used by those planners who regard the planning decision as a legislative function. These planners spell out the alternative solutions to planning problems together with their advantages and disadvantages and leave the actual choice of the plan to legislative bodies. This approach frequently leads to action because the planning decision is made by the officials who are responsible for accepting the plan and putting it into effect.

Successful land-use planning calls for recognition of the political facts of life. As long-range plans are made for the years to come, it is well and good that men of vision should speculate concerning the needs of the unfolding future and that they should pinpoint the policies needed for creating a better society. Most land-resource planners, however, must operate in terms of the present, the next decade, or the next quarter-century. They must gear their plans to the possible. Unlike the Jacobin leader of the French Revolution who proclaimed: "We will make France a cemetery rather than not regenerate it in our own way!"[10] the effective planner must be willing to adapt his goals and his plans to the political situation. He must recognize the power groups in his community; and he must always adjust his role and his techniques to the sociopolitical system in which he operates.[11]

Effectuation of planning. Many people feel that the planning process stops as soon as the planner commits himself to a given operational plan and formalizes his decision by drawing a land-use map, preparing a planning report, or issuing a policy directive. Actually, however, there is little point in planning if no action follows. Planners are always interested in the effectuation or carrying out of their plans. It is at this stage that a

[10] Quoted in H. A. Taine, *The French Revolution* [New York: Henry Holt & Company, Inc., 1881 (English translation)], Vol. 3, p. 51.

[11] Dahl and Lindblom, *op. cit.,* indicate that there are four principal systems of sociopolitical organization—the price system, hierarchy, polyarchy, and bargaining—that affect planning. When planning is subject to the controls of the price system, most planners limit their plans to decisions regarding the purchase, production, and marketing of the resources, goods, and services with which they deal. Under a hierarchical state, where the power and responsibility of government is centered in a relatively small group, planners can often indulge in "ivory-tower," visionary, and long-range planning as long as they have the sanction of the ruling group.

Public planning of a comparable type is usually less acceptable in a polyarchical state where political power is held by the citizens. Forward planning is possible under these circumstances; but the planner often finds it necessary to concern himself with grassroots problems, with popular sentiment, and with the question of what he can or cannot sell to the average citizen. A bargaining situation exists when the power of control is divided between several leaders or groups. Under these conditions, the planner must bargain and compromise with other agencies, interest groups, legislative committee chairmen, and others if he is to fulfill his function as a planner.

plan can prove itself, show need for reformulation or revision, or possibly fail.

The successful administration of any public plan calls first for a sound and reasonable proposal. Beyond this, it calls for capable and understanding administration, the cooperation of officials in other agencies and other levels of government, popular interest in the plan and its results, and continued political and public financial support.[12]

Administrative problems frequently arise concerning the recruitment and training of capable administrative personnel. Care must be taken to emphasize action and results, to avoid possible bogging down in "red tape," to keep the policy or program working in its intended way, and to prevent individuals from scuttling the program or using it as a personal stepping stone to promotion. Coordination and integration are often needed to keep individual officials or agencies from proceeding with policies that work at cross-purposes and to avoid jurisdictional conflicts over who functions where.

Considerable emphasis must usually be given to the maintenance of good public relations and to ways and means for maintaining popular interest in the fulfillment of the plan. Successful administration calls for the continued good will and support of public opinion leaders, political party officials, and the legislative bodies that control the strings to the public purse. Moral principles and other factors sometimes cause agency officials to take stands in opposition to the views held by the powers-that-be. But cordial relationships must usually be maintained because continued political and public financial support is always necessary for the carrying out of public planning proposals.

Some Examples of Land-Resource Planning

Land-resource planning takes many forms. Individual planning occurs when a farmer plans his field layout or a subdivider draws his plat map. Private group planning takes place when a neighborhood association requires architectural approval of all new houses built in the area, or when a service club develops a summer camp. Public planning occurs every time we build a highway or enact a zoning ordinance. Some of the more important types of public planning can be grouped under the headings of city and metropolitan planning; federal, state, and regional planning; and rural land-use planning.

City and metropolitan planning. Archeological findings show that the origins of city planning go back some 5,000 years. These findings suggest that directional measures have been used to provide for orderly and functional urban developments since people first started living together.

---

[12]Cf. Galloway, *op. cit.,* pp. 34-35; also Roland R. Renne, *Land Economics,* 2nd ed. (New York: Harper & Brothers, 1958), pp. 540-41.

Until recent decades, however, city planning has been limited for the most part to street layouts, the reservation of certain areas for parks and public uses, and the provision of public water supplies and systems of defense fortification. Most of the world's cities have followed a *laissez faire* pattern of growth and development. Their growth patterns have been shaped mainly by the basic functioning of cities as economic and social mechanisms and by the operation of their real estate markets in allocating lands between alternative uses, not by formal city planning.

Formal plans dealing mostly with street layout were prepared for several American cities at fairly early dates. William Penn devised a plan for Philadelphia in 1682; and plans were made for Savannah in 1733, Washington in 1791, Buffalo in 1801, and Manhattan Island in 1811. Some additional pioneering in city development came during the middle 1800s with the appointment of boards and commissions in several cities to deal with water, sanitation, park, street, and transportation problems. Yet even with these beginnings, city planning, as we now know it, did not get its start until the end of the century.

Modern city planning began with the birth of the "city beautiful" movement at the Chicago World's Fair in 1893. Visitors at the fair were deeply impressed with the beauty of the grounds and the classic splendor of the architecture. Thousands went away imbued with a desire to beautify their own drab cities. This desire blossomed into civil improvement plans in many cities shortly after the turn of the century. The central thrust of this planning effort was on municipal esthetics and improvement of the surface appearances of public buildings, parks, and major streets. Little emphasis was given to "the more deep-seated social problems which rapid urbanization entailed."[13]

A second milestone year in the history of urban planning came in 1909 with the holding of the first national conference on city planning and with the publication of the *Plan of Chicago.* This city plan had a broader orientation than the earlier city plans; and it signalled a gradual shift of emphasis from the "city beautiful" to the "city practical." This shift was implemented by New York City's adoption of the nation's first comprehensive city zoning ordinance in 1916.

City planning came of age during the 1920s as more and more cities found that they could use land-use zoning, building codes, and subdivision controls as planning tools to guide their future development. Numerous cities hired planning consultants and organized city planning commissions. Considerable progress was made in preparing "comprehensive" city plans. But at the end of the decade, most of these plans were still concerned with only six major items: civic appearance, parks and recreation, streets, transit problems, transportation facilities, and zoning.[14] Only passing

[13]Robert A. Walker, *The Planning Function in Urban Government,* 2nd ed. (Chicago: University of Chicago Press, 1950), p. 12.

[14]Cf. Theodora K. Hubbard and Henry V. Hubbard, *Our Cities Today and Tomorrow* (Cambridge: Harvard University Press, 1929), p. 109.

notice was given to the economic and social basis of the city. Important problems such as housing were largely ignored because it was felt that street, subdivision, and zoning regulations could be counted upon to produce the types of land and housing development desired.

The curtailment of operating budgets that came with the onset of the depression brought the city planning movement to a near standstill in the early 1930s. This situation gradually changed after the launching of the "New Deal" in 1933. Attention was soon focused on the role city planners could play in caring for the problems of the "lower third" of the population. Staff assistance—often financed with public relief roll funds—was made available for planning surveys and research. Federal, state, and local programs were set in motion to help cities clear away their slums, provide public housing facilities, and carry on large-scale redevelopment programs.

With these developments, the scope of city planning was again broadened. Planners began to think more in terms of the over-all city and of the changes and redevelopment work needed to eliminate blight and slums, to improve living conditions, and to raise the standards of urban life. Master plans were adopted in more and more cities to guide the future pattern of land use and to give direction to urban renewal and property conservation programs.

Considerable emphasis was still given to the problems of parks, public buildings, civic centers, and municipal aesthetics. More attention, however, was given to the economic and social base of the city, to the impact of this base on planning, and to the use of planning measures to maintain and strengthen this base.[15] Increased emphasis was given to the problems of industry and commerce, to the provision of expressways and more adequate downtown parking facilities, to the location and building of schools and shopping centers, to securing more adequate water and sewerage-disposal facilities, and to numerous other factors that bear on the economic and social life of the city.

By 1965, 92 percent of the cities of more than 10,000 people in the United States had official planning agencies.[16] The planning problem in most of the larger cities was fast expanding beyond the usual issues of urban growth and services. Complications were arising with the increasing demands of disadvantaged groups, with the continuing flight of thousands of substantial citizens to the outlying suburbs, with growing public awareness of the presence of ghettos and slums near the urban core, and with the outward sprawl and scatteration of urban-oriented developments

[15]Cf. Richard U. Ratcliff, "A Land Economist Looks at City Planning," *Journal of Land and Public Utility Economics*, Vol. 20, May, 1944, pp. 106-8; and Richard U. Ratcliff, *Urban Land Economics* (New York: McGraw-Hill Book Company, Inc. 1950), pp. 408-13.

[16]Cf. *The Municipal Year Book, 1965* (Chicago: International City Managers' Association, 1965), p. 315.

around the fringes of the cities. Instead of finding their problems neatly circumscribed by city boundaries, city planners frequently found that they were dealing with segments of the larger problems of metropolitan regions.

Most large cities are at least partly surrounded by "dormitory" communities that resist annexation but that have a definite interest in the employment, shopping, and other services provided by the central city. Taken together, these units usually have joint interests in the provision of better water, sewerage-disposal, highway, and park facilities, and in the development of coordinated land-use plans for the entire metropolitan region.

Many communities have recognized the joint nature of their land-use problems and the futility of trying to solve these problems on an individual community basis. This fact together with the offer of federal financial aids has induced many of them to work together in establishing councils of governments and metropolitan area planning commissions to plan for the better use and development of their over-all land-resource base. These planning agencies ordinarily operate on an advisory basis and find that they must use the power of persuasion to sell their proposals to local units. Some regions have extended the metropolitan approach to set up special metropolitan districts, which administer park or water and sewerage-disposal programs. A few others such as Toronto have gone further to set up metropolitan area governments with powers to deal with a wide range of metropolitan governmental problems.

Federal, state, and regional planning. Important examples of land-resource planning are also found at the state and federal levels. For the most part, these units have made little attempt to plan with the same intensity as the cities. Prior to the 1960s, most of their land-resource planning was limited to programs involving particular types of resources and the administrative planning needed in the management of public lands. This situation has since changed, and by 1970 a considerable number of states either had or were in the process of developing state land-use plans. Congressional action also was being pushed for the development of a national land-use plan.

Leading examples of state and federal land-resource planning programs are found in the public land-management plans developed and used in the administration of state forests and parks and in the administration of the holdings of the Bureau of Reclamation, the U. S. Forest Service, the National Park Service, the Bureau of Land Management, and the Bureau of Sports Fisheries and Wildlife. A somewhat similar type of area resource planning conducted on a regional basis is provided by the example of the Tennessee Valley Authority. This organization was established by Congress in 1933 as a federal corporation to serve the seven-state area included in the drainage basin of the Tennessee river. Among its objectives, TVA was designed to control floods and improve navigation on the Tennessee river and its tributaries, contribute to the national defense, develop and produce new types of commercial fertilizer, produce and distribute hydroelectric power, promote desired research, and facilitate resource development and improve the economic welfare of the people in the area.[17]

Hawaii and several other states acted during the 1960s to establish state land-use plans that provide useful benchmarks for guiding public and private resource development programs. Prior to the formation of these plans, the closest approach the federal and state governments made to providing similar types of overall land-resource planning came during the 1930s with the organization and functioning of a national and several state resource planning boards. A National Resources Board was established in 1934 to operate on an interagency basis and to take over the functions of the National Planning Board, which had been set up in the Public Works Administration in 1933. This agency was reorganized as the National Resources Committee in 1935, and again as the National Resources Planning Board in the Executive Office of the President in 1939.[18]

From the outset the National Resources Board operated more as an agency for stimulating research and study than as an actual planning board. It established several national committees that sponsored and supervised research reports on land planning, water resources, urbanism, and other national problems. Regional committees such as the Great Plains, New England, Ohio Valley, and Pacific Northwest regional

[17] In practice, TVA has built numerous dams along the Tennessee river and its tributaries to control floods, improve navigation, and produce public power. It has stimulated new economic development in the area, encouraged better farming practices, promoted soil conservation and reforestation measures, provided improved recreational opportunities, helped to stamp out malaria and other diseases, and encouraged community planning. It has produced fertilizers and nitrates for explosives and has contributed greatly to our use of atomic energy. Costwise, TVA represents a tremendous public investment. But it has justified the faith of its early proponents by demonstrating its ability to fully repay this investment cost, while at the same time contributing to the economic development of the area and to the nation's defense and welfare.

[18] As described in 1935, it was the function of this agency "to collect, prepare, and make available to the President, with recommendations, such plans, data, and information as may be helpful to a planned development and use of land, water, mineral and other national resources, and such related subjects as may be referred to it by the President, to consult and cooperate with agencies of the Federal Government, with the States and Municipalities, or agents thereof, and to receive and record all proposed Federal projects involving the acquisition of land (including transfer of land jurisdiction) and land research projects, and, in an advisory capacity, to provide the agencies concerned with the information or data pertinent to the projects." For more detailed discussion of the activities of this agency, cf. John D. Millett, *The Process and Organization of Government Planning* (New York: Columbia University Press, 1947), pp. 137-52; also Charles E. Merriam, "The National Resources Planning Board: A Chapter in American Planning Experience," *American Political Science Review*, Vol. 38, December, 1944, pp. 1075-88.

planning commissions were also organized to study resource problems. With the onset of World War II, the role of this agency became uncertain, and Congress terminated its activities in 1943.[19] Most of the state planning boards that had been established during this period were also abolished or had their functions transferred to other agencies during the 1940s.

A revival of interest in federal, state, and regional planning was experienced during the 1950s and 1960s. Initially, most of this interest was tied to single issues such as the provision of park and recreation opportunities, the management of water resources, administration of the public lands, the allocation of federal grants within states, protection of environmental resources, and the encouragement of regional and local area economic growth. By the late 1960s, however, emphasis was being given in many instances to the need for integrating and coordinating related planning efforts and for undertaking broad gauge land and water resource planning programs.

Rural land-use planning. An unusual example of land resource planning is provided by the experience of the county land-use planning program, which operated between 1938 and 1941.[20] This program was sponsored by the U. S. Department of Agriculture and the Land Grant Colleges as a means of stimulating grassroots participation in the formulation of public policies. Plans were developed for a network of community, county, and state land-use planning committees with the county committees operating as the principal cog in the planning process.

[19] Various reasons have been advanced for the demise of NRPB. Congress refused to provide funds for its continuation after 1943 on the ground that it duplicated the work of other agencies. Some writers attribute its fall to the general suspicion and hostility with which many Congressmen regarded the concept of "over-all planning" and the activities of NRPB in establishing objectives for national action. Other reasons are found in the failure of the board to clearly define its role and in its seeming inability to operate effectively as a planning agency. Millett (*ibid.,* pp. 148-49) observes that: "The board could never decide whether it wanted primarily to be a research, a propagandizing, a management, or an advisory agency. It gave most of its effort to research but tried other roles as well. The board failed to push any one line of work to effective ends, it vacillated from one role to another."

The abolition of NRPB in 1943 did not signal the end of federal interest in land-resource planning. Planning functions involving land resources were delegated to the Office of War Mobilization and Reconversion, the War Production Board, the Office of Price Administration, and various other wartime agencies. This interest in resource planning also carried over after the war with the creation of the Council of Economic Advisors and the National Security Resources Board as planning agencies in the Executive Office of the President. Presidential commissions such as the President's Water Resources Committee (1950) and the President's Materials Policy Committee (1952) also were appointed to spotlight attention on particular problems.

[20] County planning was not a new thing in 1938. More than 300 county and regional planning commissions were operating in the United States in 1935. Cf. W. E. Cole and H. P. Crowe, *Recent Trends in Rural Planning* (New York: Prentice-Hall, Inc., 1937), p. 17.

By the end of 1941, some 200,000 farm men and women were serving on planning committees in all the states except Pennsylvania. Planning committees were operating in 10,000 local communities and in 1,891 counties, nearly two thirds of the agricultural counties in the nation. These committees were made up of representative groups of farm people with the county agricultural agent and other agricultural agency people serving as ex officio members. Technical research and planning assistance was provided by various state and federal agencies. With this combination of resources, it was hoped that the county committees would (1) analyze their local problems and proceed with local remedial measures, (2) make valuable suggestions for the correlation of state and federal programs on the local level, and (3) propose desired changes and adjustments in public programs.[21]

As each county committee proceeded with its planning, it passed through three successive planning stages: (1) a preliminary or preparatory stage, (2) an intensive planning stage, and (3) a unified county program stage. Emphasis was given at the preliminary stage to general discussions, organization of committees, and laying the groundwork for more intensive planning. Committees in the "intensive planning counties" were expected to survey and classify their land-resource base, prepare land-use maps, and study the nature of and possible solutions to pertinent local problems. Once the committees passed to the unified program stage, they were expected to take an over-all view of their problems and recommend possible solutions or programs of action.

Congress withdrew its support from the land-use planning program in 1941 and the program came to a sudden halt. During its brief life, however, the program prompted the accumulation and analysis of considerable data on local problems. It focused attention on the merits of community self-evaluation and the possibilities for local remedial-action programs. And it resulted in the better integration of several state and federal programs at the local level.

Evaluations of the land-use planning program show that the planning process was quite superficial in some counties, that the idea of grassroots planning failed to catch on in many communities, and that local committees often went through the motions of planning because a map and a planning report were expected, not because they felt a basic need to plan. The program also was viewed with hostility by competing administration and farm pressure groups. Even with these defects, however, county land-use planning provided "a noble experiment in democracy." The experiences of numerous counties show that where farm people recognized that they had local problems, they often greeted land-use planning as an effective means for initiating desired action

[21] Cf. Bushrod W. Allin, "County Planning Project—A Cooperative Approach to Agricultural Planning," *Journal of Farm Economics,* Vol. 22, February, 1940, pp. 292-301.

programs.[22] This local enthusiasm caused several states to continue their local planning programs after 1941 and prompted the organization of official planning commissions in many counties.

PROGRAMS FOR BETTER LAND USE

A wide variety of public and private programs have been and are being used to bring about changes and modifications in existing land tenure and land-use situations. Individuals devise numerous strategies to attain desired goals involving the possession and use of land resources. Associations, cooperatives, and foundations frequently promote programs that can improve the management and productivity of properties of their members or clientele. Businesses and corporations seek more effective, efficient, and productive ways of utilizing land resources. Governments are also active in the development of programs designed to promote improvements in land tenure and land-use situations.

Much of the planning that takes place is self-oriented in that it is concerned primarily with the operations of the individual, group, or agency. Planning programs also are concerned with interactions with others both now and in the future and with devices for securing the cooperation or minimizing the obstacles posed by others in the attainment of specific goals. In this sense, it may be noted that considerable planning for better land-use centers on *private-private* relationships, on arrangements made between individual owners and users of land. It often involves *private-public* relationships, in which citizens delegate or assign specific responsibilities, such as the provision of a public land credit system, to government or seek opportunities to use public resources. It can emphasize *public-private* relationships, in which governments prescribe and enforce standards for individual behavior with respect to land. It can also be concerned with *public-public* relationships, which involve intergovernmental coopera-tion.[23]

Private as well as public interests and activities are involved in the land-use planning and program formulation process. Primary emphasis is given here, however, to the scope, nature, and operation of the public programs that may be used to secure better land-tenure and land-use conditions. The discussion of these planning efforts is divided into four parts: (1) identification of policy goals, (2) recognition of the range of policy measures governments can use to attain their goals, (3) an

[22] For a vivid discussion of the accomplishments of county land-use planning, cf. Howard R. Tolley, *The Farmer Citizen at War* (New York: The Macmillan Company, 1943), chap. V.

[23] Cf. chapters by Maurice M. Kelso, Marshall Harris, Kris Kristjanson and Raymond J. Penn, and Marion Clawson in Howard W. Ottoson, ed., *Land Use Policy and Problems in the United States* (Lincoln: University of Nebraska Press, 1963).

examination of the uses made of land reform programs, and (4) an exploration of some other areas in which new programs and new institutions can be used to secure better land use.

Goals in Land Policy

The goals that public and private agencies pursue in their policies concerning the possession and use of land resources ordinarily reflect the thinking and objectives of the decision makers. At times in history, these goals have stressed the aggrandizement of a single head of state or a ruling class. During recent centuries, they have tended to emphasize nationalistic ends and more recently the welfare interests of large numbers of the citizenry. With this democratization process, most nations have tended to reorient their thinking about who should control land and how it should be used.

Several nations now accept the attainment of widespread opportunities for higher and more satisfying levels of living for all of their citizens as the primary master goal of public policy. Within the framework provided by this master goal, five general goals in land policy may be identified. They are:

1. Widespread distribution of ownership, operatorship, occupancy and use rights among the citizens who wish to exercise these rights;

2. Land holdings of appropriate size and productive potential to permit a maximizing of production opportunities;

3. Orderly and equitable operating arrangements that encourage efficiency in land-resource use;

4. Arrangements that offer economic opportunities, security, and stability to land operators; and

5. Arrangements that lead to the development and conservation of land resources.[24]

[24] Other formulations of policy goals are possible. Rainer Schickele, for example, speaks of "maximization of social product over time" and "optimization of income distribution among people" as the twin master goals of economic policy. [Rainer Schickele, "Objectives in Land Policy," in John F. Timmons and William G. Murray, eds., *Land Problems and Policies* (Ames: Iowa State College Press, 1950), pp. 6-10.] V. Webster Johnson uses a less abstract approach in highlighting the following eight goals in land policy: (1) military security, (2) political stability, (3) maximum national production, (4) maximum income, (5) economic security and stability, (6) individual freedom, (7) conservation of human resources, and (8) conservation of natural resources. [V. Webster Johnson and Raleigh Barlowe, *Land Problems and Policies* (New York: McGraw-Hill Book Company, 1954), pp. 8-13.] For other formulations of goals, cf. Joseph Ackerman and Marshall Harris, eds., *Family Farm Policy* (Chicago: University of Chicago Press, 1947), pp. 9-11; John F. Timmons, "Land Tenure Policy Goals," *Journal of Land and Public Utility Economics,* Vol. 19, May, 1943, pp. 165-79; and Conrad Hammar, "The Land Tenure Ideal," *Journal of Land and Public Utility Economics,* Vol. 19, February, 1943, pp. 69-84.

Significant as this group of goals may appear, it must be recognized that the list is not all-inclusive and also that individual goals can conflict with each other. Lists of goals must be reformulated when attention is given to specific land programs such as an appraisal of a nation's public land disposal policies, the development of a public recreation program, or the devising of a program for improving landlord-tenant relations. Priorities must also be assigned to individual goals at times to indicate the direction in which programs should move when two or more goals are in conflict.

Successful program administration calls for frequent choices concerning the priorities or weights assigned to individual goals. Without broad vision in the choice of priorities, careful program planning, and willingness to act, efforts to attain particular goals can result in bitter disappointments. "Land to the tillers" and "land for the landless" have been popular slogans for land reform in many countries. Sole emphasis on these objectives, however, can lead to inefficient resource use, the creation of small holdings of uneconomic size or holdings with too little equipment or capital to function as effective production units, and consequently in wasteful and undesirable uses of both human resources and land resources.

Measures for Improving Land Use

Most of the land policies and programs found throughout the world today are the product of a long evolving process in which various measures have been devised, tested, and used to meet changing needs and conditions. The gradual development of the concept of fee simple ownership that followed the breakdown of the feudal system in England and the more recent acceptance of social controls over private property rights in the countries that accept the English common law provide a classic example of evolutionary land reform.

Here and there, particularly in areas where government leaders have resisted demands for change, new land policies and programs have occasionally been adopted as part of the aftermath of revolutionary action. Examples include the new land policies that followed the French Revolution of 1789, the Mexican Revolution of 1910, the Bolshevik Revolution of 1917, and the Egyptian Revolt of 1952. In these cases as with the examples of more evolutionary reforms, precedents either in the earlier history of the country or in other countries existed for most of the policies adopted.

Governments can choose from a wide range of possible measures in the development of new land policies and programs. The leading alternatives available to them, however, involve selections from the following list of policy measures for improving land tenure and land use conditions.

1. Legal recognition of the scope of public and private ownership rights including arrangements for sharing rights in land and arrangements for transferring rights between parties by sale, gift, inheritance, leasing and mortgaging.
2. Provision for a system of land surveys and land title registration to define the areal scope of ownership rights, minimize conflicts over boundaries, and protect property owners and operators in the possession and retention of their rights.
3. Policies for the transfer of specified public lands to private ownership and for the private settlement of these lands.
4. Programs that encourage the public or private development or redevelopment of land resources through clearing, drainage, reclamation, terracing, and area renewal efforts.
5. Provision of public credit facilities where needed to help finance property acquisition and provide necessary operating capital.
6. Provision of educational and technical assistance to land operators to instruct them in improved management techniques and under some circumstances to require their acceptance of managerial guidance.
7. Legal clarification of landlord-tenant arrangements with provisions for standardizing leasing terms, providing compensation for unexhausted improvements, and enhancing the right of tenants to security and stability.
8. Encouragement of and provision of assistance in the organization of cooperatives to deal with and provide self-help in handling production, buying, and marketing problems.
9. Creation of special government programs, boards or commissions, and districts to deal with particular problems such as the need for local area planning, the provisions of parks and waste disposal facilities, the regulation of grazing areas, and the operation of irrigation and resource conservation programs.
10. Taxation of landed property, its annual rents or total values and/or the incomes derived from them to provide revenues for government operations and at times to influence and direct the uses made of lands.
11. Enactment of government regulations (e.g. zoning ordinances, building codes, provisions limiting the minimum and maximum sizes of land holdings, rent controls and land price ceilings, and controls over eligibility to buy or own lands) to direct the uses made of land resources.
12. Provide for the public's exercise, when needed, of the right to take private lands with or without compensation for desired public purposes.
13. Public management and operation of specified areas of educational, forest, military, park, and other lands in the public interest.
14. Use of public grants and subsidies as inducements to get private land operators and owners and other governmental units to carry out desired land-use practices.

The above list is not necessarily all-inclusive. It indicates, however, that a wide assortment of land-use policies can be used for the modification and improvement of existing land-tenure and land-use situations. Some of the alternatives involve mild reforms while others may be characterized as radical in that they may require the overturning of existing institutional arrangements. Both classes of measures can be brought into use through either evolutionary or revolutionary means.

Far-reaching reform programs and programs involving an intermixture of mild and more radical reforms often are needed, particularly in developing countries, to bring about desired adjustments. Revolutionary approaches are sometimes endorsed as the quickest way to bring about change. This approach, however, can bring major disruptions in national economies and open political wounds that take years to heal. The weight of history generally favors use of a more evolutionary and gradualistic approach. Far-sighted leaders can recognize and promote needed adjustments in land-use policies. More emphasis can be given to the evaluation of objectives, to the testing of policies, and to learning from past mistakes. As long as a nation really follows through on its commitment to develop and carry out improved policies, a policy of gradualism can often produce more permanent accomplishments, more stability, and less disruption than the use of revolutionary approaches.

Land Reform

Considerable attention has been centered in recent decades on the use of land reform measures as a means for alleviating undesired economic and social conditions in rural areas and at the same time triggering economic development. The demands for these reforms come from many sources. Some come from groups who feel outraged by the inequities found in society and who demand reforms to reduce the disparity of opportunities and privileges enjoyed by landlords as compared with tenants and landless workers. Some see reforms quite rationally as a necessary first step toward providing better living conditions for large masses of the citizenry. Others argue that reforms are needed to implement industrialization and to better incorporate rural people into the stream of national life, while still others see the espousal of land reform measures as a road to political power and a means for punishing political enemies.

This combination of interests has served to make land reform a burning issue in many parts of the world. As an action program, it has been new to many areas. Yet the problems that give rise to land reform are not new. They have existed for centuries in many cases. Only the technique and will for action are new. History is filled with accounts of peasant revolts and other attempts of rural people to throw off or at least lighten the yoke of slavery, serfdom, or peonage. Most of these strivings for agrarian reforms have failed, but some have succeeded and have brought added advantages or privileges to peasant populations. The first successful large scale land reform movement of modern times followed the French Revolution and led to a general freeing of land-tenure conditions in western Europe. Land reforms spread to central and eastern Europe following the popular uprisings of 1848, the Russian peasant uprisings of the period before 1861 and again in 1905-06, and the armistice of 1918. Land reform became an issue of worldwide significance following World War II when the demand for reform programs spread from the more developed nations to the developing regions of Africa, Asia, and Latin America.

Meaning of land reform. Differences of opinion exist as to the scope and meaning of the term "land reform." In a broad technical sense, any program that leads to a change, presumably for the better, in the manner in which rural or urban land resources are held and used may be described as land reform. Common practice, however, has limited the usage of this term to programs designed to bring improvements in agricultural economic institutions. This is the sense in which the term "land reform" is used here and in which it was used by the United Nations' Department of Economic and Social Affairs in 1951.[25]

Doreen Warriner, a noted authority on land reform, rejects this definition. In her view, "land reform means the redistribution of property or rights in the land for the benefit of small farmers and agricultural labourers."[26] Still other observers limit their definitions to reform programs of which they personally approve or tend to identify land reform with radical measures such as expropriation of land holdings that they oppose. As a means of clarifying this confusion over the meaning of land reform, Johnson and Kristjanson have recommended the use of three terms: land distribution, land reform, and agrarian reform. Land distribution would involve programs designed to either break up or combine existing land holdings. Land reform would involve "the rearrangement of ownership rights and other institutions associated with land in the interests of the many rather than the few." Agrarian reform would "include overall improvements of rural life and improved relationship of rural people to the land."[27]

Significance of land reform. Two goals are frequently cited for land reform. One of these centers on improvement of the lot of the average land operator or worker while the second emphasizes the possible contributions of reforms to national economic development.[28] Both of

---

[25] United Nations: Department of Economic and Social Affairs, *Land Reform: Defects in Agrarian Structures as Obstacles to Economic Development* (New York: United Nations, 1951), p. 89.

[26] Doreen Warriner, *Land Reform in Principle and Practice* (Oxford: Clarendon Press, 1969), p. xiv. A comparable definition is accepted by Edmundo Flores, "The Economics of Land Reform," *International Labour Review*, Vol. 92, July, 1965, p. 30.

[27] Cf. V. Webster Johnson and Baldur H. Kristjanson, "Programming for Land Reform in the Developing Agricultural Countries of Latin America," *Land Economics*, Vol. 40, November 1964, p. 355.

[28] Erven J. Long, "The Economic Basis of Land Reform in Underdeveloped Economies," *Land Economics*, Vol. 37, May, 1961, pp. 113-24.

these spring from the fact that many countries are trying to implement a rapid "transition from a subsistence agrarian economy of status to a market economy in which varying proportions of the gainfully employed are engaged in agriculture."[29] Many of them seek to establish agricultural economies similar to those of western Europe. Unlike Great Britain, however, where the shift from an earlier agrarian feudal economy to the present situation was accomplished through several centuries of gradual change, they hope to realize similar progress within the lifetimes of present land operators.

The most urgent need for land reform is found in the less developed areas of the world where the great majority of the people are dependent upon agriculture and where outmoded tenure systems have tended to support the selfish interests of small classes of owners rather than the general welfare of the workers and the nation. Most of the rural population in these areas live in the traditional way of their ancestors. Typically, they look to land for their livelihood; they are no more than moderately productive; their incomes are low; and they contribute little to the market economy. The rights and opportunities they enjoy usually reflect their "relationship to the ownership and use of land and their place in the kinship or family group."[30]

Frequently the rural people in these areas are exploited by large landowners or merchants who are able to use their positions to live in comparative luxury while substantial numbers of small operators, tenants, and landless workers live on a near subsistence basis. Possession of ownership rights determines the individual's economic, political, and social status. Changes in the tenure institutions can open doors to new opportunities. As Raymond J. Penn has observed:

> . . . the ownership of land carries with it ownership to government—the right to tax, the right to judge, the power to enact and enforce police regulations. It dominates every crucial decision about investments in social capital—education, transportation, hospitals, power projects.
>
> To the campesino, ownership of land is more than a source of wealth. It is the source of prestige and political power and social justice. It gives him the right to build his own house in which to raise his family. It gives him, too, the right to tax himself to build a school. It lets him share in the bundle of rights which have so long been a prerogative of the large landholder and denied to the landless.[31]

[29] Kenneth H. Parsons, "Land Reform and Agricultural Development," in Kenneth H. Parsons, Raymond J. Penn, and Philip M. Raup (ed.), *Land Tenure: Papers of the First Conference on World Land Tenure Problems* (Madison: University of Wisconsin Press, 1956), pp. 4-5.

[30] *Ibid.*, p. 8.

[31] Raymond J. Penn, "Understanding the Pressures for Land Reform" in *Economic Developments in South America,* Hearings Before the Subcommittee on InterAmerican Economic Relationships, 87th Cong., 2nd Sess., May 10, 1962, p. 15.

Land reform is significant in that it provides a necessary bridge that large segments of the population in some countries can use in shifting to a position where they can utilize their available resources to greater advantage, contribute more to national production, and share more in the bounties of modern life. Its potential as a tool for enhancing the worth and well-being of individuals as well as for facilitating national economic development has received more recognition in some countries than others. The recognition process has been facilitated since World War II by developments such as the creation of the United Nations, the phasing out of colonialism, the extension of economic technical assistance and medical aids to developing areas, and the promotion of economic development programs, which have helped raise the aspirations of average citizens. Almost from the beginning, however, it has been obvious that

> . . . traditional agrarian structures and especially land-tenure institutions through-
> out a large part of the nonindustrialized world are a major obstacle to the kind
> of development postulated by the United Nations. The increased incomes and
> other benefits of technological progress do not reach the majority of the rural
> people. No mass markets are generated in the countryside to support dynamic
> industrial growth. Food production lags, further slowing industrialization. The
> vicious circle of poverty is not broken in rural areas. The peasantry cannot
> organize and participate actively in national affairs. Somehow these traditional
> social structures have to be changed before real rural development can proceed. [32]

Land reform programs. A broad range of land reform programs have been adopted in different countries.[33] Some of these involve single reforms while others embrace combinations of reforms. Some provide for mild adjustments while others are more sweeping in their effects.

A variety of mild reforms has been used both in the more developed and in the less developed countries to secure particular tenure policy objectives. Early examples are provided by the Ordinances of 1785 and 1787 under which the United States prescribed a policy for surveying its public lands, offering them for sale to settlers at a nominal price, providing government for newly settled areas, and opening the way for these areas to eventually be admitted as states to the union. Denmark made itself a nation of small land owners in the 1800s by granting liberal long-term low-interest loans for the tenant purchase of farms and by

[32] Solon Barraclough, "Why Land Reform?" *Ceres,* Vol. 2, November-December 1969, p. 23.

[33] A considerable number of accounts have been published that describe the land reform experiences of different countries. Several of these appear in various issues of *Land Economics.* The experiences of several nations are covered in Parsons, Penn, and Raup, *op. cit.*; in various reports published by the Food and Agriculture Organization of the United Nations; and in the publications of the Land Tenure Research Center at the University of Wisconsin.

encouraging the organization of farmer cooperatives. Great Britain used another type of mild reform in 1870 when it enacted a Landlord and Tenant Act which greatly enhanced the bargaining position and security of farm tenants and facilitated their purchase of the lands they operated. Holland and Italy have carried on large scale land drainage and settlement programs that have provided homesites for many operators. Other prominent examples of mild reforms include the provision of agricultural extension programs, the development of reclamation projects, and the establishment of voluntary land consolidation commissions.

Nations have frequently gone further with their programs to use regulatory measures to attain particular land tenure and use goals. Western Germany and Holland have stringent land use regulations that determine the uses owners can make of their lands. Germany, Switzerland, and Great Britain had policies during World War II that authorized local boards to evict ineffective managers of farm lands and replace them with operators who could contribute more to national food production. Israel has encouraged the organization of cooperative farming settlements (*kibbutzim*) in which land is held and worked by families in common. These settlements operate alongside other cooperative villages (*moshavim*) and villages of private farmers.

France, Holland, and Italy have established agricultural rent controls and in some cases have specified legal maximum rental rates for certain sharing arrangements. The United Arab Republic adopted an Agrarian Reform Law in 1952 that limited rents, if paid in cash, to not more than seven times the real estate tax and share rents to 50 percent of the crop. Agricultural rents were limited to a maximum of 37.5 percent of the crop in Nationalist China in 1949. Similar laws requiring sizeable reductions in farm rents have been enacted in Japan and Pakistan.

Parcellation of farm holdings has been discouraged in Czechoslovakia, Denmark, Israel, and Switzerland by laws that specify minimum farm areas below which further subdivision cannot take place. Programs for the mandatory consolidation and rationalization of existing holdings have been undertaken in countries such as France and Western Germany. Some of these projects involve extensive programs for rural renewal and contain provisions for the relocation of roads, canals, buildings, and utilities as well as the creation of smaller numbers of operating tracts.

Limitations on areas and types of farm ownership provide another example of land-reform measures. Czechoslovakia limited private land holdings following World War II to a maximum of 50 hectares; owner-cultivators have a 7.5-acre limit in Japan; a 33-acre limit applies in East Pakistan; a 15-hectare limit in Poland; and a 100-feddan (103 acres) limit in the United Arab Republic. Holland and the Philippines have regulations that give tenants the first right to buy farm land if it is offered for sale. France, Germany, and Sweden prohibit sales of farm land to foreigners, nonfarmers, speculators, and investment "hedgers."

Some of the most far-reaching land reforms have called for the expropriation of certain land holdings with their redistribution in smaller-sized tracts to actual farmers. Land expropriation and redistribution programs were carried out in most of the nations of Eastern Europe following World War I. A large program of this type was started in Mexico during the interwar period and large-scale programs have been carried out in Japan, India, Pakistan, Iran, Italy, Algeria, the United Arab Republic, Kenya, Bolivia, and Cuba since World War II. Some land owners have been divested of all of their holdings while others have been allowed to retain specified maximum areas. Compensation has been paid for the expropriated lands in most countries.[34] A notable exception has existed in the Iron Curtain countries where the properties of former landowners were often confiscated without compensation.

Land expropriation programs have usually been followed by a redistribution of the acquired farm lands among tenants, landless workers, and small peasant proprietors. Forest and other nonfarm holdings have often been retained in public ownership, and estate holdings with extensive building improvements have sometimes been retained as a unit and used for educational, research, and cooperative purposes. Individual allotments of the redistributed lands have usually been small, and recipients have normally been required to make some payment for their lands. Purchase payments have ranged from nominal charges equal to the value of one or two years' crops to the current market value of the land. Long-term credit and liberal repayment schedules have been provided to accomodate the new owners.

Another variant of land expropriation has been applied on a large scale in the Soviet Union, Communist China, and some other countries. Collectivization rather than private ownership programs are used in the administration of agricultural properties in these countries. Two types of programs are in use in the Soviet Union. Most of the farm land is operated in state-controlled collective farms (*kolkhoz*) while some areas are administered in large state farms (*sovkhoz*). Residents of the collective farms work together in farming the properties held by the collectives together with possible additional areas leased from the state. Through

[34] Several variations in compensation arrangements have been used. Some countries, such as Finland, have paid their expropriated owners in bonds based on current or recent land values. The United Arab Republic based its compensation on pre-World War II values. The expropriated landlords in Mexico received long-term bonds for 110 percent of the assessed value of their land. Italy's program calls for compensation based on the tax assessed value of the land two years prior to expropriation. The payments made to expropriated owners in India and Pakistan were graduated according to the income-producing value of the expropriated areas. In the United Provinces, for example, large zamindars received a nominal compensation equal to as little as twice the value of their annual net rents. Zamindars with small holdings, however, were authorized to receive payments up to the equivalent of twenty times the annual value of their net rents.

their joint efforts, they benefit from higher quality management and from the use of more farm equipment and capital than presumably would be available to them if they operated as individuals. Workers have individual houses and family garden plots and share in the income produced by the collectives in proportion to their labor inputs.

Consequences of land reform.[35]   Almost every nation has enacted land reform measures of one type or another in recent decades. As one might expect, these measures have been popular with most rural constituencies. Indeed, reform programs of a palliative nature have often been pushed by public officials who have wished to capitalize on the political fervor for land reforms without greatly disturbing existing conditions.

Overall, the effects of most land reforms may be regarded as favorable. They have often contributed to individual and family well-being, added to their dignity as individuals, and fostered actions such as the cooperative use of machinery or sinking of wells, the provision of operating credit, or the lowering of rents, which have added to their productivity as workers and to their welfare as individuals. Opportunities provided by land reforms have given millions of people reasons to hope for a better future. In many countries such as Japan, Mexico, Nationalist China, Pakistan, and the United Arab Republic, they have generated programs that are creating a more productive agriculture plus economic development.

In practice, it must be recognized that land reforms can help create favorable political institutions. They can generate individual and social well-being. They can add to individual and national productivity. They can further the processes of capital formation and economic development. Whether or not these objectives will be achieved depends upon the nature of specific reforms, the quality and enthusiasm of the leadership they attract, and the support they receive in the form of complementary programs and actions.

Evidence from various countries indicates that past land reforms have helped to create viable rural institutions and have paved the way for the

[35] For other discussions of this topic cf. Warriner, *op. cit.*; Philip M. Raup, "The Contribution of Land Reform to Agricultural Development" in Herman M. Southworth and Bruce F. Johnson, eds., *Agriculture and Economic Development* (Ithaca: Cornell University Press, 1967), pp. 267-314; Erich H. Jacoby, *Interrelationship of Agrarian Reform and Agricultural Development,* Food and Agriculture Organization Agricultural Study No. 26 (Rome, 1953); John W. Mellor, *The Economics of Agricultural Development* (Ithaca: Cornell University Press, 1966), chap. XIV; V. Webster Johnson, *Man and the Land* (Bangkok, 1970); V. Webster Johnson and Baldur H. Kristjanson, *loc. cit.*; Folke Dovring, "Land Reform and Productivity in Mexico," *Land Economics,* Vol. 46, August, 1970, pp. 264-274; and Solon Barraclough, "Alternative Land Tenure Systems Resulting from Agrarian Reform in Latin America," *Land Economics,* Vol. 46, August, 1970, pp. 217-228. Another valuable source is provided by the U. S. Agency for International Development, *A.I.D. Spring Review of Land Reform* (Washington, 1970). The twelve volumes of this report include several background papers together with individual analyses of the land reform programs of thirty nations.

establishment of a commercial agricultural economy. Reforms have brought about better housing and farm production conditions in many areas. They have prompted the cultivation of larger areas and brought more intensive use of those properties whose former owners had limited interests in farming. They have encouraged operators to be more productive, to apply innovations in their work, and to adopt conservation practices. By adding to rural production and incomes and by diverting landlord interests from investments in land to investments in industrial, commercial, housing, and other urban enterprises, they have also helped to generate economic development.

Yet the case for land reform is not entirely one-sided. Some so-called reforms have involved palliative measures that have done little for rural people. The breaking up of large holdings has sometimes destroyed economies of scale, created voids when services provided by landlords have not been forthcoming from other sources, and sometimes resulted in an initial decline in marketable surpluses as operators have elected to care for their own consumption needs and have had little incentive to produce the marketable surpluses formerly needed to pay their rents.[36]

Land reforms have a considerable potential for bringing about desirable objectives; but there is no guarantee of these results. They can improve the lot of one generation of land operators only to be swallowed up in the problems created by rising population numbers if they are not associated with industrialization and urbanization movements that draw people off the land. They can add to the self-esteem of farm operators, but this may be a hollow attainment if operators are left to "lift themselves by their bootstraps" without additional steps being taken to involve them in the workings of modern society. They can provide a basis for a more democratic society; but this process must be implemented with educational programs and measures to create democratic institutions. One of their greatest potentials lies in the role they can play as a catalyst for economic development; but this process involves the interplay of many factors, many of which are just as necessary for success as land reform.

Other Programs for Securing Better Land Use

It is frequently asserted that the United States and Canada have little need for land reform. This is a valid assumption if one is concerned primarily with possible measures for the redistribution of agricultural holdings. The

---

[36] Doreen Warriner indicates (*op. cit.,* p. 54) that reforms are most apt to lead to increased production when they are implemented rapidly, provisions are made for operating units of economic size, and the reforms are desired by the peasants. Production is apt to decline when periods of uncertainty bring delays in the application of reforms, units of uneconomic size are created, no provisions are made for replacement of functions formerly performed by landlords, or the peasants lack incentives for increasing production.

underlying problems that call for land reforms and land redistribution in many parts of the world are of little significance in these two nations. When land-tenure and land-use problems are viewed in a wider context, however, it is obvious that a variety of programs can be used to bring about more rational land-tenure and land-use conditions.

Nonagricultural reform programs have been used on numerous occasions in recent decades to promote the attainment of urban housing and land-use goals. Examples include federal insurance of housing loans, public support of the residential mortgage market, encouragement of public housing, the provision of rent control and rent subsidy programs, the outlawing of racial discrimination in housing, increased emphasis on the need for area planning, and federal support for highway construction, urban renewal, and open-space acquisition programs. Definite progress has been realized with most of these programs. Yet much remains to be done. Strong programs are needed in both urban and rural areas to promote and insure orderly and efficient land use.[37] Action programs are needed to upgrade both the urban and rural environment, to establish agricultural and natural area reserves in which lands will not be available for suburban and urban uses without public consent, to preserve open space and green-belt areas, to acquire and develop lands for public recreation, to improve the quality of both existing and new housing, and to forestall the development of slums.

Coupled with the attainment of these objectives is a need for more enlightened attitudes regarding the rights and responsibilities of property owners. The traditional concept of fee-simple ownership under which owners were free to use and abuse their properties with little regard for others is now sadly out of place. Individual owners must consider the impact of their actions in using their properties upon others and upon society at large. The old doctrine of *laissez faire* is giving way to a doctrine of *savoir faire*.[38] Land ownership is becoming a public trust under which private owners enjoy certain usufructary rights in their properties which they must exercise in a manner commensurate with the public interest.

Time alone can tell how far the United States and Canada will move in limiting private ownership rights in the public interest. With increasing urbanization, rising population numbers, and the passing of time, however, it appears probable that these two nations will follow the examples of several western European nations in exercising stronger controls over private land use. With these developments, privately owned lands may well be treated as a type of public utility, as resources that individuals must use in accordance with public regulations. Regulations

[37]An example of the type of action that should be considered is suggested by Great Britain's programs for controlling the shifting of rural lands to urban uses. Cf. G. P. Wibberley, *Agriculture and Urban Growth* (London: Michael Joseph, 1959).

[38]Cf. John E. Cribbett, "Changing Concepts in the Law of Land Use," *Iowa Law Review*, Vol. 50, Winter, 1965, pp. 245-78.

may be adopted concerning the maximum and minimum sizes of various types of individual holdings, their sales prices, the determination of possible buyers, and possibly the uses to which certain properties must be put. Steps may be taken to open beaches, forests, and other privately held properties for limited public use and to limit the rights of private owners to modify or destroy publicly-enjoyed scenic or amenity features of their properties without public consent.

Whatever course of action is followed, careful planning and consideration should be given to the techniques and consequences of a wide array of alternatives for securing better land use. In this process, it should be recognized that the property rights people hold in land represent one of our most respected and most stable institutions. Analysis of past developments shows that this institution has often been modified and adjusted to meet changing needs and demands. Further adjustments may be needed in the future if the nation's land resources are to be used in an optimal manner to serve the needs of a highly urbanized population.

—SELECTED READINGS

Chapin, F. Stuart, Jr., *Urban Land Use Planning,* 2nd ed. (Urbana: University of Illinois Press, 1965).

Galloway, George B., *Planning for America* (New York: Holt, Rinehart and Winston, Inc., 1941).

Johnson, V. Webster, and Raleigh Barlowe, *Land Problems and Policies* (New York: McGraw-Hill Book Company, 1954), chap. I, XIV-XV.

Ottoson, Howard W., (ed.), *Land Use Policy and Problems in the United States* (Lincoln: University of Nebraska Press, 1963), chap. XI-XVII.

Parsons, Kenneth H., Raymond J. Penn, and Philip M. Raup (eds.), *Land Tenure: Papers of the First Conference on World Land Tenure* (Madison: University of Wisconsin Press, 1956).

Renne, Roland R., *Land Economics,* 2nd ed. (New York: Harper and Brothers, 1958), chap. XXII-XXIII.

Southworth, Herman M., and Bruce F. Johnston (eds.), *Agriculture and Economic Development* (Ithaca: Cornell University Press, 1967), chap. VIII.

Warriner, Doreen, *Land Reform in Principle and Practice* (London: Clarendon Press, Oxford, 1969).

17

Public Measures
for Directing Land Use

When individuals, private groups, and governments plan for better land-resource use, it is normally assumed that they have some ability to follow through with their plans. This "follow through" process logically starts with the individual or agency that does the planning, particularly when the plan concerns the management or organization of resources that the planner controls. Much of the land-resource planning in today's society, however, involves the activities of other people and resources over which the planner lacks direct control. In these cases, effective planning usually calls for directional measures that can guide, limit, or control the activities of others.

Various directional measures can be used to guide and control the uses made of land resources. The simplest of these involve exercise of the rights of ownership. Private owners ordinarily control the uses made of the properties they hold throughout their lifetimes. These uses can be limited by easements, deed restrictions, or conditions of title. Owners can use deed restrictions and covenants to direct the future use of the lands they sell or otherwise transfer to others. They can write conditions into their inheritance arrangements. They also can donate properties to the public or to various private organizations with the stipulation that they be used for educational, religious, or other purposes.

Individuals frequently work together on a formal or informal basis to secure particular land-use objectives. They can join with others in formal associations to require specific architectural standards in local residential construction, to control the transfer of neighborhood properties to new owners, or to create country clubs or private hunting or fishing domains. Acting informally, but collectively, they can use public opinion and social pressures to influence the land-use decisions and practices of other individuals and of various levels of government.

Formal and informal approaches also are used by governments in their efforts to direct land-use practices. Informal powers are used when public officials use persuasion, gentlemen's agreements, and opportunities to influence public opinion to secure desired ends. Under appropriate circumstances, they may go further to exercise certain formal powers that their levels of government have over use rights in land. These formal controls include the police, eminent domain, spending, proprietary, and taxation powers of government. The exercise of the first four of these powers in the United States provides the subject of the discussion that follows.

POLICE-POWER MEASURES

Of the several powers the state and federal governments hold over landed property, the police power is often regarded as most important. The full extent and meaning of this power has never been defined; but it centers in the inherent right of governments to legislate for the advancement, preservation, and protection of the public health, safety, morals, convenience, and welfare. As one court has observed, the police power:

> . . . is of vast and undefined extent, expanding and enlarging in the multiplicity of its activities as exigencies demanding its service arise in the development of our complex civilization. It is a function of government solely within the domain of the legislature to declare when this power shall be brought into operation, for the protection or advancement of the public welfare.[1]

In many respects, the doctrine of police power is a singular American institution. No mention of this concept appears in the federal Constitution. The doctrine has evolved instead as a product of judicial interpretation. The term "police power" was first used by the Supreme Court in 1827.[2] Its recognition as a potent source of legal authority came two decades later when Chief Justice Taney defined it broadly as "the power of government inherent in every sovereignty . . . to govern men and things

---

[1] *Motlow v. State,* 125 Tenn. 547, 589 (1911).

[2] *Brown v. Maryland,* 12 Wheaton 419 (1827). Chief Justice Marshall used the term in passing to indicate the residual powers—in addition to the eminent domain and taxation powers—held by the states.

within the limits of its dominion."[3] From Taney's time on, the courts have gradually expanded the scope of what can be accomplished under the police power to permit an ever-widening latitude of social action in areas involving the public interest and welfare.

Since its judicial beginnings during the middle 1800s, the police power has been recognized as a residual power of the states, which the federal government can also exercise in its administration of federal territories and as a delegated power incident to its commerce, postal, taxation, and war powers. It has provided the principal legal basis for a wide variety of public measures that limit or regulate vested property rights. But while the courts have accepted an expanding concept of the police power, they have held rigorously to the view that every exercise of this power must be reasonable, that it must enhance the public welfare, that it not be arbitrary or discriminatory, and that it not deprive persons of their rights without "due process of law" or of their rights to "the equal protection of the laws."[4]

The police power can be employed in many different ways to influence and direct the use of land resources. Particular attention is given here to zoning ordinances and subdivision regulations as two leading examples of the application of this power in the United States. It should be recognized, however, that the police power can be used for many other land-use directional purposes. It provides the legal basis for area building codes, for fire protection and sanitation regulations, and for ordinances covering the abatement and control of pollution practices. Special district

[3]*License Cases,* 5 Howard 504, 583 (1847). In another leading case decided four years later, the Massachusetts Supreme Court defined the police power as "the power vested in the legislature . . . to make, ordain and establish all manner of wholesome and reasonable laws . . . for the good and welfare of the commonwealth, and the subjects of the same." *Commonwealth v. Alger,* 7 Cushing (Mass.) 53, 85 (1851).

Mason and Beaney indicate that the police-power doctrine was developed as a "juristic expression of popular sovereignty." Throughout the early years of the Republic, the courts emphasized a doctrine of vested rights and even went so far as to argue that the protection of property rights was the main function of government. This stand was shaken by the rise of popular sovereignty—"the notion that the will of the people is to be discovered at the ballot box, not merely in a document framed in 1787"—during the 1820s and 1830s. Several states liberalized their voting requirements and acted to remove constitutional safeguards for economic privilege during this period. Chief Justice Taney, appointed in 1837, endorsed this new philosophy when he argued that: "The object and end of all government is to promote the happiness and prosperity of the community by which it is established. . . . While the rights of property are sacredly guarded, we must not forget that the community also has rights and that the happiness and well-being of every citizen depends on their faithful preservation." Cf. Alpheus T. Mason and William M. Beaney, *American Constitutional Law,* 4th ed. (Englewood Cliffs, N. J.: Prentice-Hall, Inc., 1968), p. 300.

[4]The "due process" and "equal protection" restrictions against state action were adopted as part of the Fourteenth Amendment to the Federal Constitution following the Civil War in 1868. These provisions were designed ostensibly for the protection of individual civil rights. In practice, however, they have often been used as a check against the police power of the states.

regulations can use the police power to provide for weed eradication, the acceptance of flood control measures, or the adoption of conservation practices. The police power can also be used for such diverse purposes as instituting residential rent controls, requiring the spacing of oil wells, providing forest cutting regulations, or applying agricultural production controls.

Use of Zoning Ordinances

Zoning provides a foremost example of the use of the police power to direct land use. Far from being a complicated concept, zoning "merely means the division of land into districts having different regulations."[5] It involves the designation of specific land-use districts within which various regulations and restrictions apply concerning the use of land; the height, size, and use of buildings; and the density of population. Zoning is a tool for carrying out a land-use plan, not a substitute for planning; and its worth-whileness and general effectiveness always depend on the character of the planning upon which it is based.

Beginnings of zoning. Land district regulations have been used sporadically in urban areas since ancient times. Fire districts permitting the construction of wooden buildings in some areas but not in others were established at an early date in many cities. Some of our colonial villages banned the manufacture and storage of gunpowder from their built-up residential and business sections for fire protection and public safety reasons. Massachusetts passed a law in 1692 that authorized certain towns "to assign places in each town, where least offensive, for slaughterhouses, stillhouses, and houses for trying tallow and currying leather."[6]

Zoning regulations were adopted in several California cities during the late 1800s, primarily as a means of restricting the location of Chinese laundries.[7] Other cities followed with regulations that controlled certain practices viewed as nuisances or near-nuisances. Police power measures gained acceptance as a means for protecting residential neighborhoods from the undesired environmental impacts associated with the operation of such businesses as slaughterhouses, brick kilns, dairies, livery stables, stone-crushers, and carpet-beating establishments.[8]

---

[5] Edward M. Bassett, *Zoning* (New York: Russell Sage Foundation, 1940), p. 9.

[6] Erling D. Solberg, *Rural Zoning in the United States,* U.S. Department of Agriculture Information Bulletin No. 59, 1952, p. 2.

[7] Laundries and washhouses were regarded as a public nuisance in these instances because of their frequent dumping of wash water in the streets, because of the fire hazard associated with their often flimsy construction and their storage of inflammable materials, and because of the moral hazards arising from the congregation of large numbers of people in these establishments.

[8] Robert A. Walker, *The Planning Function in Urban Government* (Chicago: University of Chicago Press, 1941), p. 56.

The chief emphasis with these early examples of zoning was on safety measures and nuisance controls. Little attention was given to the possible use of zoning as an instrument of planning for orderly community growth. A first step in this direction was taken in 1904-5 when the Massachusetts legislature established two types of building-height districts in Boston— one with an 80-foot height limit and the second with a 125-foot height limit. Los Angeles followed in 1909-11 with a series of zoning ordinances that identified seven industrial districts and designated the remaining area of the city as a residential district from which certain uses were excluded. The "building-height" and "land-use" regulations adopted in these two cities represent our first real use of zoning for land-use planning purposes.

Acceptance of comprehensive zoning. New York City adopted the nation's first comprehensive zoning ordinance in 1916. This ordinance had its beginnings with the appointment of a Commission on Heights of Buildings in 1910 to investigate the impact of skyscrapers on community health and safety. A commission report recommending regulations to control the height, bulk, and use of buildings in different districts of the city was issued in 1913. Legislative approval was secured the next year for a change in the city charter to permit district regulations; and a special commission was appointed shortly thereafter to prepare a districting resolution and map.

New York City at this time provided a glaring, but typical, example of the need for land-use regulations. As Bassett indicates:

A building could legally rise to any height whatever, assume any form, be put to any use, and cover 100 percent of the lot from the ground to the sky. Tenement houses were the only structures that might not cover the whole lot. High office buildings not only covered their entire lots and had the same floor space in their top stories and their first stories, but cornices projected into the street from eight to fourteen feet. Buildings of this sort in the southern part of Manhattan made dark canyons of narrow streets, but what was perhaps even more harmful they produced chaotic building conditions. The first skyscraper to be erected in a block would cover the entire lot up to the roof and open its windows on neighboring lots. A high building so erected prevented other similar buildings . . . in its immediate vicinity . . . [and thus] obtained a virtual monopoly of the light and air.

. . . Improper uses caused injury to homogeneous areas and were especially productive of premature depreciation of settled localities. One-family, detached home districts, possessing trees and lawns, were invaded by apartment houses occupying nearly their entire lots. These in turn were damaged by the building of stores, garages, and factories. Localities of one-family detached homes and apartment houses were invaded by sporadic stores that sought to short-circuit the neighborhoods by utilizing eligible corners among the residences. Soon other stores were built on the opposite corners, and before long the nearby residences began to depreciate. . . .

Invasion of apartment houses by stores on their ground floors lessened the desirability of neighboring apartment houses because of the increase of noise, vehicles, fire hazard, litter, and street congestion. Business streets lined with retail stores were invaded by factories, garages, and junk shops. Localities devoted to light industry, perhaps employing women and children, were invaded by heavy industries producing noise, smoke, and fumes. No land owner in any part of the city could erect a building of any sort with assurance that in ten or twenty years the building would not be obsolete by reason of an unnecessary and undesirable change in the character of the neighborhood. Sometimes these changes left a blighted district behind.[9]

This being the situation, it was obvious that the public welfare called for some system of regulations that would control the height, area, and use of buildings and also stabilize the land-use patterns found throughout the city. Several land- and building-use regulations were suggested as an appropriate means for achieving these ends. These districting—later called zoning—regulations provided for height and area restrictions on new building construction and for reserving some areas for single-family dwellings, some for multifamily housing, and others for commercial, industrial, and other uses.

Questions were raised at this point concerning the probable unconstitutionality of the proposed regulations. Comprehensive zoning was a new thing; and many eminent lawyers felt that the proposed regulations involved an illegal use of the police power. They argued that the limitation of private property rights under zoning constituted an illegal taking of property for public use and that the proposed zoning plan should be accomplished under the eminent domain power.[10] This alternative was rejected because of: (1) the high cost and "clumsy and ineffective" nature of the eminent domain approach; (2) the conviction that effective zoning could not be accomplished in this way; and (3) the feeling that there was more than an even chance that the courts would uphold comprehensive zoning as a legal use of the police power.

A full decade passed following the adoption of the New York City ordinance before the legality of comprehensive zoning was finally established in the courts. During this decade, provisions were made for zoning in 43 states and the District of Columbia; zoning ordinances were enacted in some 420 municipalities; and several important decisions, mostly upholding but some rejecting the constitutionality of zoning, were rendered in the state courts.[11]

The constitutionality issue was finally settled by the Supreme Court in

[9] Bassett, *op. cit.*, pp. 23-25.
[10] Cf. *ibid.*, pp. 26-27.
[11] Cf. Walker, *op. cit.*, pp. 48-77, for a popular account of the more important court cases associated with the legal development of zoning law.

Village of Euclid v. Ambler Realty Company in 1926.[12] In his majority opinion, Justice Sutherland observed that:

> The line which separates . . . the legitimate from the illegitimate assumption of [the police] power is not capable of precise delimitation. It varies with circumstances and conditions. A regulatory zoning ordinance, which would be clearly valid as applied to the great cities, might be clearly invalid as applied to rural communities. . . . Thus the question whether the power exists to forbid the erection of a building of a particular kind or for a particular use, like the question whether a particular thing is a nuisance, is to be determined . . . by considering it in connection with the circumstances and the locality. . . . A nuisance may be merely a right thing in the wrong place,—like a pig in the parlor instead of the barnyard. If the validity of the legislative classification for zoning purposes be fairly debatable, the legislative judgment must be allowed to control. . . .
>
> There is no serious difference of opinion in respect of the validity of laws and regulations fixing the height of buildings within reasonable limits, the character of materials and methods of construction, and the adjoining area which must be left open, in order to minimize the danger of fire or collapse, the evils of overcrowding, and the like, and excluding from residential sections offensive trades, industries and structures likely to create nuisances.

Justice Sutherland then indicated that the police power could be used to exclude industries "which are neither offensive nor dangerous" from designated areas. The serious question, as he saw it, involved "the validity of what is really the crux of the more recent zoning legislation, namely, the creation and maintenance of residential districts, from which business and trade of every sort, including hotels and apartment houses, are excluded." After reviewing the impact of these establishments on fire, traffic, and noise conditions and the parasitic effect they have in destroying "the residential character of the neighborhood and its desirability as a place of detached residences," he concluded that

---

[12] 272 U.S. 365 (1926). The *Euclid* case concerned the constitutionality of a zoning ordinance in Euclid, a suburb of Cleveland, Ohio. At the time this case was appealed to the Supreme Court, many friends of zoning felt that the facts at issue were such as to make an adverse decision almost inevitable. Several members of the National Conference on City Planning, however, argued that the case would provide a leading precedent and that every effort should be made to secure a favorable decision. Arrangements accordingly were made for Alfred Bettman to submit a brief *amicus curiae* on behalf of the Conference. Owing to an unfortunate oversight, Mr. Bettman was not advised of the time of the court hearing and thus was not heard by the Court. He reported this situation to Chief Justice Taft and was granted the unusual privilege of submitting his brief at a rehearing of the case on October 12, 1926. It is understood that a majority of the Court had decided against the validity of zoning after the first hearing. After the second hearing, however, the Court held six to three for the constitutionality of comprehensive zoning. Cf. *ibid.*, pp. 77-78; and Alfred Bettman, *City and Regional Planning Papers* (Cambridge: Harvard University Press, 1946), pp. xv, 51-57, and 157-93.

"apartment houses, which in a different environment would be not entirely objectionable but highly desirable, come very near to being nuisances."

Much of the dicta in the decision is phrased in terms of the law of nuisances. But the Court indicated that zoning can be used for a broader purpose than merely the control of nuisances. With its endorsement of this view, the Supreme Court opened the door for the widescale use of zoning as a tool for the effectuation of land-resource planning.

The zoning process. Following the adoption of the New York zoning ordinance in 1916, several cities tried to zone under their home-rule powers. These efforts were usually rejected by the courts on the ground that they involved the exercise of a power vested in the state legislatures that could not be legally used without legislative authorization. State zoning enabling legislation was thus recognized as a necessary first step in the zoning process. Enabling legislation was soon passed in most states; and by 1970, every state had zoning enabling legislation that authorized some or all cities to enact zoning ordinances. Approximately three-fourths of the 3,000 counties in the United States along with townships and other minor civil divisions in some states also had received authority to zone. [13]

The details of the zoning process vary somewhat from state to state. In general, however, they follow the pattern recommended by the Advisory Committee on Zoning, which Secretary of Commerce Hoover appointed in 1921 to draft a standard zoning enabling act. Assuming that a city, county, or other local unit has authority to zone, the zoning process begins with the decision to appoint a zoning board or commission. This action is usually initiated by the city council, county board, or other local governing board. It may also be initiated under the enabling acts of some states by petitions signed by given proportions of the number of eligible voters.

Once appointed, the zoning commission has the responsibility of drafting a zoning ordinance and preparing a map that shows the boundaries of the various districts or zones within which different regulations apply. The typical zoning ordinance prepared by this commission includes six principal items: (1) a statement of purposes, which usually correspond closely with those listed in the enabling act; (2) general provisions including definitions of terms, a clause prohibiting the construction or alteration of buildings or the use of land or buildings except in conformity with the provisions of the ordinance, and a recognition of the right of property owners to continue nonconforming uses; (3) a statement that identifies the different classifications of districts—residential, business, industrial, or agricultural—and that either describes the boundaries of each district or establishes them as set forth

[13] Cf. Erling D. Solberg, *The Why and How of Rural Zoning,* U. S. Department of Agriculture, Agriculture Information Bulletin No. 196, revised 1967, p. 2.

on the zoning map; (4) a detailed description of the regulations that apply in each district; (5) provisions for administration and enforcement including requirements for building and occupancy permits, arrangements for possible appeals, and a declaration that violations are misdemeanors punishable by fine or imprisonment; and (6) provisions for possible changes and amendments of the ordinance.[14]

Zoning commissions are usually appointed as independent bodies, though their functions are sometimes delegated to planning agencies. In either case, the process of drafting a zoning ordinance calls for a type of land-resource planning, for decisions concerning the types of land-resource development and use that should be encouraged in different districts. This situation makes it desirable for zoning commissions to note any planning done in their communities and to supplement these plans with such additional planning as may be needed to provide a reasonably sound basis for their zoning recommendations. Like other planning agencies, these commissions function best when they operate without secrecy and when they feel free to consult with property owners and citizen groups.

Once the zoning commission has tentatively formulated its recommendations, it must hold public hearings at which affected property owners can voice their opinions. The commission then considers these opinions in the preparation of the proposed ordinance, map, and final report, which it submits to the local governing body.[15] This body is usually required to advertise and hold a second set of public hearings. Following these hearings, the local governing boards are ordinarily free to debate and either accept or reject the proposed ordinances. Some enabling acts provide, however, that this decision be made by the local voters at a regular or special election. Still others permit action by the local governing board but provide that a given proportion of the eligible voters can petition for a popular referendum on the board's action.

Zoning commissions often disband following the submission of their reports. Provisions may be made, however, for their continuation as bodies charged with the responsibility of considering possible future changes and amendments. This arrangement provides a means for keeping zoning ordinances up to date and in tune with changing needs and conditions. But although adjustments are needed from time to time, frequent changes are a sign of poor planning or weak and vacillating administration. Some enabling acts discourage frequent or hasty changes by providing a check known as the "20 percent protest." This provision

[14] Cf. Frank E. Horack, Jr., and Val Nolan, Jr., *Land Use Controls* (St. Paul: West Publishing Company, 1955), pp. 46-48.

[15] Some states have enabling-act provisions requiring that the zoning commission submit its proposals to a county or state agency for review and approval before they are officially submitted to the local governing board. This review process can be used as a check against faulty ordinances and as a means of preventing the conflicts that could develop between governmental units if adjacent areas were zoned for noncompatible uses.

makes it possible for 20 percent of the property owners affected by a proposed change to protest the change and thereby require a two-thirds or three-fourths majority of the governing board before the change can be adopted.

With the adoption of a zoning ordinance, it is necessary to appoint a board of appeals or adjustment whose purpose is that of applying "the discretion of experts to exceptional instances where permits are desired not strictly conforming to the regulations."[16] These boards hear and decide on appeals made from the actions and orders of the administrative officials who enforce the zoning ordinance. They can reverse the decisions of the enforcing officers and authorize minor modifications of the rules to fit individual needs and convenience.

The courts are inclined to question the legality of any zoning ordinance that is not adopted in strict conformance with the procedures specified in the state enabling act. Since this process is time-consuming, communities often find that they cannot zone fast enough to prevent imminent objectionable uses. This problem has caused some states to authorize *interim* zoning ordinances. These ordinances are often adopted hastily by local governing bodies as stop-gap measures to provide a type of zoning for limited time periods. They are frequently criticized because of their hasty and sometimes faulty construction. But they often play an important role in preventing undesirable types of land or building use during the weeks or months it may take to draft and adopt a standard zoning ordinance.

Another important aspect of the zoning process concerns the treatment of *nonconforming uses.* Most zoning ordinances involve existing non-conforming land and building uses that would be prohibited if they were initiated after the ordinance went into effect. The police power can be used to stop these uses if they constitute public nuisances; and some communities have taken steps to use their spending and eminent domain powers to buy out these uses. As a general rule, however, nonconforming uses can continue as long as they are not expanded or abandoned and as long as the nonconforming structures are not altered, repaired, or reconstructed.[17] They are normally regarded as established uses, which must be accepted for the time being but which will eventually be discontinued. Administrative action is needed with every ordinance to list these nonconforming uses and to take such future action as may be appropriate to insure their eventual discontinuance.

Zoning regulations in urban areas. Zoning ordinances are now used in all but a few of the nation's larger cities and in most smaller cities as well. As was the case in earlier years, zoning is still used to prevent "growing congestion, impairment of access to air, light, and sunshine, and invasion

16 Bassett, *op. cit.,* p. 117.
17 Cf. Horack and Nolan, *op. cit.,* pp. 151-63; also Bassett, *op. cit.,* pp. 105-16.

by improper uses."[18] It also plays a more positive role both within and outside city limits in promoting orderly resource development, stabilizing and preserving desired land-use patterns, and giving meaning to master plans for the future.

Four principal types of zoning regulations are used in most cities. These include (1) regulations concerning the uses permitted in different districts, (2) provisions controlling the size of lots and the proportions of their surface areas that can be covered with buildings, (3) maximum height and bulk restrictions for buildings and other structures, and (4) population density requirements. Most municipal zoning ordinances recognize three major classes of use districts—residential, business, and industrial. Additional classifications—such as agricultural, recreation, or unrestricted—may also be used when a city or village includes agricultural lands it wants to retain in their present use, areas it desires to have used for particular purposes, or areas it wishes to leave unrestricted until its future needs are more clearly defined.

Residential districts are ordinarily divided into three subclasses—single-family, two-family, and multiple-family districts. Single-family districts represent a most exclusive type of zoning. All other types of residential, business, and industrial uses are excluded from these districts. Provisions are ordinarily made, however, for the possible location of schools, churches, humanitarian institutions, parks, playgrounds, golf courses, and sometimes even farms in these districts. A two-family district permits all the uses of a single-family district plus two-family residences and duplexes. Multiple-family districts go still further to allow three- and four-family residential units and apartment houses.

Business districts frequently fall into two classes—local shopping centers and central business districts. Local shopping districts permit retail and service establishments but exclude industrial uses. Apartment houses are often permitted, and new residential construction may be either permitted or excluded. Central business districts provide for retail and service businesses and usually permit light industries. They may exclude heavy and nuisance industries and sometimes new residential construction. Apartment houses are frequently permitted, particularly when the ground-floor areas are used for business purposes.

Industrial districts also fall into two classes—light industries and heavy industries. Districts designated for light industrial uses frequently permit all uses except heavy or nuisance industries and sometimes residences. Heavy industrial districts are sometimes zoned for this use alone but may also permit all uses or all nonresidential uses. Exclusive industrial districts in which all uses other than industrial developments are prohibited have become increasingly common since 1950.

Building-height regulations vary from city to city. A maximum height of 2½ stories or around 35 feet applies in most single- and two-family

[18] Bassett, *op. cit.*, p. 45.

residential districts. Higher structures are permitted in the multiple-family, business, and industrial districts of most large cities. Building-bulk and set-back regulations are used in combination with height regulations in many central business districts to prevent individual skyscrapers from infringing upon the rights of other property owners for reasonable access to air and light.[19] Building-height regulations are also applied in most areas adjacent to airports.

Area regulations are frequently used to specify the maximum density of population permitted in an area. These regulations may limit the number of families housed per acre, require a minimum number of square feet of lot area or building space per family, or require minimum lot sizes or frontages. Comparable area regulations may be used to prevent owners from building on more than some given proportion of their lot area; to require minimum building set-back lines from the front, sides, and rear of lots; to establish minimum sizes for inner or rear court areas; or to prescribe minimum off-street parking requirements.[20]

Rural zoning. Zoning has somewhat less appeal and less application in rural areas than in cities, mainly because the problems that give rise to zoning are less acute in these areas. Problems exist both in the unincorporated suburbs found around urban centers and in more strictly rural areas, however, that call for land-use directional measures. Most of the state legislatures have recognized the existence of these problems and the desirability of authorizing local authorities to deal with their problems through the enactment of appropriate zoning ordinances.[21] Hawaii has gone further than the other states by authorizing a statewide system of land classification and districting, which amounts to state zoning.

Two distinctly different types of rural zoning are now in use. Several counties and townships use a suburban type of comprehensive zoning that involves regulations very similar to those used in cities. Wisconsin pioneered this type of zoning with an enabling act (1923), which

---

[19] Some older ordinances specify that once buildings reach a certain height they be set back a given distance for each additional foot of height. These regulations have given way in most cities to controls that prescribe a maximum ratio between building bulk or total floor space and the area of the lot. These controls permit flexibility in building form but normally require sufficient spacing between and around buildings to insure access to daylight for every window.

[20] Since area and building-height regulations often vary from one type of use district to another, *transition* zoning is frequently used to soften the transition from one use district to another. Where a residential and a business district come together in the middle of a block, for example, the business establishments may be required to observe the same set-back and height regulations in their portion of the block as the residential properties.

[21] Cf. Solberg, *The Why and How of Rural Zoning,* and William J. Block, *Rural Zoning: People, Property, and Public Policy,* ESC-563, U. S. Department of Agriculture Federal Extension Service, 1967, for general discussions of the case for rural zoning.

authorizes counties to use comprehensive zoning measures. In the more populous counties and townships, this type of zoning is hardly distinguishable from the zoning carried on in cities. In the more rural areas, however, provisions are usually made for agricultural, forestry, grazing, and recreation districts as well as for residential, business, and industrial districts.

A second type of zoning known as open-country zoning was also pioneered in Wisconsin when that state amended its county zoning enabling act in 1929 to authorize the use of zoning to "regulate, restrict, and determine the areas in which agriculture, forestry, and recreation may be conducted." This type of county and township zoning emphasizes land-use regulations but makes little, if any, use of building-height and area restrictions. The first open-country zoning ordinance of this type was adopted in Oneida county in northern Wisconsin in 1933. This ordinance and the ordinances that followed in numerous other counties in the northern Lake States region recognized three principal types of use districts—forestry, recreation, and unrestricted (or agricultural) districts.

Most of these ordinances provided that the forest districts could be used for various forestry purposes and for seasonal recreation but not for agriculture or year-round residence. The recreation districts—sometimes divided into restricted recreation and commercial recreation use districts—permitted resorts, recreation properties, year-round residences, and most forestry uses (and hotels, dance halls, taverns, service stations, and other auxiliary businesses in the commercial recreation use districts). New agricultural developments, sawmills, planing mills, and most other industries were excluded from these districts. Agriculture was the dominant use in the remaining unrestricted districts, but provisions were sometimes made for separate business and industrial districts.

By the end of the 1930s, every county in Wisconsin's northern and central "cutover" and forest region had a zoning ordinance. But the zoning movement in these counties did not spring from an initial enthusiasm for land-use controls. It came rather because the leaders in these counties saw an opportunity to use restrictions against year-round residence as a means of checking the back-to-the-land movement and reducing local governmental costs. By prohibiting year-round residence in isolated areas of limited economic opportunity, the counties and other local units were able to reduce their costs for providing public relief, reactivating and maintaining once-abandoned schools, and providing other public services. It was only after several years of experience with rural zoning that some local leaders came to accept it as a desirable means for directing land-resource use and for discouraging the settlement of areas poorly suited for agricultural use.

Much may be said concerning the need for additional rural zoning. Many rural land owners still view zoning with considerable suspicion. Yet the impact of industrialization and urbanization on rural areas is such that it may be reasonably assumed that zoning techniques will be employed to a far greater extent in rural areas in the future than in the past. They will be used to guide and promote more orderly suburban developments around cities, to protect individual property rights and community values from rural slums and other undesirable developments, and possibly to reserve farm lands for permanent agricultural use. Rural zoning may also be used to an increased extent to promote conservation practices, to prevent human residence in flood-plain areas, and to control the roadside environment.

Some problems with zoning. Zoning can be used in many ways to promote socially desired goals. But like many other public powers, it can be and sometimes is abused. The courts are inclined to accept a broad concept of zoning as long as it involves reasonable regulations that protect or promote the public health, safety, morals, comfort, convenience, or welfare.[22] They have taken a strong stand, however, against the improper use of zoning. They have objected to spot zoning and to the use of zoning for racial- and economic-class-segregation purposes. They have usually agreed that zoning cannot be used retroactively to prohibit already existing uses. And they have held that, though aesthetic factors such as scenic beauty or architectural uniformity should be considered, zoning cannot be justified on aesthetic grounds alone.[23]

Several zoning ordinances have been voided by the courts as arbitrary and unreasonable for (1) excluding uses not regarded as nuisances, (2) providing use regulations that create monopoly rights for a few property owners, (3) restricting land areas to uses for which they are definitely not suited, (4) creating small island districts that are more restricted than the properties around them, (5) excluding uses that are incidental to permitted uses and that do not conflict with the purposes of the zoning plan, and (6) unfair or discriminatory administrative practices.[24]

By and large most of our experience with zoning can be characterized as successful and desirable. On the discord side, however, many communities have learned to their regret that the decision to zone can be

[22]Cf. Robert M. Anderson, *American Law of Zoning,* 4 volumes (Rochester: Lawyers Cooperative Publishing Company, 1968); Curtis J. Berger, *Land Ownership and Use: Cases, Statutes, and Other Materials* (Boston: Little Brown, and Company, 1968); Jacob H. Beuscher, *Land Use Controls,* 4th ed. (Madison, Wisconsin: College Printing & Typing Co., Inc., 1966); Clan Crawford, Jr., *Strategy and Tactics in Municipal Zoning* (Englewood Cliffs, N. J.: Prentice-Hall, Inc., 1969); Horack and Nolan, *op. cit.*; and Herbert H. Smith, *The Citizen's Guide to Zoning* (West Trenton, N. J.: Chandler-Davis Publishing Company, 1965) for more detailed discussions of the legal aspects of zoning.

[23]Anderson, *op. cit.,* Vol. 1, pp. 520-30, indicates that while the courts have softened their earlier position to accept aesthetics as a strong secondary objective of zoning, they still hold that zoning cannot be justified for aesthetics purposes alone.

[24]Cf. Horack and Nolan, *op. cit.*, pp. 166-67.

postponed too long if they hesitate to act until undesired situations arise. Some have zoned too little or too much land for particular purposes. Several have abused the concept of zoning by using it to freeze existing situations without really trying to plan for the best future use of their land resources. Many have seen the stability suggested by their ordinances whittled away as local officials have failed to take a firm stand against demands for amendments and exceptions. And some have allowed special interest groups to use or change zoning ordinances for selfish purposes. [25]

Many communities face a real problem in trying to keep their zoning ordinances up to date and in tune with changing conditions. Zoning ordinances tend to be relatively fixed and inflexible. As set up in the past, they have seldom had any built-in mechanism for adjusting to the changing conditions and needs of a dynamic society. Attempts have been made to itemize all permitted or excluded uses; but these lists have often failed to allow for the unexpected. In facing up to this problem, most communities find that they must reexamine and reappraise their zoning plans from time to time with the avowed intent of making such adjustments as are needed to keep their ordinances up to date. Some are also abandoning their use-oriented regulations and substituting in their place performance standards that deal with noise, smoke, odor, noxious gas, glare and heat, fire hazard, industrial waste, traffic and parking conditions, and that emphasize the attainment of aesthetic and psychological as well as simple land-use goals. [26]

A review of the nation's experience with zoning shows that far too many communities have been prone to accept zoning as a negative or defensive measure used primarily to prevent undesired developments. More emphasis should definitely be given to its use as a part of a larger, more positive, more dynamic plan for attaining better land-resource use. This more positive approach calls for the integration of zoning with other measures for the social direction of land use. It recognizes that zoning should be treated as a tool of planning and that a comprehensive area plan is fundamental for sound zoning. Going further, it recognizes that there is

[25] Cf. Richard F. Babcock, *The Zoning Game* (Madison: University of Wisconsin Press, 1966) for an irreverent view of zoning that highlights many of its weaknesses.

[26] Cf. Dennis O'Harrow, *Performance Standards in Industrial Zoning* (Columbus, Ohio: National Industrial Committee, 1954). Performance standards can be used to promote more harmonious types of area development than are currently attainable with many area-use regulations. They recognize that industrial, business, and even residential uses vary a great deal in character and that harmony in area development often depends more upon the character of individual uses than the type of use. Instead of segregating all factories into industrial districts, performance codes recognize that some of our modern, single-story, enclosed, air-conditioned, and well-landscaped plants can be a real asset in many residential districts.

Performance standards have one important fault. They are harder for the average public official to administer than arbitrary use regulations. Measurement techniques have been developed, however, which can be used in specifying and enforcing the performance standards desired in different area districts.

no magic in planning. We have some good planning and some planning that is best characterized as bad, insufficient, or incompetent. It is not enough that zoning be merely tied to a land-use plan. For best results, it must be tied to a comprehensive, realistic area plan that is geared to a thorough and continuing study of the resources, goals, and potentialities of the area.

Land Subdivision Regulations

Land subdivision regulations represent a second important use of the police power for the social direction of land-resource use. Our experience with these controls can be traced back to the careful, but often unofficial, planning associated with the selection and laying out of the original townsites of many villages in the American colonies. Controls of a comparable nature were later applied with the planning of several new settlements along the frontier and with the public surveying and laying out of some 2,500 townsites on the public domain.[27] The controls used in these instances ordinarily applied only to the original townsite. Once a townsite was settled, little effort was usually made to regulate new subdivisions, and even the plans for the original townsite were often ignored. A free-enterprise spirit prevailed; and most subdividers found themselves free to operate pretty much as they wished.

The present system of subdivision controls started during the 1800s when Wisconsin (1849), Michigan (1873), and some other states acted to require the surveying, registration, and later the public approval of subdivision plats. During the 1920s New York and several other states passed enabling acts, which authorized cities and other local units to regulate new subdivisions. As late as 1928, a California study committee reported a nation-wide survey in which it "found a frank recognition of subdivision control only in the states of Michigan, New York, Ohio, Wisconsin, Texas, and Maryland."[28] Since then all of the states have either enacted or strengthened their subdivision controls with the result that every state now has some type of subdivision regulations.

The increasing emphasis given to subdivision controls since the middle 1920s reflects the general public's appreciation of the necessary role they play in good resource planning. Cities have found that the original layout of their residential, business, and industrial areas often has an indelible effect upon their future character and development. Some of our most perplexing urban and suburban problems—inefficient and undesirable land-use patterns, traffic congestion, insufficient open space, high public maintenance costs, needed improvements and redevelopments, and spreading slum conditions—are directly traceable to the manner in which

[27]Cf. Beuscher, *op. cit.*, p. 216.
[28]Quoted in *ibid.*, p. 217.

subdivisions are laid out. Haphazard and poor subdivision planning can blight an area from the start by dooming it to substandard types of development.

Subdivision controls can play a vital role in promoting and protecting the interests of the community, the buyer, and the subdivider. They can enhance the value, desirability, and long-time worth of the areas developed.[29] Everyone benefits when the lots in a new subdivision are sufficiently attractive to favor a high standard of development. Yet everyone can lose when individual lots are too narrow or too deep for effective use, when water-supply or sewerage-disposal conditions create health problems, when building sites are subject to periodic flooding, when streets are too narrow to handle fire fighting equipment or to permit reasonable parking, or when the street design contributes to traffic hazards or general inconvenience.

Communities suffer from uncontrolled subdividing when they find themselves compelled to provide a vast array of public services for blighted or partially developed subdivisions that offer little promise of ever providing sufficient tax revenue to pay their way. Subdivision controls can help protect lot buyers and home builders from the declining property values and broken hopes that often come when neighborhoods fail to develop as expected. They can help subdividers by discouraging them from investing in undesired developments that could leave them "holding the bag," by encouraging improved subdivision designs that enhance their prospects of profit, and by protecting them from the possible use of substandard subdivision practices on neighboring plats.

Nature of subdivision controls. Subdivision controls vary somewhat depending upon the type of legislative authorization, the powers granted to local governing boards, and local administrative policies. Two principal types of statutes are in use. Several states have mandatory requirements affecting all subdivisions, while several others have enabling acts that authorize cities—and sometimes towns, townships or counties—to adopt subdivision regulations. Some states with mandatory requirements have also acted to authorize cities, and sometimes other local units, to map future improvements and supervise subdivision developments within (and sometimes around) their corporate limits.

Most of the mandatory state laws provide for certain exemptions. Several apply only to subdivisions in which four or more lots are offered

---

[29]For other discussions of subdivision controls and their value, cf. Marygold S. Melli, "Subdivision Control in Wisconsin," *Wisconsin Law Review,* 1953, pp. 389-457; *Suggested Land Subdivision Regulations* (Washington: Housing and Home Finance Agency, revised 1960); Anderson, *op. cit.,* Vol. 3, chap. XIX; *Control of Land Subdivision* (Albany: New York Office of Planning Coordination, 1968); and Roger A. Cunningham, "Land Use Control—The State and Local Programs," *Iowa Law Review,* Vol. 50, Winter, 1965, pp. 367-457.

for sale in any given year; some apply only to lots that are less than 1½ acres in size; and some specifically exclude tracts of five acres or more that are sold for agricultural use. State enabling acts are also selective in that they frequently apply only to cities or to cities of certain sizes. Some states authorize extraterritorial powers permitting cities to regulate subdivision developments for distances ranging from ½ to 10 miles from their municipal limits.

Most subdivision regulations require that new subdivisions be surveyed by licensed surveyors, that plat maps be prepared to show the location and boundaries of every lot and the location of the streets and other areas dedicated to public use, that the subdivision plat be approved by certain officials, and that it be officially registered. The plat must usually be approved by the local planning commission or the governing body of the local unit. Some states also require the approval of the county road commissioners or state highway commission (when they must administer the streets dedicated to public use), the state or county board of health, a county plat board, or certain state officials.

Subdivision controls vary considerably. They can be used to prevent developments in areas regarded as unhealthful because of flood hazards, improper drainage, or other conditions. They may require that a subdivider conform to an over-all street plan, provide right-angle inter-sections with through streets, or avoid jogging street connections. Minimum construction standards, maximum grades, and definite widths are usually specified for streets and street rights-of-way. Lots of minimum size and depth are often required. Regulations or administrative guidance can also be used to discourage plats involving a single row of long narrow "rifle-range" lots along an existing road, blocks of insufficient width to permit two rows of lots, dead-end streets that are more than 500 feet in length, or long blocks with infrequent cross-street connections to parallel streets.

City subdivision ordinances usually require the subdivider to provide a complete water-supply system or water-main connections to the city system. Sanitary and storm sewers must be provided; and the subdivider may be required to pave the streets, provide sidewalks and street lamps, and plant trees along new streets. Subdividers are sometimes required to dedicate or reserve minimum areas in addition to streets for public uses. When a city maps the streets, parks, and other public improvements planned in an undeveloped area within its jurisdiction, it can usually require future subdividers to adhere to its plan. Cities do not secure ownership of the areas mapped for public use until they are acquired by dedication, purchase, or eminent domain. But the courts have held that they need not compensate owners for buildings and other structures built on areas that have previously been mapped for public use.[30]

[30]Cf. Beuscher, *op. cit.,* chap. V.

Subdivision regulations have been accepted as a valid use of the police power. In the various cases that have come before them, the courts

> ... have upheld as reasonable requirements that streets be much wider than the adjoining portions of the same streets, that park areas be dedicated, that land be dedicated to widen abutting streets, that improvements such as grading streets and installing utilities be made, that a bond be filed to cover such improvements, and that fees be paid to cover the cost of examining and checking the plat.

> From these cases it appears that ... the limits on what conditions can be required for approval of a plat are very broad. But they must be imposed for the good of the community as a whole and not for the sole benefit of the surrounding property owners.[31]

Administration of subdivision controls. Like most land-use regulations, the real test of the usefulness of subdivision controls comes in their administration. Some communities have made far more effective use of these controls than others. Among the states with mandatory regulations, some officials who must approve plat proposals have treated their function as an automatic formality. Others have been more inclined to press for standards that protect or promote the public health, safety, and welfare.

Subdivision controls are used most effectively when they are integrated into a larger planning program. In this way, they can be used to help carry out the provisions of an area master plan. They cannot be used to force the reservation of open spaces; but they can be used to outline a pattern of orderly development that fits in with the public welfare. Planning agencies and local officials can often help this cause along by counseling with local subdividers and by reviewing and helping to improve their subdivision plans.

Since the process of surveying, registering, and developing a full-fledged subdivision always involves time and cost, it is probably only natural that many land owners should try to circumvent the usual requirements. This avoidance process is encouraged by the exemptions provided in some laws and by the tendency of many property owners to sell nonplatted building lots. These practices can be discouraged by (1) revising state platting laws to require registration of all plats involving two or more properties, (2) prohibitions against the use of unregistered plat descriptions in the legal transfer of properties, (3) more rigid requirements affecting metes and bounds transfers, and (4) use of the state's licensing of real estate brokers to discourage this type of subdividing.[32]

Local units have two potent powers they can use to discourage unauthorized subdivision developments. They can refuse to grant building

---

[31] Melli, *loc. cit.,* pp. 398-99.

[32] Cf. *Local Planning Administration,* 2nd ed. (Chicago: International City Managers' Association, 1948), pp. 253-55; and Horack and Nolan, *op. cit.,* p. 214.

and occupancy permits for structures built on lots that fail to measure up to their subdivision standards. And they can refuse to provide unauthorized lots with public services such as access to city water and sewers, street maintenance, and sometimes access to public streets or roads.

Prevention of premature subdivisions. Land booms have been a frequent phenomenon in American history; and they have often left a harvest of excessive and premature subdivisions in their wake. During the 1920s hundreds of speculators staked out subdivisions in and around cities and in recreation areas in anticipation of quick profits. Some of these subdivisions were well planned and involved extensive improvements. Some, however, involved hundreds of small, narrow, poorly planned lots and often a minimum of development. Building lots of all types were supplied in far greater numbers than the demand situation warranted.

Thirty percent of the lots in Chicago were vacant in 1928; and 69 percent of those in Cook County outside Chicago were still unused.[33] Several large cities had enough vacant lots within their environs to care for more than a doubling of their populations. New Jersey had sufficient unused lots in 1938 to accommodate a population of four million persons, more than the total population of the state at the time.[34] The large number of vacant lots around Cleveland, Detroit, Los Angeles, New York, St. Louis, and numerous other cities caused some writers to observe that their absorption would be measured in generations rather than years.[35]

With the drying up of the market for building sites during the depression years, many unsold lots reverted back to farms, to citrus groves, and in some instances to forests. But where lots had been sold and built upon, occasional home owners often found themselves surrounded by acres and acres of "dead land." Thousands of lots tax-reverted to the government and hundreds of others ended up with divided ownerships, confused titles, and high tax obligations, which seriously limited the few prospects they did have for development. Many of these lots were absorbed during the building boom after World War II. Yet even after a decade of postwar building, hundreds of narrow, poorly planned, and

[33]Cf. Herbert D. Simpson and John E. Burton, *The Valuation of Vacant Land in Suburban Areas,* Institute for Economic Research Monograph No. 12 (Chicago: Northwestern University, 1931), p. 12.

[34]Cf. *Land Subdivision in New Jersey, Its Extent, Quality, and Regulation* (Trenton: New Jersey State Planning Board, 1938), p. 18. For a vivid description of the speculative use of subdivision practices in one community, cf. Alvin T. M. Lee, *Land Utilization in New Jersey–A Land Development Scheme in the New Jersey Pine Area,* New Jersey Agricultural Experiment Station Bulletin 665, 1939.

[35]Cf. President's Conference on Home Building and Home Ownership, *Planning for Residential Districts* (Washington, 1932), Vol. 1, p. 2. For other discussions of this problem cf. Philip Cornick, *Premature Subdivision and Its Consequences* (New York: Institute of Public Administration, Columbia University, 1938); and Miles Colean, *American Housing* (New York: Twentieth Century Fund, 1947), chap. I.

partially developed lots still awaited the development anticipated three decades earlier.[36]

Along with FHA credit restrictions, subdivision controls provide one of the most effective means for discouraging any future recurrence of this premature-subdivision problem. Local governments lack the power to prohibit excess subdivisions. But they can insist upon high development standards and the posting of bonds to cover the costs of these developments. With these requirements and their opportunities to counsel with subdividers, local officials can often convince subdividers of the wisdom of maintaining a reasonable balance between the supply of new lots and the market demand for building sites.

EMINENT DOMAIN

Eminent domain provides a second important power governments can use in their social direction of land-resource use. This concept, which literally means "highest authority or dominion," involves "the power of the sovereign to take property for public use without the owner's consent."[37] It is rooted in the ultimate authority of the state over property and is commonly accepted and exercised in many countries as an inherent right of government.

As a social control over property, eminent domain can be exercised alone or in combination with the police, spending, and proprietary powers. Regardless of how it is used, it frequently plays an essential role in our society in facilitating the orderly acquisition of the sites needed for highways, streets, utilities, and other public improvements. Without the exercise of this power, individual property owners could block the will of the majority simply by refusing to sell the land needed for desired public developments.

Scope of Eminent Domain

The American concept of eminent domain does not come from the English law but originated rather in the natural-law movement. The term "eminent domain" was first used by the Dutch statesman-philosopher, Hugo Grotius, in his *De Jure Belli et Pacis* (1625) to describe the power of the state over all private property within its bounds.[38] As used by Grotius

[36]The Cook County (Illinois) Housing Authority reported that in March, 1950, there were 250,000 parcels of "chronically tax delinquent and abandoned land in Cook County." Cf. *Dead Land—A Report to the Illinois State Housing Board,* 1950. Many similar tracts were found in a suburban land-use study near Detroit in 1957.

[37]Julius L. Sackman and Russell D. Van Brunt, *Nichols' The Law of Eminent Domain,* rev. ed. (New York: Matthew Bender and Company, 1964), Vol. 1, p. 4.

[38]Cf. *ibid.,* pp. 6-7; also Arthur Lenhoff, "Development of the Concept of Eminent Domain," *Columbia Law Review,* Vol. 42, April, 1942, pp. 596-638. The term

and later writers, this natural-law concept had two important facets. It envisaged the state as the only taker of property; and it assumed the age-old doctrine of immunity of the sovereign from liability for the taking of property.

"Eminent domain" was first mentioned by the American courts in 1831.[39] Up until then, there were few examples of the public taking of private property; what few cases there were dealt mostly with roads and mill pond flowage areas; and no particular effort was made to develop a legal philosophy to justify the public taking of land. Following its recognition by the courts, the power of eminent domain was soon accepted as an established feature of American law subject to three important modifications: (1) the federal and state governments can delegate this power to other units of government and to public and private corporations; (2) the power must always be used for a public purpose; and (3) just compensation must be paid for all properties taken.

Like many legal concepts, eminent domain has a somewhat elastic scope. Almost from the start, the state legislatures regarded eminent domain as a power that they could delegate to private corporations and groups as well as to state agencies and local units of government. The courts did not object to these delegations and for several years tended to regard the meaning of "public purpose" as a legislative question. As a result, the concept of public purpose was stretched to include all types of land-resource developments. Eminent domain powers were soon delegated to railroads to help them acquire rights-of-way for their tracks and spur lines, to mill-dam owners to acquire flowage rights and acreages, to mine owners to acquire land for their tramways and other surface facilities, and to drainage districts for their ditches and drains.

With the rising tide of American industry during the 1840s and 1850s, it soon became evident that the eminent domain power could be abused. Fears were expressed concerning the increasing political power wielded by some corporations and the possibility that they might secure grants of eminent domain that they could use to seize the property of competitors and others who stood in their way. At this point, the courts gradually assumed the prerogative of deciding what is "public use." And in the process of distinguishing between public and private uses, many courts narrowed the meaning of "public use," particularly in cases involving private users, to mean use by the public.[40]

This judicial limitation of the concept of "public use" resulted in

---

"eminent domain" is not used in English law. But it is matched with a somewhat comparable concept known as "compulsory purchase."

[39] Cf. *Beckman v. Saratoga and Schenectady Railroad,* 3 Paige (N.Y.) 45, 73 (1831).

[40] Cf. Philip Nichols, Jr., "The Meaning of Public Use in the Law of Eminent Domain," *Boston University Law Review,* Vol. 20, November, 1940, pp. 615-41.

complications, uncertainties, and some legal inconsistencies. Several courts reversed their earlier precedents; some made special exceptions; and a minority continued to hold for a fairly broad interpretation of public use. In the resulting confusion, some courts held particular uses as private while others regarded them as public. As late as the 1930s some courts still questioned the public nature of the use of eminent domain to condemn slum areas for housing redevelopments. But most American courts during recent decades have tended to agree with Justice Holmes that "use by the public" is an inadequate test of public purpose.[41] The federal courts have taken the stand that any federal use that is legal can properly be construed as a public use. And except for those states with rigid constitutional definitions of public use, most of the state courts now interpret "public use" as including uses involving the public interest as well as active use by the public.

With this liberalized concept of "public use," the courts have recognized that "the promotion of beauty or national sentiment may warrant the exercise of the power of eminent domain where it would not warrant the exercise of the police power."[42] They have upheld use of eminent domain to acquire sites for airports, to clear slum areas for public housing developments, and to take blighted and open areas for urban redevelopment projects.[43] This power has been used in Puerto Rico to acquire farm land holdings from absentee owners for redistribution in smaller tracts to resident operators. As one legal journal puts it:

> It is now established that a private corporation or individual may be granted the power of eminent domain as long as the general objective of the use of his power contributes to the public welfare and advantage. A logging railroad to serve a single lumber company, an irrigation system primarily for one land-owner's benefit, and an aerial bucket line for a private mine have been held sufficient public uses to warrant the use of eminent domain for their construction. Approval of condemnation of property for slum clearance and rehousing typifies the liberal view, the legitimacy of the purpose as a whole rather than the intended use of the particular property being the criterion almost universally adopted by the courts.[44]

The requirement for just compensation was well established in many jurisdictions some decades before our judicial acceptance of eminent domain. Provisions for just compensation were written into many of the early state constitutions between 1776 and 1800 and were included in the

[41] *Mt. Vernon Woodbury Cotton Duck Co. v. Alabama Power*, 240 U.S. 30 (1916).

[42] Ernest Freund, " Eminent Domain," *Encyclopedia of the Social Sciences* (New York: The Macmillan Company, 1931), Vol. 5, p. 494.

[43] Cf. *Berman v. Parker,* 348 U.S. 26 (1954).

[44] "Public Land Ownership," *Yale Law Journal*, 1943. Reprinted by permission of the Yale Law Journal Company and Fred B. Rothman & Company from *The Yale Law Journal*, Vol. 52, p. 634.

Bill of Rights as part of the Fifth Amendment to the federal Constitution in 1791. Going behind these provisions, it may be noted that the right of compensation is really rooted in the natural- and higher-law concepts of "reasonableness," "natural equity," and "dictates of natural justice."[45] These concepts were accepted by the courts of those states without constitutional provisions as sufficient grounds for requiring compensation with the result that the right of compensation was well established before the enactment of the Fourteenth Amendment. Since the enactment of this amendment, all legislative acts calling for the taking of property without provisions for payment have been held violative of due process.

A line must be drawn with this requirement for just compensation between the police and eminent domain powers. The distinction between these two powers is often blurred and is frequently one of degree. The police power can be used up to a certain point to limit and sometimes take private property rights in the interest of public health, safety, morals, convenience, and welfare without infringing on due process or creating a duty for compensation.[46] But once one crosses the sometimes-shifting, legally determined line between these two powers, any taking of property calls for eminent domain and the payment of compensation. As Justice Holmes observed:

> As long recognized, some values are enjoyed under an implied limitation and must yield to the police power. But obviously the implied limitation must have its limits or the contract and due process clauses are gone. One fact for consideration in determining such limits is the extent of the diminution. When it reaches a certain magnitude, in most, if not all, cases, there must be an exercise of eminent domain and compensation to sustain the act.[47]

Use of Eminent Domain

From a public point of view, eminent domain may be regarded simply as a necessary power that must be used from time to time to facilitate the acquisition of particular sites for desired public purposes. But numerous problems are associated with the exercise of this power. Individual owners often find that they are called upon to give up land resources they need to maintain their economic scale of operations or resources intimately

---

[45]Cf. Lenhoff, *loc. cit.,* pp. 599-600; J. A. C. Grant, "The 'Higher Law' Background of the Law of Eminent Domain," *Wisconsin Law Review*, Vol. 6, 1930, pp. 67-85; and Emily Dodge, "Acquisition of Land by Eminent Domain," in Beuscher, *op. cit.,* p. 525. In his treatment of eminent domain, Grotius recognized that the sovereign has a right to take property but argued that this taking involves a moral obligation to pay compensation for the property taken.

[46]Compensation is sometimes allowed with the police power in instances such as the compulsory slaughter of diseased animals. This compensation, however, is paid as a matter of equitable treatment, not as a matter of duty.

[47]*Pennsylvania Coal Co. v. Mahon,* 260 U.S. 393, 413 (1922).

associated with their hopes, aspirations, and way of living. Certain administrative procedures must be followed in the property condemnation process. And emphasis should always be given to ways and means of protecting the interests of the owners whose property is taken as well as the interests of the taker.

Five important problems arise in the use of eminent domain. These include: (1) the initial decision to take property for public use, (2) a proper delegation of authority for this purpose, (3) compliance with the prescribed condemnation procedure, (4) determination of just compensation, and (5) the question of how much property can legally be taken.

The question of whether eminent domain should or should not be used in particular instances calls for a weighing of public versus private interests. This weighing process starts with the initial justification and authorization of the proposed development; and it reaches its climax when decisions are made concerning the actual location of the development. At this stage, public considerations ordinarily override private interests. Before this final choice is made, administrative attention should always be given to the relative merits and costs of alternative development plans and sites.

Once a final decision is reached regarding the location of a highway, power line, canal, or some other proposed development, steps must be taken to acquire easements or ownership rights to the properties affected. Except for a few cases such as military uses and some highway developments, these rights must ordinarily be acquired before construction begins. This means that the needed areas must be surveyed; an appraisal must be made of their value; the owners must be contacted; and definite offers must be submitted for their purchase.[48] If an owner refuses to accept the terms offered, condemnation proceedings must be started to force the sale. But before an agency can exercise eminent domain, it must have a proper delegation of eminent domain authority from Congress or the stage legislature. It must follow the procedures and operate within the limitations of its grant of power; and its use of eminent domain must be for a public use.

There is no simple standardized eminent domain procedure. Every legislature is free to outline its own method; and it can vary its requirements in its delegations of eminent domain power to different agencies and groups. Some states have acted to require a single procedure. But as late as 1943, some 320 eminent domain procedures were in use in 55 jurisdictions.[49] Despite these variations, however, all condemnation

[48]Some jurisdictions such as the city of Detroit have followed a different procedure under which they have made it a practice to acquire all the properties needed for new public developments by condemnation without submitting purchase offers to the affected owners.

[49]Cf. David R. Levin, *Public Land Acquisition for Highway Purposes* (Washington: U.S. Government Printing Office, 1943).

procedures call for court action. The property owner must be informed that condemnation proceedings have been started against him; he is entitled to a legal hearing; and the determination of compensation is ordinarily made either by a jury or a group of commissioners who hear legal evidence and who may visit the property being condemned.[50]

Determination of just compensation. The question of what constitutes just compensation often provides a controversial problem in property valuation. Individuals frequently complain that they are forced to sacrifice properties at less than their true value. Public agencies in turn often feel that they are required to pay more than fair market value. Most of this problem stems from different standards of measurement. Owners who do not wish to sell are naturally inclined to think in terms of "value to the owner" while public officials tend to base their calculations on the going free market prices paid for comparable properties.

In their determination of what constitutes just compensation, most courts reject the concepts of "value to the taker" and "value to the owner." Just compensation is usually defined as "fair market value" or "the price a willing buyer would pay a willing seller."[51] Payment is ordinarily refused for consequential damages such as expense of moving, personal inconvenience, interruption of business operations, or loss of goodwill. Yet while payment is normally denied for consequential damages, compensation may be allowed for any severance damages associated with a diminution of the market value of the holding left with the owner.

Condemnation awards ordinarily range between the lowest estimate of value provided by a qualified witness and the price claimed by the owner. Some courts and condemnation commissions are more liberal in their awards than others; and some apparently make allowances in their calculations of fair market value for personal inconveniences while others do not.[52] Differences also exist in the land-acquisition policies of

[50] Cf. Glenn Lawrence, *Condemnation: Your Rights When Government Acquires Your Property* (Dobbs Ferry, N. Y.: Oceana Publications, Inc., 1967) for a popular discussion of the law and procedures of eminent domain.

[51] Cf. Lewis Orgel, *Valuation Under the Law of Eminent Domain*, 2nd ed. (Charlottesville, Virginia: Michie Company, 1953) Vol. 1, p. 56; and Dodge, *loc. cit.,* pp. 531-38. In contrast with the emphasis placed on payment of just compensation for the value of property taken, some Latin American nations use valorization taxes assessed against expected increases in the value of affected properties, including those that give up land, to help finance street-widening and other public improvement projects. Cf. William G. Rhoads and Richard M. Bird, "Financing Urbanization in Developing Countries by Benefit Taxation," *Land Economics*, Vol. 43, pp. 403-12; and Rhoads and Bird, "The Valorization Tax in Colombia," in Arthur P. Becker, ed., *Land and Building Taxes* (Madison: University of Wisconsin Press, 1969), pp. 201-37.

[52] Legislative action has been taken in some states to authorize compensation of property owners for some types of consequential damages. Michigan, for example, modified its highway eminent domain procedures in 1965 to permit nominal payments to owners for moving expenses.

different agencies, with some agencies giving far more consideration to the owners' problems than others.

The Tennessee Valley Authority provides a good example of a public agency that operates on the premise that "the land owner should be at least as well off after taking as he was before."[53] In its determination of the purchase prices it offers for land, TVA considers not only the market value of the land but also what it would cost to re-establish the owner at some other location with no impairment of his economic position. As a TVA staff member has indicated:

> The farmer who lives in a reservoir area does not usually want to sell. The loss of his land imposes a burden upon him even if he receives a fair price. He must find a new place to live, move his household furniture, move or dispose of his farming equipment and stock, and frequently make other substantial adjustments. If he wants to relocate in the same general area, he must buy his new farm in a seller's market in which he is competing with other prospective buyers whose farms have been acquired for the same reservoir project. These factors are taken into consideration by TVA and an attempt is made to leave the land owner in as good a financial position as he occupied before his land was purchased. This policy is required by considerations of fairness to the land owner and we are satisfied that it pays off in dollars and cents.[54]

This procedure applies only as long as the owner is willing to accept what TVA considers as a fair purchase price. When an owner refuses to sell, TVA presses for condemnation at the court-accepted price of what a willing buyer would pay a willing seller. Thus

> TVA may offer $10,000 for a farm. If the land owner rejects this offer, the case is heard by a commission. TVA may then present evidence to show that the land is worth only $8,000 or the figure that selected witnesses will testify to be its fair market value.
>
> In addition, the land owner is not allowed to remove his buildings, for which a reasonable salvage value is deducted, if property is acquired by condemnation.
>
> Among the reasons advanced for this shift to a willing buyer-willing seller concept under condemnation are (1) a belief that the courts generally favor the land owner as against the Government, (2) a desire to discourage litigation, and (3) a feeling that it is under no obligation in litigation to offer anything other than just compensation as defined by the courts.[55]

Allowance of compensation for severance damages often poses unique

[53] Kris Kristjanson, *TVA Land Acquisition Experience Applied to Dams in the Missouri Basin,* South Dakota Agricultural Experiment Station Bulletin 432, 1953, p. 9.

[54] Charles J. McCarthy, "Land Acquisition Policies and Proceedings in TVA," *Ohio State Law Journal,* Vol. 10, Winter, 1949, p. 56.

[55] Kristjanson, *op. cit.,* p. 10.

problems in condemnation valuations. In theory, whenever the act of taking property from an owner greatly reduces the productive value of his remnant holdings, he should receive sufficient compensation in excess of the market value of the property taken to "leave him whole." Differences of opinion often arise, however, as to the actual extent of severance damages. Some of the problems that arise can be illustrated by an example, such as that depicted in Figure 17-1, in which a right-of-way is condemned across properties *A, B, C,* and *D* for the construction of a limited access highway.

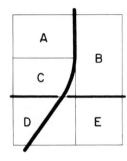

FIGURE 17-1. Illustration of impact of condemnation of a right-of-way for a limited access highway on five properties.

In the calculation of just compensation, it is hard for the owners of properties *A* and *B* to claim more than the market value of the acreages they lose. A case for severance damages can be made only if they can show that their marginal losses of land area have a disproportionate effect in reducing the economies of scale at which they can operate. A stronger case for severance damages can be made with property *C* because the owner is left with a small severed tract that is isolated from the principal tract. Acquisition of the severed tract for later use or disposal by the acquiring agency can often entail lower costs to the public than procedures that call for simple acquisition of the right-of-way plus payment of severance damages. A still stronger case for severance damages arises with tract *D*. Here, the owner's holding may lose its economic viability as it is split into two tracts of uneconomic size. Combination of the two severed tracts with those of neighboring properties may provide the most practicable solution for all concerned. If construction of the highway results in the dead-ending of the road that formerly ran between properties *B* and *E* and *C* and *D,* it may also add to the operating costs of property *E*. The fact that this operator now finds it less convenient to travel to a nearby shopping center, however, gives him no claim to severance damages because none of his property is taken by condemnation.

Excess condemnation. Questions are frequently raised concerning the amounts of land that can be taken by eminent domain. Is this power limited to the taking of only the land necessary for a proposed development, or might it be extended to cover additional areas? The requirement of "public use" has often been interpreted as limiting all takings to the land areas needed for specific projects. But circumstances and good administrative management often favor the condemnation of additional areas. Several states—California, Massachusetts, Michigan, New York, Ohio, Pennsylvania, and Wisconsin—have constitutional provisions that expressly authorize excess condemnation; and the courts in many other states now accept excess condemnation when its use appears reasonable.

Excess condemnation can be justified as (1) a means of protecting the values associated with resource developments, (2) the best way to handle the problem of remnant tracts, and (3) a means of cost recoupment. With highways, recreation areas, and certain other developments, it is often desirable to acquire buffer tracts, which can be used for project-protection, aesthetic, or safety purposes. Buffer strips can be used to separate playground areas from busy streets and to preserve the natural scenery along highways and around recreation areas. Tracts along highways can sometimes be landscaped or developed as roadside parks. In some instances they may be leased or sold back to farmers or others with restrictions against billboards, the cutting of trees, or practices that destroy the rustic beauty of the countryside. Restrictions may also be used to control roadside developments and prevent those uses that prompt the gradual conversion of through highways into hazardous streets.

When only those lands needed for highways or other projects are taken, owners often find that they are left with small, odd-shaped remnant tracts that have little value by themselves. Some states authorize the taking agencies to acquire these extra tracts and either sell them to adjacent property owners or regroup them with other remnants to form units of greater economic value. This type of excess condemnation can often pay for itself by bringing in sales revenues and by preventing legal claims for severance damages that may actually exceed the original taking price of the remnant holdings.

Excess condemnation may also be used as a means of recouping all or part of the costs of a new resource development. With this approach, a public agency may acquire more land than it needs for a new street, highway, or reservoir and then resell the extra land as building sites after the project is completed. This approach is used in the regrouping and sale of remnant tracts; and it has been used on a more commercial scale by a few cities. On the whole, however, it has received only limited use, partly because of the fear that it may be rejected by the courts as a use of eminent domain for private purposes, partly because of the traditional notion that all profits arising from eminent domain should accrue entirely to private owners, and partly because of objections against public agencies engaging in the real estate business.

In contrast to these arguments, many people feel that excess condemnations (or special tax assessments) should be used wherever practicable to help recoup the costs of project developments. After all, it makes more sense for the public to use the increase in adjacent property values associated with public projects to help pay for these projects than to allow them to accrue entirely to a few fortunately situated landowners.

SPENDING AND PROPRIETARY POWERS

Among their other powers, Congress and the various state legislatures can spend money for the general welfare and provide for the acquisition, management, and disposition of public properties. Unlike the police, eminent domain, and taxation powers, these spending and proprietary powers do not represent direct controls over property. The experience of recent decades demonstrates conclusively, however, that these powers can be used quite effectively to influence and direct land-resource use.

Both of these powers are broad in scope. The Supreme Court has held that Congress can spend public funds for almost any purpose as long as its spending is for the public welfare.[56] It has also held that the federal government's power to own property includes not only the right to acquire, manage, and dispose of properties but also the right to carry on production and marketing programs in competition with private operators. Powers of a comparable nature are held by the state legislatures subject to the possible limitations imposed by their various constitutions. Local governments in turn enjoy all those spending and proprietary powers granted to them in their charters and enabling acts.

Use of the Spending Power

Public expenditures have been used since the beginnings of organized government to provide property owners with fire, police, and military protection. They have also been used to provide a variety of land-resource development and public works programs ranging from the building of aqueducts, fortifications, pyramids, and roads to the construction of elaborate drainage and irrigation systems. Numerous examples, both ancient and modern, can be cited to show how the power of the purse can be used to direct land-use developments and practices. Some of our best

[56]Questions concerning the constitutionality of the federal spending power have been raised in numerous court cases. Prior to 1936, the Supreme Court always disposed of these cases on other grounds—frequently on the ground that the litigant's interest in the questioned expenditure was too small to give him legal standing in court to insist upon adjudication of the issue. In *United States v. Butler*, 297 U.S. 1 (1936), and *Helvering v. Davis*, 301 U.S. 619 (1937), however, the Court recognized the wide and almost unlimited scope of the federal spending power. Cf. Glick, *loc. cit.*, pp. 618-21; and Mason and Beaney, *op. cit.*, pp. 311-42.

examples are provided by the current and recent activities of the federal government.

During recent years, the United States has used its spending power in five important ways to direct land-use practices. It has used public funds to (1) acquire lands for various public purposes, (2) carry on public resource developments, (3) provide public credit facilities, (4) subsidize desired private practices, and (5) finance part of the cost of various state and local projects.

The federal government has used its spending power on numerous occasions to acquire (and reacquire) title to land. The Louisiana Territory, Florida, southern Arizona, Alaska, and the Virgin Islands were acquired directly by purchase. Payments of various types have been used to extinguish the claims of Indian tribes, foreign nationals, and foreign governments to considerable portions of the public domain. The federal spending power has been used along with eminent domain to acquire land for public buildings, roads, and military sites. Some 11.3 million acres were bought up and retired from agricultural use under the submarginal land purchase program of the late 1930s. Large areas have been purchased for national forest, wildlife, and other purposes. Altogether, slightly more than 25.8 million of the 755 million acres held by the federal government in 1970 was "acquired" land.[57]

Federal funds have been used to finance several types of land-resource developments. They have been used to construct public buildings and highways, provide for river and harbor improvements, and dig the Panama Canal. They have provided the basic financing for TVA and for numerous reclamation, power, flood control, and multipurpose projects. They have also been used for public research, reforestation, and range-improvement purposes and for the development of recreation facilities.

Thousands of farm and home owners have benefited from the public credit facilities provided through the federal spending power. The federal government provided the initial capital used to set up the federal land bank system under the Farm Loan Act of 1916. It established the Reconstruction Finance Corporation in 1932 (disbanded in 1954) to make loans to corporations and businessmen. A Federal Home Loan Bank Board was created in 1932 and the Farm Credit Administration in 1933 to promote better credit arrangements. Provisions have been made for agricultural production credit, loans to farm cooperatives, loans and rehabilitation grants to disadvantaged farmers, loans to small businessmen, and loans to victims of floods and other disasters. The FHA-mortgage insurance and VA-loan guarantee programs also have been set up to help prospective owners acquire residential properties with liberal credit terms and nominal down payments.

[57]Cf. Public Land Law Review Commission, *One Third of the Nation's Land* (Washington: U.S. Government Printing Office, 1970), pp. 327-34.

Government subsidies are used from time to time to placate certain groups and to promote particular practices. Subsidies were paid to sugar producers under the McKinley Tariff Act of 1890. Public funds have been used to promote low-rent public housing. Consumer subsidies are used in the federal food stamp and school lunch programs. Government-owned plants, cost-plus contracts, and other subsidy arrangements were used during World War II to stimulate industrial promotion. Federal commodity purchase and loan programs have been used to buoy up and support farm market prices. Public funds are used to finance the soil bank and conservation reserve programs. And subsidies have been used with the Agricultural Conservation Program since 1936 to provide farmers with benefit payments for accepting conservation practices.[58]

Despite their element of subsidy, ACP payments may also be characterized as a type of cost-sharing arrangement under which the federal government pays part of the cost of securing desired land-use practices. Congress has authorized use of this cost-sharing approach to help finance a variety of state and local projects that meet specific federal standards. Federal aid has been granted to the states for the construction of approved highway projects since 1916. Under the Federal Aid Highway Act of 1956, the federal government pays up to half the cost of highways located entirely within states and up to 90 percent of the cost of those highways and expressways classified as parts of interstate systems (up to 95 percent in states with large acreages of unappropriated and unreserved public lands or nontaxed Indian lands). Provisions are made in the Watershed Protection and Flood Prevention Act of 1954 for federal assistance to local communities to facilitate the development and operation of small watershed programs.[59]

Federal assistance for slum clearance and public housing projects has

[58]ACP payments have been made mostly as an inducement to get farmers to accept and use good conservation practices. During the early years of the program, however, they were used primarily as a supplement to farm incomes. In 1939, the peak year in ACP payments, some $807 million was paid to farmers. This represented almost 10 percent of the total cash income to farmers (including payments) received in that year and accounted for almost a fourth of the cash incomes of farmers in four states. The program was renamed the Rural Environment Assistance Program in 1971, terminated by the Administration the next year, and then reinstated a year later as the Rural Environmental Conservation Program with funding of $90 million for 1974.

[59]This program is designed to bridge the gap between the conservation programs carried on on individual farms and the flood control programs used on major rivers. It represents an attempt by the federal government to help local groups plan and install water management and flood prevention programs that could not be installed by individuals acting alone or in small groups. Cf. Harry A. Steele, "Economics of Small Watershed Development," *Agricultural Economics Research*, Vol. 8, January, 1956, pp. 17-23; Virgil C. Herrick and Philip M. Raup, *Organizational Programs in Developing the Small Watersheds of Minnesota*, Minnesota Agricultural Experiment Station Bulletin 437, 1957; also John Muehlbeier, *Organizing for Watershed Development*, South Dakota Agricultural Experiment Station Circular 133, 1957.

been available to cities since 1937. The National Housing Acts of 1949, 1954, and 1956 authorize the federal government to finance two-thirds of the cost of approved local urban renewal projects. Later Housing Acts authorize the Department of Housing and Urban Development to pay up to 40 percent of the cost of local open space land acquisition programs and 80 percent of the cost of model city projects. Federal agencies also make grants to state agencies for acquiring recreation land holdings, for paying substantial portions of the cost of state, regional, metropolitan, and local planning efforts, for planning public works, for facilitating regional economic development programs, and for providing waste water treatment facilities.

Use of the Proprietary Power

Public administrators have long since found that they can exert more influence over the uses made of land resources when they are held in public ownership than when they are held by private owners. By and large, the United States has not made as much use of its proprietary powers in this regard as many nations. But even with its somewhat limited experience along this line, it has found, particularly in recent decades, that this power provides a potent tool for securing desired land-use objectives.

Public land ownership in the United States. Around 39 percent of the surface land area of the United States is held in public ownership—more than 33 percent by the federal government and around 5 percent by the states and 1 percent by counties, municipalities, school districts, and other local units of government. Almost 40 percent of this total area is found in Alaska. The remaining areas are used mostly for forestry and grazing uses and are concentrated mostly in the 11 western states, where they account for around 60 percent of the land area.[60]

Approximately 30 percent of the forest land and nearly half of the grazing land in the 48 contiguous states are held in some form of federal, state, or county ownership. Public ownership also accounts for 1.5 percent of the cultivated farm land—half of it held as Indian land and the balance used for experimental purposes or operated in connection with penal or public welfare institutions. It also accounts for between 30 and 40 percent of the area of the average city; for substantial areas used for transportation, military, park, wildlife refuge, and other service areas; and for a sizable residual area of barren and waste land.

Considerable portions of the land area of the United States have been held in public ownership ever since the birth of the nation. Yet it was not until the 1890s that much attention was given to the development of

[60]The amount of federal ownership by states in 1970 ranged from 0.3 percent of the area of Connecticut and 0.6 percent of Iowa to 66.5 percent of Utah, 86.4 percent of Nevada, and 95.3 percent of Alaska.

long-range public land management programs. Up until that time, it was more or less assumed that practically all the public domain would pass into private ownership—that the plow would follow the axe across the wooded frontier and that the farmer would soon supplant the cattleman on the western range.

Two factors prompted a change in this philosophy. The gradual awakening of public interest to the need for forestry and other land-resource conservation measures led Presidents Harrison, Cleveland, McKinley, and Theodore Roosevelt to reserve 192 million acres of forest, mineral, park, and other lands from public disposal. And the painful experimentation and bitter failure of thousands of high-hearted settlers in the cutover and range areas finally convinced the general public that these areas were not physically suited for agricultural development under current cost and price conditions.

With this change in outlook, the state and federal governments gradually reoriented many of their public land policies. Instead of handling their lands on a temporary caretaker basis, emphasis was given to the development of long-term management programs. New agencies such as the Forest Service, Grazing Service, Fish and Wildlife Service, and the various State Conservation Departments were established to administer the public lands. These agencies were authorized to buy and exchange lands—and in the case of the states, to use tax-reverted lands—in blocking up their holdings. This acquisition program brought the creation of a "new public domain," which accounts for approximately 10 percent of the lands held in federal ownership in the 48 contiguous states and for well over half of the public lands administered by many states.

No attempt will be made here to discuss the many administrative problems associated with the use and management of public lands.[61] Suffice it to say that the public lands represent a vitally important segment of the nation's economy. Streets and highways, parks, public buildings, and public service areas involve some of our most intensively used land resources. Public forests, grazing areas, mineral lands, and reclamation and power facilities are providing an increasingly important source of public revenues. They provide raw materials and employment opportunities for a significant number of operators and workers; and they are operated for the most part in the interests of the general public.

Public ownership and the direction of land use. Prior to 1900, only limited use was made of the proprietary power as a means of directing land use. This situation changed with the rise of the Conservation Movement. Since then, the proprietary power has been used in many ways to secure particular ends in land-resource use. It has been used with

---

[61] Cf. *One Third of the Nation's Land;* and Marion Clawson and R. Burnell Held, *Federal Lands: Their Use and Management* (Baltimore: Johns Hopkins University Press, 1957).

various programs to (1) emphasize public rather than private objectives, (2) promote resource developments and provide examples of how land resources can best be used, and (3) give direction to the future use of land resources returned to private ownership.

The federal government has used its proprietary powers over the public domain to reserve large areas of forest, mineral, grazing, and other lands that might otherwise have been homesteaded or sold to private operators. Together with the states and local units, it has reserved and acquired substantial areas for park and recreation purposes. Along with these other units, it has established numerous public forests and undertaken re- forestation projects, partly to get land areas back to their highest and best use, partly as an example for private operators, and partly because it was feared that private operators could not or would not do the job needed for the nation's future welfare.

The federal and state governments have joined with private operators to organize grazing districts and draw up regulations for the orderly and efficient use of their combined range holdings.[62] They have undertaken reclamation and range improvements to shift large areas to higher and better uses. The federal government has used its spending and proprietary powers to shift submarginal farm lands to more appropriate uses and to promote other desired land-use adjustments.[63] It has used its spending and proprietary powers to develop single- and multipurpose flood control, power, and reclamation projects—projects that have often come closer to representing the optimum scale of development than those that probably would have been constructed by private enterprise.

The proprietary power has been used in many urban areas to provide public water, transportation, power, and housing facilities. It is used together with the spending and eminent domain powers in the clearance of slum and blighted areas for urban redevelopment and renewal programs. Most of the lands acquired for these programs are sold again for private redevelopment. But in the sale of these lands to private redevelopers, restrictive covenants are ordinarily used to insure future compliance with the over-all redevelopment plan for the area.[64]

Unlike some other nations, the United States has made little effort to nationalize properties or to use the threat of nationalization to influence the uses owners make of their land resources. For the most part, it

[62]Cf. C. W. Loomer and V. Webster Johnson, *Group Tenure in Administration of Public Lands,* U.S. Department of Agriculture Circular No. 829, 1949; and Layton S. Thompson, *Montana Cooperative State Grazing Districts in Action,* Montana Agri- cultural Experiment Station Bulletin 481, 1951.

[63]Cf. Loyd Glover, *Experience with Federal Land Purchases as a Means of Land Use Adjustment,* South Dakota Agricultural Experiment Station, Agricultural Economics Pamphlet 65, 1955.

[64]Cf. Charles Ascher, "Private Covenants in Urban Redevelopment," in Coleman Woodbury *et al., Urban Redevelopment: Problems and Practices* (Chicago: University of Chicago Press, 1953), pp. 225-309.

has also steered away from the Scandinavian and Germanic policy of encouraging cities to own large areas both within and outside their municipal boundaries.[65] Both of these policies run counter to our prevailing philosophy regarding the desirability of private ownership. Widescale municipal ownership does have a certain amount of practical appeal, however, in that it gives cities a tremendous opportunity to plan and direct land-use developments in their environs.

— SELECTED READINGS

Anderson, Robert M., *American Law of Zoning,* 4 volumes (Rochester, N. Y.: Lawyers Cooperative Publishing Company, 1968).

Bassett, Edward M., *Zoning* (New York: Russell Sage Foundation, 1940).

Beuscher, Jacob H., *Land Use Controls,* 4th ed. (Madison, Wisconsin: College Printing & Typing Company, 1966).

Horack, Frank E., Jr., and Val Nolan, Jr., *Land Use Controls* (St. Paul: West Publishing Company, 1955).

Public Land Law Review Commission, *One Third of the Nation's Land* (Washington: U.S. Government Printing Office, 1970).

Solberg, Erling D., *The How and Why of Rural Zoning,* U. S. Department of Agriculture, Agriculture Information Bulletin No. 196, revised 1967.

Walker, Robert A., *The Planning Function in Urban Government* (Chicago: University of Chicago Press, 1941), chap. III.

[65] Most cities in the Scandinavian and Germanic countries of northern Europe have held large tracts of land in municipal ownership almost since feudal times. Many cities in Finland hold title to their sites with restrictions against the alienation of full titles to others. In 1926, the Finnish towns still owned 96.5 per cent of their corporate area. Stockholm acquired some 20,000 acres (five times its original area) between 1904 and 1937, mostly for housing developments; and the next five largest Swedish cities owned between 47 and 80 per cent of their corporate areas. Oslo, Norway, Copenhagen, Denmark, The Hague, Netherlands, and Vienna, Austria, owned large areas; and Berlin owned 75,000 acres (around a third of the total area) within its city limits and another 75,000 acres outside. The average German city of over 50,000 owned 23.6 per cent of its corporate area (exclusive of streets and public service sites) in 1935 plus holdings of comparable size outside its corporate limits. The areas held outside the cities were ordinarily used for park, agricultural, or forestry purposes pending their possible future need for urban development. Cf. Harold S. Buttenheim, "Urban Land Policies," in *Urban Planning and Land Policies*, Vol. 2 of the Supplementary Report of the Urbanism Committee to the National Resources Committee (Washington: U.S. Government Printing Office, 1939), pp. 228-29, 312-20; and Roy J. Burroughs, "Should Urban Land Be Publicly Owned," *Land Economics*, Vol. 42, February, 1966, pp. 11-20.

18

Taxation
of Landed Property

"Nothing in life is quite so certain as death and taxes." This old adage is as timely and as meaningful now as ever; and it is particularly apropos in the case of land resources. Land owners in the United States pay an annual property tax as a condition of continued ownership. They pay an assortment of sales and commodity taxes on the inputs they use with their land. They pay income taxes on the returns they derive from their properties. And finally, as if this tax load were not enough, either they or their estates usually end up subject to capital gains, transfer, gift, or inheritance taxes at the time their properties are transferred to others.

Emphasis is centered in this chapter on three highly important aspects of the land-tax problem. Attention is first given to the scope of the taxing power and to the effects of taxes on land-resource use. With this background, consideration is then given to the operation of the general property tax and to some possibilities for its improvement.

SCOPE OF THE TAXING POWER

No government could long exist without the power to levy and collect taxes. As the Supreme Court of the United States has observed: "The power to tax is the one great power upon which the whole national fabric is based. It is as necessary to the existence and prosperity of the nation as the air he breathes is to the natural man. It is not only the power to destroy but also the power to keep alive."[1]

The taxing power provides the means by which governments collect the major portion of the revenues they use to finance their many operations and functions; and it also provides a tool they can use for various nonfiscal and regulatory purposes. But great and important as this power may be, it always has its limits. Most governments are limited by constitutional principles or provisions that specify the conditions under which the taxing power can or cannot be exercised. And even in the absence of these limits, every government is limited in an ultimate sense by the fact that it cannot tax property beyond the point of confiscation or tax its citizenry beyond the point at which they will rise up in rebellion.

Throughout the United States, the taxing power is vested in the legislative branch of the government and cannot be delegated to other agencies.[2] Except for constitutional restrictions, every legislature is free to tax the persons or property subject to its jurisdiction at rates of its own choosing. The courts have held, however, that all taxes must be levied for public purposes and that they must be levied in an equitable and reasonable manner. Except in those cases in which constitutional limitations apply, legislatures can group or classify particular persons, properties, privileges, or incomes for taxation purposes. But these classifications "must be reasonable, not arbitrary, and must rest upon some ground of difference having a fair and substantial relation to the object of the legislation, so that all persons similarly circumstanced shall be treated alike."[3]

In addition to the general limitations listed above, the taxing powers of the federal, state, and local units of government are limited by various constitutional provisions. Under the federal system, the national government and the governments of the various states are sovereign within their respective spheres. Neither level of government has a right to infringe upon or interfere with the other's legitimate functions and neither can tax the agencies or instrumentalities of the other. The federal government has only those taxing powers delegated to it by the federal Constitution. State and local governments in turn have only those taxing powers not

---

[1] *Nicol v. Ames,* 173 U.S. 509, 515 (1899).

[2] For more detailed discussions of the scope of the taxing power in the United States cf. William J. Schultz and C. Lowell Harriss, *American Public Finance,* 8th ed. (Englewood Cliffs, N.J.: Prentice-Hall, Inc., 1965), chap. VII; Harold M. Groves, *Financing Government,* 5th ed. (New York: Henry Holt and Company, 1958), chap. XIX; and Ansel M. Sharp and Bernard F. Sliger, *Public Finance* (Homewood, Illinois: The Dorsey Press, 1964), chap. XIII.

[3] *F. S. Royster Guano Co. v. Virginia,* 253 U.S. 412 (1920).

prohibited by the federal Constitution and not limited by state constitutional provisions.

Congress has the power under the federal Constitution "to lay and collect taxes, duties, imposts, and excises." This broad grant of power is subject to five specific limitations. (1) No tax or duty can be laid on the exports from any state. (2) Except for income taxes, which are provided for by the Sixteenth Amendment, all direct taxes must be apportioned among the states according to population numbers. (3) All direct taxes must be applied uniformly throughout the nation. (4) Discriminatory taxation measures cannot be used to deprive any person of his "life, liberty, or property, without due process of law." And (5) from the standpoint of purpose, taxes can be collected only "to pay the debts and provide for the common defense and general welfare of the United States."

The provision that taxes can be collected for "the general welfare" both expands and limits the scope of the federal taxing power. In practice, few questions are raised about those taxes whose revenues go into the general fund of the federal treasury because the courts ordinarily refuse to question the character of the expenditures made from this fund. When a tax is used for regulatory purposes or when its receipts are earmarked for some particular activity or function, however, the courts may consider the nature of the tax and its objectives to determine whether or not it actually provides for the general welfare. When a court decides in the negative—as the Supreme Court did in the case of the processing tax, which was used to finance the crop reduction program under the Agricultural Adjustment Act of 1933—the tax is declared unconstitutional.

Except for its requirement that no state can levy import, export, or tonnage taxes without the approval of Congress, the Constitution makes no direct reference to the taxing powers of the state and local governments. Indirectly, however, these units are limited in their taxing powers by the federal constitutional requirements that they (1) pass no laws, "impairing the obligation of contracts," (2) treat federal treaties as "part of the supreme law of the land," (3) take no action to discriminate against the citizens of other states, (4) grant "equal protection of the laws" to all persons, (5) deprive no persons of "life, liberty, or property without due process of law," and (6) adhere to the judicial doctrine of noninterference with interstate commerce.

Most state constitutions contain provisions that limit the taxing power of the state and local governments. One of the most widely accepted provisions is that of "uniformity" or "equality" in taxation. This requirement usually applies primarily to property taxes, although it can be applicable to other taxes as well. As usually applied, it requires that all properties, or all properties of the same class, within any taxing district be taxed at the same millage rate and according to the same assessment-value ratio. State constitutional provisions are also used at times to provide that (1) all taxes be for public purposes, (2) property be assessed at its "fair market value," (3) tax levies be limited to specified maximum millage rates, and (4) property not be subject to double taxation.

EFFECTS OF TAXES ON LAND-RESOURCE USE

Land resources are affected both by the collection and by the spending of tax revenues. Almost every tax tends to reallocate wealth and resources by taking capital from the taxpayer to finance the functions of government. In this reallocation process, a high proportion of the funds collected through land taxes are used for purposes that benefit the taxpayer and his family or that enhance and protect property values. In this sense, taxes often have a favorable effect upon land resources. This measure of benefit varies from taxpayer to taxpayer. Some receive benefits far in excess of their tax contributions while the reverse situation applies with others.

On the collection side, land taxes always represent compulsory contributions on the part of property owners. As such, they involve a claim of government against either the income associated with land resources or the value of the property itself. The actual effects of these taxes on land resources vary somewhat depending upon the type of tax used, the amount of the tax, the uniformity with which it is applied, the extent to which it can be shifted to others, possible benefits and penalties associated with its application, and the role it plays in influencing operator decisions.

Emphasis is centered in this section on three important aspects of the effects of taxes on land resources and their use. Inasmuch as these effects vary from tax to tax, consideration is first given to a brief description of the principal land taxes now used in the United States. Attention is then focused on the question of who actually pays these taxes and on an examination of a number of ways in which tax measures can be used to direct land-resource use.

Principal Taxes Affecting Landed Property

When one speaks of land taxes, most Americans think of the property tax. This tax is far and away our most important tax on landed property. Yet it is only one of several taxes that affect land resources. In addition to the property tax, land resources are subject to special assessments, capital gains taxes, inheritance and gift taxes, documentary taxes, severance taxes on forest and mineral products, and a variety of less direct taxes.

Property taxes. The general property tax, or the ad valorem (according to value) property tax as it is often called, involves an annual charge against the assessed value of all the nonexempt properties located in a taxing district. These properties fall into two classes: personalty and realty. When one deals only with the tax on personalty, it is customary to speak of the personal property tax. The tax on realty is usually referred to as a real property tax, real estate tax, or simply as the property tax. Real property taxes apply to all classes of realty except public properties, churches and other properties expressly exempt by law, and properties handled under possible alternative taxing arrangements.

As a part of the property taxing process, all nonexempt properties are supposedly valued or assessed at some set percentage of their true market value. These assessed values are then multiplied by a uniform tax levy or millage rate to determine the actual tax payments due. If these taxes are not paid within a specified period of time, the property is said to be tax delinquent. Continued nonpayment ordinarily leads to the owner's forfeiture of his property rights.

More detailed attention will be given to the real property tax in a later section of this chapter. At this point, however, it should be noted that this tax is more or less indigenous to the United States. Its chief precedents are found in the English land and property tax concepts the early settlers brought to the American colonies and in the annual quitrents which the settlers in some colonies paid to agents of the Crown.[4]

As it exists today, the property tax differs from these precedents in three important respects. Unlike some early taxes, which related property tax liability to individual abilities and other non-real property items, it has become a tax on property rather than on persons. It has shifted from the early use of arbitrary rates to the taxation of all properties within each taxing district at a uniform proportion of their assessed value.[5] And unlike the annual payments enacted under the quasi-feudal quitrent system, taxes are collected as a matter of government right and not as a symbol of superior tenure status.[6]

[4]Cf. Jens P. Jensen, *Property Taxation in the United States* (Chicago: University of Chicago Press, 1931), chap. II.

[5]Most of the shift to uniformity in property taxation—use of uniform tax rates and proportionate assessed values—came after 1800 at a time when the federal government's monopolization of the revenue from custom duties forced the states to shift to greater reliance upon property taxation. Prior to this time most property tax rates were more or less arbitrary. In 1645, for example, Virginia taxed land at a rate of 4 pounds of tobacco (tax collected in kind) for every 100 acres. North Carolina taxed land at 2.5 shillings per 100 acres in 1715; and New Hampshire taxed land (within fence, meadows or marsh, mowable) at 5 shillings per acre in 1680 and at 10 shillings per acre in 1742. Cf. *ibid.*, pp. 28-33.

[6]Under the quasi-feudal tenure system first adhered to in many American colonies, the nominal owners of land held their occupancy or "ownership" rights subject to the seigneur rights of the Crown or some proprietary lord who was a vassal of the Crown. Specified payments, varying from token gifts such as a red rose to cash payments, were supposedly paid each year to agents of the Crown for the privilege of continued occupancy. These payments served a multiple function in recognizing the operator's inferior tenure status, in quitting or cutting off the seigneur's right of rent for the year,

Special assessments. Special assessments are usually regarded as a type of tax although they may also be described as a public fee. In any case, they represent "compulsory levies imposed upon owners of property for the purpose of defraying the cost of specific public improvements likely to enhance the value of assessed property."[7] Like the property tax, they constitute a claim against the property rather than the owner; and they are ordinarily added to and collected with the property tax.

Special assessments have a long history which goes back to the great fire of London in 1666. Throughout the United States, they are widely used in cities and subdivisions to finance the construction and provision of streets, sidewalks, sewers, water mains, parks, and other improvements. They are also used extensively by *ad hoc* units of government to finance drainage, levee, irrigation, and other projects. Prior to the 1930s, special assessments were used to a considerable extent in many rural areas to finance highway construction and improvements.

From the standpoint of tax theory, special assessments supposedly affect only those properties that benefit from area improvements; and they never exceed the value added by the improvements. Problems arise, however, in the allocation of costs among taxpayers. At best, special assessments are presumably allocated according to estimated benefits; yet they often overcharge some taxpayers while they undercharge others. In some cases, as when a home owner is required to pay his share of the cost of converting a quiet residential street into an express thoroughfare, they can lower the value of property for the purpose for which it is held.

Since special assessments are supposedly allocated in proportion to benefits received, it is only proper that the allocation system should differ with different types of projects. The cost of a water main may best be allocated on a house- or lot-unit basis, the cost of a drainage or levee project on an acreage basis, the cost of sidewalks on a foot-frontage basis, and the cost of some other projects on an assessed-value basis. With some types of projects such as a public park or the provision of an express street, the radius of benefit often covers a considerable area. Several zones of benefit are often designated in cases of this type with the costs being allocated between the properties in each zone somewhat in proportion to the benefits realized from the improvement.

Special assessments have provided a real service in financing local improvements in the past. There is no reason why they should not continue to function for this purpose in the future. A word of caution,

---

and in producing public revenue. The quitrent system had little application in New England but persisted in Maryland and Virginia until the time of the Revolutionary War. Quitrents were unpopular in most areas and were frequently evaded or ignored by many owners.

[7]E. H. Hahne, "Special Assessment," *Encyclopedia of the Social Sciences* (New York: The Macmillan Company, 1937), Vol. 14, p. 276.

however, is in order. Special assessments often create a considerable tax burden on property; and they can represent unwise or premature expenditures that have no immediate value to the property owner. These problems sometimes assume acute proportions, as they did in many areas during the late 1920s; and they can lead to wholesale tax delinquency when they are associated with depression conditions such as those of the early 1930s.

Taxation of capital gains. It has been argued that special assessments are often inequitable and that local improvements should be financed instead by a value increment tax, which would be levied after the improvement is made.[8] This proposal would tax away the increment of increased value that results from improvements. Thus far, no attempt has been made to apply this proposal. But the capital gains tax associated with the federal and most state income taxes does represent an attempt to tax the gain in property values that operators realize when they sell real estate, securities, and other types of property.

Between 1913 and 1921 capital gains from the sale of real estate and other types of property were taxed by the federal government as regular income. Since 1921, however, a distinction has been made between long-term and short-term gains. Under the Federal Internal Revenue Code of 1954 as amended by the Tax Reform Act of 1969, all gains or losses associated with capital investments held for six months or less are treated as "short-term" gains or losses and are treated along with regular income. Gains or losses associated with capital investments in real estate and other properties held for more than six months are treated separately as "long-term" gains or losses.

Under this arrangements, a long-term capital gain realized from the sale of real property—the operator's net selling price less his initial cost plus the cost of any permanent improvements he has made—can be taxed in either of two ways. The operator can add one-half of his long-term gain to his regular taxable income and have it taxed at the applicable rate; or if he is in a high income bracket, he can use an alternative method of computation under which he pays a tax equal to 32.5 percent of his capital gain. Provisions are also made for the deduction of up to $1,000 in capital losses from an operator's other taxable income and for allowing some carryover of losses to other years.

Most capital gains involving landed property come from one of three sources: (1) the owner's efforts to improve his property, (2) an appreciation in property values attributable to community growth or the discovery of unexpected resources such as oil, or (3) the effects of

---

[8]Cf. Edwin H. Spengler, "The Increment Tax Versus Special Assessments," *Bulletin of the National Tax Association*, Vol. 20, June, 1935, pp. 258-61; Vol. 21, October, 1935, pp. 14-18; Vol. 21, March, 1936, pp. 163-67; and Vol. 21, May, 1936, pp. 240-44.

inflation in reducing the unit value of money. A capital gains tax on the first of these sources can be easily justified on the ground that this gain is closely akin to personal income and should be taxed accordingly. Gains from the second source fall into the unearned increment class and provide a logical subject for taxation.

Real questions can be raised concerning the justification for taxing the gains associated with inflationary trends. In a real value sense, these gains are often fictitious because the operator often has no more and sometimes less buying power when he sells his property than when he acquired it. Under these conditions, the capital gains tax becomes a tax on property transfers; and as such, it can be used to discourage property sales. The taxation of these gains during the inflationary period that followed World War II often penalized those owners who sold their properties with the plan of buying newer, larger, or more productive properties. Congress recognized the inequity of this situation as it applied to home owners in 1951; and since then, rural and urban home owners have been exempt from this tax as long as they use the proceeds from their sales within a specified time period to build or buy homes of comparable or higher value.

Inheritance and gift taxes. Property owners can avoid the capital gains tax by giving their properties to others or by allowing them to pass by devise or inheritance to their heirs. With each of these alternatives, the properties remain subject to taxation. Death taxes of various types are used by the federal government and all of the states except Nevada; and gift taxes are used by the federal government and around a fourth of the states.

Federal estate taxes are levied on all estates with a net value of $60,000 or more after deductions are made for expenses, debts, contributions, and exemptions.[9] The tax rate on these estates is steeply graduated from 3 percent on the first $5,000 above the $60,000 exemption to 77 percent on any value above $10,060,000. Credits are allowed, however, for state inheritance tax payments.

With this credit arrangement, most states have found it advantageous to enter the inheritance tax field either by using an estate tax, a tax on inheritances, or a combination of both. Ten states use estate taxes while 37 tax the inheritances received by individual heirs. These taxes vary somewhat in their rate structure but usually start with lower exemptions than the federal estate tax. In most cases, they use the graduation principle with their rates. With inheritance taxation, they usually tax direct heirs at a lower rate than heirs of more distant relationship.

Most inheritance tax laws are interpreted to include deathbed gifts and gifts made in contemplation of death. Gift taxes are also used, however, as

[9]Estates passing to a surviving husband or wife enjoy a marital exemption of up to half of the value of the estate. Charitable bequests are also exempt from this tax.

a supplementary measure to tax substantial transfers of property between persons and to discourage the use of large-scale gifts to avoid inheritance taxes.

The federal gift tax is supposedly paid by the donor, with the tax not being counted as part of the gift. Each donor has a lifetime exemption of $30,000, which he can use all at one time or over the period of his life. In addition, he is allowed an annual exclusion of $3,000 for each donee; and marital deductions are permitted on gifts between husband and wife. Gifts in excess of these exemptions are subject to tax rates that approximate three-fourths of the estate tax rate.

State gift taxes usually bear the same relationship to the state estate or inheritance tax that the federal gift and estate taxes bear to each other. Some states levy their gift taxes on the donee rather than the donor; and some use a graduated tax rate that favors gifts to a spouse or direct descendant or ancestor as compared with persons of more distant relationship.

Documentary or recording taxes. The Federal Revenue Act of 1932 specified that all deeds, instruments, or writings under which "lands, tenements, or other realty sold shall be granted, assigned, transferred or otherwise conveyed to, or vested in, the purchaser or purchasers, or any other person or persons," shall be taxed at the rate of 55 cents "when the consideration or value of the interest or property conveyed, exclusive of the value of any lien or encumbrance remaining thereon at the time of sale, exceeds $100, and does not exceed $500" plus 55 cents "for each additional $500 or fractional part thereof." This tax was repealed in 1965. Documentary taxes of a comparable nature, however, are used by many states. Some of these state taxes apply to the recording and registration of deeds, some to mortgages, and some to both deeds and mortgages.

Under these taxes, any person who grants a deed or other taxable instrument must affix and cancel the required number of revenue stamps and pay the required state tax or fee. The receipts from these taxes are ordinarily small and represent a relatively insignificant souce of public revenues. The taxes themselves are important to property owners, however, in that they add to the costs and paper work associated with property transfers.

Severance taxes. Several states levy severance taxes on the privilege of harvesting, mining, extracting, or otherwise severing natural resources such as timber, metallic ores, coal, petroleum, natural gas, salt, and sulphur. These taxes normally involve either a fixed charge against each unit of product severed or a percentage charge against the gross receipts or gross market value of the raw products produced.

As a taxing device, severance taxes are sometimes combined with and sometimes used in lieu of property taxes. When used in addition to the general property tax, they are often justified on the ground that the resource owner is exploiting a free gift of nature and that he should share his profits with society. With this purpose in mind, several states levy taxes involving specified charges on every thousand board feet of lumber, every ton of coal or ore, or every barrel of oil produced within their jurisdiction.

When severance taxes are substituted for property taxes, they are usually justified as being more equitable and more favorable to conservation practices than the property tax. Realistic assessments for taxation purposes are almost impossible in the case of hidden resources such as oil. And even when the total value of a forest or a mine can be estimated, its annual taxation at its full assessed value often encourages the owner to exploit or liquidate his resource as soon as possible. With commercial forest holdings, for example, high property taxes can favor "cut out and get out" policies which leave little room for sustained-yield management.

Several states have substituted severance taxes for property taxes on oil, mineral, and other underground resources. This approach is also used to a considerable extent with forest holdings.[10] Approximately a third of the states now have optional or compulsory forest-crop taxation programs that use the severance or yield tax principle. These laws usually involve a nominal annual land tax—between 5 and 10 cents per acre in most states—plus yield taxes that vary from 3 to 12.5 percent of the value of the forest crop at the time it is harvested.

Other taxes affecting land resources. Several other taxes have an important though less direct impact upon land resources. Among the more important of these, mention should be made of custom duties, income taxes, sales taxes, and business taxes. Tariff regulations such as our custom duties on sugar and wool are often used to favor domestic industries that might prove unprofitable without protection from foreign competition. Income taxes represent a claim against the income from land resources. Sales taxes affect the inputs used with land in the production process. And business taxes can favor or discourage the organization, location, and expansion of particular business enterprises.

Shifting and Incidence of Land Taxes

With most taxes, questions are often raised concerning: Who actually pays the tax? Is the tax absorbed by the person from whom it is collected? Is it shifted forward to some eventual consumer in the form of higher prices; or might it be shifted backward in the form of lower prices for raw

---

[10] For more detailed descriptions of these taxes, cf. Groves, *op. cit.*, pp. 308-17; Ralph W. Marquis, *Forest Yield Taxes,* U.S. Department of Agriculture Circular No. 899, 1952; and Warren A. Roberts, *State Taxation Of Mineral Deposits* (Cambridge: Harvard University Press, 1944).

materials, lower rent to the landlord, or lower wages to labor? In discussions of this type, economists ordinarily use the terms "shifting" and "incidence"—*shifting* meaning the transfer of the tax burden from the original taxpayer to someone else, and *incidence* referring to the persons or things that bear the actual tax burden.

The question of tax incidence always has an important bearing upon discussions concerning the effect of any given tax on land resources. When a tax can be easily shifted, the taxpayer functions mostly as a tax collector for the government. But when the tax is only partly shifted or when it cannot be shifted at all, the taxpayer invariable suffers a reduction of income. With land taxes, this reduction of income can lead to lower property values. It may cause an operator to live in a smaller or less pretentious house than he otherwise would. It may cause him to use his land more intensively or possibly exploit his available stock of resources. It may cause him to move his enterprise to a lower-taxed area; or it may even lower his income to the point at which he finds it uneconomic to continue his operations or impossible to pay his taxes.

Whether or not a tax will be shifted "depends on (1) the nature of the tax, (2) the economic environment in which it is levied, and (3) the taxpayers' practices in taking advantage of any possibility of shifting."[11] Some taxes are much more shiftable than others. A uniform tax on each ton of iron ore produced may be shifted on and on until it is fairly evenly diffused throughout the economy. A tax on the land rent received from the use of land resources, on the other hand, may be virtually nonshiftable.

Incidence of property taxes. According to the "pure" theory of tax incidence, a property tax on bare land is nonshiftable while a tax on land improvements can usually be shifted over time, even though it may be nonshiftable at particular moments in time. This theory assumes a simple model such as that depicted in Figure 18-1 in which bare land is viewed as a nonreproducible resource with no cost of production. The market values of the better grades of land reflect the capitalized values of their land rents and the amount of tax levied is assumed to be directly proportional to the levels of market value and land rent. Land at the extensive margin of use pays no rent, has no capitalized value, and accordingly pays no tax. With these assumptions, the raising or lowering of a tax— the taking of a larger or smaller portion of the land rent as taxes— in no way affects the owner's operating decisions. An increase in the tax rate has no effect on the location of the extensive margin, on the total amount of land used, or on the market price of the products produced. The higher tax cannot be

[11] Shultz and Harriss, *op. cit.* p. 142. For other discussions of this subject, cf. Groves, *op. cit.*, pp. 129-32; Dick Netzer, *Economics of the Property Tax* (Washington: Brookings Institution, 1966), pp. 32-66; and Herbert A. Simons, "The Incidence of a Tax on Urban Real Estate" in Richard A. Musgrave and Carl S. Shoup, ed., *Readings in the Economics of Taxation* (Homewood, Ill.: Richard D. Irwin, 1959).

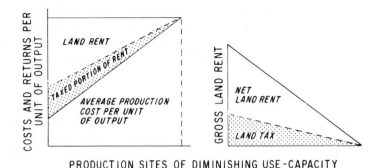

PRODUCTION SITES OF DIMINISHING USE-CAPACITY

FIGURE 18-1. Land rent models assumed with "pure" theory of land tax incidence.

shifted to others.[12] It simply takes a larger share of the land rent, which otherwise would stay with the land owner.

In contrast with this situation, it is assumed that a tax on buildings and other property improvements can usually be shifted over time because these properties ordinarily wear out and must be replaced. This type of property always competes with other investment alternatives for new investment capital. When high property taxes depress the comparative investment values of these properties, new capital is withheld from these uses and the existing supply of reproducible properties tends to wear out faster than new investments are developed. Under free market conditions, this situation supposedly leads to higher product prices, higher rental rates, the reattraction of investment capital to these uses, and some incidental shifting of the tax burden.

This two-part theory of property tax incidence applies to some extent under real-life conditions. In practice, however, its application is often complicated by differences between its assumptions and the conditions of the real world. The lack of any clear-cut distinction between the concepts of land and improvements, for example, often makes it unrealistic to apply these theories to those land resources that represent a combination of bare land and improvements. Other problems arise when properties are used primarily for consumptive purposes and when there is no expectation of replacing improvements as they wear out.

A principal weakness of the "pure" theory of land tax incidence centers on the simplicity of its assumptions. It assumes a single land use and visualizes the tax on land as a relatively uniform proportional tax on the capitalized value of land rent. A different set of conditions prevail in the real world. Land areas are subject to many competing uses. Few uses are carried on to their actual extensive margins. Individual uses tend instead to be displaced at or near their margins of transference by other uses that can utilize lands of lower use-capacities to greater advantage. (Cf.

[12] Cf. Jensen, *op. cit.,* pp. 61-62.

Figure 6-12, p. 180.) The transference and extensive margins for most uses are supramarginal for other uses and thus have considerable value for taxation purposes. This situation is further complicated by the fact that the land area of the United States is distributed among some 82,000 taxing districts, each of which has its own assessment levels and taxation rates. Moreover, property taxes are often regressive in the sense that they have a heavier proportional impact on lower-valued than higher-valued properties.

With this combination of factors at work, it may be argued that the situation depicted in Figure 18-2 is more descriptive of what happens with land taxes than that of Figure 18-1. Far from having land of no taxable value, operators at the transference and extensive margins for most uses find that their sites are valuable for other uses and that they still have a tax to pay. Payment of the tax represents an additional cost of production and insofar as production does take place to the extensive margin, product prices must rise enough to cover production costs at this margin if land is to continue in its assumed use. This situation does not mean that prices must rise sufficiently at the transference margin to permit a complete shifting of the tax. However, when taxes are regressive in their application or when productive sites at the extensive margin for a given use (use *B* in Figure 18-2A) are subject to high local tax levies, the price of the product of this use must rise sufficiently to cover the tax cost. This price increase permits all of the *B* users to shift much of their tax and may even bring windfalls to operators in low tax areas. The effect of the tax on the transference margin *ab* also necessitates an increase in the price of the product of *A,* which permits some shifting of the tax burden from the *A* use producers to the consumers of the product of the land.

When one discusses the actual shifting and incidence of real property

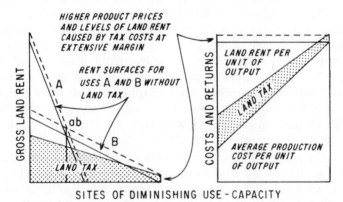

SITES OF DIMINISHING USE-CAPACITY

FIGURE 18-2. Illustration of impact of a land tax on production costs at the extensive margin for an assumed use of land (use B) and its probable effect upon the shifting of a portion of the tax through higher product prices on higher grades of land.

taxes, it is best to distinguish between the types of properties involved and the conditions under which they are used. Taxes on owner-occupied homes and other properties used for personal or family consumptive uses are usually considered nonshiftable. This situation exists because individual home owners are seldom able to shift their taxes in the form of higher wages or salaries for their services or higher prices for the products they produce and sell. An exception to this situation arises when a property owner's income is geared to a cost of living index that reflects possible increases or decreases in his property tax burden.

With productive properties such as industrial plants, commercial establishments, farms, and forests, the extent to which one can shift his property tax usually depends upon the universality of the tax and the degree of control he has over his market prices. Under perfectly competitive conditions, product prices are set by the interplay of supply and demand and ordinarily correspond with the productive costs encountered at the extensive margin. A property tax that has a more-or-less universal effect on all properties used for some given purpose can thus be shifted up to the point at which it affects production costs at the extensive margin. With higher taxes in some districts than others, however, producers must usually bear the incidence of any taxes they pay in excess of the taxes paid in lower-taxed districts. This situation holds because they cannot shift these extra taxes on in the form of higher product prices and still maintain their competitive position with lower-taxed areas.

Unlike the farmers and other businessmen who enjoy little individual control over the prices they receive for their products, some businessmen are able to dictate the prices at which their products sell. In their exercise of this power, these operators can sometimes shift increases in their property taxes on to the buyers of their products, or they may even shift part of their tax load backward in the form of lower wages and lower supply prices. Even with these price-setting powers, however, these producers find it difficult to shift a tax increase if they have already set their market and supply prices at those levels that promise them a maximum net return.

It is normally supposed that all taxes on rental properties will be shifted to the tenants. Landlords are frequently limited in this shifting process, however, by personal inertia, long-term lease commitments, rent control regulations, and by uncertainties in the current rental market situation. Taxes can be shifted into higher rents rather easily in periods when the rental market is tight and when considerable competition exists between tenants for properties. But when landlords compete for tenants against other landlords who are willing to absorb all or part of a tax increase or against landlords located in other taxing districts not affected by tax increases, there is some tendency to absorb the increase rather than risk the loss of desired tenants.

Some shifting of the incidence of property taxes from buyers to sellers of property takes place with the process known as tax *capitalization*. As was pointed out in chapter 6, productive properties have an economic value equal to the sum of their future land rents discounted back to the present. Since property taxes represent a cost factor, they help to reduce the annual land rents associated with individual properties and accordingly can cause a reduction in their market values.

To illustrate the effects of tax capitalization, one might assume a property with an annual expected land rent of $1,000, which is capitalized at 5 percent to give a market value of $20,000. If the total property tax in this case is increased by $50 a year and if this tax increase appears to be permanent, cannot be shifted, and is not associated with any increase in property value or income, the annual net rent will drop to $950. Capitalization of this figure at 5 percent gives a market value of $19,000—the drop of $1,000 being attributable to the higher property tax.

As one might expect, knowledgeable buyers frequently try to capitalize out the cost of their future property taxes at the time that they acquire real estate. This is particularly true when they operate in buyers' markets and when they use an income-capitalization approach in the valuation of their properties. Insofar as the tax-capitalization process works, these future owners buy themselves free of property taxes while the current owners bear the incidence of future as well as present taxes.

Several factors limit the overall importance of this tax-shifting process. To begin with, tax capitalization works best with cases of income-producing properties and then only to the extent that the tax is not shifted through higher product prices or lower supply prices. It applies mainly to cases in which the buyer anticipates a definite pattern of future taxes with no compensating increase in property values. In this respect, it must be noted that property tax expenditures for items such as better schools, police and fire protection, or civic improvements often enhance property values and thus counterbalance any losses that may take place under tax capitalization.

Still another complication stems from the average buyer's failure to understand the capitalization principle. Many buyers ignore the tax factor until after they have acquired their properties and received their first tax bill. These buyers compete alongside the more tax-conscious buyers in most markets involving real properties; and through their bidding activities, they can force the better-informed buyers to take less tax capitalization than they might wish if they are to get the properties they desire.

Incidence of other land taxes. The incidence of special assessments varies with the circumstances. These tax payments are ordinarily associated with improvements that benefit the properties assessed. With productive properties, these benefits often lead to higher production, lower costs, or higher business receipts and thus to a shifting of the actual tax cost. Even when this type of tax shifting does not take place, property owners can shift the portion of their tax costs represented by the value of their benefits to buyers at the time they sell their properties. But insofar as the tax cost exceeds the sale value of the benefit that comes with the improvement, the incidence of the special assessment lies with the original taxpayer.

Capital gains taxes along with documentary taxes on conveyances provide excellent examples of land taxes that fall almost entirely upon the persons who sell property. Very little tax shifting is possible because the sellers ordinarily seek the highest prices possible for their properties regardless of the tax rate. With this situation, one might argue that the incidence of these taxes falls entirely upon the sellers because the prices they receive for their properties would not change even if their tax rates were doubled. It might also be argued, however, that a higher tax rate would discourage some owners from offering their properties for sale, that this would reduce the supply of properties in the market, that the resulting interaction of supply and demand would result in higher market prices, and that these prices thus include an element of tax shifting.

Gift taxes are usually paid by the donor although a few states such as Wisconsin levy this tax on the donee. In either case, the incidence of the tax is usually divided between the donor and the donee because the tax comes out of wealth supplied by the donor and because it deprives the donee of property he otherwise might have received. The incidence of inheritance taxes falls on the beneficiaries who are deprived of part of the inheritance they otherwise would have received. This incidence can also be shared to some extent by the deceased owner during his lifetime if he allows his anticipation of this future tax burden to affect his property accumulation and transfer practices.

Severance taxes ordinarily involve either a fixed charge against each unit of natural resource produced or a fixed percentage of its market value. In either case, this tax represents an addition to the operator's production costs; and it can usually be at least partially shifted in the form of higher prices.[13] This is particularly true when the tax affects all

[13]The amount of tax shifting that actually takes place always varies with market conditions. Assuming perfect competition and an elastic demand schedule, any attempt to shift the tax in the form of higher prices will lead to less taking of products in the market (cf. Figure 2-1, p. 21), a leftward shift of the extensive margin (cf. Figure 5-7, p. 152), and the withdrawal of several marginal producers from the market. Under these conditions, one could argue that the tax will be included in the costs covered at the new extensive margin. But the new equilibrium price will be somewhat below the sum of the previous price plus the tax; and the producers with the more productive properties will find that the over-all price adjustment falls short of the amount necessary to permit a complete shifting of the tax. For further discussion of the effects of different market conditions on this aspect of tax incidence, cf. Groves, *op. cit.*, pp. 105-29.

producers of a given resource or when it affects some producers including those at the extensive margin. Complications arise, however, when competing producers find themselves subject to different tax arrangements. Under these conditions, the producers in high-tax areas usually find that they must bear the incidence of their additional tax burden. Varying amounts of tax absorption also take place in those instances in which producers continue their mining, forest-cutting, or other resource-severance activities during periods when gross market receipts are inadequate to cover full production costs.

Use of Taxation Measures to Direct Land Use

Taxes are ordinarily used mostly as a means of supplying needed governmental revenues. But they can also be used as a regulatory tool to implement the attainment of public policy objectives. Land taxes are occasionally used in this manner. Leading examples include their use to (1) foster more intensive land use, (2) promote conservation and environmental goals, (3) attain particular tenure goals, (4) influence investment decisions, and (5) enhance property values.

Land taxes usually play a neutral or more-or-less routine role as far as the above categories of use impacts are concerned in that they have few noticeable effects upon individual ownership or use practices other than that of depriving owners of funds they could use for other purposes. Quite often, however, they do have important impacts on the use, ownership, or value of land resources. These effects are sometimes accidental or incidental, sometimes a result of deliberate policy. They can be either desirable or undesirable from the standpoint of society. Overall, they show that taxes can be used as a potent tool in the direction of land use.

Use to foster more intensive land use. Land taxes are often used to encourage or stimulate the more intensive use of land resources. Officials along the western frontier frequently assessed potential as well as actual farm lands at value levels reflecting their highest and best use and thereby encouraged speculators to sell, settle, or otherwise use the idle lands they were holding in anticipation of windfall profits. This same technique was used again in many forested and cutover communities to foster the clearing, sale, and agricultural development of the areas held by various land and lumber companies. Farm lands with potential value for subdivision purposes can often be pressured into this higher use if they are assessed at their going market values for residential rather than farming purposes. A comparable shifting of sites to a higher use often follows when residential lots around expanding commercial districts are assessed at their emerging values for commercial purposes.[14]

[14]Penalty taxes of a somewhat similar order are used in some Latin American countries to discourage the underutilization of land. Colombia, for example, enacted a law in 1957 that calls for official classification of all rural lands in the nation, specifies

In addition to encouraging the shifting of some lands to higher and better uses, tax pressures can cause operators to make more effective and intensive use of properties in their present use. Countries such as Finland, the Soviet Union, and Yugoslavia use incentive tax levies based upon the levels of production expected from average producers to encourage more intensive land use and superior management of resources. Similar results are associated with property tax levies when taxpayers see more intensive resource use practices as necessary if they are to pay higher taxes without lowering their present levels of net return. Under these circumstances, operators may attempt to increase production so that they will suffer no decrease in net returns while home owners may decide to rent out unused rooms because the rental income "will help pay the taxes."

Although property taxes can be used quite effectively at times to force more intensive land uses, this approach has its limitations. There is no automatic relationship between taxes and the ripening of land for particular uses. Higher taxes can favor the more intensive use of lands not used at their optimum level of intensity; but they have an undesirable effect when they encourage operators to go beyond this point. They can pressure lands into higher uses when suitable demand exists for these uses and when the lands in question actually qualify for the uses in question. But when these conditions do not exist, taxes can have an injurious effect in fostering the waste that comes with premature developments, tax delinquency, and the tax forfeiture of property rights.

Promotion of conservation and environmental goals. When a known reserve of timber, mineral ore, coal, or some other resource is taxed year after year at its full assessed value, the resource owner is sometimes impelled to follow a "cut out and get out" policy. Aside from its effect in speeding up the exploitation of these resources, this policy often leads to considerable social waste. A forest owner operating under these conditions will often use more exploitive cutting practices than an owner who is interested in reserving seed trees, saving his younger and smaller trees for future growth and harvesting, and in carrying on a long-term forestry program that will preserve the economic base of the local community. In like manner, a mine owner who is subject to a heavy annual property tax may feel that he should skim off the best of his resource as soon as possible. As a result, he may have little incentive to bother with marginal grades of ore; and in his attempt to reduce operating costs, he may use practices that make his lower-grade ore deposits actually less accessible for future use.

Several states have substituted severance taxes for property taxes in an

---

a minimum proportion of each land holding that should be in cultivation, and establishes an annual penalty tax starting at 2 percent of the cadastral value of the land in the first year and rising to 10 percent in the fifth year for holdings that fail to meet their cultivation quotas.

attempt to promote resource conservation.[15] Special forest-yield taxes are now used in some states to encourage long-term forestry practices by exempting growing forests from annual taxation and taxing the forest crop only at the time it is harvested.[16] Comparable measures can be used with other resources such as oil wells and mines to encourage slower rates of extraction and less social waste in the exploitation process.

In addition to their use of severance taxes, some states have encouraged long-term forestry by exempting growing timber from taxation or by classifying it for special treatment under the real property tax. A few others have levied a flat tax on new oil wells, partly as a conservation measure to discourage the drilling of new wells. The allowances permitted under the federal income tax for soil and water conservation expenditures may also be cited as an example of a tax policy used for conservation purposes.

The use of tax measures to promote resource conservation goals has a close parallel in the emphasis given to programs that protect and enhance the quality of man's environment. Use-value assessment programs under which rural lands are assessed at their productive values for open-space uses are used in several states, often in combination with open-country zoning and "green acres" programs, to protect land owners from the tax pressures that might impel them to offer their lands for urban-oriented developments. Tax exemptions on air and water pollution control and treatment equipment are permitted in some areas to encourage private investments in these facilities. Some communities also have taken steps to monitor and measure the volume of wastes contributed by leading polluters to municipal waste treatment systems and to assess appropriate shares of the treatment costs to the responsible parties.

Taxing arrangements are used in each of these situations to promote environmental goals. In practice, however, it must be recognized that use

---

[15]Although severance taxes can favor conservation practices, it should be recognized that they can also have the opposite effect. Since severance taxes represent an addition to production costs, they affect the location of each operator's intensive margin of operations. When the severance tax is high or when it is used in addition to other taxes, it prevents the economic use of some of the low-grade resources that would be harvested or extracted if the producer were tax free.

[16]Forest yield taxes have been authorized in approximately one-third of the states. In most of these states, the forest owner has the option of keeping his forest land under the general property tax or entering it under the provisions of a special forest crop taxation law. The number and acreage of voluntary private entries has been somewhat disappointing in most states. The existence of this taxation alternative, however, has had a beneficial effect on all forest owners in many areas in keeping property tax levies on forest lands competitive with those available under the special forest crop taxation laws. Cf. George S. Wehrwein and Raleigh Barlowe, *The Forest Crop Law and Private Forest Taxation in Wisconsin,* Wisconsin Conservation Department Bulletin 519, 1946; and Lee M. James and James G. Yoho "Forest Taxation in the Northern Half of the Lower Peninsula of Michigan," *Land Economics,* Vol. 33, May, 1957, pp. 139-48.

is being made of only a few of the tax options that might be employed for this purpose. Special taxes could be used to discourage the sale and use of potential pollutants such as nonbiodegradable detergents, hard pesticides, leaded gas, or automobiles not equipped with pollution control devices. An arrangement calling for the refunding of a portion of the federal tax on automobiles to the last owner at the time he turns his vehicle over to an official junking agency offers a possible answer to the abandoned car problem. Taxes designed to internalize externalities by clearly associating the responsibility for dealing with the social costs of air and water pollution, stream sedimentation, and landscape disfigurement with those operators who benefit from the shifting of these costs to society can provide an important step towards their solution. By more closely relating costs to benefits, such measures can facilitate more effective waste treatment practices and encourage efforts for reclaiming wastes for possible use as valuable resources.

As these examples suggest, tax policies can be used to promote conservation and environmental goals. Tax measures by themselves, however, are often inadequate to secure achievement of the desired ends. Economic considerations can easily cause operators to follow exploitive and polluting practices even when substantial tax penalties are involved if the operators are not also subject to police power regulations.

Use to attain particular tenure goals. Tax policies can have an extremely important effect upon land-tenure conditions. When taxes are uniform and equitable and when they are related to the taxpayer's ability to pay or to the benefits he receives, they often encourage capital accumulation, higher levels of living, and a wide distribution of ownership rights. But taxes are not always levied with an eye to these goals; and as a result, they often have quite different effects upon tenure conditions.

Among those peoples who have adhered to a communal village system of property ownership or who have regarded all property rights as centering in the crown, the fixing of a tax-paying duty in particular individuals has sometimes represented the first step in the evolution of individual ownership rights. This was the situation in Czarist Russia where the tax-collection rights assigned to the early *boyars* gradually ripened into the property rights exercised by the later nobility. It was also the situation in parts of India where the British authorities designated the *zamindari* as the tax collectors in the communal villages—a step that later led to their recognition as landlords. "Similarly, the Spanish colonial governments made systematic use of local native chieftains or tribal leaders as tax collectors, thus giving them powers which were later solidified into land-tenure rights, and ultimate ownership."[17]

---

[17] Philip M. Raup, "Agricultural Taxation and Land Tenure Reform in Underdeveloped Countries," *Agricultural Taxation and Economic Development* (Cambridge: Harvard Law School, 1955), p. 256.

Special taxing arrangements have been used on various occasions to favor particular classes of owners. Property tax exemptions make it possible for religious and charitable organizations to own and use properties located at some of the highest valued sites located in and near central business districts. A 5-year exemption from local property taxes provided the early buyers of public domain lands in the United States with an added boon for ownership. Federal income tax deductions for payments of interest and taxes plus exemption of the annual value of the equities taxpayers have in their homes provide a tax subsidy for home ownership in the United States. Several states have homestead exemptions, which free the owner-occupants of homes and farms from certain tax levies on the first $500 to $5,000 of their assessed property values.[18] Similar exemptions are provided in some communities for special groups such as disabled veterans, widows, the aged, and families with low incomes.

History records numerous examples of rulers who have used oppressive tax measures in their efforts to raise revenues. These taxes have often had an onerous effect upon the great mass of the population. But they have usually favored certain individuals or groups; and in doing so, they have often contributed to the aggrandizement of small privileged classes, to the debasement of the average citizen, and to the rise of new tenure institutions such as the feudal system.[19]

Discriminatory tax policies of this general type are often used in the modern world as an arm of land reform. Special tax exemptions are claimed by farming cooperatives in countries such as Czechoslovakia, India, and Yugoslavia. The Soviet Union used a highly discriminatory tax during the 1930s to break the economic position of the free peasants and to force them to join collective farms. More recently Czechoslovakia, Poland, and some other countries within the communist orbit have used a system of compulsory deliveries of farm products, paid in kind, and steeply graduated by size of farm to (1) encourage certain types of land

[18]From a tenure-improvement standpoint, homestead tax exemptions favor home ownership by reducing the small owner's tax load and by affording him some opportunity to capitalize his tax savings into higher property values. These tax savings often result in higher property tax rates on the nonexempt portion of the owner's total valuation and thus represent higher tax burdens for the owners of considerable property, for landlords, and for nonresident owners. Outside of holding out a slightly greater incentive for ownership, homestead tax exemptions usually penalize tenants by (1) increasing the tax load landlords shift to their tenants, (2) discouraging some owners from leasing land to tenants, (3) favoring a possible increase in the value of the properties tenants may wish to buy, and (4) creating a need for replacement taxes such as sales taxes, which may shift more of the tax burden onto tenants.

[19]The Danegeld tax imposed in England near the end of the tenth century is reputed to have had a crushing impact on small landholders. "The English peasant lost his freedom to his commended lord . . . who was ready to discharge the tax burden in exchange for greater service. Men were ground into the soil." Cf. D. R. Denman, *Origins of Ownership* (London: George Allen & Unwin, Ltd., 1958), p. 58.

use, (2) favor the breaking up of the larger and medium-sized farms, and (3) undermine the economic status of the more prosperous peasants. These forced deliveries really add up to a graduated tax on agricultural holdings, and, as such, represent a significant phase of the collectivization and other land-reform programs carried out in these countries.

Tax measures are also used to attain particular tenure goals in other countries. Great Britain has used death duties to break up large landed estates. Inheritance and estate taxes are used in the United States with this same result. Exemptions from land recording fees are used in Belgium to favor the consolidation of fragmented farm holdings. Graduated land taxes with provisions for higher tax rates on the larger and higher-valued properties than on smaller holdings are used in Australia and New Zealand to discourage concentration and monopolization of land ownership.

Unbridled taxation can easily become the power to confiscate and destroy. In this sense, high taxes sometimes lead to the forfeiture of individual ownership rights and in some cultures have even caused people to sell themselves or their children into bondage. Because of the unsavory nature of this approach, taxes are seldom used for the deliberate purpose of depriving people of their property rights. The experience of the United States, however, indicates that high property taxes often have an incidental effect upon tenure conditions in causing substantial areas of tax-delinquent land to shift from private to public ownership. This movement has involved considerable social waste. During the late 1920s and the 1930s in particular, it provided the means by which many states and counties acquired lands they have since dedicated to public forest and recreation uses.

Use to influence investment decisions. Taxing arrangements can be used to either encourage or discourage particular types of investment decisions. Investments in property are generally encouraged whenever tax revenues are used to provide desired services to property that exceed their costs to the taxpayer. Repressive taxes have the opposite effect. Tax incentives are used to encourage land drainage in Finland and the provision of water canals in Iran. Depletion allowances have been permitted for several years under the federal income tax that encourage investments in mining properties. Special investment credits have been used with the corporation income tax to encourage investments in plant modernization and new plant construction.

Protective tariffs—the freedom of domestic producers from a tax that affects those outside producers who compete in domestic markets—have favored the rise of many new industries and the production of numerous products in areas where such production would not have been economically feasible under freely competitive conditions. Property tax concessions involving temporary exemptions or favorable assessed valuations have been used in many states as an inducement to favor the location of new manufacturing plants at particular sites. Several communities have used tax incentives of this type to attract new industries. The over-all importance of these incentives as a factor affecting industrial location, however, is still open to question.[20]

Taxing arrangements also have been used to discourage or prohibit certain types of investments and practices. The Soviet Union has used prohibitive taxes in its virtual elimination of the free peasantry; Chile has used penalty taxes on newly planted vineyards to discourage further expansion of the areas used for this purpose; Indonesia uses a tax on tobacco production for a similar reason; the Gambians of Africa have used a "stranger farmer tax" to discourage the seasonal leasing of cropland to migrant farmers; and several American states have taxed the use and purchase of oleomargarine to discourage its use in competition with butter.

Here in the United States, the federal and state governments can use taxes for regulatory and nonfiscal purposes. But in their use of the taxing power for these purposes, they must put up a pretense of collecting revenue; and in the case of the federal government, the government cannot attempt to do by taxation that which it has no authority otherwise to do. Acting in this regard, the federal government has used tax measures to drive state bank notes out of circulation, prevent the manufacture of white phosphorus matches, discourage the sale of certain firearms to unlicensed parties, and control the importation and sale of products such as adulterated butter and cheese, marihuana, and opium. Its attempts to use taxes to control child labor and to limit agricultural production, however, were held invalid on the ground that these functions were reserved to the states under the Tenth Amendment.[21]

Enhancement of property values. Taxes can have an important side effect in either enhancing or depressing property values. Enhancement of values results when taxes are used to provide services, such as police and fire protection, garbage collections, community planning, good streets, parks, and school facilities, that property owners and prospective investors associate with high property values. As long as the benefits associated with tax payments exceed their costs and do not exceed the cost at which owners could provide satisfactory levels of services for themselves, taxing programs can contribute to rising property values.

[20]Cf. Lewis H. Kimmel, *Taxes and Economic Incentives* (Washington: The Brookings Institution, 1950), chap. VII; and Paul E. Alyea, "Property-Tax Inducements to Attract Industry" in Richard W. Lindholm, *Property Taxation: USA* (Madison: University of Wisconsin Press, 1967), pp. 139-58. New York City's practice of freezing preimprovement assessment levels for twenty-five years on residential property remodeling projects provides another example of a tax concession of questionable desirability. Netzer indicates that this practice has favored the renovation and holding of old properties in preference to private redevelopment efforts that could provide new apartments. (Cf. Netzer, *op. cit.,* pp. 83-85.)

[21]Cf. *Bailey v. Drexel Furniture Co.,* 259 U.S. 20 (1922), and *United States v. Butler,* 297 U.S. 1 (1936).

When taxes contribute to higher costs of household and business operations without providing services with compensating values, they can depress property values. At this point, the concept of tax capitalization begins to operate. Taxes become an additional cost and total property values are reduced by the capitalized amount of this cost. Taxes designed to provide new services can enhance property values only when an effective demand exists for the services provided. Experience with tax programs designed to provide public services for premature subdivisions clearly shows that these programs cannot enhance property values in the absence of consumer demands. Far from adding to property values, these programs have often complicated the ability of owners to hold their lands and have sometimes led to tax delinquencies and forfeitures.

OPERATION OF THE PROPERTY TAX

Land taxation in the United States finds its most important single example in the general property tax. In examining the leading issues associated with the operation of this tax, attention should be centered on the importance of the property tax, its administrative procedures, its breakdown in cases of tax delinquency, an evaluation of its strong and weak features, and on some possible modifications and improvements.

Importance of the Property Tax

Since its first use in the United States, the property tax has been treated almost exclusively as a source of state and local revenues. The federal government has attempted to collect a property tax on only three occasions. And on each of these, the constitutional requirement that federal direct taxes be apportioned among the states in proportion to their population made the tax both difficult to administer and hard to collect. As a result, the federal government has moved on to other sources of tax revenue and left the property tax field more or less by default to the states and local units of government.

Real and personal property taxes provided the major source of revenue for both the state and local units of government up until the early 1900s. Since then, most states have turned more and more to other sources of revenue; and several states have withdrawn entirely from the property tax field. General property taxes accounted for only 2.3 percent of the tax revenue of the states in 1970 as compared with 46.5 percent in 1913 and 71.9 percent in 1890. (Table 18-1.)

With the virtual withdrawal of the states from this field of taxation, the general property tax has become the almost exclusive province of the local units of government. Between 1902 and 1970 the real and personal property taxes collected by these units jumped from $624 million to

TABLE 18-1. **Importance of Property Taxes in the United States, 1870-1970.**

Year	Total public revenues secured from real and personal property taxes (millions of dollars)			Proportion of tax revenues from own sources secured from property taxes		
	States and local units	States	Local units	States and local units	States	Local units
1870	$ 226	55	$ 171	†	†	†
1880	314	52	262	†	†	†
1890	443	69	374	88.4	71.9	92.3
1902	706	82	624	82.1	52.6	88.6
1913	1,332	140	1,192	82.8	46.5	91.1
1922	3,321	348	2,973	82.7	36.8	96.9
1932	4,487	328	4,159	72.8	17.4	97.3
1942	4,537	264	4,273	53.2	6.8	92.4
1952	8,652	370	8,282	44.8	3.8	87.5
1962	19,054	640	18,414	45.9	3.1	87.8
1967	26,047	862	25,186	42.5	2.7	85.9
1970	34,054	1,092	32,963	39.2	2.3	84.9

†Data not available.

Source: U. S. Department of Commerce, *Historical Statistics of the United States, Colonial Times to 1957*, Series Y526, 590, and 658; and Bureau of the Census GF reports on *Government Finances in 1962, 1966-67*, and *1969-70*, Table 4.

$32.96 billion. This $32.96 billion accounted for 84.9 percent of the taxes collected by local governments for their own use in 1970.

Property tax collections increased more than 48-fold in the United States between 1902 and 1970. Yet even with this increase in monetary importance, the property tax has declined considerably in its relative importance as an over-all source of tax revenues. More than half of the federal, state, and local tax revenues came from property taxes in the years prior to World War I and again during the middle 1920s. This situation changed considerably during the 1930s; and in 1941—the last year in which the general property tax rated as the most important single source of tax revenue in the United States—property taxes accounted for only 31 percent of the federal, state, and local tax revenues. In 1970, they accounted for 12.0 percent of the nation's total tax collections.

Much of the increase in property tax collections reported in Table 18-1 has resulted from new construction and rising property values. A measure of the actual trend in real property taxation is provided by the data on farm real estate taxes reported in Figure 18-1. As this chart indicates, the average tax per acre on farm land in the United States increased almost threefold between 1910 and 1921. Tax rates then gradually increased until 1929 when they reached an index peak of 55 (1957-59=100). Between 1930 and 1934, the average acreage tax dropped to a post-World War I low of 35, then remained relatively stable until 1945 when taxes started an upward climb, which reached an index of 216 in 1969.

During this same 60-year period, the average tax on farm real property reached its highest peak in proportionate value terms ($1.52 of tax on every $100 of actual market value) in 1932. Tax reductions brought a lowering of this rate between 1933 and 1935. The rate then leveled off only to drop again during the early 1940s when the increasing property values and relatively constant tax rates of the World War II period brought a 25-year low of 77 cents in taxes for every $100 of actual market value in 1946. Increasing tax rates brought this national index up to $1.12 for every $100 of farm real estate value in 1969. The average property tax rates by states in 1969 ranged from a low of 25 cents per $100 of farm real estate value in Alabama to a high of $2.43 in Maine and in Massachusetts.

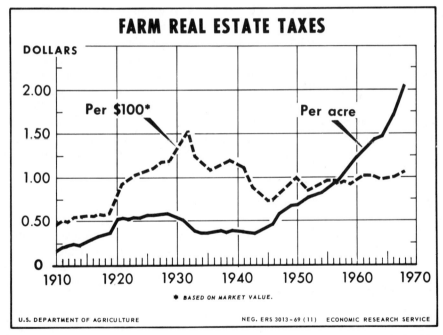

FIGURE 18-3. Trends in farm real estate taxes, United States, 1910-1970.

Administration of the Property Tax

The administration of the property tax involves a series of procedures or steps that are often described as the *property tax calendar*. These steps can be grouped under the following headings: (1) assessment of properties, (2) review of assessments, (3) equalization between assessment districts,

(4) the general tax levy and determination of the tax due on each property, (5) collection of the tax, and (6) possible appeals.

Assessment of property. As a first step in this taxation process, every taxable property must be located, listed, and appraised for taxation purposes. This procedure can be comparatively simple in some assessment districts while it is often very complex in others. Most rural properties involve holdings of several acres, which are often used for similar purposes. With these properties, it is frequently easy to locate each holding, establish who the owner is, list the owner's name and the legal description of his property on the assessment roll, and then assign the property an assessed value that measures its comparative value relative to other taxable properties. The smaller size and more heterogeneous nature of the properties found in most urban areas make the assessment process more complicated in these areas. As a result, the assessors in these areas usually work on a full-time basis and often use elaborate filing and valuation procedures in the pursuance of their duties.

Several observations are in order concerning the functioning of the assessment process. In theory, all properties should be assessed at their full market value or at some commonly accepted proportion of their market value; and all properties should be reassessed at frequent intervals.[22] Neither of these rules is rigidly adhered to in practice. Some properties are almost invariably assessed at higher proportions of their market values than others within the same assessment districts. And once an assessed value is accepted, it is often carried over year after year on the assessment rolls with only occasional adjustments for the addition of new improvements or for possible losses owing to factors such as fire. These practices naturally result in numerous inequities both within and between assessment districts.

Because of area differences, the assessment process often involves only a few days' work for a single assessor in some districts while it may call for the year-round services of a large office force in others. But regardless of when the property is visited, assessments are ordinarily made as of some uniform date. Differences also exist in the location of the assessment responsibility. This function is handled on the county level in more than half of the states; on a township, city, or village level in about a fourth of the states; and on a joint county and local basis in the remaining states. Most county and local assessors are elected to their offices. During recent

---

[22]Twenty states had statutory guidelines that called for assessment of properties at 100 percent of their full market value in 1968. Nineteen had statutory assessment ratios pegged to some flat percentage of full market value, six used locally determined ratios, three used property tax classification systems that called for assessing different classes of property at varying rates, and two were guided by the objectives of "just value" and "fair value." Cf. Paul V. Corusy, "Improved Property Tax Administration," in Arthur D. Lynn, Jr., ed., *The Property Tax and Its Administration* (Madison: University of Wisconsin Press, 1969), p. 66.

years, however, more and more cities, counties, and other units have shifted to an appointive system and to the employment of assessors who have technical training in appraisal work.

Review of assessments. After all of the properties in a given tax district have been assessed, an assessment roll is prepared and property owners are ordinarily advised of any changes in the assessed values of their properties. At this point, the property owner has the privilege of meeting with the board of review for his assessment district to protest his assessment.

This board has the power to correct assessment errors and to lower those assessments that involve the inequitable or unjust treatment of particular taxpayers. In presenting his protest to this board, it is not sufficient for the property owner to merely assert or claim that his assessment is too high. Instead he must shoulder the burden of proving that his property is assessed at a higher proportion of its fair market value than are certain other properties. In this process, the protesting owner usually operates at a disadvantage because of (1) his frequent lack of information concerning the assessed and market values of other properties, and (2) the probability that his complaints will bring higher assessments to those acquaintances whose properties he cites as examples to illustrate his case.

Equalization between assessment districts. Although the assessment review process helps to iron out inequities within individual assessment districts, it has little effect upon possible inequities between districts. These inequities exist because of the tendency of each assessment district to use its own standards in determining the proper level for its assessed values. A city, for example, may try to assess all its properties at 80 percent of their market value while five neighboring units may assess their properties at 67, 50, 40, 33, and 25 percent of market value, respectively. These differences would have little significance if every tax applied only to a single assessment district. But definite inequities can arise when school districts overlap two or more assessment districts or when each local unit is called upon to bear its fair share of a county- or state-wide property tax.

The smoothing out of these inequities between assessment districts is called "tax equalization." In those states with local assessors, the first step in this equalization process is usually carried out by a county board of equalization. This board examines the copies or summaries of the corrected assessment rolls submitted by the local units, considers such other information as it may have, and then proceeds to raise or lower the various assessment totals so that each district will come out with an equalized value that represents the same relative proportion of the market value of its properties.

These county equalized values—and the county assessed values in those states using county assessors—are in turn sent on to a state tax office where a state equalization of county assessments is usually made. State equalizations are necessary in those states that levy a state property tax. They are also used in computing the taxes applied in school and other taxing districts that overlap county lines. And they are used in some states as a basis for the distribution of certain state-collected taxes and state aids.

Levying the tax. The next step in the property taxation process involves the actual levying of the tax and the determination of the total tax due on each property. Acting under the taxing powers delegated to them by the state legislatures, the governing bodies of the various units of government (1) determine the amount of money they need for operating and other purposes during the coming year, (2) formally appropriate money for this purpose, and (3) levy a property tax for that portion of the appropriation to be financed by property taxes. The amount of this tax levy is then divided by the total assessed value of the tax district to get the tax rate for the year. A local unit with a total assessed value of $5 million and a tax levy of $60,000, for example, would have a tax rate equal to 1.2 percent of its assessed value ($60,000 divided by $5 million = .012).[23] This tax rate is frequently referred to as a millage rate—12 mills in this example—because it represents the number of mills of tax to be collected for each dollar of assessed valuation.

Once the tax rates for all the various units of government affecting a given area are known, they are totaled and a computation is made of the actual tax due on each property. A tax bill is then sent to the property owner with information concerning the various tax rates in effect, the legal description and assessed value of the property taxed, the date when the tax is due, and the period within which it can be paid without penalty.

Collecting the tax. Most state tax laws specify a date when property taxes are due. From this date on, the tax constitutes a lien on the property, which can be discharged only through payment of the tax or eventual tax sale and foreclosure. Property tax notices are usually mailed on or near the due date. Periods varying from several days to several weeks are then allowed during which the tax can be paid without penalties. Following the final payment date, all unpaid taxes are regarded as delinquent. Discharge of the tax lien against a property then calls for payment of the full tax plus interest and in many cases an additional penalty charge.

---

[23]This tax computation process is somewhat more complicated when a tax levy applies to properties included in two or more assessment districts. In a typical case, a county would "spread" its tax levy between its local assessment districts in proportion to their county equalized assessed valuations. Each local district would then divide its share of the county tax by its local assessed valuation to get its county millage rate for the year.

Many different tax payment arrangements are now in use. In times past, most states had a single final payment date—usually some date after harvest-time when the farmers were most able to pay. Approximately three-fourths of the states have since deviated from this pattern to permit tax payments in two or more installments. These payments are usually collected by the treasurers of the units of government that administer the assessment process. Once a tax becomes delinquent, however, the collection function is usually shifted from the local treasurers to the office of the county treasurer.

Possible appeals. A dissatisfied owner can usually appeal his assessment from his local board of review to a state tax agency or possibly to a court. Appeals can also be made to the courts when a taxpayer feels that a tax levy may be illegal for some particular reason. Since these appeals usually take time, the owner ordinarily finds it best to pay his tax under protest. Then if his appeal is upheld, any overpayment he has made will be returned to him.

Tax Delinquency Problems

Property taxes are levied primarily for the purpose of collecting revenue; and since these revenues are necessary for the conduct of local government, it is usually assumed that all taxes must be collected. Experience has shown, however, that many property owners fail to pay their taxes before the penalty date. Special provisions are thus necessary to cover the collection of delinquent taxes.

These provisions vary from state to state but usually allow the delinquent taxpayer a period of several months during which he can pay up his back taxes plus the accumulated interest and penalty charges. If the tax remains unpaid at the end of this period, the tax lien against the property is usually offered at a public tax sale. Outside buyers can then acquire tax certificates to tax-delinquent properties by paying a minimum price equal to the sum of the tax and its accumulated charges. With this sale, the local governments receive their tax money, and the buyer of the tax certificate acquires an interest in the delinquent property, which ripens into ownership if the delinquent owner fails to redeem his property within a specified redemption period. When no one bids on a delinquent tax, it is usually bid off in the name of the state or county.

Tax delinquency does not constitute much of a problem during prosperous times. During these periods, the legal provisions regarding the collection of delinquent taxes act mostly as a prod or incentive to get people to pay their taxes on time. Under depression conditions, however, tax delinquency often becomes a very serious problem because of the inability of many owners to meet their tax obligations. This was the situation during the 1930s when the average tax delinquency rate for the nation went up to 17 percent (1932-33) and when three-fourths or more of the taxes levied by some units went uncollected in some years.[24]

One of the chief lessons to be learned from the experience of the 1930s is aptly described by the old maxim "you can't squeeze blood out of a turnip." As many local units discovered, costly governmental services cannot be supported by an inadequate tax base. Steps were soon taken in many areas to curtail local government costs; state aids were made available to some local units; and several local functions were shifted to the states. At the same time, tax moratoria, special tax settlement arrangements, and delays in tax sales were used in most states to soften the ravages of the tax-delinquency problem. These concessions helped many taxpayers to tide themselves over the worst years of the depression. Yet even with these ameliorative measures, the tax-delinquency problem remained serious in most states until the return of better times.

Much of the confusion and indecision that surrounded the tax fore-closure policies of many states during this period gradually cleared during the late 1930s when states and counties started to take tax title to large areas of hopelessly delinquent land. As had been the general prac-tice in the years prior to the 1930s, much of this tax-reverted land was soon restored to the tax rolls. But in many cases the states and counties broke away from their earlier practice of acting mostly as land brokers in transferring property from one private owner to another. Instead, they looked upon their tax-reverted holdings as a "new public domain," which should be classified and then administered according to its best use. In their administration of this new public domain, the states and counties have sold considerable areas for private use; but they have also dedicated large areas for public forest, recreation, grazing, and other uses.

Evaluation of the Property Tax

Like most other taxes, the property tax has both its strong and weak points. These points can best be isolated and appraised when they are

[24]Tax delinquency was most serious in areas with premature and submarginal developments. Thousands of unsold lots around most major cities were sacrificed through nonpayment of taxes. A Michigan study indicates that 72 percent of the 236,000 platted lots in the area covered by 17 governmental units (7 cities, 6 villages, and 4 townships) on the northern fringe of Detroit were advertised for tax sale in 1938. Serious delinquency problems also occurred in the cutover portions of the Lake States, the Pacific Northwest, and the Ozarks; in the drained areas of the South; and in the drought-stricken portions of the Great Plains States. More than 90 percent of the rural drainage and levee district taxes were delinquent in some Arkansas counties in 1933; and 93 percent of the tax levy of the Everglades drainage district in Florida was delinquent in 1936. Several townships in Minnesota reported complete delinquency for some years. For more detailed discussion of this problem, cf. National Resources Planning Board Technical Paper No. 8, *Tax Delinquency and Rural Land-Use*

considered in light of the principal canons or criteria of a "good" tax. Important among these criteria are the assumptions that a "good" tax should (1) be related to the taxpayer's ability to pay, (2) reflect the benefits received from public expenditures, (3) have a reliable and uniform yield, (4) be both easy and economical to administer, and (5) be both familiar to the taxpayer and socially expedient.

One might argue whether property ownership has ever constituted a good measure of a person's ability to pay taxes. As late as a century ago, most of the wealth of the country was held in the form of tangible goods and properties that a tax assessor could see and touch. But even then, many property owners were "land poor" and their income potentials were such that they often forfeited their properties because of their inability to pay the taxes expected of them.

With the changes of the past century, this relationship between property ownership and ability to pay has become worse rather than better. Most of our larger personal incomes are now associated with salaries, fees, and dividends rather than with direct income from real property. Intangibles have become more and more important; and many people with high capacities to pay taxes now own very little real property. This situation has led to numerous inequities. Some property owners pay a tax commensurate with their ability to pay; some escape a major portion of their fair share of the costs of local government; and some pay a considerably larger tax than one can justify in terms of their ability to pay.

Property taxes are often more closely associated with benefits received than with ability to pay. This is particularly true when a high proportion of the collected tax is used to provide protective services and community facilities that enhance property values. A certain amount of inequity always appears, however, when one compares the relative benefits enjoyed by different properties. One might ask, for example, whether a $5,000 vacant lot receives as much fire and police protection as a $5,000 building or a $5,000 automobile? Or does a new fireproofed building with an assessed value of $100,000 receive 20 times as much fire protection as an older, more antiquated structure with an assessed value of $5,000? Going beyond these questions, it may be noted that many public funds go for nonprotective services such as schools, highways, recreation facilities, and welfare services. The benefits from these expenditures accrue more to people than to properties and often have only an indirect effect on property values.

Some of the leading arguments favoring the property tax center around

Adjustment, 1942; Raleigh Barlowe, *Administration of Tax-Reverted Lands in the Lake States,* Michigan Agricultural Experiment Station Technical Bulletin 225, 1951; and A. M. Hillhouse and Carl H. Chatters, *Tax-Reverted Properties in Urban Areas* (Chicago: Public Administration Service, 1942), chap. I.

its uniformity of yield, its ease of administration, and its long acceptance. Unlike many other taxes, the revenues collected through the property tax need not fluctuate with changes in the business cycle. Except for a possible increase in the amount of tax delinquency, tax collections can be as high during depression years as during periods of prosperity. This reliability and uniformity of yield from property taxes is naturally desirable as far as the local units of government are concerned. But as one might expect, this often means that the individual taxpayer is hit hardest at the very time when he is least able to pay.

The real property tax compares very favorably with other taxes in its ease and cost of administration. Problems naturally arise with the assessment and equalization steps. But the fixed and continuing nature of real property practically guarantees the collection of a tax once it is levied. Property taxes are seldom evaded or avoided. They are ordinarily paid on time; and the total revenues collected from this source are usually high relative to the costs of tax administration.

People are seldom very enthusiastic about paying taxes. But they are ordinarily more inclined to accept a tax with which they are familiar and to which they have long been accustomed than the unknown quantity of a new tax. In this respect, social expediency often favors the retention of a long-accepted tax such as the property tax partly because of the howls of protest which greet most new tax proposals and partly because of our willingness to tolerate those taxes that have become an accepted part of our economic system.

In addition to the various criticisms of the property tax listed above, it may also be noted that the usual lump-sum or two-, three-, or four-installment payment system makes the property tax a relatively inconvenient tax for most people to pay. Its tendency to treat residential and productive properties in the same class constitutes a burden on home ownership. Its failure to respect periods of income favors those operators who enjoy a rapid turnover of capital or inventory as compared with those who suffer from crop failures or those who invest in long-term forestry ventures. High property taxes in urban communities frequently encourage the migration of families and industries to lower-tax areas. And the separate taxation of real properties and intangible properties such as mortgages can easily result in double taxation.

Practically every tax has its weak as well as its strong points. The property tax is probably no worse in this respect than most other taxes. Our problem in tax policy is not so much that of finding the perfect tax as it is that of combining taxes in such a way that they tend to complement each other with the strong features of one tax always balancing the weak features of another. Some of the weaknesses of the property tax such as its alleged regressivity, for example, are compensated for when it is used alongside a graduated income tax.

Even if the general property tax met every criteria of a "good" tax, property owners would still have numerous grounds for complaining about the high tax cost of property ownership. These individuals are not alone. Tax burdens constitute a universal problem in our economy that most operators would like to minimize but that all must expect to share. Owners could decide to give up their properties and squander their incomes on high living, but they would still find themselves paying a considerable tax for items such as luxury goods, travel, tobacco, liquor, and entertainment.

Possible Modifications and Improvements

Few taxes have been subject to more criticism than the property tax. As one might expect, this criticism has been accompanied in many cases with suggestions for the modification, improvement, and reform of the property tax. These suggestions fall into three classes: (1) an insistence upon the need for better administration, (2) proposals for modifications in the property tax, and (3) the recommended partial or complete replacement of the property tax with other sources of revenue.

Need for better administration. As long as the property tax is accepted and retained in its present form, every effort should be made to administer it in such a way that it will work out as expected. This need for good administration is extremely important because some of the greatest inequities associated with the property tax stem directly from faulty administration.

The need for better property tax administration is nowhere more widely felt than in the case of property assessments. Many assessors do a professional job in appraising the properties in their assessment districts and in keeping their assessed values up to date. But the prevailing pattern in many districts is one of haphazard assessment practices with taxpayers sometimes reporting their own property values and with local assessors all too often limiting their function to the copying of last year's values onto this year's assessment roll.

Better administration calls for a more professional type of assessment service. This means that steps are needed to either (1) train and supervise local assessors so they can carry on their assessment function in a satisfactory manner, or (2) combine assessment districts in such a way as to permit the employment of full-time salaried assessors who have both training and experience in property appraisal work. Most tax authorities favor the use of appointed rather than elected assessors, the centering of the assessment function in a county assessor, and state assessment of properties such as railroads and public utilities.[25]

[25] Shultz and Harriss (*op. cit.,* p. 347) observe that experts unanimously favor the appointment of assessors on a civil service basis because the "elected assessor is too often a vote-getter instead of a competent appraiser and administrator, worse yet, he may be a creature of the local political 'machine' and misuse his office to further the

Assessment reform represents only one aspect of the need for better property tax administration. Improvements of a comparable nature are definitely needed in the equalization process if the taxpayers of many assessment districts are to enjoy equitable tax treatment. Steps also are needed in some areas to facilitate the collection process by making property taxes more convenient to pay. The property tax collection function should always be centralized in a single official who will collect the taxes levied by all the taxing districts. Wider use might also be made of an optional installment or pay-as-you-go method of making tax payments.

Good property tax administration is invariably tied up with the costs of local government. These costs must always be kept in line with the taxpaying capacity of the local property tax base. When a local government fails to abide by this basic rule, even the best administration breaks down. Avoidance of the conditions that foster tax delinquency thus becomes a paramount objective of good property tax administration.

Possible modifications of the property tax. Several proposals have been made for possible modifications that would limit or change the present emphasis of the property tax. Some of the more important of these involve the use of tax rate limitations, graduated property tax rates, classified property taxes, special tax exemptions, and a shift to taxes on net worth, land rents, or unearned increments.[26]

Most states have constitutional or statutory provisions that set ceilings for the tax rates levied by their various units of government. These rate limitations take many different forms. Sometimes they provide a maximum over-all rate limitation for all property taxes; sometimes they

---

'machine's' ends. Informed opinion is decidedly critical of village, town, and school district assessment. The assessment district should be large enough, in area and in taxable resources, to permit the employment of one full-time assessor and at least one assistant. Rarely, however, can a village, a town, or a school district afford a full-time salaried assessor. Too often, assessment is performed on a part-time basis at a compensation which compares unfavorably with a laborer's wage, and the function suffers accordingly. The county, or a major city, is likely to be the smallest unit for efficient assessment. Even where a small poor county cannot support an adequate assessor's office, it can at least do better than any of its subdistricts. County assessment has the further advantage of removing the assessor to some extent from the influence—not necessarily willful and pernicious, but none the less dangerous—of his immediate neighbors and electors. In larger units, personnel can specialize on particular types of property—factories, stores, homes, or personal property." Cf. also Daniel M. Holland, ed., *The Assessment of Land Value* (Madison: University of Wisconsin Press, 1971).

[26] Cf. Shultz and Harriss, *op. cit.*, pp. 365-69; Roland R. Renne, *Land Economics*, 2nd ed. (New York: Harper & Brothers, 1958), pp. 276-86; Netzer, *op. cit.*, chap. VIII; James Heilbrun, *Real Estate Taxes and Urban Housing* (New York: Columbia University Press, 1966), chap VI.; and Mason Gaffney, "Land Rent, Taxation, and Public Policy," *Regional Science Association Papers*, Vol. 23, 1969, pp. 141-53.

apply to specific levies such as the levy for state purposes; sometimes upper limits are set for each level of government; sometimes the limitations are graduated according to the assessed valuation or population of the tax district; and sometimes they specify a maximum permissible percentage increase over the tax levy of the previous year. Each of these approaches is designed to prevent excessive taxation. Except for the overall limitations, they usually allow most government units considerable flexibility and freedom in their use of the taxing power.

Over-all limitations have been adopted in several states for the specific purpose of keeping property taxes low.[27] These maximum rates can usually be boosted for specific purposes and specific time periods by popular referendum. But even with this flexibility, they are ordinarily criticized by tax and fiscal authorities because of the effect they have in cramping the fiscal activities of local governments. The adoption of these limitations in the past has often led to a rigid curtailment of government services, an increase in local governmental debt, a search for new sources of public revenue, and frequent increases in assessed valuations. On the positive side, these blanket limitations have helped to reduce property taxes and have forced many local units to look to sources other than the property tax for part of their revenues.

A second modification involves the possible graduation of the millage rates used in property taxation. Under this proposal, the owners of properties of large size or value are taxed at higher proportions of their assessed values than taxpayers with smaller or less valuable holdings. This proposal is sometimes argued as a means of discouraging concentration of property ownership. It can also be used to counterbalance the alleged regressivity of the property tax and—insofar as property ownership provides evidence of ability to pay—to collect more revenue from the owners with the greatest ability to pay. Graduated property taxes have been used with some success in Australia and New Zealand. Yet, although they have been suggested in several American states, their proposal has seldom evoked much popular enthusiasm. Tax proposals of this type have been adopted on three different occasions in Oklahoma, but in each instance were voided on technical grounds.

According to the tax-uniformity concept, all properties should be lumped together and treated alike for tax purposes. Most states have deviated from this standard by authorizing at least one of three different types of special tax treatment. Minnesota and a few other states assess

[27]Oklahoma adopted a 17-mill overall limit in 1907 and Ohio followed with a 10-mill limitation in 1911. Over-all rate limitations of a comparable nature were voted into effect in five additional states in 1932 and 1933—Indiana (15 mills in towns and cities and 10 mills elsewhere), Michigan (15 mills, cities were later exempted from this limitation), New Mexico (20 mills), Washington (40 mills with property assessments at 50 percent of market value), and West Virginia (5 to 20 mills with a 15-mill limit applying to most properties). Some of these limitations no longer apply.

different types of real property at different proportions of their market values. Approximately half of the states use a classified rate approach in their taxation of intangibles and tangible personalty; and a number of states use *in lieu* arrangements such as severance or gross receipts taxes in their taxation of forests, minerals, and railroads. These classified property taxes have some drawbacks. But they recognize the fact that (1) some types of property have greater ability to pay taxes than others, and (2) equality in tax treatment does not necessarily add up to equitable or just treatment.

Special tax exemptions provide still another means for modifying the general property tax. Under the federal system of government, public properties are always exempt from property taxes.[28] Comparable exemptions also apply to cemeteries and to properties used for charitable, educational, and religious purposes. In addition to these exemptions, many states have gone further to exempt personal properties and certain specified items and products from property taxation. Homestead exemptions and veterans exemptions are used in many states to favor particular classes of citizens by exempting them from certain taxes on the first $500 to $5,000 of their assessed valuations. Exemptions are also used in some states to foster the location of manufacturing plants.

Several valid arguments can be advanced for the granting of special tax exemptions. But experience has shown that exemptions can be abused and that they often stem from political expediency. Since exemptions ordinarily reduce the local tax base, they naturally shift an additional tax burden to those taxpayers who are not lucky enough to qualify for exemption. Sometimes this shifting of the tax is justified on equity grounds; but in many instances it merely compounds the inequities associated with property taxation.

Several proposed modifications would shift the emphasis in property

---

[28]The exemption of public properties creates only a minor problem in most tax districts. Real problems exist, however, in those districts where most of the property is held in public ownership. The federal government has recognized its implicit obligation to help support the costs of government in those areas where it holds considerable productive property. Annual cash grants are made to the government of the District of Columbia. Twenty-eight different revenue sharing arrangements were used with the nation's larger land holdings in 1970. These ranged from TVA's payment of 5 percent of its gross receipts from power sales to the units of government in which it operates, the U. S. Forest Service's payment of 25 percent of its receipts from sales of timber products, and the Department of Interior's payments of 37½ percent of the proceeds from oil, gas, and mineral leases and 50 percent of the grazing fees received from the leasing of some classes of grazing lands, to the Army Corps of Engineers' payment of 75 percent of the revenues received from acquired flood control lands. No payments were made to the state or local governments for some types of land held in federal ownership while payment-in-lieu-of-tax arrangements ranging up to the approximate equivalent of local property taxes applied with others. Several states also make payments in lieu of taxes to their local units on state lands held in forests, parks, and game areas.

taxation from a tax on property values to a tax on (1) the owner's net worth, (2) the annual land rent of property, or (3) unearned value increments. A net-worth tax would be concerned only with the equity the owner has in his property plus the value of his other assets. In many respects, this proposal appears more equitable than the present property tax. It would be harder, however, to administer, and its chief advantage disappears when one remembers that the tax on mortgages would in all probability be shifted to the mortgaged owner.

Taxes on land rents and unearned value increments have been advocated for well over a century. Henry George became a leading exponent of this approach when he championed the cause of his now famous single tax. This tax was designed to take all of the economic return to bare land without detracting from the value or income of land improvements.[29] George and his "single taxers" argued that this tax would (1) provide all of the tax revenues needed by government, (2) reduce the investment cost of property ownership, (3) encourage the owner-operatorship of rural and urban properties, (4) foster the improvement and more efficient use of land, (5) discourage land speculation, and (6) be a relatively painless tax since it would affect only the "unearned" annual rent of land.

In answer to these claims, it may be argued that (1) the single tax would provide only a fraction of the revenues now needed by government; (2) it would be difficult to administer in an equitable manner; (3) its exclusive dependence on the economic return to land would leave the economic rents of nonland factors untouched; (4) it would have little effect on former owners who have already realized their unearned land value increments through the sale of properties at their capitalized income value; (5) it would work a definite injustice on the thousands of owners who have used past savings to purchase properties at their capitalized values; and (6), elimination of the economic values ascribed to the bare land portion of real properties would reduce the incentive operators have for conserving and building up their properties and would at the same time complicate the process of allocating land areas between competing owners and uses.

Land-value taxes involving aspects of the single-tax approach have been used for many years in parts of Australia, Canada, and New Zealand. A land taxation system embracing this concept was adopted in Jamaica in

[29] Great Britain has used taxes on the actual or imputed annual rental values of property as the basis of its rates system since 1601. This system has been adopted in western Europe, India, Iran, Pakistan, Peru, and Cuba. [cf. Haskell P. Wald, *Taxation of Agricultural Land in Underdeveloped Economies* (Cambridge: Harvard University Press, 1959), chap. I] and is a tax based on annual land rents. It differs from George's proposed tax on land rents, however, in that it involves the rental value of improvements as well as bare land.

1957.[30] Several American cities such as Houston, Pittsburgh, and Scranton have also experimented with the idea of basing their property taxes primarily on bare land values while exempting all or part of the value of improvements from property taxation. Capital gains taxes and special assessments are also used in the United States and some other countries to tax the value increments associated with changing conditions and public improvements. Several strong arguments can be advanced for the taxation of land rents and unearned value increments. But these measures can hardly be justified on a single-tax basis; and there is little reason for limiting them to the income and value increments associated with bare land.

Replacement of the property tax. Some advocates of property tax reform argue that it is not enough to merely modify or patch up the present property tax. Instead of settling for modifications and administrative improvements such as those listed above, they sometimes argue for the partial or complete replacement of the property tax with other sources of revenue.

A realistic appraisal of the present situation suggests little prospect for the complete replacement of the property tax. A strong case can be made, however, for the limitation and partial replacement of this tax in the future. In this respect it may be noted that a gradual replacement process has been going on for several decades. Most states have withdrawn almost entirely from the property tax field; and many once locally supported public activities such as those that involve highways, public health, and welfare are now financed on a state basis. With this shift to new sources of revenue, the property tax accounted for only 39 percent of the tax revenues (not including intergovernmental aids) of the state and local governments in 1970 as compared with 88 percent of these revenues in 1890.

Despite this decline in its relative importance as a tax, the total property tax burden has increased manyfold. The growing demand for new and better governmental services has brought need for more and more tax revenues in most taxing districts. This demand has resulted in tax levies in some areas that could easily provoke a wave of tax delinquency under depressed business conditions. In facing up to this problem, two points bear emphasis: (1) a conscious effort should be made to limit

---

[30] For descriptions of these programs, cf. A. M. Woodruff and L. L. Ecker-Racz, "Property Taxes and Land-Use Patterns in Australia and New Zealand," and Daniel M. Holland, "A Study of Land Taxation in Jamaica," in Arthur P. Becker, ed., *Land and Building Taxes* (Madison: University of Wisconsin Press, 1969), pp. 147-86 and 239-86; and Kenneth Taeuber, "A Century of Australian Experience with Land Value Taxation" and Wilfred Chang, "Recent Experience of Establishing Land Value Taxation in Jamaica," in *1966 International Seminar on Land Taxation, Land Tenure, and Land Reform in Developing Countries* (West Hartford, Conn.: John C. Lincoln Foundation and University of Hartford, 1966), pp. 128-74 and 210-38.

property taxes to the long-run paying capacity of the properties taxed, and (2) new sources of revenue should be sought to supplement the property tax as a source of local-government and public-school finance.

—SELECTED READINGS

Becker, Arthur P. (ed.), *Land and Building Taxes* (Madison: University of Wisconsin Press, 1969).

Groves, Harold M., *Financing Government*, 5th ed. (New York: Henry Holt & Company, Inc., 1958), chaps. III-VI.

Lindholm, Richard W. (ed.), *Property Taxation: USA* (Madison: University of Wisconsin Press, 1967).

Lynn, Arthur D., Jr. (ed.), *The Property Tax and Its Administration* (Madison: University of Wisconsin Press, 1969).

Netzer, Dick, *Economics of the Property Tax* (Washington: Brookings Institution, 1966).

Renne, Roland R., *Land Economics,* 2nd ed. (New York: Harper & Brothers, 1958), chaps. XIII-XIV.

Shultz, William J., and C. Lowell Harriss, *American Public Finance,* 8th ed. (Englewood Cliffs, N. J.: Prentice-Hall, Inc., 1965), chaps. VII, XVIII-XIX.

Index